D0828515

THE NEW EUROPE

THE NEW EUROPE

Edited by JONATHAN STORY

*Politics, Government
and Economy since 1945*

NATIONAL UNIVERSITY
LIBRARY ORANGE COUNTY

BLACKWELL
Oxford UK & Cambridge USA

JN
15
N488
1993

Copyright © INSEAD, 1993

First published 1993

Blackwell Publishers
108 Cowley Road
Oxford OX4 1JF
UK

238 Main Street, Suite 501
Cambridge, Massachusetts 02142
USA

All rights reserved. Except for the quotation of short passages for the purposes of criticism and review, no part may be reproduced, stored in a retrieval system, or transmitted, in any form or by any means, electronic, mechanical, photocopying, recording or otherwise, without the prior permission of the publisher.

Except in the United States of America, this book is sold subject to the condition that it shall not, by way of trade or otherwise, be lent, resold, hired out, or otherwise circulated without the publisher's prior consent in any form of binding or cover other than that in which it is published and without a similar condition including this condition being imposed on the subsequent purchaser.

British Library Cataloguing-in-Publication Data

A CIP catalogue record for this book is available from the British Library.

Library of Congress Cataloging-in-Publication Data

The New Europe / edited by Jonathan Story.
   p.   cm.
  Includes bibliographical references and index.
   ISBN 0-631-18079-6. – ISBN 0-631-18613-1 (pbk.)
   1. European federation. 2. European Economic Community.
3. Europe – Politics and government – 1945– 4. Europe – Economic conditions – 1945– I. Story, Jonathan.
JN15.N488 1993
321'.04'094–dc20   92-8606
                                                        CIP

Typeset in 10 on 11½ pt Aster
by Graphicraft Typesetters Ltd., Hong Kong
Printed in Great Britain by T.J. Press (Padstow) Ltd., Padstow, Cornwall

Contents

Contributors

Jonathan Story

Jonathan Story is Professor of International Politics and Business at the European Institute of Business Administration (INSEAD), and writes and teaches on European and world politics and markets. He belongs to a number of professional organizations dealing with international affairs. His books include *Western Europe in World Affairs* (Praeger, 1986), with Guy de Carmoy; *Euro-communism: Myth or Reality?* (Penguin, 1979), edited with Edward Mortimer. He has written numerous case studies, articles and monographs on European and international affairs.

Henry R. Nau

Henry R. Nau is Professor of Political Science and International Affairs and is Associate Dean of the Elliott School of International Affairs, the George Washington University. He has served in the State Department from 1975 to 1977 as Special Assistant to the Under Secretary for Economic Affairs and on the National Security Council in the White House from 1981 to 1983 as senior staff member responsible for international economic issues and White House summit preparations. He is author of numerous articles and books, including most recently *The Myth of America's Decline* (Oxford University Press, 1990).

Neil Malcolm

Neil Malcolm was educated at Oxford and Birmingham Universities, has taught Soviet politics and foreign policy at Wolverhampton Polytechnic, and is head of the Soviet Programme at the Royal Institute of International Affairs in London. He is author of *Soviet Political Scientists and American Politics*, *Soviet Policy Perspectives on Western Europe* and other studies of Soviet foreign policy and policy making.

Jean-Pierre Lehmann

Jean-Pierre Lehmann is Representative Director of InterMatrix Japan and Partner of the InterMatrix Group. He is adviser to a number of European and American multinationals on their Japanese and Asia Pacific strategies and to Japanese companies on their international, especially European, strategies. He is also affiliated Professor of International Management at the London Business School. Former positions include Associate Professor of International Business at INSEAD and Director of the Centre for Japanese Studies, University of Stirling. He is the author of three books and numerous articles on Japanese and Asian affairs. He holds a BSFS from Georgetown University and a D.Phil. from Oxford University.

Hanns W. Maull

Hanns W. Maull is Professor of Foreign Policy and International Relations at the University of Trier and Co-Director of the Research Institute of the German Society for Foreign Policy in Bonn. He previously taught at the Universities of Munich and Eichstaett, and was Visiting Professor of International Relations at the Johns Hopkins University, Bologna Centre. From 1976 to 1979, he was the European Secretary of the Trilateral Commission. Among his publications are *Raw Materials*, *Energy and Western Security* (1985 for the International Institute for Strategic Studies) and *The Gulf War* (co-edited with Otto Pick).

William E. Paterson

William E. Paterson is Salvesen Professor of European Institutions and Director of the Europa Institute, University of Edinburgh; he was formerly Professor of Politics at the University of Warwick. He is also Chairman of the University Association for Contemporary European Studies, and the founder and past Chairman of the Association of German Politics. Current interests include the interaction of German and European unification and the redesign of community institutions. His latest publication is *Governing Germany* (1991) with David Southern.

Guy de Carmoy

Guy de Carmoy was born in 1907, and earned degrees in law and political science. He has worked in the French Treasury, and was Executive Director of the World Bank, and Director of the Organization of European Economic Cooperation. He is Professor Emeritus INSEAD, and has written several books on French Foreign Policy and World Energy.

Geoffrey Edwards

Geoffrey Edwards is the Alderson Director of Studies in the Centre of International Studies at the University of Cambridge. He took his Ph.D. at the

London School of Economics (LSE). After a brief period in the Foreign and Commonwealth Office (FCO), he taught in various capacities at the Universities of Essex, Kent, Southern California, and at the LSE. He has also been a Research Fellow at the Royal Institute of International Affairs (RIIA), Chatham House. His publications have been primarily in the fields of the institutional development of the European Community and its international relations, the most recent being a collection of papers co-edited with Elfriede Regelsberger (q.v.) *Europe's Global Links* (1990).

Cesare Merlini

Cesare Merlini is Chairman of the Institute for International Affairs in Rome. He has been Director of the Institute since 1970 and became its Chairman in 1979. He has also been a member of the Council of the International Institute for Strategic Studies since 1983. Trained in industrial and nuclear engineering, Mr Merlini began his career as a researcher in the Argon National Laboratory in the United States in 1963, and was Professor of Nuclear Technology at the Turin Polytechnic in 1965–85. He is the author and editor of numerous articles and books, the most recent being *Fine dell'Atomo? Passato e Futuro delle Applicazioni Civili e Militari dell' Energia Nucleare* (1987).

Elfriede Regelsberger

Elfriede Regelsberger is Deputy Director of the Institut für Europäische Politik, Bonn. She was born in 1955 and studied Political Science, Modern History and International Law in Munich. Her main field of work is European Political Cooperation (EPC), the German European policy and the decision-making processes of the EC and EPC. Her numerous publications include: *Europe's Global Links: the European Community and Interregional Cooperation* (co-editor, 1990); The twelve's dialogue with third countries – progress towards a communauté d'action?, in Martin Holland (ed.), *The Future of European Cooperation: Essays on Theory and Practice*, (1991); Foreign policy: towards a dialogue, in Helen Wallace (ed.), *The Wider Western Europe: Reshaping the EC–EFTA Relationship*, (1991).

Stephen Woolcock

Stephen Woolcock is a Research Fellow with the European Programme of the Royal Institute of International Affairs. Recent publications include: *Britain, Germany and 1992: the Limits of Deregulation*, (co-author, 1991), *Corporate Governance in the Single European Market*, RIIA, 1990 and *The Uruguay Round: Issues for the EC and US*, RIIA, 1990. He has been the Deputy Director for International Affairs at the Confederation of British Industry, (1985–8) and Paul-Henri Spaak Fellow at the Centre for International Affairs, Harvard University (1983–4).

Albert Bressand

Albert Bressand is the managing director and co-founder of PROMETHEE, a Paris-based international think-tank. Dr Bressand has served as economic adviser to the French Foreign Minister, as Deputy Director of the French Institute for International Relations and as a member of the policy planning staff of the World Bank. His publications include *Strategic Trends in Services 1989*, (co-edited with Kalypso Nicolaïdis), *Le Prochain Monde* (1985, with Catherine Distler), and articles in *Foreign Affairs*, *Politique Industrielle*, *Revue Tiers-Monde*, *Politique Internationale*, *Encyclopaedia Universalis*, etc. Dr Bressand holds engineering degrees from Ecole Polytechnique and Ecole Nationale des Ponts et Chaussées and a Ph.D. in political economy from Harvard University.

Marcello de Cecco

Marcello de Cecco is Professor of Monetary Economics at the University of Rome 'La Sapienza' and external Professor at the European University Institute in Florence. He has published *Money and Empire* in 1974, edited *Changing Money* in 1985 and, with A. Giovannini *A European Central Bank* in 1990.

Paul G. Lewis

Paul Lewis is Senior Lecturer in Government at the Open University of Great Britain, where he works on comparative politics, international relations and European studies – with particular reference to Poland and the countries of east-central Europe. His current work is concerned with the development of the region since 1945 and the role of political parties in contemporary processes of regime change.

Michael Kaser

Michael Kaser was born in London in 1926 and read Economics at King's College, Cambridge. After service as an economist in the British Foreign Service and HM Embassy Moscow (1947–51) he was in the Research Division of the UN Economic Commission for Europe until he took up an appointment at Oxford University in 1963. He is Director of the University Institute of Russian, Soviet and East European Studies, and Professorial Fellow of St Antony's college. Among his fifteen books written or edited are *Soviet Economics* (1970) and *The Economic History of Eastern Europe* (3 vols 1985–6).

Georges Sokoloff

Professor Sokoloff teaches the history of Russian and Soviet Economy at the National Institute for Oriental Languages and Cultures in Paris. He is also the scientific adviser for the Centre d'Etudes Prospectives et d'Information Internationale (CEPII), and a consultant in foreign trade relations. He is the author of two hundred articles, studies, communications and contributions to collective works on the USSR, east European countries, COMECON and east–west trade. His publications include *L'Economie Obeissante* (1976), *L'Economie de la Detente* (1973) and *Drole de Crise* (ed.) 1986. A history of contemporary Russia is in preparation.

Vojtech Mastny

Vojtech Mastny is Professor of International Relations at the Johns Hopkins School of Advanced International Studies, at the Bologna Centre. His area of expertise is diplomatic history during and after World War II, and his many publications on the subject include *Helsinki, Human Rights and European Security* (1986).

Peter Stratmann

Dr Stratmann was born in 1943 and studied political science, contemporary history and sociology at the Universities of Hamburg and Munich. He obtained his doctorate at the faculty of philosophy of the University of Munich in 1978. He has been a researcher at the Research Institute for International Affairs of the Stiftung Wissenschaft und Politik in Ebenhausen since 1967. He is the author of numerous articles on problems of military strategy and arms control, including *NATO Strategie in der Krise?* (1981).

Alexander Naumenkov

Alexander Naumenkov was born in 1961 in Moscow. He studied in the Department of International Economic Relations at the Financial Institute, and obtained his Ph.D. in international economics from the Institute of World Economy and International Relations (IMEMO), USSR Academy of Sciences, in March 1987. Since 1988 he has been a Research Fellow in the Department of Integration Processes at the Institute of Europe of the Academy of Sciences. He has written several articles, monograph chapters and reviews on Thatcherism, Britain's relations with the EC, financial aspects of west European integration, and Soviet European policies.

Ian Davidson

Ian Davidson is European columnist and Paris correspondent for the *Financial Times*. He has reported and analysed European Affairs since the early 1960s, and is the author of *Britain and the Making of Europe* (1971), and *The Cold War* (1970) with Gordon Weil.

Tables

Preface

The design of this book originated in an article of the editor's, entitled 'Western Union or Common Home?', and published in a number of the *Political Quarterly*, 'The Politics of 1992', edited by Colin Crouch and David Marquand (1990). The analysis then was that the probabilities are higher for a western European union, than for a closer pan-European association of states. Gorbachev's vision of a 'common European home' had yet to be filled out with political and market content. Russia had embarked on its second revolution, the outcome of which was unpredictable. But in the longer term, Berlin and a united Germany had the opportunity of becoming the centre of a pluralist and reconciled pan-Europe.

The general lines of argument developed in that article seem to hold up in the light of subsequent events. Europe's transformation in the 1990s is being driven by the disintegration of the former Soviet empire, the transitions underway in central and south-eastern Europe, German unity and the moves to European union. Germany is the dominant factor in European affairs, all the more so since the collapse of the Soviet Union in 1991 means that there is no great power to Germany's east. The great power has been substituted by a host of successor states, while the countries of central and south-eastern European look to Germany and western Europe for markets and support in their varied political transitions.

But equally significant in shaping Europe's future are the reorientation in US policies following the end of the cold war, the weight of Japan in world affairs, and the permanent changes underway in the world political economy. Germany may be *primus inter pares* in a diverse Europe, whose varied states and peoples remain jealous of their independence and identities. But on the world stage, Germany is dwarfed by the United States and Japan; it is bound into a global, and interdependent state and market system which it may seek to influence as best it can, but that it cannot hope to fashion on its own and after its own interests. United Germany has turned therefore to the European Community's member states as its prime partners in seeking to fashion a new Europe after the cold war, capable of holding its own in the world.

As argued in my article, there are no certainties that the powerful trends towards a more united western Europe, as the kernel for a broader entity, will win out. The new Europe opening up before our eyes is not entirely uncharted. A central theme of this book is the enduring weight of history, modified by the transformation in world affairs in particular by the complex polity built up in western Europe over the past forty-five years. The purpose is to chart its further elaboration by drawing on the distant and recent past, while covering the subject from as many angles as space permits to bring out the new Europe's main traits.

The book's organization follows from its premise. The introductory chapter places the Europe of 1985 in the context of the inherited global state and market system. This is followed by a section covering some of the major changes in world affairs as they affect Europe. Another section focuses on the linkages between the domestic and external policies of the larger European states. The fourth part deals with four aspects of western European statecraft, where the emphasis is on the reciprocal influence of European politics on Europe's relations with the rest of the world. The focus of the fifth section is on the regime and system change underway in the former communist party states, including the Soviet Union, from either political or market perspectives. The sixth section deals with the end of the cold war and the complex process, and question, of redefining Europe's architecture.

The book's aim is to chart the parameters within which policies, both government and business, are likely to evolve as the 'new Europe' takes shape. Initial drafts were presented at a conference at the European Institute of Business Administration (INSEAD) from 28 February to 2 March 1991. Our proceedings were enlivened by the comments and criticisms of our discussants John Beck; Marie Mendras; Victor-Yves Ghebali; Jean Klein; Kenneth S. Courtis; Edith Penrose; Will Hutton; Yao-Su Hu; Alfred Pijpers; Denis Lacorne; Douglas Webber; Michael Burda; Richard Gillespie.

I would like to take the opportunity to thank Dean Ludo van der Heyden, and the INSEAD research committee for their generosity in making the whole undertaking possible. My thanks go also to the Institute's staff in their support for the project. This is particularly due to Mrs Susan Treffel who managed the whole process from start to finish with her usual competence and energy, alongside her many other tasks. I would also like to thank Ritsa Panagiotou, researcher at INSEAD, for her editorial assistance and helpful comments in the final revisions of the book. Finally, I would like to thank Heidi Story for putting on a splendid party for our guests, and for putting up with me during the book's gestation.

Jonathan Story
Fontainebleau

Abbreviations

ABM	Anti Ballistic Missile
AMS	Aggregate Measure of Support
ASEAN	Association of South East Asian Nations
BDI	Federation of German Industry
BIS	Bank for International Settlements
CAD	Computer Aided Design
CAM	Computer Aided Manufacturing
CAP	Common Agricultural Policy
CBI	Confederation of British Industry
CCC	Customs Cooperation Council
CDU	Christian Democratic Union
CEPI	Centre d'Etudes Prospectives et d'Information Internationale
CES	European Trade Union Confederation
CET	Common External Tariff
CFE	Conventional Forces in Europe
CIM	Computer Integrated Manufacturing
CIS	Confederation of Independent States
CMEA/COMECON	Council for Mutual Economic Assistance
CNPF	National Council of the French Patronat
CoCom	Coordinating Committee
COPA	Committee of Professional Agricultural Organizations
CPSU	Communist Party of the Soviet Union
CSBM	Confidence and Security Building Measures
CSCE	Conference on Security and Cooperation in Europe
CSFR	Czech and Slovak Federal Republic
CSSR	Czech and Slovak Socialist Republics
CSU	Christian Social Union
DPC	Defence Planning Council
DTI	Department of Trade and Industry
EAEG	East Asian Economic Grouping
EBRD	European Bank for Reconstruction and Development
EC	European Communities

ECB	European Central Bank
ECSC	European Coal and Steel Community
ECU	European Currency Unit
EDC	European Defence Community
EDI	Electronic Data Interchange
EEA	European Economic Area
EEC	European Economic Community
EETRO	European External Trade Organization
EFA	European Fighter Aircraft
EFTA	European Free Trade Association
EMI	European Monetary Institute
EMS	European Monetary System
EMU	Economic and Monetary Union
ENA	Ecole Nationale d'Administration
END	European Nuclear Disarmament
EP	European Parliament
EPC	European Political Cooperation
EPU	European Payments Union; European Political Union
ERM	Exchange Rate Mechanism
ESCB/ECB	European System of Central Banks
ETA	Euzkadi ta Eskatasuna
ETSI	European Telecommunications Standardization Institute
ETUC	European Trade Union Congress
FCO	Foreign and Commonwealth Office
FDP	Free Democratic Party
FEN	Federation of National Education
FNSEA	National Federation of Unions of Agricultural Workers
FOFA	Follow-on-Forces Attack
FRG	Federal Republic of Germany
FTA	Free Trade Agreement
GAL	Grupos Antiterroristas de Liberacion
GATS	General Agreement on Trade and Services
GATT	General Agreement on Tariffs and Trade
GCEC	Greater Chinese Economic Circle
GDP	Gross Domestic Product
GDR	German Democratic Republic
GEMU	German Economic and Monetary Union
GNP	Gross National Product
HDTV	High(er) Definition Television
IBRD	International Bank for Reconstruction and Development
IEPG	Independent European Programme Group
IGC	Intergovernmental Conference
IMF	International Monetary Fund
IMEMO	Institute of World Economy and International Relations
INF	Intermediate-range Nuclear Forces

INSEAD	European Institute of Business Administration
IPR	Intellectual Property Rights
JETRO	Japanese External Trade Organization
LDP	Liberal Democratic Party
LODE	Law on the Right to Education
MBFR	Mutual and Balanced Force Reduction
MFA	Multi Fibre Agreement
MFN	Most Favoured Nation
MITI	Ministry of International Trade and Industry
MRP	Popular Republican Movement
MTR	Mid Term Review
NATO	North Atlantic Treaty Organization
NIC	Newly Industrialized Country
NTB	Non Tariff Barrier
OECD	Organization for Economic Cooperation and Development
OEEC	Organization for European Economic Cooperation
OIEC	Organization for International Economic Cooperation
OIRT	International Radio and Television Organization
OMA	Orderly Marketing Agreement
OPEC	Organization of Petroleum Exporting Countries
OPZZ	Official Trade Unions
PC	Personal Computer
PCE	Communist Party of Spain
PCI	Italian Communist Party
PSOE	Spanish Socialist Workers Party
PUWP	Polish United Workers' Party
RIIA	Royal Institute of International Affairs
RPR	Rassemblement Pour la Republique
SII	Structural Impediment Initiative
SACEUR	Supreme Allied Commander Europe
SACLANT	Supreme Allied Commander Atlantic
SBCD	Second Banking Coordination Directive
SDI	Strategic Defence Initiative
SDR	Special Drawing Rights
SEA	Single European Act
SNF	Short Range Nuclear Forces
TNC	Trade Negotiating Committee
TRIM	Trade Related Investment Measure
TTSS	International Institute of Strategic Studies
UCD	Union de Centro Democratico
UNGA	United Nations General Assembly
UNICE	Union of European Community Industries
UNR	Union pour la Nouvelle Republique
VER	Voluntary Export Restraint
WEU	West European Union
WIPO	World Intellectual Property Organization
WTO	Warsaw Treaty Organization

THE NEW EUROPE, 1992

NORWAY

SWEDEN

N
IRELAND

North
Sea

UNITED
KINGDOM

DENMARK

B

REPUBLIC
OF
IRELAND

Atlantic
Ocean

ISLE OF
MAN

NETHERLANDS

P

CHANNEL
ISLANDS

BELGIUM

GERMANY

BOHEMIA

LUXEMBOURG

CZECHOSLOVAK

S

FRANCE

SWITZERLAND

AUSTRIA

H

SLOVENIA

CROATIA

PORTUGAL

SPAIN

BOSNIA
AND
HERZEGOV
Y

ITALY

CORSICA

RALTAR

SARDINIA

BALEARIC
ISLANDS

Mediterranean Sea

SICILY

MALTA

PART I

Europe in the Cold War

1

Europe in the global state and market system

Jonathan Story

Europe of the 1990s has been forged by the complex dynamics inspiring the European Community's internal market programme, and by President Gorbachev's revolution from above, dismantling the Soviet Union as a single party state. Major changes, too, are underway on the world stage. As the cold war recedes, the postwar alliances have either disintegrated or undergone profound transformation. German unity, following the dramatic breaching of the Berlin Wall on 9 November 1989 turns German energies inwards to reconstruction of the former territories of the German Democratic Republic. The newly liberated peoples and states are engaged on the painful transition from party dictatorships and command economies towards market economies and constitutional governments.

In 1985, the main features of Europe were not too dissimilar from those of the early postwar years (de Carmoy and Story, 1986). Europe's division seemed set in stone. Stalin's territorial annexations and his suspicions of western motives had ended the wartime Grand Alliance against the Axis powers; led to Germany's and Europe's division; and had been a crucial factor in the creation of the two hostile alliances under the dominance of the United States and the Soviet Union. Monopoly party rule and centralized planning systems were clamped onto the satellite states. The lines of command ran through Moscow. Political pluralism and market economies prevailed in western Europe. Interdependent among each other and with the rest of the world, the states were particularly sensitive to changes in the global balance of power and in world markets. Their common affairs were managed through a complex diplomatic system, centring on four clusters of institutions: the European Communities (EC); the North Atlantic Treaty Organization (NATO); the Conference on Security and Cooperation in Europe (CSCE) between the thirty-five signatory states of the 1975 Helsinki Final Act; and the annual summits of the seven advanced industrialized countries' leaders, plus the President of the European Commission. The meetings, launched on the joint initiative of Paris and Bonn, symbolized Japan's emergence as the world's second largest, and most dynamic economy.

Yet the events of 1985 suggested a new flux in international relations.

Ronald Reagan's re-election to the Presidency in November 1984 was followed by Mikhail Gorbachev's nomination in March 1985 to the post of Secretary General of the Communist Party of the Soviet Union (CPSU). Arms talks between the two great powers, interrupted since 1983, were resumed at Geneva, where Reagan and Gorbachev met for preliminary discussions in November. In May, the annual summit was held in Bonn, where the western leaders agreed on a medium-term adjustment programme, bringing greater flexibility to domestic markets. In June, the EC launched its internal market programme to reduce non-tariff barriers on the same day as the accession treaties for Spain and Portugal were signed in Madrid and Lisbon. At the Milan EC Summit, the heads of state and government voted by majority to revise the 1957 Rome Treaty. In July, the tenth anniversary of the Helsinki Final Act witnessed disputes among the party-states over treatment of minorities, and frontiers. In September, the five leading financial powers met at the Plaza Hotel, New York, to head off protectionist pressures arising from trade conflicts between the United States, the EC and Japan. The accord was to manage a further fall in the dollar's rate on foreign exchange markets. In Seoul, US Secretary to the Treasury James Baker announced measures designed to ease the plight of the 15 major debtor countries in the developing world. At the December EC Summit in Luxembourg, the modified constitution was dubbed the Single European Act (SEA).

This contrast between the stability of the state system, and flux within it, had been a constant since 1945. The system evolved out of the collapse of its predecessor in the European civil wars of 1914 to 1945, but derived its particularities from the juxtaposition of its inherited competitiveness with the order provided by the presence of the two great powers. The postwar order was established through a prolonged process, starting in 1943, consolidated in its main features around 1955 and lasting through to the late 1960s. Its gradual transformation, accompanying the rhythm of world politics and markets, was made possible by the flowering of a specifically European state system. By 1985, its pole was western Europe which presented the Soviet Union with a political, economic and civilizational challenge in eastern Europe that it could no longer match. The change in European attitudes towards the Soviet Union in turn infused a greater assertiveness into relations with the United States (Rummel, 1990). But western Europe remained fragmented, and dependent for protection on the United States from a militarily threatening Soviet Union.

In order to trace Europe's historical evolution in a synthetic way, the first section briefly presents the broad framework for the book and for the subsequent discussion in this introductory chapter. The second section places Europe in the historical context of 1945, and brings the account forward to the end of the 1960s. The third section covers the transformation in the global state and market system, and Europe's place in it, from the late 1960s to the mid 1980s.

Some features of the European state system

In abstract form, the European state system may be said to hold four key features. It posits a condition of anarchy, where the unity of empire is absent. The political units are the sovereign states, fulfilling functionally similar tasks, but with their own particular histories, internal organization, and neighbourhoods. The western European states after 1945 developed as a society of states, complementing their traditional bilateral diplomatic relations with multilateral fora, where common norms were elaborated both for the conduct of their relations and, increasingly, for implementation in their domestic affairs. Finally, the states became enmeshed in a web of political and market interdependence, of a density that marks them out as a unique entity, but does not separate them from the global system.

(1) The European tradition of *realpolitik* posits a condition of anarchy, whose component political units – the states – submit to no government superior to themselves. They form a system to the extent that they interact with sufficient regularity to behave as parts of a whole (Aron, 1962, p. 103). Membership in the system is inescapable; all are effected differentially by events in any part of it; they are bound to the precept of self-help to tend to their own survival and prosperity (Waltz, 1979, pp. 91–2). State interest and necessity are the operating concepts of *realpolitik* (Meinecke, 1957); the balance of power in a system of self-seeking states, intent on avoiding the hegemony of any one, is the operating concept of the system. States are differentiated from the rest not only in domestic structures or values, but notably by the distribution of capabilities among them. Great powers are distinguished from the rest by the resources at their command, their relative self-sufficiency, and the respect paid them (Bull, 1980, pp. 200–29). No conflict of significance in the system may be settled without them. The actual configuration of the system's structure is conditioned by their number. This may vary between one and a few, in a gamut ranging from unipolar, to bipolar, tripolar or multipolar. Transitions from one configuration to another fundamentally alter the behaviour and expectations of all political units in the system.

The two principles of the secular state and of its bounded territoriality are one of Europe's most significant legacies to the modern world. Europe is the cradle of the secular sovereign state, and of its corollaries of competition or conflict. War and diplomacy are the two political forms through which interstate commerce is conducted. Competition invariably has stimulated the emergence of capitalism, as the most efficient way to provide the means for the state to pursue its particular purposes. Divergent performance has fed the rise and decline of powers in a constant rearrangement of their rank and status (Kennedy, 1989).

(2) The principle units in the condition of anarchy are the states. Sovereignty is the legal formula which grants a state a formal equality with all other members of the system. A sovereign political unit forms a community of people living together in a territory with their own internal organization and laws. The internal order allows for a specialization of tasks, predicated on a broad, but controversial distinction between the political domain of public policy and the private area rooted in the guarantee of individual or group rights. As a category of like units, states duplicate each other's tasks and functions (Waltz, 1979, p. 96). Internal political and market structures have their own particular arrangements, within which policy and market processes evolve. Each state conducts its affairs according to its own concept,

or rather according to the prevailing ideas among public officials about state interests. These are filtered, in that when one of a number of proposals has been selected for implementation within the territory, it becomes a binding command. The selection may be influenced by the presence and actions of other states (Waltz, p. 65). Foreign policy, however, remains in the realm of persuasion (Baldwin, 1985), as sovereigns are free to ignore a command.

(3)   The western European states after 1945 developed as a society of states, complementing their traditional bilateral diplomatic relations with multi-lateral fora, where common norms were elaborated both for the conduct of their relations and, increasingly, for implementation in their domestic affairs. The concept of a society of states stands in contrast to a system of states in which fragmentation breeds competition. A society is defined as forming a sub-set within the system, that is described by a sharing among the units of common interests and values (Bull, 1980, p. 13). The states bind themselves to cooperate in the working of joint institutions, according to a set of rules and involving the elaboration of mutually recognized norms. Membership in a society is voluntary, and implies the pursuit of joint goals according to the general rules that sustain the autonomy of each, and reduce or channel the incidence of frictions in their mutual relations. A society also presupposes that the principles of domestic political and market structures are similar. The organizing principles of western Europe are constitutional democracy, human rights, individual freedoms laced with social duties, and moderation in applying the principle of national self-determination.

A central feature of the western European society of states has been the density of relations between themselves and the rest of the world. Density refers to the growing number of actions by people impinging on other people's existence (Buzan et al., 1990, pp. 23–5). It is driven by the permanent revolution in technologies, communications and exchanges. Its prime political effect is to increase interdependence between states and societies across a wide spectrum of activities. This is particularly applicable to the modern practice of diplomacy through public officials – often in conjunction with private-sector representatives – where the western European society of states negotiate their differences and identify their common interests as sovereign states coexisting within a confined space. Bilateral and multi-lateral diplomatic channels provide public officials with the means of managing multiple linkages between domestic affairs and the external environment. No act of foreign policy is independent of an aspect of domestic politics; it requires the permanent exercise of judgement as to the appropriate balance between the satisfaction of domestic constituencies and the external requirements to achieve the best possible result for the state in the international arena. This external arena provides a host of opportunities to sustain the autonomy of the states (Nordlinger, 1981) against societal groups domestically, or to seek to export the costs of domestic policies or non-policies (Bachrach and Baratz, 1962, pp. 947–52) into interstate relations as non-negotiable items. In other words, western Europe's society as expressed through diplomatic relations rests on and sustains the states.

There is another specific feature of western Europe's society of states.

Each western European state is the point of intersection between its own cluster of domestic, European or global ties. No clear distinction may be made between European and global relations. This derives from the condition within anarchy in which the boundaries between the system and society of states are controversial. The United States, for instance, is a participant within Europe's society through bilateral relations with all member states, as well as through such multilateral fora as NATO and the Conference on Security and Cooperation in Europe (CSCE). But the EC's expressed aspiration 'to speak with one voice' implies a distinction between the EC as one cluster within the western European society of states, and the United States. The lack of distinction also follows from the practice of sovereign states within western Europe to use relations within the global state system to sustain the state's autonomy against the demands of other states, either outside or within western Europe's society. All western European states are 'Trojan horses', within the society's figurative walls. Nowhere is the web of outward-looking diplomatic relations between western European states, and between each one of them and the rest of the world, so dense. All the other states in the world system participate to some degree in European society, either through bilateral relations or through their presence in – or their accreditation with – the varied multilateral fora. These multilateral fora have core functions, overlapping competences and variable membership. Western Europe is the hub of world diplomatic relations, because diplomacy lies at the heart of European politics.

(4)   Finally, the states became enmeshed in a web of political and market interdependence, of a density that marks them out as a unique entity, but does not separate them from the global system. The conditions for complex interdependence are provided with the existence of multiple channels for exchanges between societies and complemented by extensive consultative networks, which are indicative of the overlap between domestic and foreign policy characteristic of relations between developed industrial countries (Nye and Keohane, 1977). States are still seen as the central pillars of the system, but their ability to pursue their particular ideals through intermediate policies which are aimed at increasing the Community's productive power and culture have been undermined by the workings of the established domestic principles.

Two competing interpretations derive from this contestable observation. One holds that transnational transactions imply wide areas of discretion for citizens to conduct their affairs with others (Merle, 1984). Such transactions tie local into global markets, over which no single authority exists. The dynamics in markets is provided by competition between state policies, but more substantially over technological leadership between corporations (Strange, 1988), where a crucial determinant is the differential ability of states and societies to harness human capital, innovativeness, information and financial resources to the common pursuit of productive power and culture. There is therefore a crucial interaction between the domain of the state's resources and transnational transactions. Three key relations are thereby identified between states (Merle, 1984, p. 170): diplomatic relations, transnational interactions at the level of societies and markets, and interactions between states and their domestic domain of the transnational arena.

The second interpretation holds that public officials are overwhelmed by the transformation of domestic society and by the volume of interstate transactions (Wallace, 1971). With universal suffrage, the political process has become more complex. A widening scope of government activities has introduced a host of divergent interests into the domain of public policy. Policy coherence is an arduous task. Interdependence has broken down the older boundaries between external and internal affairs. Domestic matters have been externalized, ending the monopoly of foreign ministries in the daily conduct of a state's foreign policy. Multilateral organizations in the European society of states have been created with a view to managing common concerns. State interests therefore no longer provide clear criteria for the conduct of affairs in the state system. This has had two effects: first, government departments, interests or political parties build coalitions across frontiers; second, a multitude of centres of power seek to coordinate their own domain at the level of the state, the multilateral fora, interstate or transnational exchanges. Overall, these multiple centres become mired in a tangle of complexity. Only a chosen few make decisions. Complexity derives from the multitude of tasks and interests involved.

Strategies to break out of complex interdependence have been multiple. But all require the cooperation of the states, which remain jealous of their prerogatives and position in the global state and market system. Proponents of state prerogatives focus on the interactions of policy with their domestic domain of the transnational arena. They argue that the conditions of complex interdependence severely restrict the efficiency and effectiveness of common policies agreed and enacted on by states (Nau, 1990). Policy actions applied within the boundaries of a sovereign state have infinitely greater chance of taking effect. But interactions between states are transmitted through transnational flows. Incompatible domestic policy actions may be avoided through negotiations, or they may be accepted as the price to pay for policy in conditions of anarchy. In the latter case, the key variable is the impact of the domestic policy actions of the predominant regional or global power that is transmitted through transnational channels into the domestic domain of the dependent states. The politics of complex interdependence is thus about the distribution of costs in policy and market adjustment between states. It does not escape the logic of the state system, in which states are distinguished by their capabilities.

Bipolarity and the postwar order, 1943 to 1967-8

Whatever the details of a possible peace settlement, five events in the course of 1945 prefigured the pattern of postwar Europe. One was the strained nature of relations between the western allies and the Soviet Union, particularly over the future of eastern Europe and Germany. This had become evident in the differences that had emerged over Poland, well before Marshall Zhukov's army groups entered the suburbs of Berlin in April 1945. Another was the plight of Germany and former German occupied territories, after the deprivations of war and exactions of Hitler's regime. Liberation by the armed forces of the wartime allies had exacted its own toll of sufferings. A third was formed by the draft Charter of the United Nations, signed by fifty-one states at the San Francisco Conference of April–June. The United Nations Charter tokened to a liberal vision of a world, with defined responsibilities of the great powers in the Security Council, the sovereign equality of states in the General Assembly, and geared to opening access for all participants in world markets. The fourth was the revelations by the advancing allied armies of the concentration camps, and the industrial organization of mass murder. Human rights were subsequently written into constitutions, and received institutional expression as core values for western Europe in the European Convention of Human Rights of 1950. The fifth event was the dropping of the atomic bombs by the United States on the Japanese cities of Hiroshima and Nagasaki on 6 and 9 August. Stalin immediately ordered research and development of a nuclear capability (Holloway, 1984). The advent of nuclear weapons heralded a fundamental break in the nature of warfare, as their possessors could initiate war with absolute violence against an enemy (Howard, 1983, pp. 59–73). The year 1945 marked a deep rupture in Europe's past.

The European balance of power

The origins of the European state system may be traced to the years 1492 and 1494. From inception, its cardinal feature was the dialectics between extra- and intra-European dynamics. The first date marks the fall of Granada, and the unity of Spain under Ferdinand and Isabelle. The Genoan venturer, Colombus, set sail in his quest for the Indies, leading to the Spanish crown's claim of general sovereignty over the Americas, and exclusive rights of navigation in the Caribbean and the Pacific. In 1494, the rivalry between the Italian city states pulled Charles VIII of France into the peninsula, and later Spain and the German empire of Charles V. Machiavelli's hopes to find a prince with the wit to unite Italy by stratagem, and then to preserve that unity through the creation of a civic polity, were dashed. France succeeded to Spain as the power with hegemonial ambitions in Europe. The Treaty of Westphalia, signed in 1648, consecrated Spain's demise, as well as Germany's fragmentation into a multitude of petty states. Britain established its extra-European supremacy over France in 1759, the 'year of victories' in India and North America. Pitt the Younger's alliances with Russia, Austria and Prussia, checked, and then defeated Napoleon's continental system. Britain became the world's prime manufacturing centre, and herald for free trade. Prussia's response was to organize the northern German states within a customs union, and then win unity by force of arms against Austria in the battle of Sadowa in 1866. Defeat of France in 1870 was celebrated in January 1871 by the proclamation of the German Empire in the palace of Versailles. Germany's subsequent rise to eminence was made possible by the conversion of savings through the new commercial banks into long term financing for Germany's new industries. Social democracy was held at bay through the Prussian aristocracy's hegemony in the Federal Council. The Diet, elected by universal suffrage, had little weight in shaping public affairs. There were consequently two dimensions of the 'German problem' between 1870 and 1945: its domestic organization, and the incorporation of a united Germany into Europe (Calleo, 1978).

Divergent performance fed the rise and decline of powers in a constant rearrangement of their rank and status. Settlements involved the digestion of the smaller or weaker states. Allies were sought after with a view to accumulating external resources, in addition to those that could be raised internally. But the price of alliance could entail for the weaker states a sacrifice in the choice of market specialization, as evidenced for instance by Portugal's abandonment of textiles manufacturing following the conclusion of the 1704 Methuen Treaty with Great Britain in defence against Spain. The same logic inspired Friedrich List, in his *National System of Political Economy*, written as a rejoinder to British free-trade policy. The British, he argued, sought to make 'Germans humble themselves to the position of hewers of wood and drawers of water' (List, 1977, p. 388). Accumulated wealth was the outcome of past policy, and not the result of an abstract interplay of supply and demand in cosmopolitan markets. The national community's productive power was best enhanced through manufacturing, and the state's major task was to pursue this through commercial policy. Germany subsequently developed an organized capitalism, characterized by cartels and combines. It contrasted notably to the small firms and open markets prevailing in liberal Britain.

European states traced their own particular path through time. Spain, France, the Netherlands and Great Britain attained statehood in the sixteenth and seventeenth centuries. Poland, after centuries as a major power, was partitioned between Prussia, Austria and Russia in the late eighteenth century, to re-emerge as a sovereign state in 1918. Italian and German unification were acts of statecraft, implemented according to the traditional criteria of European *realpolitik*. But they were also informed by the twin ideals of liberalism and nationalism, emerging from the British, American and French revolutions. Liberalism proposed the internal transformation of monarchical or oligarchic states, to allow for the participation of citizens in public affairs. Individualism was the guiding tenet of political, as of market liberalism. Private property rights were to be assured by a state with functions limited to maintaining internal order and external security. Nationalism referred to the geographic or cultural bounds of community under the law. Shaping a nation's future enjoined a drive to statehood, portending the disintegration of pre-existing political entities, notably the multinational empires of central and south-eastern Europe. It required the political activation of mass publics, bringing a host of formerly excluded forces into the domain of public policy, while the multiplication of sovereigns representing a heterogeneity of cultures raised the incidence of competition between states. As the French revolution introduced conscription for war, so nationalism democratized diplomacy, and transformed the state system.

The different paths to statehood accentuated the diversity in domestic organization between the European states. Each state developed its own political structures that evolved out of the manner of insertion into world markets. In the late nineteenth century, the development of long distance transport brought low cost cereals and beef from the Americas and Australasia to Europe (Tracy, 1982). Population pressure ensured an elastic demand for cheap foods. Responses by producer interests to competition from non-European sources ran along state lines. Denmark and the Netherlands developed their farm cooperatives to add value through the import of foodstuffs to domestic production for sale in British and German markets. German rye producers in Prussia opted for protection, harming the trade from eastern Europe, but securing their position through alliance with German steel producers. France adopted the Méline tariff, perpetuating existent peasant farming to the benefit of low cost producers in the Paris bassin. Italy and Spain followed suit. Great Britain stuck to the 1845 repeal of the Corn Laws. The result was the collapse of land prices, the fatal weakening of the landed interest, and the creation of a cheap food system geared to imports from the Americas and Australasia. These different policy adjustments of the late nineteenth century provided the points of departure for the creation of the EC's agricultural policy in the 1960s.

The interaction between the competition between states and technological progress compounded Europe's lead over the rest of the world. Technologically backward areas of the globe were incorporated into Europe's balance of power struggles, with the allocation of non-European territories used as a means to settle inter-European disputes. Over time, this expansion of the European states transformed the world into a states and markets system of global dimensions. The process, initiated with the inclusion first of the United States, and then of the Latin American republics, was accentuated with the rise to world position of the United States and the Soviet Union, and with the dissolution of the European and Japanese colonial empires in Africa, the Middle East, and Asia. By 1985, the number of states in the global system had multiplied from the fifty-one which signed the San Francisco Treaty in 1945, setting up the United Nations Organization, to over 160. The multiplication of the number of states was accompanied by an accentuation in the divergence between the capabilities of the political units in the system.

The European civil wars of 1914 to 1945 dealt a crippling blow to the Eurocentric state system, predicated on the maintenance of the balance of power between the European great powers. For the first time in the four centuries prior to 1918, the Versailles Treaty reversed the pattern of concentration in the number of states. The idea of national self-determination was applied to the multinational empires of Russia, Austria-Hungary and Turkey, leading in the direction of fragmentation. It was not applied to Austria, in that the victors prohibited its joining the new Germany. After 1945, the experience of fragmentation was not repeated in, but outside of Europe. Neither of the two world powers were European. The main European states were dwarfed. Europe formed a sub-system in the global system. The member states, with few exceptions, could not ensure their own security, depending for protection on one or other of the two extra-European powers (Deporte, 1979). Warfare had been revolutionized by the exponential progress of technologies, and by new types of revolutionary struggle. The scope of the state system was on the scale of the two dominant powers. All states risked being caught in a global war. All were enmeshed in the web of world markets. Modern communications and transport shrank the boundaries of distance. As the rivalries of the great powers were global in scope, decisions of global significance were taken outside Europe, and the results felt within (Northedge, 1981, p. 74). Europe had become an object of world politics, with the shots being called by the great powers.

The reluctant allies

War was the cement between the three great powers, and once victory was achieved, it was inevitable that the incompatibilities between their respective economic and political systems would come to the fore. Churchill, Roosevelt and Stalin, meeting at Yalta in the Crimea in February 1945, toasted their victory, but as Stalin told Churchill, 'an alliance against the common enemy is something clear and understandable. Far more complicated is an alliance after the war for securing lasting peace and the fruits of victory' (Churchill, 1954, p. 317).

Since its foundation, the Soviet Union as a party-state had seen the world through a dialectical prism (Ulam, 1974; Levesque, 1987). Socialism survived in fundamental hostility to capitalism, and diplomacy was one tool among others to exploit the contradictions between capitalist states. Germany had been a constant source of anguish. Following the German social democrats' vote for war funds in 1914, hopes vested by socialists in the working classes as a force for international peace had been shattered. Lenin split with the social democrats. The German high command smuggled him to Petrograd in 1917, and then imposed a Carthaginian peace, consecrated at the March 1918 Treaty of Brest Litovsk, where Lenin surrendered immense tracts of territory to extract Russia from the war. Lenin's dream of winning Germany to the revolution in 1919 failed, as the German social democrats established the Weimar Republic and signed the Versailles Treaty. The treaty branded Germany as guilty of the war and imposed heavy reparation payments. Germany and the Soviet Union, as the two outcasts of the postwar settlement, concluded the Rapallo Treaty of 1922 enabling the German armed forces to train on Russian territory in avoidance of the treaty clauses, which had restricted the size of German armed forces.

State foreign policy took early precedence over party foreign policies. With the military defeat, and then the collapse of the central empires of Germany and Austria-Hungary, the Russian leaders sought to organize the revolutionary movements across Europe. The Comintern was to be a world-wide party, whose national branches would be the local branches. At the July–August 1920 congress, the constitution was laid out in the form of the '21 Conditions', whereby the delegates were required inter alia to accept: near military discipline under centralized leadership, the supranational authority of the Comintern, the defence of the Soviet Union, the advocacy of the dictatorship of the proletariat, the vilification of reformists as class traitors, communist penetration of trade unions, support of colonial revolts, and the establishment of parallel, paramilitary organizations in preparation for underground activity. The resulting split in working-class organizations thus came to run between the communists, and the social democrats. The latter adhered to social reform through parliamentary methods. In 1927, Stalin declared that the social democrats in Germany were the communists' principal enemy, opening the way to the National Socialist seizure of power in 1933.

Stalin launched the first Five-Year Plan of forced industrialization in 1928, entailing in time the expropriation of the peasantry, famine, the consolidation of the labour camps and the deaths of millions. In Europe, communist parties then were mobilized to form 'anti-fascist' alliances, winning over socialist parties to form 'popular fronts'. But conservative governments in Britain and France were scared away from dealings with Moscow, while Italy, Germany, and Japan – now deeply engaged in its China conquests – formed in 1936–7 the anti-Comintern Pact. When Britain sought to maintain its positions in Asia through a temporary deal with Hitler at Munich in 1938, Stalin drifted towards rapprochement with Germany, confirmed in the pact of August 1939, where the two powers agreed to divide up Poland, with large tracts being absorbed into the Soviet Union. Hitler created the infamous general government in the rump Poland, and in June 1941 launched the Barbarossa campaign on the Soviet Union. Continental Europe's labour, farms and factories were harnessed to Hitler's war machine. European Jewry, along with gypsies, and other opponents of the National Socialists, were rounded up into the concentration camps and annihilated in the flames of the Holocaust.

The turning point in the war in Europe came in 1943, with the surrender of the remnants of the Sixth German army at Stalingrad, followed by the collapse of the Wehrmacht's tank divisions at the battle of the Kursk salient in July 1943. Churchill and Roosevelt finally informed Stalin at Teheran in November 1943 of their plans for Operation Overlord, launched onto the Normandy beaches on 6 June, 1944. As the Red Army rolled towards Germany, and into Rumania and Bulgaria, there was little that the United States and Great Britain could do to prevent the Soviet Union's domination of central and south-eastern Europe. Indeed, at Yalta in February 1945, Stalin agreed to enter the war against Japan, in return for possession of the Sakhaline, and the Kurile islands. He also agreed to a treaty with Chiang Kaï-Chek, Roosevelt's protégé. By the time of Germany's surrender in May, 1945, the Red Army occupied the area stretching from the Baltic, through Poland and eastern Germany, to Hungary, Austria, Rumania, and Bulgaria. Yugoslavia was in the hands of Tito's communist partisans. Greece fell under British influence, but civil war broke out there in 1944. The communist guerrilla movement refused to surrender arms, and turned against the government. It took the Greek government – with British military backing – a year to re-establish control over the territory. The world powers thus met simultaneously in Europe and the Pacific.

The United States came to its legacy as the world's greatest power with a vastly different history and outlook to the Soviet Union (Aron, 1973). The revolution of 1776 was also a victory in the struggle for independence against a European monarch. Self-determination of nations and individual rights for life, liberty and property against an overweening government were the twin ideals, manifested in foreign policy through swings from isolation to an assertive national purpose to bring the American message to a corrupt world (Osgood, 1953). The advice of George Washington's farewell address not to become entangled in foreign alliances had been heeded, with energies devoted to the continental expansion of the United States from sea to sea. Since 1865, the United States had never suffered the cataclysm of social revolution and war on its own territory. Involvement in the war in 1917 had been presented by President Wilson to the American and European public in terms of the relevance of the US experience to the old Europe. A world safe for democracy was to be built on the principles of self-determination,

the rights of small nations, and a League of Nations to adjudicate differences. But the disintegration of the Austrian–Hungarian and Turkish empires into their successor states, French insistence on pinning a guilt clause
to Germany as the cause of war in 1914, and the US Senate's repudiation
of the Versailles Treaty ended Wilson's hopes of mending Europe's ways.
The United States retreated into detachment, and then after the 1929 Wall
Street financial crash, to massive tariff protection. As the United States had
become since 1914, the world's prime creditor, tariff protection made debt
repayment impossible. The world was dragged into America's monetary
vortex. It was not Roosevelt's New Deal policies of the 1930s that pulled the
United States from the depression, but the United States entry to war in
response to the Japanese air attack on Pearl Harbor in December 1941.

Japan's forceful bid for supremacy in the Pacific in the sea battles of
1941–2, dealt a fatal blow to Europe's colonial interests throughout the
region. But the application to devastating military effect of US industrial
might culminated in the nuclear attacks on Hiroshima and Nagasaki.
The United States emerged from the war in vastly better condition than the
Soviet Union, which had borne by far the largest burden of war against
the Axis powers. Compared to the Soviet Union, the United States suffered
minimal losses in human lives. It was later conceded that the Soviet Union
lost twenty-six million lives during the war, not counting the wounded or
the material destruction. Victory confirmed the United States as a truly
global power, with armed forces in Europe, Asia Pacific, the Mediterranean
and the Gulf. It enjoyed a monopoly on nuclear weapons. Industrial output
had soared, making the United States the world's main producer of military
and consumer goods. It was the world's bread-basket. The United States
held two-thirds of the world's gold stock. The dollar, convertible at $35
dollars an ounce, was the world's key currency. It was the prime world
exporter, so that globalist views that the causes of the 1930s depression lay
in trade protectionism, competitive economic policies and restricted access
to raw materials, neatly dovetailed with US business interests in opening up
world markets to prevent a postwar recession. It was only slowly that
Washington moved away from aspirations to establish a new world order
predicated on the United Nations – and its ancillary organizations such as
the International Monetary Fund, the International Bank for Reconstruction
and Development (IBRD) and then the General Agreement on Tariffs and
Trade (GATT) – towards a US hegemony that emphasized the incompatibilities
with the Soviet Union's domestic order and external ambitions.

The third power in 1945 was Britain. France and Germany had succumbed to defeat. France's economy had stagnated in the 1930s. Riven by
political and class rivalries, it drifted to 1940 and the ignominy of defeat.
Reliance on Britain as a counterbalance to Germany was revealed as
worthless, when the allied armies folded in front of the compact attacks of
German tanks, aircraft and infantry. The war then turned to a struggle
between Britain, on its home base, the Balkans and the Middle East, and
Germany as the dominant power on the European mainland. Both had
stagnated in the vulnerable international economy of the 1920s. But both
had shown marked revival in the 1930s, as their arms race accelerated.
Britain's rapid growth of new industries in the decade was then coined by
1940 into a 50 per cent greater output than Germany in aircraft, as well as

in tanks (Kennedy, 1989, p. 441). Neither won a decisive advantage in their air warfare, and peripheral battles. Only with the boost in arms production in 1943 under Speer as Economics Minister, did Festland Europa overtake Britain in arms output. This massive German industrial machine was shorn of one-quarter of its productive capacity by war or dismantlement, leaving the remainder to fuel the Federal Republic's economic revival in the 1950s.

The central point of Britain's position was not economic decline, but a conscious act of policy to merge Britain's future security in alliance with the United States. Inevitably, the 'special relationship' was as the United States' junior partner, but one with considerable means. New industries had been adopted on a grand scale. The new economics of Keynes provided a theoretical framework for fiscal and financial policy. All parties were committed to social reforms. Financial aid was forthcoming from the United States; lend-lease enabled Britain to be supplied without immediate payment asked in return. Many dominions had achieved self-government and India was well on the way there prior to the war. The process was accelerated by the signing of the Atlantic Charter between Roosevelt and Churchill in August 1941. The ideals of self-determination, individual freedoms, and access to world markets proclaimed the crusade around which the United Nations formed in January 1942. Churchill's Grand Alliance was cemented by the creation of combined chiefs of staff along with economic boards. This co-operation culminated in the United Nations organizations, and then in the regional economic and security arrangements of the late 1940s.

Britain's weakness was financial. During the negotiations setting up the IMF, the British had sought to lay the foundations for an Anglo-American leadership in international financial affairs. But the United States bore no equal. As soon as the war against Japan was over, President Truman terminated lend-lease to Britain. As a major debtor, the newly elected Labour government could have withheld payments unless US markets were opened to British products. But Commonwealth countries had built up claims on the Bank of England, denominated in sterling. Labour wanted to continue domestic expansion, so the terms of the December 1945 loan agreement negotiated by Keynes with the United States provided for an early return of Britain to free trade within the Commonwealth markets, and sterling convertibility (Gardner, 1980). The short experiment underlined the difficulty Britain would have to coexist with a continental European economy: sterling convertibility in 1947 exhausted the newly replenished British reserves, as the continental Europeans rushed from sterling to dollars to keep their economies running. Convertibility was suspended in August, and Britain lined up with the other European countries for Marshall aid to cover its needs in dollars.

Germany and Poland

The incompatibilities between the three powers (McNeill, 1953; Fontaine, 1965–7) came to the fore most clearly over Poland, whose independence Britain had vainly gone to war to defend in 1939. President Roosevelt had also to take account of the seven million Poles in the United States. Stalin's priority was to consolidate a sphere of influence in central Europe.

In August–September 1944, the Red Army stood on the Vistula, while five German divisions massacred the Polish resistance in Warsaw, linked to the London exile government. The pro-Soviet Polish National Liberation committee was created, and installed at Lublin. The conferences of Yalta in February 1945, and at Potsdam in July–August barely concealed the tensions. The three leaders agreed to compensate Poland with a western extension of territory running along the Oder-Neisse rivers. Final settlement would await a peace conference with Germany. The Lublin government was to be 're-organized on a broader democratic basis'. Each power would occupy a zone of Germany; a fourth was assigned to France. A joint control commission for Germany was to be established in Berlin. Its general principles were defined. It was agreed that a conference should be called at San Francisco to draft a Charter for the United Nations. The Declaration on Liberated Europe committed the powers to facilitate 'the earliest possible establishment through free elections of governments responsive to the will of the people' (Grenville, 1974, pp. 226–34).

In the period 1945–7, wherever the Red Army had entered, Stalin used intimidation or force to impose the primacy of communist parties or flanking organizations within broader coalition governments. Yugoslavia and Czechoslovakia were the exceptions. Tito's partisans had acquired complete power by their own exertions. The Czechoslovak leaders, Mazaryk and Benes, gave priority in relations to Moscow. They were comforted in this by the memory of the 1938 Munich accords, where France and Britain had betrayed the country's independence to Hitler. The Czech communists were the strongest party. As with Poland's expulsion of the Silesian Germans, Czechoslovakia's expropriation of the Sudeten Germans bound them to the Soviet Union in fear of a revived Germany placing territorial demands. But Prague also aspired to act as a bridge between western and eastern Europe. Stalin could hope that détente would lead to a gradual shift of the balance of forces in favour of the western parties in government in Rome or Paris, while keeping open the prospect of western aid in the reconstruction of the Soviet Union.

Europe's division was precipitated by events in the Gulf, the Mediterranean and in Germany. President Roosevelt's meeting with Saudi Arabia's King Ibn Saud, had laid the groundwork for the special relation between Washington and Riyadh. US action in 1946 stalled Stalin's ambitions to annex the northern provinces of Iran. In August 1946, Stalin demanded from Turkey the control of the Straits, and restitution of territory taken from the Soviet Union in 1918. The United States moved warships into the eastern Mediterranean. Simultaneously, the Greek civil war broke out again, with the communist partisans receiving strong support from Yugoslavia. In February 1947, the British government invited the United States to provide economic and military aid to the Greek government. Meanwhile, it had become clear that the powers could not agree on Germany's future. The United States and the Soviet Union suspected one another of seeking to pull Germany into its own sphere. France opposed any recreation of a central government. Britain sought to limit the costs of occupation. The British and US occupation zones were merged in January 1947. At the March–April Moscow conference, the powers failed to settle their differences.

The US policy of containment ended the search for cooperation with

Stalin. No negotiated settlement would be possible until the Soviet Union had changed. Its inherent hostility to the western powers required a policy of strength. There were two variants. One stressed US support for Europe's economic revival. The other proposed military preparedness (Gaddis, 1982). The balance moved from the first towards the second. In March 1947, Truman announced US aid to anti-communist forces in Greece and Turkey, promising to 'support free peoples who are resisting attempted subjugation by armed minorities or by outside pressures'. Within a few weeks, communist party participation terminated in the governments of France, Italy, Belgium and the Scandinavian countries. In June 1947, Secretary of State Marshall launched the idea of a long-term US undertaking to grant aid in support of a cooperative regional effort to achieve a rapid reconstruction in Europe. 'Its purpose', Marshall declared, 'should be the revival of a working economy in the world so as to permit the emergence of political and social conditions in which free institutions can exist'. Germany would be an evident beneficiary. Its inclusion would pull Europe's prime industrial power fully into the western camp.

The doctrine of the world as divided into two camps was expounded in September 1947 by Zhdanov, Stalin's chief lieutenant. There was no third way between the imperialist camp under the leadership of the United States, and the democratic camp, headed by the Soviet Union and backed by 'fraternal communist parties in all countries', and by 'all progressive and democratic forces'. Prague and Warsaw were subsequently ordered to desist from participation in the Marshall Plan. This, and the Czechoslovak communists' sole seizure of power in Prague in February 1948, prompted Britain, France and the Benelux countries to sign in March the Brussels Treaty pledging military aid and economic cooperation. This was one prelude to involving the United States directly in Europe's defence. The other was the three western powers' decision in March to unify their occupation zones; to call a constitutional assembly, and to introduce the currency reform, establishing the deutschmark (DM) in June. Parallel steps were taken in East Germany. The Soviet Union's attempt to blockade Berlin was answered by an allied airlift in relief of the city. The North Atlantic alliance came into existence in April 1949. In May, the Soviet forces lifted the blockade around Berlin. The German Democratic Republic (GDR) was created in October 1949, one month after the constitution of the Federal Republic of Germany (FRG).

The preamble to the constitution committed the Federal Republic to seek reunification by peaceful means. Human rights were written into the text, and a complicated system sketched out in which administration was located mainly in the regional governments and legislation in Bonn, the new capital. Berlin retained a special status, where the four powers retained responsibility. The client party-states across central and south-eastern Europe took Moscow as a model. Their economies were cast into the Soviet mould, entailing the bureaucratic allocation of resources through the means of a central plan. Land reforms were imposed, and priority given to heavy industry. Finland managed to secure Stalin's acquiescence in a neutrality status in the Treaty of 1948, while Yugoslavia broke with Moscow in the same year, when Tito refused to accept Stalin's tutelage. Moscow's hegemony over the satellite party-states took the form of bilateral treaties, with strong controls being exerted through political and military channels. In 1949 a multilateral economic organization, the Council for Mutual Economic Assistance (CMEA, or COMECON), acquired a shadowy existence. Only after 1957 did COMECON gain some significance.

The Washington Treaty, setting up the Atlantic alliance, constituted a broad, but unspecified commitment, by the United States, Canada, and the ten European founding members (Belgium, Britain, Denmark, France, Iceland, Italy, Luxemburg, The Netherlands, Norway, and Portugal) to come to their mutual protection. The assumption was that the provision of an adequate military shield served to convince Moscow that aggressive actions would not go unopposed. In the longer term, economic recovery in western Europe would provide the means for self-help. Those were the sole conditions on which the US Senate could be brought to sign an entangling alliance (Osgood, 1962) with European states, reserving each member state's right to determine its course of action in the light of circumstances. Such a minimal commitment failed to alleviate fears in France and elsewhere that, in the event of an invasion of Europe, the light forces available would have to retreat, leaving the continent open again to the terrors of liberation by war. The alternative, stipulated by Congress, was 'an integrated defence of the North Atlantic area', involving a specialization of tasks between signatory states and a civilian and military command structure.

Alliance assumptions on the adequacy of a military shield composed of the US monopoly on nuclear weapons, and the ready compatibility of economic recovery with security were shattered by two events. One was the explosion of a Soviet nuclear device in August 1949. Anxiety about nuclear war rose steadily over the coming years. With the strains of rearmament aggravating economic and political problems in alliance countries, the 1952 Lisbon Atlantic Council proposal for a quadrupling of member states' divisions, and a substantial surge in aircraft, remained a dead letter. The United States in October 1953 decided that the main deterrent of an aggression against western Europe by the Soviet Union would be the use of its atomic forces in the form of massive retaliation aimed at the Soviet Union's cities. In other words, NATO Europe imported US nuclear protection on the cheap, as western nuclear and technological superiority readily compensated for any superiority in numbers possessed by the Soviet Union's armed forces. Equally, though, as the Soviet Union's nuclear diplomacy developed, NATO Europe's concerns of Soviet military incursions waned, while worries about US nuclear retaliation waxed.

The second event to shatter western complacency was the entry of the Chinese communists to Beijing in October, 1949. Communist predominance on the Eurasian landmass seemed confirmed with the conclusion of a Sino-Soviet treaty in February 1950. The State Department's NSC 68 memorandum of April 1950 urged a political, economic and military strategy for the security of the free world (Acheson, 1987, pp. 373–81). In June 1950, North Korean troops invaded the south, with Chinese and Soviet support. President Truman thereupon announced military intervention in the Korean conflict, United States naval protection for the Chinese nationalists on Taiwan, and support for the French forces opposing the communists in Indochina. In September 1951, the United States signed a peace and security treaty with Japan. Japan subsequently devoted its resources to industrial expansion under US military protection, and entered Asian markets as European colonial tariff schemes were dismantled. US predominance in the Asia-Pacific region provided the context in which the Asia-Pacific economies were to prosper.

The Korean war proved crucial to Europe's later development: it opened two decades of US foreign policy, predicated on global military containment. The US military positions in Japan, Korea, the Philippines, and then in Indochina, were supplemented by a network of alliances and military bases, complementary to the North Atlantic Treaty Organization, and strung around the periphery of the Soviet Union in Asia and the Middle East. For the United States, Asia was the scene of two major wars over Korea and Vietnam, informed by the policy of containment. The Korean war ended in 1953, and was followed by negotiations with Moscow or Beijing over Germany, Austria, Korea and Indochina. Of the three, only Austria escaped partition. The interactions between events in the Pacific and Europe were intensified by the fact that both the United States and the Soviet Union were Pacific and European powers. The dynamics of the Pacific balance came to affect the central balance between the great powers and European relations with both of them. The rhythm of US global policies was set by fluctuations in the domestic political definition of the Soviet threat, which in turn set the tone for demands in budget allocations for military purposes. The domestic politics of the world's key state became a central consideration for European states. US policies were punctuated by massive surges in military spending that placed severe strains on the national or international economy, followed by attempts to curtail outlays or to have them financed at minimum cost to the cohesiveness of US society. US commitments regularly tended to outrun the means to sustain them (Osgood, 1981, pp. 465–502).

In Europe, the Korean war hastened the creation of an Atlantic command structure, with General Eisenhower's appointment in December 1950 as Supreme Allied Commander Europe (SACEUR). The Atlantic Council, attended by Foreign and Defence Ministers, was presided over by a European secretary general. Its role was to define arms policies and defence strategies on the recommendation of the SACEUR. His authority extended from the North Cape and North Sea, to the Mediterranean, and from the Atlantic seaboard to the eastern border of Turkey. The command included US land, air and naval forces, notably the Second Fleet in the Northern Atlantic and the Sixth Fleet in the Mediterranean. Some European armed forces were assigned in peacetime to NATO commands, but remained also under national control. US bilateral ties were reinforced with Turkey and Greece, and the two countries entered NATO in 1952. In October 1953, the United States concluded the Madrid Pact with General Franco's Spain, securing the Atlantic approaches to the Mediterranean.

On the outbreak of the Korean war, Adenauer's suggestion of a German military contingent as a contribution to forward defence in Europe prompted the US State Department in September 1950 to propose the creation of ten German divisions to be placed under NATO command. Paris in October advanced the idea of a supranational European army, under effective French control. This conflict between the German search for equality, and France's demand for security was resolved by Bonn and Paris agreeing in 1951 to equality, implying the dissolution of a French military identity in a European army under SACEUR. The Paris treaty providing for a European Defence Community (EDC) was signed in May 1952, in parallel to the Bonn Treaty terminating the occupation statute (Fursdon, 1979). The United States saw a European army as a means to reduce the US troop presence, but French opinion turned against the idea, which was rejected by the National Assembly in August 1954. The result was a British scheme for German participation in NATO. The Paris accords of October 1954 enlarged the 1948 Brussels Treaty membership to include the FRG and Italy. The German government agreed not to acquire atomic, bacteriological or chemical weapons. In return, Germany's sovereignty was affirmed, and the allies pledged anew their support for the German objective of national unity. Britain promised to maintain forces on the continent. The Federal Republic was admitted in May 1955 into the Atlantic alliance, and its nascent armed forces were placed under NATO command.

Stalin sought to counter western strategy by his offer in March 1952 of German unification. The price was neutrality and abandonment of the Federal Republic's claims to the lands east of the Oder-Neisse. Adenauer rejected it, insisting that a united Germany be able to chose its own alliances. With Stalin's death in March 1953, an alternative route was followed by the police chief, Beria, whom First Secretary of the CPSU Khrushchev later alleged had planned to drop the East German regime, in exchange for Germany's neutrality (*Neues Deutschland*, 14 March, 1963). Whatever the truth, the general strike of June 1953 in East Germany revealed the strength of anti-communist sentiment in the population. The subsequent crackdown by Soviet troops contributed to Adenauer's electoral victory in the general elections of September 1953, confirming wide public support for his western policy. Moscow moved to integrate the GDR into its own system. But greater latitude was granted to the client party-states to pursue their own economic 'roads to socialism', while in May 1955, a few days after the Paris Treaties, the Warsaw Pact was signed. The 'treaty of friendship, cooperation and mutual assistance' established a supreme command for the member states, based in Moscow. The Supreme Commander was a Red Army officer.

With both spheres of influence in place, a policy of détente predicated on mutual recognition of the interests of the other could develop. The limits to accommodation were defined by the incompatibility of political systems. The western powers rejected the Soviet Union's offer of July 1954 for a European security conference, excluding the United States, and intended to establish a collective security system, predicated on cooperation between the participant states. The United States was the pillar of the Atlantic alliance, and the western powers were committed to free elections for the whole of Germany. They were not prepared to recognize the GDR. But Germany was de facto divided, with the Federal Republic's sovereignty still restricted by the continued responsibilities of the wartime allies for the whole of Germany. The Soviet Union illustrated satisfaction with this modus vivendi in signing the Austrian State Treaty with the western powers in May 1955. Occupation forces were withdrawn, in return for an Austrian guarantee of neutrality. The treaty excluded any political or economic union with Germany. Austria and Finland – as well as Switzerland, Sweden and Ireland – thus remained on the margins of the western alliance.

The essential features of the postwar world were now in place. The United

Nations proclamation of self-determination and state sovereignty as the organizing principles of world politics had accelerated the retreat of the European powers from their extra-European colonial possessions. The British withdrew from the Indian sub-continent in 1947, and subsequently from Asia, the Middle East and the Gulf. The Dutch reluctantly conceded independence in Indonesia. In 1948, both the United States and the Soviet Union backed the creation of the state of Israel under the auspices of the United Nations. The Arab national revolution in Egypt in 1951 marked the beginning of the end of the British presence on the Suez canal, and undermined the French positions in North Africa. The French left Indochina in 1954, following their defeat at the hand of the Vietnamese communists at Dien Bien Phu. Demands for independence were sweeping into Africa. At the April 1955 conference of Bandung, in Indonesia, India and China took the lead in rallying the newly independent countries of Asia and Africa to a policy of peace, outside of the power blocs. At the Geneva Conference in July 1955, the four powers with ultimate responsibility for Germany celebrated their new modus vivendi. The powers acquiesced in the status quo, without renouncing their mutually exclusive ideals. The bipolar system would be characterized by a triple dialectics of competition, emulation and subversion between the two Germanies, the two alliances and their two great powers. The 'spirit of Geneva' proved short lived.

Expectations for change within the Soviet bloc prompted the Poles, and then the Hungarians to defy the authority of the party-states. The uprisings were duly crushed. In October 1956, while the Soviet Union was facing popular revolts in Poland and Hungary, the French and British, with Israeli military support, launched their expedition to seize back the Canal, which the Egyptian leader Nasser had nationalized. The French went on to fight the colonial war of 1958–62 in a vain attempt to maintain Algeria as a French province. The Algerian war brought General de Gaulle to power in France in 1958. Britain opted to accelerate the pace of decolonization. These two extra-European developments contributed to unravelling the precarious economic peace settlement, negotiated by the western European states in 1950.

Economic reconstruction and European integration

The early postwar hopes placed in the United Nations organization to construct a new world order predicated on commerce and law, had foundered on the divergent political objectives of the former wartime allies. The deliberations at the 1944 Bretton Woods Conference had been an Anglo-American affair, whence Italy, Germany and Japan were absent. The participants aimed at preserving the world from the monetary disorders of the interwar years. Three ideas informed their deliberations. Currencies were to be convertible on current account. Member states had to assume obligations to maintain stable exchange rates and to avoid unjustifiable devaluations. In the event of a 'fundamental disequilibrium' in the current account, member states could chose between devaluation or internal retrenchment, but the International Monetary Fund (IMF) reserved the right to pronounce on the measures. The International Bank for Reconstruction and Development

(IBRD) was to provide long-term funds for the reconstruction of the industrialized regions ruined by war.

Congress was the first to intrude on this design. In ratifying Bretton
Woods, it insisted that its approval would be required for any change in the
dollar's parity. This measure altered the sense of the IMF statutes to avoid
rigidity in exchange rates and gave Congress the final say in any multilateral
realignment of parities with respect to gold, as stipulated in the statutes.
These included no practical measures against chronic surplus countries, the
United States being the only candidate for that condition in 1945. Congress
also wanted its money back, and cancelled lend-lease to Britain and the
Soviet Union as soon as the war was over. US export interests clamoured
to break down Britain's 'imperial preference' system of 1932, while clinging
to the Smoot Hawley tariffs of 1930. The short experiment of the December
1945 loan agreement led to Britain's suspension of sterling convertibility in
August 1947, and a more determined British policy to preserve Commonwealth trade, accounting for nearly two-thirds of British exports and imports
until the early 1960s. But British volume export growth in 1950 to 1960 was
under 2 per cent per annum, in contrast to western European volume trade
growth of 7 per cent (Maddison, 1962).

What were the reasons for this formidable surge in west European postwar growth? The one central factor was Germany. The United States aimed
to integrate the Federal Republic westwards, as a step towards global free
trade and convertibility. France opposed the idea of free trade, where its
steel industry would be sacrificed to Germany's, and its agriculture to US
exports. Britain refused to ditch the sterling area, and take the lead in
creating an 'integrated' European economy. The two institutions that laid
the foundations for European interdependence came as a response to the
relative failure of the Marshall Plan. Britain sought protection against US
pressure to return to a multilateralization of payments, and supported the
creation of a European Payments Union (EPU) in 1950, facilitating the
coexistence of the sterling area with a managed system of commercial
payments in western Europe. France devised the European Coal and Steel
Community (ECSC) to establish a common market, but subject to a complex of jointly administered regulations. This set the precedent for the
European Economic Community, and the French-centred Common Agricultural Policy (CAP) (Milward, 1984).

The Marshall Plan's main success was to help finance European imports
of capital goods. It also contributed to shifting the fulcrum of European
governments towards the centre-right. The US policy debate was infused
into European conditions. There were three components to the policy mix:
governments were to pursue discretionary, but conservative counter-cyclical
fiscal and monetary policies; national factor markets in labour, capital and
products were to be made as efficient as possible; moves were to be made
towards freer trade, and currency convertibility (Nau, 1990, pp. 8–10,
99–128). Productivity was to be promoted through the dissemination of
scientific management principles. Capital accumulation was to be fostered
by keeping wages low, and by sustaining profits at a high level. Output and
income would rise together, thereby satisfying the demand for policies of
growth and full employment. Private corporate initiative would provide the
means to finance government commitments on health, education and welfare.

The Paris conference of July–August 1947, with representatives from 16 countries, revealed the limits to interpreting US policy into practice. Britain and France proved resilient to US pressures for 'integration'. The Organization for European Economic Cooperation (OEEC) was set up in April 1948, but funds voted by Congress came under the more direct supervision of the European Cooperation Agency. The United States also reached a series of bilateral treaties with European states to foster freer trade and protection of US property rights. But by 1949, the continued European boom widened the demand for dollar imports at a time when a new US Congress had grown more reluctant to vote funds. Nor could the Europeans agree on their distribution. United States exporters thus faced recession, without the prospect of relief from export markets. They were saved from recession by the revolution in the Truman administration's policy, leading to the global containment strategy defined in NSC 68. Marshall aid programmes were now merged into the global security policy, and US defence spending surged from 5 per cent GNP in 1949 to 13 per cent in 1953. Federal spending went 84 per cent on defence outlays (*Economic Report of the President*, January 1987, p. 245).

With Marshall Plan funds scarcer, most OEEC member country currencies were devalued in 1949 against the dollar. A device was then conceived for European countries to extend reciprocal credits within limits. The European Payments Union (EPU) was set up in 1950, to operate as the agent for European central banks through the Bank of International Settlements (BIS) at Basel, Switzerland. The EPU functioned as an official multilateral clearing mechanism designed to promote intraEuropean trade and payments. Funds were recycled from surplus to deficit countries, allowing intra-European trade to expand apace. The United States accepted protection against its exports as contributing to European reconstruction. But once the continental European central banks had reconstituted their reserves, US diplomacy resumed the push for freer trade on world markets. The terms of the Bretton Woods accords were cited to end their discrimination against the dollar. The EPU was dismantled in December 1958 thereby ending the notion of a distinct monetary zone in Europe. Private foreign exchange markets, centred on London, came to substitute for the official clearing mechanism.

The other institution was the European Coal and Steel Community (ECSC), launched in May 1950 by France's Foreign Minister, Robert Schuman (Grosser, 1978, pp. 154–63). The key condition was that European coal, iron and steel industries would be subject to a supranational authority, in exchange for which a common market would be established in those sectors. The proposal was presented as a major step to Franco-German reconciliation, which would make war impossible and would create a common base for economic development. The idea was immediately welcomed by Chancellor Adenauer of West Germany. It satisfied German national aspirations for equality of treatment, opened the path to reconciliation with France, and helped bind the young republic into the Atlantic alliance. The initiative therefore received the enthusiastic backing of the US State Department. Great Britain declined the offer to join in order to protect the nationalized coal and steel industries and out of hostility to supranational ideals.

The main divide in the debate over the desirable shape of European institutions was over state sovereignty. The differences emerged at the Congress of the Hague in May 1948, attended by over 700 delegates and representing the multiple strands running through the movement for European unity. The Congress settled for a consultative assembly, to be elected by national parliaments. In May 1949, the ten founding states signed the statute creating the Council of Europe, with a Council of Ministers whose decisions were to be taken on unanimity, and a Consultative Assembly. The Council was based at Strasbourg, to symbolize Franco-German reconciliation. The statute thereby encapsulated the idea that a political community among states may only rest on shared values and compatible domestic institutions. Those institutions derive their authority to enact public policy through commitment to political freedoms and the rule of law. Diplomatic relations between governments facilitate the extension of the area of freedoms available to private citizens. The council came to be identified specifically with the European Convention on Human Rights, signed in November 1950. It signified the commitment to human rights as binding on sovereign states.

For those aspiring to create a Europe beyond the states, the council was entirely inadequate. The spread of democracy over the previous hundred years had transformed the European states from within. Nationalism was seen as the cause of Europe's fragmentation and its terrible wars (Lipgens, 1983). The debate about appropriate institutions for a European entity encapsulated three different ideas: sectoral integration; global integration and federalism. Sectoral integration implied that member states pool resources in the joint administration of a particular sector, such as in the ECSC, the Euratom treaty of 1957 for a European civilian nuclear industry, or the Common Agricultural Policy (CAP) set up in the 1960s. The global approach informed the Rome Treaty, signed in 1957, which set up the European Economic Community (EEC). Its principal stated objective was the creation of a customs union, capped with institutions capable of promoting a general European policy, but that would represent specific national interests. The Commission was charged with sole responsibility for establishing the Common External Tariff (CET), thereby becoming a crucial negotiating partner for the United States on trade liberalization. European federalists hoped that the process of policy making within the EEC between Commission, Council of Ministers, Parliament and Court of Justice would lead to a European polity resembling that of the United States (de Carmoy and Story, 1986, pp. 39–43).

The terms of debate on the ordering principle of European institutions in the western European society of states were thereby set. The permanent feud has been between those who espouse close cooperation between sovereign states in all spheres of public concern, and others who look forward to an overcoming of the inherited state system through the development of common supranational or federal institutions (Robertson, 1966; Gerbet, 1983). Supranationalists contend that common institutions must be powerful in order to master Europe's diversity, and to allow Europe to assume its place in world affairs as a single entity. The federalists favour common institutions, whose tasks would be those which could not be effectively handled by the states or by their local authorities. Their disagreement is over the degree of desirable centralization. Both differ from those favouring cooperation, in that the latter wish to retain the voluntary nature of relations, while the former stress the need for binding rules. The idea of binding rules was written into the Rome Treaty, setting up the EEC. The cooperative principle informs all other European institutions.

These western European ordering principles stood in strong contrast to the idea of 'proletarian internationalism', informing the policy of the communist parties and states (Royen, 1978). The parties claimed to be the vanguard of the proletariat. Their doctrine of Marxism–Leninism justified their monopoly of power over the states which they had come to rule. Dissent was outlawed. For communist parties operating in the capitalist world, the 'road to socialism' could vary from acceptance of the parliamentary route to office in coalition with other political parties and interests, through to the use of terror. The parties reserved the right to choose according to circumstances. Communist propaganda could therefore flourish in the open societies of western Europe, but penetration of western values into the societies of the party-states was severely restricted in the name of the right of states to non-intervention in their internal affairs. The single common denominator between the competing western and communist systems was therefore state sovereignty. East–west relations were restricted to balancing competition between the two systems, with the delineation of restricted areas of cooperation.

The language and symbols of western European integration failed to sink popular roots. This had become evident as early as 1952–4, when General de Gaulle, in alliance with the French communists and with the discreet support of Great Britain, scotched plans for the EDC. The failure of the EDC was interpreted by the pragmatists, surrounding Jean Monnet – the instigator of both the ECSC and the EEC – as counselling more supple methods in pursuit of the desired objective of eventual European union: hence the accommodations to national susceptibilities included in the Rome Treaty. These delimited majority voting in the Council of Ministers to market liberalization measures, without extending the commission's powers into the fields of non-tariff barriers, taxation or money. Western European security matters, after the EDC saga, were left to NATO and to the United States. The Rome Treaty failed to mention monetary matters, as financial stability was provided by the dollar. Dismantlement of the EPU in 1958 was accompanied by an early move to trade liberalization in the EEC.

Germany was a major beneficiary of this complex European settlement. Of the total Marshall Plan aid disbursed between 1948 and 1952 – which amounted to $12.9 billion – $4.4 billion went to the Federal Republic (Francois-Poncet, 1970, pp. 97–100). The 1948 currency reform, and the realignment of European currencies in 1949, undervalued the deutschmark. Foreign demand for German goods helped put to work the massive German industrial machine built up during the war. European governments were determined to facilitate private investment, with the example of the US consumer's cornucopia in mind. As the German boom gathered pace, the economy became the locomotive for trade expansion in western Europe. No tariffs were erected between the two Germanies, in compliance with the one-Germany policy. Growth rates in the 1950s averaged 8 per cent volume growth. Government policy stimulated savings and investment, keeping private consumption low and export volume growth high. Labour costs were held down by the constant inflow of refugees through Berlin, and East

Germany. Germany's percentage of world market shares rose from 6 per cent in 1950 to 15 per cent in 1960, whereas Britain's at 20 per cent in 1950 fell to 14 per cent (Scammel, 1983, p. 64). Britain's trade pattern minimized the benefits from the European boom, while the 12 per cent Gross National Product (GNP) devoted to defence during the Korean war diverted resources from the expanding consumer goods markets. France's promotion of ECSC and the Rome Treaty would make the Federal Republic, not Britain, its principal partner in Europe.

Polycentrism in the blocs

There were two dimensions to the gradual weakening of the two blocs, as they had been constituted in the 1950s. The one was the expansion of world business, along with a gradual undermining of the postwar policy mix in the Atlantic alliance that had yielded almost unbroken expansion for over twenty years. The other related to the disruptive effect of nuclear weapons diplomacy, and the complementary policies of France and China towards the United States and the Soviet Union.

When US diplomacy resumed the drive for a liberal world economy in the late 1950s, it did not share Britain's fear of the EEC as a continental bloc, splitting the OEEC countries. Little concern was shown in Washington over Paris's decision in November 1958 to break off negotiations between 11 OEEC members with the six over the creation of a European free trade zone; also, there was lukewarm support for Britain's promotion of the European Free Trade Association (EFTA), composed of the Nordic countries, Finland, Austria, Switzerland and Portugal. EFTA established a light secretariat at Geneva, with the task of promoting tariff reductions on manufacturing goods. The small, export-dependent states of the EEC joined with the manufacturing interests of Germany to back the US and UK initiatives to develop the multilateral trading system in the framework of GATT. In 1961, the OEEC membership was expanded to include the United States, Canada, Australia and New Zealand; Japan and Spain joined subsequently. The OEEC became the Organization for Economic Cooperation and Development (OECD), indicating the dual trend of western economies to promote national economic growth simultaneously with global market integration among industrialized countries.

Into the early 1960s, international conditions for expansion had never been so favourable. The continued reduction of tariffs transformed western Europe into an open and maritime economy. The port at Rotterdam became the hub of tanker traffic for imported oil as a main energy source. Primary energy imports to Europe in the 1960s rose by a multiple of four, displacing indigenous coal resources. Consumer prices were kept low, through the oligopolistic structure of the oil market, dominated by the seven major Anglo, Dutch and US companies, with extensive downstream facilities in Europe. Changes in US tax incentives had encouraged the companies to increase their liftings from the oil-rich region of the Gulf and the Middle East. A number of consequences flowed from these events. Cheap oil stoked world growth. The conversion to oil extended the dollar's primacy, as the key commodity currency. Europe became dependent on political conditions in the main supplier countries. In 1960, oil-producing countries in the Middle East, Africa and Latin America, created the Organization of Petroleum Exporting Countries (OPEC) with the aim of dismantling the concession regime in order to gain control over production and pricing policies (Maull, 1984; Chevalier, 1973).

With high growth and accelerated interdependence came a weakening in the consensus on western economic policy (Boltho, 1982), that had informed Atlantic relations since the late 1940s. In parallel, Britain, Eire, Denmark and Norway lodged their candidacy for EEC membership (Camps, 1964). All were variously effected by French determination to take the lead in a continental peasant coalition to establish a protectionist EEC agricultural policy, that threatened to exclude US farm exports from the lucrative West German markets. The full scope of US policy to promote an outward-looking EEC was spelt out by President Kennedy in his July 1962 speech at Philadelphia, calling for an Atlantic partnership between the United States and a uniting Europe, hinging on an EC that included Britain. The President also won Congressional support for a Trade Expansion Act, granting the executive extensive powers to negotiate down world tariffs, notably those of the EEC.

The first leg of the post-1947 policy mix to be challenged was adherence to cautious fiscal and monetary counter-cyclical policy. The major change in conditions was provided by the shift from the dollar scarcity of the immediate postwar years, to the dollar overhang as the United States moved to overall deficit on balance of payments. In parallel, the Federal Republic's permanent trade surpluses in Europe could no longer be offset through the mechanisms of EPU. One way of reducing the transatlantic and intra-European trade deficits was to stimulate demand in surplus countries. The OECD proved an appropriate forum for disseminating the gospel of deficit spending. Governments proved attentive, as evidenced by Bonn's adoption of a Stability and Growth Law in 1967, empowering the government to plan for expansionist growth beyond the one-year fiscal cycle written into the Federal Republic's constitution, the Basic Law. Electoral shifts across Europe brought centre-left parties to power. Cautious fiscal and monetary policies were gradually abandoned in favour of more ambitious plans to stimulate growth. Budgets slipped into permanent deficit. Inflation rates ratcheted upwards. These strains on national markets were then translated into tensions on the exchange rates.

The second leg of the post-1947 policy formula was the promotion in national economies of competitive labour, capital, and product markets. These, too, were gradually called into question. High rates of employment shifted the balance of power in labour markets away from management towards trade unions. Income policies proved weak instruments in the face of full employment and rising expectations. Wages began to rise faster than productivity, and governments, towards the end of the decade, conceded wage indexation, more income maintenance, and changes in redundancy laws. With corporate profits falling as tariffs declined, European states began to elaborate mutually competitive industrial policies, with a view to promoting 'national champions', notably in high-technology sectors. National procurement was deployed as a means to defray research and development costs, and to keep national corporations in business. Funding for national governments and corporations was typically shifted away from budgets, to captive national capital markets. Meanwhile, the expansion of the Eurodollar markets provided abundant sources of funds for multinational corporations, which governments scrambled to attract through tax holidays or interest rate subsidies.

The third leg was the promotion of open markets, and the maintenance of stable exchange rates. De Gaulle used US demands for trade liberalization to push through French policy to establish a Common Agricultural Policy (CAP) (Willis, 1965, pp. 312–65). Paris agreed that the commission represent the EEC in the Kennedy Round of trade talks, under the auspices of GATT. Negotiations lasted from 1963 to May 1967, and confirmed the EEC as a major trade power, capable of negotiating on equal footing with the United States. The results were recorded in an agreement for extensive cuts in industrial tariffs over five years, prompting a leap in the growth rates of world trade. Within the EEC, France forcefully used its veto right to trade an opening of markets for manufactured goods in exchange for German implementation of the CAP. This entailed the establishment of common farm product prices, EEC preference for local producers, a common budget, and provisions for export subsidies on third markets. But de Gaulle rejected the Commission's proposals to link the EEC's own revenues to an increase in the powers of the European Parliament. Nonetheless, the key cereal price was established below costs of production in Germany, but considerably above French levels. The result in the longer term was to have output grow faster than consumption, moving the EC towards self-sufficiency by the end of the 1970s. Meanwhile, the institutions of the ECSC, the Rome Treaty and Euratom were fused in 1965, thus creating a single Commission, Council, Parliament and Court of Justice for the European Communities. The EC, strengthened through the extension of its commercial powers, negotiated trade preferences with the former African colonies, and with Mediterranean non-member countries to ensure that their products had continued access to EC food markets.

France's dual vetoes on Britain's entry in 1963 and 1967 were informed in part by the strains in the Atlantic alliance over balance of payments deficits. The continental European states, in comfortable surplus, urged Britain and the United States to reduce domestic consumption, while the latter sought to reduce EC trade discrimination against their exports. As neither side was ready to concede, dollars and pound sterling accumulated in central bank reserves and irrigated the nascent offshore dollar markets in London. In February 1965, de Gaulle attacked the whole monetary system as highly inflationary, and called for a return to payments discipline on agreed rules (de Carmoy, 1967, pp. 469–71; Kolodziej, 1974, pp. 176–221). The Anglo-American response was to push for an increase in world liquidity through the creation of special drawing rights for central banks on the IMF. But the Anglo-American deficits continued, with consumption in the United States fuelled by budget deficits, compounded by expenditures on the Vietnam war. The war's unpopularity was gauged by President Johnson's refusal to ask Congress to finance the war through taxation. Attempts by the US Federal Reserve to manage the economy through manipulation of interest rates only served to accentuate flows in and out of national monetary systems. Meanwhile, France began converting its dollar holdings into gold, while the

Federal Republic desisted after US warnings against following the French example. With its gold stock shrinking further, the United States in March 1968 arranged with its major European partners – in France's absence – to signal the de facto non-convertibility of dollars into gold. The series of currency realignments between the pound sterling, the franc and the deutschmark in the years 1967 to 1969 augured a move away from the stable parities of the past.

Britain allowed the formation of the EC and CAP to undermine its Commonwealth and sterling system. Both main political parties supported the policy of extensive overseas military commitments, trade liberalization, active promotion of capital exports, a reserve currency status for sterling and the restoration of London as an international financial centre. Such priorities, linked to the desire to maintain the wartime consensus on welfare and full employment, placed too many strains on the economy. The authorities alternated between periodic doses of deflation and reflation, until they abandoned attempts to defend sterling's parity with the dollar and the role of sterling as a major reserve currency. Fear of a continental trading bloc being created at its expense drove it to negotiate on terms that de Gaulle insisted should involve the sacrifice of the Commonwealth agricultural system. Devaluation in 1967 of the pound sterling, which had held its parity with the dollar since 1949, was followed by the completion by 1969 of Britain's withdrawal east of Suez, begun in the 1950s.

French and British nuclear diplomacy were strongly conditioned by relations between the Soviet Union, the United States, and China. A central problem in the Soviet Union's policy towards the western powers was whether to opt for bloc consolidation at the cost of an improved climate in relations with the west, or for détente with the west at the cost of control over the client states, and of relations with China. As the Moscow leadership came to live with two Germanies embedded in their own political systems, a new policy had to be defined that reconciled the two dimensions inherent to the foreign policy of the Soviet Union as a party-state. The unifying aim was the encouragement of centrifugal forces in the Atlantic alliance, with the party and state assuming two distinct, and, in the long run, contradictory, lines of policy. The state policy was to secure the Soviet Union's equality with the western powers in world politics, while its contribution to promoting disintegrative tendencies in the Atlantic alliance would be conducted through the instrument of nuclear diplomacy. Party policy was to promote ideas of peaceful coexistence and national liberation around the world, while maintaining the Soviet Union's claim to leadership in the international communist movement. That meant support for a more polycentric communist movement in western Europe, but continued close control over the party-states in central-eastern Europe.

Khrushchev's reformulations of party doctrine in February 1956, at the Twentieth Congress of the Communist Party of the Soviet Union (CPSU), proved a landmark in the history of the international communist movement. His proposal for a policy of peaceful coexistence with the capitalist world ditched Stalin's precepts on the inevitability of war between the two systems. The explosion of a hydrogen bomb in August 1953 had ended any immediate concern of Germany as a military force. The Paris Treaties of 1955 indicated that the western powers, too, could be relied on to oppose the German acquisition of a nuclear weapon. But in October 1957, the Soviet Union successfully launched the Sputnik, a satellite whose launch vehicle reflected an intercontinental ballistic missile capability. The launching preceded by a few months a similar launching by the United States. With both great powers in a situation of reciprocal deterrence, doubts emerged in Washington about the policy of massive retaliation, in view of the vulnerability of US territory. This raised the problem of US readiness to engage nuclear forces in the forward defence of the Federal Republic, and posed the question of Bonn's co-decision in nuclear strategy. Bonn, along with other NATO capitals, welcomed US tactical nuclear weapons on European soil in 1958.

Khrushchev's response was to deliver in November 1958 an ultimatum contesting the western allied position in Berlin. His aim was to reach a modus vivendi with the United States, based on recognition of the GDR and a guarantee by the powers that the Federal Republic would not acquire nuclear weapons. But Krushchev's vaunting of the Soviet Union's technological prowess prompted public readiness in the United States to support the huge space programmes of President Kennedy, elected to office in 1960. Kennedy was also prepared to negotiate with the Soviet Union, though not at the Federal Republic's expense. Adenauer was not convinced. The NATO allies' passivity in response to the erection of the Berlin Wall in August 1961 compounded Adenauer's distrust of Washington's motives. De Gaulle backed the Chancellor, but indicated that a German unity would have to be within the territory of the two existing states. This was the context in which France in October advanced the 'project of a treaty establishing a (European) union of states'. The Fouchet Plan preserved the unanimity principle, and proposed the inclusion of foreign and security policy (Silj, 1967). Decisions on nuclear policy were indivisible; there could be no sharing between Paris and Bonn. The plan met with vigorous opposition from the Dutch and Belgians, anxious to avoid a Franco-German condominium in Europe and supportive of Britain's entry to the EC. The talks on the Fouchet Plan ground to a halt in April 1962.

Divisions in the Atlantic alliance over nuclear strategy also proved fatal for Kennedy's proposal of an 'Atlantic partnership'. In May 1962, Defence Secretary McNamara expounded the US preference for a nuclear monopoly in the Atlantic alliance. The Europeans would provide the conventional forces, leaving the ultimate decisions on use of nuclear weapons in the hands of the United States. De Gaulle's response was that both great powers could destroy the other, so that 'nobody knows today neither when, how, nor why one or the other of these great atomic powers would use its nuclear armament'. France would have to retain autonomous use of its nuclear weapons.

Britain, though, was moving towards technological dependence on the United States. It had announced purchase of the US Skybolt air-launched ballistic missiles in exchange for giving the United States the use of Holy Loch, Scotland, for Polaris missiles submarines. But in December 1962, McNamara dropped Skybolt in favour of sea-launched missiles. At Nassau, in the Bahamas, the US President agreed to provide Britain with Polaris submarines assigned to NATO and targeted according to the plans of the organization (*American Foreign Policy Documents 1962*, 1966, pp. 635–7).

The Nassau agreements provided a central reason for de Gaulle's 14 January, 1963 veto of Britain's EC candidacy. With Britain's membership, Europe would merge into a huge Atlantic alliance under US dominion. On 23 January de Gaulle and Adenauer in Paris signed the Franco-German treaty, based on the same principles as the Fouchet Plan. But the Bundestag modified the protocol, with a view to confirming the Atlantic over the European dimension of German foreign policy, notably a commitment to promote trade liberalization in the GATT (Camps, 1966).

In October 1962, overwhelming US conventional superiority in the Caribbean, and a giant lead in nuclear weaponry, had forced Khrushchev to step back from his attempt to have missiles installed in Cuba. The crisis in the Caribbean was a moment of truth, revealing the continued disparities between the United States and the Soviet Union. Khrushchev drew the lesson: the Berlin ultimatum was withdrawn. His failure prompted the signing in August 1963 of the Test Ban Treaty on nuclear weapons by the two great powers and Britain. The Soviet Union enhanced its military build-up in the conventional, naval and nuclear fields, while Khrushchev was removed from power in October 1964. Meanwhile, the US proposal floated four years earlier to create a NATO multinational force composed of nuclear submarines had run into strong resistance (Kissinger, 1965). The idea was to have Germany participate in some form in the making of allied nuclear policy. But Denmark and Norway were opposed. The British Labour government, elected to office in October, was cool. The US Congress was opposed to a proliferation of weapons. In December, President Johnson withdrew the proposal. A new formula had to be found to fit a non-nuclear Germany's security needs into the Atlantic alliance.

The limits to autonomy within Moscow's sphere of influence had been revealed in 1956 when Khrushchev's denunciation of Stalin's crimes, coupled with a modest relaxation of police controls, raised expectations of further changes in Poland and Hungary. The brutal suppression in November of the Hungarian uprising left no doubt as to the determination of the Soviet leadership to maintain its sphere of influence, if need be by force. Nor was Moscow prepared to tolerate challenges to its claim to leadership in the international communist movement. The ideological disputes between the two party-states had sharpened with Chinese attacks on the Soviet Union for seeking accommodation with the United States and reducing support for revolution in the third world (Griffith, 1964). Moscow's relations with Beijing deteriorated into open rivalry in the course of 1963. Like France, China refused to adhere to the test ban accords and later the Non-Proliferation Treaty, patronized by the two great powers. China's first nuclear device was exploded in October 1964. And like France's challenge to the United States in western Europe, China sought to counter the Soviet Union's efforts to promote economic integration in COMECON by encouraging Romania in declaring independence of Moscow. But the Soviet Union provided the bulk of military support for North Vietnam, in the war against the south and the United States.

After the self-imposed isolation of the cultural revolution from 1966–8, China then became anxious about the Soviet military build-up along the disputed 7,000-kilometre border, and about Soviet diplomatic efforts to encircle China through closer relations with its neighbours in North Korea,

North Vietnam and India'. The Chinese leaders' concern grew at the prospect of a US retrenchment from the Asian mainland, following the US set-
back in the war in Vietnam, leaving the Soviet Union as the predominant
military power. This convergence of Chinese and US interests in the containment of the Soviet Union in Asia held the additional attraction for the
United States of hobbling communist activities around the world, as national
parties fractured along the lines of the Sino-Soviet conflict, or emulated
China in contesting Moscow's claim to leadership in the communist
movement. Khrushchev's demise – which marked a swing in favour of
conservative forces in the CPSU – prompted the Italian communists to take
the lead in western Europe for greater autonomy from Moscow. The trend
was accelerated in August 1968, when the Czechoslovak communists' attempts
to introduce reforms were crushed by the Warsaw Pact's military action.
The Soviet Union opted for the status quo in the party-states, at the price
of relations with the western European parties.

Meanwhile, the Soviet Union was becoming entangled in the politics of
the Middle East (Carrère d'Encausse, 1975). Arab nationalists had never
accepted the creation of Israel, and the accompanying expulsion of the Arab
Palestinians from their homeland. The wars of 1948 and 1956 had ended in
Israeli victories, which in turn enflamed nationalist sentiments and opened
opportunities for the Soviet Union to champion the Arab cause. Egypt
benefited from Soviet military and economic aid, and in 1964 a Soviet fleet
entered the Mediterranean. The aim was to have a say in the resolution of
conflicts in a region which Moscow considered essential to its interests
because of the adjacency of its borders. Support was provided to the Algerians
against France, the Syrians against Israel and later Libya against the Anglo-
American presence. But Israel triumphed again in the six-days war of June
1967, during which it took control of the Sinai Peninsula from Egypt, the
Golan Heights from Syria, the West Bank from Jordan and the Gaza Strip,
which had been under Egyptian administration. Both territories were
populated by Palestinians. France adopted a stance favourable to the Arab
cause. The United Nations Security Council resolution 262 of November
1967 called for Israeli withdrawal from the occupied territories, but in
ambiguous terms. The result was to draw the Soviet Union deeper into the
affairs of the whole region, and notably to radicalize the Palestinians, whose
1968 Charter called for Israel's 'liquidation'. In turn, the US concerns
intensified for western access to oil supplies and Israel's security. But the
policy of containment had been breached.

The rifts in the Atlantic alliance over security and economic policy duplicated the fractures in the communist movement. US and NATO policy
moved towards a policy of flexible response, based on escalation. The fighting,
in case deterrence failed, would escalate from a conventional battle to a
tactical response and lastly to strategic reprisals. France stuck to a strategy
of massive retaliation, arguing that the limits on the size of its nuclear
armoury enjoined an immediate riposte of 'the weak to the strong', in the
event of any major military action against the homeland. In March 1966, de
Gaulle announced the withdrawal of French forces in Germany from NATO
command, and the closure of NATO facilities in France. France, however,
remained in the alliance, and a bilateral cooperation agreement was concluded between the allied command and the French military authorities.

French troops remained in Germany. In 1967, NATO officially adopted the doctrine of flexible response. The future tasks of the alliance were spelt out in the Harmel report of that year, which argued that military security and détente policy towards the Soviet Union and the Warsaw Pact were not contradictory, but complementary. The process of great power détente was launched in 1968, when Moscow and Washington with 35 other states signed the Non-Proliferation Treaty. The Soviet Union insisted that any move to intraEuropean détente had to be preceded by Bonn's signature to the NPT. For the Federal Republic, renunciation of access to nuclear weapons would have to be conditional, and accompanied by a permeability of frontiers to make division tolerable (Kaiser, 1968).

By the late 1960s, both blocs had survived the centrifugal forces at work within them. The feuds over Europe's future shape between the protagonists of an Atlantic partnership, a federal Europe, or a Europe of the states had resulted in a delicate set of compromises. Europe of the late 1960s was a complex fabric of interdependent markets, and a mosaic of states cooperating together in a number of functional areas with their own institutions, overlapping competences and differing memberships. The Soviet Union's control over the satellite states remained precarious, resting on force. The communist parties of western Europe sought to distance themselves from Moscow's policies in eastern Europe, while making common cause with Moscow in promoting a policy of peaceful coexistence from within the western European states. France's detachment from NATO left Germany a pivotal role in establishing the framework of European security, predicated on a recognition of the results of the world war. The United States, disillusioned with the turn of events in western Europe, was moving towards acceptance of Europe's and Germany's division, while edging towards a deal with China to contain the Soviet Union in Asia. The boundaries between intra-European and extra-European affairs were permeable and changing, leaving the region vulnerable to the massive changes occurring in world politics and markets.

The transformation of the postwar system

The new configuration of world politics began to take shape around the end of the 1960s. Richard Nixon was elected to the US Presidency, and inaugurated an extensive reassessment of US foreign policy towards the Soviet Union in Europe and around the world. The world was moved onto a dollar standard, with the United States world power operating as central banker. Leonid Brezhnev emerged as the Soviet Union's leader, and embarked on his dual policy of arms talks and competitive peaceful coexistence with the 'capitalist' world. The contradictions in this policy eventually helped to undermine public support in the west for détente, but also for NATO's Harmel doctrine. In western Europe, the forces operating to weaken the Marshall Plan formula of cautious macroeconomic policy, competitive factor markets and international trade with stable exchange rates were strengthened by protectionist labour market measures, expansive budgetary and monetary policies, and the emergence of Japan as a major industrial and exporting force on world markets. The western stabilization policies of

1979–82, mediated through the markets under sway of the Bundesbank's preferences, locked Europe into stagnation. A third attempt at relaunching the EC since 1969 was undertaken at the Milan EC Summit in June 1985.

Atlantic relations, China and the Middle East

The broad lines of US foreign policy were defined by President Nixon and his adviser, Henry Kissinger. The key to the new team's redefinition of US policy lay in Pacific Asia. The Nixon–Kissinger strategy of an opening to Beijing and détente with the Soviet Union was predicated on the idea that the two communist powers could be contained at lesser cost to the US economy (Osgood, 1973). The decisive factor was to exploit the Sino-Soviet split. Peace for the countries of the maritime Pacific was now to be assured by US retrenchment from military engagement on the Asian mainland, and by US encouragement of foreign direct investment into the region. The Pacific became, more than ever, a dollar-based economy.

The rhythm in relations between China, the Soviet Union and the United States set the pace for détente in central Europe (de Carmoy and Story, 1986, pp. 14–16, 27–31). Moscow, fearful of encirclement by an alliance under US leadership, responded favourably to Bonn's overtures for a peace settlement, while expanding its own network of allies in Asia to encircle China. Nixon's visit to Beijing in February 1972, followed by China's move to improve relations with Japan and all western European states, came in counterpoint to the signing in May 1972 of the Strategic Arms Limitation Talks (SALT) by Nixon and Brezhnev. In January 1973, the Paris accords ended the war between North Vietnam and the United States, thus consecrating the continued division of Vietnam. In June 1973, the two powers signed the Agreement on the Prevention of Nuclear War, implying joint action against third parties whose policies might jeopardize nuclear peace. Talks on mutual balanced force reduction talks opened in Vienna, and preliminary discussions were opened in Finland on the Soviet Union's cherished aim to hold a pan-European security conference. But confidence in the United States in the policy of détente was already dented when in April 1975 North Vietnam conquered the south. By 1978, the Soviet Union had established a bridgehead in Afghanistan, and in early 1979 Vietnam formally entered the Soviet Union's socialist camp. China, meanwhile, had moved closer to Tokyo and Washington, leading the call for a worldwide alliance against the 'social imperialists' in Moscow.

From the late 1970s on, the public mood in the United States swung away from détente to a renewed emphasis on containment of the Soviet Union, and of US leadership in the western alliance. One reason was the concern about the relentless growth of Soviet military forces, which had proceeded apace throughout the decade. The SALT I agreements of May 1972 had left open competition in ballistic missile systems. Both sides armed apace. By 1979, a majority could not be found in the US Senate to ratify the SALT II treaty. The Soviet Union's invasion of Afghanistan in December thus accelerated the third major surge in US military spending in the postwar period. The conservative swing was fuelled by the evidence of Soviet support for third world revolutions stretching from Indochina, through the Persian Gulf to Africa and Central America. 'The Kremlin leaders do not want war, they want the world' (Nitze, 1980, pp. 82–101). As Washington–Moscow relations reached their nadir in the early 1980s, China moved backed to a policy of equidistance. It opposed the Reagan administration on the matter of arms sales to Taiwan, and in 1984 achieved negotiations with Britain on the return of Hong Kong to Chinese sovereignty by 1997. Talks were resumed with the Soviet Union on frontiers. With the revival of the containment spirit in the United States, China could turn to its true priority of internal development, cut the military budget, and introduce market mechanisms. By 1985, China was setting the pace for reform in centrally planned economies.

Another initial element of the Nixon–Kissinger policy was 'benign neglect' towards the Gulf and the Middle East. Although the Arab states might look to the Soviet Union for arms against Israel, local communist parties were regularly persecuted; moreover, in July 1972 Egypt evicted its Soviet military advisers. In OPEC, Libya and Iran pushed for higher oil prices in negotiations with the oil companies in September to April 1970–1. The price rises were intended to last for five years. Western Europe and Japan, rather than the United States with its low dependence on oil from the region, would be affected (de Carmoy, 1971). Indeed, the Nixon administration took steps to develop domestic sources of energy, and to reduce dependence on imported oil. The economy had been primed for growth, with federal budget and trade deficits on the rise. Nixon was not prepared to stabilize the US economy, and on 15 August 1971, he announced the end of the dollar's convertibility to gold. A number of consequences flowed from this momentous decision. The relative value of the dollar to other currencies would be set over the coming years in the light of US domestic macroeconomic policy, and the price of oil that OPEC could sustain on the world markets. A temporary surcharge on imports to the United States was imposed, with a view to extracting trade concessions from Japan and the EC. In December the dollar was devalued to a new rate against the yen and the deutschmark; but the dollar's convertibility was not reinstalled.

The October 1973 war revealed Europe's reduced place in Arab–Israeli and world affairs. Oil producing countries that winter raised prices by a factor of 3.5 in dollar terms. The second price surge occurred in 1979 in the aftermath of the Iranian revolution. On both occasions, one motive was to ensure the purchasing power of their dollar resources (de Carmoy and Story, 1986, pp. 129–31). The dollar's hegemony on world markets had been secured by a number of key decisions in the course of 1974. The raising in January 1974 of all restrictions on foreign loans by US banks opened the way to the recycling of funds through the Eurodollar markets to oil importing countries in balance of payments difficulties. In September, the Federal Reserve Board initiated an expansion of the US money supply. The banks' sovereign lending to Latin America and the party-states in eastern Europe grew by leaps and bounds. The United States also concluded agreements with Iran and Saudi Arabia on weapons sales and on the placement of their dollar surpluses in US Treasury bonds.

The subsequent five-year boom in the United States was sustained on a diet of fiscal deficits, easy money and cheap energy. The dollar depreciated on the foreign exchange markets. But after the second surge in oil prices, the Federal Reserve Board tightened monetary controls in October 1979, stabilizing the world economy (Calleo, 1982). The resulting high world interest rates led to a rapid decline in the OPEC dollar surplus, as world oil demand fell away. Debtors were figuratively strangled by the high interest rates.

During the October 1973 war, most European countries and Japan leaned towards the Arab countries, and sought to restrict US overflight and landing rights for the supply of Israel. At Copenhagen in December, the EC heads of state and government adopted a statement of intent 'to speak with one voice'. But these remained words. As the predominant power in the Mediterranean, the Middle East and the Gulf, the United States played a double role, sharing common interests with European partners in the Atlantic alliance, but pursuing its own interests as a world power. The United States excluded the Europeans from participating in the search for a peace solution in the Middle East, where their interests were directly involved. National responses in Europe varied from energy savings measures to bilateral trade deals, including armaments, with the oil producers. Alternative sources of supply were developed around the North Sea, through major investments in nuclear fuels, and by diversification of oil imports from the region, which, nonetheless, in the mid 1980s held over one-half and one-quarter of oil and natural gas reserves respectively.

The war also underlined that events in the region would prove to be a constant source of divisiveness in the Atlantic alliance. After Egypt in 1975 had turned to the United States to reach a settlement on Israel and the occupied territories, the EC member states favoured an agreement affirming the rights of all parties – including the Palestinians – to be guaranteed by the great powers. The position was reaffirmed at the 1980 EC European Council meeting at Venice. The United States and the Soviet Union moved in that direction in the course of 1977, but in October President Carter changed tack and took advantage of the Egyptian President Sadat's visit to Jerusalem in November to initiate the Camp David trilateral talks between Washington, Tel Aviv and Cairo. The March 1979 Washington Treaty between Israel and Egypt, co-signed by the United States, provided for the return of the Sinai Peninsula to Egypt. But the provisions concerning the Palestinian people in the West Bank and Gaza were not implemented. The whole region was figuratively set alight, by a sequence of events: the new revolutionary power in Iran promptly pledged support to the Palestinians, Moslem activists assassinated Sadat, and the Soviet Union supplied arms to the Arab opponents of the Washington Treaty.

The December 1979 Soviet invasion of Afghanistan tolled the knell of great power détente in Europe. Many in the United States assumed that the Soviet Union was making a bid for hegemony in the Gulf. Forces were duly deployed to guard against the eventuality, and the US alliance with Saudi Arabia was complemented by the creation of a Gulf Cooperation Council. But the labyrinthine politics of the region could not be boxed into a simple cold war scheme, rooted in postwar European conditions. Moscow feared the spread of religious revivalism among its Moslem population; Washington shared Saudi Arabia's concern at the Iranian leader, Ayatollah Khomeini's intent to rid the region of foreign powers. In September, Iraq declared war on Iran, funded on dollars from the Gulf states to buy arms from the Soviet Union and France. Israel supplied Iran, and invaded Lebanon in June 1982 to destroy the PLO and keep Syria at a distance. In September, the United States created a multinational peace force for Lebanon, to which British and French forces were detached. But the force had no clear mandate, and was withdrawn in February 1984, after the US marines had suffered severe losses at the hands of suicide volunteers driving lorries laden with explosives. The episode raised the question whether it was riskier to be absent from the region, like the Europeans, or to intervene, like the United States. Moscow and Washington reached tacit agreement to downplay the region's salience in their own relations. Europe, though, became the target of a wave of terror actions, launched by Syria, Libya, or Iran.

Dilemmas and contradictions in peaceful coexistence

In 1969, Leonid Brezhnev emerged as the Soviet Union's leader. The contradictions inherent in the search for recognition of status as a great power while acting rhetorically as a revolutionary force in world affairs derived from Marxist–Leninist dogma. As a party, the Soviet Union legitimated its own absolute hold on power on the grounds of fundamental hostility between socialism and capitalism. As a state, the Soviet Union claimed the rights and obligations in equality with the United States to shape the world order emerging from the victory of 1945. The two goals proved to be incompatible. On the one hand, by proclaiming itself a revolutionary party aiming to transform the world order, the Soviet Union jeopardized its credibility as a partner for other states. On the other, when acting as a great power aiming to uphold the status quo, it risked its reputation as a leader of world revolution. The Soviet leadership's attempt to combine the two strands of policy helped to bring on the 'second cold war' (Halliday, 1983), and led the Kremlin to fear in the early 1980s that the world was on the brink of a nuclear catastrophe.

A central objective of the Soviet Union was to win western recognition of postwar Europe's territorial status quo (Mayall and Navari, 1980). The western failure to react to the Warsaw Pact's invasion of Czechoslovakia in August 1968, and the readiness of Chancellor Brandt's new government of 1969 to sign the NPT seemed to confirm the west's readiness to accept Germany's and Europe's division. The Soviet Union also sought recognition of the new borders established after 1945, including the Oder-Neisse line separating Poland from the GDR. Arms talks with the United States were opened that year, with the Soviet Union ratifying United States leadership in the Four Power Agreement on Berlin in September 1971. The wartime allies kept their responsibilities for the former German capital, thereby recognizing continued limitations on the Federal Republic's sovereignty. The high point of Soviet–US détente came in May 1972, with the signing of the SALT accords in Moscow. A joint statement was also issued on the Basic Principles of Relations between the United States and the Soviet Union that referred to the concept of equal security.

NATO's Harmel doctrine, whereby defence and détente were complementary, also took firm political shape with the development of the Federal Republic's relations with the Soviet Union and its eastern neighbours. *Ostpolitik* was designed to alleviate political tensions between the two German states, and also between the Federal Republic and the Soviet Union (Griffith, 1978; Haftendorn, 1983). But there were two conditions: Bonn's opening to the party-states was predicated on continued German dependence on the US alliance, and Bonn was determined to keep its long-term commitment to unity. The NPT was ratified in 1968 with a vote by the Bundestag preserving the possibility of European unification. Treaties between the FRG and Poland, signed in 1970, were ratified in 1972 after the four powers responsible for the status of Berlin (the United States, Britain, France and the Soviet Union) had signed in 1971 an agreement according to which the Soviet Union guaranteed free access to West Berlin and recognized the special links between that city and the Federal Republic. The Basic Treaty between the two German states was signed in November 1972, leading to their admission to the United Nations Organization. Germany's division was confirmed de facto; de jure, the Atlantic alliance and the Federal Republic remained bound to the goal of German unification.

The four-power Berlin accord also implied the Soviet Union's acquiescence in the United States' continued presence in Europe. This opened the way to US agreement to the Soviet Union's proposal for a European Conference on Security and Cooperation. The Soviet Union responded by agreeing to US proposals for force reduction talks. Both sets of talks opened in 1973 in Helsinki and Vienna. In June 1974, the Atlantic alliance conference at Ottowa formally recognized the deterrent value of the French and British nuclear strike forces. The Helsinki Final Act, signed by thirty-five states in 1975 – including the United States and Canada – ratified the settlement, giving solemn confirmation to the agreements. The Federal Republic became the centre of gravity of east–west relations in Europe. *Ostpolitik* came to be accepted by all political parties, and as the kernel of German foreign policy. As Chancellor Schmidt stated: 'For us in West Germany, the German question remains open: we are called to achieve the reunification of Germany. But the German question cannot and must not have priority over peace. This is a contribution of the Federal Republic of Germany to stability in Europe' (Schmidt, 1978, pp. 9–17).

According to the Soviet Union, the road to recognition as a great power also ran through the development of a military capability comparable to that of the United States. The military build-up pursued since the setback over the Cuban missile crisis brought rough parity by the end of the 1960s. Détente between the powers wilted rapidly as competition continued around the world and in armaments. Higher ceilings on the number and weight of missiles were agreed on in 1974 to set the guidelines for SALT II. Moscow then began to deploy the intermediate-range missiles, SS-20s, and the Backfire bombers with ranges covering the whole of Europe and the Mediterranean. Warsaw Pact conventional forces, benefiting by numerical superiority in tanks and standardization in equipment, tactics and organization, were consistently strengthened. The Soviet navy, too, was expanded with a view to countering western seaborne nuclear forces and to securing the local exits to Soviet fleets in the Norwegian Sea, the Baltic Sea and the Turkish Straits. Military air-transport facilities were deployed to effect during the October 1973 war, and again in 1975 in Africa for the convoy of Cuban troops to Angola.

Brezhnev announced his Peace Programme at the Twenty-fourth CPSU

Conference in March 1971 (Holloway, 1978, pp. 49–76). Beneficial conditions for socialism were to be fostered through promoting a peace campaign in favour of nuclear disarmament and of international trade. A central feature in the move to greater European security was France's policy of détente and cooperation with the Soviet Union. But the promotion of peace also meant support for alliances between communists and socialists in Europe to advance the interests of the socialist camp. 'Détente', Brezhnev stated at the Twenty-fifth CPSU Congress in February 1976, 'does not in the slightest abolish nor can it alter the law of the class struggle. . .We see détente as the way to create more favourable conditions for peaceful socialist and communist construction'.

The contradictions between seeking to maintain leadership in the international communist movement, while allowing each national party to take its own 'road to socialism' became increasingly apparent over the decade (Filo della Torre et al., 1979). The communist parties had to elaborate policy within the context of national politics, while the states' diplomatic autonomy to maintain the balance between defence and détente remained unimpaired. In France, the communists entered a joint Programme of Government in June 1972 with the socialists, calling for an abolition of the French nuclear force. But the Soviet Union favoured the conservative parties' candidate, Giscard d'Estaing in the April 1974 presidential elections. A radical programme for change in a key state such as France may have initiated a violent reaction, such as had occurred in September 1973 in Chile with General Pinochet's bloody intervention against President Allende's United Front government. Fear of a right-wing coup also induced the Italian communist leader, Berlinguer to propose in autumn 1973 an 'historic compromise' on the governance of Italy with the Christian Democrats. A compromise had to be reached between the two main parties, representing the Catholic and secular traditions in Italian political culture. Subsequently, the collapse of the dictatorship in Portugal prompted the Portuguese communists in 1974–5, and with substantial East German aid, to attempt to establish a party dictatorship in Lisbon. The Italian, Spanish and French parties distanced themselves from the Portuguese, and at the East Berlin conference of European communist parties in June 1976, they convinced the Soviets to recognize the principle of autonomy of national parties, subject to solidarity with the Soviet Union in international politics. The Italian communists declared their accord for Italy's membership in NATO, and the French communists in 1977 veered round to support for the French nuclear strike force.

Solidarity with the Soviet Union for western European communist parties by 1977 was restricted to the anti-imperialist struggle in the third world, and hostility to NATO's nuclear weapons plans. As the Spanish communist leader, Carrillo, pointed out in his book, *Eurocommunism and the State*, there were serious deficiencies in the Soviet Union's political system. The Soviet model was not transferable to the advanced industrial societies of western Europe (Carrillo, 1977). The signal for the launching of the European peace movement was given by President Carter's statement to Congress that he would invite the European governments to decide if they wanted deployment of a neutron, or enforced radiation bomb, highly effective as an anti-tank weapon. In March 1978, Carter decided against production on the grounds that western Europe's political leaders were opposed (Carter, 1982, pp. 225–7). Chancellor Schmidt then stated that the Federal Republic would accept the neutron bomb if other NATO countries agreed to station the weapons. One source of this sensitivity was the rapid development of the European peace movement since the previous August (Alting von Geusau, 1982, pp. 29–32). Western communist parties decided unanimously to support the campaign to 'Halt the neutron bomb', hinging on the Dutch Inter-Confessional Council for Peace, with close ties to Europe's socialist parties.

The Carter administration's readiness to exclude the SS-20s and Backfire bombers from the SALT negotiations, and the neutron bomb incident, seemed to indicate a US trend to disengagement from Europe's defence. Simultaneously, the SS-20s provided the Soviet Union with a first-strike capability in Europe, without endangering US territory. The ensuing debate in NATO led allied governments to recommend the deployment in Europe of US weapons comparable to the new Soviet missiles. Bonn's conditions for accepting the installation of the Pershing II and Cruise missiles was that they be land based and under sole US command, that other non-nuclear allies should participate in the operation, and that the United States should negotiate with the Soviet Union on the limits to new weapons on the basis of adequate reciprocity. The December 1979 Atlantic Council thus reached a 'double decision', involving the allies as well as negotiations between Washington and Moscow. A deadline was set for end 1983, after which the missiles would be installed (Lellouche, 1980). France stood aside from the decision, and sought to maintain a dialogue with the Soviet Union. The British and Italian governments agreed to the eventual installation of the missiles on national territory. But the Dutch and Belgian governments were constrained by christian democrat and socialist opposition to express their reservations.

With the collapse of détente, the peace wave swept across Europe (Lellouche, 1983; Volle, 1981–2, pp. 77–91; Johnstone, 1984). Both strategic and intermediary arms talks were, in effect, broken off. A number of themes emerged. One was that western European states were determined to preserve détente, giving prior emphasis to the continuation of arms control talks over rearmament. European differences with the US were thereby accentuated, as Washington seemed reluctant either to negotiate or to ratify SALT II. The pre-existing public support for the Harmel formula of defence and détente was undermined. In 1980, the Dutch Socialists campaigned for the denuclearization of the Netherlands in the context of pan-European negotiations and in the NATO framework. The British-based European Nuclear Disarmament (END) proposed the creation of a nuclear-free zone in Europe, while the Labour party opted in 1982 for unilateral nuclear disarmament, closure of the US bases and no installation of the missiles in Britain. The German Social Democrats by 1983 came round to rejecting the installation of missiles under the 1979 'dual' decision, though a majority was found in the Bundestag to vote in favour. But in May 1984, the party maintained its commitment to the Atlantic alliance, recommending the gradual replacement of nuclear deterrence by a defensive conventional strategy. Across Europe, government and opposition parties supported the renewal of discussions with the Soviet Union.

Another theme of the peace movement was that both great powers were to blame for the breakdown in relations. The world crisis of 1980 was the first postwar example where conflict between Moscow and Washington did not lead to their affirming control over their allies. Rather, the argument ran, Europeans on either side of the divide rallied verbally to their leaders, but distanced themselves in deed (Bender, 1981). Their main concern was to keep the crisis from their continent, and to preserve détente. Unlike former cold war crises, the early 1980s saw a modest improvement in relations between the two Germanies, both exposed to the danger of becoming a 'globally German' battlefield. The temporary crushing of the Solidarity trade union movement in Poland in December 1981 underlined that Europe's division was coming to an end. The party-states, mouthing an empty ideology and dependent on western trade, were mere dictatorships, fearful of domestic dissent. Their predicament was to look to Europe to preserve the peace, but to trust on the Soviet Union to maintain their position.

Yet there was one area where the difference between President Reagan and the European peace movement was one of emphasis, rather than of substance. American opinion, too, had been long opposed to exposing US territory to nuclear devastation. The 1960s McNamara strategy for NATO of flexible response depended on the threat to use tactical weapons immediately, but Washington proved evasive on the matter (Bundy, Kennan, McNamara et al., 1982, pp. 754–66; Kaiser, Leber, Mertes et al., 1982, pp. 1,157–1,170). Indeed, the Reagan administration offered to resume arms talks in November 1981 with the Soviet Union on the basis of a 'double zero' – a dismantlement of intermediary nuclear weapons on both sides in Europe. The Strategic Defence Initiative, launched by President Reagan in March 1983, was intended to isolate US territory from any possible nuclear attack. Reagan later offered to share the technology so that both sides would not be tempted to strike first. The aim, Reagan declared, was to 'liberate the world from nuclear war'. The offer was picked up by Gorbachev with the accord in 1985 for negotiations to cover strategic arms, intermediate missiles and space.

There was also a difference in emphasis between the Reagan administration and the Europeans on policy towards the party-states. The German reaction to the December 1981 coup d'état in Poland betrayed a sense of relief that inter-German détente had not been placed in jeopardy. Washington saw the event as one more example of the Soviet Union's readiness to crush the liberties of the captive nations in eastern Europe. The contradictions came to the fore in June 1982, when the European governments refused to comply with Reagan's decision to block the sale of technology for the gas pipeline under construction, and linking Siberia to Europe. The matter was quietly shelved. More importantly, the Reagan administration's thesis on the basic incompatibility of the Soviet Union's domestic political system with western values came to be shared overtly by the Italian communist party. The party-states represented a menace to peace, and the Warsaw Pact was an ideological–military bloc, 'governed by the logic of power politics'. A similar conclusion was reached by the members of the European peace movement, as they reflected on nuclear deterrence. Eastern European political liberties came to be seen as essential to the consolidation of a pan-European détente, ensured by other means than peace through nuclear terror (Thomson and Smith, 1980, pp. 58–9).

The Polish crisis of 1980–1 destroyed any vestige of legitimacy possessed by the party-state, and further deepened the rifts among European communist parties (Ascherson, 1982; Griffith, 1989). Debates on the 'contradictions' of socialism began in the Soviet Union prior to the death of Brezhnev, and continued under the short reign of his successor, Andropov. The Polish case had indicated that the party of workers was divorced from the daily concerns of people. The KGB's industrial spying illustrated the Soviet Union's growing backwardness in applying and developing the products and processes associated with the new industrial revolution sweeping the world economy (Goldman, 1987).

The installation of Cruise and Pershing missiles in western Europe from late 1983 on pointed to the failure of the Soviet Union's previous policies. Indeed, the East German party leader, Honecker, announced in 1984 his intention to continue inner-German détente, despite the neo-Stalinist freeze in Moscow under the feeble leadership of Chernenko. This demonstration of autonomy by a state so dependent on the Soviet Union's military protection derived less from confidence bred by economic success, than from economic failure. East Germany received a DM 1 billion loan from the Federal Republic to sustain minimal living standards. Hungary, Bulgaria and Romania, too, sought to preserve their ties with Germany. These frictions between the satellite states and Moscow ended in March 1985, when Gorbachev's arrival paved the way to a new, and generalized détente.

The United States, too, was more than ever reluctant to maintain forces in Europe. The proponents of sea power held that the United States devoted too many resources for NATO. The alliance had adopted the United States' concept of Follow-on-Forces Attack (FOFA), whereby military targets deep in enemy territory could be attacked through high precision electronic equipment. The advantage, in US eyes, was that the nuclear threshold would be held high. The disadvantage in European eyes was that it underlined the US retreat from flexible response, and promised to be expensive. As the European public was averse to raising defence expenditures, the two options were to encourage the Soviet Union to talk disarmament, or to spread the costs of developing weapons systems through joint production and more open defence procurement policies. The Europeans already provided 90 per cent of the ground forces and 80 per cent of NATO's tanks and aircraft. France and Britain had both embarked on the modernization of their nuclear arsenals, providing the Soviet Union with the prospect of a formidable indigenous nuclear deterrent in western Europe by the 1990s. In 1984, on French initiative, the WEU Treaty was amended to drop discriminatory clauses concerning the FRG. In April 1985, France launched a joint Europe-wide space research programme under the name of EUREKA.

Western competition in interdependent world markets

In western Europe, the forces operating to weaken the postwar formula of cautious macroeconomic policy, competitive factor markets and international trade with stable exchange rates were strengthened by three new linkages between world politics and national conditions. One had direct effect on labour markets, through the changes wrought on political ideas and legislation. The second altered the exchange rate regime, and derived from the shifts in US macroeconomic and trade policy. The third was the eruption of Japan as a major industrial and exporting force on world markets. The swing back to the old policy formula gathered pace from 1979 on.

The first linkage, affecting labour markets, came in the mid 1960s with the development of the Soviet Union's policy of peaceful coexistence and the changes in the churches. The cause of peace was to be served by communist parties leaving their cold war ghettos, to form alliances with left socialists or christians on the basis of broad platforms for change from within the capitalist states. In parallel, Pope John XXIII launched the *aggiornamento* of the Catholic church. The Vatican Council, ending in 1963, condoned political pluralism and the separation of church and state. Radical changes ensued. Catholics demanded an extension of worker rights in works councils and a greater social control over corporate investment decisions. A similar evolution occurred in the protestant churches. The churches also embarked on their distinct initiatives to overcome Europe's and Germany's division, or at least to mitigate some of the suffering caused. This was paralleled by the Federal Republic's move in 1966 to establish closer bilateral relations with its eastern neighbours. Moscow's suspicions were aroused, and in August 1968 the Warsaw Pact invaded Czechoslovakia to crush the 'Prague spring'. Brezhnev's reimposition of monopoly party control under Moscow's tutelage prompted the new social democrat–liberal government in Bonn, elected in 1969, to achieve the same objectives through reaching agreements with Moscow, in effect recognizing the postwar territorial status quo. The resulting easing of east–west relations provided a more amenable climate in west European countries for closer cooperation or heightened competition between socialist or communist parties and trade unions.

The political constellations on the left of the national spectrums underwent extensive realignment. All Nordic social democratic parties had shifted leftwards in 1965–6 in response to left socialist or communist criticisms on their failure to move beyond political to economic democracy. The Danish, Norwegian, and Swedish parties subsequently adopted similar platforms, calling for a greater state role in credit allocation, worker co-determination in industrial and financial enterprises, and wage earner funds run by trade unions. In Italy, the divisions of the socialist parties between 1966 and 1969, and a series of strikes by semi-skilled workers in the northern industrial cities, brought the communists and christian democrats into competition as champions of worker rights. In 1971, the Statute of Workers extended worker rights to all industrial sectors, ensured employment for those in work, and launched the major public and private corporations on a decade of financial losses, funded through privileged access to capital markets. In France, a revived socialist party entered the June 1972 Common Programme with the communists, calling for extensive nationalizations and hitching the fragmented trade union movement to the electoral struggle. In Britain, the trade unions rejected income policies or legislation on curbing their power as proposed by both parties. Union membership expanded, along with militancy for higher wages. In 1973, a joint Labour party and trade union political programme was drawn up, proposing extensive dirigiste measures, involving nationalizations in the industrial as well as financial sectors. In

Spain, Portugal and Greece, the clandestine communist parties took the lead in opposition to the three dictatorships.

The second linkage was relayed through foreign exchange markets. Nixon's financial diplomacy of late 1971 presented the Europeans with an option to maintain stable exchange rates or retain currency autonomy, and float separately against the dollar. Central banks agreed to maintain parities within narrow margins. In October 1972, at Paris, the EC leaders declared their common objective to complete a monetary union by 1980 (Tsoukalis, 1977; Kruse, 1980). The EC was to move in January 1974 from exchange rate alignment to coordinating budgetary policies. But dollars flowed into deutschmarks. Inflation rates rose, as the Bundesbank tried to stop the flood. The smaller countries around Germany endured similar experiences. Furthermore, the advances of left parties or the militancy of trade unions prompted governments in France, Italy and Britain to go for growth. Italy, then Britain, dropped out of the combined float. Wage costs and prices soared across Europe. In March 1973, the German authorities clamped down on domestic demand. The trade surplus began to expand even before the oil price rises of 1973–4. Highly dependent on oil imports, France dropped out of the joint float with the deutschmark against the dollar in January 1974.

It was a chastened Europe which emerged in 1974 into a world of floating exchange rates. The Federal Republic was confirmed as Europe's foremost exporter, industrial power and key currency country. The compression of domestic demand accompanied an expansion of the German trade surplus with all of Europe, the United States, and the oil producing countries. Neighbouring small countries hitched their currencies to the deutschmark, as a means of exerting a price discipline on their economies. In Italy, Britain, France and the smaller European Mediterranean countries, government deficits leapt, with the surge in transfers for local government or social policy outlays. Wage costs soared. The moment of truth came in 1976, when the financial markets withdrew their confidence. Stabilization policies were introduced. But the United States embarked anew on a growth path, with a further flight into the deutschmark in the winter of 1977–8. The Bundesbank entered the markets to keep the currency down, prompting a rapid growth of the deutschmark as an international reserve currency (Brown, 1979). Eventually, the United States moved to stabilize the dollar in the winter of 1978–9, when the Shah's fall precipitated another currency panic.

Meanwhile, the Federal Republic had found a new partner in France to establish 'a zone of monetary stability' in Europe (Ludlow, 1982). The lesson learned from the 1976 franc devaluation was that there was no option to aligning domestic economic policies with those of West Germany. But it was only with the victory over the left parties in March 1978 that the conservative French government had freer hands to join Bonn. The European Monetary System, conceived as a Franco-German initiative in April 1978, was launched in March 1979. It amounted to an organization of foreign exchange markets on the basis of stable but adjustable exchange rates. The common discipline, it was hoped, would encourage a convergence of domestic economic policies. Italy was granted wider margins of fluctuation in the EMS, to make allowance for its chronic financial difficulties. Britain retained its option to join, but showed no willingness to make parity changes for sterling a matter of EC concern. In June, Chancellor Schmidt agreed to stimulate the German economy, which entered the second wave of oil price rises on an expansionist path. The deutschmark weakened, as the current account turned to deficit.

The third linkage between world politics and national conditions in Europe was the emergence of Japan as a major industrial and exporting force on world markets. Japan had been absent from the Kennedy Round of trade negotiations in the mid 1960s, when its economy successively outgrew those of Italy, Britain, then France and finally Germany. Over half of Japanese exports went to the United States and western Europe. Penetration of foreign markets was made possible by constant improvements in value added, as Japanese exports moved away from labour to capital intensive production. On the import side, the pattern differed considerably from those of OECD competitors, in that manufactured imports accounted for one-quarter compared to two-thirds in other industrialized countries. The bulk of imports were energy and raw materials (Hanabusa, 1979). The result was that Japan's traditional trade deficit with the United States moved to surplus in 1965. Its trade with the EC moved into surplus in 1969, with over two-thirds of exports in machinery and equipment. The main feature was the speed of growth in specific sectors, notably consumer electronics, cars and ships. Its share of industrialized country exports rose from 4.8 per cent in 1960, to over 9 per cent in 1973. The two oil shocks of 1973–4, and 1979–80 were followed by a large current account deficit, rapidly made good by a surge in exports. By the early 1980s, Japan accounted for 13 per cent of industrialized country exports (IMF, 1984). About one-fifth of total exports were in the broad category of electronic products (GATT, 1985).

The contrast between the performances of Japan and western Europe prompted a growing number of critical observations. Unemployment rates in Europe, edging upwards from the late 1960s, were at 2.5 per cent of the work force in 1973. The wage explosion that followed the oil shock of 1973–4 was accompanied by a surge in social security expenditures, and labour legislation that raised the cost for employers of hiring. While the United States created 15 million net jobs and Japan 4 million from 1973 to the early 1980s, none were created in Europe. Private and government consumption rose in Europe, while in Japan the notable feature of the period was that savings and investment rates remained high. Tax rates stayed modest, with the Ministry of Finance tapping public savings through bond issues to promote economic activity. The limited government outlays in Japan on transfers enabled public investment rates to be sustained. By the early 1980s, government outlays in western Europe were in the range of 45 per cent of national income, as against under one-third in the United States or Japan (OECD, 1985a). Corporate investment and profitability had fallen off, and Europe's trade in high-technology products seemed in jeopardy.

Japan's trade offensive was a prime cause, along with the EC's agricultural policy and preferential trade agreements with Mediterranean and African countries, for President Nixon's aggressive trade policies. Another multilateral trade round opened officially in September 1973, but it was only in January 1978 that negotiating positions of the three major trade powers were placed on the table at Geneva. The 'new protectionism' had been fostered by the oil price rises, currency fluctuations, recession and harsher competitive conditions (OECD, 1985). Governments in Europe turned to direct subsidy or EC protection in response to the problems in the textile, steel, shipbuilding or automobile and light engineering sectors. Tariff reductions in previous negotiations had laid bare the importance in international competition of different institutional features between national economies (Spero, 1981, pp. 92–8). The negotiations were concluded in April 1979. Japan's tariffs on manufactured products – still 40 per cent for automobiles – were reduced; new codes were agreed to regulate the use of non-tariff barriers, such as procurement or export subsidies. World farm trade, however, which amounted to 20 per cent of world trade, was consistently excluded, and the EC insisted on keeping safeguards against surges in exports from developing countries.

Japan's prowess in trade symbolized the revolution sweeping through the world economy. Starting in the 1960s, Japan's mixture of 'administrative guidance' and highly competitive markets launched the nation into a vigorous assault on the lead electronics sector. The Japanese challenge hit US and European producers in the late 1970s, and left the rigid Soviet economy standing. Chief of Staff Marshall Ogarkov's blunt criticism in May 1984 of Soviet technology for not being able to provide up-to-date weaponry provided an indication of the dimensions of the economic restructuring required of the Soviet Union. Meanwhile, Japan had become the US's prime creditor, thereby cementing a competitive industrial and financial duopoly across the Pacific. With Europe stagnant, there was the prospect of a Pacific economy displacing the centre of world political and economic gravity from its postwar Euro-American moorings. Furthermore, Japan's corporations were driving European competitors into the nooks and crannies of the crucial North American markets. A central component therefore of an EC revival was to place external relations with Japan on a stronger footing.

In May 1979, the British conservatives were returned to power with a programme to sweep away the state-assisted *laisser-aller* that had hampered the British economy since 1945. Tight monetary conditions were imposed. The conservative government in France gave priority to a stable franc, refusing to reflate in order to reduce unemployment. In June, the leaders of the main industrialized countries agreed that the oil price rises of that year would not be accommodated by easy credit, as in 1974. The Federal Reserve Board tightened monetary controls in October, setting the pace for a worldwide rise in interest rates. The Euromarket rates jumped to a high and volatile plateau of around 16 per cent in 1980 and 1981. Borrowers faced real long-term interest rates of 7–8 per cent. With the Reagan administration's inauguration in January 1981, foreign exchange intervention to keep the value of the dollar as agreed in 1979 was ended. Funds flowed back, and the dollar revalued sharply. In February 1981, the Bundesbank countered by tightening the lead deutschmark rates. The Bank of Italy followed suit in March. The socialist government elected in France in April and May had to raise interest rates from 12 to 18 per cent, in order to stabilize the franc. Both franc and lira were realigned downwards three times by March 1983. The Bundesbank moved to the fore as Europe's de facto central bank.

With the hard currency doctrine on the virtues of sound money, the OECD countries initiated a competitive race to attract funds. OPEC countries were less prepared to invest in dollars after the 1970s depreciation, and looked for alternative homes. In March 1980, both Germany and Japan modified domestic regulations to increase the attraction of investments in yen and deutschmark. With the suspending of US intervention on foreign exchange markets in early 1981, funds flowed to a more assertive United States. Given Germany's exposed geopolitical position in the second cold war, savers moved out of deutschmarks to dollars as a refuge. The Bundesbank's tightening in February 1981 raised the commercial banks' lending rate to the corporate sector, and made them unwilling to finance a government reflationary package. This precipitated a change in the governing coalition, and the confirmation in the general elections of March 1983 of a christian democrat–liberal coalition more ready to assume restrictionary policies. Thereafter, Germany's trade surplus with the EC widened, notably in machinery and transport equipment. But the Bundesbank's hopes to win independence of US interest rates was not fully realized. West German savings, as in Japan, flowed to the United States, where savings were low and government or corporate demand high. The US thirst for world savings was revealed in 1984 with the removal of the US withholding tax on interest earned by non-residents on US paper. The Bundesbank responded promptly, and abolished withholding tax. Tokyo was encouraged to ease restraints on capital outflows.

The global stabilization of the early 1980s internalized trade expansion within the OECD (de Carmoy and Story, 1986, pp. 144–50). Developing countries in Latin America and Africa were precipitated into recession that lasted throughout the 1980s. The Reagan administration's easing of monetary and fiscal restraints in late 1982, combined with an upward surge in the dollar on the foreign exchange markets, then turned the United States into the world's locomotive, sucking in imports. In 1985, the United States became a net debtor to the rest of the world for the first time since 1914. Oil prices, edging down after 1983, plummeted in 1986. Nothing could be expected from a pick-up in the demand for western European production in surrounding markets. The African continent faced famine, debt repayment and chronic low growth. Middle East and Gulf markets were dwindling as oil revenues declined, and the Iran–Iraq war continued. Latin American states strangled domestic growth in order to raise export revenues in vain efforts to repay debts incurred during the recycling of the previous decade. The party-states in central-eastern Europe faced debt repayment and sullen populations.

The United States therefore became the main target for European exporters. This subjected the world trade system to extreme tension. Restrictions were placed on European steel and Japanese car exports. In 1982, anti-dumping and countervailing duty petitions multiplied. The US delegation to the GATT ministerial meeting in November met with EC stonewalling on proposals to liberalize trade in agriculture and services, and to include industrial subsidies for high technology in discussions. Then with the high dollar and the solitary US boom, US-based producers lost price competitiveness. The United States moved into trade deficit with all its major partners. The US trade balance deteriorated in every category of manufacturing. Growing external debts whittled away the surplus income on services, implying a longer-term deterioration on current account.

By 1985, the Reagan boom had lost its gloss. Signs accumulated of a downturn in the United States, and calls were heard anew for western Europe to 'pick up the slack'. The question was posed whether the EC as the world's major importer could take over from the United States as the 'engine of growth'. Two formulas were proposed. One advised extensive deregulation of national markets in order to accentuate European integration. European savings would be provided with incentives to stay closer to home. The other looked to a conscious reflation by Germany. Neither were likely to yield early results. Deregulation of internal markets could only be achieved by lengthy and arduous negotiations between governments. Any idea of reflation would run the gauntlet of a vigilant Bundesbank, more than ever Europe's de facto central bank. The alternative was for the United States economy to continue to be financed on a capital inflow from the rest of the world, at the risk of further trade deficits and mounting debts. Europe seemed to be locked into a position of becoming a reluctant net creditor to its reluctant defender, the United States.

From one EC relaunch to another

By the EC summit at the Hague in December 1969, the concept of co-operation within the EC had prevailed over the more ambitious aims of creating a federal Europe, to which the states would be subordinate. The Rome Treaty of 1957 had outlined a detailed timetable to achieve the customs union and to dismantle internal tariffs and quotas. The timetable was completed in 1968, with the establishment of the agricultural policy and the moves in GATT to reduce tariffs negotiated in the Kennedy Round. Meanwhile, Britain, then France and finally Germany had embarked on an attempt to improve relations with the Soviet Union. The Federal Republic moved away from an exclusive focus in foreign policy on prior relations with the United States and integration within the EC, to the development of its *ostpolitik*. At the Hague, Chancellor Brandt balanced his diplomatic overtures towards Moscow by backing French proposals to 'deepen' the EC through the establishment of a European monetary union, based on stable exchange rates.

At the Hague, Chancellor Brandt and President Pompidou also agreed to balance the EC's 'deepening' with its first enlargement. France, concerned about the political evolution in West Germany, dropped its opposition to Britain's entry into the EC, which had been facilitated by the agreement to stall majority voting in the Council of Ministers. The Commission thereby became engaged in a never-ending series of trade negotiations with outsiders seeking to preserve access to an enlarged EC through membership, associate status or preferential trade agreements. The negotiations – which spanned the period from 1969 to 1985 – absorbed EC energies, disrupted the compromises of the 1960s in the EC on which its partial external trade and farm policies had been based, and accentuated the trend to a reinforcement of the Council of Ministers in EC mechanisms. Britain, as well as Ireland, Denmark and Norway had little intention of abandoning sovereign powers to a European entity. The Norwegian electorate voted by referendum in 1972 against entry. The first extension of the EC's membership from six to nine was followed by the events of 1973–4, inevitably complicating the EC's bureaucratic decision-making processes.

The fall of three Mediterranean dictatorships in 1974–5 in Portugal, Spain and Greece opened the prospect of the EC's enlargement to the south. Accession was favoured by all members on the general grounds that once in the EC, the new democracies would be strengthened by their participation in the club. Greece joined in 1981 while negotiations with Spain and Portugal were concluded in March 1985. The further expansion of the EC from 10 to 12 member states, with distinct political traditions and often conflicting economic interests, threatened either to bring the cumbrous EC mechanisms to a halt, or to oblige them to resort to majority voting.

At the Hague, too, the heads of government launched an arrangement whereby the member states' foreign ministries, under the name of European Political Cooperation (EPC) (Pijpers et al., 1988), came to consult regularly on foreign policy matters. Unlike the Fouchet Plan, it was agreed that the foreign ministries would consult the Commission and European Parliament, wherever their competences were affected. Intergovernmentalism was thus incorporated closer into the Community's operations. A key objective in setting up the EPC was to elaborate common positions on world affairs. But the member states retained their autonomy, and limited their engagement to consultations, while retaining their own external representations. No permanent secretariat was set up to lend consistency to the process. The states, too, remained jealous of their powers in the key areas of military, tax, currency, and foreign aid policy. Nonetheless, the habit of consultation was developed between the foreign ministries. By 1981, it was possible for the states to agree on an obligation to consult with their partners, prior to undertaking an initiative.

The Hague meeting also marked the first step to establishing the summits of heads of state and government on a regular basis. The next was held at Paris in October 1972, where an ambitious programme for an enlarged EC was sketched out. This included a commitment to economic and monetary union, a regional fund, a social action programme, an industry and technology policy, a definition of the EC position on the forthcoming GATT round, and a strengthening of political cooperation. The deadline for establishing a European union was earmarked as 1980, with 1975 as the date for initiating final discussions on the union's institutions. But the crucial details on the institutional balance between intergovernmental meetings and EC procedures were left vague, as became apparent at the December 1973 summit at Copenhagen where the nine member states' capacity 'to speak with one voice' in the great affairs of the world was subjected to the harsh test of events.

The major problem for the EC was to define a common position towards the United States. By the late 1960s, US support for EC integration had waned. Failure of the Europeans to support the United States in Vietnam, as had been the case in Korea, fostered the view that the Europeans should pick up more of the burden for their defence. The EC was seen as competing with the Atlantic community. Once the eastern treaties had been signed, though, it became evident that the United States had no intention of abandoning its leadership position. As Kissinger stated in his April 1973 speech, the United States alone had global responsibilities, while Europe's were purely regional. The member states, under French and British urging, sub-sequently subscribed to a definition of a European 'identity', but added that there was no alternative to the United States' protection. The US blocked EC efforts to participate in a Middle East peace settlement, and demanded that the west elaborate a common energy policy, through the creation of an International Energy Agency, attached to the OECD. US dollar diplomacy, furthermore, had disrupted the EC's timid bid for monetary union. At Ottawa in June 1974, the European allies termed the US contributions to the common defence as 'indispensable' and 'irreplaceable'.

A prime source of conflict between US and European interests lay in the Mediterranean, the Middle East and the Gulf. The EC had multiplied pre-ferential trade agreements with the Mediterranean non-member states, but had not been able to reach any agreement on a 'global' policy on account of divergent trading interests and differences over the Arab–Israeli conflict. But the events of 1973 brought the member states to align their position closer to that of France, as outlined at the EC Copenhagen summit of December where the member states called for recognition of the legitimate rights of the Palestinians and proposed a direct dialogue between the EC and the oil producers. This ran into US opposition, so that when the Euro-Arab discussions opened in 1975, the agenda was restricted to economic discussions. The EPC process, nonetheless, proved effective in facilitating the regime changes in Portugal, Spain and Greece. In June 1977, the EC summit suggested that talks without preconditions be opened on the Middle East. The EC position was restated at Venice in June 1980, to little effect.

The events of 1973–4 had highlighted, as the Commission pointed out at the time, the EC's 'weaknesses and dependence' (Grosser, p. 356). In the first five months of 1974, the political leaderships in France, Germany and Britain changed. In December, Chancellor Schmidt and President Giscard d'Estaing decided to make the summits between heads of state or government a regular feature of the EC's calendar and to link coordination of economic policy between member states with cooperation on foreign policy (Morgan, 1976; Bulmer and Wessels, 1987). The idea was to associate the Community and inter-governmentalism. The heads of state were to meet three times a year in the European Council, placed over the Council of Ministers and the Commission. The European Council was to act as the European executive and to provide the driving force behind any progress in the EC. Subsequently, it patronized direct elections to the European parliament, the launching of the European Monetary System (EMS), the enlargement negotiations, es-pecially with Spain, the reforms of the early 1980s in agricultural policy, and in June 1985, the calling of an inter-governmental conference, on a majority vote, to introduce revisions in the Rome Treaty.

There was broad support across western Europe for NATO's policy of defence and détente on the basis of the Harmel doctrine, and high expec-tations among western corporations on the prospects for business with Comecon countries. These were reciprocated in the Soviet Union, where a major plank of Brezhnev's peace programme was to ease access to western technologies through improved political relations. Poland in particular embarked in December 1970 on a bold programme of economic expansion, where external borrowing on the Eurocurrency markets was to finance the import of capital goods, which in turn would generate the export revenues from sales on western markets to repay debts. The party-states were thus vulnerable to western influences on a number of scores. The EC refused to recognize Comecon, with its headquarters in Moscow, as an equal, preferring to encourage the party-states to negotiate separately with the Commission. More competitive conditions on western European markets restricted their foreign currency earnings and ability to repay debts. The EC foreign ministries elaborated a complete policy towards the party–states during the 1973–5 negotiations on the CSCE.

The Helsinki Final Act also confirmed the Soviet Union's hegemony over its satellite states by recognizing existing borders, but undermined it in the longer term. The Act held three components, or 'baskets'. The first dealt with security matters, where Romania won western support in confirming respect for the sovereignty of states and non-intervention in their internal affairs as the organizing principles of inter-state relations across Europe. The Federal Republic, with EPC backing, established the principle of the inviolability of frontiers, keeping open the possibility of eventual German unity through peaceful negotiations. The second basket concerned economic and technological cooperation between states. At the time of the signing of the Helsinki Final Act the boom in east–west trade had peaked, accounting for under 3 per cent of world trade in 1975. The third basket pertained to human rights and the free movement of people and ideas. EPC insistence eventually won the party-states round to accepting a chapter referring to the 'respect for human rights and fundamental freedoms, including the freedom of thought, conscience, religion or belief'. The states confirmed 'the right of the individual to know and act upon his rights and duties in this field'.

The terms of the Final Act, officially published and distributed by the party-states, became the basis for the claims of dissidents in eastern Europe and the Soviet Union. Their demands threatened the parties' monopoly and touched the foundations of their state power. Consequently, the party-states from late 1976 on, intensified their ideological cooperation, cracked down on dissident groupings, and countered western support for human rights as contrary to the Final Act clauses on non-intervention in the affairs of other states. Repression in turn fostered hostility to the Soviet Union in western Europe, weakened the support for détente, and complicated the Soviet Union's propagation there of its policy of competitive 'peaceful coexistence'. Western Europe by the end of the 1970s, as ideological and economic stagnation enveloped the party-states, presented them with a challenge which they could not match. This became evident in Poland when the party's decision to raise consumer prices in June 1980 led to a general strike, and the signing of the Gdansk agreements in August, recognizing the trade union, Solidarity. Two months later, Reagan was elected to the presidency. Any military intervention by the Soviet Union in Poland would have united the western allies, and been in flagrant violation of the Helsinki accords, as the EPC pointed out. It could also have damaged the vital trade with western Europe. General Jaruselski's coup d'état of December 1981 was therefore the best possible solution for the Kremlin, but it stripped the regime of any semblance of legitimacy.

The European Council was also conceived as helping to set a European agenda in preparation for the yearly summits of industrialized countries, initiated at Rambouillet in November 1975 (Merlini, 1984; Putman and Baynes, 1984). These discussions confirmed the dollar's status as the world currency. The leaders' deliberations at Rambouillet opened the way for the ratification in January 1976 of the modified Articles of Agreement of the IMF. The Special Drawing Rights (SDR) as numéraire was to be valued not in gold but in terms of a basket of currencies where the dollar weighed one-third. Governments were to counter disorderly conditions on foreign exchange markets essentially by giving priority to domestic price stability in their national economies (de Vries, 1976, pp. 577–605). The summits of 1977 and 1978 in London and Bonn, including the Commission President, involved pressure on Germany to reflate. A deal was cut whereby Chancellor Schmidt agreed to stimulatory fiscal measures against a promise by Carter to introduce legislation to reduce US oil imports. This eased the way to conclusion of the GATT round of trade talks. In Tokyo, the following year, the industrialized countries agreed to stabilize the world economy. At Venice, the 1980 summit inevitably dealt with the need to promote energy conservation, while in the early 1980s the agenda was filled by the problems of world trade, debt and domestic adjustment policies. The May 1985 Bonn Summit, like that of June 1978, represented an ambitious package not of reflation but of agreed microeconomic measures.

Similar ideas inspired the Commission in its ceaseless campaign to overcome the EC's stagnation following the events of 1973–4. Its prime concern was to restrict member states' protectionist propensities and to open up intra-EC markets, as the precondition to strengthening its negotiating position against non-members. The Commission therefore elaborated a principle, based on a Court of Justice ruling, whereby a good could be freely exported to another member state when produced and commercialized in accordance with the regulations of the exporting country (Timmerman, 1982; Mattera, 1980, pp. 505–14). Its interpretation into policy required wider scope for majority voting, thereby enabling more Council decisions to be taken on the basis of Commission proposals. The principle of mutual recognition was encapsulated in the June 1985 White Book, setting out in detail the measures to eliminate internal barriers to trade within the EC by 1 January, 1993. The policy to relaunch the EC was elaborated at the three European Councils of Brussels, Milan and Luxemburg in the course of 1985 and early 1986. Treaty revision included widening the scope for majority voting on matters relating to the internal market.

The German and Italian foreign ministers, Genscher and Colombo, presented their plan for a 'European Act' to the European Parliament in November 1981. Their main idea was carried over by the christian democrat–liberal government, formed in March 1983 at the height of the crisis in the Atlantic alliance over the installation of the Cruise and Pershing missiles. At the Stuttgart European Council in June, the heads of government subscribed to a Solemn Declaration on European Union, indicating an intention to extend EC domains into 'the economic and political aspects of security'. The German Presidency made the successful completion of the Iberian entry negotiations a precondition to the release of additional funds for the EC budget. The move underscored Germany's status as Europe's prime economic and political power. It obliged member states to speed agreement on control of farm surpluses, to conclude Spain's EC entry negotiations in

March 1985, and to win member state support for the Commission's internal market programme, from which Germany had most to gain. The Genscher–Colombo plan lent its name to the Single European Act (SEA), amending the Rome Treaty, and agreed on at the Luxemburg European Council of February 1986.

French policy moved in parallel. France's Minister for European Affairs, Chandernagor, advanced a 'memorandum on the relaunch of the European Community' in October 1981, suggesting the need for a European 'social space' and for a tougher external trade policy against Japan and the United States. But President Mitterrand's domestic economic policy of extensive nationalizations, reflation and redistribution was at odds with any forceful French lead in the EC. The moment of truth came in March 1983, when Mitterrand was forced to ditch his initial policies. The President opted for the franc's stabilization within the EMS, rejecting counsel to move to national protection. In November, the French government submitted a further proposal to the European Council on an EC-wide industrial policy, internal free trade and more effective external protection (*Agence Europe*, 16 September 1983). Mitterrand's full substitute policy, announced in two key speeches in early 1984 at The Hague and at Strasbourg, was European unity. This implied a prior agreement on agricultural policy reform, Spain's EC entry and new budgetary funds. French–Spanish bilateral negotiations paved the way for the conclusion of Spain's entry negotiations in March 1985; the subsequent European Councils witnessed the EC's relaunch. France, and French opinion, became a champion of European integration.

The European Parliament added its suggestion for a federal Europe, in its resolution of July 1982. Inspired by the veteran Italian federalist, Spinelli, the parliament proposed a European Union the objective of which would be the promotion of a greater sense of solidarity among the European peoples. The Commission was to play a central role as the executive. The Parliament and Council would share legislative and budgetary powers, with the Parliament exercising control over the Commission. This scheme was then elaborated in the form of a proposal for a treaty, and voted by large European Parliament majorities in 1983 and 1984. Some of these ideas, along with the other suggestions, were taken on board by the committee, appointed by the heads of state and government at the June 1984 Fontainebleau summit to propose improvements to the EC institutions. The interim report, published in December, pronounced in favour of a 'true political entity'. Key objectives would be the achievement of a single internal market and of a single currency. The report also proposed incorporating security matters in the Community domain, a strengthening of Commission and Parliament powers, and that an inter-governmental conference be put forward with a view to negotiating a treaty for European union.

Finally, the British government supported the EC relaunch. With reform of the farm policy underway, and EC enlargement negotiated, there was a chance to promote free market ideals as a positive contribution to EC integration. Indeed, by introducing deregulation to the centre of EC activity, the new policy would go well beyond the old negative freeing of trade between the states to actually dealing directly with non-tariff barriers within the states themselves. While this would lead to inevitable resistance by protected interests, the policy could be expected to appeal to a wide public throughout western Europe. It offered a free market solution to low growth that complemented the prevailing tide of liberal thinking in the 1980s. The policy would also serve to loosen up further the coalitions of producer interests nestling into the centre or centre-right parties, and that had under-pinned the governments of the 1950s or 1960s. But a liberal policy applied to labour markets also ran the risk of confronting entrenched trade union interests. For this, the British government suggested that the Rome Treaty sufficed.

The majority of member states, though, considered that negotiation of such a complex process, entailing a mutual disarmament pact on non-tariff barriers, required a strengthening of the EC policy mechanisms. The Single European Act, finally ratified by all member state parliaments in June 1987, restricted the extension of majority voting to matters pertaining to the internal market. It both amended and incorporated into the Rome Treaty, the institutions and practice that developed alongside. It served as an example of 'cooperative federalism' (Bulmer and Wessels, 1987), in that the inter-governmental institutions of the European Council and European Political Cooperation were incorporated officially among Community institutions. Cooperation in fiscal, monetary and also security issues were evoked, but the first two fell expressly within the rule of unanimous voting while European security policy was made primarily within NATO, but also in the deliberations of the EPC. On the other hand, the SEA strengthened the federalist elements in the Community. It fully associated the Commission with the proceedings of political cooperation, and confirmed the Commission's status as a twin pillar with EPC in the elaboration of the EC's external policies. It extended majority voting in the Council of Ministers to include financial services, capital markets and legislation concerning the internal market, previously solely under the unanimity rule. This opened wide areas of discretion for the Commission, which could frame policies in such a way as to bring them under the majority voting rule. A new procedure allowed the European Parliament to amend a Council position; the Parliament also had an effective veto over new applicants for membership, and especially over the ratification of trade agreements with third countries. The Act, in short, strengthened the Commission within the Community, and reinforced the Community as a negotiating partner for third parties. The states retained the legislative power in Council.

Conclusion

By 1985, there were still many features of the world state system in place that were inherited from the period of the immediate postwar years. The most notable continuity was Germany's division, and the failure of the Soviet Union to implement the terms of the Declaration on Liberated Europe, agreed on at Yalta. But the transformations in the structure of the world had been extensive. In 1945, the structure was close to unipolar, but the United States could not or would not prevail in implementing the vision of a One World, associated with the principles and institutions of the United Nations. Forty years later, Europe was fashioned by four elements of the world structure: bipolarity in relations between the two world powers, conditioning the military system; tripolarity in trade and industry, between the leading centres of the world economy – the United States, western Europe and Japan; unipolarity in the dominance of the dollar as the key state-produced currency commodity on world markets; fragmentation of the world polity into over 160 political units.

The dynamics in all four elements impinged on Europe. The global rivalry between the two world powers, informed by incompatible views of political community, preserved the European divide. Competition on markets between states and corporations bound western Europe into interdependence with the United States and Japan, whose rivalry in the key electronic sectors posed a fundamental challenge to the Soviet Union's planned economy. A rich western Europe exerted a strong attraction on its poorer eastern neighbours. The United States as the world banker had to reconcile management of the national, with the world economy, setting the world interest rate and the context for exchange rate regimes. Fragmentation ran along and within the divide in Europe. Bilateralism was evident in eastern Europe through the prevalence of what amounted to barter trade, while the strands of military and political authority ran through Moscow. In western Europe, diversity in political and market institutions was coined into distinct security policies within the framework of the Atlantic alliance, often competing or exclusive industrial policies and national currencies and capital markets.

The rhythm of world and European politics and markets had been set by the interaction between these dynamics. The bipolar system, set in place over the years 1943–55, was subsequently modified by fragmentation through the medium of decolonization, de Gaulle's challenge and the Sino-Soviet rift of the 1960s. Nixon's inauguration as president in 1969 embarked the United States on a redefinition of foreign policy, continuing the policy of containment, but taking into account the formation of the EC and Japan as partners *and* competitors while forging the Sino-US alliance in the years 1972–8. The Soviet Union's concern with China opened the way for the Federal Republic to launch its *ostpolitik* in 1969, while the aggravation of Sino-Soviet rivalry in 1978–9 contributed powerfully to swinging the United States back into a hard containment policy in the line of the NSC 68 paper of 1950. The second cold war, though, occurred in a world in which the tripolar industrial and commercial system had taken shape. The commercial rivalry it entailed, coupled with the Soviet Union's active presence in the Middle East and the more assertive posture of OPEC on world oil markets, informed Nixon's August 1971 decision to take the dollar off gold. As world banker, the United States nudged the world onto a dollar standard, inflated the world economy, and then moved to stabilization in October 1979. The European states prevaricated between maintaining their autonomy in macroeconomic policy, and moving towards union in the EMS. Germany by the early 1980s was clearly the hinge on which European security, markets and monetary conditions depended.

The gradual transformation of the world state and market system, accompanying the rhythm of world politics, was made possible by the flowering of a specifically European society of states, characterized by a density of complex political and market interdependence marking it off from the rest of the world. Once the military boundaries had been staked out between the two powers and the two alliances in 1955, competition between the two systems broadened into the incompatible policies of détente and peaceful coexistence. Détente spelt relaxation of party-state controls in eastern Europe, and dialogue with the western alliance or its members. Peaceful coexistence meant making Europe safe for socialism, involving a gradualist strategy to transform the western political and market system. But the extension of the ideological struggle into a politically fragmented western Europe, which cohered on fundamental principles of political community, contributed to the disintegration of unity in the international communist movement. The cost for western Europe was to have to absorb the ideological struggle into the domestic and Atlantic sources of inflationary growth in the period 1965 to 1978. But the European move to stabilization in the late 1970s, preceding the US global stabilization of October 1979, paralleled the export into the party-states of the values subscribed to in the Helsinki Final Act. The events in Poland in 1980–1 showed clearly that western Europe presented the Soviet Union with a political, economic and civilizational challenge in eastern Europe that it could no longer match.

The evolution of the European society of states was accompanied by a partial, contradictory reconciliation between France and the Federal Republic, successive enlargements of the EC, and the demise of the British Commonwealth as a specific trading and currency system. Its bilateral and multilateral network of relations, tying European states and markets to each other and into the rest of the world, developed first within the blocs. But the centrality of the two world powers to Europe extended the membership of COMECON and the Warsaw Pact beyond Europe, and ensured the opening of the OECD to include Japan. The Council of Europe, with its European Convention of Human Rights as a pendant to the UN Convention, was the sole inclusive western European organization. In external trade relations the functions of the EC were shared with the GATT, whose membership became widened to about one hundred states in the world, and with the BIS in Geneva, which served as the club for central bankers and included the United States. The maturing of the European society of states came in the years 1974–7, with the creation of the European Council, the signing of the Helsinki Final Act and the institutionalization of the seven-power annual summits. Heads of state and government were included into the EC's business, with the Commission as co-pillar. The bicephalous nature of the EC was recorded in the SEA, relaunching the Community in 1985–6.

The change in European attitudes towards the Soviet Union in the 1980s infused a greater assertiveness into relations with the United States. Détente was a European policy, designed in part to keep war away from Europe by binding the United States into a policy of flexible response that became increasingly irksome for Washington to sustain. As the flow of funds from Europe and the world to the United States was the counterpart to the assertion of US policy priorities in the early 1980s over European concerns, western Europe became a reluctant creditor to its reluctant defender. The US became the world's, and western Europe's main export outlet. As the costs for the United States rose of extending its deterrence over western Europe and keeping its markets open, the tensions in the Atlantic alliance were played out in trade conflicts and over nuclear policy. Stabilization as conveyed through high interest rates and relayed through the Bundesbank's primacy in the EMS was less divisive, as external constraints on policy in western European states served to restrict the upward movement of real wages and government transfers. The rub came with Reagan's coupling of his vision to free the world of nuclear weapons, and US backing of dissidents in eastern Europe. The one represented a step towards US withdrawal of nuclear protection from western Europe; the other cut across the western European governments' proclivity to identify the maintenance of détente with good relations between governments, rather than the subversion of the party-states.

The relaunch of the EC, culminating in 1985, coincided with Gorbachev's promotion to the post of Secretary General. The EC's analysis saw Europe's excessive fragmentation as a source of vulnerability to military, monetary or technological initiatives taken in Washington, Moscow or Tokyo. That vulnerability had been particularly visible, too, in 1973–4 and 1978–9, when plans to move to unity had been shredded by political events in the Middle East and Gulf, leading to the two oil shocks. The creation of an 'internal market' and the strengthening of EC institutions was a prerequisite for the Commission to be able to negotiate more forcefully with the United States and Japan. But it meant challenging domestic interests in member states, while extending EC competences deeper into the sphere of social, monetary and security policy. Gorbachev's programme for *perestroika* and *glasnost* likewise drew on an analysis of the inheritance of stagnation in the Soviet economy, tying the process of restructuring to moves to greater freedom of expression. But the policy reconfirmed the leading role of the party, and Moscow's hegemony over the party-states. The Warsaw Pact in April 1985 was renewed for 20 years. Gorbachev then strode on to the world stage with his competing vision to Reagan's to rid the world of nuclear weapons. It included the concept of a 'common European home'.

The novelty in Europe in 1985 was that three visions for its future were now on the table for discussion. The EC's pointed towards more union between the 12 member states; Gorbachev's opened the prospect of a new détente among the 35 signatories to the Helsinki conference; a world 'freed of nuclear weapons' meant at the very least a transformation in the political and psychological support for Europe's inherited security system, and therefore of Germany's place in its centre. This book seeks to analyse the dynamics inherent to the competition between the three visions, and its impact on Europe and the world. It emphasizes the continuing dialectic between extra- and intra-European developments, or the relation between the balance of power and the balance of trade (Liska, 1964) in a world of states.

REFERENCES

Acheson, Dean 1987: *Present at the Creation: My Years at the State Department*. New York: Norton (original edition 1969).
Alting von Geusau, Frans 1982: Die Niederlande und die Modernisierung der Kernwaffen. *Europa Archiv*, 2, 29–38.
Aron, Raymond 1962: *Paix et Guerre entre les Nations*. Paris: Calmann-Lévy.
Aron, Raymond 1973: *Republique Imperiale: Les Etats Unis dans le Monde, 1945–1972*. Paris: Calmann-Lévy.

Ascherson, Neil 1982: *The Polish August: the Self Limiting Revolution*. New York: Viking Press.

Bachrach, Peter and Baratz, Morton 1962: Two faces of power. *American Political Science Review*, 56, December, 947–52.

Baldwin, David 1985: *Economic Statecraft*. Princeton: Princeton University Press.

Bender, Peter 1981: *Das Ende des Ideologischen Zeitalters, Die Europisierung Europas*. Berlin: Severin und Siedler.

Boltho, Andrew 1982: *The European Economy: Growth and Crisis*. *Oxford*: Oxford University Press.

Brown, Brendan 1979: *The Dollar–DM Axis: On Currency Power*. New York: St Martin's Press.

Bull, Hedley 1980: *The Anarchical Society: a Study of Order in World Politics*. London: Macmillan.

Bulmer, Simon and Wessels, Wolfgang 1987: *The European Council: Decision-Making in European Politics*. London: Macmillan.

Bundy, Kennan, McNamara et al. 1982: Nuclear weapons and the Atlantic alliance. *Foreign Affairs*, 60(4), 754–66.

Buzan, Barry, Kelstrup, Morten, Lemaitre, Pierre, Tromer, Elzbieta and Weaver, Ole 1990: *The European Security Order Recast: Scenarios for the Post-Cold War Era*. London: Pinter.

Calleo, David 1978: *The German Problem Reconsidered: Germany and the World Order, 1870 to the Present*. Cambridge: Cambridge University Press.

Calleo, David 1982: *The Imperious Economy*. Cambridge: Cambridge University Press.

Camps, Miriam 1964: *Britain and the European Community, 1955–63*. Princeton: Princeton University Press.

Camps, Miriam 1966: *European Unification in the Sixties: From the Veto to the Crisis*. New York: McGraw-Hill.

Carrère d'Encausse, Hélène 1975: *La Politique Sovietique au Moyen Orient, 1955–1975*. Paris: Fayard.

Carrillo, Santiago 1977: *Eurocommunismo y estado*. Barcelona: Editorial Critica.

Carter, Jimmy 1982: *Keeping Faith*. Toronto/New York: Bantam Books.

Chevalier, Jean-Marie 1973: *Le Nouvel Enjeu Petrolier*. Paris: Calmann-Lévy.

Churchill, Winston 1954: *The Second World War. (Vol. VI): Triumph and Tragedy*. London: Cassell.

de Carmoy, Guy 1967: *Les Politiques Etrangères de la France*. Paris: La Table Ronde.

de Carmoy, Guy 1971: *Le Dossier Europeen de l'Energie: les Marches, les Industries, les Politiques*. Paris: La Table Ronde.

de Carmoy, Guy and Story, Jonathan 1986: *Western Europe in World Affairs: Continuity, Change and Challenge*. New York: Praeger.

Deporte, Anton 1979: *Europe Between the Superpowers: the Enduring Balance*. New Haven: Yale University Press.

De Vries, Tom 1976: Jamaica, or the non-reform of the International Monetary System. *Foreign Affairs*, 54(3), 577–605.

Filo della Torre, Paolo Mortimer, Edward and Story, Jonathan 1979: *Euro-Communism: Myth or Reality*. Harmondsworth: Penguin Books.

Fontaine, Andre 1965–67: *Histoire de la Guerre Froide*. Paris: Fayard.

François-Poncet, Jean 1970: *L'Allemagne Occidentale*. Paris: Sirey.

Fursdon, Francis 1980: *The European Defence Community: a History*. London: Macmillan.

Gaddis, John L. 1982: *Strategies of Containment: A Critical Appraisal of Post-War American National Security Policy*. New York: Oxford University Press.

Gardner, Richard 1980: *Sterling–Dollar Diplomacy in Current Perspective: the Origins and Prospects of Our International Economic Order*. New York: Columbia University Press

GATT 1985: *Le Commerce International, 1984–5* (Table A 24).

Gerbet, Pierre 1983: *La Construction de l'Europe*. Paris: Imprimerie Nationale.

Ghebali, Victor-Yves 1989: *La Diplomatie de la Détente: La CSCE, 1973–1989*. Brussels: Bruylant.

Goldman, Marshall 1987: *Gorbachev's Challenge: Economic Reform in the Age of High Technology*. New York: W. W. Norton.

Grenville, J. A. S. 1974: *The Major International Treaties, 1914–1973: a History and Guide with Texts*. London: Methuen.

Griffith, William 1964: *The Sino-Soviet Rift*. Cambridge: MIT Press.

Griffith, William 1978: *The Ostpolitik of the Federal Republic of Germany*. Cambridge: MIT Press.

Griffith, William (ed.) 1989: *Central and Eastern Europe: the Opening Curtain?* Boulder: Westview Press.

Grosser, Alfred 1978: *Les Occidentaux, les Pays d'Europe et les Etats Unis depuis la Guerre*. Paris: Fayard.

Haftendorn, Helga 1983: *Sicherheit und Entspannung, zur Aussenpolitik der Bundesrepublik 1955–1982*. Baden Baden: Nomos Verlagsgesellschaft.

Halliday, Fred 1983: *The Making of the Second Cold War*. Thetford: Verso.

Hanabusa, Masamichi 1979: *Trade Problems Between Japan and Western Europe*. London: RIIA.

Holloway, David 1978: Foreign and defence policy. In Archie Brown and Michael Kaser (eds) *The Soviet Union Since the Fall of Khrushchev*. London: Macmillan.

Holloway, David 1984: *The Soviet Union and the Arms Race*. New Haven: Yale University Press.

Howard, Michael 1983: *Clausewitz*. Oxford: Oxford University Press.

International Monetary Fund 1984: *Direction of Trade Statistics*. Washington DC.

Johnstone, Diana 1984: *The Politics of Euromissiles, Europe's Role in America's World*. Thetford: Verso.

Kaiser, K., Leber, G., Mertes, A. et al. 1982: Nuclear weapons and the preservation of peace: a German response to no first use. *Foreign Affairs*, 60(5), 753–1170.

Kaiser, Karl 1968: *German Foreign Policy in Transition: Bonn Between East and West*. Oxford: Oxford University Press.

Kennedy, Paul 1989: *The Rise and Fall of the Great Powers: Economic Change and Conflict from 1500 to 2000*. London: Fontana.

Kissinger, Henry 1965: *The Troubled Partnership: a Reappraisal of the Atlantic Alliance*. New York: McGraw-Hill.

Kolodziej, Edward 1974: *French International Policy Under de Gaulle and Pompidou: the Politics of Grandeur*. Ithaca, New York: Cornell University Press.

Kruse, D. C. 1980: *Monetary Integration in Western Europe: EMU, EMS and Beyond*. London/Boston: Butterworths.

Lellouche, Pierre 1980: *La Securité de l'Europe dans les Années 1980*. Paris: IFRI, Economica.

Lellouche, Pierre 1983: *Pacifisme et Dissuasion*. Paris: IFRI, Economica.

Levesque, Jacques 1987: *L'URSS et sa Politique Internationale, de Lenine à Gorbatchev*. Paris: Armand Colin, 2nd edn.

Lipgens, Walter 1983: *Die Europäische Integration*. Stuttgart: Europa Union Verlag.

Liska, George 1964: *Europe Ascendant: the International Politics of Unification*. Baltimore: Johns Hopkins Press.

List, Friedrich 1977: *The National System of Political Economy*. Fairfield, NJ: A. M. Kelley.

Ludlow, Peter 1982: *The Making of the European Monetary System*. London/Boston: Butterworths Scientific.

Maddison, A. 1962: Growth and fluctuation in the world economy, 1870–1960. *Quarterly Review*, Banco Nazionale del Lavoro, June, 127–95.

Mattera, A. 1980: L'arret 'Cassis de Dijon', une nouvelle approche pour la realisation et le bon frictionnement du marché intérieur. *Revue du Marché Commun*, Paris, 241, November, 505–14.

Maull, Hanns 1984: *Energy and Western Security: Studies in International Security*. London: Macmillan.

Mayall, James and Navari, Cornelia 1980: *The End of the Post-War Era: Documents on Great Power Relations 1968–75*. Cambridge: Cambridge University Press.

McNeill, William 1953: *America, Britain and Russia: Their Cooperation and Conflict, 1941–1946*. London/New York/Toronto: Oxford University Press.

Meinecke, Friedrich 1957: *Machiavellism: the Doctrine of Reason of States in Modern History*. London: Routledge & Kegan Paul.

Merle, Marcel 1984: *La Politique Etrangère*. Paris: Presses Universitaires de France.

Merlini, Cesare 1984: *Economic Summits and Western Decision-Making*. New York: St Martin's Press.

Milward, Alan 1984: *The Reconstruction of Western Europe 1945–51*. London: Methuen.

Morgan, Annette 1976: *From Summit to Council: Evolution in the EEC*. London: Chatham House, PEP.

Nau, Henry 1990: *The Myth of America's Decline: Leading the World Economy into the 1990s*. New York: Oxford University Press.

Nitze, Paul 1980: Strategy in the 1980s. *Foreign Affairs*, 59(1), 82–101.

Nordlinger, Eric 1981: *On the Autonomy of the Democratic State*. Cambridge: Harvard University Press.

Northedge, Frank 1981: *The International Political System*. London: Faber.

Nye, Joseph and Keohane, Robert 1977: *Power and Interdependence: World Politics in Transition*. Boston: Little, Brown.

OECD 1985a: *OECD Economic Outlook*, 37, June, 163.

OECD 1985b: *Costs and Benefits of Protectionism*. Paris.

Osgood, Robert 1953: *Ideals and Self-Interest in America's Foreign Relations*. Chicago: Chicago University Press.

Osgood, Robert 1962: *NATO: the Entangling Alliance*. Chicago: Chicago University Press.

Osgood, Robert 1973: *Retreat from Empire? The First Nixon Administration*. Baltimore: Johns Hopkins Press.

Osgood, Robert 1981: The revitalisation of containment. *Foreign Affairs*, 60(3), 465–502.

Pijpers, Alfred et al. 1988: *European Political Cooperation in the 1980s: A Common Policy for Western Europe?* Dordrecht: Martinus Nijhoff.

Putnam, Robert and Baynes, Nicholas 1984: *Hanging Together: The Seven-Power Summit*. Cambridge: Harvard University Press.

Robertson, A. H. 1966: *European Institutions: Cooperation, Integration, Unification*. London: Institute of World Affairs.

Royen, Christoph 1978: *Die Sowietische Koexistenzpolitik gegenuber Westeuropa: Voraussetzungen, Ziele, Dilemmata*. Baden Baden: Nomos Verlagsgesellschaft.

Rummel, Reinhardt (ed.) 1990: *The Evolution of an International Actor: Western Europe's New Assertiveness*. Boulder: Westview Press.

Scammel, W. M. 1983: *The International Economy Since 1945*. London: Macmillan.

Schmidt, Helmut 1978: The Alastair Buchan Memorial Lecture 1977. *Survival*, January–February, 9–17.

Schulz, Eberhard 1980: Charakteristika Sowjetischer Westpolitik und Ihre Auswirkungen auf die Entspannung. In J. Fallenbuch and E. Schulz (eds) *Entspannung am Ende?* Munich: Oldenburg Verlag.

Silj, Allessandro 1967: *Europe's Political Puzzle: a Study of the Fouchet Negotiations and the 1963 Veto*. Cambridge: Harvard University Press.

Spero, Joan Edelman 1981: *The Politics of International Economic Relations*. London: St Martin's Press 2nd edn.

Strange, Susan 1988: *States and Markets: an Introduction to International Political Economy*. Oxford: Basil Blackwell

Thomson, E. P. and Smith, Dan 1980: *Protest and Survive*. London: Penguin Books.

Timmerman, Christian W. A. 1982: La libre circulation des marchandises, in *Trente Ans de Droit Communautaire*, Collection Perspectives Européennes. Commission des Communautes Europeennes, Brussels, pp. 283–5, 295–6.

Tracy, Michael 1982: *Agriculture in Western Europe: Challenge and Response 1880–1980*. London: Harvester Wheatsheaf.

Tsoukalis, Loukas 1977: *The Politics and Economics of European Monetary Integration*. London: Allen & Unwin.

Ulam, Adam 1974: *Expansion and Coexistence: Soviet Foreign Policy 1917–1973*. New York: Praeger.

Volle, Anjelika 1981–2: Innere Wandlungen in Westeuropa: eine neue Generation mit

Veranderten Werten. *Die Internationale Politik*, Jahrbücher der Forschungsinstituts der Deutschen Gesellschaft für Auswärtige Politik. Munich: Oldenbourg Verlag, 1984, pp. 77–91.

Wallace, William 1971: *Foreign Policy and the Political Process*. London: Macmillan.

Waltz, Kenneth 1979: *Theory of International Politics*. Reading, MA: Addison-Wesley.

Willis, Frank Roy 1965: *France, Germany and the New Europe, 1945–1967*. Stanford: Stanford University Press.

PART II
Changes in World Politics

Editor's introduction

This section covers some of the major changes in world affairs as they affect Europe. The Atlantic partnership, built up over the past decades, has rested on the purposeful creation of community based on shared political purposes. The broad framework of economic policy has supplied the content of debates among the western allies, yielding an impressive record with respect to the spread of political rights and economic well-being. Whether this record continues into the future depends in part on the choice of policies pursued.

But the challenges should not be understated. Russia's historic impulse has been to alternate between westernization or isolation. The momentous changes within the Soviet Union since Gorbachev's advent to power in March 1985, and the collapse of the party dictatorships in central and south-eastern Europe in late 1989, have altered Europe's political map. Russia in the early 1990s is closer to Europe than it has been since 1917. Will it move closer or will the pattern of history return as Russia veers to isolation?

There is also the Japan factor. Japan has developed a formidable industrial and commercial empire. It dominates the Pacific Asia in a way that a united Germany cannot hope to in Europe. The significance of the dynamism evident in Pacific Asia is measured in political, market and cultural terms. The most plausible future is the continued priority given in Tokyo to the crucial relationship with the United States. How European industry meets the Japanese challenge will be the key test for the region. Japan has demonstrated that modernization is compatible with the preservation of more traditional values.

Finally, the Atlantic partnership faces the challenges of global interdependence. The prime engine of change is technological innovation, and its evolution is accelerating. Political arrangements are subject to unprecedented strain, as evidenced in the collapse of the stagnant communist party-states. Indeed, the former east faces many of the problems associated with the developing countries of the south. The west–south dimension of the global agenda is now more critical than any other.

2

Europe and America in the 1990s:
no time to mothball the Atlantic partnership

Henry Nau

As Europe and the United States enter the post cold war world, they should remember one thing. Their partnership over the past forty years has overseen one of the most prosperous and peaceful eras of modern history. Today, for the first time since Catholicism ruled in medieval Europe, all of the major industrial powers share a common value – namely, open pluralist, democratic institutions. Increasingly, eastern European and many developing countries do so as well. Even the transitions underway in the former Soviet Union illustrate the struggle to become more open. What is more, economic growth in the postwar era has been more rapid and – what many analysts forget – more equitable than in any previous period for which we have data. From 1950 to 1980, per capita income in some sixty middle-income developing countries grew twice as fast in real terms as it did in the industrial world (Nau, 1990, pp. 20–5). The spread of economic development today is by no means satisfactory but it is wider than ever before.

Keeping these facts in mind is essential if Europe and America are to meet the challenges ahead. The 1990s offers the opportunity to expand the postwar community of prosperous and democratic states to include the peoples of eastern Europe, developing nations who have decided to abandon authoritarian and centrally-controlled economic policies, and perhaps even the old Soviet Empire. It also brings with it threats of new conflicts, however – war in the Middle East, repression in China, the frustration and hopelessness that breeds terrorism, migration and violence in the third world, and perhaps even renewed conflict with Japan. No chance exists to meet these new opportunities and threats unless the Atlantic partnership holds together. The stakes are much larger than preserving an American habit of spending more than it saves or a European nostalgia for small farms. The stakes are nothing short of peace for generations to come. For one fact (and perhaps only one fact) we know from the research of my profession of political science. Historically, open democratic states have rarely fought against one another (Small and Singer, 1982). The challenge of the 1990s is to seize upon and nurture this hopeful trend toward democracy and peace.

There will be those in Europe (some in this volume) and the United States who will object to the idea of a continuing Atlantic partnership. They see the Atlantic alliance of the past forty-five years as a marriage of convenience that can now be safely ended. Europe can declare its independence of both superpowers and claim sole responsibility for reuniting east and west Europe. The United States can stop paying a disproportionate share of security costs for Europe (and Japan) and start paying more attention to its own economic interests in competition with former allies.

These attitudes are understandable but unhelpful. They assume that cultural and historical differences among nations – in this case between Europe and America – are unbridgeable. They interpret postwar events primarily in terms of traditional interstate politics and see the Atlantic partnership as largely a euphemism for the dominance of American power. But international politics is about much more than permanent national differences and unending conflicts of power. It is also about the shaping of international community and the improvement of human economic well-being. To put US–European differences *and* partnership in perspective, we need a more dynamic model of international politics – one that allows for the possibility that political cultures and economic markets change and indeed converge. After all, this is the dynamic that is shaping the formation of a new United States of Europe. It is also the dynamic that has shaped the Atlantic partnership over the past forty years and brought the United States and Europe closer together today than they have ever been in the past.

A voluntarist, choice-oriented model

A model of international politics that allows for change cannot be governed exclusively by laws of history. (See chapter 1 in this volume.) It has to allow for voluntarist choice that changes historical circumstances. My recent research suggests that there are two important sets of choices that societies make that have significantly influenced postwar history: (1) the way western societies defined their political personalities or what I call their national purpose; and (2) the large economic policy choices they made to influence the efficiency of resource use – macroeconomic, microeconomic and trade policy choices (Nau, 1990a, ch. 1).

National purpose

How nations define themselves is what we mean by national culture. A critical element of national culture is politics – how societies choose to organize their political relationships with one another. These choices involve two basic issues: (1) What aspects of political life in any given group, country, or international system are going to be reserved for private decision making and initiative? (2) How are those aspects that remain public to be decided? The first issue concerns the central question of human and civil rights in political life; the second involves the question of whether the voting franchise for public decision making will extend to all or most individuals or only to a small, politically privileged elite.

Over the centuries, groups and nations have made different choices with respect to these issues of public and private rights and democratic institutions. Some have chosen to centralize power in the hands of the state; others have chosen democratic systems. Out of these varying choices arise contemporary confrontations between totalitarian and democratic societies. Countries with differing domestic political personalities will face limits in their international relationships with one another and will compete to decide how issues of human rights and political participation are resolved at the international level.

What is impressive about the situation in the world today is that all major industrial countries (some twenty-four countries altogether), for the first time ever, are democratic states. These nations share an important element of national culture, namely a political commitment to basic human rights and popular political participation. This fact is not trivial, and it is the underlying empirical and historical basis for asserting that there is much more of a partnership among western nations today than has ever been true in the past. Whatever differences persist between European and Atlantic nations, they share a common political personality.

Large economic policy choices

Just as societies choose their politics, they also choose economic policies. Some societies organize their economies centrally with little role for private activity; others emphasize private entrepreneurship and ownership, with governments limiting their role to broad macroeconomic, infrastructure and trade policy choices.

Table 2.1 identifies factors that influence economic outcomes. While more deterministic approaches to international politics emphasize the role of relatively long-term and deep-seated institutions or social coalitions in economic policy, my approach emphasizes the role of more immediate government policies that affect directly the price of goods and capital assets in international exchanges (see the fourth column of table 2.1) and that seek to place broad limits on the behaviour of governments in areas where institutional differences exist (see the third column of table 2.1, e.g. limits on subsidies to state-owned firms).

Economies converge toward or diverge from one another depending upon the policy and institutional choices each country makes. If policy or institutional differences become too large, countries cannot achieve significant economic exchanges. For example, if governments pursue diverging exchange rate policies, as they did in the 1930s and to a lesser extent in the 1970s and early 1980s, they discourage stable trade and investment flows. Or if countries differ too greatly in domestic traditions and institutions, as eastern and western countries have done in the postwar period or as some analysts now claim the United States and Japan do, they may be unable to accept common rules on more immediate government policies to maintain, for example, convertible currencies or liberalize trade.

According to this perspective, therefore, Europe and America have developed intensive economic interdependence with one another because they have adopted converging economic policies and institutions. Economic interdependence is not something that dooms Europe and America to

Table 2.1 Factors affecting international economic competition

Endowments	Infrastructure	Domestic institutions	More immediate government policies
Natural resources	Transportation	State/society relations	Domestic policies
Population	Roads	Role of private vs public actors in various activities	Macroeconomic
Climate	Ports	Production	Fiscal
Land	Railroads	R&D	Monetary
	Airlines	Consumption	Overall regulatory (e.g. antitrust)
		Finance	Microeconomic[a]
	Communications		Labour regulations
	Telecommunications	State policymaking	Sector-specific policies (e.g. for agriculture, financial services, etc.)
		Degree of centralized vs decentralized administration	Subsidies to industry
	Energy and power		
		Society networks	Exchange-rate policies
	Human capital	Market structures (e.g. competitive vs oligopolistic)	
	Literacy/education	Corporate structures (e.g. large vs small, management–labour–bank relations, etc.)	Trade policies
	Nutrition		Tariffs
	Health		Non-tariff barriers (e.g. health and safety standards)
			Financial market and official exchange reserve policies

[a] Microeconomic policies are also commonly referred to as structural policies. We use both terms in this study but the term *structural* should not be confused with the term *structuralist*, which refers to broad conceptual approaches to international economic relations discussed in Nau 1990a.
Source: Nau, 1990a, p. 36, reproduced by the kind permission of Oxford University Press.

economic partnership. It is something they have chosen jointly and something which they can in the future reject.

Learning from the past

Interpreting the recent past from a dynamic, voluntarist perspective on international politics may yield new insights. It may help to explain how convergence toward democracy has occurred at the same time that America's relative power has declined, a fact which realist perspectives are unable to explain (Kennedy, 1987). It may also help to explain the variations in growth performance in the postwar period. Conventional explanations attribute growth either to favourable circumstances beyond the influence of policy (Gilpin, 1987) or to social compromises after the war that have not changed and hence cannot account for variations in postwar performance (Ruggie, 1983). In what follows, we try out this new choice-oriented perspective first to explain the origins of the cold war and then to explain more broadly the evolution of the postwar world economy.

Origins of the cold war

Conventional theories offer two explanations for the origins of the cold war – a clash of fundamental political ideologies and a vacuum of power. These ideological and realist explanations, however, offer at best, only a partial understanding. The realist view that World War II left a vacuum of power in central Europe that had to be filled by conflicting US and Soviet security and economic interests does not tell us why US and Soviet interests differed. Even if American and Soviet interests had been irreconcilable in central Europe, it was not inevitable that they should lead to conflict, particularly military conflict. Differences, if recognized, can be managed – most safely by mutual attention to balancing competitive military and economic capabilities or, alternatively, by careful and delicate diplomacy to identify sufficient overlapping interests (especially in a nuclear age, for example, to avoid mutual destruction).

Similarly, idealist or ideological views that attribute the cold war to fundamentally opposed domestic political systems in the United States and the Soviet Union do not tell us why these domestic differences had to lead to severe economic and military conflict. The ideological characteristics of a country do not lead to predictable diplomatic behaviour. In 1945, for example, Wilsonian ideology led the United States to withdraw precipitously from Europe both economically and militarily. But, in 1950, containment or anti-communist ideology caused the United States to recommit itself to Europe. Ideology, in short, explains little about how specific economic and political efforts from 1945 to 1950 failed to find some common middle ground of accommodation between the United States and the Soviet Union.

The true origins of the cold war can be found between the Wilsonian and containment phases of US policy. After leaving Europe in 1945 to pursue a globalist solution to world order – through the UN and Bretton Woods institutions – the United States expected European states to undertake the task of national economic and political reconstruction. The only country expected to require US assistance in this task was an occupied and divided Germany. But how was Germany to be reintegrated politically to promote economic reconstruction? The wartime allies agreed on the de-nazification of Germany, but they disagreed on whether pluralist or communist political and economic principles would replace nazi socialism (Pollard, 1987). The Yalta agreements gave the west hope that the Soviet Union would accept pluralist political institutions and free elections, initially in Poland, Czechoslovakia and other east European countries, and eventually in the whole of Germany. The same agreements led the Soviet Union to believe that the west accepted the coexistence of competitive political systems in central Europe and might even tolerate the ascendancy of communist parties in western European political systems.

The conflicting expectations about domestic political developments in Germany and more broadly in Europe as a whole did not have to lead to growing mistrust and military conflict between the United States and the Soviet Union. As long as the two countries were able to communicate with one another politically (as they were, for example, during the war) and possessed roughly comparable capabilities to exert economic leverage, they might have waged a kind of peaceful symmetrical competition to decide the fortunes of communism and democracy in Europe. The capabilities for leverage, however, were asymmetrical. The Soviet Union (and communist parties in Europe) possessed political advantages that derived from the relatively closed and collusive, if not conspiratorial, manner in which communist parties operated and from the view in many quarters at the time that communist systems represented the wave of the future. These political advantages were reinforced in eastern Europe by the presence of large Soviet military forces, which had not been withdrawn as had US forces in western Europe. The United States, on the other hand, was the only industrial power to emerge largely unscathed from World War II and possessed significant economic advantages. What happened from 1945 to 1947 is that the United States and democratic parties in western Europe came to fear the political and military advantages of the Soviet Union in eastern Europe, particularly the potential appeal of communism in western Europe under prevailing circumstances of economic stagnation. The Soviet Union, in turn, came to fear the economic advantages of the west, particularly as the west began to use that advantage to launch economic recovery in the western zones of Germany and western Europe more generally.

The asymmetries in capabilities between the Soviet Union and the United States were compounded by differing perceptions of the links between these capabilities. The shapers of the Marshall Plan in the United States believed that their efforts were aimed primarily at poverty and not against a particular form of government (i.e. communism) (Price, 1955). They hoped to separate economic from political considerations. Some planners believed that once European states recovered economically, they would retain or choose pluralist democratic political systems. Others, however, such as George Kennan, did not consider that either necessary or desirable (Kennan opposed, for example, imposing western style democracy on Germany) (Kennan, 1967). Not perceiving linkages between economics and politics, American planners did not anticipate that the Soviet Union would reject participation in the

Marshall Plan nor that the Soviets would react militarily (i.e. the Berlin blockade) to monetary and economic reforms in the western zones of Germany. The Soviet Union, by contrast, saw military and political capabilities as closely linked and both as a primary means of gaining economic leverage. The Soviets were using their political and military control of institutions and resources in eastern Europe to extract reparations for economic reconstruction in the Soviet Union.

This choice-oriented view of the origins of the cold war suggests that what countries are politically (that is, their choice of national purpose) has a lot to do with what they can accomplish together diplomatically (that is, their choice of economic and other relationships). This perspective does not mean, however, that ideologically opposed powers must inevitably clash. They can manage peace but must do so largely through a careful balancing of military, political and economic advantages. Imbalances will give rise to mutual suspicions because the two powers do not have sufficient access to and understanding of one another politically to avoid such suspicions. At the same time, the perspective developed here suggests that international politics does not stop with the balancing of mutual power. The objective is eventually to create community based on shared political purposes. The competition among national purposes is the means to define this common community. Debates about whether to organize political society along free or totalitarian lines are not, therefore, the source of conflict in international politics; they are ultimately the source of community. Indeed, community beyond the balance of power is not possible without these debates. They do not threaten peace as long as states observe the need to balance mutual advantages while they compete politically.

With this understanding, it is possible to investigate what choices have been made in the postwar period that have contributed to the building of political community among states (initially, among industrial states that had been erstwhile enemies – France and Germany, the United States and both Germany and Japan – and today among a wider group of states including developing and former communist states) and to the promotion of unprecedented economic growth and prosperity. The following analysis looks at these choices of national purpose and economic policy in the United States and other major industrial countries.

Building political community

As noted earlier, national purpose defines a nation's approach to the two key dimensions of international political society – the internal or domestic dimension that defines the scope of individual (human) rights at the global level, and the external or diplomatic dimension that establishes the global decision-making mechanisms (inter-governmental agreements, universalist organizations, etc.) by which all other decisions that are not reserved for individual or private action are made in world society.[1]

In the postwar period, the United States projected various national purposes summarized in table 2.2. Before World War II, the United States placed exclusive emphasis on the domestic dimension of international politics to the exclusion of any active interest or involvement in the diplomatic dimension.

Table 2.2 Varying definitions of US national purpose

Dimensions of international political community	Isolationism pre-World War II	Wilsonianism 1942–6	Containment 1947–67	Detente 1967–79	Reagan policies 1979–87	Era of liberalization 1988–?
Domestic content	Uniqueness of American politics	No basic differences	Freedom versus communism	Coexistence and possible long-term convergence	Freedom vs communism	Deepening liberalization in western Europe and initial liberalization of eastern societies toward more pluralist and competitive standards
Diplomatic construction	Non-involvement	Functional problems	Military alliance and economic integration within the west	Web of political and economic interdependence capping military race and possibly demilitarizing international relations	Military and economic strength of the west leading to balanced arms reductions, including possible denuclearization of east–west relations	Reduction of military forces, including possible denuclearization of central Europe and integration of eastern countries into the international economic system

Source: Nau 1990a, p. 28, reproduced by the kind permission of Oxford University Press.

Isolationism defined America as a unique society with no obligations or role towards the outside world. In 1945, the United States went to the opposite extreme and entertained a universalist–utopian vision of world community which stressed diplomatic relationships structured around common functional problems – food, health, money, trade, etc. – that completely ignored differences in the domestic content of political society (e.g. democratic versus totalitarian definitions of human rights). This conception failed to win wider social acceptance, particularly in the Soviet Union, and, although some global institutions were established which included the Soviet Union – the United Nations and Bretton Woods organizations – these institutions were unable to agree on and implement substantive political or economic programmes. Even on a bilateral basis among the western countries, widely differing conceptions of property rights – between the ruling Labour Party in Great Britain and a conservative Republican Congress in the United States – prevented successful implementation of international economic cooperation to rescue the British pound or to initiate postwar European economic reconstruction. International politics drifted toward conflict and the postwar economic institutions and reconstruction languished.

Eventually, as noted earlier, differences between east and west concerning the domestic political organization of society in central Europe (Germany, Poland, Czechoslovakia) sharpened diplomatic conflicts in 1947–8 and gave rise to the cold war. American policy shifted to containment which clearly expressed the free world's concept of political society rooted in individual freedom and mobilized diplomatic mechanisms (e.g. NATO, which was originally a purely political organization) to defend that concept in central Europe. A heightened sense of common political purpose facilitated a convergence of economic goals and policies, both within western Europe (the Franco-German reconciliation and the initiation of western European economic integration) and within the Atlantic community (the Marshall Plan). Regional institutions were created to develop more competitive and interdependent markets and, once these markets existed, some of these institutions actually disappeared (e.g. the European Payments Union, the Economic Cooperation Administration, etc.). The Soviet Union constructed counterpart diplomatic and economic mechanisms (Warsaw Pact and COMECON) in the east which operated on different principles of monolithic party control and command economies. While it was not inevitable that these political and economic differences would lead to military confrontation, it was also not surprising. The Korean war in 1950 militarized the diplomatic division in central Europe.

Understandably, Europe was never comfortable with its own division and militarization. Having lived with totalitarian political traditions of its own, western Europe was also less offended by internal repression in the east and more eager to coexist with and to build diplomatic bridges to the east. Already in the early 1960s, French President de Gaulle began to project an alternative definition of political society in central Europe, one which stressed international political and economic contacts and interdependence that might eventually permit the reduction of military forces and bring about a convergence in fundamental political values between east and west. Known as détente, this concept of political society in central Europe weakened the rationale for western European and Atlantic economic integration. It encouraged experimentation with more aggressive interventionist policies in western economies (see next section of this chapter for evidence) and with institutionally rather than market-driven relationships between east and west (e.g. subsidized trade and credits). Cartelization of oil markets by OPEC countries extended this new 'institutionalism' in diplomatic relations to north–south relations as well (the era of the 'new international economic order').

Détente gained ascendancy in Europe in the late 1960s as America extended the militarization of the east–west conflict to Vietnam and third world countries and, in the process, appeared to undercut the original political rationale of containment by aligning with societies that were less than free (e.g. South Vietnam). Détente also inspired expectations of convergence between domestic systems in east and west. While western countries experimented with more interventionist economic policies, the Soviet Union and eastern European countries tested some modest market-oriented reforms. Both experiments proved less than satisfactory. The Brezhnev doctrine and priority expenditures for the military sector suppressed both political liberalization and economic growth in the east. Meanwhile, the Soviet Union undertook its own militarization of the cold war in central Europe through deployment of intermediate range nuclear missiles and in third world countries through interventions in Ethiopia, Angola, Indochina, and, ultimately, Afghanistan. The decade ended with neither diplomatic bridges nor domestic reform between east and west.

Afghanistan triggered a renewed awareness of continuing differences between totalitarian and free societies in world affairs. The United States and other western countries reasserted the principles of free societies and competitive markets and initiated the deployment of counterbalancing intermediate-range nuclear forces (INF) and a reversal of inflation and regulation (intervention) in western markets. In the Soviet Union, meanwhile, the Brezhnev era ended, and Mikhail Gorbachev launched the Soviet Union and eastern world on an apparent new course of internal political and economic liberalization and external demilitarization.

In the early 1990s, a potential new era of liberalization in east–west relations opened up. For the first time in the postwar period, decisive economic reforms are being implemented in eastern Europe and hope continues that, despite reversals, liberal reforms may still gain the upper hand in the former Soviet Union. Meanwhile, western Europe is deepening its internal commitment to liberal economic policies (Europe 1992), although the west as a whole (US–EC–Japan) may be on the verge of breaking up into regional blocs with the delayed conclusion of the Uruguay Round of global trade negotiations.

The convergence of domestic political and economic systems creates a new and firmer basis for construction of peaceful and prosperous international relations between east and west. Already, the superpowers have negotiated significant arms reduction agreements (INF and CFE), eliminating the central military threat that endangered NATO security for forty years (i.e. a massed Warsaw Pact conventional thrust through central Europe). The Conference on Security and Cooperation in Europe (CSCE), bringing together the members of NATO, the Warsaw Pact and neutral countries in

Europe, met in Paris in November 1990 to formalize a potential new arrangement to manage continuing disputes in Europe on the common grounds of shared human rights and democratic institutions. The EC is engaged in negotiating new association agreements with both the EFTA countries and the frontline states of eastern Europe – Poland, Hungary and Czechoslovakia – and has simultaneously launched new inter-governmental conferences to work out the terms of further economic and monetary union among the twelve and to define a new political and security community in Europe – a community with still undefined relations to NATO, on the one hand, and neutral European countries, on the other.

The possibilities are enormous because, unlike during the period of détente, domestic and international reforms may be working in the same direction. Much depends, therefore, on the success of liberal reforms in eastern Europe and the Soviet Union, the stability and energy of democracy in a reunited Germany, and the ability of the democratic triumvirate of the United States, European Community and Japan to remain open and accessible to one another, not only economically but politically (see concluding section of this chapter).

There will be continuing debate in the west about how all of these hopeful developments came about. Some, especially in Europe, will argue that the détente openings of the 1970s were decisive, creating the human rights watchdog mechanisms of the CSCE and encouraging liberal reformers in the Soviet Union and eastern Europe. Others, perhaps more often in America, will argue that the military, economic and political revitalization of the west in the 1980s was key, demonstrating to the Soviet leadership that they could neither intimidate nor compete with the west using their traditional, repressive military and economic policies.

From the perspective of this chapter, both détente and western revitalization were essential. In its domestic dimension, détente expressed the human freedoms that lie at the heart of western political societies (although some expressions of détente, such as the joint ideological statement of the West German Social Democratic Party and East German Communist Party in 1987, blurred the conventional distinctions between social democracy and communism (Larrabee, 1989). But, in its diplomatic dimension, détente expected too much from a growing web of economic and political interdependence between east and west. It neglected the need to continue to balance military and economic advantages between societies that practised fundamentally different political principles at home. Policies of revitalization in the 1980s looked after these balances (e.g. deploying INF weapons) and created the opportunity for eastern societies to reconsider and choose alternative directions for their domestic evolution.

Building economic prosperity

Building political community is only one side of the equation, however. Related is the ability of states to create economic wealth and well-being. The postwar era has been extraordinarily successful in this respect. From the voluntarist perspective of this essay, these outcomes can be explained in terms of conscious economic policy choices.

As we noted earlier, the Bretton Woods institutions created in 1944 did not initiate postwar recovery in the west. They established an institutional process of policy coordination but did not supply an efficient policy content for this process. The IMF agreement, while calling for fixed exchange rates, did not insist on domestic economic policies of fiscal and monetary discipline or market flexibility that would have helped to ensure stable prices (and hence stable exchange rates). Nor did it call for lowering trade barriers even though Europe at the time was choking under the grip of over two hundred bilateral, managed trade agreements (i.e. quotas). As a result, postwar reconstruction languished from 1945 to 1947 (Nau, 1990a, ch. 3)

The policy content for efficient economic growth was supplied by the Marshall Plan consensus of 1947–8. That becomes evident, as we look at indicators of economic policy choices in the major industrial countries from 1947 to 1987. These indicators focus on the three large economic policies identified earlier that can plausibly be related to efficient economic growth: macroeconomic (fiscal and monetary) policies, microeconomic (structural) policies and trade policies.

Tables 2.3, 2.4 and 2.5 offer a summary statistical snapshot of correlations between economic policy choices and outcomes among western countries for different periods from 1947 to 1987. While the indicators of economic policy are aggregate and crude, they show very strong correlations between policy choices and economic performance for the first two periods, from 1947 to 1967 and 1968 to 1980, that can be fully explained in terms of classical economic theory. In the first period, restrained macroeconomic and microeconomic policies (table 2.3) combined with the significant liberalization of trade policies (both quotas and tariffs – table 2.4) to produce (correlate with) the highest levels of growth and lowest levels of inflation and unemployment in the postwar period (table 2.5), including the period from 1945 to 1947 (not shown in the tables) when inflation and unemployment in Europe were rampant and growth stagnant. In the second period, highly stimulative macroeconomic policies, a rapidly growing public sector, and creeping trade protectionism produced (correlated with) significantly higher inflation and unemployment and slower growth. These relationships in both periods are exactly what classical economic theory would predict.[2]

Since 1980, the relationships are more clouded, reflecting the reversal of some inefficient economic policy choices after 1980, but the continuation and even acceleration of others. Monetary policy, for example, was noticeably tightened on average in the western countries, particularly in the early 1980s in comparison to the late 1970s (compare numbers in parentheses for 1977–9 and 1980–2 in columns 2 and 3 of table 2.3). Similarly, on average, microeconomic intervention in western economies was sharply reduced and even reversed, especially after 1983 (numbers in parentheses in column 4 of table 2.3). On the other hand, fiscal policies expanded even further after 1980 (numbers in parentheses in column 1 of table 2.3), and trade policies became more noticeably restrictive, particularly through the growth of quotas or voluntary restraint agreements (table 2.4). Performance, not surprisingly, was mixed (table 2.5). Whereas inflation declined significantly overall, unemployment continued to climb in Europe and growth failed to recapture the levels of even the 1970s, let alone the 1950s and 1960s. Only in the

Table 2.3 Economic policy indicators, 1947–1987

Countries or groups of countries	Macroeconomic policy — Fiscal: Budget deficit (avg.[a] annual as % of GDP)	Macroeconomic policy — Monetary: M_1 (avg. annual % change)	Macroeconomic policy — Monetary: M_2 (avg. annual % change)	Microeconomic policy — Public sector: Government expenditures as % of GDP (avg. % point change per decade)
	1947–67	**1947–67**	**1947–67**	**1947–67**
US	−0.2	2.5	5.3	1.6
G4[b]	−0.7	11.0	12.5	−0.5
G5[c]	−0.6	9.3	11.0	0.0
G7[d]	−0.9	9.6	10.7	0.5
Quad[e]	−0.9	9.5	11.2	0.8
DCs[f]	−0.9	5.2	7.9	NA
LDCs[g]	NA	11.5	14.9	NA
	1968–80	**1968–80 (1977–9)**	**1968–80 (1977–9)**	**1968–80**
US	−2.0	6.4 (7.9)	8.8 (9.4)	1.9
G4	−2.1	11.1 (11.2)	12.9 (10.5)	6.0
G5	−2.1	10.1 (10.5)	12.0 (10.3)	5.1
G7	−3.1	11.2 (11.7)	13.3 (12.7)	5.4
Quad	−2.9	10.7 (11.6)	12.8 (12.5)	7.7
DCs	−2.2	9.0 (9.9)	11.4 (11.4)	5.8
LDCs	−3.0	25.0 (28.3)	28.1 (33.8)	4.3
	1981–7 (1983–7)	**1981–7 (1980–2)**	**1981–7 (1980–2)**	**1981–7 (1983–7)**
US	−4.6 (−5.0)	9.3 (6.7)	9.0 (6.2)	−0.9 (−4.6)
G4	−3.6 (−3.4)	9.7 (7.3)	10.5 (10.9)	−1.6 (−4.0)
G5	−3.8 (−3.7)	9.6 (7.1)	10.2 (10.0)	−1.4 (−4.1)
G7	−5.2 (−5.3)	10.7 (7.6)	10.0 (10.8)	0.2 (−4.2)
Quad	−6.4 (−6.3)	10.7 (7.1)	11.1 (10.3)	1.4 (−6.0)
DCs	−4.9 (−5.0)	8.7 (6.6)	9.4 (8.9)	0.3 (−3.3)
LDCs	−4.9 (−4.8)	39.1 (30.5)	44.4 (35.0)	3.2 (3.0)

[a] Averages calculated from individual country tables compiled from sources. Averages in columns 1, 2, and 3 do not include all years for every country. Averages in column 4 are standardized on per decade basis

[b] G4 = G5 without United States

[c] G5 = France, Germany, Japan, United Kingdom, United States

[d] G7 = Canada, France, Germany, Italy, Japan, United Kingdom, United States

[e] Quad = European Community, United States, Canada, and Japan. From 1947 to 1967, EC = 6 (Belgium, France, Germany, Italy, Luxemburg, Netherlands); from 1968 to 1980, EC = 9 (plus UK, Ireland, and Denmark); from 1981 to 1987, EC = 10 (plus Greece)

[f] DCs = Industrial countries as found in IMF, *IFS Yearbooks*

[g] LDCs = Developing countries as found in IMF, *IFS Yearbooks*

Source: Nau, 1990a, pp. 374–5, reproduced by the kind permission of Oxford University Press.

Table 2.4 Trade policy indicators, 1950–1985

Country	Non-tariff barriers (NTBs)[a] — % private trade freed[b]			NTB products (timeline 1970–1985)	Expiration date[c]	Tariffs[d]					% change 1965–85
	1950[b]	1955[b]	1960[b]			1965	1970	1975	1980	1985	
Canada				Textiles →	1991	7.95	5.66	5.46	4.62	3.25	−59.1
				← Footwear →	1985						
France	53	76	95	← Autos →	Indefinite	6.05	2.33	1.43	1.07	0.78	−87.1
				← Autos →	Indefinite						
				Electronics →	Indefinite						
				← Footwear →	Indefinite						
				← Motorcycles →	Indefinite						
Germany	47	90	93	← Autos →	1984	4.64	3.04	2.36	1.81	1.80	−61.3
Italy	54	99	98	← Footwear →	Indefinite	5.94	4.66	0.57	0.78	0.89	−85.0
				Electronics →	Indefinite						
				Autos →	Indefinite						
				← Motorcycles →	Indefinite						
Japan	← Autos (discretionary licensing) →			Textiles →	Indefinite	7.55	7.05	2.96	2.46	2.13	−71.8
UK	57	84	97	← Autos →	1991	5.97	2.76	2.25	2.17	1.45	−75.7
				← Footwear →	Indefinite						
				← Electronics →	Indefinite						
					Indefinite						
US				Textiles →	1991	6.75	6.08	3.79	3.08	3.05	−54.8
				← Footwear →	1983						
				Electronics →	1984						
				← Autos →	1989						
				Carbon ← Steel →	1989						
				← Specialty steel →	1987						
				← Motorcycles →	1988						
EC				← Steel →	Indefinite						
				Carbon Steel	1991						
				← Textiles →	Indefinite						
				← Autos →	1986						
				← Electronics →	1986						
				← Motorcycles →							
OEEC/OECD	56	84	94			6.79	5.05	3.32	2.43	2.13	−74.9

[a] Includes, in addition to quotas, various restrictive arrangements with various countries, including basic price systems, OMAs, and VERs

[b] These columns show per cent of private trade freed from quotas (quantitative restrictions) by 30 June of indicated year

[c] Column does not reflect all renewals since 1935

[d] Receipts from customs and import duties as percentage of value of imports

Source: Nau, 1990a, pp. 376–7, reproduced by the kind permission of Oxford University Press.

Table 2.5 Economic performance indicators, 1947–1987

Countries or groups of countries	Growth Real GDP (avg.[a] annual % change)		CPI Inflation (avg. annual % change)		GDP deflator Inflation (avg. annual % change)		Unemployment Wokforce unemployed (avg. annual %)	
1947–67	1947–67		1947–67		1947–67		1947–67	
US	3.6		2.7		2.9		4.7	
G4	6.6		3.7		4.4		2.0	
G5	6.0		3.5		4.1		2.5	
G7	5.9		3.8		4.7		3.4	
Quad	5.3		3.5		4.6		3.8	
DCs	4.3		2.5		2.8		3.1	
LDCs	5.0		8.6		8.5		NA	
1968–80	1968–80		1968–80		1968–80		1968–80	
US	2.6		7.2		6.9		5.9	
G4	3.8		8.4		8.6		3.1	
G5	3.5		8.1		8.2		3.7	
G7	3.7		8.5		8.9		4.2	
Quad	3.9		8.3		8.7		4.4	
DCs	3.3		7.9		7.9		4.4	
LDCs	5.7		16.5		17.2		NA	
1981–7 (1983–7)	1981–7	(1983–7)	1981–7	(1983–7)	1981–7	(1983–7)	1981–7	(1983–7)
US	2.8	(4.0)	4.3	(3.3)	4.6	(3.3)	7.8	(7.5)
G4	2.8	(2.8)	4.8	(3.4)	4.2	(3.6)	7.8	(8.2)
G5	2.8	(3.0)	4.7	(3.4)	4.3	(3.6)	7.8	(8.1)
G7	2.7	(3.1)	5.7	(4.4)	5.5	(4.5)	8.5	(8.8)
Quad	2.1	(2.4)	7.0	(5.5)	7.4	(6.3)	9.1	(9.5)
DCs	2.7	(3.2)	5.2	(3.9)	4.9	(4.0)	8.2	(8.7)
LDCs	1.8	(1.7)	37.0	(40.4)	41.3	(48.4)	NA	NA

[a] Averages calculated from individual country tables compiled from the preceding sources. They do not include all years for every country
Source: Nau, 1990a, pp. 378–9, reproduced by the kind permission of Oxford University Press.

United States did growth after 1983 exceed earlier levels and unemployment plunged almost to the levels of 1947–67 (5 per cent in early 1989 compared to 4.7 per cent for the period from 1947 to 1967).

Some explanations of postwar economic growth that trace recovery back to the New Deal and interventionist policies of the war and early postwar period (1945–7) incorrectly identify the policy choices of the period from 1947–8 (Maier, 1977; Ruggie, 1983). They miss the important shift of economic policies that occurred in 1947–8 towards conservative or neo-classical policies, in both the United States and Europe. Rather than supporting continued inflationary and interventionist policies, the consensus in the United States shifted in 1946–7 sharply towards moderate Keynesian fiscal policies (the standard being a slight budget surplus at maximum, not full, employment), a monetary policy aimed at stable domestic prices (rather than at low interest rates), a 'truce' on microeconomic intervention, and freer trade policies (Stein, 1984; Collins, 1981). This consensus, adumbrated in the Employment Act of 1946, became the basis for US Marshall Plan programmes in Europe and served to reinforce and, in some cases, initiate policy changes in the same moderate Keynesian direction in Europe (Hogan, 1987). It was this policy shift, according to the interpretation offered in this essay, that ignited the era of rapid growth after 1947.

Conventional explanations also underestimate the inefficient consequences of economic policy choices after the mid 1960s. In the late 1960s, according to these explanations, the favourable postwar circumstances for growth – pent-up demand and abundant labour and other supplies – disappeared. The oil crisis compounded the unfavourable situation (Gilpin, 1987). Economic policies throughout the industrial and developing world shifted to more stimulative and interventionist objectives largely to offset the recessionary impact of higher oil prices. Thus, the policy shifts recorded in table 2.3, according to these interpretations, followed rather than led a slowdown in economic performance, with the latter caused largely by a shift in circumstances outside the control of policy.

The evidence in this essay, reinforced by work of the Organization for Economic Cooperation and Development (OECD), suggests otherwise. As tables 2.6 and 2.4 show, shifts towards more stimulative macroeconomic, especially monetary, policies and more restrictive trade policies clearly preceded the first oil crisis. The OECD concluded that these shifts had at least as much to do with creating the underlying inflationary conditions that permitted the quadrupling of oil prices as the latter had to do with reinforcing unfavourable policy circumstances (OECD, 1977). At the very least, it is difficult to pass these policy shifts off as either irrelevant for deteriorating economic performance in this period or as mere consequences of the oil crisis.

Policies shifted again in the late 1970s. Monetary and microeconomic policies reverted to the non-inflationary and non-interventionist standards of the earlier postwar period, whereas fiscal and trade policies, especially in the United States, continued in the expansionary and restrictive directions respectively of the 1970s. Conventional explanations (that is, those which emphasize circumstances rather than policy choices) interpret these shifts as evidence of the limits of neo-classical market policies in a world of complex interdependence and diffused power. According to these ex-

Table 2.6 Economic policy shifts after 1967

| | Macroeconomic policy | | | Microeconomic policy |
| | Fiscal | Monetary | | Public sector |
Countries or groups of countries	Budget deficit (avg. annual as % of GDP)	M_1 (avg. annual % change)	M_2 (avg. annual % change)	Government expenditures as % of GDP (avg. % point change per decade)
	1961–7	1961–7	1961–7	1961–7
US	−0.8	3.5	7.5	1.7
G4	−0.9	11.2	12.6	0.7
G5	−0.9	9.6	11.6	0.9
G7	−1.2	10.3	11.6	1.1
Quad	−1.4	9.7	11.1	1.2
DCs	−0.9	6.4	9.4	4.0
LDCs	NA	15.1	16.6	NA
	1968–74	1968–74	1968–74	1968–74
US	−1.1	6.1	8.3	−1.6
G4	−0.7	11.2	14.5	4.0
G5	−0.8	10.2	13.2	3.2
G7	−1.5	11.4	13.9	3.8
Quad	−1.4	10.5	13.1	4.1
DCs	−1.1	8.9	11.4	4.3
LDCs	−2.6	20.5	28.1	5.7

Source: Nau, 1990a, p. 380, reproduced by the kind permission of Oxford University Press.

planations, Reagan's policies of extreme monetarism (tight money) and supply-side tax cuts (loose fiscal policy) pushed up interest rates and the dollar, precipitating an enormous inflow of capital and imports which ultimately forced Reagan's market-oriented policies 'back to the centre' (Nye, 1988; Oye, Lieber and Rothchild, 1987). Exchange market intervention, restrictive trade policies, and prospective tax increases – all became necessary once again to cope with the complexities of interdependence.

The conventional explanations account for the shortcomings of Reagan policies better than for the successes of those policies. Conventional explanations, for example, overlook the dramatic improvement in manufacturing productivity in the United States in the 1980s (3.6 per cent per year from 1981 to 1990, three times higher than in the 1970s and 33 per cent higher than the 2.7 per cent per year from 1948 to 1973; for recent confirmed statistics, see Bureau of Labour Statistics, February 1991 and related article in *New York Times*, 5 February, 1991, p. A1). They ignore the unprecedented high rates of real investment in the US economy, not wanting to give any credit to supply-side tax policies;[3] and they generally attribute the conquest of inflation to the policies of Paul Volcker, chairman of the Federal Reserve Board from 1979 to 1987, ignoring the steady and substantial support which Reagan gave Volcker in the fight against inflation (Stockman, 1988; Anderson, 1988).

By the criteria in this chapter, Reagan's policies get credit for important improvements in economic performance in the 1980s, as well as blame for failing to follow through and complete the transition back to the neo-classical premises of the earlier postwar policy consensus, particularly in fiscal and trade policy areas (Huntington, 1988–9). And, although time will eventually run out, it is still possible, according to this interpretation, that policy changes to reduce the budget deficit and reinvigorate the multilateral trading system could overcome current problems in economic performance and usher in a more sustainable period of noninflationary growth.

Looking ahead to the future

The interpretation of the postwar US–European partnership offered in this essay suggests three critical policy issues for this partnership in the future:

1 The most critical one perhaps is the course of liberal reforms in the territories of the Soviet Union and eastern Europe, and the evolution of democratic identities in a reunited Germany, a uniting Europe, a politically defensive Japan, and a retrenching America.
2 The second is the ability of the western nations, especially Europe and the United States, to maintain a consensus on economic and military relations with the former Soviet Union and with countries engaged in conflicts outside Europe, illustrated by the 1990–1 war in the Persian Gulf.
3 The third is the willingness of the western nations to maintain and expand open, competitive economic and trade relations with one another, accommodating the newly emerging market-oriented countries of eastern Europe and the third world.

Liberal reforms in the east and democracy in the west

The most decisive constraints on progress towards democracy and prosperity in eastern Europe are still the pace and stability of reform in the Soviet Union. A reassertion of oppressive power in the Soviet Union's main successor states will, at a minimum, freeze and most likely reverse liberal movements in the Baltic and other ex-Soviet republics. Such oppression, or the consolidation of authoritarian regimes would also cast a long shadow once again over eastern Europe, not in the same form of a Soviet military presence but in the concern that eastern European countries will have to demonstrate that their own further liberalization and association with the west will not threaten a more repressive eastern power or confederation. If the gulf in the direction of domestic reforms widens between the ex-party-states, they will experience the same difficulties in bridging this gulf through diplomacy alone that the west experienced with the Soviet Union throughout the cold war years, especially in the 1970s. Domestic change and the emergence of community based on shared domestic values (national purpose) are essential if countries are to get beyond military and economic balances in their diplomatic relations.

Europe and America have so much at stake in this transition in both eastern Europe and the former Soviet Union that it would be tragic indeed if they failed to coordinate their expectations. The first step they must take is to ensure that they remain mutually open to one another and to Japan. At the moment, they may be drifting apart. Europe may be tempted again to believe that it can manage its relations with the Soviet Union on its own. America, in turn, may be tempted to believe that it has no continuing stake in Europe, now that Soviet armed forces are on their way out of Europe and the European allies seem unwilling to accept any common interests or responsibilities with the United States outside Europe. Europe is less inclined to become involved with the third world and Japan. America is growing increasingly tired and frustrated with its third world responsibilities and Japan.

As a consequence, the three great democracies are eyeing one another with greater and greater suspicion. Already revisionists in the United States charge that Japan is not a democracy (van Wolferen, 1989). The Persian Gulf war, although in many respects a model of western cooperation, also revealed continuing suspicions between Europe and the United States, especially in the case of Germany which hesitated to contribute to the war effort and whose companies supplied Iraq with critical war materials. The erosion of the common political identity of the western democracies could be serious. It calls for more dialogue and exchanges among western societies, as much now as in the past, if the west is going to hold together to nurture the spread of democracy and prosperity in other countries.

Consensus towards the ex-Soviet Union

The linchpin of European and global stability remains the west's relationship with the former Soviet Union. While the Soviet Union struggles to reform its domestic life, differences persist with western societies. These differences can lead to suspicions and misunderstandings unless there is an atmosphere of mutual confidence based on stable balances of military, economic and political power.

The situation in Europe is marked by potentially destabilizing imbalances. In 1991, the Soviet Union remained a potent military power, even as it began the process of military withdrawals from central and eastern Europe. In recent years, it had continued to invest heavily in modernization of its nuclear and military forces and in early 1991 was still attempting to define and position conventional military units in ways that excluded them from agreed CFE reductions. The United States delayed submitting the CFE Treaty to Congress for ratification, and the United States and the Soviet Union continued to move slowly on START negotiations to reduce strategic weapons.

These developments suggest that thoughts of weakening NATO are unquestionably premature. NATO remains the bedrock of western security, as well as the only acceptable means of providing nuclear cover for a reunited Germany. Neither the CSCE nor the EC has any prospect of substituting for NATO, perhaps not in the 1990s decade or longer. The Soviet veto of a CSCE meeting to consider the Baltic crisis in January 1991 suggests the fragility of this institution for dealing with serious political and security issues in Europe. And, although the EC responded imaginatively to the Yugoslavian crisis in June 1991, it is divided internally on its future security role and may require a long time to square the circle of its link to NATO (through nine of its members participating in the western European union) and its desire to include eventually neutral and eastern European states as full members in the community.

Managing military balances prudently is even more essential given the serious economic and political imbalances in Europe today. The ex-Soviet Union is shattered both economically and politically, and the eastern European states are struggling back slowly from a collapse of political legitimacy and economic viability under the ousted communist parties. Meanwhile, western Europe and particularly the EC are riding the crest of political and economic self-confidence, surging ahead toward further internal political and economic union.

These political and economic imbalances place a constraint on what the western powers can do to assist political and economic reforms in eastern Europe and the former Soviet Union. If the west seeks to play a large and direct role, as it did in 1947–8 when it invited eastern European countries to join the Marshall Plan, it may reawaken fears and insecurities in the successor states, particularly if they fail to move forward with domestic reforms. On the other hand, the west has too much at stake to ignore the needs of eastern Europe or the ex-Soviet Union.

Managing these economic and political imbalances in Europe will demand extraordinary skill. For the moment, it requires emphasizing those forms of assistance that are least interventionist in the affairs of the reforming countries. Technical assistance (know-how transfers in all areas of market operations) and especially access to western markets would be most helpful. The EC and the western democracies more generally are going to have to find a way to include the eastern European countries in agricultural, textile, steel and other markets in the west. This commitment to accept exports in those sectors where eastern Europe is most readily competitive is even more important than balance of payments support to promote convertibility of currencies. For financing imports in the short term makes little sense, unless the market access for exports has been assured.

The group of twenty-four mechanism to coordinate western aid to eastern Europe is the appropriate vehicle. Leadership is shared by the European Community and the United States, and Japan is included. The mechanism is sufficiently low key (unlike the high profile Marshall Plan) to avoid appearances of interference, but it is also so low key that it may miss opportunities to reward dramatic policy initiatives in eastern European countries. The hesitation of the European Community to open its agricultural, steel and textile markets to Poland, Hungary and Czechoslovakia is a case in point.

Consensus towards out of area conflicts

The 1990–1 Persian Gulf war sharpened the debate among western powers about burden sharing. Even more so, however, it raised the question of common or conflicting goals among the western democracies in areas outside Europe. This issue of goals will decide the issue of burden sharing, for burden sharing makes no sense except in the context of shared goals.

If the question of out of area conflicts was a divisive one in the alliance during the cold war, it should not be in the post-cold war era. The threat which out of area conflicts posed to Europe in the cold war was two-fold: drawing resources out of the European theatre and provoking Soviet retaliation in Europe. Neither of these threats is as likely in the post-cold war era because the immediate Soviet threat in Europe is transformed (again assuming force withdrawals continue roughly on schedule and that the transition from Soviet to Russian control of nuclear weapons proceeds smoothly). The frontiers of conflict have moved, at least partially, outside Europe as political community has grown between east and west inside Europe. All European countries, including the ex-Soviet Union, and the United States have a stake in out of area conflicts. This was evident in the Persian Gulf crisis.

The UN or at least the Security Council in the UN may prove to be the most appropriate organization to coordinate the politics of out of area disputes. As long as great power cooperation is possible, the UN has shown that it can work – but not without aggressive leadership on the part of the United States, Britain and France. Moreover, if out of area conflicts in the future threaten to turn into north–south confrontations, the UN is a far better place to temper these confrontations than NATO or some other organization (e.g. CSCE) that does not include developing countries.

As hopeful as the role of the UN was in the Persian Gulf war, however, the real test of UN cooperation toward the new world order lies in the postwar effort to win the peace in the Middle East. The great powers and particularly the western democracies have yet to mount a major political and economic effort to rebuild Kuwait and construct a wider political and economic community in the Middle East (Nau, 1991). This will be a decade- or decades-long effort, and will require continued contributions and burden sharing among the United States, Europe and Japan. Some mechanism will have to be found, like the group 24, to coordinate this reconstruction effort. At the very least, this mechanism will need to be more efficient and low key than the ad hoc procedures pursued during the early days of the Persian Gulf sanctions and war effort. The US Secretary of State meeting episodically one on one with German, Japanese or Saudi ministers to hammer out highly visible and contentious burden-sharing formulas is likely to do more to fragment the western democracies than to help rebuild the Middle East.

Maintaining economic unity within the west

The fact that the western democracies have new obligations in the Middle East now that the war is over, to go along with their existing obligations in central and eastern Europe and the ex-Soviet Union, underscores the need for these countries to preserve the efficiency of post-World War II economic arrangements. After World War II, it would have been impossible for the west both to recover economically from the war *and* to rebuild western defences without integrating western economies through the Marshall Plan, EC and the GATT. So too, today, the west will not succeed in meeting its dual obligations in Europe and in the Middle East (and other developing country regions) without preserving and enhancing global markets and multilateral free trade.

One wonders if this point was sufficiently appreciated by trade ministers meeting in Brussels in December 1990, and again in winter 1991, to complete the four-year-old negotiations of the Uruguay Round. Apparently it was not. The meeting broke up over indescribably petty (when viewed from the perspective sketched in this chapter) conflicts over agriculture, services and intellectual property issues. No one country is to blame. They are all to blame, and none can escape responsibility by pointing the finger at the other.

As this analysis suggests, the western democracies have to make only a few key economic policy choices to return to the path of most efficient growth for the 1990s. But these choices are very large ones and hence difficult to make politically. The United States has to solve its budget problem; the EC must follow through on its internal restructuring of the single market to include agriculture, telecommunications and other protected sectors; and Japan has to open up not just its markets but its entire society (so that foreigners as well as more of its own citizens can participate in, and benefit from, Japanese markets). Making these adjustments would put the western democracies back on the course of disciplined macroeconomic policies, flexible microeconomic policies and freer trade policies that sparked the unprecedented growth and integration of world markets in the 1950s and 1960s.

The US deficit soared again in 1990 and 1991 (estimated) to more than 5 per cent of GNP. It hangs like a Damocles sword over an economy in recession and a dollar that, although rising in the first half of 1991 in the face of political uncertainties in Europe and the Middle East, is still vulnerable to foreign capital inflows. The Federal Reserve can manage the economy alone only so far. Eventually, its efforts to rejuvenate growth may reignite inflation and weaken the dollar, particularly if other western countries, such as Germany and Japan, increase their demand for foreign capital.

Europe too has got to look anew at its spending priorities. As it enters the new post-cold war era and incurs new obligations to finance central and eastern European development, as well as Soviet and Middle East recovery, it can no longer afford wasteful agricultural and telecommunications policies. It has got to follow through on its commitment to liberalize microeconomic structures in European markets. If subsidies and technical and other barriers have hampered efficiency in many industries, they also hamper efficiency in agriculture, telecommunications and aviation. None of this needs to be done quickly, but the commitments have to be made. The most disappointing aspect of the agricultural negotiations in the Uruguay Round is the unwillingness to make a long-term commitment, especially when the eastern European and many developing countries need precisely this assurance of long-term commitments to help them through the difficult short-term problems of democratic transition.

Japan has perhaps the largest economic responsibilities and yet the least political capacity to make decisions to put the western countries on the path of most efficient growth. For this reason, Japan is likely to attract uncompromising pressure from the outside to continue to open its markets and society. In Japan's case, it is not only a question of accepting more imports and foreign investment; it is a question of inviting foreigners to be a part of Japanese society in a way that has never been true in the past (Nau, 1990b). Japan has never integrated itself socially and culturally with the rest of the world, unlike the political and economic integration among the Common Market countries or the ethnic integration of the races and immigrants in the United States.

Above all, the western democracies must preserve the practice of multilateral free trade. About half of the world's trade today is between regions. If the western democracies break up into regional trading blocs, this proportion of world trade will shrink. If the entire pie is growing rapidly, this proportional shift will not matter, but if global trade talks stagnate and regional trade agreements move forward, regional integration will come at the expense of global markets. And since regional markets are less efficient, global growth will suffer. The west will not find the resources to meet both its own needs and the needs of the newly emerging democratic countries. The world will lose its historic opportunity to establish a world community of shared democratic values.

Conclusion

Some analysts may conclude that the task of the Atlantic partnership in the postwar world has been completed (Fukuyama, 1989). The United States and Europe have led one of the most successful periods in human history. From the perspective in this paper, however, the past forty years have been but a prelude to the historic opportunity that lies ahead. For the first time ever (because the universal authority of the Catholic church was always confined chiefly to Europe), the world may be able to find a common, universal basis for allocating authority in international society. The achievement of more open and representative domestic societies in both the east and south could assure peace for generations. As the cradle of democracy, Europe and the United States have unique responsibilities. This is no time to mothball the Atlantic partnership.

NOTES

1 The focus here on *national* purpose does not imply a status quo, state-centric, rationalist approach to world politics. Nations are the main actors in contemporary world politics, but they have not always been in the past, nor are they always likely to be in the future. They are merely the most prominent current manifestations of choices about how to organize political society for individual benefit. The terms international and world society are used interchangeably to mean society at the global level rather than to designate the principal actors at that level (i.e. national or universal organization).
2 The explanation is straightforward: disciplined macroeconomic policies helped to preserve price stability and a stable environment for long-term investment and trade. Restrained microeconomic policies in turn facilitated the flexibility of labour and capital markets and the movement of resources in a timely manner from declining to advancing industries. Finally, freer trade ensured that broad competitive markets, not governments, picked the advancing and declining industries and promoted the globalization of production and technology, both between industries (inter-industry trade) and among them (intra-industry trade).
3 Real investment as a percentage of real Gross National Product stood at 12.72 in the second quarter of 1985, higher than in any previous quarter in the postwar period. See John A. Tatom, US investment in the 1980s: the real story, The Federal Bank of St Louis *Review*, 7(27), March–April 1989, p. 11. Supply-side tax policies clearly failed to raise the national savings rate and tax revenues sufficient to cover the budget deficit, but they very likely had something to do with the higher rates of real investment.

REFERENCES

Anderson, Martin 1988: *Revolution*. San Diego: Harcourt, Brace, Jovanovich.
Collins, Robert 1981: *The Business Response to Keynes*. New York: Columbia University Press.
Fukuyama, Francis 1989: The end of history? *The National Interest*, 16, 3–19.
Gilpin, Robert 1987: *The Political Economy of International Relations*. Princeton: Princeton University Press.
Hogan, Michael J. 1987: *The Marshall Plan: America, Britain, and the Reconstruction of Western Europe 1947–1952*. Cambridge: Cambridge University Press.
Huntington, Samuel P. 1988–9: The US: decline or renewal? *Foreign Affairs*, 67(2), 76–97.
Kennan, George 1967: *Memoirs, 1925–1963*. Boston: Little Brown.
Kennedy, Paul 1987: *The Rise and Fall of the Great Powers*. New York: Random House.
Larrabee, F. Stephen 1989: From reunification to reassociation: new dimensions of the German question. In F. Stephen Larrabee (ed.) *The Two German States and European Security*, pp. 22–3. New York: St Martin's Press.
Maier, Charles 1977: The politics of productivity: foundations of American international economic policy after World War II. *International Organization*, 31(4), 613–15.
Nau, Henry R. 1990a: *The Myth of America's Decline: Leading The World Economy into the 1990s*. New York: Oxford University Press.
Nau, Henry R. 1990b: Commentary on Super 301 and Japan. In Jagdish Bhagwati and Hugh T. Patrick (eds) *Aggressive Unilateralism*, pp. 232–41. Ann Arbor, MI: University of Michigan Press.

Nau, Henry R. 1991: Winning the peace. *National Review*, 43(5), 35–7.

Nye, Joseph S. Jr 1988: Understanding US strength. *Foreign Policy*, 72, 105–30.

OECD 1977: *Towards Full Employment and Price Stability*. Report by Paul McCracken, et al. Paris: OECD.

Oye, Kenneth A., Lieber, Robert J. and Rothchild, Donald 1987: *Eagle Resurgent?: the Reagan Era in American Foreign Policy*. Boston: Little, Brown and Company.

Pollard, Robert A. 1987: *Economic Security and the Origins of the Cold War, 1945–50*. New York: Oxford University Press.

Price, Harry Bayard 1955: *The Marshall Plan and its Meaning*. Ithaca, New York: Cornell University Press.

Ruggie, John 1983: International regimes, transactions and change: embedded liberalism in the postwar economic order. In Stephen D. Krasner (ed.) *International Regimes*, pp. 195–233. Ithaca, New York: Cornell University Press.

Small, Melvin and Singer, J. David 1982: *Resort to Arms*. Beverly Hills: Sage Publications.

Stein, Herbert 1984: *Presidential Economics: the Making of Economic Policy from Roosevelt to Reagan and Beyond*. New York: Simon & Schuster.

Stockman, David 1988: *The Triumph of Politics: Why the Reagan Revolution Failed*. New York: Harper & Row.

van Wolferen, Karel 1989: *The Enigma of Japanese Power*. New York: Alfred A. Knopf.

3

The Soviet Union and Europe

Neil Malcolm

Located on the European periphery, Russia has had a difficult and ambivalent relationship with its historically more highly developed western neighbours. It has seen them on the one hand as a military and a cultural threat
and on the other as a model of success which must be imitated to some
degree simply for the sake of survival over the years. Impulses to westernization and to isolationism have tended to alternate in Russian government
policy. However, as time passed, technological change and improvements in
communications made the former more compelling. During the nineteenth
century the educated part of society in the main embraced western values
and looked for ways of overcoming the economic backwardness, super-
stition and bureaucratic despotism which in their eyes represented Russia's
persisting 'Asiaticism' (Vihavainen, 1990, pp. 1–21).

Like previous Russian military defeats, defeat in World War I appeared at
first to have opened the way to a new round of westernization, but the very
radicalism of the 1917 revolutions provoked new tensions in Soviet–European
relations. Under Stalin traditional nationalism, militarism and xenophobia
returned with full force. Soviet rulers practised an unblinking realism in
their dealings with the other European countries. In internal debates they
declared that, encircled as it was by hostile and aggressive imperialist states,
the USSR must give absolute priority to accumulating military strength.
In the meanwhile they practised a flexible policy of building alliances and
exploiting differences between potential enemies, while striving to mobilize
communist-organized fifth columns in the capitalist camp.

After World War II the USSR acquired new strategic assets: a protective
glacis of satellitized east European states, a divided Germany, nuclear weapons. Western Europe was displaced by the United States as the principal
threat, and as the principal interlocutor. This helps to explain the lack of
progress in Soviet–European relations during the forty years after 1945.
European members of NATO found themselves being used primarily as a
communications channel with Washington, and as a lever on American
policy; their own interests tended to be disregarded.

A second obstacle to progress was Moscow's perception of rivalry and conflict as the main feature of relations between the western powers. Soviet spokesmen dismissed the possibility of any kind of sustained (capitalist) international cooperation among capitalist states. At first they seriously underestimated the potential of the European Community. When in the 1970s they began to acknowledge the emergence of western Europe as a 'power centre' in world affairs, this was as an element in a larger pattern of sharpening 'inter-imperialist struggle' with the United States and Japan. Before Gorbachev, Soviet leaders never seem to have understood the strength of transatlantic solidarity, especially in the security sphere, and a counter-productive anti-Americanism persisted in their approach to western Europe.

The main problem, however, and the reason why from the 1970s onwards the hopes vested in détente and the Helsinki process were obstinately dis-appointed, arose from a central contradiction in the Soviet policy of peace-ful coexistence with the west. Total isolation and unqualified hostility had been rejected as too costly and too dangerous. Pressures for more economic interaction and arms control agreements were mounting. Yet powerful interests in Moscow were bound up with maintaining the military com-petition, stimulating ideological vigilance and shoring up economic barriers. In some spheres this helped to perpetuate the sense of a Soviet threat and made the west reluctant to cooperate; in others it simply obstructed coop-eration. It was clear that the existing Soviet 'command-administrative' system with its military and political superstructure could not 'engage' with the European and wider western systems; only its erosion could open the way to real change (Dallin, 1981; Malcolm, 1990).

'New thinking' and Europe

The accession to power of a new generation of political leaders in Moscow in 1985 came at a time of growing impatience for change, even in the upper reaches of the state and the Communist Party. There were pressing reasons, for example, to look again at foreign policy. Existing strategy was bankrupt: NATO unity had been consolidated around the leadership of the most hos-tile US administration since the 1950s; the military challenge from the west was bigger than it had ever been; trade and technology transfer was under-developed and hampered by political restrictions at a time when economic problems at home were threatening to provoke social and political crisis; in several of the east European satellites the crisis had already arrived.

In a surprisingly rapid ideological turnaround the main principles of Leninist foreign policy doctrine were at first pushed into the background, then openly cast in doubt. 'Interdependence', 'balance of interests' and 'all human values' officially displaced concepts such as class war and anti-imperialist struggle. Previous Soviet intransigence and reliance on military strength were publicly deplored (Gorbachev, 1987; *Politicheskii doklad*, 1986; *Izvestiya*, 3 November 1987). Amid all this change, two new lines of thought intersected to suggest a new approach to Europe. The first concerned the nature of east–west relations, and the second concerned changing patterns in west–west relations.

When international relations was perceived predominantly as a zero-sum game in which the 'balance of forces' between socialism and capitalism was calculated more in political and military than in economic terms, it was natural for decision makers in Moscow to focus attention first and foremost on the rival superpower, the United States; western Europe was perceived mainly as a more or less reliable part of the system of 'US militarism'. But by the end of the seventh decade of Soviet rule, and after forty years of peace in Europe, the threatening and militaristic image of capitalism enshrined in Lenin's theory of imperialism was losing credibility in Moscow. Simultaneously, faith in the Soviet system's capacity to prevail in the *underlying* socio-economic dimension of east–west competition was dwindling. The benefits to be gained from fuller participation in the world economy were becoming more and more evident. A new kind of genuinely cooperative relationship with the western world seemed (1) possible; and (2) in conditions of increasing relative weakness much more congenial than a confrontational one. Europe was the region in which previous attempts at cooperation, especially in the economic sphere, had had the most success. This dictated a shift of emphasis towards Europe.

As for west–west relations, Soviet writing on international affairs in the 1970s and the 1980s reflected the preoccupation of western authors with the changing configuration of economic power in the world, with the rise of Germany and Japan, and the questioning of American leadership. As in the west, there was no consensus about the exact balance of forces between Europe, the United States and Japan, or about medium-term trends. Yet there was a substantial degree of agreement: firstly, that over the decades the United States' dominance was set to decline; and, secondly, that any lessening of the relative importance of the military dimension of international relations automatically worked to the benefit of its European and Japanese rivals, who as a rule had smaller investments in arms technology and who incurred economic penalties because of their reliance on American military guarantees.

Soviet economists who favoured the new thinking in foreign policy did not, however, make apocalyptic predictions about inter-regional conflict in the light of these changes. Instead they drew attention to the growing unity of the world economy, and warned against underestimating continuing American technological and financial power (Malcolm, 1989, pp. 14–34). Yet Europe, whatever its role in the international system, was regarded as the natural place for Moscow to begin its campaign for reintegration into the world community. This region was close to the country's main centres of population and industry. Trade and economic cooperation with it were long established and had been relatively unaffected by the ups and downs of political relations. The European Community had pioneered regional economic integration: the system of institutions which it embodied could conceivably be adapted to embrace a wider geographical area. Central Europe was the main seat of east–west military confrontation. It was thus the obvious place to set about improving east–west political relations. What is more there was clearly a hope that Russia could expect favourable treatment from its western neighbours because of its cultural/ethnic 'Europeanness' (Smolnikov, 1990b, p. 100).

Internal factors also played their part. Support for external détente traditionally went along with support for domestic reforms which favoured civilian as opposed to military production, and reflected intelligentsia 'secularism' as opposed to apparatus dogmatism. Opening up to the west, in other words, went hand in hand with attempts to westernize Soviet society. The reaction against Stalinist and neo-Stalinist isolationism was in full flood. For many in the newly confident and influential Soviet intelligentsia, with their access to the ear of the leadership and to the mass media, 'Europe' had a special significance as a symbol of modernity, just as it had for their predecessors. (It should be said that it is not, in this understanding, a concept which excludes the United States, or 'western civilization' in general.) In the words of one member of the Foreign Ministry Planning and Assessment staff:

> By Europe we should understand not only the political phenomenon, but also a definite method as to how to live, think, communicate with other people... The Common European House is the home of a civilization of which we have been on the periphery for a long time. The processes that are going on today in our country, and in a number of socialist countries in Eastern Europe, have besides everything else a similar historical dimension – the dimension of movement towards a return to Europe in the civilized meaning of the word. (Dawisha, 1990, pp. 22–3; Norgaard, 1990, pp. 57–83; Snyder, 1987–8; *Pravda*, 1990, pp. 1–24)

Matters, of course, were not so simple. A full 'return to Europe' implied a revolutionary transformation of Russia itself. Reading Gorbachev's *Perestroika* (1987), it is obvious that he saw himself as committed to the project of 'Europeanizing' his country. Yet his conception of what this entailed and of how it could be achieved in Russian circumstances was obviously a rather hazy one. It appeared to be compatible, for example, with the preservation of 'socialism' at home and the 'socialist community' abroad. The goal explicitly set by the Soviet leadership was a *reform* of their system and of the European system. Not surprisingly, as the return to Europe gathered momentum, increasingly serious problems began to confront Gorbachev and his colleagues, both in eastern Europe and at the interface of domestic and foreign policy.

The idea of radically reforming communism was based on a mistaken assumption that the coercive and terroristic practices which played a central part in the system could somehow be replaced by voluntary consent and cooperation, all within roughly the same institutional framework. In reality, when the underpining of coercion was removed, the political structures built by Stalin at home and abroad inevitably began to crumble. Faced with the choice of accepting change or returning to the old methods, Gorbachev in most cases allowed events to take their course. He strove to preserve formal continuities and to moderate the speed of change, but in the end he seemed to learn from events and to accept, however awkwardly, the revolutionary consequences of his reformist initiatives.

The question is often posed, was Gorbachev's gradualism due to illusions about the possibility of reform, to the belief that Russia could find its own, 'third way', or was it due to a prudent regard for the sensitivities of still powerful military and bureaucratic elements in Moscow, whose powers he was seeking to subvert stage by stage? Was it temperamental caution and hard negotiating tactics deployed by an individual determined to salvage as much of 'communism' as possible, or was it part of a rhetorical smoke-screen designed to allay the fears of the oligarchy while he slowly dismantled the old system? In regard to the loosening of Soviet control in central eastern Europe, for instance, it has been argued variously that the Soviet withdrawal and the unification of Germany on western terms were (1) foreseen relatively early in Moscow as an acceptable scenario; (2) conceded philosophically once the situation was correctly understood; (3) wrenched out reluctantly only because the alternative would have been large-scale conflict and the wrecking of recent improvements in east–west relations. Gorbachev's flexibility, his political agility and his mastery of ambiguity make it difficult to select confidently between these alternatives. Certainly the wholeheartedly westernizing line being taken by the Soviet leader (and even more strikingly by those who were his closest associates in 1985–90) in the middle of 1991 suggested either that there was a great deal of ideological camouflage employed in the early years or that Gorbachev passed through an extremely rapid learning process. But in any case, as Gorbachev's retreats and manoeuvres earlier in the same year demonstrated, it would be a mistake to dwell over much on the preferences of one individual. Broader social and political forces will have their way in the end.

Whatever the initial expectations of the Soviet leadership, small changes led to bigger ones, and from 1989 onwards events appeared to get more and more out of the Kremlin's control. What began as incremental change es-calated into the transformation of international relations in Europe and incipient revolution at home. Policy developed through a series of more and more radical and uncomfortable adjustments and adaptations until by the end of 1990 – as the citadels of apparat power came under threat – signs of obstinate resistance to further change began to emerge inside the Soviet Union.

The body of this chapter will consider the sequence of Soviet policy in-novations – at first proactive and imaginative, and later increasingly desperate – as Gorbachev and his colleagues were obliged to come to terms firstly with the depth of west European mistrust of the Soviet Union and the strength of the Atlantic solidarity which mistrust helped to reinforce, secondly with the determination of the central and east European peoples to break free from Soviet control, and finally with the growing threat inside the Soviet Union to Russian and communist dominance. The final section will consider how internal political factors may interact with outside influences to affect the future of European relations with the ex-Soviet Union.

Stage 1: rebuilding détente

Europeanism or Atlanticism?

In one of his first statements after taking office Gorbachev announced that, although Soviet–American relations were important, 'We do not view the world solely through the prism of these relations, we understand the im-portance of other countries' (*Pravda*, 8 April 1985). Western Europe, he declared during his first official visit abroad to Paris, was 'at the centre of attention in Soviet policy' (*Pravda*, 2 October 1985). This shift had a double significance. By activating its west European diplomacy the Soviet government took the first step in its long-term strategy of diversifying away from a superpower-oriented military focus of policy. At the same time it set in motion a tried and tested short-term tactic – using rapprochement with the United States' European allies to rekindle interest in detente in Washington, at a time when Soviet–American relations were at a low ebb. This second aspect turned out to be the most important. Only in a better overall east–west climate, it soon became clear, could any durable improvement occur in the European area.

Certain highly placed Soviet officials in the mid 1980s embraced a sharply anti-American tone, implying that if Washington was not prepared to cooperate then it could well be ignored. Future Politburo member and Gorbachev adviser Alexander Yakovlev stated his conviction that 'centrifugal tendencies' predominated in the west, and that in the foreseeable future they would bring sharper and sharper conflicts, leading to 'the further disintegration of the postwar monocentric capitalist world' (Yakovlev, 1984). In particular, he wrote in 1986, western Europe was increasingly impatient with American war-mongering, and with its forty-year old subordinate role in the Atlantic community (Yakovlev, 1986; Hough, 1984–5, pp. 38–41). This tendency of thinking was reflected in the first section of the General Secretary's Report of the Twenty-seventh Party Congress in 1986 with its stress on 'contradictions' between the three main centres of imperialism (*Politicheskii doklad*).

But the record of Atlantic alliance relations in practice scarcely justified such a view. Cruise and Pershing II missiles had been deployed with energetic European backing. Restrictions on exports to the USSR had been tightened and credits reduced. A large programme of conventional arms modernization in NATO was under way. Brushing aside Soviet protests, west European governments, led by West Germany and the United Kingdom, had endorsed the SDI project and were seeking to become involved in the associated research and development work. By 1986 some Soviet foreign affairs advisers were even expressing the view that in the light of continued American technological, financial and political dominance in the west, it had perhaps been premature to talk of the appearance of a new west European power centre (Davydov, 1986, p. 9). In such conditions a separate Europe-oriented diplomatic course held few attractions. There seems no reason to doubt *Izvestiya* commentator Alexander Bovin's statement in 1985 that Soviet policy was designed 'to make use of western Europe's potential via the transatlantic channel to meet the evident deficit in common sense on the part of the current administration in the USA' (*Izvestiya*, 25 September 1985).

Superpower rapprochement

But it was not just a matter of exerting leverage on Washington in the old way – the overall policy context had changed radically. There was a genuine effort, especially marked from 1987, to reach agreements with the administration in Washington even if these required large concessions on the Soviet side, agreements which could form a stepping stone towards a non-confrontational east–west relationship. Despite earlier rebuffs the USSR showed great persistence in this regard (Adomeit, 1990a, pp. 247–51).

Whereas Gorbachev's much-publicized trip to Paris proved to be his only full-scale visit to western Europe in four years as leader, he attended four superpower summits during the same period, and his Foreign Minister met with the American Secretary of State approximately thirty times. The result in the end was a rapid transformation in Soviet–American relations, of which the most dramatic immediate consequence was the unprecedented agreement reached in the autumn of 1987 to remove all SS-20s and Cruise and Pershing II missiles from Europe (Haslam, 1988, pp. 38–42).

Another new element was the evidence in Soviet policy of an understanding that a careful balance had to be kept between 'Europeanism' and 'Atlanticism'. The early anti-American colouring of the Soviet 'Common European House' campaign ('someone else's house' as far as Washington was concerned, wrote *Pravda* in November 1985) was succeeded by attempts to reassure the Europeans that they did not have to *choose* between better relations with the USSR on the one hand and continuing close alliance ties with the United States on the other. In 1986 and 1987 the Soviet leadership was at pains to emphasize to west Europeans that, notwithstanding its long-term goal of dissolving blocs in Europe, for immediate practical purposes it saw it as essential to strengthen them. 'The historical relationship between western Europe and the United States', stated Gorbachev, 'or, say, between the Soviet Union and the European socialist countries, is a political reality. It may not be ignored if one pursues a realistic policy' (*Soviet News*, 27 May 1987).

Yet too close a Soviet–American relationship could also alarm the Europeans. After the Reykjavik superpower summit meeting in October 1986 which opened the way to the 1987 deal to remove all Soviet and US intermediate-range missiles from Europe, increasing concern was aroused in Moscow by what were described as symptoms of 'nuclear addiction' in France and the United Kingdom, and over signs of moves to closer west European military cooperation (Anglo–French, Franco–German, the revival of the WEU). It was understood that, as a senior Soviet official later expressed it, intensified arms diplomacy with the United States had been perceived by its allies as 'an attempt by the two great powers to by-pass the Europeans and to reach some form of agreement behind their backs'. By 1988 Soviet Foreign Ministry personnel were openly admitting that the European dimension had 'not been paid the attention it deserved', and had been 'pushed to the sidelines by our activity towards the United States' (Afanasyevsky et al., 1988, pp. 22–33; Vybornov et al., 1988, pp. 36–7; 'Perestroika, the Nineteenth Party Conference and Foreign Policy', 1988, pp. 10, 37).

Stage 2: lowering barriers in Europe

By the end of 1987 a further change of emphasis in Moscow's policy towards the west was clearly overdue. Despite the self-critical remarks just cited, progress towards building a more multifaceted diplomacy had already been made in 1986 and 1987. This affected several parts of the world. Gorbachev's Vladivostok speech in July 1986, for instance, marked a reactivation of Asian diplomacy. But Europe was the main focus. While efforts to involve the British and French in the nuclear arms control process made little progress, unexpectedly quick results emerged in 1986 from CSCE-sponsored negotiations in Stockholm on new military confidence-building measures, largely because of a striking new Soviet readiness to accept intrusive verification conditions.

An even more momentous shift was implied by the CMEA approach to the European Community in 1985. The Soviet Union abandoned its long-standing demand that the CMEA should maintain control over all east–west economic contacts. It proposed instead a joint declaration 'to create more favourable conditions for the development of relations *between member countries separately* and the EEC' (*Le Monde*, 3 February 1986). Thus, several years before the 'Brezhnev doctrine' was formally revoked, the Soviet Union was already prepared to contemplate a substantial loosening of its control over eastern Europe. Bilateral talks between Brussels and east European capitals duly got under way, and the main points of a joint declaration were swiftly agreed in the spring of 1987.

But up to 1987 this regional diplomacy was still in a low gear compared to what was to come. The litmus test was the state of Soviet–German relations, and it was obvious that the Federal German government was being systematically cold shouldered. Soviet officials and journalists referred repeatedly to the old threats of German 'militarism and revanchism'. There was violent criticism of Bonn's loyal support for SDI and for NATO modernization, and of its supposed plans to subvert socialism and to establish a new hegemony in eastern Europe (Yakovlev, 1985). When in 1987 and 1988 signs began to emerge of a turn for the better in Soviet–West German relations, this marked the beginning of the avalanche-like process which culminated in the recasting of the whole European system in 1989 and 1990.

Reasons for the turn to Europe

The turn to a more active policy in Europe from 1987 was encouraged by a combination of circumstances. First of all, it was clear that better superpower relations and the prospect of a reduction in the American military presence might perversely act to stimulate west European defence cooperation, and create, in Soviet eyes, a new military threat to the USSR. Moscow strove, therefore, to use the momentum generated by the INF treaty process to build agreement on an overall lowering of the level of military confrontation. This meant conventional weapons negotiations, which would entail close consultation with the principal west European powers.

Inside the USSR Gorbachev was engaged in 1987 and 1988 in a fierce struggle with conservative forces in the Communist Party in the lead-up to the Nineteenth Party Conference. He had every incentive to produce evidence of the success of his new de-ideologized foreign policy strategy. It was important, too, to be able further to undermine the 'enemy image' of the west which was such an important weapon in the hands of his opponents.

Soviet economists drew attention to plans in western Europe for political union and for the creation of an EC single market by 1992, and to the progress being made in research and development cooperation. Meanwhile the USSR's trade with the region (80 per cent of all its trade with the west) had been in absolute decline since 1984. The first years of perestroika had failed to generate any lasting improvement in Soviet economic performance; the technological lag seemed likely to remain as wide as ever. Old theoretical revisionist arguments about the need to participate fully in 'the world division of labour' and to share in global technological progress had now acquired a hard practical relevance.

Europe was not just seen in Moscow as the most appropriate point of engagement with the world economy. It occupied a special place in the world view of Soviet advocates of new thinking, as an example of how deeper interdependence could work to make armed conflict between the nations concerned virtually unthinkable. In this sense it represented a test bed and a point of crystallization for the new, more humane style of international relations which Gorbachev advocated. It represented an alternative kind of security at a time when military means were being dismantled (Artem'ev and Halliday, 1988). The Soviet Union thus had even more urgent reasons than the region's other economic partners for not wishing to 'miss the European boat'.

The problem of eastern Europe

Yet Soviet power in eastern Europe represented a serious obstacle to normalization of relations on the continent. What hope could there be of getting agreement to talk about a 'Common European House' if half of its potential inhabitants were held prisoner by a heavily armed neighbour?

In the decades following World War II, the 'socialist commonwealth' of eastern Europe had been regarded by the USSR as a valuable asset: a bulwark against imperialist aggression, a partner in the 'socialist world economy', and a demonstration in practice of the superiority and adaptability of the Soviet model. By the 1980s such a view had become difficult to sustain. The military reliability of countries such as Poland and Hungary in an east–west conflict was at best doubtful. International economic cooperation in COMECON had been difficult and unrewarding. The individual economies of its member states had lost the dynamism of the postwar reconstruction period and had become dependent on cheap energy and raw materials supplies from the USSR. The sorry picture of repression, economic stagnation and social decay, and of regimes propped up in power only by the threat of Soviet intervention did little to advertise the benefits of socialism.

The new relations being built between the EC and the CMEA opened the way to transforming the region into something more like a bridge than a buffer between east and west. Closer economic ties with the European Community, according to such a scenario, would attract capital, technology and know-how in order to carry through a process of re-equipment which the USSR was in no position to resource. They would also blur the east–west European economic boundary and lessen the danger of Soviet isolation. In the autumn of 1987 all these arguments were apparently being put forward in discussions inside the Soviet Ministry of Foreign Affairs (MccGuire, 1991, pp. 357–9).

Like the plans to make cuts in conventional weapons, any move to relax controls in eastern Europe faced enormous domestic political obstacles in the USSR. Both struck at the foundations of Soviet security policy as it had become entrenched over sixty years. It seems to have been hoped by the Soviet leadership that, just as its own policies of *perestroika* and democratization could revive popular support for the regime, so communist governments in eastern Europe which were forced to rely on their own efforts for survival would find ways of revitalizing socialism. East–west economic cooperation and military détente would deepen, but the two political blocs would persist. Conservatives in Moscow were (rightly as it turned out) not persuaded by such arguments. They persisted in harping on revanchist tendencies in the West German leadership. But Soviet policy had shifted decisively. East German President Honecker's long-delayed visit to the west was allowed to take place in September 1987, and two months later Gorbachev distanced himself even further from the Brezhnev doctrine which had been used to justify previous interference in eastern European politics, declaring 'The days of Comintern and Cominform and even the days of binding international conferences are over' (*Izvestiya*, 3 November 1987).

Building a partnership with Germany

During 1988 and 1989 the second phase of Gorbachev's foreign policy towards Europe got under way. The primary impetus to change came from the Soviet Union, but western goodwill and constructiveness was an essential precondition, above all in the case of West Germany, which emerged more and more as the principal partner.

The USSR was mainly responsible for the situation where for the preceding four decades the Germans had been divided into two states, had been deprived of access to their natural hinterland in central and eastern Europe, and had found themselves at the focal point of a huge and dangerous concentration of military power. Now that the USSR was negotiating seriously on disarmament in central Europe and on opening up channels of economic contact with the east, the Bonn government began to come under powerful electoral and other pressures to seize the opportunities which were being offered. A common preoccupation with questions of economic development and reconstruction meant that Soviet and German preferences concerning the future shape of Europe were converging more and more (Waever, 1990).

Urged on by Foreign Minister Hans-Dietrich Genscher, Chancellor Kohl gradually shifted his ground on disarmament issues during the summer of 1987, aligning himself with the Soviet preference for removal of all ground-based nuclear missiles from Germany, to accompany the INF agreement. In October Gorbachev transmitted a personal message of gratitude to the German Chancellor, and invited him for talks in Moscow. Simultaneously, Soviet spokesmen began to drop hints in public that some relaxation of restrictions on inter-German contacts was being considered (*Guardian*, 7 April 1987; Kautsky, 1987). As early as April 1987 proposals were being discussed in West Germany for a new east European 'Marshall Plan', and for the accelerated development of trade ties with the USSR. A new era was beginning, as Soviet journalists were fond of saying, in Soviet–German relations.

The push for change: disarmament

At the top of the European agenda in 1987 was the subject of conventional disarmament. In May 1987 the Warsaw Pact suggested reducing armed forces in Europe to a level 'where neither side in ensuring its own defence would have means for a sudden attack on the other side or for carrying out offensive operations in general' (*Pravda*, 31 May 1987). Speaking to the United Nations General Assembly in June 1988, Eduard Shevardnadze proposed a three-stage programme of disarmament in Europe, leading to a purely defensive disposition of forces on both sides. In December of that year Gorbachev created a sensation in the same forum by revealing Soviet unilateral undertakings to reduce military manpower over the following two years by half-a-million men, roughly 10 per cent of the total. Six tank divisions and 50,000 Soviet troops would be removed from Central Europe. All forces would be restructured on a defensive basis (*Guardian*, 8 December 1988).

In March 1989 the Conventional Forces in Europe (CFE) talks opened in Vienna. It became clear that the Soviet side was now offering to make the kind of massive asymmetrical cuts in tanks, armoured vehicles and artillery required to reach rough parity at something below current NATO levels. Frictions persisted over the scope of the agreements, and over associated issues such as NATO plans for modernizing short-range nuclear weapons. But by 1990 confidence was growing that the forty-year-old military confrontation in central Europe was on the way to being effectively dismantled.

Economic rapprochement

From 1988 onwards economic contacts between the USSR and western Europe multiplied rapidly. An EC–CMEA agreement was initialled on 9 June and the first bilateral trade cooperation deal, between Hungary and the Community, three weeks later (*Christian Science Monitor*, 26 June 1988). On 18 December 1989 Moscow signed its own bilateral agreement with Brussels, covering economic ties, scientific and technological cooperation and joint work on protection of the environment. During the ceremony Eduard Shevardnadze emphasized the political significance of the document and hailed it as a contribution to the process of 'forming an integral economic complex on the continent' (*Guardian*, 21 December, 1989).

It was clear that West Germany would play a central part in any such future integral complex, both because of its economic weight and because of its dominant position in east–west European economic relations. By 1990 the Federal Republic accounted for around 5 per cent of all Soviet foreign trade and for a third of all high-technology imports to the USSR from OECD states (Adomeit, 1990b, p. 19). When Helmut Kohl eventually arrived in Moscow on 25 October 1988 for the first German–Soviet summit meeting since 1983, he brought with him five cabinet ministers and 50 bankers and businessmen. The German Chancellor called publicly for NATO to ease CoCom restrictions on the sale of high, technology goods to the east (*Guardian*, 22 and 25 October, 1988). This is not to say that the other west European states were disinclined to cooperate. By October 1988 British and

French banks had, like their German counterparts, extended substantial new credit lines to the USSR. But Germany was the most consistent and largest-scale collaborator. It was playing for much bigger stakes.

Loosening the ties in eastern Europe

Progress towards disarmament, wider European economic cooperation and improving Soviet–German relations both depended on and encouraged a process of disengagement in eastern Europe. The May 1987 Warsaw Pact meeting which called for defensive deployments in Europe also established a commission to consider the implications of Soviet military withdrawal from eastern Europe by the year 2000. In the middle of 1988, as Hungary's treaty with the EC was being signed in Brussels, Soviet security experts were discussing scenarios involving the total withdrawal of troops from Czechoslovakia and Hungary (MccGuire, 1991, p. 359).

Soviet domestic politics pushed in the same direction. In the course of *perestroika* its supporters had consistently looked for lessons in the earlier east European attempts at reform. Now the tide began to flow in the other direction, as the crumbling of neo-Stalinism in the USSR made the continued existence of regimes such as those of Honecker and Ceausescu appear more and more anomalous.

It was in June 1988 that the long-delayed Nineteenth Conference of the CPSU confirmed the principle of free electoral choice. Gorbachev made it plain that the principle of self-determination applied abroad as well as at home: 'In this situation the imposition of a social system, way of life or policies from outside by any means, let alone military, are dangerous trappings of past epochs' (*Soviet News*, 6 July 1988). The consequences in practice were not long in coming. In August 1988 General Jaruzelski of Poland, faced by yet another outbreak of industrial unrest, moved to initiate round-table negotiations with Solidarity and other opposition organizations, something that undoubtedly required Soviet approval. In the spring of the following year, in the wake of the first even partially contested Soviet election to take place since 1918, the Polish government announced that it would permit free competition for 161 seats in the Sejm. Of these seats, 160 were won by Solidarity, and communist rule in Poland was effectively over by August. In Hungary, likewise, 1989 saw the piecemeal but relentless demolition of the system of party rule.

In July 1990 Eduard Shevardnadze was to claim that he and his colleagues had been well aware of the likely consequences of their permissiveness in eastern Europe: 'Yes, we had in principle predicted all this ... we sensed this, we knew this.' (Shevardnadze, 1990, p. 22). But the foreign minister's 'in principle' is a hint that the foresight was of a very imprecise kind. It is difficult to pinpoint at what stage the Soviet leadership began to be overtaken by events. Up until the autumn of 1989 they still seemed to be acting with confidence, although it was becoming obvious that once the populations of the ex-satellite states were given the choice they would not by any means necessarily opt for 'renovated socialism'. In June Gorbachev signed a declaration in Bonn which encouraged German hopes for 'self-determination'. In October in Helsinki he praised the relationship that had grown up between his country and Finland, calling it a model for relationships between large and small states (*Independent*, 26 October 1989; Roberts, 1989, p. 165; Adomeit, 1990, p. 5).

There was evidence of a degree of wishful thinking in Moscow at this time. The Foreign Ministry warned that 'any Finlandization in reverse' was unacceptable to the Soviet Union. The east European states must adhere to the 'international obligations' contingent on membership of the CMEA and the Warsaw Pact. Apparently, hopes persisted that the international security dimension could somehow be insulated from domestic political change. It is clear with the wisdom of hindsight that this was always an unrealistic expectation, and it was demolished by the collapse of the East German regime at the end of the year. By 1990 a new stage in Soviet–European relations was under way.

Stage 3: coping with disintegration

As the structures of communist power in eastern Europe fell apart during the winter of 1989–90, the Soviet leadership faced a sizeable challenge to its skills of negotiation and manoeuvre. Those in the west who argued that Gorbachev was swept along by events, and those like Shevardnadze who claimed that everything was foreseen in Moscow, were both right in different ways. The unification of Germany, the rapprochement of eastern Europe with the European Community, the withdrawal of Soviet troops behind the USSR's own frontiers and the dismantling of the Warsaw Pact – all this was undoubtedly part of Gorbachev's scenario for the future. When *Pravda* welcomed the breaching of the Berlin Wall on 9 November 1989 as 'a step towards the Common European House', this was quite consistent with Soviet thinking. The problem was one of timing and balance. In the preferred Soviet vision of the future the events just listed were to unfold over a long period, alongside similar moves to military disengagement on the western side, the creation of all-European security structures, and decisive moves to integrate the USSR into a single European political and economic system.

The German question

It became a matter of urgency to find an interim solution that would limit the domestic-political damage caused by the 'loss' of eastern Europe while avoiding any going back on the improved east–west relations in Europe. The key issue was German unification, and the future Germany's military status. Throughout the hard negotiations of the first half of 1990, the Soviet side, conscious of its weak bargaining position, strove to exploit to the full areas of common interest which it shared with Bonn. These centred on achieving the kind of settlement which as far as possible reduced the military presence in central Europe and opened up the scope for political and economic cooperation (*Soviet News*, 10 October 1990; Gorbachev and Genscher, 1990).

Now Soviet leaders reversed the logic of their previous stance and argued that bringing Germany together would bring Europe together – the very act of German unification, declared Eduard Shevardnadze, 'created a load-bearing structure' of the Common European House. The Federal German government for its part repeatedly stated its willingness to cooperate in reconstructing the Soviet economy, and it campaigned throughout the second half of 1990 for greater economic assistance from the west to the USSR When the Soviet government finally assented in July 1990 to a united Germany's membership in NATO, it also announced a string of agreements with Bonn. The Germans agreed to recognize the permanence of postwar frontiers in Europe, to abjure chemical and nuclear weapons, to reduce substantially the combined armed forces of the expanded state, and to provide DM 20 billion to the USSR in aid, credits and troop maintenance and relocation costs over the next few years. Soviet commentators compared the new partnership with Germany to the one between Germany and France that had healed the postwar divisions in western Europe and laid the foundations for its prosperity (Smolnikov, 1990a, p. 28).

The future of the blocs

Both Moscow and Bonn went to great lengths, of course, to reassure the NATO member states that the two of them were not plotting a Rapallo-style realignment in Europe. The Germans reaffirmed their loyalty to the Atlantic alliance and committed themselves to further consolidation of the European Community. The Soviet Union, for its part, re-emphasized the line which it had adopted in the late 1980s, that any Common European Home must inevitably include the United States (*Pravda*, 7 July 1989). As Shevardnadze expressed it in February 1990: 'Our aim used to be to oust the Americans from Europe at any price, now we are putting our relations with the USA on a different footing' (*Izvestiya*, 20 February, 1990).

The principal arenas of negotiation in 1989 and 1990 involved both the USSR and the United States – the Conventional Forces in Europe (CFE) talks, the 'two plus four' meetings on the future status of Germany and the rapidly multiplying specialized CSCE forums. Both sides, for opposite reasons, enforced a tight linkage between progress in arms control and progress in strengthening all-European institutions. For the Soviet Union the promise of a 'new European order' was a vital incentive to persist with the kind of arms control reductions which aimed for a balance between alliances, despite the fact that its own alliance was beginning to crumble away. The west, accordingly, agreed to hold a CSCE summit meeting in the second half of 1990 only if a CFE treaty had been signed.

As it became clear that NATO had no intention of following the lead given by the Warsaw Treaty Organization when it declared its intention in August 1989 of transforming itself into a 'political' institution, far less of dissolving itself, and that the NATO states envisaged a fairly limited security role for the CSCE, Soviet energies became focused on the shorter-term goals of lowering the level of military confrontation in central Europe and building better relations with NATO itself. The NATO 'London Declaration' of July 1990 and the Two Plus Four Treaty in October went part of the way to meet Moscow's requirements, with promises of substantial force reductions and redeployments on a defensive pattern, with the offer of a peace declaration and institutionalized representation at NATO for the Warsaw Pact states. The CSCE, it was agreed, should be endowed with a permanent secretariat and an office to monitor elections, a conflict-prevention centre and a parliamentary assembly of Europe.

In Paris in November the CFE I agreement and the new peaceful relationship between NATO and the Warsaw Treaty Organization were endorsed. Much was talked about all-European cooperation and about the future of the CSCE. But it was clear enough to the participants that the key institutional actors would be those established ones, mainly based in the west, which had already demonstrated their viability. In the security sphere this meant the Atlantic alliance. By 1991 several central-east European states were seeking some kind of formal relations with NATO, and establishing closer contacts with the alliance was being described in the Soviet press as the most promising first step towards a collective security solution in Europe (Gladkov, 1991, p. 23; *Izvestiya*, 29 May 1991).

The signing in December 1989 of a trade and economic cooperation agreement between the USSR and the European Community coincided with the exhaustion of any illusions in Moscow about a continuing role for the CMEA (finally laid to rest just over a year later). The Soviet leadership began to engage more actively with the community as a political entity. Eduard Shevardnadze declared that the projects for an EC-centred 'European Confederation' put forward by the French and the Belgian governments fitted well into his conception of a common European house (*Izvestiya*, 19 January 1990). In September 1990 the Soviet Foreign Ministry mounted a joint foreign policy initiative with Brussels asserting a common position on the Persian Gulf crisis and undertaking to cooperate in solving other Middle East problems (*Izvestiya*, 17 September 1990).

Yet the European Community was not about to welcome the Soviet Union as a member in its present form and in the foreseeable future. Indeed, from 1989 there were signs that the Soviet leadership, aware that there was no single comprehensive 'docking point' for their country in Europe, were engaged in an exploratory campaign of contact building, picking up opportunities for integration and cooperation as they presented themselves.

The high point of Gorbachev's European tour in 1989 was his visit to the Council of Europe in Strasbourg in July. Here in a significant adjustment of Soviet expectations about economic relations he acknowledged that an 'all-European economic zone' would have to be constructed on the west's terms: for the Soviet Union it would entail 'transition to a more open economy . . . similarities in the functioning of economic mechanisms'. He also proposed setting up an all-European ecological centre, a European institute of human rights and a 'European legal framework' (*Pravda*, 7 July 1989). In the spring of 1990 Shevardnadze announced the USSR's intention of seeking full membership of the Council of Europe, which he described as a crucial institution for building 'a common European political and legal space'. Its parliament and its foreign ministers' meetings could, he suggested, evolve into all-European institutions in the CSCE structure (*Moscow News*, 1990, no. 8–9).

Moscow's pragmatic, functional approach continued throughout 1990. The Soviet Union participated in the European Energy Community project. It began to collaborate with the European Environment Agency and it became a member, albeit under temporary constraints, of the European Bank for Reconstruction and Development (EBRD). The Soviet leaders appear to have arrived at a conception of the European process as something open-ended and loosely organized, with participation *à la carte*. This suited a power which was perceived, and indeed undoubtedly saw itself in many contexts, as half in Europe and half outside of it. It had a string of special interests in different parts of the globe, some connected with its large territorial presence in Asia. The emphasis put by Soviet diplomats on regional interests in Europe was intended to draw attention to a genuine running down of global ambitions. But the country remained a superpower willy nilly: 'We and the United States are doomed to be tied together . . . it is the guiding axis of international relations', said President Gorbachev in May 1991 (*Sunday Times*, 12 May 1991).

In so far as his country became more closely associated with a more confident and independent-minded Europe, it would be less dependent on the United States. In the meanwhile, however, it needs American cooperation if it is to complete its disengagement from regional disputes, if it is to have a say in any Middle East settlement, if it is to achieve its goal of establishing a new security geography in the Asia–Pacific region, and if it is to establish a useful relationship with global financial institutions, such as the IMF and the World Bank. The importance of the United States in Moscow's foreign economic policy was well illustrated by the intensive diplomatic contacts with Washington which preceded and followed the Group of Seven summit meeting in July 1991. All this sets definite limits on the intensity of 'Europeanism' in Soviet foreign policy.

Internal problems

The signing of the 'Charter of Paris' in November 1990 marked the culminating point of Shevardnadze's European diplomacy. One month later the foreign minister had resigned, protesting about a 'drift to dictatorship'. Shevardnadze had been under fire throughout the year from conservatives and representatives of the armed forces, who declared that too high a price had been paid for a settlement in Europe. The military also expressed their resistance directly, removing equipment and reallocating forces in such a way as to evade the full impact of the CFE I agreement and to block further progress in arms control. By December the conservative counter-offensive in Soviet politics was in full swing. Gorbachev explicitly adopted a policy of 'consolidation': substantial economic reforms were postponed in favour of a tightening of administrative controls; hopes of self-determination for the republics were disappointed as troops went into action in the Baltic states; the Communist Party international department published a report regretting the loss of influence in eastern Europe. Government spokesmen, such as the head of the KGB, the prime minister and even the president, began to echo the old language about western subversion in order to discredit internal opponents. Old economic and political structures based on administrative control and fear of punishment fell apart without any properly functioning market mechanisms, or any fundamental civic consensus or respect for law to take their place. Shortages, political deadlock and ethnic conflicts were sapping faith in the reform project.

After Gorbachev's agreement with the leaders of nine Soviet republics in April 1991 on the principles of a new looser union of sovereign states, it seemed that some of the old reformist momentum had been regained. Subsequently, after the debacle of the conservative coup attempt in August, and the discrediting of the Communist Party, important political obstacles to progress seemed to have been removed. Yet the deeper-lying obstacles to Europeanization presented by the established political and economic culture remained in place. In order to form an idea of what Russia's future relationship with Europe might look like, it is useful to consider more closely how events might evolve inside the country and in its relations with other ex-Soviet republics.

The future of Europeanization

In Russian historical perspective Gorbachev's strategy is a radically westernizing one, albeit based initially on a rather unclear vision of the full implications of westernization. More than any previous regime, his has courted and relied on the support of the westernized intelligentsia. Occasional threats and backslidings apart, he has steadily expanded freedom of communication internally and externally; he has striven to establish law and constitutional procedure in the place of traditional arbitrary rule and bureaucracy; he has encouraged the adoption of western economic practices, and opening up to the world economy. Yet progress has been slow and uneven. By 1991 the Soviet leader was being criticized at home and abroad for his indecisiveness and attachment to old forms.

Gorbachev responded by defending his own 'reformism', rejecting what he called 'neo-Bolshevik' anti-communist radicalism. This was clearly a matter of temperamental preference for him. It also seemed to reflect, firstly, an awareness, common to generations of Russian westernizers, of the special requirements of his society (*Sunday Times*, 12 May 1991), and secondly a sense of the need to preserve as broad as possible an elite consensus, especially including the forces of order, during a difficult transition from authoritarianism to democracy. These considerations implied keeping maximum institutional continuity and promoting gradual change rather than bringing about a revolutionary break. They also encouraged a pragmatic approach to innovation, a willingness to 'try out' different solutions. The problem was that piecemeal reform provoked social and economic dislocation which threatened to derail the whole project. As in foreign affairs, loosening of control from above released increasingly powerful pressures from below. Gradualism came to seem more and more of an unaffordable luxury.

To Soviet radicals, Gorbachev's centrism looked like irresolution in the face of the urgent need to clear away remnants of the command-administrative system blocking the way to the full emergence of European style civil society and to a workable relationship with the non-Russian nationalities. To the conservatives it looked like unwillingness to impose order and to use a firm hand against destructive forces. The two sides made a persuasive case for emerging from chaos either through consistent reform or through consistent retrenchment, and sizeable political forces consolidated in 1990 and 1991 behind these extreme positions. The clashes of August 1991 were a vivid expression of these tensions.

It is a measure of the flexibility of Gorbachev's strategy and of his ability to appear all things to all men that the 'putschists' believed that he could be pursuaded to accept an authoritarian seizure of power as a fait accompli, while the victorious democrats subsequently felt able to work together with him to dismantle the old regime. Gorbachev's dramatic shift of line in August highlighted a wider change in the political climate. By the autumn of 1991 a consensus on the need to push ahead with modernization and democratization, to 'rejoin Europe', appeared to be shared by almost the entire active political community in Moscow. It seemed as if the long-awaited revolutionary break had finally come about.

Yet the path ahead was by no means smooth or predictable. Those east European states which had thrown out their communist leaders in 1989 and 1990 were already struggling with difficult problems of transition. And, despite initial reports, it was not the mass of the Russian population which made the anti-communist revolution: the authentic voice of 'people power' still had to make itself heard. There was no guarantee that it would echo the westernizing preferences of the radical intelligentsia.

The new regime had to deal with the same problem that faced Russian revolutionaries in 1917 – how to cobble together workable new political and economic mechanisms on the ruins of the system which had collapsed more from exhaustion than because it had been pushed aside by new forces and structures. It was easier to suspend the operations of the Communist Party than to root out the power of officialdom in a society where new democratic and market-oriented institutions, expectations and patterns of behaviour were only just beginning to be formed, and where talented and honest administrators were in desperately short supply at all levels. By the autumn of 1991 angry debates were already under way between authoritarian-inclined 'democrats' and defenders of the existing powers of the representative soviets. The old regime had repressed national enmities and allowed them to fester: it had provided little experience of negotiation and compromise. It was easier to keep on good terms with the leaders of other republics when there was a common enemy in the union and a common goal in eroding its powers than it was once that enemy had been defeated, once it became necessary to divide the spoils and liabilities and to work out a new system of horizontal relations. It was easier to criticize the old bureaucratized economic system than to introduce markets, revalorize the currency, reduce huge budget deficits, build industrial competitiveness and modernize the derelict agricultural sector.

Each of these three spheres taken on its own would have posed difficult challenges to Yeltsin and his supporters. Taken together, administrative incompetence and sabotage, nationalist fears and ambitions, and conflict over painful economic adjustments could interact with the most destructive consequences. Yet the very fluidity of the situation which followed the coup attempt, and the unprecedented character of the changes underway meant that it was no more possible to make confidently gloomy predictions than it was to make sanguine ones. The three medium-term scenarios which follow are intended to illustrate the range of possibilities and the implications which alternative lines of development would be likely to have for relations with Europe.

Scenario 1: a democratic community of nations

One can envisage many different patterns of economic and political relationships emerging between the ex-member states of the Soviet Union. What is important is not so much the degree of institutionalized consolidation, or the balance between multilateralism and bilateralism, as the quality of these relations and the atmosphere in which they develop. It is difficult to imagine a successful programme of modernization being carried through in conditions of even low-level military conflict and economic warfare. Harmonious and cooperative relations between Moscow and the capitals of the larger republics would permit faster progress in economic reform and would help to prevent political activity being diverted into nationalist channels.

In the best case the various democratic factions would reach the compromises necessary to construct an effective executive power in the Russian Federation. The executive would in turn refrain from abusing the extra prerogatives accorded to it and would respect the rights of representative institutions and the mass media. The party system would mature, and the activities of opposition groups and trade unions would largely be incorporated in a constitutional framework. Progress would be made towards reforming the administrative machine and tailoring it to its new tasks. In the economy, technical assistance from the west would, play an important part. There would be decisive moves to introduce convertibility of the currency and to give greater freedom to exporters and importers. A start would be made on breaking up and privatizing state monopolies, and the state and collective farms would be handed over to individual farmers or otherwise commercialized. An effective mix of private and public enterprise would be arrived at. Careful targeting of investment and know-how would ensure that in exchange for the sacrifices being demanded the population would begin to sense an early pay-off, for example in improved supplies of food and consumer goods.

As governments put into practice the kind of reforms proposed at the end of 1990 in the European Community and Group of Seven-sponsored reports on the Soviet economy, and as a democratic Russia established a clear division of rights and responsibilities with the other republics, the way would open up to a flowering of economic relations with the west. In view of the size of the ex-Soviet Union's economic problems, coordinated assistance would have to come from all the OECD states, and the IMF would probably play a leading role, but Europe would be the region most closely involved. The ten-year trade and economic cooperation agreement with the European Community signed in December 1989 could be fully implemented. The promise of a grand accord between Moscow and Brussels, based on article 235 of the Treaty of Rome, which was made by the European Council in December 1990 (*Europe*, 16 December 1990), could conceivably be fulfilled, providing the Soviet Union with the political attributes of associated status with the EC in the mid 1990s. Energy and environmental cooperation would develop rapidly, and foreign private investment and know-how transfer would accelerate as economic stability returned.

The successor states of the Soviet Union (or any political union which remained, plus a number of independent republics) would move towards full membership of the Council of Europe, while either a strengthened CSCE or more likely a more and more cooperative NATO–Soviet/Russian relationship would emerge. As disarmament in Europe proceeded and confidence increased, Moscow would have less difficulty in accepting closer association with NATO and/or European-centred defence structures for the central-east European states, especially if Russia itself was simultaneously engaged in a military rapprochement with western institutions.

A Russia of this kind would focus attention in the west of the continent even more acutely on the vexed question of where and how firmly to draw the eastern boundaries of 'European' entities. If Poland is to be allowed to look forward to eventual full membership of the European Community, for example, then why not Lithuania? If Lithuania, then why not Ukraine? Yet to include little Russians and exclude great Russians might seem not only difficult to justify but also dangerously provocative to Moscow. Whatever the balance of arguments, German interests would no doubt ensure that the eastern frontier of the community remained reasonably open and that Russia did not have cause to feel shut out (Weaver, 1990). Attempts would undoubtedly be made to develop multitier European structures – confederations, communities, spaces and so on – designed to facilitate both widening and deepening, but it is difficult to envisage rapid or stress-free solutions.

Scenario 2: authoritarian nationalism

If relations between Russia and the other ex-Soviet republics should begin to deteriorate, and if this should be accompanied by an upsurge of resentment in Russia about the real or imagined mistreatment of the 25 million Russians who live outside the borders of their own republic, the nation's fledgling democracy could be an early victim. A reforming government would already be struggling with painful policy dilemmas as it strove to control public spending and to modernize industry. Prolonged large-scale unemployment, inflation and social upheaval would create good conditions for the rise of demagogic nationalist politicians able to identify scapegoats and ready to offer easy solutions. This would pave the way to a slipping back into traditional Russian authoritarianism.

Natural supporters of a new authoritarian nationalist regime, and necessary allies in its effort to retain power, would be conservative elements in the armed forces and the security apparatus. Such groups tend to hold unionist views. They particularly dislike the idea of separate armies being established in the other republics. They would be likely to back any moves to put pressure on these states, for example, by asserting the right of Moscow to take steps to 'protect' the local Russian population. A nationalist government in Moscow could well lend its support to the idea of a 'Greater Russia', embracing large parts of Ukraine, Kazakhstan and possibly Moldova. Another group which would gain in influence would be the leaders of the heavy/military–industrial sector, those most threatened by a reorientation of the economy to civilian needs. They might well be able to appeal for backing to certain trade unions. The outcome would not be a return to communism, but rather the adoption of a corporatist economic policy justified by patriotic and workerist rhetoric and focused on short-term goals.

The western states would be inclined to view such a government with suspicion. While its limited resources would force it to direct any aggressive impulses against enemies close to home, it is not difficult to imagine how conflicts between even the major ex-Soviet republics could escalate rapidly into armed confrontation on the Yugoslav pattern. Internal disputes could generate tensions and perhaps even clashes with southern neighbours like Turkey and Iran. At the same time, military and military-industrial circles in Moscow might be tempted for political and economic reasons to renew and extend the kind of contacts which they cultivated in 1990 and 1991 with congenial regimes in other parts of the world: for example, in Belgrade and Baghdad. An eastern Europe itself prey to ethnic conflict and economic discontents could offer fertile ground for low-profile trouble making.

Relations with the European Community and the Council of Europe would be distant. Moscow's foreign policy rhetoric would be more likely to emphasize defensive-nationalistic or third world themes than the 'common European house'. Conditions would not favour further institutionalization of the CSCE, but would rather give NATO a new lease of life. They would also encourage whatever tendency there was for the European Community to develop a defence identity and for the western defensive umbrella to be extended to cover central-eastern Europe. Most likely would be the emergence of what Ole Weaver calls a 'French' Europe, stretching from Brest to Brest and acquiring increasingly state-like characteristics (Weaver, 1990).

Scenario 3: disorder

Experience since the passing of communism in eastern Europe and in the smaller republics of what was the USSR seems to indicate that when ethnic rivalries and nationalist feelings are aroused rational calculations about the economic advantages, say, of compromise and cooperation lose their power to persuade. Yet the inhabitants of the Soviet Slav republics had up till the end of 1991 behaved with relative moderation. It is conceivable that, even if harmonious progress towards a new model of political and economic partnership fails to materialize, and if conflicts persist on the outskirts of the old empire, reasonably civilized relations can, nevertheless, be maintained on the whole between the Russians and the other larger nationalities. This would permit the continuation of democratic politics and economic reform.

Political life would be marked by oscillations between phases of executive dominance, arbitrary rule, and bending of legal safeguards on the one hand, and phases during which the population reasserted its preferences, through parliamentary activity, strikes and demonstrations on the other. One aspect of the general disorder would be a marked differentiation not just between republics, but also between policies applied in particular regions, 'zones' and even cities.

Untidiness and geographical diversity would hamper economic reconstruction. There would be republic and local restrictions on competition, on the movement of commodities and labour. Ways would be found of propping up unviable production units, and monopolies would be protected. In the end, growing unemployment, falling living standards and continuing inflation combined with a sense that little progress was being made towards a long-term solution would demoralize reform-inclined elites, antagonize the population and increase the likelihood of a switch to something resembling scenario 2.

Scenario 3 would pose the most acute problems for the west European states. Weakness and disarray in Russia and the other republics would widen the scope for external intervention. The tendency which was already evident in 1990 and 1991 to look to the advanced countries for easy solutions would no doubt strengthen. The west, for its part, would perceive the ex-Soviet Union more and more as a source of potential dangers which had to be averted – civil war, possibly involving nuclear weapons, ecological disaster, large-scale population movements, inflaming of hostility between the Christian and Moslem worlds. It would therefore be unlikely to stand aloof. Fears of instability would make it appear all the more urgent to push ahead with the disarmament process, to try to bolster living standards and to interfere in order to stack the cards against extremist groups. Yet there would undoubtedly be fierce disputes concerning, for example, the scale, types and timing of economic assistance, and the conditions to be attached to it.

It has been argued that the fragmentation of the USSR into smaller units would increase its 'digestibility' for Europe. What is more, those newly independent republics which are apprehensive about Russian imperial ambitions are anxious to acquire what they see as the guarantee of continuing autonomy which association with European institutions would help to provide. As for the Russian republic itself, it was already noticeable in 1991 that its spokesmen were more consistently Europeanist in foreign policy statements than their union counterparts ('Russian diplomacy reborn', 1991, pp. 128–9). Any rift with the Asian republics would no doubt increase this tendency. Yet disorder and uncertainty would hamper the formation of pancontinental economic and political ties. It would strengthen the case of those in the west who advocate consigning the states of the ex-Soviet Union to the outermost of Europe's concentric circles, focusing assistance and political attention on their more manageable western neighbours.

Of course, neither the Gorbachev–Shevardnadze team nor any conceivable successors could have an absolute commitment to Europeanizing the Soviet Union as an end in itself. Since 1985 Europe has been seen in Moscow, however, as a relatively accessible entry point to the world system. Gorbachev and his reformist associates, moreover, saw some variant of European social democracy (adapted in a pragmatic way to local circumstances) as an appropriate evolutionary step away from Soviet communism, and they hoped to transmute the ties of military confrontation in the region into ties of political and economic cooperation. The new governments in Moscow and Kiev appear intent on pursuing an even more energetic westernizing policy. Yet it should be remembered that the history of Russian social thought, not to mention historical practice, contains many examples of projects of modernization which lay more stress on the country's specific, non-European features. As recently as early 1991 certain writers were emphasizing Russia's 'Euro-Asiatic' characteristics, which, they argue, dictated a more statist, authoritarian approach to reform (*Literaturnaya Rossiya*, 22 February 1991; Kurginyan et al., 1990; *Independent*, 20 February 1991). Alternative policies were available should the new relationship with Europe prove unsustainable. But by that time events since 1985 had already brought about a profound social and cultural transformation, as the upheavals later in the year were to demonstrate. Russia had come 'closer' to Europe than at any moment in the previous seventy years. There even seemed to be a chance that it might be able to break out of the old cycle of attraction and repulsion and settle at last into what its reformers called a 'normal' relationship with the rest of the continent.

REFERENCES

Adomeit, H. 1990a: The impact of perestroika on Soviet European policy. In T. Hasegawa and A. Pravda (eds) *Perestroika: Soviet Domestic and Foreign Policies*. London: Sage/RIIA.
Adomeit, H. 1990b: Gorbachev and German unification. *Problems of Communism*, July–August, 1–23.
Afanasyevsky, N., Tarasinkevich, E., Shvedov, A. 1988: Between yesterday and today. *International Affairs*, Moscow, 5, 22–3.
Artem'ev, I., Halliday, F. 1988: *International Economic Security: Soviet and British Approaches*. London: RIIA Discussion Paper 7.
Dallin, A. 1981: The domestic sources of Soviet foreign policy. In S. Bialer (ed.) *The Domestic Context of Soviet Foreign Policy*. London: Croom Helm.
Davydov, Yu. 1986: Dva 'tsentra sily' v mirovoi politike i problema razryadki. In Yu. Davydov (ed.) *SShA – Zapadnaya Evropa i problema razryadki*. Moscow: Nauka.
Dawisha, K. 1990: *Eastern Europe, Gorbachev and Reform*. Cambridge: Cambridge University Press, 2nd edn.
Gladkov, P. 1991: Requiem for the treaty. *New Times*, 9.
Gorbachev, M. 1987: *Perestroika. New Thinking for Our Country and the World*. London: Collins.
Gorbachev, M. and Genscher, H.-D. 1990: Joint statement reported in BBC, *Summary of World Broadcasts*, SU/0687, p. A1/11 (10 February).
Haslam, J. 1988: Soviets take fresh look at western Europe. *Bulletin of the Atomic Scientists*, May, 38–42.
Hough, J. 1984–5: Soviet perspectives on European security. *International Journal*, 15(1), 20–41.
Kautsky, E. 1987: Are Soviet attitudes towards Bonn changing?, *Radio Free Europe Background Report*, no. 194 (22 October).
Kurginyan, S. et al. 1990: *Postperestroika: kontseptsual'naya model' razvitiya nashego obshchestva, politicheskikh partii i obshchestvennykh organizatsii*. Moscow: Politizdat.
Malcolm, N. 1989: *Soviet Policy Perspectives on Western Europe*. London: Routledge/RIIA.
Malcolm, N. 1990: Destalinization and Soviet foreign policy. In Hasegawa, T. and Pravda, A. (eds) *Perestroika: Soviet Domestic and Foreign Policies*. London: Sage/RIIA.
MccGuire, M. 1991: *Perestroika and Soviet National Security*. Washington, DC: Brookings Institution.
Norgaard, O. 1990: New political thinking east and west: a comparative perspective. In Harle, Iivonen (eds) *Gorbachev and Europe*, pp. 57–83. London: Pinter.
Perestroika, the Nineteenth Party Conference and Foreign Policy 1988: *International Affairs* (Moscow), no. 10.
Politicheskii doklad Tsentral'nogo Komiteta XXVII s'ezdu KPSS 1986: Moscow: Politizdat.
Pravda, A. 1990: Introduction: linkages between Soviet domestic and foreign policy under

Gorbachev. In Hasegawa, T. and Pravda, A. (eds) *Perestroika: Soviet Domestic and Foreign Policies*. London: Sage/RIIA.

Roberts, W. 1989: A new status for eastern Europe. *The World Today*, October, 165–6.

Russian Diplomacy Reborn 1991: *International Affairs* (Moscow), no. 3.

Smolnikov, S. 1990a: Novaya logika evropeiskogo razvitiya. *Mirovaya ekonomika i mezhdunarodnye otnosheniya*, 6.

Smolnikov, S. 1990b: The Soviet economy's Eurovector *International Affairs* (Moscow), 8.

Snyder, J. 1987–8: The Gorbachev revolution: a waning of Soviet expansionism? *International Security*, 12(3).

Vihavainen, T. 1990: Russia and Europe: the Historiographic Aspect. In V. Harle, J. Iivonen (eds) *Gorbachev and Europe*. London: Pinter.

Vybornov, V., Gusenkov, A. and Leontiev, V. 1988: Nothing is simple in Europe. *International Affairs* (Moscow), 3, 36–7.

Weaver, O. 1990: Three competing Europes: German, French, Russian. *International Affairs*, 66(31), 477–93.

Yakovlev, A. 1984: Imperializm: sopernichestvo i protivorechiya – voprosy teorii. *Pravda*, 23 March.

Yakovlev, A. 1985: Opasnaya os amerikano-zapadnogermanskogo militarizma *SShA: ekonomika, politika, ideologiya*, 7, 3–15.

Yakovlev, A. 1986: Mezhimperialisticheskie protivorechiya – sovremennyi kontekst. *Kommunist*, 17, 3–17.

4

Japan and Europe in global perspective

Jean-Pierre Lehmann

Europe, to paraphrase Dean Acheson, having lost its empires after World War II, has taken several decades to define its role. Since 1986 especially, and with the build-up to '1992', the process seemed to be accelerating, albeit not without profound and recriminatory disagreements. The configuration of the 'European space' has been further complicated by the disintegration of the Soviet formal and informal empires. De Gaulle's dream of a 'Europe from the Atlantic to the Urals' may in the long term be fulfilled, but perhaps with a sequence of many nightmares in the short term.

In the four decades following defeat in World War II and having had to abandon ambitions to be a military and geopolitical power, the Japanese were quite content in carving out a purely commercial empire. On the political front, Tokyo adopted a 'low profile', while generally following, although from a distance, the American lead. Since the mid 1980s, however, as Japan's economic might grew to daunting proportions, the outside world, Washington in particular, began urging the Japanese 'to assume their international responsibilities'. The three pillars of the Japanese establishment – the ruling Liberal Democratic Party (LDP), the bureaucracy, and big business – along with intellectuals and opinion leaders, are grappling with the task of defining what Japan's role in the world should be. This has become all the more urgent in the wake of the Gulf war and at the dawn of what has been euphemistically (and perhaps naively) called the 'new world order'.

While relations between perhaps virtually all states and regions are clouded with uncertainties and contradictions, it is the case that the Euro-Japanese relationship remains especially ill-defined. The conclusion to this chapter will seek to identify various scenarios for Japan's relationship with Europe. Beforehand we will analyse the key issues, forces and trends within the global environment that will set the framework for and impact upon the relationship. We start by examining the development and current state of American–Japanese relations, as these will clearly dominate the course that Japan will follow in global affairs.

American–Japanese relations

Former American Ambassador to Tokyo Mike Mansfield has described the relationship between Japan and the United States as 'the most important bilateral relationship, bar none'. Certainly, in what has commonly come to be referred to as the 'Triad', the US–Japan relationship has been the focus of far more attention, far more controversy, vitriolic or otherwise, than either of the other two bilateral relationships, Euro-American or Euro-Japanese.

The 'special relationship' between Japan and the United States emerged from the ashes, the settlements, and the changing global and specifically Asia Pacific geopolitical environments of the immediate postwar era – decolonization in South-east Asia, the cold war, the communist takeover in China, the Korean war. Whereas initial American occupation policy had been to 'de-militarize, de-industrialize and democratize' the country, by the late 1940s and early 1950s the main effort was to assist in its economic reconstruction.

Following the end of the occupation in 1952, the United States and Japan signed a 'Security Pact', according to which Japan was to benefit from American military protection. The American 'nuclear umbrella' over Japan was made all the more necessary in that according to Article 9 of the new Japanese constitution, drafted by American authorities and promulgated in 1947, Japan forever renounced the sovereign right of declaring war and, to that end, undertook not to maintain land, sea or air forces. Being 'freed' from military commitments, Japan was able to focus all its attention on industrial and commercial development.

The rest, as the saying goes, is history.

By the late 1950s and early 1960s the Japanese economy had entered an unprecedented boom, leading to what came to be labelled the 'Japanese economic miracle'. It was also at this time that Japanese goods came to be more noticed on international markets. There was some grumbling on the American side that cheap Japanese products, especially from smoke-stack and labour-intensive industries, e.g. steel and textiles, were being 'dumped' on the American market and thereby menacing American industry. On the whole, however, throughout most of the 1960s Japan tended to be ignored or not to be taken seriously.

While Japanese industry was accelerating at full velocity, successive governments in Tokyo sought to maintain a harmonious relationship with the United States primarily by following Washington's lead. For example, Tokyo refrained from establishing diplomatic relations with Beijing, and thereby recognized Taipei as the legitimate government of China, until the Nixon–Kissinger initiative changed the course of America's China policy. Then Prime Minister, Kakuei Tanaka, visited Beijing and toasted Mao Zedong only *after* Richard Nixon had paid his visit and his respects. The Japanese sought to avoid so far as possible becoming entangled in complex international issues. At the time of the Vietnam war, and thanks to the country's 'peace constitution', Japan was able to remain aloof, nor did Washington demand that Japan 'assume its international responsibilities'.

By the early 1970s however, the relationship began to sour. President Richard Nixon delivered what were referred to as a series of unexpected 'shocks' to the Japanese. These included the unilateral imposition of punitive tariffs on Japanese textile imports, the flotation of the US dollar – leading to the first rapid appreciation of the yen from the hitherto fixed rate of ¥360–$ – and undertaking his 'historic' visit to Beijing without prior consultations with Tokyo. Under the administration of Jimmy Carter, the relationship further deteriorated, mainly as a result of a rapidly growing American trade deficit with Japan, which in turn led to increasingly acerbic trade negotiations. Throughout most of the 1970s, however, the Tokyo–Washington exchange was able to remain outside of the limelight, as many other international issues – the OPEC crises, war in the Middle East, Iran, the Soviet invasion of Afghanistan – attracted attention and remained paramount in American policy.

By the late 1970s, Japan's industrial advance was re-enforced, while the American economy fell into the doldrums. A number of American academics, consultants, journalists and businessmen began perceiving Japan as possibly a 'model' for American industry. The publication by Harvard University Professor, Ezra Vogel, *Japan as Number One: Lessons for America* (1979), was both a major landmark and a major shock. Japan as 'number one'? For the Japanese, hitherto accustomed to being in the shadow of the United States, the possibility of being 'number one', let alone having lessons to teach Americans, was tantalizing. For Americans, still unaccustomed to having to eat industrial humble pie, the fact that the Japanese might play the role of teachers was disturbing. In the course of the early 1980s, 'learn from Japan' books, articles, seminars, conferences, etc., proved to be quite a growth industry.

The Reagan years saw a number of divergent trends in the US–Japan relationship. Ronald Reagan enjoyed a seemingly particularly close personal relationship with then Japanese Prime Minister, Yasuhiro Nakasone. For one (symbolic?) thing, the relationship marked the first time that an American president and a Japanese prime minister addressed each other on a first name basis. This came to be called the 'Ron–Yasu' relationship. At a rhetorical level, Reagan withstood growing and increasingly strident demands from Congress to impose protectionist measures against Japanese imports. In reality, however, Washington and Tokyo increasingly ignored the broader multilateral framework of the General Agreement on Tariffs and Trade (GATT) as more and more bilateral 'grey' measures were adopted to 'manage' the trading relationship: e.g. the 'Voluntary Export Restraint' agreement (VER) on Japanese automobiles, the 'Orderly Marketing Agreement' (OMA) in semiconductors, etc. The 'Ron–Yasu' relationship might have been flourishing, but, increasingly, Japanese industry was made to dance to an American protectionist tune. The point, though, was that Japanese industry danced extremely well. All American measures against the Japanese seemed to backfire, leading Japanese industry to re-enforcing, rather than weakening, their positions.

Nor did American exports to Japan fare well. As Americans argued that Japan maintained trade barriers, the Japanese countered that American failure to penetrate the Japanese market was due to poor quality, inability to meet delivery schedules, unwillingness to adapt products to the standards and tastes of the Japanese market, the fact that American businessmen could not transact business in the Japanese language, etc.

A major turning point occurred in September 1985 on the occasion of the New York Plaza Hotel agreement of the Ministers of Finance from the Group of Five (G5) leading industrial nations. In the course of the early Reagan years the yen had dropped as low as 260 to the dollar. The Plaza Hotel agreement rapidly resulted in the massive appreciation of the yen, which by late 1988 had risen to 120 to the dollar, subsequently falling and 'hovering' in the 130–40 range. The depreciation of the dollar against the yen was supposed to result in decreasing Japanese export competitiveness, consequently rising American competitiveness, and, hence, inter alia, a reduction in the American trade deficit with Japan. Once again, however, the 'game-plan' misfired. Not only did the trade deficit not decrease, but indeed the sudden massive 'dollar enrichment' of Japanese corporations and individuals led to an intoxicating buying spree of American companies and real estate. With the acquisition by Sony Corporation of Columbia it appeared in American eyes that nothing was sacred anymore – as *Newsweek* put it in very emotional terms, the Japanese had thereby acquired a 'piece of the American soul' – and the purchase shortly afterwards by Mitsubishi Real Estate of Rockefeller Center was seen as a further devastating blow to national dignity.

In the year that Ronald Reagan became President the US trade deficit with Japan was just over $10 billion; by the year he left the presidency it was close to $60 billion.

The term 'friction' came to punctuate all aspects of the American–Japanese economic relationship. Initially confined to trade, friction has since proliferated into many areas. 'Investment friction' intensified as more and more Japanese manufacturers located plants in the United States. These came to be perceived in certain quarters as an industrial 'fifth column' or as 'Trojan horses'. 'Acquisition friction' assumed, as noted earlier, highly emotional overtones. Economic tension spilled over into 'political friction'. With Japan generally suspected of not being a reliable ally of the United States, the 'proof' seemed to occur when it transpired that Toshiba Machine, a subsidiary of Toshiba Corporation, had been transferring sensitive military-related technology to the Soviet Union.

Combined political and economic friction generated 'technological friction'. This particular dimension came to a head in what became known as the 'FS-X controversy', a US–Japan cooperative venture in the joint development of a new generation of fighter aircraft, code-named the FS-X. The deal included a two-way technology transfer. A number of Congressmen, however, objected in that the risks for the United States of technological leakages to the Japanese were unacceptably high: consequently American industry would be jeopardizing the future of one of the few sectors of industry, aerospace, in which it had so far been able to maintain leadership over the Japanese. The controversy was ultimately resolved, albeit not without having left a considerable amount of frustration and resentment on both sides.

As the 1980s came to a close, relations between Japan and the United States seemed to reach their nadir. Japan (along with India and Brazil) was specifically cited in new trade legislation enacted by Congress, under the 'Super 301' clause. This amounted to an official accusation of Japan as an 'unfair trader'. Terms such as 'unlevel playing field' became increasingly in usage in describing Japanese attitudes to trade and other forms of economic exchange. The Japanese, it was held, approached economic relations from an 'adversarial' perspective, and refused to accept the principles of reciprocity.

A growing number of American government officials, academics, and other opinion leaders have become preoccupied – some obsessed – about the United States losing its position as 'number one' to Japan. This has given rise to a proliferation of books, articles, speeches, etc., emanating from what has been termed the 'revisionist school' on the US–Japan relationship. Whether focusing on technology, trade, industrial policy, politics, etc., the theses tend to converge in the view that Japan is 'different' and, thereby, 'unfair'. While the focus, gist and substance of their arguments vary, they advocate the view that American attitudes towards Japan need to be revised, that the policy of 'appeasement' must cease: in a word that Washington must become 'tough' with Japan. In mid 1991 the publication of a CIA sponsored study labelled the Japanese as racists, amoral and bent on world economic domination.

At the same time, more Japanese have been 'revising' their own vision of the bilateral relationship and consequently engaging in some 'America bashing' of their own. The most notorious, but by no means isolated, example of the latter has been the publication by the right-wing politician Shintaro Ishihara and Akio Morita, of Sony Corporation, *The Japan That Can Say 'No'* (1989).

At a policy level, the 'Japan is different' view has led to the conclusion that improvements can only be achieved by recognizing and thereby rectifying Japanese cultural or 'structural' impediments to its economic relations with the United States. Hence, the 1989–90 round of bilateral negotiations between Washington and Tokyo has been labelled the 'Structural Impediments Initiative' (SII). The SII, in principle, is a two-way street. Thus, on the Japanese side, apart from castigating Washington for the unacceptably high level of its budget deficit, suggestions have also been made to the Americans which include: improving the level of American education, developing more long-term oriented corporate strategies, introducing the metric system, etc. For their part, American negotiators have focused on such issues as Japan's labyrinthine distribution system and the lack of management transparency held to be inherent in the *keiretsu* industrial organization.

Tensions were further exacerbated during the Gulf war. Japanese public opinion tended to see the Persian Gulf and the events taking place as being very distant from Japan and as a primarily American affair in which they should studiously avoid becoming involved. After some prevarication, the Japanese government again manifested its desire not to alienate Washington, particularly as American criticism that Japan had been enjoying a 'free ride' on the back of the United States became all the more acute. Eventually, the Japanese contribution of $11 billion mollified Washington, especially since it now appears that the United States actually made a profit out of the war!

Other issues (e.g. the opening of the rice market) are bedevilling and will continue to bedevil the US–Japan relationship. With the collapse of the Soviet Union and the consequent ending of the threat to American military security,

Washington will become increasingly obsessed with its economic security: and Japan is and will remain for the time being the major threat to American economic security.

At the same time, however, no matter how high emotions may ride on both sides of the Pacific, it remains the case, as will be made clearer at the end of this chapter, that the economic interdependence between the two countries is deep and constantly intensifying. More Japanese productive investment will flow into the United States, leading to job creation, technology transfer, and contributing to the American external account as Japanese products made in the USA are exported. The vice-minister of the Ministry of International Trade and Industry (MITI), Yuji Tanahashi, has announced that MITI will 'encourage' Japanese companies to assist their American counterparts in achieving revitalization. Also, for all the belly-aching, indeed gnashing of teeth, in Washington, attitudes on the part of American consumers and many producers, as well as those of state governments seeking Japanese investment, remain far more positive.

Certainly, as the twentieth century comes to a close, while this 'most important bilateral relationship, bar none' may not be the only show in the 'global town', it will undoubtedly play the more prominent and influential role in the evolving economic and geopolitical environment.

Implications for Europe

Much of what is said and written about the US–Japan relationship either excludes or only makes brief passing references to Europe. From a Japanese perspective, in the course of the postwar decades Europe has been relegated to a second-possibly even third-fiddle position. Japan's global economic and political priorities have focused firstly and primarily on the United States, followed in somewhat distant second position by neighbouring Asian countries, along which, or possibly even after which, has come Europe. For its part, Washington has tended not to involve Europe in its dealings with Japan. Not only is the United States–Japan relationship 'the most important, bar none', but it is pretty much strictly a bilateral affair from which third parties, including Europe, are excluded. The absence of Europe from the American–Japanese table will have repercussions on the global trading environment, which are unlikely to prove to be in Europe's interests. These will be looked at more closely in the concluding section. Prior to addressing more specific Euro-Japanese issues, one needs to consider the Asia Pacific dimension.

Japan and the Asia–Pacific region

The ambivalence with which Japan has viewed Asia since the mid nineteenth century remains a prominent phenomenon in the late twentieth century. The ambivalence is more than reciprocated by Japan's Asian neighbours. There are two elements that strongly influence the Japan–Asia Pacific interface.

The first is *economic*. The rapid economic growth over recent decades of a number of the east Asian economies notwithstanding, it still remains the

fact that by and large Japan is the rich kid in a relatively poor neighbour-
hood. Japan's GNP per capita is roughly four times that of the Republic of
Korea, approximately twenty times that of Thailand, seventy times that of
China. Japan's position in virtually all the east Asian economies is dominant:
it is the metropolitan power *par excellence*, with the Asian countries as its
satellites.

The second is the *historical legacy*. Throughout most of its history, Japan
sat *in statu pupillari* at the feet of its two main Asian neighbours, China and
Korea: with Japan learning and 'importing' religions, philosophies, writing,
architecture, administration, craftsmanship, etc. However, when in the mid
nineteenth century, Japan, hitherto sealed off from the outside world for
over two centuries, was 'opened' by the western imperialist industrial powers,
it soon emerged unique among Asian nations in adopting a policy of 'if you
cannot beat them, join them'. In the wake of its socio-economic revolution,
referred to as the Meiji Restoration (1868), Japanese government officials,
entrepreneurs and intellectuals set about learning from and emulating the
west in virtually all domains.

As Japan responded positively, indeed aggressively, to the western challenge through a combined policy of administrative modernization and industrialization, the other Asian nations floundered. The great Chinese empire,
in particular, suffered ignominious blows at the hands of the western imperial powers and collapsed into a state of virtually unceasing civil wars.
The contrast between industriously energetic Japan and decadent China
was glaring.

In the course of the last decade of the nineteenth and first decade of the
twentieth centuries, Japan imposed itself on its Asian neighbours. It fought
a victorious war against China (1895), colonized Taiwan (1895) and then
Korea (1910), and rapidly extended its economic and military sphere of
influence over north-east Asia. Having also in the process beaten the Russians at war (1905), by the time of World War I it was, along with the major
western nations, a prominent imperialist power in Asia. In the inter-war
period, Japanese encroachments on the Asian continent increased, including the colonization of Manchuria (1931), ultimately leading to all out war
with China from 1937 to 1945. Following the attack on Pearl Harbor, Japanese
armed forces moved to south-east Asia. The American and European imperialist powers were ejected from their colonies, but with the Japanese
assuming the role of overlords. In 1945 the greater east Asia co-prosperity
sphere collapsed.

While defeat led the Japanese to abandon their military ambitions in Asia,
on the economic front things were rather different. From the late 1950s
onwards, Japanese industry returned to Asia en masse. The Japanese industrial presence and investments in Asia were driven by a number of forces,
but which in aggregate certainly gave the appearance that much of Asia was
in the process of being re-colonized, albeit through economic means. Not
unnaturally, Asian resentment against Japan grew, until in the early 1970s
it blew up, including violent demonstrations on the occasion of a 'goodwill'
visit in 1972 by then Prime Minister, Kakuei Tanaka, to a number of south-
east Asian capitals.

In the meantime, however, significant economic and political developments
were occurring in Asia. In the late 1960s hitherto reciprocally antagonistic

states of south east Asia renounced belligerent goals and proceeded to form
the Association of South East Asian Nations (the ASEAN). By the early
1970s, the United States had withdrawn from Vietnam. In China the Great
Proletarian Cultural Revolution was brought to an end, Mao's revolutionary
zeal seemed to have mellowed, and relations were being renewed with most
of the western nations. In South Korea, under the economically 'enlightened'
despotism of President Park Chung-hee, the country's 'economic miracle'
was well under way. While Taiwan was finding itself abandoned and ostracized on the diplomatic front, it too was engaged in a successful accelerated
push to industrialization. In Hong Kong the entrepreneurial drive was in
full throttle. The changing geopolitical and economic landscape required
Tokyo to take Asia more seriously and attempts were made to 'patch up' the
various relationships.

By the late 1970s and early 1980s the Asian ambivalence towards Japan
was illustrated in it being seen as both a 'menace' and a 'model'. As Malaysia's
Prime Minister, Datuk Seri Mahathir Mohammad, turned against the United
Kingdom, he simultaneously adopted his 'Look East Policy', a main thrust
of which consisted of looking for Japanese tuition. Deng Xiaoping, in
launching the economic reforms in China, publicly stated that China stood
to gain from learning from Japan. Explicitly or implicitly, Asian governments
and entrepreneurs sought to transfer elements of the Japanese economic
management model to their own environments. Also, in the mid to late
1980s, not only was the quantity of Japanese industrial investment in Asia
increasing, but its quality was improving. Through investment in more value
added manufacturing, Japanese industry was contributing to the countries'
industrial development and to boosting their exports.

While the climate has improved, it is by no means one of unblemished
sweetness and light. Access to the Japanese market for Asian exporters, with
the exception of raw materials and semi-finished products, remains limited.
Japanese exports, especially of capital goods and components, on the other
hand, continue to increase. Korea, Taiwan, Thailand, Hong Kong and
Singapore have huge and seemingly endemic trade deficits with Japan. Asians
also complain that the Japanese are insufficiently positive in terms of
transferring technology. The economic frictions have been further fuelled
by the Japanese penchant for 'historical revision'. Tokyo's Ministry of
Education, through the censorship of school history textbooks, has sought
to play down the aggressive role and the atrocities committed in the course
of Japan's wars and colonization in Asia. This has resulted in quite strong
emotional responses especially in China and Korea.

In terms of future trends and prospects in Asia, two points can be made.
The first point is that the buoyancy of the Asia Pacific economies is likely
to be sustained well into the next century. The score card will vary country
by country, as it has to date. The continued growth of individual countries
will be further sustained by the dynamics of intra-regional economic activity, including trade, investments, technology transfer, and tourism. Hitherto
existing ideological political barriers are being torn down by pragmatic
economic forces. South Korea's trade with the People's Republic of China
has spiralled, as have Taiwanese investments in the 'mainland'. Informal
sub-regional groupings will form de facto even if not de jure. The 'triangle
of growth' encompassing Singapore, Johore in Malaysia and the island of

Bataan in Indonesia is one example. What has been referred to as the Greater Chinese Economic Circle (GCEC), encompassing Taiwan, Hong Kong and the south eastern maritime provinces of the People's Republic of China, is another, and one that may well become a major regional hub of industrial activity within the next few years.

The second point refers to both Japan's regional and global position. Japan has recently played a more active role in the region. It has, for example, been the major source of foreign aid to Asian countries for at least a decade. In 1988 Prime Minister Noboru Takeshita sought to promote the economic interests of the Asian Newly Industrialized Countries (NICs) at the Toronto Summit, while at the 1990 Houston Summit Toshiki Kaifu was instrumental in the 'rehabilitation' of China following the Tiananmen events of the preceding year. Potentially very significant has been the Japanese initiative in seeking to end the isolation of North Korea. While Japan's role in Indochina–China has been neither particularly energetic nor effective, certainly as Vietnam emerges from its quagmire, Japanese industry can be expected to play a substantial part in the country's economic reconstruction. Japan, much more than Europe or America, will continue to benefit from Asia's economic buoyancy.

At the same time, Japan remains and will remain in an Asian class of its own. As the only Asian economic global power, Japan is far less vulnerable than other Asian countries to whatever protectionist forces may emanate from North America or Europe. Following strategic overseas direct investments in the course of the 1980s, major Japanese corporations are now firmly ensconced in all of the world's major markets. Not only in comparison with other Asian nations, but also when compared to North America and Europe, it currently stands, *ceteris paribus*, in a pre-eminent win-win position. The Japanese commercial empire is very robust indeed.

Implications for Europe

In recent decades, generally, Europe has tended to be perceived as somewhat on the periphery of Asian affairs. In the years that followed the French defeat at Dien Bien Phu and the British and Dutch departures from their various Asian colonies, the European presence and influence in most of Asia have been on a course of rapid eclipse. With the exception of the oil companies, the major chemical groups, and luxury products, European industry tends to be more conspicuous by its absence. Cultural ties have been loosened. There is a tendency among Asians, especially of the postwar generations, to perceive Europe not as menace, nor as a model, but more as a museum.

While there is awareness of the growing markets and industrial developments of Asia in European business circles, comparatively little action has ensued. In new investment in Asian countries, Europeans tend to rank not only after Japanese and Americans, but they also are trailing well behind other regional players such as Taiwan, Korea, Hong Kong and Singapore. European industry has increasingly accepted as a fait accompli the premise that the Asia Pacific is Japan's 'back yard'. On the basis of current trends, European industry's presence and role in the region will continue to diminish. Hence Europe is unlikely to derive the benefits from Asia Pacific's sustained growth that more aggressive and less Euro-centric strategies would ensure.

Asian concern with Europe, however, has recently taken on a more acute urgency and this in the context of trade. From the mid 1980s, greater attention has been directed to Europe by Asian producers. This shift has been driven by a number of forces, including, of course, the prospects of '1992'. Increasingly, however, it came to appear in Asian eyes that Europe is in the process of constructing an internal fortress, with its siege towers directed primarily against Asia. Furthermore, the erection of a fortress in Europe is leading, or encouraging, Americans to follow suit and to establish their own trade stockade. The stalemate in late 1990 of the Uruguay Round added force to the alarmist view.

Recently, therefore, a number of Asian or Australian inspired proposals on establishing some form of Asia Pacific intra-regional organization have seen the light of day, with the Malaysian government putting forward the concept of an East Asian Economic Grouping (EAEG). The point to stress in this context is that the initiatives are primarily defensive in nature: in other words, it is because Asians perceive Europe and North America engaged in forming exclusive blocs that they feel compelled to devise one of their own. Thus the Asian perception of 'fortress Europe' could in due course act as a catalyst for the creation of some form of Asia Pacific bloc. The main beneficiaries would obviously be the Japanese, who, on the one hand, would consolidate their position in Asia, without, on the other, losing their well entrenched presence in Europe and North America.

Japan and the Soviet Union

While the former Soviet Union is in Asia, as a Eurasian power, until recently a 'super-power', and with policy having been formulated in Moscow, it clearly stands in a category of its own.

As the Czarist Russian empire pursued its 'manifest destiny' across the Asian continent, towards the late eighteenth and early nineteenth centuries the grand vision extended as far as the largely uninhabited island of Hokkaido. The Japanese Meiji government in the 1870s pre-empted any further Russian design by colonizing the island. Russo-Japanese territorial competition then switched to the Asian mainland. By defeating Russia in war in 1905, Russian Asian ambitions were further thwarted, and indeed the Japanese victory was a not insignificant cause behind the revolution that occurred a dozen years later.

Throughout most of the inter-war period, contact between Japan and the Soviet Union was minimal. With the outbreak of World War II, the Soviet Union remained outside the Asian theatre and only joined the allies against Japan at the very end of the war. Japan, thereby and among other things, escaped being divided into two occupation zones. The Soviets, however, did grab four islands to the north of Hokkaido, which Japan has ever since claimed as its territory. The two countries have still not signed a peace treaty. In the postwar decades relations between the Soviet Union and Japan were limited to little more than a 'dialogue of the deaf'. Tokyo would regularly demand that the northern islands be returned to Japan, while Moscow invariably responded that particular item was not on the agenda.

It is also the case that the Kremlin had been more Atlantic than Pacific oriented. In the course of the mid to late 1980s, Gorbachev and his foreign minister, Eduard Shevardnadze, began to pay more attention to Pacific affairs. In the summer of 1986 Gorbachev delivered what was then hailed as a major speech in Vladivostock in which a 'vision' for Soviet–east Asian relations was articulated. With the major exception of Soviet relations with South Korea, however, not much has significantly changed yet. Moscow's relations with Beijing have marginally improved, whereas with Pyongyang they have significantly deteriorated, and with Hanoi they are at a standstill. With other east Asian capitals, such as Jakarta, Bangkok, Kuala Lumpur, Singapore, whatever *rapprochement* has occurred can best be described as lukewarm.

In April 1991 Gorbachev paid an official visit to Tokyo. This was a landmark in the sense that it was the first visit to Japan by a Soviet head of state, but in every other respect it proved to be an anti-climax. Gorbachev wanted Japanese investment and technology, but he was not able to deliver anything concrete in regard to the northern islands. Since the islands are part of the Russian republic, and in light of the election of Boris Yeltsin and the deep transformation underway in the former Soviet Empire, it would appear reasonable to have expected some breakthrough on this highly sensitive issue.

Whatever the ultimate outcome of the northern islands dispute, it is unlikely that a very marked change in Soviet–Japanese relations will occur in this decade. A return of the islands, followed by the signing of a peace treaty, would 'normalize' relations and probably lead to more Japanese financial assistance to and economic activity in the former Soviet Union. A stalemate on the issue would see the situation remaining much as before. In any event, neither a dramatic amelioration, nor a major deterioration in the relationship would seem to be on the cards.

With the end of the cold war, the former Soviet Union is no longer a military threat, but simply a weak and awkward power. It is not an economically viable proposition, especially now with all the confusion arising in its economic management. The potential of Siberia's rich mineral resources notwithstanding, Japanese investment in the USSR or its successor states is likely to remain minimal. The collapse of the Soviet Union clearly enhances Japan's power. Apart from the issue of the northern islands, the former Soviet Union is not a priority on the Japanese agenda.

Issues in the Euro-Japanese relationship

The Japanese impact on Europe has taken various forms. Following an initial export-driven thrust into European markets, more recently Japanese corporate strategies have focused on direct investments. Today, not only do the Japanese run automobile, motorcycle, electronics, zipper, etc., factories in Europe, but they also own hotels, restaurants, resorts, golf courses, *haute couture*, vineyards, and so on. Without the Japanese tourist trade, such notable European institutions as the Crazy Horse, the Moulin Rouge, Madame Tussaud, etc., would find it difficult to survive. The Japanese presence in Europe may not be as dramatically conspicuous as it is in the United States – e.g. they have not bought the Eiffel Tower or Trafalgar Square, yet – but it, is nevertheless, undoubtedly there, and growing.

While there have been some very vocal European reactions to the *défi Japonais*, with the French, in particular, getting, if not on their chariots, certainly on their high-horses, there has been little genuine debate on the subject and the European economic presence in Japan is weak. The European business community in Japan, certainly in comparison to Americans, tends to be small and uninfluential. American corporations account for 50 per cent of foreign investment in Japan. As to Europe's investments in Japan, the star par excellence is Switzerland, which at not quite $1 billion corresponds to almost double the UK figure and more than four times that of France. Indeed, Japanese investment in Luxembourg alone is greater than total European investment in Japan. With very few exceptions, European captains of industry have shown relatively little interest in Japanese industry, technology, or the market, and therefore tend to steer clear of the country, or, at best, only make very brief periodic visits.

There have been a number of more recent developments. Jacques Delors paid an official visit to Japan in May 1991 – though the fact that this was the first official visit to Tokyo by a President of the European Commission since 1986 speaks for itself. Japan and the European Community have indicated an intention of signing a joint political declaration, comparable to the one signed earlier by the Community and the United States. The European 'Japan-basher' par excellence, Edith Cresson, was appointed Prime Minister of France in 1991. Her short tenure of under one year saw little abatement of her anti-Japanese invective.

Prior to seeking to determine what course the Euro-Japanese relationship may take, the historical background and the key issues need to be assessed.

The historical background

Whereas Japan was 'opened' by the United States navy in 1854, as a result of the ensuing American Civil War and various other internal preoccupations, the United States subsequently played a somewhat minor role in Japanese affairs. During the first decades of the Japanese industrial revolution, the model and mentor was the United Kingdom. Indeed, as the Japanese industrial revolution picked up steam and Japan developed a first class navy – also under British tuition – by the latter part of the nineteenth century it became fashionable to refer to Japan as the 'England of Asia'. In the early twentieth century, Britain emerged from splendid isolation to sign an alliance with Japan (1902–22), which, as pundits declared, joined the empire of the rising sun with the empire over which the sun never sets!

In the years following World War I, however, Japanese industry was already emerging as a competitor, indeed as a 'threat', to British industry. Market share was being taken by the Japanese away from the British not only in 'neutral' markets such as China, but also within the boundaries of the British Empire. Britain's erstwhile championship of free trade began wearing thin. In the course of the 1930s the relationship further deteriorated, imperial rivalry became more intense, and, finally, after the Japanese attack on Pearl Harbor, Hong Kong was invaded, the British were defeated in Singapore, and the war followed its brutal course. While Dutch colons were imprisoned in Indonesia, and the French surrendered to the Japanese in Vietnam, Britain is the only European country that fought against Japan in World War II.

France's role in Japan was far more minor than Britain's. Napoleon III's emissary in Edo (the former name for Tokyo), Léon Roches, connived with the Tokugawa Shogun against the imperial forces behind the Meiji Restoration, but, in so doing, backed the loser, and consequently France's potential political influence was aborted. The French *mission civilisatrice* was not totally absent from the Japanese scene, in that, for example, Japanese officials responsible for developing a modern system of jurisprudence did derive inspiration from the Code Napoléon. The writings of French eighteenth-century philosophers (e.g. Rousseau) and nineteenth-century writers (e.g. Victor Hugo) were considered required reading for the newly-emerging elites. France's major contribution to Japan's industrial development was in the transfer of sericultural technology. And indeed the silk industry provides the first example of the Japanese students catching up with and surpassing their western tutors, in that by the beginning of the twentieth century French producers heavily lost market share against their Japanese rivals. Essentially, however, in the latter part of the nineteenth century, whatever prestige France may have had in Japanese eyes was lost following the country's defeat at the hands of Prussia.

It was indeed in the newly unified Germany that the Japanese found their most appropriate military and political mentor. Bismarck was much admired by Japanese officials, and Japan's first modern constitution of 1889 – scrapped by the Americans after World War II and replaced by their own version – was carefully drawn up on the basis of the Bismarckian model. The Japanese Imperial Army received guidance and instruction from its German counterpart. In engineering, the natural sciences, medicine and the social sciences, Germany's influence on Japan was also significant.

In World War I Japan was on the side of the Allies, although actual fighting was limited to a few minor skirmishes. Japan and Germany did come together in the years leading up to World War II, although it was, in many respects, a strange alliance. At the ideological level, while both nazi Germany and Japan shared certain characteristics, e.g. in their racism, it was nevertheless somewhat uncomfortable for the nazis to preach doctrines of Aryan racial superiority on the one hand, and be allied with Asians on the other, while Japan's own racist doctrines contained a strong anti-western element. At the military level, the Germans stuck to Europe and the Japanese stuck to Asia. The fact that Japan did not go to war with the Soviet Union allowed Joseph Stalin to concentrate his forces on the western front. Germany and Japan, however, now both share the stigma of their wartime belligerence and atrocities, the effects of which continue in many different ways, and are illustrated, among other things, by their respective positions and attitudes in the Gulf war and the fact that neither are permanent members of the Security Council of the United Nations.

Japan's relations with other European countries either go back to the far more distant past – e.g. with the Iberians, mainly via missionaries, in the sixteenth century, or with the Dutch from the seventeenth to the mid nineteenth centuries, when the Netherlands was the only country allowed to maintain a small commercial presence in Japan during its long period of enforced isolation – or are of only very marginal importance.

Following Japan's defeat in 1945, and in the course of the postwar settlement, the historical legacy of Europe's relations and involvement with Japan was essentially negative. Anti-Japanese feeling was strong in Britain and the Netherlands in particular. The European allies, including Britain, were only minimally involved in the occupation and postwar reconstruction of Japan. The general feeling was that this was essentially an American affair. Europeans had other priorities.

Trade

The overriding European concern regarding Japan, on the basis of prewar alleged Japanese predatory trade practices, was to seek to prevent that particular phenomenon from recurring. Suspicious and obstructive vigilance was definitely the order of the day. Only very slowly, reluctantly, and as a result of considerable American pressure did the British and other European governments allow Japan to join the GATT, and even then initially on the basis of restrictive conditions. The 1960s, characterized by high growth among all industrialized countries, witnessed a more liberal international trade environment. Even then, however, a series of bilateral 'agreements' were imposed limiting Japanese access to European markets.

Generally, however, the 1960s and early 1970s were not a period when Europeans took the Japanese very seriously. The illustrative example often cited is that of President Charles de Gaulle referring to Japanese Prime Minister Hayato Ikeda, as 'ce petit marchand de transistors'. 'Petit marchand' indeed, as by 1970 Japanese exports to Europe of transistor radios amounted to no more than ¥19 billion. [It was to quadruple to ¥83 billion within five years.] In the 1960s, 'Made in Japan' still conveyed an image of cheap goods definitely not up to European standards of technical sophistication and quality. The British motorcycle industry, for example, still stood supreme. Japanese automobiles were sneered at – and indeed by 1970 exports to Europe were a meagre ¥17 billion. Honda's initial attempt to penetrate the European markets in automobiles failed. Toyota was especially laughed at in France in that the third syllable of the name of one of its first exports to Europe, the Toyopet, rhymes with the French for 'fart', thus Japanese cars were dubbed as no more than 'little farts'.

In the early 1970s the situation changed, indeed with hallucinating speed. From 1969 to 1972 Japanese exports to Europe sky-rocketed from $1.4 to $3.3 billion. Japanese imports still represented a small percentage of Europe's total imports, but they were nevertheless highly visible and seen to be attacking European industry in especially sensitive sectors. The export of ¥17 billion worth of cars for 1970 increased to ¥191 billion by 1975. The Japanese were accused from various European government and business circles to be engaging in 'laser-beam' exports. The Director General for External Relations of the European Commission, Sir Roy Denman, referred to the Japanese as 'workaholics living in rabbit hutches'!

With unemployment and inflation rising dramatically, corresponding to the era of 'Euro-sclerosis', Europe's defensive trade posture vis-à-vis Japan intensified. As European countries sought to promote the fabric and bear the costs of their welfare states, the perception of Japan as a land of exploitative labour conditions implied the necessity of protecting the European workforce from the blistering winds of 'unfair' Japanese competition. Europe frequently resorted to anti-dumping measures. Further bilateral 'agreements' were reached in a wide spectrum of products. In automobiles, the United Kingdom restricted Japanese imported cars to a reasonably 'generous' 10 per cent of the market, as against 3 per cent for France and no more than 2,500 units for Italy. In 1972 Kakuei Tanaka, at the time Minister of International Trade and Industry, announced that Japanese electronic manufacturers would set VERs on tape-recorders, television sets, and other products. In the ensuing twenty years Japan and Europe have remained locked in a trade embrace that violates both the GATT and the Treaty of Rome.

The European defensive position and policies notwithstanding, Japanese exports continued to make rapidly increasing inroads. From 1972 to 1977 Japanese exports to the European Community increased by 264 per cent to $8.7 billion and in that year the Japanese surplus stood at $4.5 billion. Within another five years (1982), both Japanese exports to and the surplus with the Community rose to $17 billion and $9.5 billion respectively. Within the next five years (1987) the same pattern emerged, with exports at $37.7 billion and the surplus at $20 billion. Since 1987 Japanese exports have grown by more than another $10 billion, but so have imports from Europe, hence the Japanese surplus continued to hover around the $20 billion mark. Recently, however, the Japanese surplus with Europe has once again experienced a significant increase: in 1991 Europe's trade deficit with Japan may surpass that of the United States.

As the process to the single European market accelerated, European trade policy towards Japan has remained at a stalemate and with significant internal dissensions between the member states. The issue par excellence has been that of automobiles. As noted above, various European countries have established and maintained independent bilateral agreements restricting Japanese market penetration. The critical (yet unresolved) question is whether and how these restrictions should be applied on an EC-wide basis, and for how long. As the agreements in principle referred to imports, the matter, however, has become further exacerbated now that Japanese manufacturers have established transplants in Europe, primarily in the United Kingdom. Another automotive trade 'hot potato' is whether cars imported into Europe from Japanese transplants in the United States should or should not be included in the restrictions. The automobile, therefore, has come to represent a Japanese industrial cat among the European trade pigeons.

Trade policy vis-à-vis Japan in general and the Japanese automobile industry in particular strikes at the heart of what the Single European Act is supposed to be all about. It has painfully raised questions regarding European solidarity, or lack thereof, the ability of European industry to compete, even on its own turf, and, even more so, what kind of market Europe will be.

Europe and 'le défi Japonais': investments, technology and strategic alliances

Euro-pessimism was driven by the apparent de-industrialization of Europe. Europeans were rapidly losing in such 'strategic' industries as steel, ship-building, machine tools, automobiles, electronic equipment, consumer electronics and electronic components, information technology, telecommun-ication equipment. A major thrust, therefore, behind the Single European Act was to reverse the trend of de-industrialization and, instead, hasten the process of *re*-industrialization. Thus, the industrial success or otherwise of the 'new' Europe will to a significant extent be judged in terms of how European industry will measure up to the Japanese challenge. There remains a high degree of divergence on what the responses to the challenge should be. Confrontation, competition, collaboration, and many shades in between, are promoted by different interests, different industries, different corporations, and, indeed, different countries.

In terms of national responses, the emphasis in France – with Italian support – has been on confrontation, the emphasis in Germany on competition, and in the United Kingdom on collaboration. It should be clear that the three options are not necessarily mutually exclusive. Thus in the case of France's consumer electronics industry, for example, Thomson has fostered collaboration with Japanese companies in, for example, video tape-recorders. The French are also trying to beat the Japanese to the higher definition television (HDTV) post, hence seemingly actively pursuing competition. As to the Germans: while, for example, their machine tool industry has made a successful come-back in fending off Japanese competition, such major companies as Siemens, Daimler Benz, BASF, Hoechst, Bayer, and others, have pursued strategic collaboration with Japanese companies. But recently it is the United Kingdom which has most enthusiastically adopted the policy of collaboration.

The responses of the three major European countries reflect their own economic standing. With Germany as the economic strong man of Europe, the competitive approach illustrates, among other things, both the country's strength and sense of self-confidence. France has tended to adopt a far more entrenched position, not only vis-à-vis Japan, but vis-à-vis practically every other industrialized or newly-industrialized state. Confrontation in regard to Japan is, therefore, a somewhat 'natural' reaction. Britain, as the economic sick man of Europe has, as critics allege, nothing to lose in collaborating with the Japanese. Certainly the Thatcher government did perceive Japan as a potentially very important player in the country's re-industrialization.

Thus the British government has been particularly active, and to date singularly successful, in attracting Japanese manufacturing investment. Currently, it ranks second only to the United States and has by far the lion's share in Europe. Japanese investment has, for example, revived Britain's television industry, and the same objective is being sought in automobiles. Japanese corporations have also been active in Britain's computer industry. The earlier collaboration between Fujitsu and ICL resulted in 1991 in the purchase of the latter by the former.

While the British government has been energetically seeking to attract

Japanese investment to Britain, it has also taken a far more positive stance than any other European government in encouraging British industry to get into the lucrative Japanese market. In 1988 the then Secretary of State for Trade and Industry, Lord Young, launched what came to be known as the 'Opportunity Japan Campaign'. Since then the Department of Trade and Industry (DTI) has sustained efforts at getting British exporters to focus attention on the Japanese market. The DTI has embarked on a new campaign, entitled 'Priority Japan', aiming both at encouraging British industry to transfer technology from and to invest in Japan. While the European Commission has also initiated a number of projects aiming to facilitate European industry's understanding of Japan's business environment and penetration of its market; in comparison to Britain no other individual European government has adopted as positive a profile.

Conclusive lessons from the British experiment are not easy to draw. Japanese inward investments have certainly made a contribution to job creation and to the balance of payments. On the other hand, Britain's possible failure fundamentally to benefit from the potential of Japanese industrial invigoration would appear to have been self-inflicted. In her eleven years as Prime Minister, Margaret Thatcher would seem to have made the somewhat classic mistake of having sought to promote economic growth at the expense of social development and infrastructure. Britain does not offer a technical or engineering base comparable to that of other more 'advanced' European countries. The deterioration of the infrastructure may in the longer run impede future inward investment from Japan – or anywhere else. Furthermore, whereas the Thatcher years saw a considerable expansion of the services industry, the performance of the manufacturing sector has remained unimpressive. It is questionable how much British managers in industry have actually learned from their Japanese counterparts: the not-invented-here syndrome remains an opaque barrier. There is a risk that Japanese investment ultimately will not so much have contributed to the re-industrialization of the United Kingdom, but rather merely provided a brief interlude in its inexorable de-industrialization.

Strategic alliances between European and Japanese corporations is another controversial issue. Whereas to some, Euro-Japanese corporate collaboration implies a dynamic process of industrial and technological globalization, to others the term rather conjures up a more sinister, quasi-'Quislingesque' interpretation. In the latter scenario, 'lean and mean' Japanese corporations use, indeed exploit, their more flabby European 'collaborators' in order to conquer and 'occupy' European markets. A somewhat more moderate position also put forward on the subject is that in the context of European industrial integration the 'Euro-patriotic' thing to do is to foster Euro-Euro collaboration, as opposed to consorting with foreign interlopers. In most cases, however, pragmatism and necessity will have to be applied: hence, even Edith Cresson had to back down following her abortive attempt to block NEC from purchasing 5 per cent of Bull!

Whatever the merits or demerits of Euro-Japanese corporate collaboration may be, two points can be made. The first is that attempts at collaborative arrangements between European and Japanese companies have been proliferating. The second point is that the number and size of Euro-Japanese corporate partnerships pale into insignificance when compared to those between American and Japanese companies. If collaboration with the Japanese does provide a major fillip to corporate competitiveness, then European enterprises may risk falling behind both Japanese and American competitors.

The strategies of a number of European corporations in regard to Japan have increasingly been influenced by the recognition of its role as a technological power-house. In 1990 Japan had spent not quite 3 per cent of its GNP in R&D, as opposed to the European average of just over 2 per cent. As about 80 per cent of Japan's R&D is financed by the private sector, compared to the European average of 50 per cent, Japanese innovation comes far more quickly to the marketplace. Japan's output of new products and new ideas is bound to increase at an ever brisker pace. A number of European companies such as ICI, Hoechst, Rhône–Poulenc, the BOC Group, L'Air Liquide, etc., have developed technology driven strategies vis-à-vis Japan. These include various forms of collaborative arrangements and the establishment of R&D centres in Japan. In the course of the last two years, the globalization of R&D has led Japanese companies to locate R&D facilities in the United States and Europe.

Again, however, in their approach to Japanese technology there is a tendency among Europeans either to be far more timid or indeed more arrogant than the Americans. The number of European companies with R&D centres in Japan and the size of their facilities pale in comparison with American R&D operations there. In contrast to Americans who are increasingly coming to fear Japanese technological competition and possible dominance, there is still in Europe the sniggering view that the Japanese are imitators, not innovators. European pusillanimity in comparison with a somewhat more rugged American response can also be illustrated from the human resource dimension: far fewer European scientists and engineers than Americans study Japanese. European failure to plug effectively into the Japanese science and technology network will ultimately prove to be a source of weakness.

Ultimately Europe's response to the *défi japonais* will be determined to a considerable degree by those Europeans who are the main transmitters of information from Japan, namely the European expatriate community. The European business community in Japan is in fact very small. It is infinitesimal in comparison to the size of the Japanese community in Europe – roughly a ratio of one to fifteen – and small in comparison to the size of the American community. There is also the qualitative dimension to consider. In recent years, American multinationals have started to appoint to Tokyo their first division executive players. These people have clout both in Japan and in their respective head offices. With very few exceptions, such is still not the case with European companies. Thus, the European expatriate community in Japan cannot function as an effective or influential conduit for processing information and interpretation back to Europe.

The Japanese 'vision' of Europe

The Japanese know Europe well, certainly far better than Europeans know Japan. Most Japanese have studied European history at school, European classic and modern authors, painters, sculptors, architects, cineastes are familiar names. The Japanese 'love affair' with European classical music has been intense and borne much fruit, with many Japanese musicians achieving international recognition. More recently European luxury goods have become the prized possessions of Japanese from many different walks of life. French gastronomy has taken the fancy of innumerable Japanese palates, and Japanese home-grown chefs are reckoned to be among the world's best. More cognac is drunk in Japan than in France. The taste for European goods and customs has been accompanied by a veritable boom in 'education', ranging from detailed articles in the media on the origins and history of perfumes, to a proliferation of wine tasting academies. And today many Japanese, almost one million per annum, travel to Europe.

The Japanese may *know* Europe well, but it does not follow that they *understand* Europe. While from a European perspective much is often made about the cultural barriers in Japan, the cultural barriers in Europe for the Japanese are no less formidable. The Japanese must contend not only with differences and rivalries between the national characters of the different European countries, but also between, say, the Catalans, Basques, Andalusians, etc., in Spain, the French and Dutch speaking Belgians, Catholic and Protestant Irishmen, and so on. The 'tribes' of Europe appear as an anthropological goulash. The multiple European structures and cultures in such areas as labour–management and government–industry relations, distribution systems, etc., leave the Japanese confused.

So long as Europe consisted of a mosaic of detached, independent pieces, the pieces could be dealt with individually. The coming together of the mosaic has added considerable confusion and indeed apprehension. There is the suspicion in many quarters that a united Europe will be a Fortress Europe whose architects are motivated by an anti-Japanese conspiracy. Many Japanese corporations and organizations have located intelligence monitoring posts near the European Commission, but the situation is not made any easier by the fact that lobbying is far less the transparent art in Brussels than it is in Washington.

The recent sea-changes that have occurred in central and eastern Europe have not helped matters. As these nations joined the capitalist camp, the view was expressed in various European and American quarters that undoubtedly Japanese enterprises would rush in. In fact, apart from numerous industrial intelligence gathering type junkets, Japanese corporate approaches to these nations have been characterized by caution. This is partly due to sheer economics, i.e. the markets are not that alluring and infrastructure is weak, but also to cultural barriers. Western Europe may be an anthropological goulash, central and eastern Europe are a cauldron.

Thus, just as it is an exaggeration to suggest that the European Single Act is an anti-Japanese conspiracy, similarly, it is more than an exaggeration to suggest that the Japanese are about to 'conquer' European markets. While Japanese direct investments in Europe have been growing significantly over the last five years or so, they remain very limited in comparison to those of the United States. IBM alone employs more Europeans than all Japanese manufacturing investors put together. Few Japanese companies have the status of good corporate European citizenship, something quite a few American companies achieved many years ago.

For their part, the Japanese have shared, indeed perhaps inspired, the general Asian perception of Europe as a 'museum'. The one European nation and its industry for which the Japanese business community retains a considerable degree of respect, however, is Germany. A *rapprochement* between the German and Japanese economies is a possibility. German and Japanese industrial structures and corporate cultures bear certain strong similarities: the role of banks in the industrial sector, the privileged relations between manufacturers and their sub-contractors, the tendency among large companies in both countries to practise 'lifetime employment', the emphasis on technical skills, the generally long term oriented nature of their companies' strategies. Germany is Japan's third biggest trading partner, while German exports to Japan are equal to those of France and the United Kingdom combined. Germany may be the more credible and powerful opponent to European anti-Japanese protectionism.

With the European Community emerging as a market of 340 million consumers, along with the possible 'annexation' of the 120 million or so central and eastern Europeans, Japanese corporations can be expected to persevere and allocate significant resources to increasing and/or consolidating their presence in Europe. If the response of European industry in the face of the Japanese global challenge is to retrench into Europe, rather than expand into third markets, and especially in Asia, then the emerging introverted Euro-centric Europe will become economically and culturally a poorer and less dynamic Europe. And it is perhaps for that reason that one should be talking not so much about a *défi japonais*, but a *défi européen*.

Scenarios for Japan and Europe in the global environment

In the scenarios that follow, emphasis is placed on the global environment and on the outstanding importance of the US–Japan relationship. This is not to say that Europe is not a master of its own fate, nor that its role is doomed to be a passive one. Far from it. Nevertheless, it must be clear that issues in the Euro-Japanese relationship cannot be addressed, let alone resolved, from a purely bilateral perspective.

In looking at the decade ahead, three assumptions have been made. The first is that the Japanese economy will continue to grow at a briskest pace. On the basis of both driving forces and current trends the average annual growth rate of Japan's GNP over the next decade should be sustained in the region of 3.5 to 4 per cent. The second is that Asia Pacific's economic dynamism will also be sustained. The third is that there will be no dramatic shift in Japan's relations with the former Soviet Union. On the basis of these assumptions, the scenarios are the following.

Euro-American-Japanese dynamics and harmonious 'ménage à trois' Scenario

This would require that the GATT Uruguay Round be revived by concessions being made by all sides on a number of issues, including agriculture.

The multilateral framework will need to be restored and respected, hence grey areas and the proliferation of unilateral acts by Washington such as Super 301 will have to cease. Protectionist forces must be deflected. Economic growth, though still higher in Japan than in either the United States or Europe, should be reasonably robust among all three major economic players. Both American and European companies will have to be more energetic in the flourishing Asia Pacific environment in order to benefit from its fast growing markets. The process of learning by American and European companies from state of the art Japanese manufacturers must be enhanced. The emphasis must be on competition and collaboration, not on confrontation.

Japan's recent market opening measures will have to expand significantly. Also, Tokyo needs to define a plausible and acceptable role for itself in the world. Its economic management must become more transparent and greater efforts made in establishing genuine dialogue with its trading partners. For its part, Europe will have to take initiatives, reflecting a global rather than Euro-centric vision. It will have to formulate a clear liberal trade policy vis-à-vis Japan. It implies that whoever is French Prime Minister, their anti-Japanese vituperations would have been silenced by other European leaders.

American–Japanese exclusive 'ménage à deux' scenario

This scenario sees Europe becoming more introverted as the three major European countries fail to solve their difficulties. In Britain, rising unemployment, inflation and trade deficits continue through the Conservatives' fourth term of office, following the election victory of April 1992. As to Chancellor Kohl, he bit off more than Germany can chew. The economic morass of former East Germany, the social problems and rising neo-Nazi political violence force the German government to concentrate on purely domestic matters. While the situation in France is hardly any better, the disarray in Britain and Germany allow Paris to influence European trade and industrial policy: French protectionist interests keep adding bricks to the European fortress. The Commission, divided on these issues in any case, has to fight a rearguard battle. Washington is alienated, Tokyo is ostracized.

In spite of persisting differences between Washington and Tokyo, both recognize that one cannot survive without the other. The American economy remains battered, but the Japanese, even if reluctantly, sign the necessary cheques. Progress is achieved in opening the Japanese rice market, and concessions are made in Structural Impediment Initiative (SII), etc. The marriage may be of the shotgun variety, but a marriage, and a monogamous one to boot, it is. Recognition, grudging or otherwise, is given in the United States to the fact that it is indeed the 'most important bilateral relationship, bar none'. Europe in this scenario remains the proverbial wall-flower.

The 'Rambo/Edith Cresson confrontation' scenario

This would imply not only that emotions have run very high in Washington, but also that Tokyo has refused to make any significant concessions.

American domestic economic problems continue to escalate, the trade deficit with Japan remains high, the Uruguay Round has got bogged down, SII has reached a stalemate. Thus, pugilistic protectionists are definitely in the ascendant on Capitol Hill, in Foggy Bottom and, finally, in Pennsylvania Avenue. Anti-Japanese trade and investment legislation is enacted. Washington acts in 'Rambo-esque' fashion, aiming at a show-down with Japan.

Washington may act unilaterally, but under certain circumstances Europe may join in the fray. As it may be recalled it was Edith Cresson, at the time French Minister of European Affairs, who labelled the Japanese 'the common enemy of Europe and the United States'. Others would presumably add their voices and seek to lead Europe in a Washington conducted anti-Japanese chorus.

The 'Pax Nipponica' scenario

Here Japan emerges as quite simply in a league of its own, not just a, but *the* geo-economic superpower. With both the United States and Europe having failed to keep up a comparable level of productive investments, Japanese industry forges ahead. Although both America and Europe engage in various protectionist measures, Japanese corporations, nevertheless, successfully circumvent these and in the process deepen their presence and clout in all of the world's major markets. More and more European and American industrial and cultural assets are purchased by the Japanese. Japan's geopolitical role remains somewhat ill defined, but indirect financial clout allows it effectively to use the still predominant American military as mercenaries protecting Japan's global economic interests.

Scenarios are scenarios and clearly imperfect analytical instruments. In all likelihood reality will not correspond in any way precisely to any of the scenarios indicated above, but more probably to a combination of several.

Elements of the fourth (*Pax Nipponica*) scenario will be pervasive in all of the other scenarios. However, the *Pax Nipponica* scenario per se, i.e. Japan replacing the US as world leader, must for the time being be relegated to a fairly high degree of improbability. For one important thing, it would not seem that the Japanese are much nearer to defining a global role that will enjoy both domestic support and international acceptability. A number of recent events, but especially the Gulf war, have shown that Japan's global policies remain reactive, rather than pro-active.

The first (*ménage à trois*), while clearly the ideal, also appears implausible. Even if not all of the conditions needed absolutely to be met, it nevertheless remains a pretty tall order: seemingly altruistic enlightened self-interest would be required of all three parties. Enlightenment is not necessarily the order of the day among any of them. On the basis of current trends the Europeans are unlikely to get their act together vis-à-vis Japan. Euro-Japanese relations will remain the weak link in the Triad, hence preventing the formation of a *ménage à trois*.

Variations along the third (Rambo/Edith Cresson) scenario represent a remote possibility. However, while the Edith Cressons of Europe may huff and puff, the actual transformation of this one-woman act into a joint Euro-American anti-Japanese crusade is unlikely to correspond to one of the more plausible variations of this particular theme. Other European leaders may fail to provide leadership or direction in regard to Japan, but they are unlikely actively to follow any Cresson initiative. Nor has there been much evidence that the Americans are interested in bringing the Europeans on board whether in their crusade against or their cavorting with the Japanese. The only way in which the 'Edith Cresson' scenario could become reality would be if the Japanese were to embark on an overtly aggressive trade policy. This has so far most definitely not been the 'Japanese way'.

The unilateral Rambo variation of scenario three has assumed with each recent passing year a greater degree of plausibility. Emotions in the United States are clearly running very high. The atmosphere between Japan and the United States will remain somewhat poisoned for the time being. In order to placate the anti-Japanese lobby, it is probable that more Super 301 or SII type unilateral actions will be taken. Saber rattling may become more cacophonous. The spirit and letter of the international trading system will erode, bilateral grey areas will proliferate, the United States will increasingly act the bully in matters of trade, and negative effects will spill over to the entirety of the world trading community.

Nevertheless, the most plausible scenario remains the second, the US–Japan *ménage à deux*, with elements of the third and fourth conspicuous by their presence. The United States has far too many vested interests in Japan. Many American jobs depend on Japanese enterprises in the United States The United States is dependent on Japanese finance. American leading corporations, including highly strategic ones in areas related to space and defence, are dependent on Japanese technology and components. A number of major American corporate players reap significant profits from the Japanese market. The tourism industry of Hawaii, California, New York, and other states would be devastated without the Japanese. Japan is the United States' biggest market for agricultural produce. Hence, while it may be true that Americans, in their economic relations with Japan, have had a certain proclivity to shoot themselves in the foot, it is reasonably safe to assume that they will refrain from shrinking their wallet.

The second, incorporating a vivid hue of the third and an increasing dimension of the fourth, corresponds the closest to the no-change scenario. The 'exclusive' nature of the partnership clearly reveals that Europe will be, indeed will continue to be, left out and that it will wallow in self-centredness. In the longer term, some time in the middle of the 1990s, the impact will be significantly negative. Europe will have failed to position itself effectively in the most dynamic region of the world, it will have failed to face, let alone meet, the cultural, industrial and technological challenge that Japan and a number of its Asian neighbours poses. With the exception of certain remaining pockets of entrepreneurial activity, Europe may indeed become an industrial museum.

While these prospects, arising from current trends, may appear depressing, it should be noted that no trend is irreversible. It would not take all that much for Europeans to reverse the trends. The European house needs to be put in order, kept open, and invigorated. For example, in comparison with

Japan, education in Europe leaves very much to be desired and critical skills are lacking. Competing with the Japanese industrially will require a willingness to compete with Japan educationally. Also, far more Europeans, especially scientists, engineers, and managers, need to learn the Japanese language, as well as about Japanese and other Asian cultures. If Japan and its Asian neighbours are to be penetrated commercially, industrially and technologically, they also need to be penetrated culturally.

A greater quantity and a better quality of European businessmen are required in Japan and in the other Asian markets. Forceful professional thrusts are necessary to penetrate the market or expand market share, to forge strategic alliances, to engage in technology transfer, etc. To accomplish forceful thrusts, forceful personalities are required: forceful, both vis-à-vis the Japanese and/or Asian markets and vis-à-vis the head office. European corporations need to be committed to meeting the *défi japonais* not simply in Europe, but more so in global markets and especially on the Japanese domestic market. Commitment will remain no more than rhetorical until and unless European corporations actually commit appropriate financial and human resources to the Japanese and Asian markets.

A question that arises is what kind of government support European enterprises should be given in Japan. There is a view that the best thing for government is to stay out. Proponents of this view point to Switzerland, the most successful European country in Japan, whose companies have succeeded on the basis of no government support, but simply through good Swiss businessmen selling good Swiss products. Nevertheless, there would seem to be a role for European official institutions to assist European enterprise at the level of information collection and diffusion. Information is a strategic weapon which the Japanese government has turned to very considerable advantage. A primary role of MITI is simply to inform Japanese enterprises of what is going on in specific markets, sectors, etc. In the earlier days of Japanese industry's expansion into export markets, MITI's foreign arm, the Japan External Trade Organization (JETRO), played an immensely useful role in gathering all sorts of intelligence on foreign markets for Japanese companies. Europe should establish a European External Trade Organization (EETRO) in Japan, and possibly from there expand its operations more widely.

Indeed, perhaps more in Tokyo than elsewhere, the fragmented, and consequently rather ineffective European effort sticks out like the proverbial sore thumb. Why there should be twelve separate and expensive to run embassies in Tokyo, each with their understaffed commercial section, is a question the perceptive Martian might well ask. A Single European House in Tokyo, including all the embassies, with a professional and linguistically capable staffed EETRO, would appear to make much more sense on all fronts.

At virtually every level there is a great deal that Europeans could benefit from learning from Japan. This is by no means to suggest that Japan is anywhere near a perfect model. But Japan has been successful in many of its industrial pursuits and a selective transfer from Japan, comparable to the selective transfer the Japanese made from Europe in the last century, could indeed serve to reinvigorate the old continent into the 'new' Europe. The trends could indeed be reversed.

NOTE

I should like to express my thanks to Quinn Riordan for interesting material and perspectives. Kenneth Courtis acted as commentator on an earlier draft presented at a symposium at INSEAD. His comments were, as always, extremely helpful and welcome. Considerable benefit was derived from insights given to me by Ezra Vogel. Jonathan Story provided excellent editorial and intellectual guidance.

REFERENCES

Abegglen, James and Stalk, George 1985: *Kaisha: The Japanese Corporation*. New York: Basic Books.

Beasley, William 1972: *The Meiji Restoration*. Standford: Stanford University Press.

Beasley, William 1987: *Japanese Imperialism, 1894–1945*. Oxford: Clarendon Press.

Benedict, Ruth 1946: *The Chrysanthemum and the Sword*. Boston: Houghton.

Boltho, Andrea 1975: *Japan: An Economic Survey, 1953–1973*. London: Oxford University Press.

Dove, Ronald 1973: *British Factory, Japanese Factory*. Los Angeles: University of California Press.

Ishihara, Shintaro and Morita, Akio 1989: *The Japan That Can Say No*. New York: Simon & Shuster.

Johnson, Chalmers 1982: *MITI and the Japanese Miracle: the Growth of Industrial Policy 1925–1975*. Stanford: Stanford University Press.

Kahn, Herman 1970: *The Emerging Japanese Superstate: Challenge and Response*. Englewood Cliffs, NJ: Prentice-Hall.

Lehmann, Jean-Pierre 1978: *The Image of Japan: from Feudal Isolation to World Power, 1850–1905*. London: Allen & Unwin.

Macrae, Norman 1975: Pacific country, 1975–2075. *Economist*, 4 January, 15–35.

McCraw, Thomas (ed.) 1986: *America versus Japan: a Comparative Study of Business–Government Relations*. Boston: Harvard Business School Press.

McMillan, Charles 1989: *The Japanese Industrial System*. Berlin: de Gruyfer.

Pempel, T. J. 1982: *Policy and Politics in Japan*. Philadelphia: Temple University Press.

Reischauer, Edwin (ed.) 1990: *Japan: the Story of a Nation*. New York: McGraw-Hill.

Sautter, Christian 1987: *Les Dents du Géant: le Japon à la Conquête du Monde*. Paris: Olivier Orban.

Scalapino, Robert 1977: *The Foreign Policy of Modern Japan*. Berkeley: University of California Press.

Smith, Robert 1983: *Japanese Society: Tradition, Self and the Social Order*. Cambridge: Cambridge University Press.

Stockwin, James 1982: *Japan: Divided Politics in a Growth Economy*. London: Weidenfeld & Nicholson.

Suziki, Yoshio 1987: *The Japanese Financial System*. Oxford: Oxford University Press.

van Wolferen, Karel 1989: *The Enigma of Japanese Power: People and Politics in a Stateless Nation*. New York: Alfred Knopf.

Vogel, Ezra 1979: *Japan as Number One*. Cambridge: Harvard University Press.

Wilkinson, Endymion 1983: *Japan versus Europe: a History of Misunderstanding*. Harmondsworth, Penguin Books.

5

Europe and the changing global agenda

Hanns W. Maull

It will not be the end of history: rarely has a prediction been falsified more rapidly, and more dramatically. With the war over Kuwait and the use of force against the Baltic states in the Soviet Union, the world moved from the anni mirabiles of 1989 and 1990 back into history with a vengeance. While the full scope and meaning of the sea-changes in international relations during the 1980s remain to be fathomed, it already is clear that those changes are truly revolutionary: the international system is undergoing a fundamental transformation, comparable to that in the late 1940s and early 1950s. While the world then moved into the framework of the cold war, it now has already moved out of it. Europe has been, and will continue to be at the forefront of those changes – as it was at the beginning of the cold war.

The new situation could be labelled, in the laconic phrase coined by Jürgen Habermas (admittedly in a somewhat different context), *'die neue Unübersichtlichkeit'* (the new obscurity). The following chapter will try to bring some clarity into this obscurity by identifying some of the changes which have taken place during the second half of the 1980s, and to mould them into a hopefully coherent picture of systemic change. In this picture, technological innovation appears as the prime engine of change, as the stimulus which profoundly affects, and thus forces responses from, economic, social, political and cultural structures around the world, albeit to vastly differing degrees and in ways which have been highly complex, ambivalent and even contradictory in their effects. In those responses to technological change, cultural adjustment is seen here as ultimately the probably most decisive element, although over the short and medium term this may not be apparent. Cultures adapt differently to technological change, just as economic, social and political structures take their specific forms and content from the culture in which they are embedded. This differential and ambiguous impact of technological change has produced new cleavages in international relations whose dialectics are likely to dominate the future evolution of international relations, and the responses of Europe to this evolution.

Technological acceleration: the force in the background

Technology – the systematic linking of scientific research, social purpose and organization – has since its inception around the turn of the century (some would argue: during World War I[1]) played a critical role in shaping international relations by its principal qualities: the ability to solve problems and to provide material benefits, and the creation of new risks and uncertainties. During the 1970s and 1980s, the pace of technological innovation seems to have accelerated substantially, and to have produced cumulative effects which add up to profound and far-reaching changes in at least four critical areas: economic productivity; transport and communications; the ecology; and military power.

Technological innovation is, of course, not just a one-way street of implanting new inventions in an economy and society: the very term, properly used, refers to the absorption of an invention within a social context (such as a firm). The acceleration of innovation in this sense is thus a complex social phenomenon which may be gauged by using two types of indicators: indicators referring to inputs, and those related to outputs of processes of technological innovation. Some measure of the exponential development of the former is the fact that 85 per cent of all scientists of the entire history of mankind live and work today (Wriston, 1988–9, pp. 63–75). One measure of technology output is the number of technology-related payments and receipts, which has been expanding rapidly during the last decade.[2]

Technological innovation has thus clearly received substantially enhanced attention and resources. At the same time, the 1980s was also a period in which the impact of new technology spread rapidly, producing far-reaching changes in at least four major areas:

The most obvious area is *industrial production*. Firms are at the same time the major source of innovation, and its beneficiary or victim – depending on the viewpoint. Technological innovations, especially progress in information technology, has allowed vast increases in data collection and processing; their impact has spread throughout industry, pushing up overall rates of productivity growth. The following statement by Robert Noyce, one of the founding fathers of the modern electronics industry, puts this change into perspective: 'Today's microcomputer . . . has more computing capacity than the first large electronic computer. It is 20 times faster, has a larger memory, is thousands of times more reliable, consumes the power of a light bulb rather than a locomotive, occupies $\frac{1}{30,000}$ the volume, and costs $\frac{1}{10,000}$ as much' (Simpson, Love and Walker, 1987, p. 3).

This was in the mid 1970s; today's microcomputer capabilities dwarf those of that time as dramatically as they, in turn, towered over their predecessors: the characteristics of high-performance microcomputers showed a twenty-fold increase in capabilities between 1981 and 1987 (GATT International Trade, 1990). Advances in computer science are estimated to double the total amount of information available to mankind every eight years (Sussman, 1989, pp. 60–5); the cost of information processing has fallen by 65 per cent in the decade from 1975 to 1985, and probably more during the 1980s. The personal computer, which hardly existed at the beginning of the past decade, has become the symbol of this potent change. While the first industrial revolution resulted in an increase in productivity by a factor of about 100, the microelectronic revolution offers to enhance productivity in the information sector by a factor of one million (Wriston, p. 64). Those innovations have created new industries with an explosively expanding turnover; they have also transformed, often beyond recognition, a whole range of traditional industries.[3] One crude indicator for this is the number of robots used in industrial production: it grew from 1,255 (1980) to 22,534 (1989) in the Federal Republic of Germany (FRG), and from 14,000 to 275,000 in Japan at end of 1990.

A substantial role in this dramatic impact of technological innovation on industrial production was played by innovations in *transport and communication*. If the symbol of new productivity in information gathering and processing has been the personal computer (PC), in communications it has been the fax. The number of fax subscribers in western Europe and Japan increased ten-fold in the second half of the 1980s (from 120,000 to 1.2 million in western Europe, and from 40,000 to 400,000 in Japan), while in the US there was a five-fold increase from 0.5 to 2.5 million (GATT International Trade, 1990). But the arrival of the fax has been but one element in a dramatic enhancement of communication and transportation facilities. The world has been moving rapidly towards a single vast global information and communication network which offers everybody the opportunity to communicate with anybody else in all corners of the globe, and to retrieve information from a virtually unlimited pool of data. The unit cost of transportation and communication has continued its secular decline, and has thus contributed to the rapid intensification of communication around the globe. One example illustrating this development is the increase in the number of international telephone calls during the 1980s: the annual growth rate of such calls has been around 20 per cent for most industrialized countries and well over 40 per cent for some of the newly industrializing economies.

These enhanced opportunities for exchange across national borders, in turn, have resulted in two major developments:

Economically, they have opened up dramatic new opportunities for transnational corporate activities. Transnational corporations were pushed into 'going global', into restructuring their activities to become 'good national citizens in any country of major corporate activity'. This implied at the same time globalization and localization of their internal organizational structures: companies had to operate with a worldwide perspective, yet respond closely to local circumstances.

Socially, new channels of communication such as satellites and cables (and the concomitant rise of new media as suppliers of information) have further perforated national sovereignty over information and in many ways created a 'global village' in which television coverage in real time around the globe becomes routine.[4] This information revolution has no doubt affected human behaviour across the globe, stimulating social mobilization and social change.

Technological innovation indirectly has also had profound effects on the global *ecology*. The cumulative impact of economic activity on the forests, land and water, on the ozone layer and the world's climate is moving uncomfortably close to critical thresholds beyond which huge and irreversible damage may be inevitable. The reactor accident of Chernobyl in 1986 has underlined the worldwide risks of radioactive pollution. Technological innovation has also played a major role in changing the demographics of our societies by stimulating migration, by enabling developed countries to support an ever older population, and by supporting the population imbalances in large parts of the south.

Finally, technological change has also affected *national power* in many ways. One aspect of this has been that technological prowess in itself has come to be considered as an attribute of a state's status and influence in international relations; another, the role technological assets may play in supporting economic strengths. Yet a third aspect of technology's influence on national power has been its impact on military capabilities. On the one hand, weapons acquired new range, precision and destructiveness, thus creating a continuum of conventional selective military options which tends to blur the traditional 'firebreak' between conventional and nuclear weapons (Welch, 1990, pp. 111–20). Innovations in armaments also came to be driven by innovation in civilian sectors of the economy, such as electronics and materials research (Pilat and White, 1990, pp. 79–91). This seemed to shift military advantages decisively in favour of the western industrialized countries – and Japan. Concern about the implications of a new, technology-driven twist in the arms race seems to have been an important factor behind the 'new thinking' in the Soviet Union: Moscow worried that the SDI initiative, even if it failed to achieve its defined objectives of developing comprehensive strategic defence systems, would produce decisive American military advantages simply through spin-off effects of vast R&D expenditure on the Strategic Defence Initiative (SDI), as well as through mobilizing 'spin-on' effects for military purposes (Adomeit, 1989, p. 46).

On the other hand, proliferation of technologies of mass destruction widened and accelerated during the 1980s, thus creating new uncertainties and threats. Military power in some sense thus became more diffuse, rather than less, and the vulnerability of complex industrial societies to disruptions – what some observers have termed 'the structural inability of highly developed industrial societies to wage war' – accentuated this diffusion of power. On balance, the utility of military power in efforts to secure national interests and coerce other actors appeared to continue its decline, while its destructive potential kept increasing.

The impact of technological change on international relations

The enormous dynamics of technological innovation produced three major results for international relations, whose cumulative force dramatically surfaced in the second half of the 1980s. Firstly, they caused a pronounced and qualitative rise in interdependence between national economies, societies and states. Secondly, the meaning of the term 'national security' changed, thereby weakening the traditional security dilemma which formed the core of the modern state system. And thirdly, they produced deepening tensions between a highly dynamic and rapidly changing socio-economic international context, and the relatively rigid and static world of the international political system, with its emphasis on national security, autonomy and territorial stability.

The *rise of interdependence* during the 1980s is often erroneously seen as a predominantly or even exclusively economic phenomenon; this is misleading. A broader view reveals that the growing perforation of national boundaries has developed in at least four major areas – security, economics, ecology and society – and that it has been interwoven with a growing interdependence between state and society *within* national borders (vertical interdependence).

Security interdependence has been a major factor in international relations since the effective advent of MAD (mutual assured destruction). The situation of 'existential deterrence', which this created, tamed the east–west confrontation, and turned it into an almost ritualistic effort by both superpowers to win without a fight – by outracing the adversary in arms procurements in the vain hope of securing a decisive political advantage, and by competing for influence in the third world (an expensive and ultimately fruitless endeavour, as both superpowers came to learn). The phenomenon of 'nuclear winter', postulated as the result of a major nuclear exchange in the early 1980s by a group of American scientists and fiercely disputed in some of their conclusions, perhaps best symbolizes the potential destructive effects of major war – the monstrous risks involved in such efforts to unilaterally protect national security demonstrated that national security could no longer be achieved without taking into consideration the security of the adversary. Thus, the 'London Declaration' of NATO heads of state and government unequivocally declared: 'We know that in the new Europe the security of every state is indivisibly tied to the security of its neighbours' (Europa Archiv, 1990).

War decisively lost its utility as a means to settle conflicts between the major powers, and the threat of common suicide pushed both superpowers into developing forms of cooperation to contain the risk of such a war breaking out. But as major war receded into the background, and as the superpowers shifted their relationship from 'collaborative competition' to 'competitive collaboration' (as they did in the second half of the 1980s), security concerns in the western industrialized countries also began to incorporate new issues such as threats from international terrorism, global environmental degradation, drugs and migration – i.e. to problems of social insecurity closely related to intensifying transnational processes,[5] as well as more traditional security concerns outside the mainstream east–west competition ('out-of-area conflicts').

The deepening of *economic interdependence* is a well-documented phenomenon. Its dynamics have shifted from trade in manufactures to capital movements and the development of technological links in the broadest sense across national boundaries. International trade during the 1980s – and especially in the second half of this decade – continued to show growth rates which were significantly higher than the evolution of world output. But those growth rates paled by comparison with those of foreign direct investment (Julius, 1990), other capital flows and (though this is more difficult to pin down statistically) of 'strategic alliances' and other forms of link-up between firms of different nationalities. Those networks of international interdependence in trade, capital and technology have become important, perhaps the most important, incubators of economic growth and prosperity across the globe.

If deepening economic interdependence reflects the relentless search for wealth and welfare, growing *ecological interdependence* shows up the negative side of this drive for prosperity. The degradation of the global environment has reached levels where its implications threaten the present and future quality of life for millions, even billions, of people across the globe. Although the effects of environmental degradation will be distributed unevenly, they will in many cases not be confined to the source of pollution. To contain and reverse the destruction of the environment in areas such as water, soil and tropical rain forest resources, and of the ozone layer, and to halt climatic changes with dramatic and potentially irredeemable consequences will require international cooperation on a wide scale (McNeill et al., 1990). Indeed, one of the remarkable diplomatic achievements of the second half of the 1980s has been progress towards such cooperation.

Lastly, *interdependence between societies* has been growing rapidly during the 1980s, and again particularly strongly during the second half of the decade. The growth of transnational mass communications has weakened, if not undermined, the ability of national governments to prevent 'contamination' of their citizens with outside information; images of western prosperity, individual freedom of choice and liberty have penetrated the most remote corners of the globe, triggering rising expectations and a willingness to move in search of new opportunities – but also violent revulsion and rejection of patterns of values and behaviour profoundly alien to traditional cultures. The relentless intrusion of western values and the western way of life represent a new, subtle form of cultural imperialism, and for many in non-western cultures is perceived as a continuation of western efforts at dominance.[6] Yet millions of individuals across what traditionally has been called the third world react to those intruding images with fascination and an ardent desire to enjoy a similar lifestyle. The ways to satisfy their expectations are also provided by the modern channels of interdependence: if their will is sufficiently strong, people may emigrate towards the centres of this way of life – from the countryside to the cities, from the south to the developed north. And the numbers of those who succeed are rising constantly, reaching proportions of mass migration to the urban centres within societies (thereby often causing major domestic political changes),[7] as well as across national boundaries (with similarly corrosive effects on international relations).[8]

This deepening of international interdependence across the board has profoundly affected the ability of governments to govern – to shape political outcomes in ways conducive to furthering perceived 'national interests'. What actually constituted 'national interests' was increasingly defined by developments abroad, requiring a gradual re-interpretation of the very term: viable definitions of national interest had to consider external implications of national actions and even the interests of other actors, as well – otherwise, the pursuit of national objectives could easily become counterproductive. Perhaps the most far-reaching illustration of this trend may be found in the realm of security policies, where the pursuit of strategies of unilateral security (e.g. through the development of ever more numerous counter-force options in lieu of strategies of mutual assured destruction or sufficiency) by both superpowers ultimately not only accentuated the risks of nuclear annihilation, but also foundered on the drain those strategies constituted for the national economies of both superpowers (although admittedly this drain was much more powerful in the case of the Soviet Union). The history of international economic relations in the last decade is also full of similar, if less dramatic, examples of the shrinking ability of national governments to pursue their objectives unilaterally – starting from the failure of French efforts at unilateral reflation in the early 1980s to the return of America to multilateral exchange rate coordination policies in the second half of the 1980s.

Interdependence not only affects the way national governments *define* their interests, but also the way they *pursue* them. And if patterns of interdependence can no longer be rearranged unilaterally to meet national interests at acceptable cost, then the only alternative are negotiations with other countries, often in a multilateral framework. In other words, the management of interdependence needs an expansion of political capacities to shape events at the supranational level – be it through ad hoc cooperation between governments, formalized international regimes, or the development of supranational integration.

At this point, we have to include the facts of vertical interdependence in our picture. The growing interpenetration of state and society has been characteristic of the development of western industrial countries since World War II (in fact, the war powerfully propelled this development forward). It also has been a secular trend in other parts of the world: in the eastern European countries and the Soviet Union, it has taken the form of a brutal subjugation of societies by the state, which ultimately resulted in the self-destruction of the political systems under the impact of declining performance, eroding legitimacy and social revolt. In many parts of the third world, the political repression of social demands from below (sometimes with the active support of one or the other superpower for the local regime) has led to intensified ethnic and civil strife and strong pressures for democratization. While governments worldwide have thus been besieged from within, they have also lost some of their ability to externalize domestic pressures through unilateral national actions. The nation state has thus shifted from its traditional position of supremacy to an intermediate position between sub-national and international constraints and demands. Governments thus, increasingly, are sandwiched between cross-cutting pressures from within and without, from below and from above; the art of governance has thus tended to become not only far more complex, but also different in nature.

Adaptation and resistance to change in international relations: the quest for wealth and the drive for security

As we have seen, interdependence reflects technological changes which promise huge material gains and enhanced individual freedom from natural and social constraints. But interdependence is no panacea – indeed, it may well resemble the curse of Midas: everything he touched turned into gold – so he starved amidst his material abundance. Among the losses caused by interdependence are externalities of economic growth (such as pollution and environmental degradation), and a loss of social cohesion and autonomy. People, states and international relations are forced to adapt to changing conditions because they have become vulnerable. This may threaten their values, their identity, even their human dignity. They can try to adapt – but they may also revolt, and try to resist or at least control the forces of change.

The international relations of interdependence thus imply a shift from what has been called the 'power game' nations played traditionally to the 'wealth game' (Kumon and Tanaka, 1988, pp. 64–82), but also a shift from national autonomy to vulnerability. The wealth game is the prerogative of firms, rather than countries – but states will play it, too. At the same time, however, their principal concern traditionally has been with autonomy, or sovereignty – and this power game has by no means been called off. Both the gains and losses from interdependence are, as a rule, unevenly distributed between national actors. National interests in a world of interdependence thus are of two kinds (Keohane and Nye, 1989). Firstly, interests which relate to common benefits (or avoiding common costs) from interdependence – e.g. the common interest of all countries to keep the world economy on a course of healthy expansion, to maintain an open trading system, or to prevent certain forms of global environmental degradation.

Secondly, countries will continue to consider the relative distribution of gains and costs from interdependence, as well as the evolution of their relative position in terms of crucial national assets in an interdependent world – economic competitiveness, technological dynamism, 'soft power' (Nye, 1990, pp. 177–92). They will thus strive to better their own relative position vis-à-vis other actors. Heightened interdependence may thus reduce the utility of military power in resolving conflicts and strengthen cooperative impulses, but it will imply, if anything, a multiplication of conflicts between nations, rather than their disappearance.

The processes of economic, social, political and cultural adaptation and/ or resistance to technological change are ultimately driven by values: people will respond to opportunities and threats in ways which will try to achieve or protect what they treasure. If technical advances provide the engine behind the challenges of technological change, the dynamics of social response are driven by values which will lead people to mobilize their human energies and resources. Adaptation to interdependence will be guided by the values of the modern world: the quest for escape from poverty and insecurity, the search for material benefits and greater individual freedom, and for enhanced opportunities and gratification. In the final analysis, those values turn around (mostly material) individual or group self-interest, with the tacit assumption that Adam Smith's 'invisible hands' could be relied upon to look after the collective good.

Those values to which interdependence appeals, and on which it builds, in themselves are rather deficient. First of all, the very rate of change in all major segments of the international system produces strong counter-pressures demanding continuity and security – i.e. the ability to enjoy presently valued conditions in the future. The forces of interdependence may thus clash with the desire for individual and social autonomy and dignity. Secondly, the values of interdependence provide few answers to questions such as: Who am I? Who are we as a collective? What is the purpose of freedom and wealth? And thirdly, in spite of their broader appeal, they are also the values of the west, and in that sense a manifestation of cultural domination.

Those deficiencies in terms of the speed of change, but also of defining individual and collective identities and social cohesion, of a transcendent vision, and of a historical bias, are taken up by resistance to change. This resistance will often rest on individual or collective self-interest by the 'haves' against the demands of the 'have-nots'. But it can also be built on alternative values: e.g. on exclusivistic, emotional collective identities (such as nationalism or ethnicism), on transcendent values (such as religious fundamentalism), or simply on the rejection of an alien set of values (such as anti-imperialism).

If we drop the naive assumption that the forces of change in themselves will – through the 'invisible hands' of market forces – by themselves produce a more perfect world,[9] both adaption and resistance to the changes wrought by technological advances ultimately are the task of politics as the realm in which social objectives are determined and pursued. If the adaptation to change is to retain control over our individual and collective fate, it needs to be predictable, to offer a sense of security. The provision of security against external and internal threats has traditionally been the task of the state, and it continues to be the most obvious addressee for demands for security, autonomy, and predictability.

At the most basic level, this means *national security against military aggression* from other states. While the essence of this challenge has been profoundly affected by developments towards security interdependence, the traditional national security problem has not yet been resolved – by a far cry. Until viable alternatives allow them to overcome the traditional security dilemma, states will continue to pursue their national security objectives in traditional ways, by accumulating military power. While the evidence is mounting that the use of military power no longer promises any effective contribution to national security even in a third world context,[10] let alone between the major powers, the destructive potential of modern weapons is still harnessed on a wide scale to achieve security objectives (and sometimes also others, as well).

Political *adaptation* to the pressures of interdependence in the realm of security consists in developing policies which are able to overcome the traditional security dilemma. This may be done by combining steps at the three levels of the security problem: within societies, through the guaranteeing of individual freedom, rule of law, human rights and political participation; at the national level, through the maintenance of residual military capabilities to ensure effective deterrence of military attacks; and at the international level, through negotiated regional and global security cooperation and integration (Buzan, 1983) and effective international structures of order. Successful adaptation along those lines has already taken place, and has led to the establishment of what Karl W. Deutsch has called 'security communities' (Deutsch et al., 1957) in western Europe, across the Atlantic, in Scandinavia and in North America. *Resistance* to change, on the other hand, tries to keep military force as an instrument to pursue unilaterally political objectives of a state against others. It implies the continuation of wars and national military interventions by global or regional powers.[11]

In the economic realm, *adaptation* essentially implies the development of effective structures of international economic management. In this sense, the move towards economic and monetary union in the European Community may be seen as an effort to adapt to changing conditions of interdependence. So may other efforts to build up free trade areas (as long as the objective behind them is to build *open* economic regions), the development of international economic cooperation within the framework of the G7 and the G3, and steps taken in many developing countries to bring their domestic economies in closer alignment with the requirement of world markets. *Resistance* to change constitutes the main motive behind policies of trade protection. As in the case of military security, however, the powerful realities behind the forces of economic interdependence can no longer be shut out effectively by national policies. Firstly, as interdependence deepens, it acquires powerful domestic constituencies which oppose protectionist measures (Milner, 1988). Secondly, there are ample opportunities to circumvent protectionist barriers or exploit them to one's own advantage.[12] Protectionist measures in highly industrialized countries are thus not only ineffective but also counter-productive. Yet as in the case of military security, in the absence of alternative ways to satisfy domestic pressures governments have still fallen back on unilateral measures of protection: the share of industrialized countries' imports affected by trade restrictions rose significantly during the 1980s, while the international trading regime weakened (witness the fate of the Uruguay Round) (Nikolaidis, 1990, p. 85). Again, the principal cause for those failures has been national reluctance to transfer effective authority to supranational arrangements. Contrary to the case of military security, however, economic interdependence provides gains as well as risks; the failure to accept supranational arrangements also reflected failures of governments to effectively compensate segments of society bearing the costs of interdependence through transfer payments financed by gains from interdependence.

The motive of economic security may be less obvious in the realm of high-tech industrial policies – but it lurks there, too. A sense of insecurity has traditionally been the powerful motive behind Japan's industrial policies in general, and her efforts to achieve dominance in high technology industries, in particular. The search for security also often motivated high-tech policies by the US and by the European Community (the fear of Japan's drive for technological supremacy loomed large in efforts such as Sematech, the US VHSIC project to produce very large integrated circuits, and Eureka were all inspired by such fears) (Pianta, 1988, pp. 53–79). Yet while national governments pressed ahead with such efforts, the nature of technological change and the realities of technological interdependence pushed for closer cooperation across national boundaries, producing a spate of strategic alliances between firms, and a number of highly visible international technological cooperation projects. And again, there was considerable evidence that national efforts produced at best limited positive, and significant negative effects (Eads and Nelson, 1986, pp. 243–69).

Developing countries confront particularly pronounced dilemmas in dealing with the realities of economic interdependence. On the one hand, they are often extremely vulnerable to changes (e.g. as a result of excessive dependence on raw material exports and pressing problems of poverty driven by the population explosion); on the other, their capacity to adjust is often low (e.g. due to the scarcity of capital, human skills, information and technologies to develop alternative economic activities). In addition, political structures are often ineffective, corrupt and repressive, blocking necessary policy changes (such as land and price reforms) and deploying wasteful economic instruments (such as state sector development). Economic policy adaptation has, nevertheless, taken place successfully in a number of developing countries, particularly in east and south-east Asia, and there are also hopeful signs in Latin America and parts of Africa.

Concerns over *ecological security* provide perhaps the clearest example for the dilemmas of interdependence. In more than one sense, global environmental degradation is the 'shadow' of economic interdependence: it reflects the dark side of material benefits provided by the growth of economic activity, and those detrimental effects follow the growing globalization of those activities as faithfully as a shadow. To some extent, it has been possible to externalize the ecological costs of economic activity – but the assumption that those costs could simply be pushed onto one's neighbours, or into the limitless dumps of the global commons, has increasingly fallen apart during the 1980s. To adapt to the risks of environmental degradation will require very substantial domestic rearrangements so as to internalize the costs associated with environmental degradation. It will also need substantial transfer payments between rich and poor countries to achieve optimum results. This, in turn, will require new forms and new instruments of multilateral cooperation. Effective security will be impossible to achieve without drastic steps in those directions. Yet the temptations to resist the pressures of change, or to take a free ride and dump one's own problems in front of one's neighbours, doors, will continue to loom large.

Socio-cultural adaptation to change implies the absorption of values and attitudes without which interdependence will not be able to work. This might be called 'westernization' or 'modernization' of non-western cultures. Successful cultural adaptation may be thought of as the integration of modern values with traditional cultural values and identities; modernization in this sense has taken place (highly successfully, as it seems) in east Asia. 'Westernization', on the other hand, may be thought of as unsuccessful efforts at imitating or implanting western values and attitudes. (A ready example for such a failed process of westernization is Iran under the Shah).

Resistance to modernization is probably often rooted in *social and cultural insecurity* related to psychological and socio-psychological limits to change. The pains and frustrations suffered by those exposed to the forces of technological, economic and social change will often be tremendous; and not for all affected will there be gains to compensate for the losses. Change threatens traditional values and challenges identities; it corrodes established social structures and undermines traditional social hierarchies. Opposition to change at the socio-cultural level will thus often take the form of ideologies of one kind or another – ideologies opposing change, ideologies advocating different forms of change compatible with traditional values and culture, and ideologies establishing new identities and social structures with emotional content around particularism, images of enemies and scapegoats.

Emotional (as opposed to functional) nationalism is one obvious form which such particularism may take; fundamentalism is another; the rejection of the west, of Europe as a concept, a third. Such ideologies may be understood as expressions of a desire for socio-cultural security; at the same time, however, they also may easily be turned into instruments of social control and purposeful mobilization for aggression against others. In this sense emotionally rooted ideologies such as anti-imperialism, nationalism or fundamentalism constitute the most dangerous alternative to the values of freedom and the pursuit of individual wealth and happiness, and a potentially forceful threat to the world of interdependence.

The opening gap, 1985–1990: towards a new global agenda

The accelerating pace of socio-economic change during the past decade has clearly strained existing political arrangements to provide security and stability to the limit – and beyond. At the centre of the widening gap between the dynamics of technological, economic and social change on the one hand and resistance by rigid political structures on the other has been the nation-state, which has been trying uneasily to master this ever more demanding straddling act. This gap has confronted all major groupings in the international system, albeit in different ways and to different degrees. The results have been most dramatic for those political structures least well equipped to adjust and change: political systems in eastern Europe, the former Soviet Union and parts of the so-called third world. In some other developing countries and in the western industrialized world, political structures have been able to adapt successfully to pressures for change: they have opened up to provide for wider political participation (e.g. South Korea and Taiwan), and have intensified the search for new, supranational political structures (e.g. the Single European Act of 1985, or the new regime governing the protection of the ozone layer).

The implications of the gap between socio-economic change and political stability on international relations have begun to shape the new global agenda. Put very simply, the consequence has been a profound and terminal crisis of socialist systems in eastern Europe and the Soviet Union and, as a consequence, the end of the cold war; an accentuation of efforts to enhance existing, and to develop new structures of international and supranational cooperation between major industrialized countries; and a stark differentiation of the 'third world', depending on the degree of adaptability displayed by their political structures (a capacity which probably also closely correlates with past successes in modernization efforts in those countries). Let us now look briefly at those three groups of countries and their experiences in turn.

(1) *The socialist systems in eastern Europe* constitute the most dramatic examples of failure to adjust to the pace of socio-economic change. Processes of technological innovation and their implications played an important role in the crisis of those socialist systems (Graham, 1989, pp. 36–42). On the one hand, their inability to compete with the west in implementing

new technologies was becoming ever more obvious during the 1980s. It showed up in their declining export performance in world markets, in their inability to innovate at home (with the extremely costly exception of the military sector), and potentially even in their military power vis-à-vis the west. On the other hand, the technological solutions implemented in the east were often woefully inadequate, and produced huge external costs, in particular, in terms of environmental damage.

The nuclear reactor accident of Chernobyl in 1986 put the deficiencies, indeed the bankruptcy of the Soviet technological system into sharp relief: complex modern technologies require high levels of information, voluntary commitment, freedom of choice and responsibility from its users, if their potential is to be realized and their dangers controlled. The Soviet political system, with its emphasis on controlling all aspects of individual and social activities, clearly had become incompatible with a modern economy in this sense. It also could no longer bar its citizens from information about catastrophic failures: the accident in Chernobyl was early on discovered by a private French reconnaissance satellite, and news quickly filtered back into the Soviet Union. The experience of Chernobyl apparently played an important role in the process of systemic reforms launched by the new leadership of the CPSU under Mikhail Gorbachev. The thrust of 'new thinking', *glasnost* and *perestroika* was an effort to reform the Soviet political and economic system from the top down, in order to make its political structures compatible with the requirements of a modern, high-tech economy. In the process, the Soviet Union shed its empire in eastern Europe, and offered to terminate the cold war on western terms.

If the absolute deficiencies and the relative loss of competitiveness (in the broadest possible sense of this word, including the lack of ideological attractiveness and legitimacy) had motivated reform from the top in the USSR, political change in eastern Europe resulted from a combination of social upheavals from below and reform efforts from above. The deficiencies, the brittleness and fatigue of political structures in Poland, the Czech and Slovak Socialist Republics (CSSR) and Hungary had long bred opposition deeply rooted in what remained of civilian societies in those countries; when the new Soviet leadership in effect renounced the Brezhnev doctrine of limited sovereignty, the opposition was encouraged to strengthen pressure on the governments (International Institute for Strategic Studies, 1989, p. 89). This met with a confused response by the authorities, which were divided between reform and repression. The result of the combined attack on the old political structures from within and below was their implosion: with the exception of Romania and the Soviet Union (though not all its republics), the old communist regimes were eventually ousted peacefully through general elections. In the wake of those momentous changes, the Warsaw Pact effectively folded, Germany became united and the cold war was formally ended at a CSCE summit meeting in Paris in November 1990: the joint declaration ended the ideological division of Europe by establishing a set of common values and principles of political and economic organisation, and provided, together with the results of the negotiations on conventional arms control in Europe, the outlines of a common political and security structure spanning the whole continent.

(2) *The western industrialized democracies* (including Japan) had to adjust their political structures to a world 'after hegemony'.[13] As interdependence deepened in the 1970s and 1980s, it changed the essence of power (Nye, 1990); also, differential gains from interdependence resulted in significant shifts in relative weight between the members of the western alliance system. This meant that the alliance increasingly had to rely on cooperative ways to resolve or manage problems. At the same time, conflicts over relative gains and losses from interdependence intensified as differences in national and personal wealth and individual living conditions between the US and its allies diminished. With the external threat of the Soviet Union fading, those conflicts have gained in importance.

'Project 1992' and the relaunching of European integration since 1985 in many ways respond constructively to those changes. At the beginning of this effort at revitalization was concern about the dangers of US unilateralism and the technological and economic competition from Japan. With the unification of Germany, European integration gained an additional important rationale: to tie Germany firmly into a multilateral context, and thus domesticate its potential power. In doing so, it underlined the importance of supranational responses to the problems of the 1990s: effective solutions to international challenges will ultimately often require transfer of sovereignty, as well as significant domestic changes. Supranational political structures not only facilitate the former, but could, in principle, also provide legitimacy to do the latter.

By and large, the institutions of western alliance cooperation have held up reasonably well under the strains of momentous changes – but the rafters have been creaking. The Atlantic and the bilateral US–Japan relationship have so far withstood some minor quakes, and cooperation in trilateral frameworks (such as the G7) has been expanding.

(3) The group of *countries in the south* have been affected by the accelerating changes of the 1980s in widely differing ways, as was noted above. Some countries – particularly those from the 'Confucian' world of east and south-east Asia – have coped very well, and have benefited disproportionately; others – especially those in sub-Saharan Africa, but also in Latin America – have often slid back desperately. In those regions, too, however, there have been signs of positive adaptation to changing circumstances. Perhaps the most pronounced resistance to change has been observed in the Middle East and in India. While there is thus no way to generalize the results of the experience of developing countries during the second half of the 1980s, the growing strains on political structures resulting from the dynamics of socio-economic change have been visible everywhere.

Perspectives for the future

Some of the arguments presented above may have seemed excessively optimistic, indeed imbued with a sense of historical determinism. This would be misunderstanding the thrust of the argument: the only certain thing we can say about the future is that it remains uncertain, to be shaped by human decisions and actions. Yet we live in an era of major historical discontinuities, comparable to the coming of the modern world in the sixteenth and early seventeenth century. This means that we find ourselves at a crossroads. On the one hand, we are facing an opportunity for a qualitative change in international relations towards a better, more peaceful world. On the other, if the world fails to cope with the dynamics of change, the destructive scope of our technological potential has become so large as to make major catastrophes, even a collective suicide of mankind, quite conceivable. What, then, ought to happen to steer the world into the future?

Eastern Europe and the former Soviet Union have begun to come in from the cold, and to join the mainstream of European development (Maull and von Heynitz, 1990). The east–west conflict has folded, or rather, it has now been replaced by huge differences in economic development and the quality of life, which we have traditionally associated with the north–south conflict. In many ways, the problems of the old 'south' and the old 'east' have indeed become similar; in the vocabulary of political geography, the 'north' has disintegrated, and the 'east' fused with the 'south' to reduce the coordinates of international relations to a single dimension, the 'west–south conflict'. To put it in those terms also helps to understand the crudeness of this terminology: in reality, the boundaries between 'west' and 'south' run between, as well as within societies, they are often blurred and constantly shifting.

In the east, as in the south, the destruction of the old political mould and of aspects of economic culture hostile to the use of market mechanisms has often been incomplete. Eastern Europe, the successor states to the Soviet Union and many countries in the south still need to develop viable political and economic structures, while striving to close the enormous gap in living conditions between themselves and the western world. This task is enormous, and success cannot be taken for granted – indeed, it may be extremely difficult to escape from a vicious circle in which the absence of political stability disturbs economic development, which in turn feeds social violence and political turmoil.

Simply speaking, eastern Europe, the former Soviet Union and many countries in the south thus appear to face three alternative, though not necessarily mutually exclusive, futures: turmoil, tanks or transition.

Turmoil would result from major crises in the process of 'modernization': governments under this group of scenarios would feel threatened or even in fact lose control, igniting brutal struggles for power. Violence and crime would become rampant means to deal with poverty and frustration. The civil wars in Ethiopia, or in Iraq after the war in the Gulf in 1991 provide only two of the depressingly numerous examples which might be cited here.

Under the second group of scenarios, *tanks* would be used to establish central and authoritarian political control over societies. They could be commandeered by the old elites, by army officers, or by nationalist or populist movements seizing power. Yet brutal repression alone would certainly not cure the deficiencies of those economies; the problems would quickly reassert themselves, making repression at best an unstable intermediate solution. Only if such a system could draw on strong ideological sources of legitimacy might it succeed in efforts at economic modernization. But it would almost certainly be faced with the handicap of restrictions on exchanges with the western world: were such circumstances to develop in eastern Europe or the successor states of the Soviet Union, the east–west conflict and efforts at containment could reappear. Iraq under Saddam Hussein provides an example for such scenarios: forced westernization at gunpoint not only led the regime into a permanent state of war against its own people, but also into attacking the Iranian revolutionary regime (which Saddam perceived as a dangerous political threat to his domestic rule) and then Kuwait. During the ensuing crisis, Saddam Hussein ironically tried to mobilize anti-western emotions under the banner of pan-Arabism or Islamic fundamentalism. The (for Iraq, as well as its supporters in the Arab and Islamic world) disastrous outcome of Saddam's aggression only underlined the lack of realism and futility of efforts to seek independent ways for the third world. Iraq's seizure of Kuwait represented a challenge to the prevailing regional balance of power, and the international order which she could not win: the only question was how much destruction and suffering Saddam would be able to impose on his society, and on others. Tanks – or even weapons of mass destruction – simply cannot offer an alternative to the third scenario, transition.

Transition identifies a group of hopeful scenarios under which the transformation of economic and political structures evolves successfully, opening opportunities for a virtuous circle in which western support strengthens successes in transformation, which in turn leads to closer ties with the western world, and so forth. In such successful efforts at adaptation, the European experience may well have particular relevance: 'Europe' can, in fact, be conceived as a concept for cultural modernizers.[14] The key tenets of Europe as a concept historically are the reliance on modern science and technology, on political and cultural pluralism, on market mechanisms, on the principles of human rights and the rule of law, and on effective forms of democratic participation.[15] More recently, a new, important element has been added: supranational cooperation and integration. In the past, during the era of colonialism, Europe offered a successful model of modernization to other cultures by brutally demonstrating its superiority. More recently, having shed its colonial past, its postwar successes of economic advance and political integration have given this function of role model a new meaning: Europe's successes stimulate imitation, while its huge market provides a magnet of attraction to the whole of the developing world, and thus creates a desire for closer cooperation and even association with this European experience. On the basis of a universal application of those principles of 'Europe' as a concept, other parts of the world could find their own models of successful development, and the west could gradually but effectively begin to cooperate and integrate with eastern Europe, the Soviet Union and the south, thus ultimately turning 'Europe' into a global reality.

Does such a transition of the 'south' represent a new, subtle form of European imperialism? Yes and no. Yes, because the development of modern science and technology offers no other viable path into the future but this one; no, because 'Europe' as a concept will prove capable of changing, adopting and adapting elements of other cultures into new syntheses with new opportunities for Europe itself, as well as for other cultures. Moreover, the principles associated with the rise of Europe can be varied indefinitely in their specific implementation, as the successful 'European' or 'western' cultures of modern Japan or Korea show. And lastly, the model has already proven tremendously attractive all over the world, and thus stands a good chance to find widespread approval and legitimacy in other cultures – provided, however, it can 'deliver'.

The jury thus is still out on the future of western capitalism, of the concept of Europe. The west has not won the east–west conflict – the east has lost it. To win the new conflict between 'west' and 'south' will be the real test – for no matter which set of scenarios will predominate during the coming decades, the implications for the west will, in any case be dramatic.

Under conditions of *turmoil*, western security will be threatened through an upsurge of the effects of 'destructive interdependence' on our societies. Driven by the huge population explosion overhanging the coming decades, ecological destruction and mass migration from eastern Europe and north Africa could sharply erode the quality of life in European countries and undermine the values and principles on which modern democracies are built: how could Europe stem the tide of desperate immigrants who fear for their lives without itself threatening them with death? How could democracy survive if pervasive police methods will be needed to patrol the limits to immigration? Mass migration could also cause other, old-fashioned types of security, such as tensions between countries and border conflicts (Strategic Survey, 1991, p. 37).

Scenarios of turmoil would also encourage individual attempts to escape poverty and instability through organized crime such as drug-trafficking or hostage-taking. And it seems likely to breed new incidents, and perhaps new forms, of international terrorism. And, finally, turmoil might also threaten western access to critical resources, such as oil – as evidenced by the repercussions of the Iranian revolution on world oil markets.

Such problems could also arise under scenarios of *tanks*. The use of military force at home is likely to encourage the use of tanks abroad, as well – as was the case with Iraq's Saddam Hussein who repeatedly resorted to war to achieve his political objectives. Scenarios of tanks thus contain implicit threats to regional order, as well as to international stability (others may draw the wrong conclusions from Saddam's unsuccessful efforts to develop and instrumentalize weapons of mass destruction – they may be tempted to try harder). But the most fundamental problem related to scenarios of tanks may be this: in many ways, the world has moved beyond (i.e. above and below) the state as the key unit of international relations. Yet states still maintain the effective monopoly of the use of force – and are thus able to undermine the preconditions which a successful development of interdependence requires. As long as the use of socially organized force remains taboo, the tension between the state as the key unit of international relations on the one hand, and the shift of social and economic dynamics away from the state towards regions, ethnic and religious groups and supranational organizations on the other may remain manageable. Once the taboos are broken, however, the west faces painful dilemmas: to intervene to uphold its own principles, or to lose credibility and undermine its own values in the eyes of a critical domestic audience (which, however, may quickly turn very intolerant of interventionist policies which demand a high price); to protect the notion of national sovereignty and the inadmissibility of interference in one other state's domestic affairs, or to intervene at the price of pushing aside such considerations. Nor are the choices likely to be black and white (as they were pretty nearly in the case of Iraq 1990–1). There will in all likelihood be no easy answers for Europe, once the tanks are called in to resolve political conflicts within or between countries.

Western responses to those different scenarios could unfold along three lines of response: *containment* (including emergency assistance and efforts at diplomatic resolution) will have to dominate the responses to anarchy and chaos; *conflict* (though mitigated by persistent efforts at constructive engagement) over issues such as human rights, support for terrorism and military threats using the proliferation of weapons of mass destruction would play a central role in dealing with authoritarian, ideological regimes, but also those set on an authoritarian course of modernization from above. Lastly, *cooptation* and *cooperation* should dominate western strategies towards developing countries undergoing successful strategies of transition.

In this context, Europe, the west and the international community as a whole will have to develop new policies for the future. Those policies will have to focus on the following major areas:

- *'Deepening'*, that is, consolidating and strengthening the alliance system. To have a strong core of international cooperation will be indispensable to support its expansion into new functional and geographic areas. The argument is familiar from the process of European integration, and applies in this wider context, as well.
- *Managing the 'worldeconomy'*.[16] This challenge really implies solving two different tasks: first, to prevent the world economy from 'malfunctioning', i.e. from sliding into serious crises which could undermine its ability to 'deliver', and hence the legitimacy of an open international economic order. And secondly, to secure wide legitimacy for the management structure: it would be impossible to impose if it were not seen to be fair, ecologically benign and socially equitable. This means the new concept of international economic order will have to integrate values of social equity and a healthy ecology.
- *Providing security and order*. The security of western industrialized countries will continue to be threatened, although the essence of those threats may well change substantially to include new dimensions of security such as proliferation, terrorism, drugs, and environmental degradation. Many of those threats can be met only through cooperative efforts within and beyond the western alliance, such as through a strengthening and re-orientation of international regimes, e.g. on nuclear non-proliferation. Some of the threats will continue to require responses of a military nature, however, confronting the western alliance with the tasks of adjusting and re-designing their military security structures. To be compatible with the concept of 'a new order', such interventions would have to be carried out by way of collective military action, preferably under the procedures of Chapter VII of the UN Charter.
- *Widening the range of the western political and economic system* to include eastern Europe, as well as eventually also the former Soviet Union and the south. This is obviously a long-term task, which will have to be taken up step by step. The logic of interdependence suggests, however, that there is little prospect for prosperity outside the web of world markets; that closer economic integration will also require closer political coordination and ultimately political integration, as well; and that the

western alliance system would lose credibility and legitimacy if it blocked the entry of other countries which demonstrably shared its values and showed compatible economic and political structures.

- *Defining a convincing set of universal values* to secure the required political support both within western societies and among the poorer countries for a system of international management which is bound to impose costs and some sacrifices on people in the west, and to be less than satisfactory to the horizons of expectations which have been aroused in the south and the east. In addition to the values outlined above as constitutive for the western experience, those values will have to include:

  - respect for the global environment as a value in its own right;
  - international empathy, to allow for the peaceful resolution of ethnic conflicts within states, and to develop viable supranational structures involving partial but effective transfers of sovereignty;
  - international responsibility, to gain domestic political support for internationalist policies, but also international legitimacy for individual or collective leadership by some states.

If the west were to develop policies along those lines, this could make all the difference between success and failure. Yet the principal tasks of transition and modernization will have to be met by the societies in the 'south' (i.e. in eastern Europe, the former Soviet Union and the developing countries) themselves. The experience of east Asia shows that the concept of Europe can be adapted to different cultural circumstances. Four fundamental elements, however, will have to be present to allow for effective cooperation with the west: the rule of law and respect for human rights; reliance in principle on market mechanisms and an international division of labour; political pluralism, including a firm commitment to avoid the use of military force to settle differences; and international empathy, i.e. the willingness to renounce chauvinism and the use of force as a means of settling conflicts with other countries.[17]

NOTES

1 During World War I, governments first began to shape the process of technological innovation by organizing systematic efforts to develop weapon capabilities. Cf. William R. Kintner and Harvey Sicherman, 1975: *Technology and International Politics: the Crisis of Wishing*. Lexington: D. C. Heath, p. 7. See also William H. McNeill, 1982: *Krieg und Macht*, Munich: C. H. Beck esp. ch. 8.

2 In the case of Japan, technology payments rose from $966 million in 1980 to $1,958 million in 1987, technology-related receipts from $644 million to $1,490 million.

3 For a comprehensive analysis, see OECD, *Structural Adjustment and Economic Performance*, Paris: OECD 1987, pp. 253ff.

4 See *Rapport Annuel Mondial sur le Systéme Economique et les Stratégies, 1989* (RAMSES, 1989), Paris: Dunod, part IV.

5 An amusing footnote on the 'socialization' of security policies, which illustrates the changing attitudes towards and expectations of traditional security structures harboured within developed societies is the following letter received by the NATO headquarters in Brussels:

Dear Sir,

My cousin Jeremy tells me that your organization controls a network of satellites that, though invisible to the human eye themselves, are keeping close surveillance over us. Though hard to imagine, these satellites photograph objects on the ground mere centimetres across.

The point of my letter is that last Monday 11th, someone bumped into my car as it was parked on the Prinsengracht in Amsterdam at about 9pm. Would you therefore be so kind as to look over your photographs of the area around that time, and see if you can spot a car in a collision situation with a white Skoda with a roofrack, and let me have the other car's make and colour to help me track it down. I would be very obliged.

If you have trouble identifying Prinsengracht from the air, it is the outermost of the three canals that ring the centrum. Yours in anticipation, etc.

6 The most virulent opposition today of course comes from Islamic fundamentalists. See Bernard Lewis: The roots of Muslim rage. *The Atlantic Monthly*, Sept. 1990, pp. 47ff.

7 Thus, black urbanization has perhaps been the most powerful social force eroding the structures of apartheid in South Africa. Even the highly elaborate and equally brutal efforts of South Africa's white governments to stem this movement were ultimately swept aside.

8 In Europe, the principal causes for acceleration of migration were, of course, the changes in eastern Europe and the Soviet Union, but also the rising number of asylum seekers. On this subject, see François Heisbourg, Population movements in post-cold war Europe. *Survival*, Jan.–Feb. 1991, pp. 31–44.

9 This assumption would not only ignore a host of historical evidence, but also fail to confront two fundamental issues: first, market mechanisms can only function within a political framework guaranteeing the stability of contractual arrangements; and second, market mechanisms cannot per se produce a distribution of gains and losses among social actors which will be considered acceptable and legitimate.

10 To illustrate this point, one need to mention only the failure of South Africa and Israel to achieve national security in their respective regional environments through the use of military power. The case of Iraq is also illustrative – see, e.g. the argument of Karsh and Rautsi that Saddam Hussein was pushed into the invasion of Kuwait by insurmountable internal problems resulting from the previous war against Iran – a war initiated by Saddam to dispose of threats to his rule from the Iranian revolution. See Ephraim Karsh and Inari Rautsi, Why Saddam Hussein invaded Kuwait. *Survival*, Jan.–Feb. 1991, pp. 18–30.

11 The willingness to use military force by a state (or more precisely, by a regime) against its neighbours seems related to its willingness to use force against its own citizens. Growing interdependence erodes the utility of both forms of state violence; resistance to change in that sense may therefore also result in civil war.

12 The classic example here are the 'voluntary export restraints' imposed on Japanese auto firms by the US industry. The effects of this have been closely studied, and the results of those analyses clearly show that those measures were largely self-defeating for US auto manufacturers, and economically very costly to the US consumer.

13 This is the title of a seminal book by Robert O. Keohane (*After Hegemony: Cooperation and Discord in the International Political Economy*, Princeton: Princeton University Press, 1984).

14 I am grateful to Jean-Pierre Lehmann for this insight.

15 This notion (as much of this essay) is based on William H. McNeill, *The Rise of the West: A History of the European Community*, Chicago: Chicago University Press, 1963.

16 The term was coined by Albert Bressand to illustrate the growing integration of the world economy into one single global system (Mastering the 'worldeconomy', *Foreign Affairs*, 1983, pp. 735–62.

17 These categories have been inspired by Dieter Senghaas, who developed similar categories with regard to western policies towards eastern Europe and the Soviet Union (Dieter Senghaas, *Europa, Quo Vadis?*, Neue Aufgaben für eine Politik der Friedensgestaltung, Ebenhausen: SWP Jan. 1991, p. 61 (SWP–AP 2679).

REFERENCES

Adomeit, H. 1989: Gorbachev's 'Umgestaltung' und der der 'militärisch-industrielle Komplex' der UdSSR, Militär, Partei und Rustungsindustrie im neuen ideologischen and aussenpolitischen Bezugssystem, Ebenshausen: SWP May and passim (SWP–AP 2609).

Buzan, Barry 1983: *People, States and Fear: the National Security Problem in International Relations.* Brighton: Harvester.

Deutsch, Karl W. et al. 1957: *Political Community and the North Atlantic Area.* Princeton: Princeton University Press.

Eads, George C. and Nelson, Richard R. 1986: Japanese high technology policy: what lessons for the United States? In Hugh Patrick (ed.) *Japan's High Technology Industries.* Seattle: University of Washington Press, 243–69.

Europa Archiv 1990: 17/17990, 10 September 1990, pp. 456gg.f.

GATT 1990: *International Trade, 1990,* vol. I.

Graham, Loren R. 1989: Toward a new era in US–Soviet relations. *Issues in Science and Technology,* Fall, 36–42.

International Institute for Strategic Studies 1989: *Strategic Survey, 1988–89.* London: IISS/Brassey's, 38.

Julius, DeAnne 1990: *Global Companies and Public Policy: The Growing Challenge of Foreign Direct Investment.* London: RIIA/Pinter.

Keohane, Robert O. and Nye, Joseph S. 1989: *Power and Interdependence,* 2nd edn. Glenview, Illinois: Scott, Foresman and Co.

Kumon, Shumpei and Tanaka, Akihiko 1988: From prestige to wealth to knowledge. In Takashi Inoguchi and Daniel I. Okimoto (eds) *The Political Economy of Japan. Vol. 2: The Changing Economic Context,* Stanford: Stanford University Press, 64–82.

Maull, Hanns W. and von Heynitz, Achim 1990: Europe auf dem Weg in die Postmoderne. *Europa Archiv,* 15, August, 441–52.

McNeill, Jim, Winsemius, Peter and Yakushiji, Taizo 1990: *Beyond Interdependence: A Report to the Trilateral Commission.* Washington DC: The Trilateral Commission.

Milner, Helen 1988: *Resisting Protectionism: Global Industries and the Policies of International Trade.* Princeton: Princeton University Press.

Nicolaidis, Phaedon 1990: Trade policy in the 1990s: avoiding the trap of regionalism. *World Today,* 46, May, 85–6.

Nye, Joseph 1990: *Bound to Lead: The Changing Nature of American Power.* New York: Basic Books.

Pianta, Mario 1988: High technology programmes: for the military or the economy? *Bulletin of Peace Proposals,* 1, 53–79.

Pilat, Joseph P. and White, Paul S. 1990: Technology and strategy in a changing world. *The Washington Quarterly,* Spring, 79–91.

Simpson, David, Love, Jim and Walker, Jim 1987: *The Challenge of New Technology.* Boulder: Westview.

Strategic Survey 1991: London: IISS, 37.

Sussman, Leonard R. 1989: The information revolution. *Encounter,* 61, 61–65.

Welch, Thomas J. 1990: Technology change and security. *The Washington Quarterly,* Spring, 111–20.

Wriston, Walter B. 1988–9: Technology and sovereignty. *Foreign Affairs,* 61, 63–75.

The Major Countries and Europe

PART III

The Major Countries
and Europe

Editor's introduction

This section focuses on the linkages between the domestic and external policies of the large western European states. While their membership in the European Communities conditions policy in broad areas of political and economic activity, all European states hold their own memories and have followed their own path through time. Political cultures derive from a common root of religion and legal or state traditions, but remain specific, as do the party political systems, economic institutions or foreign policy preferences. All states in the EC have a dual status as members of the Community, and bound by its treaty obligations, as well as being sovereign members of the world system or society of states. Relations between member states are therefore conditioned in part by their common insertion in the global economy, as well as by their particular relations to non-EC member states.

The subsequent country chapters follow, where appropriate, a similar design, starting with an overview of the longer-term factors shaping policy (cultural, institutional, economic, military); the linkages between the operational environment of domestic politics, such as central government or political parties, and their external relations with other international or non-governmental organizations; the domestic aspects of interdependence as expressed through an analysis of the particular political economy, and its position and performance in the broader European context. Finally, the country is examined in the perspective of world politics along functional lines (security, finance or trade), their relations with the various European or Atlantic institutions, particularly the EC and NATO, and their relations with non-European states as they impinge on their policies within Europe.

All of Europe has been transformed by German unity, giving rise to fears of a continent dominated by its central state. The history of Europe and Germany from 1870 to 1945 is sufficiently recent to prompt analogies from the past. Whatever the political and economic difficulties may be that confront the Federal Republic in absorbing the five new regions, conditions for a successful transition are favourable. The institutions of the Federal Republic have taken deep root in the affections and practice of its citizens. The state is embedded in the western institutions, and underpinned by a strong industrial and export-oriented economy. German unity, nonetheless, confronts France with some fundamental choices in external and domestic policy. The same holds for Great Britain, which fears exclusion from a more federal Europe, but is too bound in to draw back. Italy remains supportive of both a wider Europe, and a more integrated EC, but is hobbled by its perennial problem of political logistics. Spain as a full member of the EC, and in the Atlantic alliance, is determined to gain status and wealth as one of Europe's lead powers.

6

Germany and Europe

William E. Paterson

Introduction

The universal adoption of democratic forms in nineteenth-century western Europe left Imperial Germany as a notable exception. For the next hundred years the German question was to have two aspects; the first concerned the possibility of establishing a stable liberal democratic polity in Germany. The consolidation of the Federal Republic, the increasing attachment of its citizenry to democratic values and institutions and the successful governmental transition of 1969 were all indications that the Federal Republic had become the first successful liberal democratic German state. The extension through unification of the Federal Republic to encompass the German Democratic Republic must mean that the German question in this formulation can be now regarded as settled (Paterson and Smith, 1992, pp. 9–33).

Whilst the first formulation of the German question was one which in the first instance affected citizens of Germany, the second formulation which focuses on the compatibility of Germany with its European environment had always aroused intense interest inside and outside Germany. The second formulation has been well expressed by Pierre Hassner: 'What kind of Germany would fit into what kind of Europe so as to be neither too strong nor too weak for its European environment?' (Hassner, 1982, p. 3).

Germany and Europe: is there a dominance problem?

Germany's size and geographical position has ensured that Pierre Hassner's question, with its bifocal perspective on the reciprocal interaction between the characters of Germany and its European environment, has never lost its relevance. For much of the postwar era the twin German states were in a Gulliver-like posture. There were, of course, notable differences. The GDR shared its absolute lack of autonomy with other east European states whilst the lack of the autonomy of the Federal Republic was only relative. Other West European states were often also members of the NATO Alliance and the constraints imposed by the European Community were shared by other member states. The stationing of the bulk of allied forces in West Germany, the absence of an independent planning function and the Berlin factor created a situation of German exceptionalism in the area of security, however.

West Germany's relationship with the EC was mutually reinforcing. There was a marked congruence between the economic and political versions of liberal capitalism characteristic of the Federal Republic and the EC. This is hardly surprising since they both owe much to American influence. West Germany was never too strong for the Community, since its governments resisted the temptation to try to turn its economic strength into an explicit political leadership role. Where a political leadership role was played, it was usually in tandem with France. This self-denying ordinance reflected a sensitivity to the shadow of the German past and to the domestic economic and political limitations within which other member governments operated. The major exception was in the field of monetary policy where a *lehrmeister* attitude sometimes prevailed in the Schmidt period, especially towards Italy.

The leadership avoidance reflex of successive West German governments was shared by the political class in general and was reinforced by a number of features of policy making in West Germany. The system of cooperative federalism with the premium placed on harmony between Bonn and the Länder militated against a purposive coherent national policy.

> The West Germans describe the structural features of their system of inter-governmental relations with terms such as 'cooperative federalism' or 'inter-locking politics' (*Politikverflechtung*). In the West German system of intergovernmental relations, divergent interests are brought together through a policy process that resists central reform initiatives and defies sustained attempts to steer policy developments. (Katzenstein, 1987, p. 47)

The vertical divisions imposed by federalism were reinforced by the 'sectorized' nature of socio-economic interest organization which fed in to highly specialized ministries. In effect, the ministries parcelled out responsibility for domestic and EC policies among separate policy communities, peopled by the relevant state and private interests. What was manifestly absent in the West German case was a strong coordinating power. The commitment to consensus and to coalition government meant that sectoral interests would only rarely be overruled. It could only be done by the chancellor and then only sparingly.

There was no question then of West Germany being too strong for the European Community nor could it be said to be too weak. Its economic and political stability and its readiness to contribute towards the funding of the Community were also sources of strength, although external critics sometimes drew sharp contrasts between the size of the West German trade surplus with its Community partners and its budgetary contribution. This is, of course, still a major issue.

Does unity make a difference?

> When the workmen found it was impossible for me to break loose, they cut all the strings that bound me; whereupon I rose up, with as melancholy a disposition as ever I had in my life. But the noise and astonishment of the

people, at seeing me rise and walk, are not to be expressed. (Jonathan Swift, *Gulliver's Travels*)

The negotiations on German unity (see pp. 172–177) can be viewed in different ways. It is possible to read them as a triumph for the Community institutions which proved capable of responding to the challenges and which contrived to set a European roof on unity whilst not upsetting the priority of the single market programme. On the other hand, the Community's lack of impact on the process is equally striking. This is perfectly understandable given the stark imperatives that the possibility of the imminent collapse of the GDR imposed on the federal government. The key question is whether the pattern of the unity negotiations will prevail in the future.

The arguments against expecting an onset of German dominance can be set out fairly simply. The constraints already sketched out will continue to apply. The position of the Chancellor remains unchanged. Many in the Christian Democratic Union (CDU) had hoped that the December 1990 election would usher in a period of single party government with attendant possibilities for coordinating and strengthening the coordination of European policy, reducing the functional ministries' *Ressort* autonomy and pursuing a more purposive policy. These hopes were cruelly disappointed by an election result which left the CDU in its old position while strengthening the FDP significantly. Paradoxically, a clear cut victory for Chancellor Kohl would probably not have led to Germany playing a more dominant role. Kohl's consistent policy was to support progress in the two inter-governmental conferences (IGCs) towards a deeper level of integration and a greater pooling of sovereignty.

There is little indication, as yet, that a more assertive policy would be backed by domestic public opinion. One of the most striking features of the achievement of unity was its lack of nationalist euphoria and the absence of *Überheblichkeit*. Repeated surveys, have indicated that the German public after unity has an even smaller appetite for a leading German role than hitherto, rather it aspires to a Swiss-like status where it should be left alone to get on with the uncomplicated business of accruing wealth. There are also considerable reservations among German elite opinion about Germany playing a manifestly assertive role.

The federal dimension

Pierre Hassner's formulation is especially apposite in relation to the federal nature of the German system; a different kind of Germany organized along unitary lines would clearly be in a much stronger position to exercise purposive dominance. The Länder were able to utilize the ratification of the Single European Act in 1986–7 to extend their powers, and an agreement was reached in December 1987 providing for formal consultation of the Länder where their exclusive powers are affected by EC proposals.

Federalism after unity

Federal pressures have, if anything, increased after unity. The eastern part of Germany has been refederalized and it is difficult to envisage that someone like Kurt Biedenkopf, in his new role as Minister President of Saxony, will not use it to play a role in European policy.

The Länder governments became extremely active in preparations for the two IGCs. At the Ministerpräsidenten-Konferenz on 7 June 1990, the eleven minister presidents demanded that the Länder be given extensive rights to participate in the negotiations for European union and that the principle of subsidiarity be included in the new treaties in an enforceable manner. Further demands included the creation of a new European Council of Regions and amendment of art. 173 (EEC) to allow the Länder to bring legal actions before the European Court. At the Bund–Länder Besprechung of 10 August 1990 the Länder representatives met with the federal government who made clear that it could accept three of the Länders four demands: the right of sub-national entities to bring legal action, the establishment of subsidiarity in the treaties and the creation of an EC regional chamber. The fourth demand, inclusion of Länder representatives in the national delegation in the Council of Ministers was rejected by the federal government.

The Länder government have again been extremely active in pushing for an extension of their powers in the Maastricht ratification process.

The forces making for dominance

One set of arguments focuses on German economic strength. This view stresses that there is no overall German *Gesamtkonzept* acting as a blueprint for domination, but emphasizes that in the field of economic integration Germany has a number of minimal conditions that it will seek to impose on its partners (see chapter 14). This will, of course, also be true of other leading member states. The singularity of the German case in this argument is that German economic strength will allow Germany to prevail.

Those who argue in favour of this position then often go on to argue that the end of the cold war has reduced the displacement of 'high politics' and that Germany's competitive advantage in the economic area will now mean that it is overall in a new and dominant position since in the past it often had to accept a trade-off between its economic strength and security deficit in relations with its western partners.

A second set of arguments argued in favour of the emergence of a more dominant and purposive German European policy from Chancellor Kohl's increasingly frequent pronouncements on the urgency of European union. This argument was heard less loudly in the wake of the Gulf crisis of early 1991. But it was evident in the latter part of the year, when Foreign Minister Genscher threatened unilaterally to recognize Slovenia and Croatia, while France and the other member states preferred a more cautious approach to the break-up of Yugoslavia.

A third set of arguments focuses on a wider Europe and points to the weakness of all the east European states. Their economic condition and the collapse of the Soviet Union has compelled them to look for massive German support and in this argument they will be quite prepared to accept it on Germany's terms (Markowits and Reich, 1991, pp. 33–7).

External responses

The issue of German dominance has an external as well as an internal dimension. In an earlier section we examined the way in which the Community institutions responded to German unity and identified the strategy of the Commission. Baldly put, and unsurprisingly, the Commission's answer to the problems posed by the emergence of a larger and potentially more powerful Germany is to advocate a deepening of the Community.

The responses of the other member states fell into two broad groups, with Britain at one end of a spectrum, with all the others including Germany at the other. In the response of the other member states France has played a key role. French policy elites worry not only about a potential German dominance but about Germany's future orientation – the 'Wo liegt Deutschland?' question. The response to both issues is to advocate a further deepening of the Community. This policy enjoyed the support of the federal government and was pushed with elan by the Italian presidency. The disjointed (to say the least) response of the member states to the Gulf war clearly impeded moves towards a common foreign policy, but Maastricht envisaged progress towards a common foreign and security policy (see chapter 14). Clear differences became apparent in the response of the French and German governments to the Yugoslav crisis with the French leaning to the preservation of the Yugoslav federation whilst the Germans increasingly advocated the principle of self-determination for Slovenia and Croatia.

Britain

> A German racket designed to take over the whole of Europe...This rushed take-over by the Germans is the worst possible basis with the French behaving like poodles towards the Germans is absolutely intolerable. (Nicholas Ridley, *Spectator*, 14 July 1990)

While British policy makers refused to become excited over the questions of Germany's future orientation, anxiety about German dominance was not confined to Nicholas Ridley. The Ridley affair had an importance because it was widely believed that his views reflected those of Prime Minister Thatcher; her deeply felt and long established commitment to the preservation of sovereignty and her visceral reaction to attempts at supranational integration excluded the prospect of containing a unified Germany by deeper integration. Margaret Thatcher's preference was for a wider and looser Europe where the core issues would remain the prerogative of national governments and German dominance would be diluted by these restrictions on the scope of Community policies and the effects of further Community enlargement. Neither of these assumptions looked tenable. The attempt to implement the first left Britain dangerously isolated during the Italian presidency of autumn 1990 and the early admittance of east European states would have derailed the single market programme which the Thatcher government supported and placed intolerable pressures on the EC budget.

Under Prime Minister Major, British policy has been in a process of continuous revision. The entry into the ERM and the resignation of Mrs Thatcher were preconditions for the reduction of the gap between British policy and that of the other member states, while the enthusiasm with which many in Britain greeted the US–UK alliance on the Gulf and the loudly trumpeted contempt for the reactions of Britain's European partners pointed in another direction. The Prime Minister and the Foreign Secretary were careful not to associate themselves with these sentiments and the accent remained on stressing British commitment to making the inter-governmental conferences work, though the policies of the British government continues to be constrained by the continued reservations of a significant proportion of Conservative MPs.

The dominance issue: towards a balance

Germany's economic strength will ensure that its influence counts for more than any other single member. This will clearly be crucial in matters like defining the future policy of the EC towards eastern Europe. The Federal Republic will continue to dominate trade between the member states and its share of intra-EC trade might be expected to increase from 27.8 in 1989 to something like a third by the end of the present decade if the economic transformation of the five new Länder succeeds. There is as yet no indication that other members are unable to live with this share though they will continue to demand significant economic and political side payments. It can however plausibly be argued that they would be unable to accept it if it were combined with an assertive attempt to dominate EC policy responses. The strongest argument against expecting a German attempt at manifest dominance however relates to the situation in the five new Länder. The stability of Germany is seen as inextricably bound up with the economic transformation of the five new Länder. Such a transformation will require the continued acceptance by Germany's Community partners of massive derogations from EC rules. This is incompatible with a situation in which Germany would seek to manifestly dominate its partners.

It is impossible not to conclude that the dominance issue has been much overstressed. Germany will be the strongest member of the Community, but there will be severe limits on her economic strength as a result of unity, limits which will lead it in the future as it has done in the past to seek the help and cooperation of her European partners. Moreover the present and indeed all foreseeable future German governments are committed to the pooling of sovereignty: 'Konrad Adenauer reached the only sensible conclusion, that since power had been vested in and was being exercised by common institutions national state rivalries and the attempts for dominance by any one country would become a matter of the past' (Kohl, 1991, p. 8).

Germany and Europe

The division of Germany and the creation of the Federal Republic in 1949 left the new state with a series of extremely pressing problems. The first was the question of how to re-establish national unity. The second focused on the economic problems faced by the new government. At the time the state was established there was still a major problem of mass unemployment and German industry was still constrained by discriminatory allied restrictions on production and sales and lack of access to the markets of other developed industrial economies. The expansionist policies of the Soviet Union under Joseph Stalin posed a third problem.

The common factor in all the problems that beset the Federal Republic was that they could not be solved by the federal government acting alone. All of them required a recognition by the federal government of the contingent dependent position of the Federal Republic and the implications for Germany of global bipolarity. Konrad Adenauer, the first Federal Chancellor, therefore, concluded that the answer to all three policy problems lay in a close and unambiguous identification with the western powers. National unity on terms acceptable to West Germans, i.e. a Germany which was democratic, capitalist and not neutral, could only come about as a result of close identification with the American 'policy of strength' which would lead in the course of time to the break up of the Soviet Empire in eastern Europe and the disappearance of the German Democratic Republic. The constraints on the West German economy would be loosened by the whole-hearted participation of the Federal Republic in the various attempts to integrate western Europe, the integration of which would have the further advantage of reinforcing the pressures on eastern Europe. The security threat to the Federal Republic would be resolved by a reliance on the American nuclear guarantee.

The Federal Republic and European integration

A commitment to European integration was a central, if not *the* central, element in the policies of the Christian Democratic-led governments in the first two decades of the Federal Republic. The grounds for this centrality are fairly obvious. It is normally unwise to overstress the role of individuals and their policy preferences as an explanation but the situation of the Federal Republic was a peculiar one. It was a newly created state without an established set of policies. It was also less than fully sovereign with the western allies exercising important residual rights, especially in relation to external policy until 1955. As the sole interlocutor with the Allied High Commissioners, Adenauer was in a position of enormous strength vis-à-vis his cabinet colleagues. His electoral success in 1957, when the CDU–CSU secured the only absolute majority in a competitive election in Germany, secured his ascendancy until 1961 and the Federal Republic played a key role in the establishment of the European Communities.

Adenauer's vision of Europe had at its centre a Franco-German entente, a policy which he consistently favoured since the early days of the Weimar Republic. His policy was a novel one for a German statesman since it represented an unequivocal and unwavering choice for the west. This reflected his basic premise that Germany's traditional central position in Europe, indeed the whole idea of Central Europe, had been made obsolete by the division of Europe; a division which now cut Germany in half (Adenauer, 1967).

Adenauer's views quickly came to attract a great deal of support, although the German Social Democrats' view that efforts at reunification should take priority over European integration, led them to oppose Adenauer's policy until 1955 and the Free Democrats (FDP) was also opposed for a short time after it entered opposition in 1956. From then on there was a party political consensus on European integration. This consensus reflected a consensus among the interest groups which had prevailed since the establishment of the Federal Republic.

German support for and interest in the European Community declined somewhat under the SPD led governments of Willy Brandt and Helmut Schmidt. Brandt gave a higher priority to *ostpolitik* and the normalization of relations with eastern Europe, while Schmidt was wedded to an inter-governmental view of the Community which played down the supranational vocation of the Commission (Bulmer and Paterson, 1987, pp. 137–40).

Helmut Kohl and the CDU–CSU generally have a more ambitious view of the Communities. Kohl played a major role in launching the two IGCs on economic and monetary and political union. He has argued strongly in favour of political union and has been especially adamant about the need to expand the powers of the European Parliament.

The fit between the aspirations of the Federal Republic and the European Community is not of course without some friction, e.g. the Commission would like it to move much more quickly than at present in opening up the services sector to external competition. In general, however, the Federal Republic fits more easily into the Community framework than the other major states. Germany dominates the trading relations of the European states and the EC framework legitimates and renders acceptable this German economic preponderance. The Community also provides a more acceptable framework for a number of pressing German concerns, e.g. migration from eastern Europe, than any other conceivable arrangement. The necessity of the Community framework to Germany implies a continuance of the close Franco-German relationship despite French fears of Germany developing a too strong eastern orientation (see chapter 7).

The European Community and German unity

Few inside or outside Germany expected the GDR regime to fall apart as quickly as it did in the autumn of 1989 when the impossible became the inevitable in the month after 9 November and the breaching of the Berlin Wall.

The initial attitudes of the major EC states were hesitant, confused and divergent. The British government was notably unenthusiastic and dwelt on the difficulties which would have to be overcome and argued that it would all take a very long time. President Mitterrand, after some initial hesitation, quickly came to the conclusion that unity was going to happen. French policy henceforward concentrated on rendering unity palatable rather than throwing tacks in its progress. The preferred option, which reflected French fears of Germany as a potential loose cannon was to reanchor the emergent new Germany in a deepened Europe.

The European Community response to the developing German situation was defined in the first instance by the French and Irish presidencies and by the Commission. Some of the literature on the presidency as an institution overstresses the way in which a presidency can manage the business of the EC. By the use of strong and active verbs, it seeks to convey the impression that the particular state which occupies the presidency is in a position to carry through an agenda in a pro-active manner – or, even more ambitiously, that groups of two or three states in sequence can push through different elements of a programme. This is sometimes possible, but more often, as in life generally, we experience the play of the contingent and unforeseen, and the advent of German unity was both.

The French government nevertheless responded with speed and agility and proceeded to implement its deepening strategy at the Strasbourg Summit of 8–9 December which secured agreement to the convening of intergovernmental conferences on economic and monetary union and on political union at the end of 1990. The Council had been preceded by much talk of a Franco-German rift and an alleged cooling of German enthusiasm for political union, but to the visible disappointment of Mrs Thatcher there was no evidence of either at the summit. Chancellor Kohl remained enthusiastic about political union and in any case perceived the convening of the IGCs as part of the price of French support. Germany was not yet manifestly centre-stage at the Council and the Commission was only instructed to negotiate a trade and cooperation agreement with the GDR, but the key theme of linking German unity to European integration was established.

The communiqué issued by the European Council of 8–9 December 1989 stated:

> We seek the strengthening of the state of peace in Europe in which the German people will regain its unity through free self-determination. This process should take place peacefully and democratically, in full respect of the relevant agreements and treaties and of all the principles defined by the Helsinki Final Act, in a context of dialogue and East–West cooperation. It also has to be placed in the perspective of European integration.

The Irish presidency

Events moved very quickly in January–February 1990. The inevitability of German unification now became widely accepted, though differing degrees of enthusiasm remained among the member states, a situation which left the initiative with the Commission.

The Commission

German unity was welcomed by Jacques Delors at a very early point. Delors, like Mitterrand, quickly became convinced of its inevitability and his policy reflected three overriding aims:

1 To preserve and strengthen Germany's European vocation.
2 To avoid the derailment of the single market programme.
3 To ensure that the Commission had some influence over events in Germany.

Delors set the tone for the Commission's response, but it should be noted that Commissioner Brittan adopted a much more negative tone and expressed continuous concern at the dangers to competition policy inherent in German unity.

The European Parliament

Whilst the Commission quickly resolved that the European Community would simply expand to encompass the territory of the whole of the new state after unification, the European Parliament initially argued in favour of an accession procedure which would have required assent by national parliaments and would have accorded a major role to the European Parliament (art. 237). This was rejected by the Commission and the Council and the influence of the European Parliament on the process derived from its uncharacteristic speed of response and its well practised procedural skills.

German choices

The rejection of the accession route (art. 237) by the Commission was rendered much easier by the decision of the federal government to press for incorporation of the GDR through art. 23 of the Basic Law. This article had already been employed in relation to the Saar and simply involved an extension of the Basic Law to other parts of Germany which voluntarily acceded to the Federation as an additional Land or Länder. The opposition Social Democrats pressed for the use of art. 146. This would have involved the formulation and ratification of a new constitution. It would have dragged out unification negotiations and strengthened the case of those who argued that what was being contemplated was the accession of a new member.

Foreign Ministers Conference, Dublin, 20 February 1990

By the time this conference convened, the East German election was imminent and unification was clearly past the point of no return. There was no agreement on its implications for Europe though all by now publicly welcomed it. France, Italy and Belgium wanted a speeding up of progress towards economic and political union, whilst Britain and The Netherlands were much more reserved towards political union.

The Commission

The Commission avoided a damaging embroilment in their disputes but secured a mandate to produce a report on the implications of integrating the GDR into the EC. The Commission's policy on the issue was formulated by a so-called group of four, i.e. Delors, Bangemann, Christophersen and Andriessen. It did not include Leon Brittan who was less enthusiastic. The task force was to be headed by Commissioner Bangemann, former German

Economics Minister, an ideal candidate to realize the Commission's three aims. The Bangemann group kept very close contact with senior German politicians and officials, including Chancellor Kohl who visited the Commission in this period.

The run-up to the Dublin Summit

The European Parliament agreed on 4 April 1990 to establish a special committee in which the British Socialist MEP Alan Donnelly would act as rapporteur on the incorporation of the GDR.

The Commission issued its formal proposal on 18 April 1990 (SEC/90/57). It envisaged a three-stage process:

1   After German economic and monetary union was achieved East German law should gradually be adapted to West German and EC law.
2   After completion of German unity EC legislation should apply.
3   The total integration of the new unified German state into the EC.

The Commission proposal stressed German responsibility but Community interest in German unity. Accordingly, unity should be carried out within a Community framework and this should be expressed in any German economic and monetary union treaty. The Commission wanted to be involved in the negotiations and to keep GEMU and EMU moving in step. Reflecting the fears of Leon Brittan, the Commission wished to be informed/consulted on the granting of aid to the GDR. The Commission also argued that incorporation of the GDR would not require a treaty revision with all the ratification complications that would have entailed. The Commission paper also took a notably optimistic view of the economic prospects of the GDR which it argued would lead to increased resources for the Community. The Commission proposal was adopted at the Dublin Summit (28 April 1990) where the final communiqué states in para. 5: 'Furthermore the Commission will be kept fully informed of these discussions' (*European Report*, 1990, p. 2). This was important since it reduced the obligation on the federal government to keep the Parliament and Council informed. The Commission was now at the centre of the information flow and by being associated in this way could be relied on to defend the German government proposals.

In the wake of the Dublin Summit the Commission set up a task force for German unification, formally chaired by Secretary General Williamson, but the day-to-day responsibility lay with his Deputy, Carlo Trojan.

The European Parliament

The Donnelly Report was considered by the European Parliament on 12 July, 1990. Among the most important amendments adopted on 12 July in Strasbourg was a clause ensuring the 'rapprochement' of East German environmental norms with those of the Community, the closure of obsolete nuclear installations which had been founded on dated Soviet technology, the elimination of the CoCom quantitative restriction list (except in areas of military technology and nuclear energy). A recommendation to leave the

East German speed limit at the existing level and the request to maintain the present East German liberal legislation on abortion also formed part of the list of amendments to the report which were adopted. Other amendments stressed the need to ensure that the Community's structural funds would be efficiently distributed within a united Germany and that in the same manner, the Community's social legislation should be generally applied to the emerging East German economy, whose increasing social problems of high unemployment, rising prices, collapse of firms should be resolved in the existing Community.

The speed with which the process took place is reflected in the Parliament's criticism of the lack of consultation between the Commission and itself during the preparations for the state treaty and it asked to be consulted more fully in the future. This was very difficult given the press of time and the Commission plan was published on 21 August. It was originally scheduled to be taken in two readings in September and November, but the bringing forward of the unity date to 3 October 1990 led to the Parliament dealing with the first reading on 11 and 13 September. The common position of the Council reached it on 7 November and it was approved by Parliament on 21 November.

Institutional impact

The record of the presidencies on this issue is mixed. Mitterrand succeeded, with the help of the German government, in the Strasbourg Summit in framing the issue in a way which made it compatible with European integration. The Irish ran an efficient presidency but this efficiency partially reflected the absence of their own ideas in this area and their reliance on the Commission.

The Commission was obviously the key player throughout, though the European Parliament produced an exceptionally good report and handled the manner with some efficiency and despatch.

The major aspirations of the Commission were fulfilled; the 1992 process was not derailed and the European dimension was given a prominent, though cursory, place in the state treaty. However, although the Commission succeeded at a formal level, its impact on process was fairly minimal given the pressure under which the federal government was operating. It was informed rather than consulted and it is difficult to point to examples of where Commission negotiations prompted the federal government to take a different view from the one that they had intended to take in any case. Moreover, in difficult areas very significant concessions were made, e.g. in the food processing industry exemptions were granted for almost 80 per cent of food legislation. On state aids the Commission document talked of a 'sensitive and flexible application' with exemptions immediately granted to shipbuilding and steel. Despite calling in a number of cases the Commission took a very lenient view of mergers and takeovers. A very understanding view was also taken of difficulties in meeting environmental legislation and East Germany was given until 1996 to meet air and water quality standards. At the insistence of a number of member states, the Commission did attempt to tighten up the rules on what was to count as new and old plant. New plant had to meet current EC levels immediately but there was an obvious temptation to have all plant classified as old.

This lack of impact of the Commission on the process was not entirely novel where German interests were concerned. The Interzonal Protocol which provided for tariff free trade between the two Germanies had of course meant that inner-German trade largely escaped the supervision of the Commission. This had been the source of increasing complaints by a number of member countries, especially the Netherlands, in the years before unity and there would have been grave problems in reconciling the continued existence of the Interzonal Protocol with the completion of the single market programme.

Security

The postwar European order divided Europe into two adversary alliances each of which was dominated by an external superpower. The division of Germany into two states was a function of this superpower rivalry and both Germanies played a leading role in their respective alliances. For the Federal Republic there was only one security threat. Relations with the west had been transformed by the experience of defeat and a fear of an expansive Soviet Union, which although shared by its western neighbours, was much more intense in the Federal Republic. One-quarter of the population of the Federal Republic were of refugee origin and their experiences greatly heightened *la grande Peur*.

Adenauer looked for an answer to the Soviet threat in a complete identification with American power. He therefore responded positively to the American request to the West Germans to rearm after the outbreak of the Korean war. The proposed West German rearmament provoked internal dissensus as the opposition Social Democrats were concerned that it would cement the division of Germany. Adenauer, by contrast, held that a 'policy of strength' would eventually lead to the break up of the Soviet empire in eastern Europe.

The Federal Republic's western neighbours continued to be concerned about a resurgence of German power, and German rearmament was initially conceived as acceptable only in the context of a quasi-federal European Defence Community. The federal character of the EDC proved to be unacceptable to Britain which refused to make a commitment to the EDC. This weakened support for the proposal in France which had in any case eroded as the parliamentary balance shifted away from the Christian Democrats (MRP) and the EDC proposal was rejected by the French National Assembly in August 1954.

The Federal Republic joined NATO in May 1955 through the western European Union. Its membership of NATO was more complete than those of the other larger European members. Unlike Britain and France, all its forces were committed to NATO. It had no general staff and no independent strategic planning function. This was in a sense the second foundation of NATO which was now redesigned to contain the Federal Republic alongside its pre-existing role of deterring the Soviet Union.

German acceptance of this double containment and the circumscribed role allotted to it in the NATO framework was not only a price to be paid for the American nuclear guarantee, it was also the price of regaining full sovereignty. A major element in the singularity of the postwar German experience which has left a deep mark on its decision makers is the manner in which acceptance of the constraints imposed by European institutions and NATO and the ceding of legal sovereignty actually led to greater political sovereignty.

While the cold war and the division of Europe lasted, West German interests were accommodated without too much difficulty by NATO. Strains began to be evident from the early 1980s, however, with German public opinion according a higher value to the pursuit of détente than opinion in Britain and the United States. After the replacement of Schmidt by Helmut Kohl as Chancellor these differences in perception led to the breakdown of the party political consensus on security issues that had prevailed since the early 1960s with the Social Democrats becoming more and more reluctant to accept Alliance positions on issues like the stationing of the Cruise and Pershing missiles in 1983 and the modernization of theatre nuclear weapons in 1988–9. In the latter debate arguments stressing Germany's singular position were at the centre of the debate. The emphasis now changed significantly. Throughout the postwar period the singularity of Germany's position was seen to lie in its position on the eastern rim of the western alliance. Helmut Schmidt never tired of telling American audiences how close his home in Hamburg was to the iron curtain. In the late 1980s, it became common even for supporters of NATO in the Federal Republic to argue that German singularity lay in the risks that both Germanies were exposed to by virtue of the fact of the stationing of massive quantities of missiles in the two Germanies.

The impact of Mikhail Gorbachev

The Federal Republic's harmonious relationship with NATO rested on a perception of a clear Soviet threat. This threat perception was, as we have seen, becoming more blurred as the 1980s progressed, and was to be transformed completely by the diplomacy of Mikhail Gorbachev. Even before the annus mirabilis of 1989 German public opinion no longer clearly perceived the reality of a manifest Soviet threat.

In the last years of Stalin's rule the Soviet Union, alarmed by the prospect of a rearmed Germany, had appeared ready to countenance German unity in return for neutrality. This was not an option that Adenauer seriously considered, nor one which the western allies would have permitted. It was again an issue in 1989–90 since President Gorbachev insisted that the membership of a unified Germany in NATO was unacceptable to the Soviet Union. The United States government, the most enthusiastic backers of German unity insisted with even greater force on the necessity of continued membership of a unified Germany in NATO. This view was shared by the federal government. It was prepared to make some concessions, however, and quite early on Hans-Dietrich Genscher floated the idea that although a unified Germany should remain in NATO, the NATO front line should continue as at present, with the East German area being held by German

rather than NATO forces. Despite both the annoyance of the British government at what they saw as Foreign Minister Genscher's premature sacrifice
of what should have been a common western position and determined Soviet
resistance, the final Kohl–Gorbachev agreement on 16 July 1990 was along
these lines with Soviet forces being allowed to remain in the GDR until 1994
(Asmus, 1991, p. 61; Kaiser, 1991, pp. 179–205).

Germany and the new security environment

The withdrawal of the Soviet Union and its accelerating break up in line
with the predictions of Konrad Adenauer has paradoxically undermined
what public support there was in the Federal Republic for a policy of military strength. The vision of Germany's future held by mass and much elite
opinion is of Germany as a 'civilian power' (Maull, 1990–1, pp. 91–106). In
the absence of a Soviet threat they simply do not see the need for a traditional security policy and there is no enthusiasm for preserving NATO at a
high level of readiness in case Russia reverts to an authoritarian and aggressive stance. German opinion is in favour of massive cuts in the Bundeswehr
and in the stationing of allied troops in Germany.

This simple view is not shared by the present German government which
in common with other governments sees continuing difficulties in the area
of security but which is constrained by German public opinion and the need
to make savings to finance the budget deficit. The Defence Ministry which
has steadily lost ground since the ending of German division was identified
with continuing adherence to NATO – a politically weak position given
NATO's own difficulties in defining its own post cold war stance. The position of the Defence Ministry was strengthened by the appointment of the
ambitious Volker Rühe in May 1992 with the promise of a more flexible
policy.

The Foreign Ministry, while still committed to continuing German presence
in NATO, was very much identified with the CSCE. The CSCE, which includes
neutrals as well as member of NATO and the Warsaw Pact, was well adapted
to the period of decreasing tension which marked the declining years of the
cold war in Europe. Unfortunately, it lacks forces and institutions and seems
unlikely to be able to deal with a Europe in which intra-ethnic, border
disputes and irredentist aspirations play an increasingly alarming role in
eastern Europe. The identification of the Foreign Ministry with the CSCE
was reduced by Hans Dietrich Genscher's retirement in May 1992.

A global role?

The increased salience of Germany and uncertainties about the future role
of NATO led President Bush in 1989 to use the phrase 'partners in leadership'
as a characterization of future American–German relations. The problem
from a German point of view is that this partnership would be conceived
in global terms or at least as extending beyond Europe. As the Gulf war
demonstrated there is very little support in Germany for operations outside
the NATO area. Chancellor Kohl has announced his intention of altering

art. 87A of the Basic Law behind which the federal government sheltered during the Gulf war. This is a necessary but a far from sufficient condition since German public and much party opinion seems unwilling to conceive 'out of area' operations in terms other than a very restricted view of Blue Helmet–UN operation.

The new security partnership that Germany seeks with the United States is rather one which addresses the economic and social difficulties of east central Europe and the USSR, since they perceive potentially massive westward migration from the former Soviet Union as a major threat to security. The German government is aware that it cannot meet this challenge alone and attempts to move the United States and other G7 states in the direction of aid but so far has only had very limited success.

German political economy

The development of the postwar German economy can be divided into four phases. The first phase took place under American tutelage and with massive American aid. In this period the social market economy was introduced through the currency reform of 1948 and the policies of Economics Minister Ludwig Erhard. The external analogue of the social market economy was the adoption with US encouragement of liberal international trade policies.

The dominant theme from the mid 1950s and in the 1960s was expansion and modernization of the economy and a relatively fast overhauling of Britain and France. This expansion, aided by an undervalued mark was especially marked in terms of export share.

By the 1970s Germany and Japan were seen as key players in the international economy and the social democratic led governments undertook to boost public spending to impart a reflationary impetus to a global economy in recession after the oil price hike of 1973. This resulted in a chronic budget deficit problem which lasted till the early 1980s.

In the final phase before unification the German economy was booming. The EC – wide investment boom in the run up to the single market programme benefited Germany's traditional strengths in capital goods.

German singularities

The making of economic policy in Germany reflects a number of singular features. The most often referred to is the impact of the hyperinflation in 1923 which is reflected in a commitment to price stability as the central goal of economic policy and a relatively very independent role for the Bundesbank. A second feature is the key role of the universal banks rather than the stock exchanges in financing industry. The close collusive interlocking relationship displays some sectoral variation, but it is a very marked feature of the German economy as a whole and it is difficult to overestimate the role of the Deutsche Bank in this respect. The tight interlocking of banks and firms renders the German economy much less open in acquisition terms than the United States or Britain.

The strong export orientation of the German economy is reflected in a very high ratio of foreign trade to GNP (64 per cent in 1990) with exports typically accounting for 30 to 35 per cent of GNP. This factor gives Germany a very strong interest in global economic conditions without the capacity to determine these conditions. In the period up to the early 1970s the Federal Republic had a high level of confidence in the ability of the United States to manage the global economy. This relationship is now under some strain given American sensitivities about German enthusiasm for economic and monetary union and sharp disagreements on agriculture.

The relatively minor role of agriculture in the German GNP (1.6 per cent pre-unity) significantly underestimates the veto power of agriculture. About 6 per cent of the population is engaged either full or part time in agriculture and the balanced party situation gives them significant electoral leverage. This creates a bias in favour of a protectionist CAP which sits uneasily with Bonn's general support of liberal trading policies and has been a major casus belli in the Uruguay Round of trade talks opened in 1986 (see chapter 12).

The German economy after unity

Pre-German unity the German economy was increasingly seen as the model and mentor for other European economies and contrasts were often drawn between its sustained boom, low inflation and unemployment rates at the end of the decade with the flagging fortunes and high inflation and unemployment rates of Thatcher's Britain.

Post-unity, the situation of the German economy looks somewhat different. Interest and inflation rates have come up to the level of its European competitors. Imports have also increased sharply in the wake of unity with a corresponding effect on the trade surplus, and unemployment has soared in what was East Germany.

These indications notwithstanding, the underlying economy of what was West Germany remains incredibly strong and its industry is still competitive in nearly all the key sectors and continues to dominate European trading relations. If the EC which emerges in the course of the 1990s from the IGCs – culminating at the Maastricht Summit of 8–10 December 1991 – and from the single market programme, remains committed to open markets then it is vulnerable in the medium to long term to competitive pressures from Japan where the annual volume of investment in Japanese industry is four times that of the Federal Republic.

The manifest and dominating problem for Germany is the parlous state of the economy in the five new Länder. Pre-unity a very optimistic view had been taken by the German government of economic prospects in what were to become the five new Länder and in German economic and monetary union wages and prices were converted at parity. The effect of this decision, given the very low level of productivity in the area, was to make labour in the five new Länder relatively expensive. Difficulties on property law, the absence of a functioning administrative structure and the appalling state of communications and the environment were further disincentives to invest.

Opinion in Germany on the economic future of the area has oscillated wildly between euphoric optimism and heavy pessimism, with the future being presented in terms of two models – 'mezzogiorno' or 'miracle'.

The 'mezzogiorno' model dwells on the technological backwardness of the area and the propensity of skilled labour to move or to commute to work in the industries of the western part of Germany leaving behind a stagnant pool of unskilled labour and a community bereft of potential entrepreneurs.

The economic miracle view draws an explicit analogy between the Germany of 1948–9 and the situation of the five new Länder. This is the view endlessly recycled by the federal government, but much less widely shared by German industry.

Both conceptions are deeply flawed. Unlike the mezzogiorno, eastern Germany has a successful history of industrialization in the pre-1945 period and there is a real commitment on the part of the prosperous three-quarters to transfer massive resources into the area.

The economic miracle view on the other hand seems too optimistic. Throughout the economic miracle, West Germany derived considerable advantages from an undervalued mark. Labour was also relatively cheap and was kept cheap by the continual influx of refugees from the GDR. German economic and monetary union removed the cushioning effects of a differential exchange rate and labour costs continue to rise steadily under the twin pressures of unionization and the ease with which skilled labour can exit to the west.

A more realistic view is to anticipate a gradual catching up of the five new Länder over the next five to ten years. The massive investments in infrastructural development are beginning to have a knock on effect and unemployment seems set to fall from next year. Serious attempts have been made to remedy the deficiencies in the property law and administrative structures and staffing. The services sector has been much more buoyant than manufactures and it seems likely that the five new Länder will more easily become competitive in this area than in manufactures. Concern remains however that 2/3 of the west to east transfers goes to support the population of the east rather than in productive investments.

Conclusion: Germany's future, Germany's choices

On the fortieth anniversary of the founding of the Federal Republic in 1989 the political and economic successes of the Federal Republic were rightly celebrated. It was a celebration of the first liberal democratic German state in Germany; it was, moreover, one in which Germany's neighbours could share since this was the first German state in modern times to enjoy friendly relations with all its eastern and western neighbours. These successes had, however, taken place in a protected environment where the key external security and economic issues were matters that German governments decided within the NATO and EEC context.

This situation is only partially changed by unity. In economic matters the European Community will continue as the dominant pole of reference, and the marketization of eastern Europe will only partially alter the economic environment in which Germany operates. In one sense, unity eases Germany's relations with its partners by significantly increasing the volume of German imports. On the other hand, the costs of unity make Germany less able to shoulder the burden of sustaining an increase in the Community budget.

The contrast with the security area could not be more stark. The ending of the division of Europe and the virtual disappearance of the Soviet threat have completely transformed the German security environment. The American relationship, the touchstone of postwar German security policy is no longer self-evident and future German governments seem set to resist American urging to play a wider role. Again, neither NATO, nor the CSCE, nor the European Community, appear to possess credible security policy instruments to deal with the security problems of eastern Europe (see chapter 20). This is a serious matter for Germany since the negative effects of unrest in eastern Europe will first be felt there. Sensitivity to this factor will be increased by the move of the capital from Bonn to Berlin less than a hundred miles from the Polish border.

Paradoxically, these great external changes and the seismic shifts in German public opinion will not feed into immediate dramatic changes of German policy. It will remain important for German governments to try to maintain an American commitment to the security of Europe and this implies maintaining the NATO connection. This may be less important after the last Russian withdrawals in 1994. The transformation of the European Community into a security community is not an immediate option given British and Dutch opposition, and the CSCE is more important diplomatically than in security policy terms. Cooperation with the former Soviet Union or solo German initiatives in this area are simply unrealistic. For the present then there is less change than one might expect.

Any major change would require inter alia a sustained and coherent public discourse about the exercise of power and Germany's specific geographical interests. The traumatic history of twentieth-century Germany and the way in which the Federal Republic was embedded in NATO have created a mind set in the German political class which is likely to continue to impede such a change. The traumatic history is likely to ensure that Germany remains a civilian power. Its history also explains the self-confidence with which the German political class approaches external economic issues and the lack of confidence it displays on how to respond to security issues. The contrast between the responses of the German and British political classes to the Gulf crisis is especially striking.

Internally, the key agenda items are the forging of the unified Germany into a national community and the transformation of the economy of the new Länder. Clearly the second aim is the precondition of realizing the first, but even if, as seems likely, the transformation succeeds, it will probably take till the end of the decade to create a new and secure German identity.

REFERENCES

Adenauer, K. 1967: *Erinnerungen, 1955–59*. Stuttgart: DVA.
Asmus, R. D. 1991: *German Unification and its Ramifications*. Santa Monica: Rand.
Bulmer, S. and Paterson, W. 1987: *The Federal Republic of Germany and the European Community*. London: Allen & Unwin.
European Report. 3 May 1990, no. 1583.

Hassner, P. 1982: The shifting foundations. *Foreign Policy*, 48, 3.

Kaiser, K. 1991: German unification. *Foreign Affairs*, 1, 179–205.

Katzenstein, P. 1987: *Policy and Politics in West Germany: The Growth of a Semi-sovereign State*. Philadelphia: Temple, University Press.

Kohl, H. 1991: *Our Future in Europe*. Edinburgh: Europa Institute.

Markowits, A. and Reich, S. 1991: *The New Face of Germany: Gramsci Hegemony and Europe*. Washington: APSA.

Maull, H. W. 1990–1: Germany and Japan: the new civilian powers. *Foreign Affairs*, Winter 1990–1, 91–106.

Paterson, W. and Southern, D. 1991: *Governing Germany*. Oxford: Blackwell.

SEC 1990: *The Community and German Unification*. 57. Brussels.

Paterson, W. and Smith, G. 1992: 'German Unity' in Smith, G., Paterson, W., Merkl, P. and Padgett, S. (eds) Developments in German Politics, Basingstoke: Macmillan.

7

France and Europe

Jonathan Story and Guy de Carmoy

The year 1992 marked one further step for France's prolonged recuperation from the ordeals of occupation with its litany of deportations and affronts to national pride, followed by liberation and the ensuing internal struggle for power. Inflation, aggravated by the colonial wars, was rampant. Under such conditions, no clear line of policy could be defined in economic affairs. Foreign policy, on the other hand, was dominated throughout by the theme of Franco-German reconciliation, beginning with the Schuman proposals of 1951. The European Community became the central institution through which French diplomacy could operate to achieve its purpose of binding the Federal Republic into a political coalition, which was not dominated by the United States. Re-launched by common accord between the member states in 1985–7, the EC found a champion in President Mitterrand to extend its mandate into the domain of social affairs, monetary policy, diplomacy and security. The path from 1945 to the discussions on monetary and political union in 1991, capping the completion of the internal market programme in January 1993, was thus long and sinuous, in retrospect marked by a notable continuity in purpose to regain the status and self-respect squandered in the wake of France's collapse in 1940.

Determining factors

France had been the dominant power in Europe from the time of the Thirty Years war until the fall of the Empire in 1814. The state had been unified since the sixteenth century. The centralized administration dates to Colbert. It was reinforced by the revolution and the First Empire. The revolution purged the old abuses of the monarchy with blood, and proclaimed nationality as the principle of legitimacy for government. Its ideological heritage only triumphed in France in the first years of the Third Republic, constituted in 1870 after the disastrous defeat at the hands of Prussians. Germany, spurred by rapid population growth and the profits of the first industrial revolution, had surpassed Britain as Europe's dominant economy by the 1890s. France remained in third position, its producers coddled by tariffs and assured outlets in colonial markets. Heavy losses in the 1914–18 war were barely compensated by immigration from Poland or Italy, or the presence of one million French settlers in Algeria. French was supplanted as the language of diplomacy after the United States' entry into European affairs.

The two world wars left France deeply scarred. Germany's defeat in 1918 was possible only with the aid of Great Britain and the United States. The collapse of 1940 was the most complete in France's history since the Hundred Years war. The same Anglo-American support had to be relied on for France, after four years of German occupation, to be counted among the victors in 1945. France was present at the signing of the German capitulation, but was not invited to the Yalta and Potsdam conferences which determined Germany's future status. At Potsdam in August 1945, the Americans, British and Soviets decided to pursue the total occupation of Germany. The nation was divided into four zones of occupation, with one of them given over to French authority. As tensions multiplied between the wartime allies, the Americans, the British and the French moved to organize their three occupation zones and to oversee monetary reform in 1948 as a prelude to the 1949 creation of the Federal Republic of Germany, a state with limited sovereignty.

At the liberation in 1944 General de Gaulle, the soul of the London-based resistance, had been proclaimed chief of the provisional government recognized by Britain and the United States. Determined to re-establish France's status as a great power, he sent an expeditionary force to Indochina before resigning in January 1945 in opposition to the political parties' determination to reinstate a parliamentary regime. But the message of national liberation swept the world, leaving Paris to opt eventually for negotiations in 1954, following the expeditionary force's defeat at Dien Bien Phu. The two protectorates of Tunisia and Morocco won their independence from Paris in 1955 and 1956 respectively. Rebellion broke out in Algeria in November 1954. The statute of 1947, following a policy of assimilation but never truly applied, was suspended. Armed force could only ensure order in the cities. The settlers finally appealed in 1958 to de Gaulle, who declared himself ready to assume the powers of the Republic.

De Gaulle's investiture by the National Assembly occurred on 4 June 1958. He disposed of the right to propose a new constitution, as well as full powers in Algeria. But in September 1959, de Gaulle proclaimed the Algerians' right to self-determination. Negotiations began in May 1961 with representatives of the rebellion on the grounds of independence–association. The Evian accords were concluded on 18 March 1962. A referendum of 8 April approved the accords by a massive majority. Algeria proclaimed its independence on 3 July. The abandonment of the organic statute for the European community prompted the exodus of the French from Algeria. De Gaulle then launched his ambitious policy of cooperation with the countries of the Maghreb and with the overseas territories south of the Sahara. The constitution of 1958, in its article XII, established a Community between France and her overseas territories willing to belong to it. But during negotiations in 1959, the Community, as a presidential regime, was transformed into a confederation, with every member state allowed to opt for independence without renouncing membership in the Community. The independence option won the day and 11 African and Malgache states, sponsored by France, were admitted to the United Nations on 21 September 1960.

Decolonization necessarily affected France's European policies. The central question for France's future in a divided Europe was Germany, amputated, occupied, disarmed, swollen with an influx of refugees from the east, and endowed with a powerful industrial infrastructure. The first signal of the French government for reconciliation with Germany was the declaration of 9 May 1950, inspired by Jean Monnet and enacted by Robert Schuman. The object was to place all French and German coal and steel production under a high authority that would be open to the participation of other European countries. The treaty creating the European Coal and Steel Community was signed on 28 April 1951 between six member states. A second initiative proved less fruitful. One year after the signing on 4 April 1949 of the North Atlantic Treaty which recorded the United States engagement in the defence of western Europe, the question of German rearmament came to the fore. Would Germany participate in an integrated European force, or reconstitute a national German army? At the French government's request, the Atlantic Council took a position favouring the first alternative. The treaty for the creation of the European Defence Community (EDC), a supranational organism, was signed on 27 May 1952. Political opinion in France divided on account of Great Britain's absence, opposition to Germany's rearmament, and the assignment of part of the armed forces for the defence of overseas territories. This argument became preponderant following the loss of Indochina. General de Gaulle was among the leading opponents of the EDC, as he was of the ECSC. In August 1954, the National Assembly rejected the treaty. Germany was admitted into the Atlantic alliance. The fear was that the EDC's failure would compromise Europe's construction.

With the route towards a military as well as a political Europe barred indefinitely, there remained the path towards an economic Europe. The initiative of 'relaunching Europe' was taken by the Benelux countries, in the form of a general common market. The means were developed in the Spaak report, drawn up after the conference of Messina in 1956. The report served as the basis for discussion in the national parliaments. The French requests tended to facilitate the transition from protectionism to liberalism. Partisans and opponents of the project denounced the French economy's weakness. In parallel to these debates on a general common market, another was opened on a common organization for the peaceful development of atomic energy. The treaties creating the European Economic Community and Euratom were signed in Rome on 25 March 1957 and ratified on 10 July 1957 by the National Assembly. The vote was 342 in favour and 239 against, including 16 out of 21 social republicans (Gaullists).

Thus two tendencies in French European policies were delineated: the federal route enunciated by Monnet–Schuman, and the route towards co-operation of states promoted by de Gaulle upon the advent of the Fifth Republic. The legacy of foreign policies under the Fourth and Fifth Republics traced an uneasy juxtaposition between the two.

After President Eisenhower had declined de Gaulle's secret memorandum of 24 September 1958 for the creation between the United States, Great Britain and France of 'a tripartite organization to take joint decisions extending to the whole world', the French promoted France as leader in a continental coalition of states. Britain's bid for entry to the EC was barred in January 1963, and again in November 1967. Paris agreed that the Commission represent the EC in the Kennedy Round of trade talks, under the auspices of GATT. Within the EC, France forcefully used its veto right to trade an opening of markets for manufactured goods, for German implementation of the Common Agricultural Policy (CAP). This entailed: the establishment of common farm product prices; EC preferences for local producers; a common budget, and provisions for exports on third markets. But de Gaulle rejected the Commission's proposals to link the EC's own revenues to an increase in the powers of the European Parliament. The key cereal price was established below costs of production in Germany, but considerably above French levels. The EC then negotiated trade preferences with France's and Belgium's former colonies, and with Mediterranean non-member countries to ensure their products continued but regulated access to EC food markets. British entry was allowed once the CAP was in place.

De Gaulle held the Federal Republic as an indispensable partner. But there was to be no sharing of nuclear policy with Bonn. The protocol, written by the Bundestag into the January 1963 Franco-German Treaty, instituting biannual meetings between Paris and Bonn, confirmed the Atlantic over the French dimension of German foreign policy. France came to occupy a unique position in the Atlantic alliance, detached from the integrated command of the North Atlantic Treaty Organization (NATO) (de Gaulle's press conference 24 February 1966). French forces in the Federal Republic no longer depended on the inter-allied command based in Brussels, but on a Franco-German accord established at the request of the German federal government. French divisions would no longer participate in the defence of the German front. But France remained in West Berlin. This status conveyed equal rights and responsibilities on the three western powers who exercised benevolent tutelage over their respective zones, while the Soviet Union imposed its will in the east.

The counterpart to de Gaulle's policy of 'free hands' was support for German unity, but within the territory of the two existing states. This required a lessening of cold war tensions, symbolized by de Gaulle's 1966 visit to the Soviet Union, to promote 'understanding, détente, and cooperation' (*Combat*, 21 May 1966) with Moscow. But the Soviet invasion of Czechoslovakia in August 1968 froze Europe's divide for two décades, and prompted the Federal Republic to embark on its own *ostpolitik*, predicated on prior understanding with Moscow and Washington. At the EC summit at the Hague in December 1969, Chancellor Brandt balanced his overtures to Moscow by a deal with President Pompidou, de Gaulle's successor. Regular foreign policy consultations were initiated between EC member states' foreign ministries. With British membership negotiated, and the Federal Republic's *ostpolitik* in place, the Paris summit of October 1972 laid out an ambitious programme for an enlarged EC of nine.

Divergent economic policies between Paris and Bonn in the course of 1973, followed by the jump in world oil prices that winter, undermined the Paris summit's ambitious plans. In December 1974, President Giscard d'Estaing and Chancellor Schmidt decided to institutionalize EC summits in the form of the European Council. The Council may be seen, over and above the regular meetings under the 1963 Treaty, as of evident Gaullist lineage, preserving the de facto power of each head of government or state to veto policies. But it has also acted as the European executive: patronizing direct elections to the European Parliament; the launching of the European Monetary System; the enlargement negotiations, especially with Spain; the reforms of the early 1980s in agricultural policy; and in June 1985, the calling of an inter-governmental conference to introduce revisions in the Rome Treaty, launching the Single European Act. The European Council's launch was followed by the signing of the Helsinki Final Act in August 1975, between the thirty-five states, including the United States and Canada. The Helsinki process had been adapted by the EC member states as part of the European Political Cooperation (EPC). The European Council was also conceived as helping to set the European agenda in preparation for the yearly summits of industrialized countries, initiated in 1975. Finally, the European Council presided over the initiation of the Lomé Convention, originally between forty-six former French and British colonies of Africa, the Pacific and the Caribbean. At the heart of this global span of diplomatic and trade relations was the Franco-German entente, 'the cornerstone', as Giscard d'Estaing stated, 'of all progress in the constitution of Europe' (*Le Monde*, 5 February 1977).

The operational environment

Under the Fifth Republic, the Presidency has emerged as the touchstone of national politics. To de Gaulle, French ailments under the Third and Fourth Republics were rooted in the weakness of parliamentary institutions and the lack of executive authority. His proposals for 'a free nation under a strong state' (de Gaulle, 1959, pp. 496–502) outlined at Bayeux in 1946, were put into effect on his return to power. The constitution of 4 October 1958, gave the president broad powers. The president, elected for seven years, names the prime minister who may select the other members of the government. He is the chief of the armed forces, and negotiates and ratifies treaties. However, most treaties must be ratified or approved by legal instrument. In particular, he may dissolve the National Assembly – a power recurrently invoked. De Gaulle also appropriated foreign affairs and defence as the president's reserved domain. The government may invoke article 49.3. to have the majority coalition accept a bill, as long as the opposition had not filed a motion of censure. Voter participation in the referendum on the constitution was extremely high at 85 per cent. Roughly 80 per cent of the population of metropolitan France voted in favour.

With the end of the Algerian war, de Gaulle proposed the use of the re-ferendum procedure on 28 October 1962 to revise the method of election of the President of the Republic from nomination by electoral college to selection by universal suffrage. De Gaulle's election on 21 December further tilted the ambiguous balance under the 1958 constitution in favour of the president, as the *élu de la nation*, while retaining the parliamentary tradition of the government's responsibility before the Assembly. As de Gaulle stated in his January 1964 press conference, 'the Head of State elected by the nation, must be the source and holder of power'. General de Gaulle's successors maintained, and often extended, the concept of a reserved domain. The prime ministers have not hesitated to make use of article 49.3 of the constitution.

Both Fourth and Fifth Republics have been served by an elitist and hierarchical administration. Recruitment into the *grand corps de l'Etat* runs through the competitive examinations for entry to the Ecole Nationale d'Administration (ENA) or the Polytechnique. Their reach extends into the nationalized banks and industries, as well as into the extensive para-public sector. The Ministers of Foreign Affairs and Defence fall under the direct tutelage of the President of the Republic. De Gaulle's successors also brought the Ministry of Finance into the reserved domain. The Ministry exercises tight control over the Bank of France through the Directory of the Treasury. Both Treasury and Bank are responsible for monetary policy, the budget and the flow of funds for public and private investment. The Treasury rationed major bond issues on the capital markets, until the reforms of the mid 1980s. The Ministry's tutelage extends over the Ministries of Industry, Agriculture and of Commerce through the Directory of Foreign Economic Relations.

The other major department of state, the Ministry of the Interior, presides over three levels of local administration: the communes, the departments and the regions, the latter created in 1982 as a major reform of the Mitterrand presidency. The result is multiple levels of administration: 36,394 communes compared to the Federal Republic, where the number was reduced from 24,778 in 1968 to 8,504 in 1989, and 22 regions compared to the Federal Republic's 16 Länder. Local government responsibilities in the conduct of economic and industrial policies developed, with over 75 per cent of public capital outlays made at regional or local level. This trend, in line with the evolution in continental Europe, accentuated party political competition for office in local government as a stepping stone for achieving majority status in Paris. Equally, this multi-tiered administration sustained a surge in personnel expenditures. General government outlays averaged 50 per cent of GNP over the 1980s, seven points over the 1970s.

De Gaulle's reconstitution of executive authority initially dealt a crushing blow to the political parties of the Fourth Republic: the third force of the Fourth Republic (Radicals, SFIO and MRP) and the PCF (Communist party of France), the most important party with roughly one-quarter of the vote. But presidential politics and close ties between central and local administration stimulated a revival of political parties in the electoral competition for higher office or for positions in local government. Professional organizations, whether farm, industrial or labour, were swept into the service of one or other of the political armies struggling for high office. Above all, the electoral mechanism rewarded whichever candidate won over 50 per cent of the votes cast in a second ballot, dividing France into two camps. Bipolar politics became the norm for presidential races in 1965, beginning with the first challenge to de Gaulle by François Mitterrand. The pattern continued when Georges Pompidou was elected in June 1969 with 58 per cent of the vote; in May 1974 when Valery Giscard d'Estaing won by a hair's breadth over Mitterrand; in May 1981, when Mitterrand won over Giscard by 3.5 per cent of the vote, marking the first alternance in power under the Fifth Republic; and again in May 1988, when Mitterrand won the second ballot against Jacques Chirac, with 54 per cent of the vote. With an electoral horizon stretching to 1995, Mitterrand had time on his side to supervise the direction of policy adumbrated in his 1988 New Year's speech: 'France is our *patrie* but Europe is our future' (*Le Monde*, 2 January 1989).

By contrast, the party political landscape underwent kaleidoscopic changes. Both de Gaulle and Pompidou based their majorities in the National Assembly on the Union pour la Nouvelle République (UNR) with an extensive working-class electorate. Mitterrand's strategy for conquest of France's highest office was to be enthroned in 1971 as secretary general of a revived socialist party, and then to embrace the PCF and later the left radicals in a union of the left, whose successive victories at local, regional and national elections punctuated the 1970s, driving the conservative parties back onto their traditional electorate; reducing the PCF to a junior partner; and opening Mitterrand's way to the crucial centre vote. In the vote of 21 June 1981 the Socialist Party (PS) won an absolute majority in the Assembly. But the centre voters' disillusion with the left orientation of Mitterrand's first two years in office gave the conservative parties a small majority in legislative elections of March 1986.

Mitterrand invited the leader of the Rassemblement pour la République (RPR), Chirac, as Prime Minister. Chirac had created the RPR in 1976, to replace the UNR, moving from an anti-German and pro-growth stance in the late 1970s, to a liberal market stance in a Europe of the states in the 1980s. Both competed for primacy in foreign policy during the two years of cohabitation. Mitterrand, nonetheless, won the presidential elections of May 1988 as champion of 'a social democratic, humanist future for Europe', 'based on liberal economic policies combined with generous social ones' (*Le Monde*, 18–19 April 1988). In the June 1988 elections to the National Assembly, the conservative parties enjoyed a slight majority, while former Prime Minister Barre's Union du Centre won forty-one seats. The domestic foundation for this priority to European policy was fragile. Polls recorded the parties' modest popularity. Immigration had become a major divisive issue. European federalist ideas were contested in the National Front, the PCF, and to a lesser extent in the RPR and the Socialists.

Another bastion of centralization embedded in a society undergoing rapid economic and technological evolution was the Ministry of Education. The Ministry runs all levels of the educational system conjointly with the Federation of National Education (FEN), whose membership amounts to 40 per cent of the Ministry's 900,000 employees. Successive 'reforms' by ministers to decentralize responsibilities while keeping central control over appointments and purse strings were absorbed within the sprawling organization, beset by periodic teacher or student strikes. Complaints about the limited relevance of secondary education to the requirements of the labour market were compounded by high unemployment among school drop-outs. Successive governments offered financial incentives to firms hiring first time employees. But this failed to address the problem of professional education, under the Ministry's monopoly. The prospect of 1,400,000 students out of 60 million inhabitants by the year 2000, ensured that pressures for decentralization in organization, budgets and personnel would mount in the 1990s.

The Ministry of Agriculture, too, is run conjointly by its own administration and by the National Federation of Unions of Agricultural Workers (FNSEA). The farm lobby is a formidable organization. Counting related industries, the sector represents about 12 per cent of GNP, about 20 per cent of employment and a similar volume of exports. The FNSEA, claiming 700,000 members, has retained its hold on representation as the principal interlocutor of government. It dominates the elections to the local chambers of agriculture, and also the government institutions responsible for price maintenance and land purchase. What is more, as the rural population has declined, farm representatives' influence in local government has risen. The Crédit Agricole, the farmer's own bank, is one of the world's largest. It monopolizes the distribution of loans or subsidies, by the government or from EC funds, for farm equipment and modernization. It has promoted the French agro-food sector, and fostered French farm exports in line with successive governments' export promotion efforts. In the EC, the FNSEA is a member of the Committee of Professional Agricultural Organizations (COPA) and plays a central role in the defence of the CAP.

Successive governments sought to promote business or trade union representation as instruments of policy, but with little success. The principal peak association representing business interests in France is the National Council of the French Patronat (CNPF), established in 1945. In the 1940s and 1950s, employers cooperated with the state, using the Planning Commission as an effective channel to express their varied interests to the state, and within the framework provided by the protection of domestic markets and government plans. The CNPF's influence reached a high point in the 1960s, as its leadership came to represent the interests of larger industrial enterprises at a time that the government sought to discriminate in their favour, with a view to promoting growth and accelerating France's industrialization. But the statutory reform of 1969, formalizing the CNPF's representative role, coincided with the political mobilization of small firm representatives in favour of legislation to protect them against the government's drive for efficiency and the opening of domestic markets to international competition. The CNPF's problems of the 1970s in representing an increasingly heterogeneous population of firms, united only in their hostility to the victory of the left parties, was resolved in 1981–2, when Mitterrand's extensive nationalizations curtailed its scope of representation to championing the interests of smaller businesses, with their own pre-existing organizations and their immediate concern to survive in the marketplace. The 1980s saw the CNPF as the defender of a private enterprise economy. It was also affiliated with the umbrella organization for employers in Brussels, the Union of European Community Industries (UNICE).

The trade unions endured a similar fate, despite or because of successive government policies. Unionization barely exceeded 20 per cent of the labour force, with unions represented in various strengths in widely different sectors, rising to 40–60 per cent in the public sector. The five recognized unions were represented by the Commissariat du Plan, the Economic and Social Council and the boards of nationalized industries. But their different party alignments and strategies to firms reduced their value to governments as a relay for public policy in such areas as incomes or labour legislation. The possible exception was the Auroux statute of 1981, promoting co-determination rights of worker representatives in working hours and training. But the low strike record of the 1980s was accompanied by the rise in unemployment levels to a peak of 10.7 per cent in 1987, falling to 9.4 per cent by 1990, and rising again in 1991. The extension of holidays and the systematic raising of the minimum wage added to labour costs, dissuading employers from hiring. Management engaged relations directly with the permanent workforce. The growth of interim work, the rise in the number of small firms benefiting by the varied incentives on large firms to sub-contract, and the application of new technologies, fractured the unions further. The non-communist unions, too, looked to their membership in the European Trade Union Confederation (CES) as a means to augment through the EC their diminished position in France.

One of the most notable developments over the longer term was the growth in the social wage. How had this occurred? The Ministry of Health presides over a maze of separate funds for families, old age, and sickness. The state administers the family fund; the old age funds are administered by man-agement and union representatives; sickness funds are a battleground be-tween the medical profession, the pharmaceutical companies, and the unions. A general regime covering most of the population exists alongside a host of special, autonomous and complementary regimes for particular categories and classes. Financing comes from employer and employee contributions, with the split heavily in favour of employees. Overtime, outlays have risen with the universalization of benefits, the ageing of the population, and the rise in medical costs. Overall, government taxation rose from 38 per cent of GNP in 1974, to 44 per cent in 1980, and averaged 46.5 per cent of GNP over the 1980s. Four fifths of the new tax burden was due to the rise in social security outlays, whose variety, decentralization and policy processes ensured greatly complicated central government efforts to control their growth. In 1988, social benefits amounted to 40.5 per cent of households' gross disposable income (OECD Economic Surveys, *France*, 1989–90, p. 72).

In summary, the Fifth Republic provided France with a stable regime, more presidential than parliamentary but incontrovertibly pluralist. As France entered the 1990s, the administration remained powerful, but with two weak points in education and social security. Fissiparous political parties and interests were dispersed but entrenched at different points across the increasingly complex regulatory archipelago. The EC's expanding com-petences made it by the 1990s the prime focus of French and European affairs.

The political economy and 'Europe'

The public discourse of French economic policy from 1945 to 1978 pro-claimed two objectives: industrial expansion, and from 1957 on, the open-ing of domestic markets to competition within the EC. Jean Monnet's experience as the head of the French Plan Commissariat in the First Plan set the tone for the coming decades by defining the choice confronting the country as one between 'modernization or decadence'. 'Expansion, produc-tivity, competition, concentration', de Gaulle declared, 'these, evidently, are the rules which henceforth the French economy, traditionally circumspect, conservative, protected and dispersed, must impose on itself' (de Gaulle, 1970, p. 142).

The principal instrument in national industrial policy for both Fourth and

Fifth Republics was provided by the extensive nationalizations of 1945 in the energy and transport sectors, and the state's complete control over the major credit establishments and the three largest insurance companies. French economic growth, already high under the Fourth Republic, was surpassed between 1960 and 1973 only by Japan. Per capita incomes came to equal German. Gross fixed investment rose from 20 to 25 per cent GNP. This rapid modernization of the capital stock was accompanied by a high rate of corporate self-financing, and abundant labour supply with the arrival of new generations onto the labour market, the return of the settlers from Algeria, and immigration from Mediterranean countries.

The French franc was stabilized in 1958–9, and trade was accelerated. French trade diversified away from captive colonial markets to concentration on western European markets. By 1973, 74 per cent of French exports were in western Europe. Non-oil developing countries took over 17 per cent of French exports, with the communist party-states and the United States taking 3.6 and 7.6 per cent respectively. With French government policy geared to production for domestic consumption, exports of manufactured goods stagnated at about 73 per cent as against 90 per cent for Germany, while imports of manufactured goods rose sharply. Concentration on European markets made France particularly vulnerable to the down-turn in the western European economy in 1973–4. Trade deficits with Germany, the United States, Japan and OPEC were in part compensated by state promotion through export credits to developing countries and the party-states, as well as by a strong surplus on services. Over the 1970s, the amount of investments by foreign corporations in France tripled; payments deficits were covered by opening Paris's financial markets to international investors. Foreign exchange reserves by 1981 topped 14 billion dollars.

Governments of the Fourth and Fifth Republics experienced the greatest difficulties in mastering inflation. In January, 1945 de Gaulle rejected a stabilization policy proposed by Pierre Mendes-France, who resigned from his position as Minister of Finance. The policy of growth at the price of successive devaluations led to the franc's depreciation by 90 per cent against the dollar between November 1944 and December 1958. Momentary respite was gained by the stabilization plan of 1958, accompanied by a further devaluation. But the money supply continued to expand, and France went into a further stabilization in 1963. Growth slowed. Liberalization measures between 1965 and 1968 to facilitate more autonomous bank lending, to encourage equity markets, and to free foreign currency and gold markets, were cut short by the effect of United States financial policy on European foreign exchange markets and by the events of May 1968. The student revolts and worker occupations of factories scared the government into conceding inflationary wage claims, and the franc was devalued a year later. Pompidou's presidency was characterized by another round of inflationary growth, repeating the cycle of an initial thrust in exports, a weakening external balance and a devaluation in January 1974. It was only when the reflationary package of September 1975 led to a prompt run on the franc in March 1976, that President Giscard d'Estaing decided to edge towards a hard currency policy. In April 1978, Giscard d'Estaing and Schmidt launched their joint initiative, leading to the creation of an EMS based on fixed but adjustable exchange rates.

The state's energies and resources in economic policy were deployed with a long-term view to promoting industrialization. But there was no direct correlation between the opening of markets and the redeployment of the state's activities. Political controversies and changing circumstances conditioned a sinuous path to partial retrenchment, followed by renewed state activism. The years from 1965 to 1968 saw the disengagement of the Treasury from the detailed regulation of financial flows; public and private enterprises were to rely less on budgetary transfers; industrial and bank concentration was to be encouraged, and inefficient farms or retailers allowed to go to the wall. After the May 1968 scare, policy was dictated by the *impératif industriel*, involving the further emphasis in bank and industrial concentration, an ambitious policy of negotiated contracts in the public sector, and attempts to introduce quantitive controls on banks to restrict the explosion in loans. After 1974, a flurry of committees, sectoral plans and special funds were created to confront the impending economic slow down, while the president personally directed a surge in public sector investment.

The period from 1978 to 1983 witnessed an uneasy coexistence between the hard currency option and the central government's industrial activism. Prime Minister Barre sought to marry a hard franc policy with partial liberalization in domestic policy. His premiership introduced a battery of measures to improve corporate finances, promote equity markets, and to restore competition. But equally, the surge in public sector investments, notably in the defence, transport, energy and high-technology sectors, were financed by borrowing on the international markets. Private sector investment tailed off. With Mitterrand's electoral triumphs of April–May 1981, the new government launched France on an expansionist course at the moment that the Federal Republic, early in 1981, moved to restrictive policies in line with the United States. French export markets suffered from stagnation in western European, developing country and party-state markets. There ensued three further devaluations of the franc within the EMS. Meanwhile, Prime Minister Mauroy's government nationalized forty-nine firms in industry and banking, with a view to providing the state with a *force de frappe* on world markets, with Japan, not Germany, as the model. The new public sector accounted for nearly one-third of French industrial exports at the moment of nationalization. State capital was to be injected to absorb the losses of sectors in crisis, and to increase investments in the sectors of the future. Production was to be concentrated in a few publicly owned groups.

The Mauroy government's decision of March 1983 marked a major reversal in policy. One camp advised giving priority to growth, statist industrial policy and the reduction of unemployment. This pointed to a weakening of the franc, a rise in the imported price of goods, and further devaluations. The franc would have had to drop out of the European Monetary System (EMS), with protectionist barriers being raised to stabilize the trade deficit. The end of the road could have meant a severe stabilization, driving unemployment rates much higher. It would also have meant France turning back on European integration, and seriously undermining relations with the Federal Republic. The route taken was for Finance Minister Delors to negotiate a parity realignment in the Exchange Rate Mechanism (ERM), and to return to the hard franc policy initiated in 1976.

All subsequent governments followed the broad lines of policy flowing from the decision of March 1983 to keep the franc in the ERM. Budgets were moved towards balance, and monetary laxity was eschewed. Growth rates fell to an average of about 1 per cent between 1983 and 1987, well below the French economy's potential. As the world economy picked up in 1988, French growth rates rose to 3 per cent. Price controls were ended; wage indexation was eliminated; and conditions eased on companies to lay off workers. Profits were reconstituted, with the corporate sector leading a surge in investment, averaging 19.8 per cent GNP. Quantitive controls on bank lending, that had been resumed in 1972 to control monetary growth while channelling funds for investment, were removed. Instead, interest rates were kept high to maintain the parity with the DM, and to encourage French firms to control costs. Inflation rates fell from a 14 per cent annual average in the early 1980s to about 3 per cent by 1990. The interest rate differentials with the Federal Republic narrowed, as the franc's reputation as a hard currency gained ground among market operators. Government deficits fell, as did the external debts. But the tax burden remained heavy. Public debt by 1990 was one of the lowest in the OECD, at 25 per cent GNP.

With subsidies and inflationary financing barred, alternative means had to be found to foster the competitiveness of French firms. As in 1965–8 and 1978–80, the emphasis was given to corporate profitability. Nationalized firms were allowed to sell off firms, acquire others, and to invest abroad. Influenced by the tide of liberal market ideals flowing out of the United States and Britain, the Chirac government set about reducing the number of committees and funds in the armoury of the state's industrial policy. An ambitious plan was unfolded in August 1986 to privatize sixty-six public enterprises, worth a total of 300 billion French francs (Bauer, 1988, pp. 49–60). The pledge was to make France a nation of shareholders. But the programme was cut short by the October 1987 crash in stock markets, when fourteen industrial and banking firms had been sold for a total of 70 million francs. Though the number of small shareholders quadrupled, one quarter of holdings on most firms were sold to ten institutional shareholders, and a discretionary limit was placed on foreign share purchases.

Re-elected in 1988, François Mitterrand held fast to the position he had described several months earlier in his 'Letter to the French': neither nationalization nor privatization. In fact, Mitterrand opted for another version of the mixed economy. Public and private groups (such as UAP and Suez, AGF and Paribas) maintained their close cooperation, facilitated by the continued flow of managers across the boundaries between the publicly and privately owned corporations. To finance their acquisitions, the public enterprises had to raise private funds. To sustain their capital base, private enterprises had to turn to nationalized banks or insurance companies. The re-composition of capital was made most often on the German model, in the form of close associations between banks and firms (Credit Lyonnais–Bouygues). Bank–insurance groups were formed (UAP–BNP). The Japanese *keiretsu* model, of a pole grouping large corporations, was more rare (Saint Gobain).

These French groups accelerated their investments, mainly into other European countries. According to a Credit National study, the large French groups placed 40 per cent of their total investments abroad in 1989. The global stock of French foreign direct investments reached 311.8 billion francs by end 1988 – about one-third the British stock, but not far less than Germany's. The devaluation of the franc against the deutschmark from a parity of 1:1 in 1958 to 3.35 in 1987 meant German investment in France greatly exceeded French in Germany. Germany only absorbed 17.8 billion or 5.7 per cent of the French total (Banque de France, *Note d'Information*, July 1990), duplicating the general pattern of very low inward investment to Japan and Germany. Both countries, too, preserved their defences against foreign takeovers of firms. Britain and the United States were the main havens for inward investment by the corporations of the G5 countries, representing about 80 per cent of world investment (Julius, 1990).

French corporate policies were, nonetheless, flawed. Their weaknesses showed up in the high unit cost of production in the automobile sector, relative to best practice in Japan, as well as in the decline of the machine tool sector and the tribulations of the electronics producers, Thompson CSF and Bull. Awareness of a growing technological gap inspired the Ministry of Industry's promotion in April 1985 of the joint European research programme under the name of EUREKA. The move was sanctioned by the European Council at Milan in June. But the defects in the industrial underpinning of French defence were underlined by the experience of the Gulf war of early 1991. The war demonstrated the significance of electronics to modern warfare, and France's modest capabilities alone. Agreement was reached with Britain on 'an enhanced programme' of defence cooperation. The prospects of co-production projects with Germany were marred by the strength of opposition in the Federal Republic to the use of force in foreign policy.

The socialist government also resumed its predecessors efforts to stimulate capital markets (Cerny, 1989, pp. 169–92). Measures were taken to foster wider share ownership, and nationalized firms were authorized to issue debenture stocks and non-voting shares. New financial instruments were created. The aim was to reduce corporate dependence on banks loans or state subsidies. State subsidised loans, amounting to nearly 45 per cent of total loans through the 1970s, were curtailed. Bank finance as a proportion of new funds raised was reduced, while the Paris markets were developed by the freeing of capital movements, begun in 1984, and the creation of a financial futures market in 1986. As in London, the traditional brokers' monopoly on market-making was ended, while a surge in competition prompted Paris's development as the second financial centre in Europe. Even so, stock market capitalization in France stood at 20 per cent GNP in 1988, over four times less than Britain but similar to Germany. Furthermore, France, along with the Federal Republic remained one of the most restrictive markets for foreign purchases of firms. Continued government ownership, cross-holdings, and prior clearance regulations for foreigners ensured that Paris would remain a tightly knit financial–industrial fraternity, subject to the discrete tutelage of the Ministry of Finance.

There were two casualties of this post-1983 policy linking the hard franc and corporate restructurings. Unemployment remained one of the highest in the EC. The reasons were multiple: deficient training, minimum wages, high immigration. Germany numbered 1.8 million apprentices against France's 215,000, with German employers spending over seventeen times more every year on their trainees, than French employers. Minimum wages provided an incentive for employers not to hire new entrants to the labour market, unemployment for under twenty-five-year olds averaging 38 per cent over the 1980s. In addition, France continued to count a foreign population of about 4.5 million people, 1.8 million of which were Maghrebis. With 1 million French Moslem citizens, Islam became France's second religion. Many of these occupied low-skilled jobs. Thus, the widening of inequalities over the decade and the decline of wages' share in national income complemented the rise in racial tensions in the suburbs.

The other casualty was the trade balance. All the growth in trade from 1983 to 1990 occurred within the EC. But the annual average growth of French manufacturing exports was 2 per cent lower than the EC average (OECD Economic Surveys, *France*, 1989–90, p. 36.) The French share of world exports of high-technology products was 6 per cent, compared to Britain's 8 per cent, Germany's 12 per cent, and Japan's 22 per cent. This flowed from the marked fall off of new investment between 1975–86. France's industrial sector became a net importer in 1987, with the Federal Republic accounting for two-thirds of the total trade deficit. French exports accounted for 6.0 per cent of world exports, compared to Germany's 11.2 per cent. Export revenues, furthermore, derived from a few sectors, such as aeronautics, nuclear reactors and armaments – all categories in the domain of state trading. The main foreign exchange earner was food exports, accounting for 15 per cent of the total.

In summary, France was still adapting in 1990 to the consequences of postwar policy to open its economy. The general trend had been to elaborate more market-oriented criteria for state action in an increasingly complex economy, integrated more than ever into the pattern of world, and especially European production and exchange. But the path had not been linear. Periods of partial state retrenchment were regularly followed by a return to overt dirigisme. The most sustained period of market-oriented policy was from 1983 to 1990. World markets turned down, leaving France with high levels of unemployment, race problems, a number of manufacturing sectors in a fragile position, and with the vast apparatus of state intervention still in place. The one saving grace was France's move to trade surplus with Germany over 1991, as the consumer boom following German unity gathered momentum.

The state and global politics

Mitterrand's decade in high office was lived first in the fear of a German 'shift to neutrality', and then in the shadow of impending German unity, as Europe's postwar division dissolved. French fears of a German 'tilt to neutralism' in the early 1980s prompted Mitterrand to show Atlantic solidarity. Immediately on coming to office, he declared his support for the deployment of Pershing II and Cruise missiles to maintain the nuclear balance in the region. In his speech in January 1983 to the Bundestag, he invited Federal Republic voters to opt in the March general elections for Kohl's stance in favour of nuclear deployment, in the event of a failure in western negotiations with the Soviet Union for a balanced arms reduction. This was the spirit in which the 1983 Stuttgart European Council's solemn declaration on the 'economic and security' aspects of EC affairs came to be included in the Single European Act.

Mitterrand complemented Atlantic solidarity by a careful revival of the military provisions in the 1963 Franco-German Treaty. A Franco-German Defence Commission was established in 1982. A French Rapid Action Force was formed, stationed on the border, and designed to signify France's readiness to contribute to the defence of German territory. France agreed to consult Germany before using tactical nuclear weapons on German territory. Joint exercises were initiated, and a Franco-German brigade of 4,200 men created. In January 1988, a Franco-German Defence and Security Council was set up, to be jointly chaired by president and chancellor. But French policy stopped short of establishing a consultation mechanism on nuclear questions similar to that between Germany on the one hand, and Great Britain and the United States on the other. Nor did France affirm the automatic nature of the engagement of French forces in the defence of Europe.

Another strand of Mitterrand's policy was to promote European integration along the lines of Jean Monnet. The ground was laid in the early 1980s, but only took shape during France's EC Presidency in the first half of 1984. Finance Minister Delors appointment in July 1984 to the Presidency of the Commission stood as an earnest of France's intent. In his speech to the European Parliament in January 1985, Delors stated elliptically that efficiency had to be complemented by equity, as the cornerstone of 'our common democratic and European inheritance'. This meant devising a programme acceptable to the member states based on a set of agreed rules, a timetable, and an overall goal to achieve a more efficient internal market. But the objective also was to engage the member states in a policy process, pulling the member states into ever wider areas of policy, requiring the deployment of Community powers and possible further amendments to the Rome Treaty.

There were evident contradictions between the French government's support for freeing up the internal market, and the structures of the French economy. France has been among the member states with the best record in implementing directives agreed on in Brussels to open up the internal market. There was much to gain by an easing of market access to other member states' markets. But the limits to liberalization were traced around France's own practices. This became evident during Chirac's administration from 1986 to 1988, when he agreed to preserve social policy arrangements, in view of the electorate's sensitivity to any cutbacks. A parallel development occurred in the Federal Republic. The June 1988 Hanover European Council laid the basis for Mitterrand's alliance with Chancellor Kohl in favour of a worker's charter, promising to stress 'the social aspects of progress towards the objectives of 1992'. 'Social Europe' became a key priority in the French EC Presidency of late 1989, presented by Mitterrand as an indispensable element of social cohesion along the path to European union. A general Social Charter was adopted by the European Council at Strasbourg in December 1989, and accompanied by an 'action programme' comprising twenty-six articles.

Internal market liberalization, according to Paris's conception, was to proceed along with a strengthening of the EC's external protection. The policy highlighted Paris's significance as an indispensable interlocutor for states dependent on access to EC markets. Non-member states were only too aware that previous united fronts to restrict outsider access to EC markets, and launched under French inspiration in agriculture, fisheries, textiles or steels, had tended to become non-negotiable once member states had struggled through to a minimal agreement. Hence, France's eagerness to push EC integration, generated a scramble by outsiders to either prevent the united front being formed, or to get in behind the walls before the metaphorical drawbridge was raised. Neighbours' demands for EC membership proliferated. The United States gave renewed emphasis to the parallel negotiations to the EC's internal market policy to the negotiations in the GATT on agriculture and services.

Protection was most effective in excluding imports from poorer neighbours. Mediterranean non-member countries had their access restricted with the EC's enlargement to the south. The Lomé countries share of EC markets shrank from 20 per cent when the convention was first signed to 6 per cent when it was again renewed in late 1989, between the EC and the now sixty-six signatories. Eastern European countries, with major potential as exporters, saw their EC outlets hindered in farm and lower value added products. Protectionism in products generated the conditions for exports of labour from these areas into France and the EC. At the heart of this EC protection stood the CAP, with France as prime beneficiary and premier exporter of food products. French farmers' opposition to substantial cuts in EC subsidies played a determining role in the failure of the Uruguay Round of trade negotiations in December, 1990.

French diplomacy also took the lead in Brussels in seeking to move the EC to 'speak with one voice' towards Japan. Yet the Commission could not readily form a united front among the member states. British policy was to re-develop domestic automobile and electronics industries through encouraging inward direct investment from Japan; German automobile exporters took 85 per cent of the Japan's car imports from the EC; little support was forthcoming for French proposals arguing for reciprocal access to non-member markets in exchange for the opening of EC markets. The Commission's array of policy measures, such as anti-dumping procedures or local content regulations, proved of little avail. France's one hope was therefore that Japan's rivalry with German competitors would gradually tilt Germany's weight into the protectionist camp within the EC.

France became, too, the champion of monetary union. The idea was simple: the best way to reduce policy dependence on the Bundesbank was to join it. The Bundesbank had become Europe's de facto central bank, dictating policy to neighbours and tying European economies to the growth path of the Federal Republic. The turning point came in 1987–8, when EC growth rates surged. In June, at the Hanover European Council, a deal was cut whereby France and Italy agreed conditionally to liberalize capital movements by 1 July 1990, and Germany acquiesced in a mandate for a report to study the means for achieving monetary union. At the Strasbourg European summit of December 1989, an accord was reached whereby the EC pledged support for the German people to 'refind unity through self-determination' (*Le Monde*, 10–11 December 1989), and Kohl agreed that a new intergovernmental conference be held in late 1990, with a view to incorporating monetary union into the treaties.

French enthusiasm for a more federal EC was also informed by Gorbachev's policy of decompression in central Europe. His campaign for 'fundamental reform' in the party-states, and an end to nuclear weapons by the year 2000, resonated into European, particularly German public opinion, prompting Paris, London and Bonn to revive the West European Union (WEU). The impetus to forge closer defence ties was reinforced as Washington and Moscow edged towards agreement to withdraw the intermediary range missiles in Europe. But Washington overrode Bonn's objections, while London and Paris kept their nuclear weapons for national use only. France's support in October 1987 for a joint statement by the members of the WEU, and entitled a 'Platform on European Security Issues' came too late, and offered too little. The platform reiterated the principles of NATO strategy in its emphasis on nuclear deterrence.

Two months later, the Washington Treaty of 8 December 1987, between Gorbachev and Reagan was signed. The treaty represented a major event in the history of nuclear weapons. Missiles with a range of between 500 to 5,500 kilometres were to be destroyed within three years. The territories of the two great powers were thereby sanctuarized by mutual contract. The treaty undermined whatever public support remained in Germany for the NATO 1967 Harmel doctrine. The withdrawal of the intermediary weapons within the space of three years left NATO with very short range weapons, whose use would devastate Germany in the event of war. Postponement of their modernization at the May 1989 Brussels NATO summit saw President Bush invite the Federal Republic as a 'partner in leadership', accompanied by an expression of US support for German self-determination.

The revolution of 1989 bore directly on France's status, and on European security. The prospect was of a state of 80 million people, with an industrial economy twice the size of France's, emerging as the privileged interlocutor of the world's powers, and the major trading partner for all European states gathered around it. As Mitterrand stated in May 1989, France would preserve its status as a great power and as a permanent member of the Security Council (*Le Monde*, 20 May 1989). Yet presidential anxiety at Germany's hegemonial potential burst out in his statement of September 1990 that 'France has no complexes'. 'It is not by the number of inhabitants, of square kilometres, of towns, the armed forces, nor by economic power that History will be determined' (*Le Monde*, 19 September 1990).

Diplomatic skill in anchoring Germany in a western European coalition would have to be France's compensation. France, indeed, held the Presidency of the EC Commission, the Secretary General of the OECD, the IMF and the Council of Europe, and the chair of the European Bank for Reconstruction and Development (EBRD), created on Mitterrand's proposal to channel aid to the countries of central–eastern Europe.

Kohl's series of unilateral initiatives from November 1989 through to autumn 1990 soured relations with Paris. Mitterrand protested against Kohl's ambiguity on the inviolability of the Oder-Neisse border with Poland. He met with Gorbachev in Kiev on 6 December 1989. He received Kohl's socialist opponent for the chancellor's office, Oscar Lafontaine, several days before the German elections of 18 March 1990 in East Germany. In July 1990, in the Caucasus, Gorbachev agreed to allow a reunified Germany to remain within NATO, while Kohl accepted the permanent de-nuclearization of East

Germany. The Franco-German summit of September 1990 was reported as a disaster. Mitterrand reaffirmed his defence plans for withdrawing France's 50,000 troops in Germany. The French Council of Ministers on 22 September decided to start withdrawal of the French army corps in Germany in 1991. The Franco-German brigade would stay in Germany on the request of Bonn.

Mitterrand also stuck to the inherited policy of nuclear independence. This had been defined by de Gaulle, in diametrical opposition to NATO's doctrine of flexible response. For de Gaulle and his successors, deterrence could be made to work on the principle of proportional deterrence, from the weak to the strong. This entailed threats to engage in a counter-city strike, and a refusal to accept the prospect of a conventional, let alone a tactical war. The strength of the French position was its early affirmation that both great powers could destroy the other, and that the United States' extended deterrence over the Federal Republic was a convenient fiction, finally exploded by the Washington Treaty of 1987. As Mitterrand confirmed, 'the mission of France is not to assure the protection of other European countries' (Fondation pour les Etudes de Defence Nationale, 1989, pp. 316–26). France disassociated from the July 1990 NATO summit on the 'last resort' use of nuclear weapons. Strasbourg would be the seat for a new French command, tied into the tactical nuclear strike force located at Metz, and stretching from Belgium to Switzerland. But it was difficult to see under which circumstances these tactical nuclear forces, with their limited range, could be used. In June 1992, France followed NATO policy, with the Ministry of Defence's announcement that production and deployment of battlefield nuclear weapons would be halted.

The maintenance of French nuclear independence entailed the risk of 'a strategic void' (*Le Monde*, 13 July 1990) opening in a few years in the heart of Europe, tempting Germany to acquire nuclear weapons of its own. The Soviet Union, despite internal political difficulties and strained links with its former satellites, retained a formidable nuclear armoury. The western allies would have therefore to be tied into Europe's new settlement. The July 1990 NATO summit recorded the future institutional form of the United States' relations with the new Europe. A united Germany would be associated with the European Community's 'affirmation of a European identity in the domain of security and with the strengthening of Atlantic solidarity' (*Le Monde*, 3 March 1990). Mitterrand took further steps to rapprochement with the United States, including authorization for the stationing of American troops in France. French troops were placed under US command in the Gulf war against Iraq in early 1991, and France signed the non-proliferation treaty in June.

But France refused to join multinational units integrated as corps and divisions. Such a formula would disturb the delicate consensus forged on military policy since the 1970s; and it would bring France back into a military organization, under continued US leadership. France stood aside from the creation in June 1991 of a NATO European rapid deployment force, under a British general and dependent on US logistics. The United States preserved the Supreme Allied Command. But France backed the use of the WEU as the organizational basis for a European force that could be used outside the geographical bounds defined in the Washington Treaty of 1949. The October 1991 plan, advanced by Mitterrand and Kohl, proposed that the EC member states move to a joint foreign and security policy. The plan called for the Franco-German brigade, established in 1988, to serve as the core of a future European corps. The EC would deal with defence 'wholly or partially' under the WEU. France's defence relations with Germany could thus be seen 'to cement a European pillar of the Atlantic alliance' to serve as the basis for a future European corps.

The EC's importance for France's embrace of Germany was underlined when Kohl and Mitterrand proposed political union in April 1990. The common message to the Presidency of the European Council in Dublin called for the intergovernmental conferences to include the establishment of common foreign and defence policies. The IGCs opened in December 1990. The positions of Bonn and Paris converged on the extension of Community competences from the internal market to include social or environmental matters. But in the EMU negotiations, the French state tradition was evident in the weight attached to the role of finance ministries in the Community's 'economic governance', and in France's preference for the co-ordination and not the integration of national forces. By contrast, Germany's federal tradition was apparent in Kohl's support for an increase in the powers of the European Parliament. At the Maastricht Summit of December 1991, Mitterrand, nonetheless, vetoed an increase in the number of German European parliamentarians, which would have represented the citizens of the Federal Republic's five new regions. Given that eighty-one French deputies were divided among eight different groups, a more influential European parliament would be expected to relay French interests less effectively than German.

Finally, France had United States support for the extension of the Community's foreign policy reach into eastern Europe. At the July 1989 seven-power summit of industrialized nations, held in Paris, the Commission was given the task of coordinating western aid to Poland and Hungary. Later, the Community's trade and aid functions were extended into Czechoslovakia, south-eastern Europe and the Soviet Union, tying foreign policy considerations between the EC foreign ministers more tightly than ever before into the deployment of economic policy instruments. Support for the transitions out of the old order was to be conditional on progress in marketization, and a verified return to democracy through the respect of human rights and through the implementation of free and secret elections everywhere. In the longer term, this spelt, in Mitterrand's words, associating 'all the states of our continent in a common and permanent organization of exchanges, of peace and of security' (*Le Monde*, 2 January 1990). At the Paris Summit of 19–21 November 1990, the thirty-four signatory states to the Helsinki accords proclaimed democracy as the sole legitimate system of government in Europe.

In summary, Mitterrand's policies on Europe developed empirically, but with a prevalent theme: better to promote the complex interdependencies of Europe, built up over the past forty years than to allow the nationality principle to become triumphant in Germany and Europe. France and the Federal Republic were bound 'in a community of fate' (Mitterrand, 1986, pp. 104–5). With Germany's changed setting in the 1980s, and French concern about the evolution in German public opinion, French policy took a number of forms: French security policy moved closer to NATO, without sacrificing the principle of nuclear independence; the EC's integration was promoted to galvanize the French economy, absorb Spain's entry, open

German markets further, and negotiate more forcefully on trade with Japan; Mitterrand championed social, monetary and political union among the member states. Such a European union would provide 'a pole of attraction' for a future and wider European confederation. France's status on the world stage would be sustained by its central position in a revived Europe. France's alliance with Germany was limited by the French position on nuclear weapons.

Conclusion

Three key points may be emphasized on France in Europe: the first concerns the adaptation of French institutions to the EC; the second elaborates on the relations of France to a unified Germany; and the third underlines the main features of Mitterrand's foreign policy.

(1)   Paris's renewed enthusiasm to develop the federalist strand of its foreign policies, while maintaining its rank on the European and world stage, revealed the domestic limits placed on France's ambitions. The past with its imprints of grandeur and humiliations, weighed heavily on the style and substance of French policy. France's Security Council seat, its remaining influence in Africa, its indispensability to any major deal in the EC, and its membership of the exclusive club of nuclear powers signified a lasting ambition to adapt past greatness to changing conditions towards the century's end. This implied maintaining France's centralization, and ran in contradiction to the European thrust of Mitterrand's policy. France's three levels of local government – commune, department and region – were incomparably more dependent on Paris than were the Länder in the Federal Republic on Bonn. The creation in 1982 of the regions, without suppressing the departments, added an extra level of bureaucracy. A further reform would be to reduce the presidential mandate from seven to five years, in line with the practice of most republican regimes in Europe.

(2)   Germany had been the central consideration in French foreign policies since Germany's unity and France's defeat in 1870, the wars of 1914–18, and collapse in 1940. A permanent feature of European affairs since the late 1940s had been the aspiration of both France and Germany to pursue policies of reconciliation, while preserving respective national claims on independence and unification. Two formulas prevailed in France. Jean Monnet inspired the institutions of the Community, pooling sovereign powers in the joint interest of the member states; de Gaulle and Adenauer, as two founding figures, signed the Franco-German Treaty of 1963, signifying priority in relations between Paris and Bonn in the creation of a European coalition of states. This dual heritage was subsequently elaborated between 1974 and 1981 by Giscard d'Estaing and Schmidt. Mitterrand, in turn, revived the EC as vital to France's embrace of Germany. France's full programme for the EC involved reform of the CAP, development of an EC-wide economic and social policy, combined with an effective industrial policy, internal free trade and effective external protection. The programme was rooted in France's domestic economy and institutions, as was the determination to maintain nuclear independence and a place apart in a restructured Atlantic alliance.

Indeed, the delimitation of France's integration into the EC, and of its cooperation in a European coalition of states, was the precondition for ensuring a continued US presence in Europe. Were France to move, as rhetoric occasionally suggested, to the creation of an independent European security organization, there would be no longer any certainty that the United States could be convinced to stay. A minimal west European military alliance would allow the inevitable transitions in eastern Europe and the Soviet Union to take their course. But it was not evident that such an alliance would satisfy German demands for security and stability.

(3)   The argument deployed in 1990 in France as elsewhere that the Federal Republic would be the hegemonial power in the EC suffered from time warp and oversimplification. By the end of the century Germany's unity could be consummated sufficiently for the Federal Republic to emerge as Europe's major power. Sovereignty had been fully re-established, and Germany had the potential to act as the locomotive for the French and European economies. But Germany's national situation remained delicate. Hardly had unity been accomplished in late 1990, than the Soviet Union began to disintegrate and the Gulf war broke out. Germany's neighbours in eastern Europe were embarked on a perilous transition out of communist hegemony. By contrast, about four-fifths of German exports went to western Europe, with France as its prime customer. It was greatly effected by the twists of United States world policy, but needed the United States to continue its postwar role as Europe's pacifier. The world wars were too close for Germany to aspire to act as Europe's arbiter. The Federal Republic needed partners on whom it could rely to embed Germany in a European peace system. It remained a European country with modest means in need of allies, and looked for one in France.

Contradictions between the strands of French policy abound. There are those, already adumbrated, between espousal of the EC internal market and adherence to established institutions and habits. There is the desire to form a tighter Community to absorb Germany, and the resulting pressures from non-members on the EC to undertake a new round of enlargements. EC protection from imports of poorer neighbours to the east and south promotes immigration, and mounting tensions in France's cities. France wants to embrace Germany in the EC, but its defence perimeter is drawn along the Franco-German frontier. It wants to tie the United States into the new Europe's settlement, but strives to preserve the CAP and pose as the champion of a 'European Europe' independent of the United States. French public discourse on public policy remains rooted in the school of national political economy, but its larger enterprises are acquiring a transnational spread of interests. It clings to the role of a great power, but must lean on Germany for a leadership role in Europe (Schmidt, 1990, p. 270). France prides itself on reaching German levels of price stability, but has failed to modify the rigidities in labour markets, which ensure high rates of unemployment. Yet it strives vainly to keep abreast of Japan, whose growth from 1986 to 1990 is equivalent to the size of the French economy. Not least, the espousal of a European confederation as a longer-term goal suggests limits to the amount of EC federalism acceptable to Paris. Yet the expansion of federal powers granted to the EC at the December 1991 summit points to constitutional reform of the Fifth Republic.

These contradictions form the unfinished business of France's position on the European stage, and in world affairs. They are the stuff on which Mitterrand continues to operate, with a view to cementing France's rank in the world and position in Europe.

REFERENCES

Adda, J. and Smouts, M.-C. 1989: *La France Face au Sud: Le Miroir Brisé*. Paris: Karthala.
Ashford, D. 1982: *Politics and Policy in France: Living with Uncertainty*. Philadelphia: Temple University Press.
Bauer, Michel 1988: The politics of state-directed privatization: the case of France. *West European Politics*, 11(4), 49–60.
Capdevielle, J., Dupoirier, E., Grunberg, G. et al. 1981: *France de Gauche, Vote à Droite*. Paris: Presses de la FNSP.
Cerny, Philip 1989: The 'little big bang' in Paris: financial market deregulation in a dirigiste system. *European Journal of Political Research*, 17, 169–92.
Cohen, S. 1986: *La Monarchie Nucleaire*. Paris: Hachette.
Cohen, S. and Smouts, M.-C. 1985: *La Politique Exterieure de Valery Giscard d'Estaing*. Paris: Presses de la FNSP.
de Carmoy, Guy 1967: *Les Politiques Etrangères de la France, 1944–1966*. Paris: La Table Ronde.
Couve de Murville, M. 1971: *Une Politique Etrangère*. Paris: Librairie Plon.
de Gaulle, Charles 1959: *Memoires de Guerre: Le Salut, 1944–46*. Paris: Librairie Plon.
de Gaulle, Charles 1970: *Memoires d'Espoir: Le Renouveau, 1958–62*. Paris: Librairie Plon.
Dupuy, F. and Thoenig, J.-C. 1985: *L'Administration en Miettes*. Paris: Fayard.
Fondation pour les Etudes de Defense Nationale 1989: *La Politique de Defense: Textes et Documents*. Paris.
Hall, P. 1986: *Governing the Economy*. Oxford: Oxford University Press.
Hall, P., Hayward, J., Machin, E. et al. 1990: *Developments in French Politics*. London: Macmillan.
Hayward, J. 1983: *Governing France: The One and Indivisible Republic*. Oxford: Blackwell.
Hoffman, Stanley 1978: *France: Decline or Renewal*. New York: Harper & Row.
Julius, DeAnne 1990: *Global Companies and Public Policy: The Growing Challenge of FDI*. London: Pinter.
Kaiser, K. and Lelouche, P. 1986: *Le Couple Franco-Allemand et la Defense de l'Europe*. Paris: IFRI.
Keeler, J. 1987: *The Politics of Neo-Corporatism in France*. Oxford: Oxford University Press.
Kolodziej, E. 1974: *French International Policy under de Gaulle and Pompidou: the Politics of Grandeur*. Ithaca: Cornell University Press.
Lacouture, J. 1984–6: *de Gaulle*. Paris: Le Seuil (3 vols).
Machin, H. and Wright, V. 1985: *Economic Policy and Policy-making under the Mitterrand Presidency*. London: Pinter.
Mitterrand, F. 1986: *Reflexions sur la Politique Exterieure de la France*. Paris: Fayard.
Parodi, M. 1981: *L'Economie et la Societé Francaise depuis 1945*. Paris: Armand Colin.
Pebereau, M. 1990: *La Politique Economique de la France: les Relations Economiques, Financieres et Monetaires Internationales*. Paris: Armand Colin.
Portelli, H. 1987: *La Politique en France sous la Ve Republique*. Paris: Grasset.
Ross, George, Hoffman, Stanley and Malzacher, Sylvia 1987: *The Mitterrand Experiment*. Cambridge: Polity Press.
Schmidt, Helmut 1990: *Die Deutschen und ihre Nachbarn*. Berlin: Siedler.
Suleiman, E. 1978: *Elites in French Society*. Princeton: Princeton University Press.
Thoenig, J.-C. 1987: *L'ère des Technocrates*. Paris: L'Harmattan.
Wright, V. 1989: *The Government and Politics of France*. 3rd edn. London: Unwin Hayman.
Zysman, J. 1983: *Governments, Markets and Growth*. Ithaca: Cornell University Press.

8

Britain and Europe

Geoffrey Edwards

Elements of change in Britain's relationship with the rest of Europe

Britain is usually cast as a reluctant, insular member of the Community with political and economic traditions that are not always congruent with those of the other member states. Despite a decade of reforming zeal under Margaret Thatcher, there remain many who question whether the changes in Britain's economic and social structure will stick. Past trends have persisted, not least the decline of the manufacturing base and the rise of the service sector. The involvement of the state in industry may have been reduced through privatization, but the results in some cases may simply have been to exchange a public for a private monopoly.

Indeed, efforts to 'roll back the state' appear to have resulted in little change in overall taxation and expenditure levels and the process of reorganization in some cases has led to greater centralization. Moreover, despite efforts to encourage an enterprise culture – or a return to Victorian values – attitudes appear to be changing only slowly, whether towards the welfare state or indeed towards Britain's place in the world. In external relations, for example, the tendency of a knee-jerk reaction of looking to the US – in seeking or providing support in times of crisis or for social or educational lessons that might be transposed to the British system – was common throughout the 1980s.

The British, at least until the early 1990s, also seemed to find it easier to invest in North America. The Atlantic orientation is thus still strong even if declining – and with, at elite level at least, no particularly marked generational differences. Yet changes are occurring; opinion polls suggest a more or less steady upward swing in support for closer European unity.

Britain began the 1990s with a new government under John Major, after over a decade of Conservative government under Mrs Thatcher. Despite a recession that had all the makings of being the worst for over a decade, Mr Major led the Conservative Party to electoral victory in April 1992. Externally, he had benefited by the war in the Gulf, which, nonetheless, brought home both the relative strengths and limitations of the UK's major ally, the United States. Briefly it also reawakened discussion on the type of longer-term commitment Britain might make once again 'east of Suez', before attention was refocused on the cost-cutting exercise being carried out by the Ministry of Defence in the aftermath of the revolutions in eastern Europe and the end of the cold war. But it had not just been a question of coping with change in the Soviet Union and eastern Europe, the unification of Germany had posed particularly difficult problems for Mrs Thatcher. Ambivalence had been the primary characteristic of her government's attitudes, a mixture of concern over its real and potential strength and uncertainty over the ways it might be contained. The need, especially given the Inter-governmental Conferences (IGCs) on economic and monetary union and political union which began in December 1990, to improve relations with Chancellor Kohl of Germany and other Community leaders was recognized early. The IGCs themselves appeared to provide the opportunity for some in government, but danger for others.

Key determinants

Many reasons have been adduced for the slowness of Britain's adaptation to changed political and economic circumstances in general and to member-ship of the European Community in particular, Britain's position in the latter probably being best summed up as 'semi-detached'. Much, of course, was made during the debates on membership of Britain's 'thousand years of history', variously interpreted in terms of national independence or Anglo-French conflict. Much was also made of Britain's continuing global role. In the immediate postwar period, Churchill had suggested that Britain was located within three interlocking circles: the Empire and Commonwealth; the special relationship with the United States; and, a seemingly poor third, Europe. 'With them', in the sense of a traditional alliance with European partners against a greater foe, communism, but 'not of them' in terms of participating in the various experiments in integration summed up a wide-spread attitude in Britain to the rest of western Europe.

Whatever the economic consequences of 'imperial over-reach' in attitudinal terms there was continuous debate over how a global role could or should be maintained. Decolonization may have been a relatively smooth process but it was, nonetheless, costly in both financial and political terms. The emerging Commonwealth may have been an increasingly disparate group of states with little impact on the international system, yet for many in the UK its existence continued to impede a psychological reconciliation to more modest means and goals. While 'kith and kin' arguments may have kept the old Dominions alongside Britain into the 1960s (though Suez in 1956 had been a profound embarrassment to most of them), the new radical mem-bership of the Commonwealth increasingly denied it to Britain as a vehicle for global authority. But 'kith and kin' sentiments were also strongly held within successive governments, Conservative and Labour, well into the 1960s and, indeed into the 1970s. By then, however, it had become only too apparent that links with southern Africa were untenable (over apartheid in the case of South Africa and as a result of the unilateral declaration of independence by the white regime in what was then southern Rhodesia, now Zimbabwe) and that Canada, Australia and New Zealand were looking, with varying degrees of success, towards rather more dynamic markets than those provided by Britain. The Acheson adage that Britain had lost an Empire but had not yet (in 1960) found a role was particularly prescient, not least because the continuation of the Commonwealth gave sometimes vivid reminders of former glories or evoked a sense of responsibility that could not be ameliorated within a European role.

Many in government also laid stress on the continuation of a special relationship with the United States as a means of manifesting Britain's global vocation. However special it may have been, it was not always an easy relationship. Beyond language, sentiment and nostalgia, the specialness was often rather more apparent in British eyes than in American. Of course, while the UK remained capable of pursuing a global role and saw its interests as coinciding with those of the United States, Britain was America's most valued ally. However there was a growing ambivalence in the relationship on both sides. On the part of British governments, it was a difficult transition from aspirations for partnership to acceptance of monetary and military dependence. Nor was it helped by the seemingly frequent intrusion of American domestic considerations into external policy and the tendency for American Presidents to forego consultation to provide information at best during, and sometimes only after the event. If the impact of the abrupt ending of lend-lease had been assuaged by the generosity of Marshall aid, American reactions to Suez indicated not only the extent to which US and British interests could differ but also the degree to which the pound was dependent on American monetary hegemony. But if the establishment of NATO with full American participation had been regarded as one of the major achievements of British diplomacy under the 1945–50 Labour government, that had not prepared many in the UK for Britain's nuclear and technological dependency on the US after the Skybolt/Polaris agreement signed by the Conservative government under Harold Macmillan. If under Macmillan, the British may have liked to view the relationship as one of Greece civilizing Rome, Americans tended to view it as one of increasingly impotent avuncularity.

In the 1950s and 1960s, however, as Europe began to integrate, the idea of being able to rely upon the Commonwealth and the United States and keep a distance from Europe began slowly to pall. If the Suez fiasco had been an important factor in 'bouncing' France into acceptance of the EEC, its lessons took somewhat longer to accept in the UK. British weakness and dependence it had certainly shown, but that it should mean foregoing global aspirations for a regional identity, despite American encouragement, was not immediately appreciated. For some, however, the lesson learned, especially as the Communities began to develop an external dimension, was that Europe could become a substitute means of sustaining Britain's global role and aspirations. These 'surrogate imperialists' were particularly well-placed in the Conservative party and, whatever their misgivings about economic integration, looked to the further development of the intergovernmental European political cooperation as the ideal vehicle.

The number of those in Britain who were strong supporters of federalism in Europe has always been small. Some of them, not least early members of federal union such as Lords Beveridge or Lothian, may have been influential but not in terms of Britain's European policy. Many more may have been highly active and vociferous, especially during the 1975 referendum on Britain's continued membership of the Community, yet their impact on policy has clearly been limited. It is perhaps illustrative to note the move from patron of the European movement to that of the Bruges group (the group hostile to further integration in Europe) by Mrs Thatcher which suggests that the European movement in Britain is a fairly broad church able to cater for very different attitudes towards integration. But neither have the federalists yet won rehabilitation for the very concept of federalism or for 'union' both of which remain highly suspect to British audiences. In the absence therefore of a strong political force for furthering integration, the bulk of those who supported British membership in the 1970s were those whose motto could easily have been 'there is no alternative' (a phrase later made popular by Mrs Thatcher). These were the pragmatists who recognized that there was little scope for a United Kingdom outside the Community, especially when the six had so visibly done better economically than the UK, and/or who believed that the only answer to Britain's structural problems of low investment, poor management and obdurate trade unions was the 'cold shower of competition'. Reluctance, negativism or simple discomfort were thus only too apparent from the beginning of Britain's membership.

These attitudes have, of course, been modified by nearly two decades of membership, yet elements of them remain discernible. For those who had been particularly susceptible to 'imperial overhang', 'Europe' has only partially fulfilled their hopes and aspirations. The economic strength of the Community undoubtedly exists but political leadership has been lacking in that so often the other European partners could not agree to any united action. Indeed, there was a growing alarm over the direction of any common foreign policy when there was consensus; too many member states being too ready to ignore the interests and susceptibilities of the United States. On the other hand, the United States itself was seen, despite some excesses such as the strategic defence initiative, the Reykjavik Summit between Presidents Reagan and Gorbachev or the US raid on Libya, as attempting successfully to maintain international order.

Thus, despite concern over the rise of a popular anti-Americanism during the 1980s, the British have been largely content with the idea of being America's closest European ally. Governments, especially those of Mr Callaghan and even more so of Mrs Thatcher were intent on ensuring Britain remained in a privileged position even if on several occasions – including the Libyan raid – the positive British response to the US had been at the expense of any joint European position. This renewed Atlanticist predisposition of so much of the foreign policy making elite (even if it excluded a good deal of the Foreign and Commonwealth Office) was reinforced, of course, by the close personal relationship between Mrs Thatcher and President Reagan. The prospective loss of that special relationship due to President Bush's seeming preference for dealing with Germany as America's most powerful European ally played a part in determining subsequent British policy. It is too soon to judge whether Britain's 'ever faithful' support for the United States in the Gulf war will have lasting effects, either for the relationship with the US or for Britain's acceptance of European foreign policy constraints, but the sense of coolness before the Gulf crisis has since evaporated.

It is not difficult, perhaps, to see why many of those who sought to retain a global role for Great Britain have wavered in their support for a Community that has become increasingly unrecognizable from that which they believed they were joining. It was enough for some to have joined a customs union. It had been only with difficulty, and certainly only after the settlement of Britain's budgetary problem in 1984, that they had been able to accept the Single European Act and the introduction of more majority voting in the Council of Ministers. And even then they had been persuaded by Mrs Thatcher that it had been necessary only because of the need to complete the internal market. They remained both dubious about the merits and suspicious of the principle that lay behind the European Monetary System (EMS) and hostile to the whole concept of European Monetary Union (EMU). They have tended to merge with others, both to the right and the left of the political spectrum, who were opposed to British membership on essentially nationalistic grounds and who remain hostile to any further integration. Traditional right-wing nationalists perhaps make strange bedfellows with those on the left who are opposed to the Community for its liberalism and, as they see it, its incompatibility with bringing about 'socialism in one country' (i.e. the UK) but expressions of mutual sympathy if not support have increased in the House of Commons, especially on the issue of parliamentary sovereignty. That issue has also, of course, caused difficulties for a number of those who approached the Community more pragmatically. While there has been a widespread acceptance of the need for economic integration, many, led by Mrs Thatcher, began to adopt a markedly Gaullist position on political integration – even if a Gaullism tempered by a strong Atlanticism.

That such divergent groups should coalesce around the concept of parliamentary sovereignty is of some significance: interesting even if its long term implications may be more limited. It is interesting, though, in view of the contribution of successive governments to the establishment of what one former Lord Chancellor described as 'an elective dictatorship' based on an idiosyncratic electoral system and the controls exercised by the government of the day over both its own party supporters and the parliamentary timetable. Certainly Mrs Thatcher's own style of government combined with the seemingly endless European and western summits and other meetings of heads of government (and/or of state) worked against effective cabinet and ministerial responsibility to parliament – though it is too early to say if, and to what extent, the trend will be reversed by Mr Major. Parliamentary sovereignty, in the sense that no one parliament can bind its successor, remains the formal position; it remains doubtful if in normal circumstances any government would seek to repeal the European Communities Act; it is inconceivable that parliament without government support could do so. Yet the emphasis was placed particularly strongly by Mrs Thatcher's government on this loss of the more formal and symbolic elements of sovereignty. Cynics would perhaps argue that this was because the loss of more substantive aspects of sovereignty, in the sense of governmental controls, has been actively encouraged by government either in the interests of competition or in response to market pressures.

For the more pragmatic, support for the Community became considerably easier with the settlement of Britain's budgetary problem in 1984 at the Fontainebleau European Council and the agricultural-budgetary package of 1988. The prospect of Britain becoming the largest contributor while being among the poorest of Community members was enough to unite all but the most fervent federalists. Some may have questioned the manner in which Mrs Thatcher addressed the problem; few questioned that a problem of equity and political sense had to be resolved by the Community. The Fontainebleau settlement released considerable enthusiasm, much of which was channelled into support for the 1992 process. Despite Mrs Thatcher's often well-publicized brushes with the Commission, the coincidence of a national government intent on a programme of privatization and a Community determined on deregulation and liberalization was fortuitous. The result was not necessarily a consistent approach and there have inevitably been problems en route, as over fiscal harmonization, but it has at least provided an area in which the British could be seen as being strongly *communautaire*. Indeed, Mrs Thatcher agreed to the extension of majority voting in the Council of Ministers in order to expedite progress. Yet it was widely regarded as a straightforward commercial enterprise, particularly within the Conservative leadership. It was only slowly that there was any serious recognition of the political momentum it had created or the full economic, monetary and social implications to which it had given rise or, if recognized, only accepted with the utmost reluctance.

The operational environment

The environment within which Britain pursues its Community policies is thus one in which reluctance has been tempered by only limited enthusiasm. The political goals pursued by successive British governments have been largely those of damage limitation as they have reacted to events, interspersed with efforts to reform unpopular policies – most especially, of course, the common agricultural policy – and to support liberalization within the internal market programme. There have been few indications of any profound shift in any wider aspirations towards the Community level even if there have been frequent assertions from Mr Major's government of the need to be at the heart of Community decision making.

This recognition of the possible danger of marginalization as other member states move further towards the goal of closer unity indicates not only the change of government but also a realization that Europe, including the UK, is moving into a new phase of development. When Prime Minister, Mrs Thatcher had provided one of the most comprehensive declarations of British government aspirations in Europe when she spoke in Bruges in September 1988. What she sought to lay down was a vision of a Europe of sovereign states, economically considerably more liberal, deregulated and interdependent, but a Europe based essentially on cooperation rather than integration and one which clearly looked to a continued close partnership with the United States. Her speech immediately evoked support from among the right wing of her party and among sympathetic groups outside parliament. It also caused increased grumbling from among her ministers, with ultimately fatal results for her own leadership. Yet interestingly enough, the speech became less and less a benchmark for British opinions, not simply because of Mrs Thatcher's own loss of leadership but because its relevance seemed rapidly to decline in the face of the changes in international, and especially the European environment, not least British membership of the EMS and negotiations on economic and monetary union, and the unification of Germany and an inter-governmental conference on political union as well.

Mr Major was, briefly, foreign secretary and, for a little longer, chancellor of the exchequer in Mrs Thatcher's last government. Significant changes in terms of substance should not perhaps have been expected when he became prime minister, at least before a general election. One could not assume, i.e. that he and others of Mrs Thatcher's ministers had been 'closet wets'. And yet, there were signs during 1991 that Mr Major and his government were prepared not only to shift domestic policy back somewhat to a more Disraelian concept of 'one nation' (and away especially from the poll tax or community charge, held by most commentators and ministers to be an election loser), but that he was also prepared to be very much more positive on European policy. Whatever the reasons for these signs, whether born of a new found conviction, a pragmatic response to new conditions (including of course the achievement of considerable privatization) or the necessity of fighting an election, and whether or not they become changes of substance, the point is that the Thatcherite right is no longer in the ascendancy over the Conservative party. Mrs Thatcher's increasingly hostile attitude towards Europe after she had resigned, expressed in a series of lectures in the United States during the summer of 1991, created a storm, especially when another former prime minister, Edward Heath joined the fray. Since both claimed to be supporting Mr Major, it created a certain degree of confusion about the government's position. It was clear, though, in her Bruges speech that not only was Mrs Thatcher intent upon creating a vision of the Community cast in a Conservative image but that she also believed it to be one that reflected British public opinion. In this she was perhaps encouraged by the sometimes blatantly xenophobic popular press rather than public opinion polls. There was, however, a certain circularity in this reliance on press opinion given the perhaps unprecedented closeness of her press secretary (Mr, now Sir, Bernard Ingham) and the press lobby, especially the popular press. Although ostensibly a civil servant, Mr Ingham regularly took his lead from the prime minister on European as on other policies, including domestic party politics, regardless of the 'official' position of the government. Public opinion, on the other hand, has shown increasing support both for the general concept of unity in Europe and for British participation in European union. While greater familiarity with the Community is in itself no guarantee of increased support, in the British case a loss of ignorance and suspicion has been important. Eurobarometer surveys have shown that while support in the UK for the Community has been consistently below that of nearly all its partners except Denmark, British attitudes have, nonetheless, been consistently higher in the 1980s than earlier. The settlement of the British budgetary problem as well as the public campaigns relating to 1992 have been particularly significant in determining these higher levels.

Mrs Thatcher's image of the Community, however, was one that increasingly distinguished the Conservative government from the Labour party which, after its defeat in 1987, had begun to take a very much more positive approach to the EC. Given Mrs Thatcher's brand of nationalism and neo-liberalism, it was perhaps not very difficult to appear as pro-European; the Labour party was in some ways also helped by being in opposition and therefore not faced by having to defend a policy in both Brussels and Westminster. That is not to undermine the genuine changes that have occurred within Labour over Europe, for certainly under Mr Kinnock's leadership there has been a profound learning process undertaken. It was less perhaps that British socialists learned a lesson from the abortive efforts of the French socialist government of 1981–3, but that by 1988 Mr Kinnock had been able to demand acceptance of British membership from the Labour party and thereafter for the 1989 European elections to develop a more coherent approach to the 1992 process (in which he was encouraged especially by the TUC), and, indeed, to the possibilities of British participation in an economic and monetary union. But as the Labour party began to take up the political centre after 1987, and to the extent that it became accepted as a possible alternative government, so Mrs Thatcher herself was increasingly encouraged to move still further to the right; a matter of conviction became in a sense a matter of political necessity even if ultimately it was her undoing. With the shift back towards the centre on the part of the Conservative party, and faced with decisions emanating from the IGCs, the position of Labour became more difficult and already in the summer of 1991 there were stirrings as some of the old anti-marketeers sought to make their voices heard against any Labour commitment to a single currency and political union.

The lack of any clear political consensus over Community membership and Community development has inevitably affected the adaptation of government machinery to Community membership. That the administration has adapted to the extent that it has is fairly remarkable; it is both a reflection of the need to be efficient in order to protect its own position and reputation and what is conceived to be the UK's position, and simply a reaction to the pressures of Community negotiation. It is clear that many Whitehall departments were and remain in favour of a positive British role in the Community. The Foreign and Commonwealth Office (FCO) as a result of its support has been particularly suspect, being charged with switching its allegiance to Brussels or generally representing Community rather than UK interests. But divisions over membership and further integration within the Community have created difficulties and additional burdens, whether at Ministerial or official levels. Given the sometimes hostile or sceptical environment, positions on Community proposals have had to be cleared centrally, both ministers and officials had to be 'in the same boat'. It has often meant as a result that more time has been spent drawing up an acceptable brief than on attempting to look ahead to assess the wider implications and likely consequences of any single piece of legislation. Yet, as David Williamson, the Secretary General of the Commission has pointed out, success in Brussels rests rather less on preparing beautifully considered briefs than on persuading partners to accept them in the course of negotiations.

It is clear from this that even while Community membership has created strong transnational linkages among departments and ministries, it has also placed a premium on centralized coordination. This has meant yet further accretion of responsibilities by central government, which since the mid 1970s had already been regarded as suffering from administrative overload. As more and more responsibilities were given to or taken by government so it became apparent, as one Secretary to the Cabinet put it, that there was 'a hole at the centre'; the cabinet in particular could not cope. Greater influence and responsibilities, however, accrued especially within the cabinet office, the role of the cabinet secretary in government being further enhanced; so too has the role of the deputy secretary in the cabinet office (a former incumbent being David Williamson, himself). In one sense the European secretariat is designed simply to reconcile the divergent interests of Whitehall departments. In another sense, however, it reflects the strong determination of successive governments to ensure a strong national position in the Council of Ministers. That is not to suggest that all positions are coordinated in the cabinet office for (1) the European secretariat is an extremely small body; and (2) individual ministers and their officials can deal straightforwardly with much of the detailed legislation that makes up the bulk of Community law. However, given the tendency in Community decision making to progress by means of package deals that frequently cross over sectoral issues, more than one ministry is involved in establishing a British position. And while most of the ministries involved are included in the UK permanent representation in Brussels and the FCO retains the role of assessing the chances of success for a policy options, the role of the cabinet office in ensuring a coordinated position is of considerable significance.

Even so, without a fundamental consensus on long-term goals, such centralized coordination cannot ensure either coherence or consistency. This was reinforced during the 1980s by the plurality of information sources, advice and policy making. While the input of the FCO has been important, however regarded with suspicion it may sometimes have been, there has also been a policy unit at Number 10 which, inter alia, has kept a watching brief over Community affairs. Mrs Thatcher when Prime Minister also had a foreign affairs adviser, Charles (now Sir Charles) Powell, who remained at Number 10 for the first six months of Mr Major's premiership in order to lend continuity during that initial, transitional period. Yet while it is necessary to stress the ways in which the nature of decision making straddles the traditional domestic/foreign divide encouraging a centralization of national policy making, which reinforced the personal approach to government of at least Mrs Thatcher, it is equally important to point to countervailing pressures. At the negotiating level, for example, the continued interaction of officials brings with it a better grasp of alternative positions and creates pressures and a disposition to agree. There is always a tension perhaps in diplomacy between the desire to reach agreement with fellow experts and colleagues in order to complete a dossier and the need to remain within the remit of instructions from home. In the British case, this tension is somewhat heightened by the strictness of the instructions agreed in Whitehall. Despite this, the British also tend to have the largest permanent representation of the member states in Brussels. In order to ensure further that Whitehall be adequately acquainted with opinion in Brussels, arguably of even greater importance than the extension of majority voting in the Council of Ministers, the permanent representative and other officials make weekly visits to London to brief the cabinet office and ministers – this, in addition to the army of Whitehall experts who go to and fro for the multitude of committees and working groups in Brussels. But at both ministerial and official levels, while the 'clubability' of agricultural councils may have declined in the face of mounting financial constraints from the 1970s and 1980s, there are clear transnational interests that counterbalance a national position based on wider criteria.

It is not therefore surprising to find that British interests groups have found increasing common cause with their counterparts elsewhere in the Community. The Confederation of British Industry (CBI), for example, was long a supporter of Britain's accession to the EC (as, indeed, had its predecessor the Federation of British Industry in the 1950s) and opened an office in Brussels on British entry better to monitor policy proposals. Since then, it has also played an active role in UNICE, the Community-wide industrialists group. The CBI's position on most issues taken by UNICE has been unremarkable, keeping with the consensus even on, for example, the CAP despite strong popular and governmental hostility to it, though it has to be added that the National Union of Farmers is a CBI member. The major exception has been on social issues, especially on worker participation and the social dimension of the internal market. Here the CBI has devoted considerable efforts at ensuring that UNICE has taken a firm line in opposition to Commission proposals to involve the Community in any way in the regulation of labour markets. In part, this reflects the generally more marked divide between management and workers in the UK and hostility to legislation in the area of industrial relations, but it has also been reinforced by the nature of the CBI when compared to other employers' groups. The CBI is heavily dependent on voluntary contributions from its business membership in terms of both funding and time. There is no required membership, for example, as in Germany, of chambers of commerce which spills over into membership of the CBI's equivalent, the Federation of German Industry (BDI). As a result the CBI's bureaucratic structure is relatively small and business attitudes are carried rather more directly into UNICE's discussions at least at senior levels. On the other hand, the effectiveness of the CBI in representing British business interests has sometimes been questioned, not least by its putative rival, the Institute of Directors. During Mrs Thatcher's premiership it suffered in particular from being ignored on domestic economic issues as part of the corporatist structure that Thatcherism was geared to bringing down. The principle was then reinforced by government suspicions of the CBI for its pro-Community stance, especially when in the mid 1980s it came out in favour of an early and full British membership of the EMS and its exchange rate mechanism. As a result it tended to be looked on as useful only when it could effectively supplement the government's own efforts to disseminate information, as in the information campaigns on the 1992 process, or reinforce the government's position in Community negotiations, as on the issues relating to the social charter. In terms of disseminating information on 1992, for example, it held a series of seminars on different aspects of policy, using both business managers and their own and UNICE experts. In terms of lobbying, CBI teams have tended to fly to and from Brussels leaving relatively little time to lobby either fellow members of UNICE on more general issues or the Commission on more particular topics. There have been relatively few successes for the CBI in its relation with the British government; it has not played a significant role in the formulation of British Community policy.

Similar limitations have applied to the role of trade unions in the UK. The differences within the trade union movement over British membership of the Community had meant that the TUC, like the Labour party, adopted a policy of non-participation in Community institutions before the 1975 referendum. Thereafter, it participated in the work of the Economic and Social Committee as well as becoming actively if not always particularly enthusiastically involved in the European Trades Union Congress (ETUC). Given the confederal structure of the Trades Union Congress (TUC), much was left to individual unions to do in pursuing links with their Community counterparts. There was, however, a gradual shift in opinion and this became very much more marked after the 1983 general election. With Mrs Thatcher's return to government there was both the prospect of having union rights further restricted and its opinions and expertise ignored. Community and especially Commission interest in social matters provided a welcome alternative. This was particularly so given Commission encouragement to unions to play an active part in alerting it to breaches of Community legislation, such as that on equal pay, on which a case was taken to the Court of Justice. But, above all, perhaps it was the Commission's interest in countering particularly the British government's view that the 1992 process was merely a commercial venture and its determination to press for a social charter and a social action programme that won trade union support. M Delors had a tremendous success when he spoke at the TUC annual conference in September 1988 and emphasized the social dimension of the 1992 process. The trade unions' increasingly positive approach to the Community and Britain's role in it had an important impact on Labour party attitudes, especially after its defeat in 1983 and again in 1987. While individual unions may stress particular areas of interest, and some may have taken a somewhat more cautious line on EMU than, say, the Labour party, the TUC itself has been actively encouraging a joint approach on issues such as protection and minimum standards for part time and temporary workers, minimum hours, rights of workers in multinational companies etc. This very much more positive approach was recognized by the ETUC when it elected the TUC's general secretary, Norman Willis, as president in 1991.

That individual trade unions have their own transnational links within the Community reflects the fact that peak associations such as the CBI or the TUC are far from being the only interests active in Community policy making. The necessity of being informed at an early enough stage in the policy-making process to have impact has caused sometimes marked changes in the way sectoral interests relate to government. This, again, has been reinforced since 1979 by the continued withdrawal of government from the economy in the sense of limiting if not eliminating the role of 'sponsoring departments' in the Department of Industry. This has made the involvement of such interests at the Community level of even greater moment. This again though highlights a difference between the UK and many of its partners where the UK has tended to emphasize the voluntary nature of such organization (even if it has sometimes had some governmental encouragement) rather than the more regulatory systems elsewhere. A number of new umbrella organizations within different sectors have gradually emerged to provide information for individual firms and to lobby both in Whitehall and in Brussels, such as the Food and Drink Federation and the British Bankers Association. That is not to suggest, of course, that every firm or interest group relies on such organizations. As Bressand and others have shown, the Community is made up of a multitude of cross-cutting, transnational networks, some fairly formal and others informal. British firms (national 'leaders' perhaps rather than national 'champions', under later Conservative governments) have been active in such 'Round Tables' etc., though it was considered disappointing that ICL, Britain's only mainframe computer company should have been ejected from the Information Technology Round Table when it was taken over by Fujitsu.

The political economy and Europe

The Thatcher government's decision to allow ICL to pass into foreign hands was a clear signal of its determination to maintain a 'hands off' approach to the corporate sector. The objective of 'rolling back the state', of cutting back on public expenditure, of privatizing nationalized industries as well as limiting or eliminating other interventionist and regulatory bodies has been pursued vigorously even if not always consistently since 1979. Whatever its successes or failures, 'Thatcherism' in many ways represented a radical change. It is significant, for example, that there is now more public ownership in Germany (excluding the complications of unification) than there is in the UK. But even if nationalization may be the most extreme form of intervention, the response of Conservative as well as Labour governments for much of the period since World War II was to intervene in the economy when the going got tough. This may have been particularly true during the Labour government's term of office between 1964 and 1970 when a number of new agencies were established in the interests of stimulating new, high-technology industries, and protecting and/or restructuring older 'lame duck' industries; but even so, Labour policy remained largely within the general political, Keynesian consensus, often referred to as Butskellism. Particular stress was laid on the goal of full employment and the responsibility of government to use public expenditure to counter recession. Inflation was rarely regarded as a problem.

The Heath government of 1970–4 was the first to try to break out of the resultant 'stop-go' policies of successive chancellors. However, while it dismantled some of Labour's more interventionist agencies and began to negotiate entry into the Community in part to bring about a 'cold shower' of competition to stimulate the economy more fundamentally, it was confronted by too many issues simultaneously that were beyond its control. There were few signs of renewed long-term investment to set against continued speculation and asset stripping (the latter practice leading an increasingly disillusioned Mr Heath to describe the multinational, Lonrho, as the 'unacceptable face of capitalism'), and, therefore, fewer signs of improved technological development or better industrial relations. Confronted with rising unemployment and the imminent collapse of Rolls-Royce (engines) and British Leyland, which were both taken into public ownership, Heath undertook a 'U-turn' in policy and 'dashed' for growth. It was not until Mrs Thatcher took office that a government, which both contributed to and exploited the breakdown of the old consensus, was able to set a new agenda and, by and large, to stick to it; the lady, Mrs Thatcher said of herself, 'was not for turning'.

But the major problems facing the economy were often well beyond the control of a single government. Successive governments, for example, had sought to maintain the role of sterling as a reserve currency. Whether or not the maintenance of the Overseas Sterling Area was the result of the dictates of finance capital or the miscalculation of the foreign policy elite of Britain's economic capacity to support a global foreign policy, the effects were disastrous for the British economy, especially as it was not finally wound up until 1968. There were perhaps three major consequences. In the first place, there was a 'leakage of capital' to more profitable parts of the area which left lower investment levels in the UK. Secondly, by allowing British exporters a safe export market in the sterling area, they were protected against other competitors and inefficiencies were masked if not encouraged. Thirdly, if the area was to survive, holders of sterling had to have confidence in it. Since Britain's economic performance gave little cause, especially when yet another balance of payments crisis loomed, the Bank of England and the Treasury had to re-attract at least short-term money by raising interest rates and causing yet another slow-down in the economy. In time, of course, and whenever possible before elections, interest rates were lowered, a credit boom encouraged, imports sucked in and, hopefully after elections had been held (and won), the cycle repeated itself. But as Shonfield suggested, when governments were faced with a balance of payments crisis, they cut back domestic investment 'like a blind man with a single automatic gesture at his command'.

But even if most governments had appeared to be willing 'to sacrifice the domestic economy again and again', other factors also made it increasingly difficult for British governments to cope adequately. The mainstay of the postwar system had been the United States and it too was facing growing economic and monetary problems. These, in August 1971, led to the final collapse of the exchange rate system embodied but not executed within the framework of the Bretton Woods agreements of 1944. Moreover, having shaken off a fixed exchange rate, the US administration was not particularly committed to maintaining the dollar rate agreed at the Smithsonian in 1972. By the time they revealed their commitment to floating exchange rates it was rather too late for the pound sterling which, as part of its negotiating package with the European Community, had been introduced to the 'snake in the tunnel', but within the space of weeks had been forced out again. Thereafter, with reluctance perhaps on the part of the Heath government but with considerable relief on the part of the succeeding Wilson and Callaghan governments, Britain pursued a policy of 'managed floating'. There appeared, however, to be an endemic propensity for the pound to sink rather than to float. Unilateral action in defence of a relatively weak economy (albeit one anchored in the European Community after the referendum of

1975) was not, of course, helped by the general world recession that was so exacerbated by the quadrupling of oil prices after 1974. The fact that Britain was emerging as an exporter of oil did little to help even if, as Mrs Thatcher later discovered, it usefully differentiated the pound from other Community currencies when the question of full British membership of the European Monetary System was raised. It was certainly not enough to help in 1976 when speculative pressures and persistent trade deficits led the pound to fall below two dollars for the first time. The Chancellor of the Exchequer, Dennis Healey, was forced to negotiate a loan with the IMF. As part of the agreement, the Labour government had to introduce a seriously deflationary package, to raise interest rates, cut government spending etc. The result was an increase in unemployment and a growing industrial unrest that sounded the death knell for an already politically weakened government.

The economic structure and outlook of the United Kingdom on entering the Community on 1 January 1973 was thus somewhat different from the other member states. The end of the reserve role for sterling may have contributed to a marked shift in foreign (and defence) policies but it had had little impact on the domestic economy. British capital, for example, continued to search for more profitable returns elsewhere, especially in the United States despite restrictions on capital movements. This had – and to some extent continues to have – complications not only between the international and domestic sectors of the economy but also between those geared more towards the Atlantic and those moving increasingly towards Europe. Efforts to restructure the economy seemed to benefit the service sectors without bringing about a slimmer but more competitive manufacturing sector and it created further unemployment. The result therefore was a post-industrial or de-industrializing society which was particularly open to highly competitive imports and therefore vulnerable to external influences.

The government of Mr Heath had had high hopes that Community membership would bring about much needed change in the economy. It was seen primarily in terms of a cold shower of competition, which for many might have been an uncomfortable prospect but clearly external discipline was necessary. But at the same time, the Community was looked to for assistance in the process of restructuring in the form, especially, of a new regional policy, seen as particularly important given the desirability of offsetting the costs of the common agricultural policy. The Labour government elected in 1974, however, was more preoccupied with the issue of British membership than with individual Community policies, and the German Chancellor, Helmut Schmidt, effectively reduced the size of any disbursements to the UK from the Regional Development Fund set up in 1975 to a mere fraction of what had been hoped for. Constrained by a party still largely hostile to the Community, the Labour governments of Wilson and Callaghan took few initiatives and were frequently reluctant even to react with any great enthusiasm. While the former deputy leader of the Labour party, the then President of the Commission, Roy (now Lord) Jenkins may have launched an initiative to revive the idea of economic and monetary union (EMU), the negotiation of the decidedly more modest European Monetary System (EMS) tended to be regarded as a Franco-German plot. Somehow, it seemed, the EMS would delimit Britain's freedom of manoeuvre while allowing France and Germany to retain theirs. Given the variety of arguments or excuses which were then used against becoming a full member of the EMS by both Labour and Conservative governments, it came to be seen as an important symbol of Britain's lack of European commitment.

Indeed, it took over a decade before the British finally became full members of the EMS by joining the Exchange Rate Mechanism as part of the move towards stage I of EMU that also entailed others, including the French and Italians, liberalizing their controls on capital movements. And even then it took the threatened resignations of the chancellor of the exchequer and the foreign secretary to 'bounce' Mrs Thatcher into making the decision. Her position earlier had been that Britain would join 'when the time was ripe' but since so many reasons had been given to explain why the time was not ripe – that sterling was, for example, a petro-currency or, when sterling was not over-valued, that the inflation rate was too high, or that interest rates were too high or that others were not fulfilling their obligations or even that sterling's entry would bring about the collapse of the system itself – it was clear that membership was regarded as an infringement of a government's right to use monetary policy in the interests of the state. The Mitterrand experiment notwithstanding (President Mitterrand was, after all, a socialist as well as being French), Mrs Thatcher appeared convinced that it was possible to pursue monetarism in one country. Efforts to 'buck the market' would inevitably end in tears, even if it was clear to her chancellor after 1985 that a tacit understanding with the Bundesbank as a preliminary move towards full membership of the EMS was more than desirable. While to others in her cabinet the costs of pursuing the policy outside the exchange rate mechanism became only too clear in 1988–9, Mrs Thatcher, supported by her transatlantic economic adviser, Sir Alan Walters, appeared determined to resist this formal submission to the weight of the Bundesbank. From her subsequent speeches it has become obvious that Mrs Thatcher had agreed to move to stage I of EMU only under duress. Once freed from office she clearly felt free from her past commitments and was even more outspoken in her hostility to any further moves towards EMU, including, of course, a single currency which, she had said, would happen 'only over her dead body', a nation's currency being the epitome of its national sovereignty.

That market forces should be given free rein was, of course, the primary characteristic of Thatcherism (even if, in the monetary field, market forces tended to mean short-term speculators balanced by the Bundesbank). In Community terms, however, the pursuit of deregulation and liberalization came second to an equitable settlement of the British budgetary problem. Clearly, given Britain's economic structure and its trading patterns, there was a problem that had to be resolved. The potentiality of a serious mismatch of contributions and receipts had been recognized during the accession negotiations without raising any alarm about *juste retour*. It had been only superficially dealt with during the Labour government's 'renegotiation' of the terms of Britain's entry in 1974–5, even if it had been enough to allow the Labour leadership to campaign in favour of continued membership. It was not, however, until 1984 that a seemingly lasting settlement was reached at the Fontainebleau European Council meeting. The budgetary battle may have been a costly one, though the effect on Britain's negotiating credit may have been exaggerated and Britain would probably have taken a negative position on policies such as science and technology in any event, in line with its own reduced expenditure on such programmes. But it was not until after Fontainebleau that Britain put its weight (and that of Lord Cockfield, the Commissioner responsible) behind a policy of completing the internal market.

It is, of course, highly significant that the British government has constantly talked of '1992' and completion rather than 1993 and a new beginning, and have focused almost exclusively on the commercial dimension, emphasizing, that is, the completion of the market in goods and services and the free movement of capital. To the extent, in other words, that the process has been one of deregulation and liberalization then the government was and remains enthusiastic. There have, even so, been one or two exceptions for, as Mrs Thatcher, herself, is quoted as saying: 'I didn't join Europe to have the free movement of terrorists, criminals, drugs, plant and animal diseases and rabies, and illegal immigrants'. Britain did not therefore take part in the Schengen group discussions among the original six founding members on frontier-free travel, and it was always regretted that M. Delors had been allowed to talk in terms of a 'frontier free Europe' and that 'his' social charter had been adopted despite the Prime Minister's opposition. Moreover, there were doubts about foregoing the government's discretionary powers in relation to competition policy. And it was firmly believed that national governments – or parliaments – should determine tax rates, at least, it was said, until market forces brought about alignment. But while the 1992 process meant deregulation and did not imply reregulation in Brussels it fitted well with British policy.

'Rolling back the state' was not always, however, as straightforward as monetarism and Thatcherism had implied. Public expenditure, for example, proved remarkably resilient to being cut back. In some cases 'sweeteners', later deemed illegal by the European Commission, had to be provided for otherwise not wholly convincing privatization programmes while in others private monopolies simply replaced public ones (water supplies being but one example). And while several ministers such as Nicholas Ridley during his brief sojourn at the Department of Trade and Industry (DTI) or Cecil Parkinson during his not much longer period at both the DTI and at the Department of Energy declared themselves ready to legislate their departments out of existence, a sometimes uneasy balance was struck between such free market desires and the need to ensure that the degree of regulation necessary, whether derived from national policy or Community legislation, was exercised in the public interest. There was, for example, intervention in a decidedly 'corporatist' manner in the financial sector in part to meet the demands of globalization but also to counter the decay of the City's institutions. Such intervention highlights the non-intervention in cases like that of ICL; it was, in other words, a deliberate decision by the government not to exercise any discretionary powers that might have derived from the traditional concept of 'the public interest'. As Woolcock and others have suggested, this discretionary power to intervene not only in major decisions such as takeovers but also in day to day operations makes the British system very different from others in the Community, in particular from Germany with its very much more regulated system. The approach may allow for flexibility in a national context but it has inevitably complicated the British approach to Community policy where, in the face of twelve competing systems, discretion and public interest are difficult if not impossible to interpret uniformly.

Despite therefore the determined efforts of the Thatcher governments, the key features of the British economy continue to be high inflation, high unemployment, relatively low growth and persistent regional disparities. The manufacturing sector has witnessed a continued decline with its share of UK GDP down from 25 per cent to 20 per cent over a decade and share of manufacturing world trade now 8 per cent instead of 10 per cent. While 1988–9 saw investment rising, it fell back in 1990 and again during 1991. The UK presents therefore a uniquely hostile environment for the manufacturing sector when compared to the financial or when compared to manufacturing elsewhere in the Community. And yet the government appointed by Mr Major after the election victory of April 1992, showed some signs of responsiveness to the renewed debate over the extent of government involvement in the economy. If there was a willingness to concede, in appearance at least, that establishing the general climate may not be enough, it was accompanied by a determination to follow through with the Thatcher reforms on housing, the health service, and education.

Britain and world politics

The end of the cold war and the changes in the Soviet Union and central and eastern Europe have inevitably brought about a reappraisal of Britain's foreign and security policy. If the Ministry of Defence's 1991 proposals are accepted, Britain faces the prospect of having its smallest army since 1830. Moreover, after nearly twenty years of Community membership, it would be surprising if Britain's foreign policy had not been extensively 'Europeanized'. And certainly to the extent that European institutions exist with responsibility for foreign and security policy, Britain has usually played a full part in them, even if appearances and rhetoric have sometimes suggested the contrary. It is, of course, the case that such institutions, notably European Political Cooperation (EPC) and Western European Union (WEU), are intergovernmental in character rather than supranational, even if in the case of EPC there is a growing blurring of the distinction between it and the Community proper. But few British political leaders or diplomats would argue that the European framework represents the totality of British interests; British policy is pursued alongside, supplementary to, and complementary to any European policy. Doubtless, few leaders from other member states would depart from such a position. There may well be a 'coordination reflex' but bilateral relationships built up over past decades or centuries remain. Each state brings its own perspective to European counsels even if increasingly there may be a community of information leading to a community of view and perhaps even of action.

Britain's 'historical baggage' may not be heavier than those of its partners but it has certainly caused the UK to seek out and pursue particular, individual paths. The nostalgia for Empire may now have almost totally disappeared; interestingly enough, its Commonwealth manifestation pretty much buried by a Conservative government, but odd bits of it have had a habit of reappearing to haunt even the most sceptical of governments. The

Falklands war of 1982 is perhaps the most obvious example, but there are other cases which have arisen to complicate policy: proposals for a new airport in Hong Kong have created difficulties with China in the run-up to 1997; an airport, too, in Grenada caused a momentary clash with the United States, even if it was conducted largely over the telephone between prime minister and president; the costs of stationing troops in Belize; the lengthy correspondence in newspapers such as the *Daily Telegraph* or *The Times* over whether to maintain the Ghurka regiment, the last vestige of the era when Britain's frontier lay in the Himalayas; all combine to remind the British that they have global responsibilities even if only in a regional capacity. But it needs to be remembered that, for many, Britain entered the Community because there was no alternative economically. Whatever the opportunities provided by Europe, there has nearly always been enthusiasm for working closely with the United States, as for example in the Lebanon in 1982 or the Gulf in 1991. Likewise, there was relief in 1985 that Mr Gorbachev turned out to be 'a man one can do business with', a reflection of the frequent desire to play an interlocutory role between east and west. Each has allowed Britain some autonomy of foreign policy, beyond the constraints of Europe.

Inevitably perhaps there have been differences over the degree of autonomy and the balance to be drawn. If the common picture of the UK is one of a government continuously seeking to maintain a special relationship with the US, this has in part been due to Britain's continued dependence on the US nuclear deterrence and a dependence on the US for its own nuclear deterrent. But during the 1980s it was also the result of the rhetorical, ideological and personal identification of Thatcher and Reagan. There may have been hiccups, as over Grenada or, more seriously, over the Strategic Defence Initiative (SDI) or the Reykjavik Summit – where the USSR and the US nearly reached an accord on cross-the-board arms cuts, without the US providing prior information to its allies. But, on the other hand, support was extended over the Libyan raid in 1986 and, more enthusiastically, after the Iraqi invasion of Kuwait in 1990. On each, and on other occasions, the UK was criticized for extending support at the expense of possible action on the part of the EC/twelve. But it was Europe's offer of only the possibility of action that created disillusionment, especially if, for action, the Europeans meant merely a demarché, however toughly worded. That is not to suggest that Britain has not sometimes welcomed a joint declaration rather than any attempted action or complete inaction. It did so, for example, over Cyprus in 1974 and the Middle East in 1980. But Britain has always been particularly concerned that any policy that diverged from American policy should (1) be carefully thought through; and (2) be carefully explained to the United States. In the latter case, the UK tended to see itself as the natural interlocutor, a task only occasionally (as after the Reykjavik Summit) delegated to it by the EC/twelve.

If Britain's continuous Atlanticism caused differences within the EC/twelve, it also caused friction domestically. Prime ministers and foreign secretaries have traditionally played a delicately balanced duet in British foreign policy. The growing importance of summitry within the Community, as well as globally in the western summits, compounded Mrs Thatcher's growing predilection for foreign affairs. Her first Foreign Secretary, Lord Carrington, had ultimately felt obliged to deprecate 'loudspeaker diplomacy'. But successive foreign secretaries, including Mr Major in his brief spell at the foreign office, found themselves in an uncomfortable no-man's land between official government policy and prime ministerial action – in Mr Major's case at the 1989 Commonwealth conference. However artificial sometimes the choice between the Atlantic and Europe, it was, nonetheless, an important factor in a number of domestic political disputes, as, for example, in the resignation of Michael Heseltine over the Westlands helicopter affair in 1985 and was not wholly absent in Nigel Lawson's resignation from the Treasury in 1990. Mrs Thatcher's European policy was, of course, the issue on which Sir Geoffrey Howe resigned in 1990, a resignation which ultimately led to Mrs Thatcher's own resignation after losing the contest for the Conservative party leadership.

But it would be an exaggeration to suggest that Europe was the only factor involved in these political events or that there has not been a growing range of issues on which Britain has agreed with its European partners – and, indeed, with the United States. Britain, from the beginning, has been a strong supporter of EPC, and has generally been in favour of developing it to include a security dimension, a British proposal along those lines being taken up by France and Germany in 1985. But the aim was to build on the ideas contained in the London Report of 1981, that EPC should deal with the 'economic and political aspects of security'. It was not about defence, which, in British eyes, was firmly the responsibility of NATO. However, moves to develop EPC were impossible given the opposition of Ireland, Greece and Denmark. At the same time, Britain had become increasingly alarmed at what were termed 'sub-structures' within the alliance, especially the closer relationship between Germany and France which had led to the creation of the Franco-German brigade. In order, therefore, to sidestep the constraints imposed within EPC and to broaden out (or keep under better surveillance) the Franco-German axis, Britain reluctantly supported the revival of WEU. It was also influenced in doing so by growing congressional complaints that Europe was not sharing enough of the burden of its own defence. Since then, the British have actually found WEU rather useful, especially for coordinating limited 'out-of-area' activities. It remains looked on, however, as a bridge between the Community member states and NATO, rather than as the potential defence arm of the Community as suggested by Italy and to some extent by France and Germany in their proposals to the inter-governmental conference (IGC) on political union which began in December 1990.

The IGC as a French inspired reaction to German unification was regarded with considerable suspicion by the UK. The attitude tended to be that it was bad enough that there was a conference on EMU; a second, on political union to which all and sundry would propose Treaty amendments so soon after the Single European Act, were difficult to countenance. But it was especially difficult because of the rationale behind it. Unlike France, Britain under Mrs Thatcher found it difficult to play the Community 'card'. Both may have reacted with alarm at the speed of German unification but the British tone seemed considerably more hostile, though the anti-German remarks of one minister, Nicholas Ridley, did lead to his resignation. There was much insistence on the need to anchor Germany within NATO, on the grounds first laid out by Lord Ismay that it was designed 'to keep the Americans in, the Russians out and the Germans down'. Closer integration within the Community was not regarded as an alternative option or even an attractive additional policy. And the more sensitive response of the United States under President Bush made the issue all the more problematic. The Gulf war, of course, went a considerable way in restoring Britain to the position of America's 'most trusted ally'.

Mr Major's election to the Conservative party's leadership led to some changes in policy, and not only in style. One of his first diplomatic moves was to improve relations with Germany and to declare the need for Britain to be at the centre of decision making in Europe. The seeming loss of impetus in the two IGCs during 1991 worked in his favour by delaying the need to put any new treaty to the country at a time when he was faced with the need for a general election and an economy in deep recession. But the changes that began to evolve appeared also to reduce the differences between the two major parties on a number of issues under discussion in the IGCs. That is not to predict the emergence of a broad bipartisan approach to Europe – the Community is involved in economic and social issues that will continue to divide parties on traditional ideological grounds. However, it is to suggest that an obstacle to the further integration of Britain into the Community has been removed, even if it has not yet wholly disappeared.

But even if the nationalist strand of Mrs Thatcher's platform is likely to be moderated, and the more overt displays of Atlanticism become less frequent, it is not yet certain that Britain will immediately become a comfortable member of the Community. Its economic structure remains problematic, however open and genuine the single market becomes in 1993 or however strong the pressures for convergence become in stage II of EMU after 1994. And in foreign policy terms, the tendency still to see the international system in hierarchical, power terms remains strong – few yet have begun to talk or even think about, for example, the question of the appropriateness of Britain (and France) retaining their Security Council seats. And governments, despite the economic and social legislation emanating from Brussels, whether Labour or Conservative are likely to try to continue to play the role of gate-keeper, of remaining the primary source of authority and direction in European matters. All the member states have experienced problems in their transition to multilateral decision making in an open, inter-dependent system. Britain, in some ways, is no different except insofar as it retains the perspective of an offshore island with a powerful imperial past. Even so, a thousand years of history may yet be interpreted as a thousand years of continental involvement.

REFERENCES

Brittan, Samuel 1988: *A Restatement of Economic Liberalism*. London: Macmillan.
Butler, M. 1986: *Europe: More Than a Continent*. London: Heinemann.
Butt, Alan Philip 1985: *Pressure Groups in the European Community*. London: UACES.
Byrd, Peter (ed.) 1988: *British Foreign Policy under Thatcher*. Oxford: Philip Alan.
Camps, Miriam 1964: *Britain and the EEC, 1955–63*. Oxford: Oxford University Press.
Cawson, Alan (ed.) 1985: *Organized Interests and the State*. London: Sage.
Curwen, Peter (ed.) 1990: *Understanding the UK Economy*. London: Macmillan.

Davies, Gavyn 1989: Britain and the European monetary question. *Economic Study*. London: Institute for Public Policy Research, 1.

De La Serre, Françoise 1987: *La Grande-Bretagne et la Communauté Européenne*. Paris: Press Universitaires de France.

Dunleavy, Patrick Gamble, Andrew and Peele, Gillian (eds) 1991: *Developments in British Politics 3*. London: Macmillan.

Franklin, Michael 1990: *Britain's Future in Europe*. London: RIIA/Pinter.

George, Stephen 1990: *An Awkward Partner: Britain in the European Community*. Oxford: Oxford University Press.

Gamble, Andrew 1988: *The Free Economy and the Strong State: the Politics of Thatcherism*. London: Macmillan.

Grant, Wyn and Sargent, Jane 1987: *Business and Politics in Britain*. London: Macmillan.

Gregory, F. E. C. 1983: *Dilemmas of Government: Britain and the European Community*. Oxford: Martin Robertson.

Hennessy, Peter 1989: *Whitehall*. London: Martin Secker & Warburg.

Jenkins, Roy (ed.) 1983: *Britain and the EEC*. London: Macmillan.

Jenkins, Simon and Sloman, Anne 1985: *With Respect, Ambassador*. London: BBC.

King, R. (ed.) 1983: *Capital and Politics*. London: Routledge & Kegan Paul.

Lewis, D. and Wallace, H. (eds) 1981: *Politics into Practice*. London: Heinemann.

Middlemas, Keith 1979: *Politics in Industrial Society*. London: Andre Deutsch.

Northedge, F. S. 1974: *Descent from Power*. London: Allen & Unwin.

Sanders, David 1990: *Losing an Empire, Finding a Role*. London: Macmillan.

Smith, Michael Smith, Steven and White, Brian (eds) 1988: *British Foreign Policy*. London: Unwin-Hyman.

Stopford, J. and Turner, L. 1985: *Britain and the Multinationals*. Chichester: Wiley.

Wallace, William 1984: *Britain's Bilateral Links within Western Europe*. London: RIIA/ Routledge & Kegan Paul.

Woolcock, Stephen Hodges, Michael and Schrecber, Kristin (eds) 1991: *Britain, Germany and 1992*. London: Pinter.

Young, Hugo and Sloman, Anne 1982: *No Minister: An Inquiry into the Civil Service*. London: BBC.

Young, John 1984: *Britain, France and the Unity of Europe*. Leicester: Leicester University Press.

Young, Simon 1973: *Terms of Entry*. London: Heinemann.

9

Italy and Europe

Cesare Merlini

Introduction

'Italy's presidency (of the European Community) is proving to be like a bus trip with the Marx Brothers in the driver's seat' wrote the *Economist* in October 1990. Rome's performance had started on 1 July of that year, not under very favourable auspices. When the 'flamboyant' Foreign Minister, Gianni De Michelis (to cite again the English weekly), made numerous speeches during the summer to state his objectives – ranging from generous support of the troubled east European and north African economies to the initiation of far-reaching institutional reforms – the perception in European capitals (including Rome, to an extent) was that of an over-ambitious package, lacking priorities, internal consistency, sufficient consensus and the necessary resources.

A multitude of meetings at all levels was convened, often on short notice and with little or no preparation, generating disarray in the national bureaucracies and in the EC headquarters, where – not by chance – the punchy comparison of the *Economist* allegedly originated. The British dislike was particularly strong and often took the form of pointing out the discrepancy between Italian federalist attitudes and Rome's lack of compliance and implementation of Community rules.

On top of everything else, one month after the Italian government took over from the Irish, Saddam Hussein invaded Kuwait. Just as in a Marx Brothers film, things got even more hectic, almost breathtaking. Meetings multiplied, initiatives crisscrossed. The problem of course was less organizational than it was political: the EC has never been fond of international crises. Soon the responses of the member states began to diverge and the traditionally divisive issue of the relationship with the United States, oscillating between partnership and rivalry, became prominent again.

Nevertheless, when on 1 January 1991 Prime Minister Giulio Andreotti handed the presidency over to Luxembourg he could read the balance sheet of his semester with some satisfaction. It had been the most crucial semester in the history of the thirty-two-year-old Community as it had comprised such 'minor' things as German reunification, the solemn pan-European (plus the US and Canada) gathering at the highest level, the initial handling of a first and major post-cold war international crisis (not yet the 'hot war', to be started two weeks later), the setting of a reasonable calendar for economic and monetary union (EMU) and the appointment of two inter-governmental conferences (IGCs), one on EMU and one on political union. All these events had the potential of diluting or even stopping European integration, but neither had happened – at least for the time being.

This of course was not the sole merit of the Italians, as the presidency was able to catalyse the main thrust coming from the Paris–Bonn axis, to limit the estrangement of President Jacques Delors that may have resulted from the axis, and to diffuse the opposition coming from Margaret Thatcher, who succumbed to personal defeat in the course of these European developments. Moreover, the 'odd couple' Andreotti–De Michelis had worked well, in any case better than the initial operation of the government early in the year would have suggested. Rome's complacency was further enhanced by the remark that under the previous Italian presidency – during the first half of 1985 – the Community had delivered the Single European Act, another major step in the integration process.

In the Italian domestic scene, also, the EC presidency had had a positive effect, insofar as it had helped patch together the pieces of the otherwise divided and shaky government coalition. Many predicted that after leaving the EC presidency to his successor, Andreotti's remaining term as prime minister would be measured in weeks, and that new elections would have become inevitable, with serious political and institutional implications.

The fact that this did not happen was primarily due to two reasons: firstly, because the Gulf crisis turned into a war on 16 January, with related new international responsibilities for the government, which was able to insure a militarily small but politically important Italian participation in the anti-Saddam coalition. Secondly, because of the step back – away from government eligibility – made by the Communist party (PCI). The PCI's leader, Valerio Occhetto, felt it necessary to embrace pacifist rhetoric in order not to lose more than a small fraction of his troops during the party's transition into a new political formation, whereby it was no longer called 'communist' – not a minor historical change, in its own right.

Italian navy and airforce presence in the Gulf was accompanied by political controversies, particularly in Catholic circles (which were under the influence of the Pope's almost equidistant position between the contenders) and revived prospects of dialogue between leftist christian democrats and former communists.

One by-product of the war was the coming to the forefront of the issue of a European identity in the field of security and defence, i.e. one of the dossiers of the IGC on political union. As we will see later, the Italian position on that matter has been that the EC should have a political profile covering security and that, to this end, it should absorb the West European Union (WEU) sooner or later.

The Yugoslav crisis provided the opportunity for such a profile to begin to shape up. Actually it became the crucial test for it, insofar as it was left to the twelve to handle, for better or for worse. Italy found itself in an uncomfortable position for three reasons: (1) its Adriatic coast had been already under an ambivalent limelight because of the tens of thousands of Albanian boat people: the response to this unexpected invasion was bound to set a precedent for an eventual Yugoslav refugee problem; (2) Austria gave hasty and unconditional support to the separatist movements of Slovenia and Croatia, leaving to others – i.e. to the Community – to handle the overall Yugoslav crisis; and (3) the Community itself was having a hard time to find and take a common position because of the traditional diversities and, at the same time, the complete novelty of the contingency.

Foreign Minister De Michelis, often accused of being uncautious in his words, proved to be very cautious in his deeds, as he almost personified the middle-of-the-road position among the twelve. His role was, nonetheless, very active and the 'troika' was visibly weakened when he left it at the end of June 1991 to make room for his Portuguese colleague. There were considerable pressures inside the country to take a position similar to the Austrian one, especially since such a position enjoyed a puzzling sympathy from Germany. This was particularly visible among the christian democrats, who have several strongholds in north-eastern Italy. Other sectors disguised their traditional sympathies for the Serbs under the cover of support for the army to maintain some sort of Yugoslav unity.

Meanwhile, once the impact of the Gulf war receded, the government coalition again came under severe strains, losing one of its components (the small republican party); it managed to survive only thanks to the daily threats of early elections. The three main reasons of bitter argument among the parties (particularly DC and PSI) have some relevance to Italy's European policy. In order of growing importance they are:

1   Constitutional reform (for a stronger executive branch and a more effective legislative branch).
2   Struggle against criminality (of high, if often soft-spoken concern to the EC partners).
3   Economic policy and particularly control over the public deficit.

In July 1991 the Commission issued a comparative evaluation of the economic situation of the twelve Community member states: only Greece separated Italy from the bottom position. A few days earlier the Moody's had dropped Italy from the top AAA rating for the international markets' most favoured clients, to the rather less august and rather more costly status as an AA1 borrower. Though the latter rating puts Italy together with countries such as Sweden and just ahead of Spain, the shock in public opinion was perceivable.

Thus, the expected new debate on European policies and more broadly on foreign policy as a consequence of the dramatic international change that has taken place, was once again affected, actually overshadowed by domestic political rifts, as any serious corrective measure was bound to have electoral consequences. However, Italy's situation and role will inevitably be affected by the new international and particularly European scene: but before discussing how, it may be appropriate to review briefly the historical, cultural and geopolitical determinants of Italian policies in Europe during the last forty-five years.

Short history

After the end of World War II, Italy had to fight its re-entry into an international setting that tended to marginalize it because of its ambiguous identity at the closing of the hostilities: in the eyes of the part of the world that counted, the country was partly associated with fascism and nazi Germany and partly associated with the 'Resistenza', the democratic movement linked with the victorious Allies. The process was to be long and difficult. From the United Nations and the Atlantic alliance (in the 1950s) to the summit of the seven major industrialized countries (as late as the 1970s) Italian membership met some resistance or overt opposition from the would-be partners.

The participation in the process of European integration was the only one to take place rather smoothly. This occurred despite the fact that the first European Community, the one pooling coal and steel (at the time still considered of crucial strategic importance) had its geo-economic heart in the centre-north of the continent (France, Germany and the Benelux), whereas Italy was no relevant producer of either of these raw materials. In addition, Rome had to solve a number of border issues bilaterally with its neighbours as a consequence of the expansionism of Mussolini.

On the other hand, postwar developments provided Italy with some comparative advantages. The country had not been divided like Germany, nor rendered neutral like Austria. Fascism had been wiped out, in contrast to what happened in Spain and Portugal and which resulted in backwardness and international isolation. The colonial empire had been dismantled, with the consequence of sparing the country from such painful amputations as those later suffered by France, Britain, Portugal and Spain. Finally, Italy soon lost direct geographical contact with the adverse alliance, as Yugoslavia and Albania left the Warsaw Pact and the Soviet troops left Austria: a strategic buffer layer had thus been placed at the Italian borders, reducing the defence problems that were confronting the FRG, Norway, Turkey and Greece.

It is thus with a relatively reduced threat perception that those basic choices were made in the 1950s – participation in the European Communities and in the Atlantic alliance – that have remained Italy's foreign policy cornerstones for some forty years. Such choices were no less controversial inside the country. The Socialist–Communist opposition strongly fought against taking side with the west and praised the Soviet model which was being imposed on the eastern part of Europe.

This east–west divide was superimposed on, and only to a limited extent coincided with the north–south divide, which has stronger roots in Italian culture and polity. But the latter surfaced again in the following years (the 1960s and the 1970s), when a low profile was dominant in the foreign policy of a country almost entirely absorbed by economic reconstruction first and development afterwards. High growth generated social and political tensions because of the existing social and regional inequalities and attracted most of the attention of a political leadership, which showed a high propensity for using foreign issues for domestic purposes. The foreign policy debate was thus often made of stereotypes.

One stereotype, however that had a significant background was the dilemma between European priorities and Mediterranean priorities. Important Italian circles have seen the role of the country as a bridge between Europe and the developing countries, particularly those in the Mediterranean and Middle Eastern area. Indeed, they were dominant until the 1970s, but they could not win control of Italian foreign policy because of the 'communist danger', both outside – the Soviet Union, against which the US provided protection – and inside – the PCI, against which a majority was needed which would be consistent with the international status of the country.

This current of thought is most frequently called *terzomondismo* (thirdworldism). *Terzomondismo* was visible in Catholic circles, which resisted what they saw as being an appendix of a predominantly Anglo-saxon and protestant western hemisphere. It was visible among the communists and until the 1980s in the socialist left, though in this case it was mostly instrumental for dislike of colonialist France and Britain first, and an imperialist United States later. (One interesting case study would be the attitude of the Italian left vis-à-vis Israel, but it goes beyond the scope of this paper).

Terzomondismo was also visible in the business community, especially in the state controlled sector. Particularly relevant was the role of the powerful state oil company, ENI, which has conducted a very active policy among the producing countries, especially in the Arab world. This policy has been rather effective in ensuring supply of oil and gas at good market conditions, but in the past often created embarrassment to the country, as it followed its own priorities, independently from, and at times in clear contradiction to, the government foreign policy.

Terzomondismo overlaps to an extent with nationalism but cannot be identified with it. There is in Italy a pro-American nationalism, that advocates 'special relations' with the United States to compensate for British and French haughtiness and to counteract German economic strength. There is a pro-European nationalism, that advocates joining together to replace US protection, i.e. to lift US dominance. (Again, one case study would be the Italian debate on the nuclear Nonproliferation Treaty.) One feature of *terzomondismo* is *mediation* as the main foreign policy objective as opposed to *integration*: Italy should mediate between north and south, between east and west, between the Israelis and the Palestinians, and so on and so forth.

Now, the debate between a European and a Mediterranean foreign policy has seen the prevailing of the former over the latter throughout the late 1970s and the 1980s. Joining the EC has turned out to be part of a success story. It has not been in contradiction with being an increasingly active member of the Atlantic Alliance – a recurrent concern in Italy – and has not prevented the country from achieving other national goals, like joining the G7. Twelve years separate the decision to join the European Monetary System (against the advice of important financial circles) from the vote for participation in the military operations in the Gulf. Despite the limiting conditions of such choices – the larger band in the EMS and no ground forces in the Gulf – such choices are no less important and suggest a rather consistent line in Italian foreign policy and particularly in its European policy.

But that line has often found it hard to translate itself into operation and implementation, i.e. into legislative and administrative measures. This, of course, has been particularly true in the realm of the European Communities, which – as opposed to other chapters of foreign policy – affects nearly all branches of government and thus makes it crucial that a proper coordination is in place – a major weakness in the Italian administrative system.

The dichotomy between policy line and implementation has been particularly evident in this case. Rome has been consistently in favour of strengthening the Community institutions. After the obvious conflict of positions with General de Gaulle and the 'Luxembourg compromise' (1965), which Italy accepted with reluctance, the first deepening-versus-enlarging dilemma confronted the six EC members. Since the first option was excluded by Paris, the Italians supported British entry. The hope that London was to become an ally on regional funds proved, however, to be illusory.

The institutional debate that re-emerged after the two enlargements and the first direct elections of the European Parliament (direct elections that had been strongly supported by the Italians), centred around two proposals: one more intergovernmental, the Colombo–Genscher plan, and the other more constituent, the Spinelli initiative in the EP. Both contributed to the following developments: the first vote ever in a European summit, Milan 1985, with the British government isolated; and the Single European Act, Luxembourg 1986. Both can be seen as part of the higher profile in the Italian foreign policy that has already been mentioned.

As we will see in the next chapter, however, good preaching is not matched by good practice. In fact, Community membership has had a limited and quite unsatisfactory impact on the country's legislative and administrative system, with the consequence that the credibility of the Italian role in the Community itself has been partly undermined. The same membership, on the other hand, has had an important impact on the Italian domestic political landscape and economy. Pro-European strands were the vehicle for the socialists to become eligible for government participation in the 1960s, which they did first in the *centro-sinistra* and then in the *pentapartito*, the two coalitions with the christian democrats and the small 'secular' parties that have run the country for now nearly thirty years.

The Communist Party (PCI) tried to follow the same pattern ten years later; indeed, to a certain extent, they did so even more seriously than their former fellow-comrades. The appeal to a former renegade of the party, Altiero Spinelli, well known founding father of the European Federalist Movement, to run as an independent in the national elections first and in the European elections later had a tremendous impact on the PCI's image (despite the several embarrassments caused by the real independence shown by Spinelli on nearly all major foreign policy votings). The Italian communist fraction in the European Parliament has often been praised for competent and active participation in the proceedings of this rather confused and powerless assembly and has de facto acted as the avant-garde of the reformist wing of the party in the otherwise hesitant and contradictory rapprochement with the European social democracies.

The attempt, however, was this time unsuccessful – with the brief exception of the *solidarietà nazionale* of the late 1970s, when the PCI was shortly part of the parliamentary majority, without, however, any government portfolio. A number of political, military and economic circles, that had already resisted the 'apertura a sinistra' of the 1960s even toying with coup d'état plots, came up this time much stronger, more serious and differentiated.

The security factor was decisive in determining the outcome, not only because it catalysed negative forces but also because it weakened the credentials of the PCI, whose half-hearted conversion to the west had brought it as far as voting the near unanimous parliamentary resolution of 1976 which explicitly supported the main guidelines of Italian foreign policy – European integration and Atlantic solidarity – but then failed to join in on any major implementing decision, especially as far as NATO is concerned.

Indirectly all this shows that as long as and until the European Community is not a full political union including having common security policies, it is not sufficient to identify what the Italians call *la scelta di campo*; the EC will require the complement of the Atlantic alliance in the task of helping the definition of political cleavages in the country.

Mooveover, public economic policies and corporate strategies have been profoundly affected by Community participation, in bringing about free market and competitive approaches in a 'milieu' previously often prone towards protectionist practices. Again, the dimension of western economic interdependence is such as to have borders broader than the ones of the EC, and the environment of the Italian economy can only be defined in such broader terms, although in this case there exist a 'European pillar': the EMS, the common trade policy, etc.

It is appropriate to recall in this synthetic historic survey that the industrial sector was rather negative on the Common Market when the government decided to participate in EEC in 1957, and that the central bank had several reservations about Italy's capability to stay in the EMS when the decision to join was taken in 1978, so much as to impose the request of special larger band (6 per cent) for the lira to fluctuate in. Both decisions were, nevertheless, of crucial importance, as the former forced the Italian productive system to jump into the cold pool of competition and the latter stopped the practice of distorting such competition through monetary instruments.

The operational environment

As was discussed above, Italy enjoys an increasingly solid policy line in foreign affairs, namely in European affairs – one may call it a 'strategy' – but lags behind in implementation – one may call it the 'logistics'. This is due both to legislative and to administrative weaknesses. At the political level 'Europeanism' is more a matter of principle than of practice. One casualty deriving from such an attitude is consistency with the policies followed in other fields – such as economic policy – as we will see in a next chapter.

Also European federalist pressure groups, which enjoy a respected status in the country because of Spinelli's leadership and of the solid cultural core, are more concerned with making bold integrationist pronouncements than they are with consistency and implementation. In the June 1989 European elections a referendum was held in which some 88 per cent of the Italian electorate expressed support for the country's total integration into a European federation. The impact of such a massive pronouncement on correcting policies or holding back practices that in fact tend to detach Italy from European standards rather than making it closer is nil.

The Italian delays and infringements in the field of implementation of

Community directives and laws are well known, but it is appropriate to recall here that Rome holds almost all records: the number of proceedings by the Commission for lack of implementation of its directives, the number of judgements by the Community Court of Justice, the number of judgements not executed and the number of second judgements.

A multitude of directives have still not been implemented, with negative consequences for the country both at home and abroad. Domestically, lack of implementation of important directives in the field of enterprise, labour and consumer protection retards the country's growth; abroad, infringements cloud Italy's image and weaken its negotiating position. Beside the substantial indifference of Parliament to Community rules (that contrast with the speed by which the above mentioned referendum – an exceptional practice – was convened), these infringements are due to delayed government action, the slow procedures of the Italian parliamentary system with its two perfectly equal branches, and to the failure to delegate a number of matters that could be handled more expeditiously by the executive.

To date, Community directives have been implemented through 'emergency measures': decree laws authorizing the government to deal with a variety of matters, passed whenever too many provisions for implementation have accumulated. This practice was initiated in 1957 with the law authorizing the ratification of the treaties, which empowered the executive to issue a series of decree laws to implement provisions contained in them. It has been resorted to numerous times since then: in 1960, 1965, 1969, 1970, 1982 and most recently in 1987 with law no. 183 delegating implementation of fifty-nine directives to the government. It also conferred status of law on another group of forty-one directives of a predominantly technical nature.

With the approval of law no. 86, 1989 (the so called La Pergola Law), these emergency procedures were to be replaced by a more stable and planned implementation process with fixed deadlines. The government is called upon to verify the state of conformity of the Italian order with Community law on the basis of the directives issued by Community institutions during the preceding year and to present a bill for a Community law to the Parliament. Such a law is meant to replace a short-sighted and inconclusive ad hoc practice with regular, periodic planning and to define the respective roles of government and parliament: the former proposes, the latter selects and manages the adaptation. Unfortunately, the Italian parliament did not give the bill the accelerated treatment demanded by the spirit of the reform. Consequently the impact of the provision to improve the Italian position by the end of 1990, which was strongly hoped for in order to enhance the image of the Italian presidency, did not come at all. In 1991 there has been little progress.

One structural problem which is shown by this description is the little – if any – efficiency of the ad hoc ministry that is supposed to coordinate EC matters in the Italian government. Its competences are not well defined and the position has been given in most of the cases to second rank political figures, chosen exclusively for party reasons. De facto, the authority on Community matters remains with the foreign ministry.

In the light (indeed, the shadow!) of this state of affairs, many observers, inside and abroad, imply that the nearly unanimous and unconditional support for European integration of a federal type stems to a large extent from a sense of helplessness about the capability of the political, institutional and administrative system to renew itself so as to adapt to the requirements of a modern state. Europe then represents if not a panacea, an external condition imposed upon the system to bring about such adaptation. Several precedents are often sited, such as that of the common market forcing the Italian industrial sector to jump into the pool of competition and thus becoming one of the most dynamic in the world, and of the EMS imposing monetary and economic discipline up to the point of making the lira a rather strong currency.

However, one must be aware of the risks of over-simplification. As far as the political system is concerned, it may be noted that the continuity of the government coalition throughout the decades (despite the many changes of government, that are often seen abroad as a sign of instability) has been an important factor in bringing about that foreign policy consistency and growing efficacy that was discussed above. The lack of viable political alternatives – which is often cited as the main cause of domestic political sclerosis, of corruption, of administrative inefficiency and of the estrangement of the citizens from their institutions – may be at the origin of the rather solid line Italy has followed towards Europe. Would the course of events have been the same if the Italian political spectrum had been divided in two parts as in France, each one holding the pro-European centre hostage of the extreme and unable to assemble in a government coalition?

The public administration – inefficient, corrupted and parochial – is a major handicap for Italy. The comparison with the other countries of the Community, particularly with such newcomers as Spain, is especially negative. One often-cited case is the central bank, whose standards are – by general recognition – among the most advanced in the west. The international involvement of the Bank of Italy has helped to attain such a good quality. It is not by chance that relative to the other ministries the foreign service performs rather well, especially in those branches that are working in the daily procedures of integration (EC and NATO).

The political economy

The link between domestic political economy and membership in the European Community has become crucial in the last few years. While the perspective of the 1993 fully integrated market was received in the country with the degree of enthusiasm which the widespread Europeanism would have led one to expect, soon concern was voiced as to the weaknesses of the Italian economic system in comparison with the major EC partners, particularly in the field of services. Let us look at three sectors in order of increasing difficulty as to their integrability into the Community of the 1990s: industry, finance and public administration.

The industrial complex

As is well known, Italy has a mixed economy with a high degree of state intervention: the largest holding in the country, IRI, is state owned. The private sector is made of few big companies and a multitude of medium and small firms. The role of the family is dominant not only among the latter ones, which is to be expected, but also among the former ones, as most of the large companies are linked to dynasties, either traditional like Agnelli and Pirelli, or new ones like Berlusconi and De Benedetti.

Such big industrial groups have shown a high propensity towards internationalization, out of the well-known vocation of the Italian productive system to export in order to compensate for dependency on external raw materials. However their dynamism has met with limited success.

During the first half of the 1980s, after the difficult decade of the two energy crises and worldwide recession which Italy was able to overcome resorting to its traditional resources of flexibility and adaptability, the Italian industrial complex performed well. The capital accumulation was higher than in the rest of Europe and so were profitability and productivity growth per person. The Italian share in world investment grew.

In such favourable circumstances the industrial leaders tried expansion outside national borders, particularly in France and Germany. The already mentioned disappointing outcome has been attributed to different causes, of varying importance for each case: insufficient financial strength, relative technological backwardness, absence of a national industrial strategy, external stonewalling. The intrinsic weaknesses of the Italian industrial complex became increasingly evident as the decade drew to its end.

State intervention was initiated under Mussolini to help the Italian productive sector out of the economic slump of the 1930s. It was maintained after the war and became an integral part of reconstruction – i.e. of the 'economic miracle' – as well of the political process: for instance, the nationalization of electricity production and distribution in the early 1960s coincided with 'opening to the left' and the entry of the socialist party in the government coalition, a permanent feature since then.

Today, this continuing role of the state is contested and talk of privatization is a recurring item of the political and economic debate, albeit without much of an impact. On the contrary, an attempt at partial privatization made in the late 1980s by the state-owned ENI and private Montedison to set up fifty fifty a chemical giant able to compete internationally, failed completely over the issue of control and was turned over to the national oil company in the midst of bitter controversy.

To put it in very sketchy terms, the pros of state intervention are the partial compensation for the fragmentation of the private system, as underlined above, and the support for sectors that are in a position of endemic weakness, like mining and steel production; the cons are endless subsidies with consequent distortion of competition (highly criticized abroad, particularly in the EC Commission) and – indeed, most of all – the gradual, irresistible, pervasive substitution of state with party representatives, under strict rules of political sharing, which the Italians call *lottizzazione* a word that means the division of land among the different proprietors to build their houses on.

The financial sector

The banking system has a very major asset: the Italian people's saving propensity, which is one of the highest in the world, higher than in Japan, to mention a relevant case of comparison. It seems to suffer, however, both the disease of private industry, i.e. fragmentation, and that of state control, i.e. invasion by party bosses. Most of the Italian banks are directly or indirectly owned by the state or local public authorities. If the burden of heavy labour guaranties is added, one would not be surprised at the serious concern which exists among bankers as to their ability to meet the competition of their European colleagues once full financial liberalization is achieved inside the Community.

Several attempts to generate larger and stronger banking groups have been and are being made since the liberalization of financial and capital movement was introduced in 1990, well within the time limit adopted by the Community and ever since the prospect of 1992 became clear on the horizon. Strategies are mixed and at times confused. Should one go international or not; should one absorb weaker partners or try to merge with strong ones; should one seek specialization or 'universal' capabilities? Despite the strong public control, there are almost no government guidelines. A few mergers have taken place domestically. Acquisitions or joint ventures abroad have not been easy and public control has been a major handicap – or an easy excuse for stonewalling by the interested country.

The picture is one of a difficult and long process, driven by a number of banking groups whose leadership shows a certain dynamism despite their political origin and whose management is not exempt from the traditional Italian entrepreneurship; by the wise supervision of the central bank; and by the shear perception of seeing survival at risk.

The stock market is endemically small and weak. The huge drain of savings exerted by the mountain of public debt (see below) joins in with the fragmentation and family dominance of the private sector and the public ownership of most of the banking sector to confine the Milan stock exchange to a small corner. Waiting for the Godot of privatization, the list of quotations is made of a handful of corporates and is periodically shaken by the misdeeds of a ruthless operator.

The public economic policy

The three major economic problems the Italian government is confronted with are, in order of increasing difficulty:

Energy   Since the abandonment of nuclear power in 1987, it has not been possible to formulate a sound and feasible energy policy capable of reducing the burden of imports.

Taxes   The fiscal drag in Italy is now quite comparable to the other European countries, but is unjustly distributed, so that any attempt to increase the public income in order to decrease the deficit touches upon the politically sensitive issue of seriously curbing evasion and hitting groups of taxpayers that are currently privileged.

Public expenditure and debt   Let us concentrate on the last item, which has become the critical pin-point in the process of Italy's participation in the new Community characterized by an economic and monetary union in subsequent phases. In the decade of the 1980s the debt service over GNP ratio for Italy went from 11.4 per cent to 10.2 per cent while for the other EC countries as a whole it went from 3.9 per cent to 1.1 per cent. The situation has not improved with the beginning of the 1990s.

Every autumn the domestic political debate is dominated by the issue of formulating and getting through parliament a budget for the next year which would be able to reduce the public deficit, especially in those sectors where expenditure is practically out of control because of the existing perverse mechanisms. Sweeping plans, tight measures, severe sacrifices, are regularly announced in the early phase of the debate, with the only result of mobilizing the defences of those sectors which are more affected. The government coalition is shaken and in order to keep it together some water is poured in the budgetary wine. The parliament then does the rest. The recurrent threat of breaking the coalition, wherever it comes from, has the result of keeping the option of early elections constantly open, generating an almost permanent electoral campaign, which in turn does not certainly favour tight economic policies. The vicious circle is thus closed.

In 1991 this script was played again, but the European constraint had more prominence than ever before. Although the 'Dutch memorandum', which formalized for the first time the two-speed integration concept, was rejected by other EC partners, the basic idea of a ceiling to the public debt as a condition to participate in EMU was retained, as it had the important backing of the FRG. Consequently, the perception that super-European Italy may one day be dropped out of the Community wagon because of lack of domestic economic discipline became widespread in public opinion and dominated the budgetary debate.

The debt service, as it has already been noted, is a heavy burden for the state budget. In order to attract savings, interest rates are relatively high and income from public bonds is relatively protected from fiscal drain. Such income can be as high as 5 percentage points above inflation and taxes. The perverse impact on the economy is thus double, as capitals are taken from other more productive forms of investment and interest rates are kept artificially high.

The positive effect comes from encouragement to the traditional Italian saving propensity and the attraction for foreign capital. This combines with the effort to curb inflation which had some positive results during the 1980s so that the inflation differential with Germany, increasingly the economic reference point, went down. Also because of the tenacious and wise action of the central bank, the lira is a stable currency and was able to join the narrower band in the European Monetary System in 1990.

In the last year or two, however, even these two positive factors have been weakened. The perception that the country might not be able to stay in the mainstream of European economic integration has shaken confidence in the lira. Savings are increasingly looking at Eurobonds and other investment forms that are named in ECU or foreign currencies. Foreign investment is affected by the same perception, which cumulates with the one of the weaknesses of the Italian productive system, discussed above. Consequently, such foreign investment has become very selective and the comparison with countries like Spain appear rather negative for Italy.

Optimists point out that the country has been in trouble before and has hitherto succeeded in recovering, thanks to its peculiar resources of inventiveness and flexibility. But such optimists are less and less in number, because the margins for inventiveness and flexibility, however difficult they are to measure, seem to be narrowing dramatically; moreover, the pattern and nature of international – and particularly EC – integration is such as to increasingly diminish the possibilities for special statuses and derogations, on which Italy has often tended to rely.

The new context of security

For the historical reasons discussed earlier in this chapter Italy made its basic foreign policy choices under a limited perception of threat. The motivation of *belonging* (to the new, democratic Europe, or to the alliance with the United States) was predominant over the motivation of *protection* (from the Soviet Union or other threats). Because of that perception, as well as because of the disarray and the discredit of the national military policy after the war, the country was for quite some time a 'consumer' of security and a rather passive member of NATO.

Decisions such as the deployment of nuclear weapons on national soil, taken by the alliance in the 1960s, were passed as 'technical' implementation of the obligations deriving from membership. Italian participation in such crucial strategic debates in NATO as the one on 'forward defence' was limited and marginal. It is only in the late 1970s that a new attention for security policy became evident. The debate that preceded the decision of deploying Cruise missiles in Sicily in 1979 – indeed, a crucial decision for the Alliance – was the first non-'purely ideological' debate on security issues to take place in the postwar period. In the following years, other relevant decisions were taken, such as the participation in peace-keeping forces in the Middle East, or the redeployment in Italy of the F-16 to be moved from Spain, to indicate a new, more prominent profile of foreign and military policy.

During the phase of 'basic choices' and for the reasons already mentioned Italy was part of the project of a European Defence Community that collapsed at the French Assemblée Nationale in 1954. During the phase of 'passivity' the issue of a European defence identity was not very prominent. When, later, it became more prominent, two schools of thought became evident. On one side such an identity was endorsed not only as a necessary component of a 'deepened' integration in the political realm too, but also as a way of broadening the national consensus on the new security policy, by showing that it was not identified with the one of the US only. On the other hand, there was the concern of encouraging alienation of the same United States from the defence of Europe by building an autonomous European defence.

Such two schools of thought do not coincide with any major political cleavage. They rather witness the existence of parallel concerns and often manifest themselves in government action. This was the case when in 1990 foreign minister De Michelis came out unexpectedly with the proposal of simply merging WEU into the Community (a proposal that angered the British and, outside the EC, the Americans, while it failed to win support from other partners because of lack of preparation); and then in 1991 the same minister co-signed with his British colleague a declaration that stressed the role of WEU as the European pillar of NATO.

Such apparent oscillation does not reflect so much an ambivalence of the Italian position as an inbuilt ambivalence of the very European security – or defence – identity, which is meant to be at the same time autonomous *and* linked with NATO, i.e. with the US. However, the manoeuvring of Rome is constrained by historical suspicions: thus, when its partners perform some diplomatic gymnastics with the US, with the Community and with eastern Europe, this is seen as an indication of clever and articulate foreign policy; when Italy does the same, however, observers frequently point to the traditional ambiguity and unreliability of this country.

Conclusions: Italy and three scenarios for the future of Europe

With the fall of the communist regimes, the European countries – Italy among them – have acquired a larger margin of choice and manoeuvre in the international scene. The main variable to measure how they use such a larger margin will be *integration*.

The west European countries have the option of not going any further in integrating among themselves, or even of going back a few steps insofar as the Community has not yet reached the point of irreversible integration. Let us call this scenario: *the balance of powers*, because it represents a return to the traditional power politics in European relations, a certain degree of renationalization of security policies and a growing resort to advanced forms of international economic cooperation rather than to supranational integration.

If, on the contrary, integration is accelerated, but is accompanied by the development of a rather autonomous and common profile in security policy, by protectionism and by rather defensive attitudes towards the outside world – and namely towards what one might call the 'new arch of crises' i.e. eastern Europe, the Balkans, the Middle East and North Africa – then we will have become customary to label *Fortress Europe*.

Close to this second scenario is the one of a European Community which is able to go ahead in integration, but without building political, economic, military and cultural barriers against its neighbours and partners. It is a Europe which continues the security partnership with the US and the economic partnership with North America and Japan, which opens the doors to the new democracies of the east to the degree that is allowed without endangering its cohesion, and which contributes to crisis management and to development aid. In the light of the international role thus attributed to the Community, this scenario will be called: the *European protagonist*.

Without going into any further in the discussion of these three scenarios, let us see, in conclusion, how Italy would find itself in each of them.

Italy and the balance of powers

This scenario implies a difficult 'renationalization' of Italian policy, and the virtual abandonment of its 'grand strategy', though some of its elements may be maintained. Such a model would, on one hand, be consistent with the 'logistic' weaknesses of the Italian system. On the other hand, the persistence of structural weaknesses would seriously limit Italy's capacity to present itself as an *interlocutor* of comparable, if not equal weight to that of the other European powers: i.e. it could give rise to a potential for a progressive self-imposed exclusion, associated with nationalistic tendencies proportionate to the extent of nationalism in the 'environment', which could renew the old debate of Europe v. the Mediterranean.

Within this framework based on the rules of power, Italy is not a recognized member of any major European axis – neither the 'central' Franco-German axis, nor the 'nuclear' Anglo-French axis; it is not a member of the club of the 'big' European powers (comprising two countries by virtue of military and political characteristics, and one country by virtue of economic attributes), and could therefore not even be a recognized and stable member of a possible future *directoire*. It is, of course, a valued ally. As such, it could be called upon by France (in the western Mediterranean) or by Germany (in eastern Europe – the 'hexagonal' area – and in the Mediterranean in general). But, in a balance of power scenario, these requests are likely to be in competition and conflict with one another.

This could result in a recurrence of the old Italian dilemma, i.e. the need to choose between the powers of the entente and the central empires, presented this time as a pro-German, or pro-French choice. The latter is, of course, much weaker and more unsatisfactory than the former. Among the reasons for this is the continued key role of the US in Europe and in the Mediterranean. In the balance of power model, Italy would still maintain close ties with the American protector.

Whatever the combination of possible axes, it is clear that Italy would tend to play an essentially Mediterranean role, which would be only indirectly tied to the balance of power in central Europe. This would result in greater problems specific to Italian domestic consensus.

Italy and Fortress Europe

From the Italian point of view a Fortress Europe offers significant advantages, for example:

1   A high level of security and international protection at relatively low cost (it might also lead to a collective European representation in the United Nations Security Council, at the repeated request of Italy).
2   Forestallment of difficult dilemmas, such as having to choose between France and Germany, or managing an arduous and unequal bilateral relationship with the US or with the former USSR.
3   Maintenance of a stable 'international frame of reference' for national policy choices (particularly in economy – i.e. protectionism – but also in security) to which domestic political decisions must conform, thus preventing the Italian model from 'slipping out' of the mainstream in the west and in the EC.
4   Clear confirmation of the end of the strategic distinction between Europe and the Mediterranean, offering a European cover for defensive policies against immigration.

On the other hand, this model also requires a difficult and rapid adjustment of the Italian economic and social welfare system to European, possibly even German, standards in an economic environment that is not only competitive, but protectionist and conflictual. It also requires the abandonment of an international political course of passive support, or at least 'rational' commitment in major international crises, and some degree of subordination to central European reasoning in its policy toward the Mediterranean and developing countries.

Therefore, if this model were to achieve consensus among some political forces, it would probably also give rise to sharp conflicts and could clash with the need for an abrupt change from a political model based on 'consensus' to a new model based on divisive decisions, the domestic consequences of which are difficult to predict.

Italy and the European protagonist

The European protagonist model implies the preservation of the traditional alliances and, therefore, of the major fundamental decisions Italy has made regarding its position in the alliance. European protagonist is a model that involves 'evolution'; and since it does not require a major breach in international consensus, it does not give rise to the possible divisive effects of a critical domestic debate. Furthermore, though this 'evolution' requires the continuous adjustment of the Italian system to the international one, it offers a longer timeframe and is based on parameters that are somewhat 'softer' than those of the preceding model.

On the other hand, there is in this model a lesser degree of European commitment and integration guaranteed and at the same time the need for a greater Italian disposition to make important economic, political and strategic commitments independently and voluntarily.

A European 'architecture' founded on three frameworks, one within the other – the European Community, the Atlantic–western system and the CSCE – basically corresponds to Italian requirements and preferences, provided that Italy will succeed in participating in all of them, albeit to different degrees. This points to an old problem: the institutional question of who decides and makes foreign and security policy in Italy. The question is still unresolved, because of the coexistence of various decision-making centres both within the government and administration, and within the country at large. This arrangement is consistent with the traditional Italian way of ensuring domestic political equilibrium and consensus, but makes it increasingly difficult to address complex issues and take decisions on them.

As long as there was a possibility of devolving the actual management of foreign policy to other external powers, all of this was relatively unimportant and the major foreign policy decisions therefore involved primarily a 'choice of sides'. Now that such a devolution is no longer as easy as it had been in the past, major foreign and security policy decisions have to be taken autonomously and can be hampered by what has been described here as weak Italian 'logistics'.

REFERENCES

Aliboni, Roberto (ed.) 1989: *L'Italia nella Politica Internazionale* (Yearbook). Rome: Istituto Affari Internazionali.
Bibes, Geneviève, 1974: *Le Système Politique Italien*. Paris: Presses Universitaires de Paris.
Kogan, Norman 1956: *Italy and the Allies*. Cambridge: Harvard University Press.
Kogan, Norman 1981: *A Political History of Postwar Italy*. New York: Praeger.
Lange, Peter, and Tarrow, Sydney (eds) 1980: *Italy in Transition: Conflict and Consensus*. London: Frank Cass.
LaPalombara, Joseph 1987: *Democracy, Italian Style*. New Haven: Yale University Press.
Leonardi, Robert 1987: *Italian Politics*. London: Pinter.
Mack Smith, Denis 1969: *Italy: a Modern History*. Ann Arbor: University of Michigan.
Pasquino, G. 1985: *Il Sistema Politico Italiano*. Bari: Laterza.
Sassoon, Donald 1986: *Contemporary Italy*. London: Longman.
Stuart, Hughes 1965: *The United States and Italy*. New York: Norton.
Templeman, Donald 1981: *The Italian Economy*. New York: Praeger.

10

Spain's transition to democracy

Jonathan Story

In 1992, Spain celebrates six events: the fifth centennial of Spain's unity; the world fair at Seville commemorating the fifth centennial of Columbus's voyage to the Americas; Barcelona hosts the Olympic games; and Madrid opens as the cultural capital of Europe. Spain's markets open, with a few exceptions, to competitive forces in the EC; the deadline for completion of the EC's internal market programme is set for 31 December. The celebrations record Spain's return to European counsels after a prolonged absence. The return was accomplished in the light of a constant ambition to become a full member of the first world, culminating in Spain's presidency of the European Communities in 1989. The accomplishment was that of the constitutional monarchy, confirmed in the 1978 constitution, ratified by parliament and by referendum. The process was informed by two considerations: the debates on external entanglements and commitments were woven into the politics of the domestic transitions. Their specific features were elaborated in part from the legacies of the past and of geography. The political transition entailed the conversion of the authoritarian state inherited from General Franco to a constitutional democracy, with the credentials for full participation in western Europe's society of states. The transition in economic policy was guided by entry to the EC, and the state's application of competitive principles to all factor markets. The transition in external policy entailed the elaboration of principles for action during the lengthy negotiations for Spain's full appurtenance to all key institutions of the western world.

Key determinants of policy

Since the Napoleonic invasions of 1808–13, Spain had been relegated to a backwater in European affairs, forfeiting rank among the great powers. Great Britain dominated the Straits of Gibraltar, while the Franco-German war of 1870 was prompted by France's fear of encirclement when a member of the Prussian royal family was proposed for the vacant Spanish throne.

Spain remained neutral in 1914–18. The republic was established in 1931, following the abdication of King Alfonso XIII. In February 1936, the electorate gave a majority to the left parties – the republicans, socialists and communists. In July, a military *pronunciamento* against the republic in the manner of its nineteenth-century predecessors, found prompt backing in Rome and Berlin. The Rome–Berlin axis, forged in October 1936, sent military aid to General Franco, who declared himself 'Chief of the Spanish State'. The western democracies resolved on a policy of 'non-intervention'. Only the Soviet Union supplied the Republic, but that source dried up as Stalin moved to accommodation with Hitler. Madrid fell to Franco in March 1939. The General established a corporatist state, where church, armed forces, and landowners retained their influence, alongside a docile Falange as the only accepted party. The regional autonomy of Basques and Catalans was suppressed; political parties and trade unions were crushed; universal suffrage was suspended. Franco's Spain joined the anti-Comintern pact.

Spain stayed neutral during the world war. But Franco's regime never escaped the stigma of association with the Axis powers. Franco turned down the March 1945 request of Don Juan, the Count of Barcelona and pretender to the Spanish throne, to reinstate the monarchy. In December 1946, the United Nations invited member states to break diplomatic relations with Madrid on account of the regime's origins, nature and record. Spain was excluded from Marshall Plan aid. But Franco clung to power. For him, Spain's decline and its multiple civil wars of the nineteenth century was due to the corrosive influence of liberal ideals on Spain's true, Catholic traditions. To propose that Spain adopt 'the demoliberal system of inorganic democracy' as the price for joining NATO and the EC was a prescription for decline. The regime's refusal to meet the minimum political requirements for membership in postwar Europe's prime political organizations prompted the development of an alternative external policy, as a second best to full participation in the Euro-Atlantic system. Relations were cultivated with the Moslem states and Latin America, and in the 1960s with the Soviet Union and the radical states in the developing world. Paradoxically, the policy fed on the widespread popular antipathy to the presence of the US military bases, as well as from an aversion to involvement in western affairs, arising from the history of national decline, the loss of national self-confidence and the economics of penury.

A partial escape from international pariah status was secured in 1953 through the bilateral base agreements with the United States and a concordat with the Vatican. Spain was conferred a significant role in US containment policy. The United States came to dominate the eastern Atlantic, the Straits of Gibraltar and the Mediterranean. The base at Rota, commanding the entry to the Mediterranean, forms – along with Holy Loch, Scotland, and Guam and Okinawa in the Pacific – one of the keys to US global naval and nuclear strategy. The air bases came to provide support for the US position in central Europe or as staging points for US Air Force flights through to the Middle East or to the Gulf. They were tied into worldwide control and communications systems. Iberia's geographic space was also exploited by the fact of Portugal's membership in NATO, and the US presence on the Azores; the Iberlant Command at Lisbon reports to the Supreme Allied Commander Atlantic (SACLANT), based in Virginia, and has a sub-command at Gibmed, Gibraltar. The Canary Islands lie above the Tropic of Cancer, alongside the shipping routes from the Gulf oil fields to European and North American ports via the Cape of Good Hope.

This blend in the regime's foreign posture left a central legacy to the constitutional monarchy. Opponents of the US connection sought to define a neutrality policy for Spain (Tierno Galvan, 1971, pp. 61–8; Armero, 1978, pp. 11–7). Its pre-condition was the reduction, or ideally the termination of the United States' military presence in Spain; the further development of friendly relations with the Arab states in their hostility to Israel; and the championing of southern causes in northern fora. The case was sharpened by the risks for Spain as host to US nuclear weapons, making Spain a target of the Soviet Union. The alternative was to recognize the regime's external policy as a second best, that it was not in Spain's interest to perpetuate. The protagonists of the transition to constitutional monarchy, under Juan Carlos – Don Juan's son – placed the constitution of 1978 in the lineage of its liberal antecedent of 1812. Its enactment meant the fulfilment of a long deferred promise of modernization. The internal reforms were presented and experienced by their Spanish protagonists as a recuperation of lost status and rights. Exclusion from the two leading clubs of the western world diminished Spanish prestige, and kept it on the sidelines of western economic and security relations (Ruperez, 1986; Prime Minister Gonzalez, interview, El Pais, 9 March 1986).

Another legacy of the Franco regime was that 'Europe' became synonymous with the EC and democracy, while Spanish public opinion tended to equate continuity of the Franco regime with the United States (Frey, 1988; Rodrigo, 1989, pp. 159–65). NATO suffered by association. After lengthy negotiations, a highly favourable commercial agreement was signed with the EC in 1970, opening Community industrial markets and granting access to Spain's citrus producers. The accords were to be reviewed in 1976. But Franco died in November 1975. Spain's interest was to 'integrate completely', in the words of King Juan Carlos's first speech, 'into the unity of Western nations and in all principal European institutions' (El Pais, 4 June 1976). The monarchy, Juan Carlos told the combined houses of the US Congress in June 1976, was 'inspired by the principles of democracy' (International Herald Tribune, 3 June 1976). The June 1977 elections, the first in forty years, were followed a month later by Spain's request for full membership in the EC. The political parties agreed to restrict the parliamentary agenda to the debates on the constitution, eschewing controversy on domestic and foreign policies. NATO membership was postponed to a later date, on account of extensive opposition on right and left of the political spectrum. 'Europe' provided the unifying objective around which the internal consensus for the 1978 constitution could be formed. The constitution was ratified by referendum in December 1978, with nearly 88 per cent of the 78 per cent who voted in favour, and only 7.9 per cent against.

Spain's integration into the Euro-American system was at the expense of relations with Latin America (Pike, 1971; Klaus, 1983, pp. 27–42; Escotet, 1989, pp. 52–9). Despite the Franco regime's rhetoric, the pull of the centres of power in the world economy proved stronger than cultural affinities. Spain's stabilization plan of 1959 introduced currency convertibility, linking the domestic to the international price system. Four-fifths of Spain's trade came to be with the OECD countries, whence it derived a similar proportion of technology and foreign investment. Income from tourism and worker remittances financed the trade deficit with western Europe. Trade with Latin America declined from 10 per cent in the l970s to about 3.5 per cent in the late 1980s, while capital outflows from Spain to Latin America following Franco's death, reversed direction after the eruption of the continent's debt crisis in August 1982. With Spain's entry to the EC in 1986, and GNP annual growth averaging 5 per cent, Latin Americans began to emigrate to Spain in search of work, reversing the trend that expired in the early 1960s whereby Spaniards emigrated primarily to Latin America. Nonetheless, there were 1.8 million Spanish passport holders in Latin and Central America, in addition to innumerable family ties.

A constant ambition of Spain was to establish diplomatic relations with states, regardless of the nature of their regime. The raising of the UN ban in 1950 facilitated the resumption of contacts with western states. With US support, Spain entered the United Nations in 1955, and by the early 1960s was a member of the IMF, the World Bank, and the OECD, while being a signatory to the GATT. In 1973 ambassadors were exchanged with East Germany and Mao's China. Following Franco's death in November 1975, Spain promptly entered the Council of Europe, resumed diplomatic relations with Mexico and the Soviet Union, lodged its EC candidature but postponed entry to NATO. In return, the Soviet Union favoured Madrid as the venue for the 1980 CSCE in the clear hope of encouraging Spain's neutralist tendencies. But the United States insisted on NATO entry as a precondition to the renewal of the base agreements. Spain entered NATO in May 1982 as the sixteenth member; the bilateral agreement with the United States was renewed in July. In October, the Socialist Workers Party (PSOE) won its resounding electoral victory, with a promise to hold a referendum on alliance membership. Diplomatic relations with Israel were fully resumed in January 1986, at the time of Spain's entry to the EC. The referendum on Spain staying in NATO was held in March, with the socialist government winning a narrow 52 per cent majority to stay in.

Spain, as an industrial latecomer, entered the EC in 1986 with a per capita income one-third that of the Federal Republic. Its entry pulled the EC southward into the competitive Mediterranean markets, while widening the income gap between the richest and poorest EC regions to a factor of 15:1. The agricultural land area of the Community was expanded by 30 per cent, and the farm workforce by 25 per cent. Spain was a giant competitor for non-member Mediterranean countries, particularly in olive oil and citrus, while its potential as a wine and fresh fruit producer challenged French and Italian interests. In the industrial sector, the para-statal entities such as INI or Telefonica, were flanked by multinational investment from the leading industrialized countries, with extensive ownership penetration into their Spanish sub-contractors. As entry negotiations proceeded, foreign investment poured in as the multinationals incorporated Spain into their plans to serve the wider European markets. The concomitant lowering of tariffs exposed the 99.5 per cent of Spanish firms, employing under 500, but accounting for 70 per cent of the workforce and 60 per cent of corporate investment, to the cold winds of EC competition. Such a market driven strategy meant that Spain has become a newly industrializing country, but with the benefit of being in the EC customs union.

A permanent ambition of the PSOE government was to join the leading group of member states in the EC. Spain, said Prime Minister Gonzalez in June 1985 at the ceremonies for the signing of the accession treaties, would be ready 'to advance with those who wish to advance and to wherever they wish to advance' (*Oficina de Informacion Diplomatica*, 12 June 1985). The Spanish diplomatic style envisaged the SEA, and the internal market programme, as a process requiring constant support for the strengthening of EC institutions (*Europa Archiv*, 25 October 1987, pp. 569–76). The PSOE government could thus sell the March 1986 referendum to stay in NATO as a necessary step to a more independent European foreign and security policy (*La Vanguardia*, 2 March 1986; El Pais, 9 March 1986). Prior emphasis was given in the EC to relations with Paris and Bonn (*Le Monde*, 11 February, 1988). This entailed a conscious distancing of Spain from Britain's image as a minimalist member state. Rather, Spanish diplomacy wrapped specific national interests within a broader policy, with a wider appeal to the European public. Madrid backed an EC social policy, monetary union and citizenship. Spain's recovery of status in Europe was symbolized by its tenure of the EC's rotating presidency in early 1989.

The operational environment

The western alliance provided the necessary continuity in Spain's international setting over the period of political transition, lasting from 1975 to 1986 (Tovias, 1984, pp. 158–71). Both the United States and western European governments sustained the domestic transition in multiple ways, so that priority could be given to the arduous task of internal transformation. The king played a vital part. In his speeches of 1975–7, he charted the course for a peaceful evolution to constitutional monarchy. He appointed Adolfo Suarez to implement his own programme once the June 1977 elections had been held. A considerable triumph for the king was Title II of the 1978 Constitution, that established the crown as a central institution of the parliamentary regime. The king is a symbol of 'the unity and permanence' of the state; he 'assumes the supreme representation of the state in international relations, especially with the nations of its historic community'; he exercises the supreme command of the armed forces. His decisive action on the night of 23 February 1981, when confronted with an attempted coup d'etat,[1] won him a standing ovation in the Congress of Deputies, and in 1982, he was awarded the Charlemagne prize for his contribution to European unity.

With his prestige firmly secured, the king deployed to the full his role as the new Spain's first ambassador. He advocated democratic government and human rights in his visits to Latin and Central America. He declared Spain's intent to play a full part in the western alliance before the United States Congress. His visits to China and the Soviet Union underlined the principle of universality of relations informing the constitutional state's diplomacy. His personal relations with the monarchies of Morocco, Jordan and Saudi Arabia proved a valuable asset in Spain's delicate relations with the Moslem world over oil, Israel, and the western Sahara. His family or personal relations with Europe's monarchies and presidents eased the new

Spain's path back into the European community of nations, and symbolized his status as 'the guardian and repository of Spanish liberties'. His speech of June 1986 to the European Parliament, for instance, spelt out the main lines of Spain's European policy: a united and free Europe; detente and disarmament; monetary union and the internal market; solidarity between richer and poorer parts of Europe, and of Europe with the world. (*The Times*, 15 May 1986).

The prime minister's office grew in stature as the transition proceeded. The king's first prime minister, Navarro, was still tinged by association with the Franco regime, and was overshadowed in the first half of 1976 by his foreign minister, Areilza, and interior minister, Fraga Iribarne. Suarez in May 1977 created his Union de Centro Democratico (UCD) out of fifteen different parties, ranging from centrist Christian Democrats, to liberals and social democrats. The UCD governments between 1977 and 1982 failed to chart a clear line in foreign or domestic affairs, with policies tending to fluctuate according to the changing constellation of forces. Only with the Spanish Socialist Workers Party (PSOE) October 1982 landslide victory could the main strands of policy come together in the prime minister's hands. Gonzalez gave consistent support to market liberalization, controlled ministerial appointments and played a determinant role in external policies. The trend to presidentialism was strengthened with the series of regular bilateral meetings with France, the Federal Republic, Italy, Portugal and Britain, as Spain became a full participant in Europe's diplomatic networks. Crucial foreign policy matters, such as the opening of diplomatic relations with Israel; the conduct of Spanish policy in Central America; or relations with the United States, and with the Soviet Union, were centralized.

Entry to both EC and NATO implied a reorganization of both civilian and military external policy machinery. Both congress and senate in 1977 constituted foreign affairs committees, together with a committee for human rights and IberoAmerica. Ministers were invited to present their positions to the plenary or to the committees. But the relative standing of the political parties in the electorate weighed more heavily on policy than speeches or hearings. The creation of a ministerial portfolio for Relations with the European Communities in February 1978 deprived the Ministry of Foreign Affairs of a monopoly over ensuing discussions. The Secretary of State for the European Communities was charged with 'coordinating the actions of the Spanish administration in matters relating to the Communities'. The role was accentuated with Spain's entry to the EC in 1986. The interministerial committee for economic affairs, and another on administrative affairs provided forums for information exchanges between ministries involved in EC affairs. But a scathing report by the Spanish Commissioner, Marin, on the lack of coordination between ministries, and between Madrid and the embassy in Brussels (*El Pais*, 26 June 1989) was followed by a considerable interministerial effort to tidy up bureaucratic procedures; preparation for the Spanish EC presidency of early 1989 was started in late 1987, with a close study by the Secretariat, the prime minister's office, and the foreign ministry on summit procedures. One of the acknowledged successes of the presidency was that the experience enabled the Spanish civil servants in Madrid and Brussels to become steeped in the EC policy process (*El Pais*, 26 June 1989). The daily meetings of the 'European group' in the Foreign Ministry to decide on the EPC position to be adopted that day on world affairs, definitively closed the centuries of Spain's foreign policy isolation from the centre of European affairs.

Creation of the defence ministry in 1977 was a major innovation of the Suarez administration. Franco had kept the three armed services separate, competing and under-equipped. This had led to growing discontent among the military reformers who wanted to join NATO. The new policy was to reorganize the forces; associate them more closely with western defence; withdraw them from the judicial role in civilian cases that they had played under the regime; and to completely overhaul the armaments industry. But military reforms slowed to a snail's pace. Assassinations of political and military personnel by the Basque independence movement, Euzkadi ta Eskatasuna (ETA), began in July 1977. The first serious military coup was attempted in November 1978, the most serious involving the seizure of the Congress of Deputies on 23 February, 1981, followed by at least four further recorded coups, including one alleged attempt in 1985 to assassinate the king.

The PSOE's Minister of Defence, Serra, proceeded with caution, basing his policy on support from 'modernizers' in the officer corps, favourable to the maintenance of Spain in NATO. He presented his plan for the modernization of the land army to parliament in February 1983. A new chiefs of staff was subsequently created in 1984, in a purely advisory capacity to the civilian power. The land army was territorially redeployed from the urban centres to the frontiers, with the constitution of six military regions. The key three regions were at Barcelona, covering the Balearics; the Canaries with their own command; the Straits, based on Seville (*Memoria de la legislatura,* 1982–6, Ministerio de Defensa). The military budget was increased in real terms by 4 per cent per annum, with military pay reaching parity with civil servants. Military tribunals were brought under civilian justice. A law of 1989 based the military career on expertise, and no longer on seniority, with the minister making final decisions on promotions above the rank of colonel. The reform was underpinned by Spain's membership in NATO, multiplying the contacts with the armed forces of allied countries.

Another task was reform of the Ministry of the Interior. Article 104 of the constitution defined the task of the police as the protection of the 'free exercise of rights and liberties and to guarantee the security of the citizens'. The monarchy inherited four corps, with varied statutes. The municipal police, subject to local government control, were upgraded after the sweeping electoral victory of the PSOE and the PCE in the local elections of April 1979. The Policia Armada, created in 1941 with German help, were renamed the Policia Nacional. The corps sided with the constitutional monarchy in the February 1981 coup. The plain clothes police – the Cuerpo Superior de Policia – were also subject to the Ministry of the Interior, and held a hard core of Francists. These and the Guardia Civil, subject to military command until the advent of the PSOE government, were attracted to sedition by ETA's assassinations. The promised organic law was introduced in 1986, regulating the status of the police as subordinate to central or local government authorities. But the PSOE government recruited the services of the hardliners in the Ministry of the Interior, in their battle against ETA. The terrorist Grupos Antiterroristas de Liberacion (GAL) was dissolved in 1987.

Madrid also carried its anti-terror campaign into the CSCE; the Council of Europe; through support for the EC Trevi group of Interior and Justice Minister meetings; and bilaterally, through a settlement with Paris. Sanctuary granted Basque terrorists in France under French asylum laws allowed the various Basque factions to operate with relative impunity from assured bases (*El Socialista*, July 1980; *El Pais*, 13 January 1984; *Diario 16*, 6 November 1983). Spain favoured the December 1986 European Council statement on Protection of an Open Society, and participated fully in the accompanying cooperation and exchange of information. Indeed, it joined the Schengen group of France, the Federal Republic and Benelux to end border controls in 1990, while Gonzalez expressed support for Chancellor Kohl's idea of a European federal police (*El Pais*, 7 February 1989). One of the major successes of the Spanish presidency in early 1989 was the initial EC proposal on the joint policing of external frontiers, internal movements across frontiers and cooperation on drugs, anti-terrorist measures, and tax evasion (*El Pais*, 7 June 1989).

Successive governments sought to assert the state's autonomy from church. The 1953 concordat had placed Spanish law subject to that of the Vatican (Ebenstein, 1960). The church's move in favour of political pluralism delivered a fatal blow to a regime, staking its legitimacy on the Vatican's theological patronage. One of the first powers that Juan Carlos surrendered on coming to the throne was the right to nominate bishops. The constitution only mentioned the Catholic church alongside 'other confessions', with whom the state would maintain 'consecutive relations of cooperation'. Concordats were then signed between the state and the various religious confessions, notably the Protestants and Jews. But conservative winds began to blow from the Vatican after John Paul's elevation to the papacy in 1978. The church's financial autonomy was agreed in 1979, leaving the state, either directly (through subsidies) or indirectly (through its religious tax) to contribute 90 per cent of income. The bishops nonetheless opposed the UCD's divorce law in 1980, and the PSOE's law legalizing abortion in 1983. The Law on the Right to Education (LODE) gave priority to the funding of public schools, and financed denominational schools in return for a governmental say over the selection of appointments and pupils. Both abortion and education laws were upheld by the constitutional court. But legal abortions remained uncommon, given the medical profession's aversion to the practice.

The constitution enjoins the government to maintain the sovereignty, territorial integrity and political independence of Spain. The Franco regime's suppression of regional rights had radicalized positions in the Basque country and Catalonia. Suarez moved slowly to a devolution of powers, delaying a Basque settlement until after the constitution had been sanctioned by referendum. His fear was of poisoning his relations further with Franco loyalists in the armed forces, enraged over his decision to legalize the PCE in March 1977, and determined to maintain Spain's unity. He offered all regions autonomy on equal terms, to place an upper limit on Basque and Catalan demands. A Pandora's box of regional claims was opened across the peninsula, leading to the creation of seventeen regional governments. Elections to the 'autonomous' governments were first held in 1980, but it took until November 1986 for a deal to be worked out with Madrid. Local government

revenues rose from 14 to 22 per cent of general government revenues between 1982 and 1987. The accord was to last until 1992. Funds were complemented by EC transfers. At the February 1988 Brussels European Council,
member states voted a multi-year budget until 1993, including a doubling
of the EC's 'structural' funds, going to the poorer EC regions. Within these
structural funds, Spain was allotted 35 per cent of the Community credits
for 1989–93 to be invested in underdeveloped EC regions; and over 20 per
cent of the funds earmarked for industrial problem areas (Arieto, 1989,
pp. 176–96). The EC regional funds went as additional resources of anything
between 3 to 9 per cent of revenues to the nine poorest autonomies, seven
of whose governments in 1987 were in PSOE hands (de Montbrial and
Edin, 1989, pp. 299–397). The multiplication of government layers would
not facilitate the implementation of EC legislation on the internal market.

The PSOE government's achievements were made possible by the solid
majority won in parliament in the general elections of 1982. The first landslide victory yielded 48 per cent of the votes, and 202 seats for a straight
majority in the lower house. The party was able initially to project an image
of youth, combined with responsibility and vision. Most of the membership
had joined after Franco's death; many registered as practising Catholics; the
vision was one of 'change', the maxim of the transition from Franco's regime,
and referring to the liberalization of the political system, markets and life-
styles. The PSOE's hegemony was assured by the collapse of the UCD,
following the referendum on the constitution in December 1978, and the
March 1979 general elections, yielding a plurality to Suarez' coalition. The
UCD was then rent asunder as the full political agenda of post-Franco Spain
came to the fore. The PSOE moved into the centre ground of Spanish
politics, without too much worry at being outflanked on the left by the
weakened PCE. The victory of 1982 saw the PSOE move into the heart of
the electoral territory of the centre-right parties. Any alternative majority
based on the conservative party had henceforth to move back into the centre
ground of Spanish politics, dislodging the PSOE. Equally, PSOE government
policies were made with an eye on the centre-right electorate, prompting a
loss of labour support. Electoral slippage was recorded in the narrowing
victories of 1986 and 1989. The June 1986 elections won the PSOE 44 per
cent of the vote, and 184 seats; the October 1989 elections saw the party lose
more votes, with 175 seats, just one seat under an absolute majority in the
350 seat Congress. This loss of the party's hegemony was a major factor
behind the infighting in the course of 1990 and 1991, paralysing government
action.

Foreign policy proved the most divisive aspect of the transition for public
opinion. Foreign Minister Areilza's negotiation in early 1976 for the withdrawal of Polaris submarines from Rota harbour by 1979, and the Suarez
government's accord to move slowly on NATO postponed debates on the
matter of Spain's alliances. The UCD government made NATO entry conditional on a 'national debate' (*Diario de Sesiones del Senado*, 1979, p. 1,048),
but then speeded the accession – consummated in May 1982 – in anticipation
of a PSOE victory. The PSOE promised to accept 'only a definite decision
on NATO if it is subject to consultative referendum as foreseen in the
Constitution'. The 1982–6 PSOE government then deployed its control over
the party apparatus to alter its public identification with hostility to NATO,

to one of canvassing to stay in. The use of the referendum ensured that the main debates were extra-parliamentary, conducted through the media, or in the streets. Spanish public opinion on EC entry also varied with the fortunes of the negotiations, with 58 per cent of Spaniards interviewed in April 1980 considering EC entry a 'good thing'; falling to a low in 1982, rising back to 46 per cent in favour in May 1983, and returning to 58 per cent by the end of 1984 as prospects for entry brightened (*Eurobarometre*, 1980–6). The NATO referendum, won with a 52 per cent majority, came just after the unanimous ratification by congress of the Treaty of Accession and the Single European Act. Spanish public opinion saw no major threat from the Soviet Union, and only 47 per cent considered that EC entry was good for Spain. But 70 per cent saw entry as beneficial to Spain's role in the world (Rodrigo, 1989, pp. 159–65). Public opinion's appreciation of the benefits of EC membership rose sharply in 1989 during the months of the Spanish EC Presidency.[2] After Gonzalez' successful handling of the June 1989 Madrid European Council, Spain's place in Europe was established. But as Foreign Minister Fernandez Ordonez stated, 'we are now less naive and ingenuous on the construction of Europe' (*El Pais*, 24 June 1990).

The political economy and 'Europe'

The global economic environment crucially conditioned Spain's political and market transitions. World war, and the ostracism of the United Nations, had left the Franco regime with no alternative to a policy of import substitution. All factor markets were heavily regulated. Employers secured low wage rates through the state syndicates, which offered workers a degree of job security in return. Agriculture was sustained through subsidies, and assured outlets through the state marketing networks. Interest on bank deposits and loans were set low by decree. Credit was channelled to export finance, or industrial sectors. The private banks had access to rediscount facilities. Spain in the 1960s won preferential access to world markets. Industrial exports surged. But inflation edged upwards. Tighter labour markets and workers' dissatisfaction with the state controlled syndicates prompted wage pressure. The rise in oil prices in 1973–4 tipped the current account into deficit. From January 1974 on, the governments of Prime Minister Navarro dithered between stop and go, and finally shelved expansionary plans in December 1975. In October 1976, a $1 billion dollar jumbo Kingdom of Spain loan was floated. The loan served as a signal to financial markets that the US government backed Spain's transition, in that it acted as lender of last resort for the economic costs incurred.

Spain lodged its bid for full EC membership on 25 July 1977. Madrid feared EC industrial protection, and demanded access to agricultural markets comparable to non-member Mediterranean countries. The negotiations proved a protracted affair. As the Commission pointed out in its March 1978 'Reflections' on the Mediterranean enlargement, the three new members on entry would generate an EC-wide surplus in cash crops (*Financial Times*, 3 March 1978). The initial transition periods suggested by the Commission ranged from five to ten years, but no date for entry was mentioned. The EC budget resources would have to be raised. Spain had to enter the customs union, bringing down its high industrial tariffs and restrictive quotas and align on the common external tariff. In April, the Commission indicated that Spain should participate in EC industrial 'restructuring' policies (*Le Monde*, 21 April 1978). Import quotas were imposed on Spanish steel exports. Spain was to be granted a three-year transition period to reduce industrial protection. Value added taxes (VAT) were to be introduced on the day of entry to the EC, ending the tax export subsidies available. There were to be no discussions about agriculture or the customs union, until Madrid concurred on the tax issue. Entry talks were officially opened in February 1979; Spain, said Foreign Minister François-Poncet, had to accept the 'acquis communautaire' (*Le Monde*, 7 February 1979).

The June 1977 elections were followed by the Moncloa pact between the political parties in October. The pact laid out the lines for an anti-inflationary economic policy, involving wage restraint, tax reform, and financial market liberalization. But growth rates fell from 3 per cent in 1978 to under 1 per cent on average through to 1982. Profits were squeezed, and new investment fell. Domestic savings declined, while the public sector deficit rose from under 1 per cent to 6 per cent GNP. The second oil shock then prompted a doubling of the trade deficit, with the government seeking to meet external obligations by winding down reserves. Foreign debt edged up. Successive UCD governments were unable to resist business and union clamour for corporatist policies, requiring the postponement of tariff liberalization and further subsidies to loss-making enterprises. Financial market reforms were stalled, as bank balance sheets became burdened with corporate debt. Export promotion and 'buy Spanish' policies helped move Spain to a growing trade surplus with France and Britain, while the Federal Republic was in surplus with Spain only on trade account. Enlargement slipped off the front of the EC's agenda. The Spanish business community's lack of confidence was compounded by concern about the impending electoral victory of the Socialist Party (PSOE) in October 1982.

With its majority assured, the socialist government's main task was to put Spain to work again. This meant giving priority to corporate profits, thereby renewing business confidence, investment and job creation. Macroeconomic policies were set on a disinflationary course. Consumer price increases at 14 per cent in 1982, fell to under 5 per cent by 1988, and then began to rise slightly into 1990. Unemployment rates rose from 16 per cent of the active population to a peak of 21.5 per cent in 1985, falling back to 16 per cent by 1990. Profits returned to the levels of the early 1970s. An export boom into the US markets in the first three years of the PSOE government sustained activity, while restraint in domestic consumption was registered in a fall in imports. This highly restrictive policy was modified by an expansionary budget in April 1985, a few days after the conclusion of Spain's EC entry negotiations. Growth picked up to an average of 5 per cent, raising government revenue. Public borrowing fell below 3 per cent GNP. Non-residential investment, negative since Franco's death, soared. Expansion was helped by the fall in the oil price in 1986, by a surge in the tourist business, and by a huge influx of foreign capital, equivalent to 3 per cent GNP per annum. The peseta, devalued in December 1982 by 8 per cent, remained soft until 1986, and then rose 10 per cent between 1987 and May 1989. The trade deficit quadrupled, pulling the current account into a widening deficit from 1988 on.

A vigorous industrial adjustment programme was implemented, and the public sector was purged. Spain's EC entry talks had advanced at a snail's pace until the German EC presidency of early 1983. Bonn became the PSOE's objective ally in pushing hard to complete the chapters of trade and industry in the Spanish entry negotiations (Gonzalez Sanchez, 1984, pp. 477–97). A comprehensive white paper on reindustrialization was published in 1983, becoming effective as law by December 1984 (OECD Economic Survey, *Spain*, 1986, pp. 34–41). The PSOE administration deployed the system of obligatory reserves authoritatively to effect the turnaround in the state industrial sector during its first three years in power. The policy held two key components: the improvement of productivity and the restoration of profits in sectors such as steel, shipbuilding, white goods or textiles. The policy stipulated a reordering of the inherited para-public sector through a mixture of cutbacks in the state holding company, INI; privatization, such as the sale of SEAT to Volkswagen; the creation of more coherent corporations, such as REPSOL, the energy conglomerate; and the raising of capital by para-public companies, particularly Telefonica, through listing on international stock markets. Spain became an eager participant in the EC research programmes; in the IEPG defence collaborative projects; corporate alliances were encouraged to compensate for the lack of indigenous research and development (Castella et al., 1986).

Spain became an eldorado for multinational companies. There was limited government concern about Spanish national assets being taken over (*Financial Times*, 8 October 1988). Grants and aid were forthcoming. By 1984, Ford, IBM and GM were Spain's largest manufacturing exporters. The Japanese were also attracted to Spain as a springboard into EC markets, recording a sharp jump in their stakes. EC entry saw a further liberalization of laws on foreign investment. EC investors moved up from 48 to 65 per cent of a total inward investment of 34 billion dollars between 1985 and 1988 (*Financial Times*, 16 October, 1988). The United States share fell from 20 to 13 per cent, with the Japanese at 4 per cent of the total. France and Germany led in industrial investment, especially in the motor industry with the Germans also strong in chemicals. The attractions of Spain included low wages; the laxer pollution standards; and the positive position of the government on the Single European Act.[3] For the Spanish government, the Rome treaties provided additional means to open up Spain's oil and tobacco monopolies to closer integration with the multinationals (*Tribune de l'Economie*, 31 July 1987; *Financial Times*, 31 March 1989); to design competition law on EC lines; to centralize decision on subsidies, and EC funds in Madrid; and to negotiate derogations with Brussels on aspects of the EC's internal market programme.

Financial market reform was pushed through in the favourable circumstances of the prolonged boom on world stock markets that started in 1983. The consistent agent of reform since 1974 was the Bank of Spain (Graham, 1984; *Financial Times Banking and Finance Special*, 16 June 1986, 17 July 1987, 23 June 1988 and 21 June 1989). The first steps towards reducing the political influence in government of the private bank cartel came with the lifting of restrictions on the opening of new bank outlets. Reforms were then stalled when the bank obliged the major institutions to absorb the costs of the multiple bank failures during the years 1978 to 1983, and to hold growing quantities of government debt.

Liberalization of capital markets was introduced by the PSOE administration as part of a wider package to promote non-inflationary funding of government requirements; to free up the capital markets to a share-holding public; and to extend more transparent corporate auditing. Adaptation to the anticipated EC single market in financial services served as a permanent refrain. Laws on capital markets and on companies in February and April 1988 laid the basis for the deregulation of stock markets in July 1989. Foreign financial institutions held 14 per cent of the national financial market by 1990, against under 1 per cent in 1978.

Fiscal reforms were initiated with a view to financing a more extensive coverage of social programmes. But the rise in tax pressure was not offset by an improvement in the quality of public services. Four-fifths of the tax burden in 1990 still fell on wage and salary earners. The PSOE's tax policy was restricted to tightening up on fraud, and the introduction of VAT in preparation for EC entry on 1 January 1986. In labour markets, the government modified the laws restricting rights of dismissal, allowing for part-time employment. This was not sufficient to prevent a steady deterioration in relations with the trade unions. Unemployment rates remained high. Trade unions demanded redistribution, and not just priority to profits as the motor for investment. Inflationary pressures undermined contractual commitments, as prices tended to outrun promised wage rises. Social security deficits placed severe limits on unemployment benefits or pensions. Matters came to a head when the two trade union organizations called a successful general strike for 14 December 1988, in response to a government plan to provide first jobs for youngsters at minimum wages and without contracts. The trade unions feared for job security. The government held to its position that Spain's sole comparative advantage in EC markets was low labour costs. Nonetheless, the rise in unit labour costs over the decade averaged 6.8 per cent annually, eroding Spain's comparative advantage.

Entry to the EC prompted an historic shift in Spain's external accounts. The net flow of funds into Spain through the EC budget was equivalent to 6 per cent of the 1987, and 7 per cent of the 1988 trade deficits with the EC, despite the doubling of EC funds (*Oficina de Informacion Diplomatica*). Spain's overall trade deficit in 1988 was 6 per cent of GNP. OECD Europe's share in total Spanish imports rose from 41.6 per cent in 1985 to 62.4 per cent in 1988. The EC's share of imports was 56.7 per cent, with the United States displaced to the fifth supplier after Germany, France, Italy and Britain (*OECD Economic Surveys*, 1986–90). The fall in income on services, plus the rise in royalty or dividend payments, plunged the current account into widening deficit. Spain's external accounts came to be balanced by a dependence on foreign direct investment to service EC markets; and on short-term capital inflows attracted by the high interest rates set by the Bank of Spain in its attempt to manage the public debt, and to keep inflationary pressures under control. The decision of Madrid to join the ERM in June 1989 (*El Pais*, 7 June 1989) was in part inspired by the aim to hold down the peseta, while joining a stable exchange rate zone that would set the measure for future wage negotiations. The influx of funds after 1985 provided the Bank of Spain with a cushion of currency reserves of 52 billion dollars by end 1990.

Spain and world politics

Spain's transition was conducted in a turbulent international environment, whose structure, nonetheless, remained remarkably stable. The re-ordering of Spain's defence policy lasted twelve years, from the signing of the Hispano-American Treaty of Friendship and Cooperation signed in January 1976 to 1988, with Spain's entry to the West European Union (WEU), the definition of Spain's role in NATO, and an eight-year base agreement, reducing the United States' position in Spain. This trajectory traced the initial focus of the transition predicated on a reinforcement of the US position in Iberia, entry to NATO and modernization of the armed forces, to the definition of a national defence policy from within NATO conceived of as western Europe's defence alliance which included the United States.

The starting point was the 1976 treaty. It established a council, to meet twice a year at the level of the US Secretary of State and Spain's Minister of Foreign Affairs; and it defined a combined interest zone, covering 1,400 square miles including the eastern Mediterranean and the east and south Atlantic. A combined staff was set up at Madrid to facilitate cooperation on operations, logistics and intelligence. Entry to NATO was postponed. With the treaty expiring in September 1981, the Reagan administration insisted that NATO entry and new base accords be negotiated in parallel. The government won the parliamentary debates on NATO entry of October and November, and Spain was invited as sixteenth member in December. The protocol of membership was deposed in Washington on May 30 1982. The new base accords were signed with the United States in June. But in the subsequent discussions of July–October 1982 on Spain's future role in the alliance, it was agreed that the Madrid NATO command – adapted from the former combined staff – would hold responsibility for the Canaries–Gibraltar–Balearics axis, outlined in the 1976 treaty (Lopez de la Torre, 1987, pp. 115–32). This new Allied Forces West (AFWEST) was to have the rank of a major subordinate command, equivalent to AFCENT, AFNORTH and AFSOUTH, and report like them directly to the Supreme Allied Commander (SACEUR). Following its crushing electoral victory of October 1982, the PSOE government had the base accords ratified, but Spain's membership in NATO was frozen, pending the referendum, held in March 1986. The government, in the wording of the referendum question, implied that Spain would not enter NATO's 'military' structure; that nuclear weapons would not be introduced or installed in Spain; and that the United States presence in the bases would be cut back. The terms of this conditional membership were negotiated in the subsequent three years. Spain was to develop the European dimension of its deterrence and security policy.

Finally approved in December 1988, Spain's form of participation in NATO was distinct from that of France (de Ojeida, 1989, pp. 58–90; *Independiente*, 5 March 1988). As a non-nuclear state, Spain remained in the Nuclear Planning Group, where the Europeans consult on US policy. The Spanish armed forces coordinate, rather than integrate, with the allied commands through the device of 'operative control' whereby Spanish or allied forces may fall under each other's direction within their specific zones. Spain participates in the elaboration of NATO defence plans, in that it is in the Defence Planning Committee and has observers with the allied commands. The allies agreed, furthermore, that Spain stay in the Military Committee on the grounds that it functions more like a diplomatic forum than a military structure. But above all, Spain was primarily concerned with its own strategic zone. Its specificity arises from the fact that the Mahgreb countries are Spain's most likely potential enemy, and are out-of-NATO area. The Seville regional military command, covering the Straits of Gibraltar, is thus the best equipped. In NATO, Spain's mission is conceived of essentially as a rearguard to the central area. The air force and navy have most experience of working with allied forces in the eastern Atlantic, the western Mediterranean and the Straits. Bilateral agreements exist with Italy and France on matters relating to security in the western Mediterranean.

To Spain, the British position in Gibraltar compromised its right to pursue a national security policy in that Britain's infringement of the principle of territorial integrity – condemned in a UN General Assembly vote in 1967 – could engage Spain in hostilities not of its own making (Sanchez-Gijon, 1978, pp. 61–91). Britain's case rested on the right of self-determination; any negotiation had to be preceded by a raising of the blockade on Gibraltar imposed under the Franco regime in 1969. Agreement was finally reached in November 1984 (*El Pais*, 28 November 1984): the two governments pledged to hold negotiations to resolve 'all the differences' between them, including their competing definitions of the sovereignty issue. Free movement of people was established in February 1985. The accord opened the way to a normalization of relations between the two countries (*El Pais*, 24–5 April, 1986), exemplified in King Juan Carlos's visit to London in April 1986, and in Queen Elizabeth's visit to Madrid in October 1988. Britain's claim to the Rock, based on self-determination, opened the way for Spain to win over the Gibraltar population through persuasion.

Negotiations for the reduction of the US military presence began in 1985, when the United States administration conceded the principle in the hope that it would help the PSOE government win the March 1986 referendum. Talks opened in May 1986. Spain aimed to scale down the US air force use of Torrejon, in the proximity of Madrid. After eight rounds of discussions, Madrid announced in November 1987 that the existing accords would be allowed to expire in April 1988, unless the United States conceded. Madrid's intent was multiple: it was to alter ingrained US–Spanish perceptions of the relation as one between patron and client. It was also to further limit the United States, freedom to use the facilities in Spain for out-of-NATO area actions, particularly in the Middle East and the Gulf. Not least, it was to allow the Spanish Air Force to take over some of the tasks of the USAF out of Torrejon. When Washington finally conceded to Spanish demands, negotiations were started on an eight-year bilateral defence pact. The new agreement, signed in December 1988, engaged the United States to withdraw the USAF Wing 401 from Torrejon within three years; Rome agreed to base them in Italy. But equally, the eight-year duration of the accords and their lack of military–industrial content pointed to Madrid's intent to act as an ally, rather than as a client intent on extracting the highest possible price for his services from the patron. It was as an ally of the United States that the government accepted the USAF's B-52 flights out of the military bases for the bombing of Baghdad during the war against Iraq in early 1991.

The PSOE government also edged towards a closer definition of Spain's non-nuclear status, that both reflected the hostility in public opinion to the presence of nuclear weapons on Spanish territory but assumed the obligations of NATO membership (Remoro Brotons, 1987, pp. 112–34; 1988, pp. 110–24; Herrero, 1988, pp. 51–69). During the EC negotiations in 1983 on Spain's joining Euratom, Spain agreed to sign a specific accord with Euratom and the International Atomic Energy Agency (IAEA) in Vienna to submit its nuclear installations to the same controls as member states (Gonzalez Sanchez, 1984, pp. 489–90). It explicitly recognized alliance nuclear doctrine on joining the Nuclear Planning Group in August 1986, and then signed the NPT. Spain was invited to subscribe to the October 1987 WEU document, 'Platform on European Security Issues', that reiterated NATO doctrine on nuclear deterrence and forward defence. But talks were opened only after the European allies has been satisfied that Madrid had settled bilateral relations with Washington. Spain's entry to WEU thus tokened its de facto subscription to European NATO strategy. Its commitment to prohibit nuclear weapons on Spanish territory was limited by the allied nuclear powers' denial of information on the presence of nuclear weapons in visiting warships or aircraft.

A key concern of the new PSOE government, as mentioned, was to subject the armed forces to civilian authority. It also took over and accentuated, its predecessor's efforts, to modernize Spain's military industries. The Ministry of Defence became a major economic agent. The state's industrial instrument was the INI, which controlled 70 per cent of arms production in Spain (Daguzan, 1988; Serra, 1987, pp. 69–77). INI was associated in co-production projects with major US and European armaments corporations, and co-production agreements were signed with the United States, France, the Federal Republic, Italy, the United Kingdom, Belgium, Sweden and Morocco. Offset arrangements were negotiated with a view to maximizing production in Spain. An ambitious electronics plan was launched, heavily geared to military consumption. Spain joined multi-national projects such as the European Fighter Aircraft (EFA), and the Eureka project to create Europe-wide research and development networks. Spain stayed an active participant in NATO procurement activities, and in the Independent European Programme Group (IEPG), which Defence Minister Serra presided from 1986 to 1988. Above all, production costs were defrayed by sales onto world markets, including to Chile, Libya and the Gulf states (Holland, 1988, p. 108; Rodrigo, 1989, pp. 159–65).

The Europeanization of Spain's security policy was woven into the growth of EPC. Spanish diplomacy worked closely with the fifteen NATO member 'western Group' in the CSCE follow-up conference in Madrid, opening in 1980 (Story, 1978, pp. 2–57; Sanchez-Gijon, 1980, pp. 615–24); and it was associated with EPC, in particular over the Middle East, and Poland. Entry to NATO brought Spanish–Soviet relations to a nadir (*El Pais*, 8 September 1981; *Le Monde*, 10 September 1981). With the PSOE election in October 1982, the climate of relations improved: in particular, Gonzalez in September 1983 used Spain's position as host to steer the CSCE to a conclusion.

Gorbachev's advent to power in March 1985, seen by Gonzalez as a historic opportunity to move towards an era of negotiations in east–west relations (*El Pais*, 15 March 1988), meant that the NATO referendum was held in a more relaxed climate of international relations. Gonzalez welcomed the December 1987 Washington Treaty, eliminating intermediary range nuclear weapons. Madrid favoured confidence building measures in the conventional stability talks, that opened in Vienna in March 1989. The regime changes in central and eastern Europe in late 1989 set Spain's own transition as an example, though conducted under very different conditions, for a peaceful inclusion into a European order of constitutional pluralist states.

Spain brought its own concerns into NATO and the EPC. As Gonzalez stated, the Atlantic alliance was the only forum where it was possible to oblige United States policy to take a certain European dimension (*La Vanguardia*, 3 February 1986). With 20 per cent of exports going to the countries of the southern Mediterranean, and as a neighbour of the Arab nation, Spain had an evident interest in diplomatic rather than military resolutions to conflicts in the whole region. Gonzalez stated that 'a just and peaceful solution in the Middle East will have to be based on Israel's retreat from all of the Arab territories occupied since 1967' (Armero, 1989, pp. 212–20). This did not prevent Spain condemning the Iraqi invasion of Kuwait in August 1990, dispatching a warship to the zone, and supporting the United Nations resolutions calling for an unconditional withdrawal. Similarly, Spain had regular conflicts with the Mahgrebi states over territorial claims; fishing rights; and competition among cash crop producers for access to EC markets. The Maghreb armed forces greatly outweighed Spain's. NATO membership therefore provided more security. EC entry meant that Maghreb states' main negotiating partner on cash crop markets and fisheries was no longer Madrid, but Brussels; Spain's concern on the western Sahara was moved on to the EPC's formal agenda.

As a full participant in all western Europe's major institutions, Spain would plead for a more comprehensive attitude towards Latin America in NATO (Aldecoa, 1986, pp. 242–3), and in the EC. Spain's support for democracy, human rights, and market reforms, together with other socialist or christian democrat parties, could help to marginalize the political extremes in the region, and to reduce the involvement of the great powers. Gonzalez received extensive support in western Europe, as well as in the US Congress (*El Pais*, 13 April 1985), to work for a peace settlement in Central America. The result was the October 1984 meeting in San José, Costa Rica, of twenty-one Foreign Ministers, including the five from Central America, and four in the Latin America Contadora group, the ten EC Foreign Ministers, as well as the Foreign Ministers of Spain and Portugal. Successive San José meetings elaborated a Community support for the democratization process in the area. President Bush at the May 1989 Atlantic Council meeting referred to Gonzalez' 'leadership' on western Central American policy (*El Pais*, 31 May 1989). Yet in December 1989, Spain's opposition in the United Nations was of no account in the United States' determination to invade Panama.

The substance of Spain's EC entry had been about reciprocal access to EC markets. Germany took the lead in prising open Spain's industrial markets. Spain was granted seven years to reduce industrial tariffs, but most quotas on imports had to be terminated on entry. Tariff levels were to fall by 52.5

per cent by 1989. The VAT, replacing cascade taxes, was to be introduced immediately. The results were soon visible in that Spain's bilateral net trade deficit with the Federal Republic was by 1987 equivalent to 75 per cent of Spain's trade deficit with the EC; 97 per cent of the imports from Germany were capital goods (*Oficina de Informacion Diplomatica*, pp. 165–73). On agriculture, the tone of negotiations was set by France and Italy. The final terms shackled Spain's comparative advantage: in particular, wines and olive oil were subject to production quotas; Spain's highly competitive fruit and vegetable sectors were given ten years' transition for full access; Spain's low productivity milk, beef or cereals had a limited period to adapt. On fisheries, Spain's access to EC waters was limited to 150 boats. Luxemburg grudgingly conceded free movement of labour into the EC after a seven-year transition, but subject to review after five.

Spain's entry to the EC has been accompanied by a revision of EC trade policies towards the United States and Japan, on the one hand, and to the EFTA countries and COMECON, on the other. It opened a further round in the world struggle for access to food markets between the United States, the major non-European suppliers such as Argentina and Australia, and the EC farm policy. Spanish food markets presented a major chance for France's northern cerealist and cattle interests. They managed to have the EC negotiate an increase of the Spanish tariff on maize and sorghum from the United States, from 20 per cent to 140 per cent. As Spain had sourced nearly all corn, sorghum and oilseed imports from the United States, Washington argued that the markets foregone by US exporters amounted to $400 to $600 million annually. In the first year of EC membership, Spain's farm trade moved into deficit, with the EC import share in total food imports doubling to 42 per cent (*OECD Economic Survey*, 1987–8, p. 22). The United States in 1987 won a respite from the EC for a period of four years, during which Spain agreed to import 2 million tonnes of maize, and 300,000 tonnes of sorghum per annum, thereby restricting the market for the French cerealists (*Le Monde*, 2 January 1987). The struggle for Spanish food markets would reopen in 1991.

Concluding remarks

Following General Franco's death, Spain became a full member of the first world, within which it recovered constitutional government and international status. The constitution of 1978 meant fulfilment of a long deferred promise of modernization. Political transition entailed extensive reorganization of the state apparatus and personnel. Economic transition was implemented by the PSOE governments through an assertion of state autonomy from inherited corporate interests, and with a view to opening markets to competition. Spain defined its specific status in the Atlantic alliance.

As evidenced during the IGC on political union in the course of 1991, Spain favoured a European security policy that incorporated the United States, but that upgraded the WEU as an instrument of EC foreign policy. As Gonzalez recurrently argued, German unity called for a strengthening of the EC institutions as the central pillar of the new European architecture. This meant extending further policy areas to the EC, and increasing the powers of the European Parliament. Gonzalez' particular proposal was to urge the creation of a European citizenship, thus bringing the elitist process of EC integration closer to the concerns of national electorates. But this alignment with France and Germany in the development of EC institutions, nonetheless, went along with strong logistical support for the United States during the Gulf war of early 1991, and the elaboration of a more active Spanish policy towards Latin America, after repeated disillusion over the EC's readiness to devote more resources to the countries of the western hemisphere.

Spain's holding of the EC presidency in early 1989 coincided with the transformation in the global security system. Spanish public opinion welcomed German unity, and favoured the EC's rapid development along federal lines. The anchoring of a united Germany into a European political and market entity would be the counterpart to Germany's crucial role in bringing Spain into the EC. That entity would promote the regime changes in central and eastern Europe, and be cohesive enough to associate in a variety of forms with an eventually reformed Russia.

However, there was also the concern about Spain's future in the new Europe. Would Spain count among the decisive powers shaping Europe's future, as mapped out by the heads of state or government at the December 1991 Maastricht Summit, or would Europe's transformation in the last couple of years once again place the peninsula on Europe's periphery, as Germany became introverted and the member states proved unable to reach an effective common policy in response to the 1991 Gulf war, the collapse of the Soviet Union or the disintegration of Yugoslavia? The results of the IGCs at Maastricht set Spanish eyes on the European horizon of 1997–2000 (see chapter 14 on monetary union). But the real challenges were more immediate: the world recession in the early 1990s, the soaring birth rates in the Maghreb and immigration to Spain, the renewed demands for self-determination in the Basque country and Catalonia, following the example of the Baltic states, Slovenia and Croatia. Events would show whether Spain would consolidate its position in the lead group of states urging the construction of a more federalized European Community, or be cast back to the western periphery of a Europe with its centre in Berlin.

NOTES

1 'The Crown, symbol of the permanence and unity of the fatherland, does not tolerate in any way', the King broadcast to the nation on television at the height of the crisis, 'actions and attitudes of persons who aim to interrupt by force the democratic process that the Constitution voted by the Spanish people had fixed . . . by means of a referendum'. Mensaje del Rey, El Pais, 24 February 1981.
2 ABC, 6 June 1989 reports Eurobarometre findings to the effect that between autumn 1988 to spring 1989, Spanish support for European union rose from 79 to 83 per cent; for the internal market from 59 to 69 per cent. The Social Charter, by 72 per cent, and EC environmental policies, by 86 per cent.
3 Favourable comments in the German business press abound. Examples in General Anzeiger, 17 September 1987; Handelsblatt, 21 January 1988; a favourable survey, entitled 'Preussen des Südens', Die Welt, 27 June 1989. In the French press, the theme of Spain as eldorado also caught on, viz. Le Figaro, 21 February 1989. Particularly appreciated

was 'Le bon choix', *Le Monde*, 26 December 1988, referring to the Spanish government's decision on the Madrid–Seville high-speed train, splitting the deal two ways: France's Alsthrom won construction of twenty-four trains, as well as the ownership of two Spanish engine construction companies; Germany's Siemens won construction of seventy-five locomotives. The Japanese were reported as excluded because of reluctance to transfer technology: *Le Point*, 8 January 1989. The deal was appreciated in Bonn and Paris, as an appetizer for the Spanish Presidency.

REFERENCES

Arieto, Javier 1989: Los avances en la integración europea durante los primeros meses de la precidencia española. *Política Exterior*, 3(10), Spring, 176–96.
Armero, José Mario 1978: *La Política Exterior de Franco*. Barcelona: Planeta.
Armero, José Mario 1989: *Política Exterior de España en Democracia*. Madrid: Espasa Calpe.
Castella, Manuel; Barrero, Antonio; Casal, Pilar; Castano, Cecilia; Escario, Pilar; Melero, Javier; Nadal, Javier 1986: *Nuevas Tecnologías, Economía y Sociedad en España*. Madrid: Alianza Editorial.
Daguzan, Jean François 1988: *L'Espagne: à la Croisée des Chemins*. Fondation pour les Etudes de Defence Nationale. Midi-Pyrenées: Published.
de Arenal, Celestino and Aldecoa, Francisco 1986: *España y la OTAN: Textos y Documentos*. Madrid: Editorial Tecnos.
de Montbrial, Thierry and Edin, Jacques 1989: La nouvelle Espagne. *RAMSES 90: Le Monde et son Evolution*, 299–397.
de Ojeda, Jaime 1989: El modelo español de participación en la allianza Atlántica. *Politica Exterior*, 3(9), 58–90.
Ebenstein, William 1960: *Church and State in Franco Spain*. Research Monograph, no. 8. Princeton: Center for International Studies.
Escotet, Miguel Angel and Mujal-León, Eusebio 1989: L'Espagne du Franquisme à la Democratie. *Géopolitique*, Spring, 52–9.
Frey, Peter 1988: *Spanien und Europa, Die Spanischen Intellektuellen und die Spanische Integration*. Bonn: Europa Union.
Gilmore, David 1985: *The Transformation of Spain: From Franco to the Constitutional Monarchy*. London: Quartet.
González Sánchez 1984: Las Negociaciones de adhesión de España a las communidades Europeas. *Revista de Instituciones Europeas*. Madrid, 11(2), 477–97.
Grabendorff, Wolf 1987: Die Beziehungen der Europaischen Gemeinschaft zur Lateinamerika. *Europa Archiv*, 22, 645–54.
Graham, Robert 1984: *Spain: Change of a Nation*. London: Michael Joseph.
Herrero, Miguel 1988: Contribución de España a la seguridad europea. *Política Exterior*, 2(5), 51–69.
Holland, Martin 1988: *The European Community and South Africa*. London: Pinter.
Klaus, J. 1983: Hispanidad, gestern und heute. *Europaische Rundschau*, 11(3), 27–42.
López-Rodó, Laureano 1987: *Testimonio de una Política de Estado*. Barcelona: Editorial Planeta.
Lopez de la Torre, Salvador 1987: España-OTAN: pasado, presente, y futuro. *Política Exterior*, 1(1), 115–32.
Maliniak, Thierry 1990: *Les Espagnols: de la Movida à l'Europe*. Paris: Centurion.
OECD Economic Survey 1986, 1987–8, 1989, 1990–1, 1992: Paris.
Pike, Frederick B. 1971: *Hispanismo, 1898–1936: Spanish Conservatives and Liberals and their Relations with Latin America*. Notre Dame: University of Notre Dame.
Pollack, Benny 1987: *The Paradox of Spanish Foreign Policy*. London: Pinter.
Remiro Brotons, Antonio 1987: Armas Nucleares y territorio español. *Política Exterior*, 1(3), 112–34.
Remiro Brotons, Antonio 1988: La cooperación europea en asuntos de seguridad: una perspectiva española. *Politica Exterior*, 2(8), 110–24.

Rodrigo, Fernando 1989: La opinión pública en España y los problemas de defensa. *Política Exterior*, 3(9), 159–65.

Rupérez, Javier 1986: *España en la OTAN, Relato Parcial*. Barcelona: Plaza y Janes.

Sánchez-Gijón, Antonio 1980: Spanien als Gastgeber des zweiten KSZE-Folgetreffen. *Europa Archiv*, 25 October.

Sánchez-Gijón, Antonio 1978: *España en la OTAN*. Madrid: Ediciones Defensa.

Serra, Eduardo 1987: El GEIP y la cooperación transatlántica en materia de armamentos. *Política Exterior*, 1(3), 69–77.

Story, Jonathan, 1978: Le printemps de Madrid. *Politique Etrangère*, 1, 2–57.

Tierno Galván, Enrique 1971: politica internacional. *España: 1970*. Madrid.

Tovias, Alfred 1984: The international context of democratic transition. In Geoffrey Pridham (ed.), *The New Mediterranean Democracies: Regime Transition in Spain and Portugal. West European Politics*, 7(2), 158–71.

Vilar, Sergio 1986: *La Decada Sorprendente, 1976–1986*. Barcelona: Planeta.

PART IV
EC Policy and Diplomacy

PART IV

EC Policy and Diplomacy

Editor's introduction

The fourth part deals with four aspects of western European statecraft, where the emphasis is on the reciprocal influence of European politics on Europe's relations with the rest of the world. A thread running through all chapters is the perennial efforts of the European states to preserve room for pursuit of particular policies and interests, while promoting collective approaches for common policies and concerns.

The principal forum is the European Communities, whose revival and development since the negotiations in 1985–6 launching the Single European Act, and the Maastricht European Council of December 1991, forms the substance of the following discussions. The competences of the EC have extended into an ever wider range of domains. The Communities' renaming at Maastricht as the European Union bear token to its aspirations. The accords chart out a course of action, and a timetable for further amendments, through to the year 2000.

Foreign policy cooperation between the EC member states has developed as a central element in their foreign policies, and as one pillar of the European Union. Of longer standing, EC trade policy, where the Commission takes a leading role, makes the Community a key player in international trade negotiations. With the strong backing of business interests, the internal market programme represents a large scale rethinking of international co-operation, and has far-reaching implications outside European boundaries. The move to monetary union, earmarked for 1997 at the earliest, has merged into the wider debates on Europe's future shape, following Germany's unity in the course of 1990, and the collapse of the Soviet Union in 1991.

11

European political cooperation

Elfriede Regelsberger

The second half of the 1980s: a new stage in the history of EPC

Since the Single European Act (SEA) – which constitutes the main revision of the EEC treaties and the legal codification of European Political Cooperation (EPC) – was signed in 1986, the world and Europe have changed profoundly. The rapid evolution of the EC towards the 1992 goal, German unification, the Gulf war and the revolutions and subsequent radical political changes in eastern Europe have considerably affected the European political cooperation procedures and its performance. Even more than in other phases of its history, European political cooperation has been the product and at the same time the factor of the changes in its environment and time.

Measured against these challenges – both external and internal – the period under review could be understood as a new stage in the evolution of EPC. But also with regard to the intensity of cooperation among the EC governments, the functioning of the internal mechanisms and the quality of the *acquis politique* (i.e. the final product of the twelve's common deliberations and actions) the progress achieved over the past years is obvious – all the more so compared to the earlier periods of EPC (see Pijpers et al., 1988).

Efforts to concert foreign policies among the members between 1970 and 1974 quite naturally had less spectacular results. After the Foreign Ministers of the then six EC member states had met for the first time in late 1970 to discuss matters of foreign policy, there were strong doubts that similar meetings would follow at all. The main purpose at that time was first of all to identify the potential for common ground which might develop into common positions and concrete steps later on. In this first stage EPC could best be assessed as 'procedure as substitute for policy' (Wallace and Allen, 1977, pp. 227–47). Largely at French insistence EPC was kept fully apart from the Community framework. Considerable divergences also existed both inside the then nine member states and on the part of the United States which role Europe should play internationally in the future.

In contrast, the second period of EPC (1974–9) was marked by some progress to strengthen the *acquis politique* in the traditional areas (Middle East conflict, CSCE) and to define common viewpoints on new issues, such as the third world (e.g. developments in Africa, particularly in the southern part and the conflicts in Asia, especially Cambodia/Vietnam). The EPC agenda was far more selective than in the 1980s and the participating governments were eager to preserve their *domaines reservés*. So after a period of 'running in' during the early 1970s EPC had reached a plateau, however, with only few dynamic elements.

Compared to the 1970s, the first half of the 1980s has been marked by a new quality of the *acquis* (Pijpers et al., 1988: pp. 85–103). Although this third period began with a confused reaction to the Soviet invasion in Afghanistan in 1979, EPC was marked by remarkable progress towards joint actions. As diplomacy alone proved to be insufficient to achieve the self-declared aim, the then ten (Greece joined the EC in 1981) made efforts to improve their international standing. EPC diplomacy was increasingly linked to other and particularly EC instruments. Though questionable in their effectiveness, 'negative' types of joint actions such as sanctions were used as well as 'positive' measures such as trade concessions and other forms of Community aid. Occasionally, however, the picture of homogeneity was weakened by the refusal of several governments (for example the British one in the Falkland Islands crisis) to accept joint decisions over a certain period of time. 'Vital' national interests – and not only the ones of Greece – more than once ran counter to the EPC majority. Nevertheless, EPC became accepted as 'a central element in the foreign policies of all member states' (*London Report of the Foreign Ministers*, 13 October 1981). In view of this historical evolution the basic features of the present EPC performance can be summarized as follows:

1   EPC has turned out as an extraordinarily stable structure. It has not suffered an institutional crisis despite considerable changes in composition (from six to twelve partners), in personnel (the changing of governments and the rotating of the diplomatic staffs) and in external conditions (the détente period of the 1970s, deterioration in the superpower relationship in the first half of the 1980s, basic changes in the transatlantic partnership, the emerging European architecture at the beginning of the 1990s, German unification etc.).

2   In historical terms, EPC unites countries which have fought bloody wars with one another even in the very recent past. The quasi-permanent and constantly extended consultation mechanisms (except for the core area of military security) have created an atmosphere of openness, mutual understanding and confidence in which collective policy making offers considerable gains to safeguard one's own national interests. Whether this sort of 'community building' already produces the ground for a 'European foreign policy' (art. 30, 1 SEA) remains to be seen.

3   EPC has not absorbed national diplomacy. It leaves room for the pursuit of individual national foreign policies. The past twenty years of EPC have seen occasional turbulences when 'going it alone' ranked higher in the eyes of some governments than common steps. Despite all the 'Europeanizing' tendencies in the behaviour of those taking part in EPC, the system has

not produced a shift in loyalties as the earlier integration theory had expected. EPC participants remain affiliated with 'their' state and stick to
the traditional concept that foreign policy is the domain of the sovereign
nation-state.

4 Since the 1980s, EPC is acknowledged as the second 'pillar' of
the process towards European union.[1] The days of long debates over
whether and to what extent intergovernmental procedures offer an alternative strategy to the Community method of solving common problems
are gone. As the Trevi cooperation between the ministers of the Interior/
Justice and their staffs to combat terrorism shows the habits and methods
developed in EPC even serve for problem solving in other areas of common
interest.

The provisions of Title III, SEA, thus reflect the maturity EPC had achieved
over the first fifteen years and the value the twelve attach to it. At the same
time, the careful wording of the EPC treaty – e.g. with regard to majority/
consensus positions (art. 30, 2) – and the restrictions imposed on EPC in the
field of defence (art. 30, 6) suggested that progress would be difficult in
the future. Already the goal of a 'European foreign policy' set by the twelve
themselves in 1986 seemed to become a demanding exercise in the following years.

Criteria and methods to measure the EPC performance

Every academic analysis to evaluate the pros and cons of EPC reveals a
certain methodological weakness: how to grasp the effects EPC activities
may or may not produce for the behaviour of other actors on the international scene and vice versa? And linked herewith, how can we provide a
solid prognosis on the future of a European foreign policy in view of the
constant moves of international events and the relative unpredictability of
crisis constellations?

Recourse to the achievements and failures of EPC until the mid 1980s and
to the basic guidelines set by the twelve themselves in the EPC treaty are
supposed to offer a useful approach. The following three criteria[2] served as
points of reference to evaluate the subject:

1 *Efficiency with regard to the internal decision-making structure of EPC.* Is
   there an increase, a halt or a decrease in the twelve's ability to consult
   each other and to formulate common positions? Which role can be attributed to the Presidency and to the EPC Secretariat in this respect?
2 *Effectiveness with regard to the twelve's external posture.* Have the twelve
   been increasingly able to translate common viewpoints into joint actions?
   How far do they participate in international diplomacy?
3 *Consistency with regard to the interrelations between EPC and the EC's
   external relations.* Have the EC/twelve made progress towards presenting
   themselves internationally as a unitary actor? Do they dispose of efficient
   communication channels inside? Which role can be attributed to the
   Presidency and the EC Commission in this respect?

Table 11.1 The frequency of EPC expert meetings, 1985–1990
(1st semester)

Working groups	1985	1986	1987	1988	1989	1990
Total meetings	87	76	91	87	94	50
Administrative affairs	4	1	2	2	2	1
Africa	7	7	9	6	6	3
Asia	5	5	4	6	6	3
CSCE	7	6	11	7	7	5
Communications (heads)	2	2	2	1	2	1
Communications (experts)	/	/	/	/	1	/
Consular affairs	3	3	2	2	3	1
Cooperation to combat international terrorism	4	6	6	7	4	3
Drugs	/	/	/	/	/	2
Eastern Europe	9	8	9	8	8	6
Euro-Arab dialogue	6	2	/	1	3	2
Exports of illegal arms (ad hoc group)	/	/	2	/	2	/
Human rights	/	/	/	3	5	2
International public law	/	/	/	/	/	/
Judicial cooperation	6	3	7	4	5	3
Latin America	6	7	5	7	6	4
Medical affairs	/	/	1	/	/	/
Middle East	10	10	11	10	9	4
Mediterranean	/	/	/	/	/	/
Non-proliferation	3	4	4	4	3	3
Policy planning	5	2	24	4	4	2
Precursors of chemical weapons	/	/	/	1	3	/
Protocol	1	1	3	2	3	/
United Nations	6	6	7	6	7	3
UN disarmament	3	3	4	6	5	2

Source: Own calculation according to EPC texts.

EPC in the test

Efficiency: extensive use of the EPC infrastructure and presidential overload

Remarkable growth of meetings at all EPC levels
According to EPC participants, the Single European Act spurred up the process of intensified consultation which had already started in the early 1980s. It reflects itself particularly in a more extensive use of the Coreu network, a telex system which connects the twelve Foreign Ministries, the EC Commission and the EPC Secretariat directly, and in more frequent gatherings of the EPC diplomats, the Foreign Ministers and even the heads of state and government.

As table 11.1 indicates, during the second half of the 1980s six new working groups were founded in addition to the already existing nineteen in 1986, thus 'Europeanizing' steadily an ever greater number of national diplomats. The newly created EPC bodies reflect at least partly the extension of the EPC agenda, which particularly originated from the international environment of the late 1980s, e.g. with regard to the production of chemical weapons, (illegal) arms exports, drug trafficking and human rights issues. The new gathering of other experts from the Foreign Affairs Ministries (e.g. those responsible for medical affairs) is more designed to smooth the internal administrative running of EPC and the communication among the twelve, including measures to harmonize the cooperation among the EC embassies abroad and between them and the European capitals.

The extension of working groups to new areas has been accompanied by a greater frequency of the expert meetings. The growth here is, however, not evenly divided. The figures (see table 11.1) indicate, in particular, higher numbers from 1989 onwards, while in the previous years the total numbers varied especially between 1986 and 1987. A closer look at the frequency of individual working groups suggests an intensified consultation in the groups dealing with Asia, UN disarmament, policy planning. Some dynamism is also obvious in the groups in charge of the Euro-Arab dialogue and in the one on human rights. Other 'classical' working groups, such as the one for eastern Europe, the Middle East, the United Nations and the CSCE meet at rather less regular intervals.[3]

At the other EPC levels regular meetings take place at very short, i.e. at least monthly, intervals. The numbers therefore by far exceed the minimum standard indicated in art. 30, 3a SEA.[4] Normally Political Directors meet every month (except for August) and if need be – i.e. in situations such as Iraq's invasion of Kuwait in August 1990 or the war in Yugoslavia – more often. The same applies to the ministerial level, where the calendar of the EC General Council already offers a quasi-permanent exchange of views on EPC-related issues in addition to the 'proper' EPC sessions foreseen in the SEA. Besides, informal concertation happens almost daily through the phone and the EPC-based telex system. The provisions for 'emergency meetings' (art. 30, 10d SEA), on the contrary, have been rather rarely applied over the past years – not because of disagreement, but because the already existing opportunities to gather are meant to be widely sufficient. It seems as if recourse to the crisis procedure launched with the London report of 1981 is necessary in only exceptional cases of highest political relevance, e.g. the Iraqi invasion in Kuwait, the attempted coup d'état in the Soviet Union in 1991 or the Yugoslavian crisis of 1991. As a general rule, one can say that in the case where a well-defined *acquis politique* exists already, no additional gatherings are needed. Then the Coreu network is used as the most efficient means to reach a decision very soon, i.e. within forty-eight hours and throughout the week.

Scope enlargement: Towards an almost unlimited EPC agenda

Due to the principle of confidentiality, official EPC texts reveal only part of the subjects under discussion. Apart from the 'traditional' topics of EPC such as the Arab–Israeli conflict, east–west relations and the CSCE negotiations, southern Africa, Central/Latin America – to mention but a few – during the period under review, an exchange of views was held on a range of rather new subjects such as the situation at the Horn of Africa, the Chernobyl nuclear accident, the western Sahara conflict, developments in South Korea, Haiti, Senegal, Mauritania, or Burma. In addition, the EPC agenda regularly contains numerous other issues which are not necessarily planned to lead to official statements, but are reserved for the internal debate. It is also customary to discuss relations with the friendly and allied states in a confidential way, all the more so when such a relation is not free of conflicts (take the case of Turkey or at certain times also the United States).

Compared to the early days of EPC when certain governments insisted on their *domaines réservés*, i.e. subjects to be excluded from the debate and handled individually by the EC member states, particularly emphasized by France (Black Africa) and (less so) by the United Kingdom, today EC governments favour a global agenda. Even if a subject may be a delicate one and produce controversies among the twelve, to discuss it in the EPC framework is given considerable weight. In such a situation it is more likely than not that deliberations are restricted to an internal exchange of information and views, when a common declaration or joint action seem difficult to be achieved. Such was the case, for example, in 1987 when Italy wished to define a common stance on the question of European arms exports. Massive French objections ran counter to the creation of a common position and prevented the twelve from taking a position in public. The issue of chemical weapons also turned out to be a sensitive one, requiring a lot of consultation before a collective viewpoint could be made public. German–German questions – according to the *acquis* and the practice of EPC until recently reserved for the debate among the states most directly concerned – were also not excluded during the decisive phase of the unification process. After some tensions in 1989 EPC, thereafter served to inform the partners about the development (particularly at ministerial level) and if agreed to by all, even went as far as to define a European position.[5]

The extension of EPC to the field of security (art. 30, 6 SEA) deserves special attention. Contrary to the fears issued during the drafting of the EPC Treaty (de Ruyt, 1987, p. 235) the twelve's legal commitment to coordinate their viewpoints on the 'political' and 'economic' aspects of security[6] did not produce a deadlock. Those governments traditionally in favour of extending the twelve's deliberations to cover defence matters, like the Italian[7] or the German ones, cautiously invaded this grey zone.[8] As long as such debates remained confidential – both foreign ministers and the heads of state and government preferred to raise such sensitive issues in their Gymnich-type meetings/fireside chats – no reservations were made on the part of those EC governments who opposed earlier attempts to include also military aspects of security into EPC. Even the most concerned Irish EPC participants are said to show a remarkable openness to participate in such informal debates on security issues in this broader perspective. To the extent European decisions are to be taken which refer to European defence – such as the sending of troops to the Persian Gulf in the course of the Iran–Iraq war, the Iraqi annexation of Kuwait in 1990, or the establishment of EC monitors/ troops to help solve the war in Yugoslavia in 1991 – other fora with European participation were so far preferred. The Western European Union, reactivated since 1984 to compensate for the weaknesses of EPC in the field of security and defence, was used in such situations. So far however, it did not entirely fulfil the expectations of its protagonists, nor did it endanger the status of EPC as the central body for consultation on matters of international politics among the Europeans. The changed security patterns in Europe as well as the EC's new responsibilities towards the resolution of conflicts both inside Europe and elsewhere made the issue of European security a main point for the Intergovernmental Conference on Political Union[9] in the course of 1991.

The institutional set-up: limits to the efficiency of EPC

Compared to the heaviness of the Community bureaucracy, the smooth running of EPC has been attributed to its light structure and to the homogeneity of its participants. Moreover, in the second half of the 1980s and despite the enlargement from ten to twelve, EPC functioned pretty well. The ever-growing catalogue of responsibilities both with regard to the internal management of EPC and the execution of the joint decisions meant a considerable workload for the presidency. The Single European Act and the ministerial decision adopted at the signing of the Single European Act in February 1986 which specifies the treaty provisions, tries to alleviate those burdens through admittedly modest procedural innovations and the introduction of an auxiliary body, the EPC Secretariat (art. 30, 10g).

With regard to the former, the proposal to hold EPC meetings at the seat of the Secretariat in Brussels deserves special attention. It was born out of the simple need to secure sufficient consultation procedures among a steadily extended and geographically distant group of participants. So far, however, it has only been implemented at the working group level, while the Political Directors and the Foreign Ministers continued to meet in the country holding the presidency. Meanwhile, the force of events and particularly the need for consistency between EPC and the Community's external relations seemed to work towards an increased use of the EC sites for EPC meetings also at those levels.[10]

With regard to the twelve's external representation the past years have also revealed shortcomings. The twelve's increased attractiveness as a dialogue partner for third countries brought about a considerable involvement of the Foreign Ministers and their diplomats in an ever-growing series of contacts with the outside world. Given the double responsibilities of the Foreign Ministers and their high-ranking advisers to act both as representative of their own country and in the name of the twelve they were occasionally forced to delegate tasks to their deputies. Such practices did not necessarily please the dialogue partners who wished to speak to the political authorities of the twelve for reasons of status and influence, and not to lower-ranking personnel.

Compared to previous times, in the past years EC governments with only limited diplomatic staff were increasingly forced to entrust the preceding or incoming presidency (troika) with tasks they were unable to fulfil themselves. Such as distribution of spokesman activities to other partners was already foreseen in the London Report of 1981, however seldom applied, because each government wished to conduct 'its' presidency alone. However, the twelve's increasing joint actions – particularly their involvement in the daily diplomatic business, and all the more so when a small country with a small diplomatic service is represented – forces the EPC spokesman towards more 'burden-sharing'. The performance of the Irish presidency in 1990, during which EPC positions had to be frequently represented by diplomats from the incoming Italian presidency, is a good example. But even during the Spanish term of office in 1989, 30 demarches out of 239 had to be carried out by other troika members because of a lacking Spanish presence in some regions.

The application of the troika formula may help to secure internal efficiency. It may, however, also be counter-productive with regard to the twelve's effectiveness towards the outside. One may wonder whether this formula does not cause considerable confusion on the side of the addressees as to who is speaking on whose behalf in the name of the twelve. To act as a coherent force may have to do partly with personal continuity and even with the identity of the persons acting in the name of Europe.

The other important and tangible new element in the twelve's decision-making process which was introduced with the Single European Act is the creation of the EPC Secretariat (da Costa Perrera in Pijpers et al., 1988, pp. 85–103). The decision concerning its final nature and duties – i.e. to 'assist' the presidency in preparing and implementing the activities of EPC and administrative matters – was preceded by a long and controversial discussion over whether or not it should be more than a 'mere' effective administrative centre working under the authority of the EPC spokesman. After more than four years of experience the balance of the Secretariat's work is, in total, a positive one, even in the eyes of its earlier critiques among the twelve. EPC participants unanimously underline the important role the Secretariat plays with regard to the technical/organizational side of the EPC business. Helped by individual presidencies today the Secretariat is also able to do conceptual work. It has been asked to draft texts to be submitted to the various EPC bodies, to prepare the speeches of the President-in-office for the UN General Assembly and to draft the EPC responses to the questions from the European Parliament.

There was a certain concern among the twelve over the Secretariat's attempts to loosen its bonds with the presidency and gain a greater autonomy. The most tempting areas for the Secretariat to do so are those where it acts as an interlocutor for the outside world. The Ministerial Decision of February 1986, which defined the Secretariat's functions in greater detail, signalled a restrictive course. In rather vague terms – and as the last item on the list of the Secretariat's functions – it offered the Secretariat's assistance to the presidency when contacts with third countries were concerned. Moreover, no indications were made as to whether the Secretariat would be allowed to establish links with the European Parliament and the press. In EPC practice, these provisions were soon felt as a straitjacket by the Secretariat staff, who by the simple virtue of their presence in Brussels were approached by those interested in EPC from outside. It would appear, however, that in the meantime the twelve have undergone a 'learning process' and are now open to a widening of the Secretariat's functions in this direction.[11]

The twelve's external posture: progress and set-backs in the effectiveness of EPC

If one takes the number of EPC statements, and the variety of the items already referred to as a yardstick for the twelve's effectiveness 'to speak with one voice', a remarkable dynamism during the second half of the 1980s is

Table 11.2   Number of EPC declarations, 1985–1990

1985	1986	1987	1988	1989	1990
52	54	63	81	99	115

Includes joint communiqués with groups of states, the reports on European union, the ones on the twelve's human rights activities, the annual speech at the UN General Assembly and some major speeches at the CSCE. The reporting to the European Parliament (EP) and other UN activities are excluded.

obvious: while in the early 1980s only twenty statements were passed per year, they amounted to more than fifty in the mid 1980s and by the late 1980s they had almost doubled (table 11.2).

On the other hand the period under review also witnessed situations whereby the twelve's effectiveness was hampered by the inability to agree upon common viewpoints within short periods of time. As early as 1988, Commission President Delors – who, contrary to his EPC colleagues, heavily criticized the twelve's cooperation on certain occasions – rightly reminded the EC governments to speed up the definition of a European stance in the field of east–west relations. For a long time, it appeared to be very difficult to bridge the gap between those who favoured a positive stand vis-à-vis Gorbachev and those that were more reluctant to do so. The same can be said for the twelve's posture towards Yugoslavia in 1991: even though numerous declarations were passed, the wording could hardly disguise the diverging views among the EC governments on how to react to the declaration of independence from Croatia and Slovenia.

Moreover, some of the twelve's credibility was lost during the course of endless internal EPC controversies about the 'right' approach towards the apartheid regime from 1985 onwards. On the one hand, the twelve managed to develop a remarkable catalogue of general principles on which relations with South Africa should be based. On the other hand, attempts to refine this *communauté de vues* and even to translate it into a *communauté d'action* created considerable tensions: while the EC governments might have been able to agree upon a package of positive measures, e.g. political and financial assistance to the non-white population in South Africa, including an adaptation of the Code of Conduct, they were split over the restrictive measures. It was only after lengthy and highly controversial debates that decisions on the latter were reached. The British–German tandem, joined by Portugal in 1986, consistently and vigorously opposed the EPC majority, in favour of substantial economic sanctions against South Africa. The revision of the twelve's policy in response to the South African President's apparent will to reform in the early 1990s turned out to be equally difficult. This time the UK tried to convince the other EC partners to lift the sanctions as soon as possible – with only limited success. The compromises finally agreed upon did little to enhance Europe's image and its desire to become a 'decisive force' (art. 30, 3d SEA) in international politics.

Another traditional issue which was of major concern to the twelve was the Arab–Israeli conflict. Over the past few years this could be tackled with comparative ease, due to both external (moderation of the PLO) and internal (moderate Greek and Spanish behaviour) events. Based on the *acquis* of the early 1980s, the common positions could be adjusted according to the development of the conflict. The twelve were able to present themselves as an interesting dialogue partner and could at least partly play a mediating role through their joint 'voice'.

The Gulf crisis of 1990–1 is also illustrative of the potential and the limits of the twelve's effectiveness: While they were able to produce joint statements immediately after the Iraqi invasion of Kuwait and even before the UN Security Council took a decision, the value of individual actions – as opposed to collective ones – seemed to increase as the crisis sharpened (with the taking of hostages and the subsequent individual national activities to release them) and as it became evident after 15 January 1991, that military measures would be the sole instrument of policy. Negative effects for the twelve's profile had also to do with delays in the implementation of the EPC *acquis* through EC legislation. The solemnly announced aid programme for the countries most directly concerned by the Iraqi invasion produced different views both among the twelve and between Council, Commission and the European Parliament, e.g. in the concrete amount of the money and the nature of it.

The twelve's representation at international organizations (art. 30, 7 SEA): the twelve's improved profile at the United Nations

From the very inception of EPC, the concept of 'speaking with one voice' at international fora has been of major concern to the EC member states. EPC participants confirm today that art. 30, 7a SEA is highly respected by the twelve: 'In international institutions and at international conferences which they attend, the High Contracting Parties shall endeavour to adopt common positions on the subjects covered by this title'. A look at the twelve's voting patterns on the resolutions of the United Nations' General Assembly confirms this positive assessment even though it does not mean that the twelve's effectiveness in the UN framework could not be improved further. Not only do they vote in common on a wide range of issues; in the eyes of the other UN member states the twelve have presented themselves as the principal representative of the western world and as a 'privileged *interlocutor*' (de Schoutheete de Tervarent, 1990, pp. 11–18).

As table 11.3 indicates, today unanimity is achieved in almost 50 per cent of those UN resolutions put to a vote compared to the first half of the 1980s when the ten managed to agree only in 30 to 40 per cent of the votes. However, the progress achieved between 1986 and 1989 has been somewhat slowed down by the southern enlargement of the EC. But even in the old group of the former nine the percentage of unanimous votes in the second half of the 1980s would have been smaller compared to the average already reached in the second half of the 1970s.

Much of the twelve's increased cohesiveness over the past years has to do with a considerable moderation of Greek policy and a smooth adaptation of Spanish and Portuguese voting patterns to those of the other EC member states. Today Greece can no longer be considered to be the 'bogy man', as it finds itself in line with other EC countries which on specific occasions may be unwilling to join the EC mainstream. This group of 'non-conformists' often includes France and the United Kingdom, as well as

Table 11.3   Survey of the total and common EPC votes on (parts of) resolutions and amendments in the UNGA, 1973–1989

Year	Total votes	Common votes	%
1973	77	36	46.8
1974	92	54	60.9
1975	101	66	65.3
1976	108	61	56.3
1977	113	67	59.3
1978	145	95	65.5
1979	162	97	59.9
1980	130	68	52.3
1981	159	76/104[a]	47.8/65.4
1982	178	74/100	41.6/56.2
1983	176	54/87	30.7/49.4
1984	189	66/104	34.9/55.0
1985	195	81/107	41.5/54.9
1986	157	64/79	40.1/50.3
1987	146	73/86	46.8/58.9
1988	157	74/84	47.1/53.5
1989	116	55/66	47.4/56.9

[a] The numbers behind the slash indicate the votes excluding the votes of Greece, 1981–9, and the votes of Portugal and Spain, 1985–9.
Source: Bartali, Silvia and Thijn, Ingeborg: The EPC in the General Assembly of the United Nations: one voice or twelve voices? Bruges 1990 (unpublished), p. 45.

Ireland and Spain. France and the United Kingdom, both with the privileged status of being permanent members of the UN Security Council and nuclear powers, prefer to act outside EPC in matters related to security/disarmament issues and matters of decolonization. British votes on South Africa and related issues as well as on the Falklands also tend to diverge from those of the EPC majority. Greek and Spanish minority votes focus on issues related to the Middle East conflict. Irish neutrality and the country's progressive stance on decolonization issues are also factors which reduce the chances of achieving a single voice. On the contrary, the Benelux countries, Italy and even Denmark constitute the core of countries whose foreign policy interests are completely covered by the *acquis politique*.

Furthermore table 11.4 indicates that from the 42nd UN session in 1987 onwards the EC member states have been able to multiply their joint representation at various UN fora. The positive trend visible in the First (Political and Security) Committee confirms again that the twelve have managed to agree on a wider range of issues of high political relevance. At the same time, these figures also reveal where effectiveness could be improved. The twelve's difficulty to speak with one voice on disarmament matters is obvious. Table 11.4 confirms what has been said elsewhere concerning the previous years (Stephanou, 1985; Stadler, 1988, pp. 181–90): the existence of a rather loose *acquis politique* in this field, which allows for a collective stance only at irregular intervals. The same can be said for the European presence at the UNESCO: as was the case in the Disarmament Commission, several EC countries – and in particular France – preferred to act individually, according to their specific needs.[12]

Table 11.4 The twelve's joint representation at the UN (speeches, explanation of votes etc.), 1985–1988

	1985	1986	1987	1988
General Assembly	16	13	6	18
First (Political and Security) Committee	7	14	14	17
Special Political Committee	8	5	8	6
Second (Economic and Financial) Committee	–	2	8	16
Third (Social, Humanitarian and Cultural) Committee	8	16	10	18
Fourth (Trusteeship) Committee	1	1	1	3
Fifth (Administrative and Budgetary) Committee	14	4	11	14
Sixth (Legal) Committee	8	4	9	8
Commission on Human Rights	–	–	–	–
Disarmament Commission	–	–	3	–
ECOSOC	1	4	10	2
UNESCO	1	–	–	–
Total	64	63	80	102

Source: Calculated according to: European Political Cooperation Documentation Bulletin 1985–8, Luxemburg 1987 onwards.

The twelve's commitment to exercise their combined influence 'through the implementation of joint action' (art. 30, 2a SEA)

To measure the twelve's capacity for joint action requires first of all a brief look at the instruments available to them.

It follows from the nature of EPC as collective diplomacy that its means are first and foremost declarations which are passed and brought to the attention of the outside world. EPC has constantly received strong criticism for its 'merely' declaratory policy. Compared to previous periods, in the second half of the 1980s, the twelve have been able to improve their international profile through a sophistication of their diplomatic means (e.g. demarches, fact-finding missions, negotiator in crisis situations such as in Yugoslavia) and – even more important – to link their genuinely EPC instruments with those of the European Community.

The most well-known, although not necessarily most efficient examples of such a combined approach, are those where EPC statements are coupled with economic sanctions. Depending on the area to which such restrictive measures should be applied, but also on the different and sometimes changing interpretations of the 'right' legal basis to be chosen according to the EC member states, EPC decisions were implemented with the help of EC and/ or national legislation.[13]

During the period under review the twelve have also made extensive use of actions resulting directly from the nature of their joint diplomacy. They can be summarized in two main categories: less formalized diplomatic activities and the twelve's institutionalized political dialogues (Regelsberger, 1991).

The twelve's institutionalized political dialogues with third countries and regional groupings (art. 30, 8 SEA)

Compared to the other forms of the twelve's diplomatic business, this type of regular meeting at ministerial and/or directorial level may serve information purposes from an EPC point of view, and/or may also offer a forum for the exchange of mutual perceptions and influence. This latter purpose is particularly underlined by the dialogue partners of the twelve who wish to be associated with the EPC as closely as possible and to be accepted as equals. Initially designed to inform the 'friendly and allied states' of the outcome of the EPC discussions and – if need be – to water down misunderstandings between the Europeans and the Americans about the role of the former in international politics, today the dialogue partners (in total twenty-six countries in 1990) come from both western Europe and North America as well as from Asia, the Mediterranean and even eastern Europe. Depending on the importance the twelve attach to a third country and to a certain degree also on the interests of the dialogue partners to be associated with the twelve, individual formats are chosen. Dialogue structures at ministerial and/or directorial level signal the relevance of a third country as does the level of the twelve's representation. Full participation of all twelve governments and the troika formula are to be understood as a sign of political relevance compared to the sole presence of the presidency.

Compared to the consultations with individual third countries, the political dialogue with other groups of states ranks politically higher in the twelve's joint diplomacy. It is seen as a genuinely European means to foster political stability and to reduce conflicts in other parts of the world. Through the establishment of permanent links, the twelve wish to encourage integration/ cooperation efforts in regions outside Europe. Here, the EC enjoys great respect as a valuable interlocutor, helping to put a certain distance between traditional colonial/superpower bonds – e.g. in the case of the Central/Latin American states against the US – and offering ways to overcome economic underdevelopment (Edwards and Regelsberger, 1990).

As both sides wish to demonstrate their coalition building to the international public, the formats of these political dialogues are very different from the ones mentioned before. The presently existing ten dialogues consist of regular meetings at ministerial level. In order to guarantee 'highest visibility', full representation of the partners on both sides is desired but increasingly impossible for the twelve, mainly due to the time constraints on the European side but also due to a certain scepticism regarding the appropriateness of the chosen procedures. In some cases – such as the dialogue with the signatories of the Lomé Convention or the Euro-Arab Dialogue – for political reasons a restrictive course was preferred, and a positive answer to the request from outside was given only with a certain cautiousness. The importance attached to such a group by EPC reflects itself again in the dialogue structures (e.g. the composition of the delegations – full EPC presence or the three troika members?) and the density of the contacts. Towards other groupings such as the Rio Group/Group of Eight Latin-American Countries or the Gulf Cooperation Council, an intensive dialogue and its 'high visibility' expressed in the participation of all twelve EC governments was strongly favoured by the twelve. On the contrary, the constant growth of these dialogues and the other EPC activities absorb considerable forces on the part of the presidency, also because each of these group-to-group relations has, in one way or another, an EC-related dimension which requires intra-European coordination.

Less formalized diplomatic activities
Through a series of daily diplomatic business the twelve are massively involved in international politics. Among the instruments which have proven
their value for joint actions, the following three categories[14] can be mentioned:

(1) *Demarches*: Demarches usually serve a two-fold purpose. The one most
frequently associated herewith are the interventions the twelve undertake
against human rights violations in non-EC member states. Even if human
rights questions have long constituted an issue of major concern for the
European Community and its member states, during the period under review the European profile and the capacities to act were further improved.
The Netherlands have played a leading role particularly during their presidency in 1986 when a declaration of principles was drafted,[15] in which the
EC/twelve clearly state that their relations with other countries will be strongly
determined by the human rights issue. It was also the Dutch government
which introduced the practice of reporting regularly to the European Parliament on the twelve's activities and efforts to achieve a worldwide recognition of human rights[16] issues.
The second approach to undertake demarches is a broader one, and
generally echoes European support or disapproval of the policy of a
third country. The number of such measures, which may be undertaken at
either diplomatic or political level – or both, depending on the political
relevance of an issue – is impressive. The Spanish presidency of 1989 during
which 239 activities of this kind were undertaken is not an extraordinary
case.

(2) *The reception of political leaders from third countries*: This instrument
has been developed quite recently in the course of the twelve's policy towards the Middle East. In this case it was designed to demonstrate solidarity with political figures involved in the Arab–Israeli conflict. The most
generous offer was made to the King of Jordan in early 1988, when he was
invited to Bonn to attend a meeting of the Foreign Ministers of the twelve
during the German presidency. At that time, EPC wished to demonstrate to
the international public European support of the Arabs' policy to seek a
solution to the conflict. Other examples of such high level reception diplomacy were the visit of PLO leader Arafat to Madrid to meet the Foreign
Ministers' troika and the (refused) invitation to the Iraqi Foreign Minister
to come to Luxembourg in January 1991 in the course of the Gulf crisis.

(3) *Fact finding missions*: High level European presence 'at place' has evolved
into a useful instrument in EPC since the early 1980s. Fact finding missions
of either the troika or the presidency alone are said to have some impact at
least on the behaviour of the parties in a given conflict. More frequently and
more realistically however they seem to serve internal EPC purposes, such
as information gathering and promoting the evolution of a *communauté de
vues* among the twelve. As was demonstrated with the fact finding missions
to southern Africa in 1985–6, such actions had to be interpreted also as the
lowest common denominator between the EPC majority favouring sanctions against South Africa and a much more reluctant EPC minority, wishing to exploit any diplomatic means before taking any other decision.

The requirement of consistency (art. 30, 5 SEA): widely fulfilled

Article 30, 5 SEA has established the principle that EPC and the external policies of the EC 'must be consistent'. The logic inherent in this postulate needs no further explanation: if Europe were to establish efficient internal structures and to play its international role effectively, the potential of EPC – or as the critiques of EPC would argue, the declaratory policy of the twelve – had to be merged with the EC instruments.

The course of international events and the responses Europe had to give in the second half of the 1980s contributed much more to increased EPC/EC interactions than intra-European considerations and pressures. To the extent EPC and the EC's external relations became intertwined because of the nature and complexity of the issues to be dealt with on either side, a rapprochement of the two institutional set-ups was inevitable. Article 30, 5 SEA confirms what had emerged in the 1980s as a common conviction: the more EPC and EC affairs and instruments could be combined, the better Europe's international profile could be served.

Gone are therefore the days when EC governments feared that EPC might become too integrated through establishing links with the EC framework. However, gone are also the days when Commission representatives followed a rather restrictive course which was based on the scepticism that the more EPC and the EC would interfere, the greater the danger would be that the intergovernmental approach would 'invade' EC mechanisms and reduce the Commission's role of initiative in EC affairs. The more both sides realized the gains of such a joint approach for Europe's international profile, the greater the reduction of 'doctrinal approaches' became, particularly since 1988 (Nuttall, 1988, pp. 104–17).

Consistency of the EC's external relations and EPC expresses itself in different ways. Less obvious from outside, consistency finds its way into the internal debate of both EPC and Community circles. Political guidelines agreed upon in EPC may constitute a valuable point of reference for Community decisions and vice versa. Here, as on other occasions, 'the Presidency and the Commission, each within its own sphere of competence, shall have special responsibility for insuring that such consistency is sought and maintained' (art. 30, 5 SEA).

In a more formal way consistency expresses itself in the twelve's declarations where the global approach to a given problem is indicated by reference to 'the European Community and the member states'[17] instead of a mere mentioning of the EPC bodies alone.

The most important expression of a cohesive force, however, has to do with Europe's capacity to act. Consistency in such a more substantial way refers to the habit of combining the political statements of the twelve with EC instruments, on the occasion of very specific international events and crisis situations. The following cases can be regarded as examples of a successful implementation.

1 The EC's and the member states' collective approach towards the reform processes in central and eastern Europe are regularly referred to as the 'pilot projects' to demonstrate Europe's determination to enter and shape a new area of all-European cooperation and integration. Over the past

years the EC/twelve's strong engagement reflected itself, e.g. in a policy of political support,[18] emphasized more than once in statements by the European Council and other EC/EPC bodies. This was combined with the offer to conclude cooperation agreements at a first stage, followed by much more far reaching association agreements between the EC and the individual countries in eastern Europe, as well as other measures of economic assistance. The multilateral aid programmes of the west launched in the course of the Seven Power Summit of Paris in 1989 should be mentioned in this context as well. There the European Community with the EC Commission in the lead plays a decisive role which has been entrusted upon it by the other members of this group of twenty-four, and which reconfirms the anchor function of the EC – Europe in an all-European perspective.

2 The freezing of the negotiations in 1989 between the European Community and Romania – which were to extend the existing trade agreement to cover economic and commercial cooperation as well – illustrates additional instruments, such as sanctions and restrictive measures, with which the EC/twelve are able to emphasize their disapproval of Romanian policy, particularly with regard to massive human rights violations.

3 The package of positive and restrictive measures to the political opposition in South Africa and the Front Line states to emphasize the twelve's disapproval of apartheid since 1985.

4 EC assistance to the population in the Occupied Territories and preferential access to the EC markets for products from there to protest against Israeli policy since 1988.

5 The freezing of contacts between EC and EPC representatives with Chinese authorities and European opposition to multilateral financial aid to China in the course of the Chinese policy of violence against peaceful demonstrators in 1989.

6 EC export controls on various chemical products which could be used to produce chemical weapons in the course of the debate on European participation in establishing a plant in Libya in 1989.

7 Full trade embargo to protest against Iraqi invasion of Kuwait coupled with emergency aid and other measures of financial assistance to the countries most directly concerned (Egypt, Jordan, Turkey) in 1990–1.

The new spirit in EPC: its evolution and its limits in light of the Intergovernmental Conference on Political Union

One of the fundamentals governing EPC from the very beginning, and which is central to the governments' commitment to coordinate their foreign policies at all, is the consensus principle. Aware of the consequences the requirement for unanimity could and had produced, the EC governments, nevertheless, refused to move towards some sort of majority decisions during the negotiations on the Single European Act. Alien to their understanding of national sovereignty, the twelve insisted to stick to consensus decisions as a general rule. At the same time, however, it was acknowledged that the twelve's self-set goal to become a 'cohesive force in international relations' (art. 30, 2d SEA) would be given priority over individual national interests, except for cases of high importance. Article 30, 3c SEA cautiously indicates that this new flexibility would be indispensable to implementing joint actions at very short intervals after the definition of principles: 'In order to ensure the swift adoption of common positions and the implementation of joint action, the High Contracting Parties shall, as far as possible, refrain from impeding the formation of a consensus and the joint action which this could produce'.

As had been the case in previous years, in the late 1980s solidarity among the twelve was not unlimited. 'Vital' national interests defined individually have, at certain occasions[19] slowed down the decision-making process and impeded the twelve from 'speaking with one voice' to third parties. However, measured against the impressively sophisticated *acquis politique* of the twelve of today, the aforementioned examples of a collision of national interests and the EPC majority can therefore be judged as exceptional cases. In contrast to earlier periods of EPC, today the participating governments are more careful in weighing the gains and losses in a short-term and longer-term perspective. The past years are marked by an increased consciousness of those involved in the daily EPC business of the importance to belong to this 'club'. It seems as if the legal codification of EPC has not created but reaffirmed the general conviction that collective foreign policy making at the European level offers greater profits for one's own international standing. The Single European Act has therefore again underlined the centrality EPC enjoys in the context of national foreign policy.

EPC is rarely regarded as a straitjacket, but rather as a guide for the EC member states' behaviour in international affairs. The *esprit de corps* EPC produced both between the twelve capitals and abroad (Tomkys, 1987) has essentially contributed to confidence building among the EC governments and has helped to bridge divergent views over the years. Until recently (1990) the view was generally held – and in particular among the twelve – that the system widely served the interests of the participating governments.

The observer may then ask why the debate to revise the ECP treaty provisions has started already, in fact much earlier than foreseen in art. 30, 12 SEA. One explanation has to do with the EC's internal dynamics. The progress visible in the field of European economic and monetary integration needs a complement in the political field, it is said. European political union would be incomplete without a foreign and security policy of a genuine character which, according to its proponents, implies the introduction of Community-like principles and decision-making structures.[20] The second – and for some even more convincing – motive emerges from the turbulences in eastern Europe and in particular of German reunification. The arguments put forward by this line of argumentation focus on different aspects: the EC's/twelve's 'anchor function' both in political and economic terms for the new democracies in eastern and central Europe; the challenge of new EC enlargements and possible impacts on the 'deepening' of the EC/EPC; changing threat perceptions and new security requirements; changes in the European–American partnership; new instabilities in Europe (ethnic conflicts); concern over a united Germany, etc. The Gulf crisis of early 1991 seems also to confirm that the twelve's capacity to act in unison can be improved even if the immediate diplomatic reaction to the crisis and the collective offers for aid should not be downgraded.

Contrary to earlier times the models/proposals discussed in preparation of and during the Intergovernmental Conference on Political Union in 1990–1 contain both short-range practical steps and far-reaching suggestions for a qualitative leap. Even though the outcome of the negotiations on the reform of the EC and EPC, and the implementation of the final outcome achieved at the Maastricht European Council in December 1991, remained to be settled, the reform of EPC towards a 'Common Foreign and Security Policy' focused[21] on the following core areas:

The definition of the scope of a common foreign and security policy of the political union

Linked to this aspect is the fundamental question concerning the relationship between national foreign policies, and policies transferred to the European level. Given the unpredictability of international events and the general conviction that a collective approach carries considerable advantages, a broad EPC agenda has been preferred thus far. In connection with the consensus rule, such an open-ended agenda (to which each of the twelve governments could add subjects which may be of vital interest to it but not necessarily to all the partners) could also produce negative effects and prevent the twelve from setting priorities. Out of this experience the proposal to define 'essential interests' – e.g. with regard to east–west relations, the CSCE or human rights – was born. Though the existence of such priority fields of interest was not denied, different views existed as to whether their insertion into a new EPC treaty was useful compared to a rather general definition of the goals of the future foreign policy, and/or whether one should look for procedural arrangements enabling e.g. the European Council to define a matter of vital interest in a given international situation.[22] As a result of the IGC, a general clause was preferred[23] against a strict enumeration of specific issue areas. This was included in a separate declaration of the Maastricht European Council annexed to the new treaty, thus having a different legal quality. In rather general terms this text refers to selected issue areas[24] where the twelve share essential common interests and may be dealt with procedurally through joint action (see below).

In connection with the scope, clarification was also needed with regard to security and defence. Contrary to previous times, in 1991–2 it seemed as if an extension beyond the existing limits of the political and economic aspects of security was desired by all even though views differed as to whether it should be limited to collective steps in international fora, e.g. the participation in UN peace-keeping forces and common steps with regard to arms exports, or enter the military field including a mutual acceptance of the obligations of the WEU treaty.[25] Understandably, such a far-reaching approach raised concern not only in neutral Ireland; several other EC governments, like the British and Dutch, feared that the evolution of such a defence dimension of the future political union might weaken the existing defence structures. Progress during the Intergovernmental Conference had been rather modest in this matter and it was therefore up to the heads of state and government in December 1991 to settle the issue. They decided in favour of strengthening WEU as an intergral part of the political union (Article D and Declaration of the EC member states also being members of WEU passed at the Maastricht European Council). This does not mean a dissolution of the WEU structures but stronger coordination in between them and those of the political union.

Improvement of the twelve's internal efficiency

Apart from a series of concrete and more practical proposals – e.g. harmonization of preparatory work, unified decision-making body at Foreign Ministers' level, Brussels as the centre of EPC meetings, proposals for a burden sharing to alleviate the presidency, a reorganization and enlarged definition of the Secretariat's functions[26] – the consensus principle and its full or limited application in the future was a core question of the Intergovernmental Conference. Considerations to move away from the consensus requirement by abstention competed with more far-reaching proposals to introduce majority voting, at least for certain kinds of decisions, e.g. measures to be adopted in the course of basic guidelines which would still depend on the consensus of all. Those who favoured such a fundamental change in EPC do not necessarily interpret it as being identical to EC practice. A qualified majority in EPC would imply the consent of at least eight member states. At the same time as in the field of Community policy, majority voting had to be seen in relation to the existence of 'vital national interests', i.e. to define the rules and responsibilities in case of derogation being necessary as well. Given the centrality of this issue much of the debate in the Intergovernmental Conference and during the Maastricht Summit had to be devoted to it. The compromise reached in the end (art. C and declaration on possible areas for joint action) has to be understood as a very first step towards majority decisions. The wording is vague enough to leave for different interpretations and for long debates in the Council as to whether the issue should be translated into a joint action.

Improvement of Europe's external effectiveness

Here the reform debate focused on procedural and institutional elements which have to do with the twelve's external profile. They refer to the continuation of the existing models of outside representation through the presidency, the troika and Commission participation; they do not, however, include the introduction of one single actor (as desired by Commission circles), intensified coordination among the Embassies of the EC member states in third countries, or the use of different instruments partly related to EPC, the European Community and the national level. Compared to the aforementioned aspects, the latter ones are less controversial and widely settled soon during the IGC (see arts E,F,H,J).

Prognosis on the real impact of the new treaty provisions on the twelve's external provisions remains divided. Some directly involved in the Intergovernmental Conference show optimism that consultations and joint actions on international events will be determined by the new spirit inherent in the treaty and also by the force of law. Other, more cautious, voices argue that international events and particularly the Yugoslav crisis have not been dealt with by the twelve in a qualitatively new way already. Of course, formally the new provisions would come into force in 1992 at the earliest after ratification in the twelve member states. Existing behavioural patterns may however be understood as a first indicator. They suppose that progress towards a European identity in foreign and security policy will be limited and will develop only stage by stage.

NOTES

The chapter is partly based on earlier research conducted by the author and Wolfgang Wessels on EPC.

1   See e.g. the *Solemn Declaration on European Union* of 17 June 1983 and Title I, SEA.
2   Also used as a yardstick in the present debate on the EC's institutional reform. See e.g. *The Conclusions of the European Council*, Dublin, June 1990, and subsequent official documents.
3   The Mediterranean Group, on the contrary, is blocked since the entry of Greece into EPC. As the Athens government intended to monopolize the debate on issues related to Turkey, the other participants willing to discuss other Mediterranean related problems had to consider different ways of communication.
4   Foreign Ministers are to meet 'at least' four times a year and may gather on the fringe of the EC Council. The Political Directors come together 'regularly' (art. 30, 10 c SEA).
5   As happened in 1989 in the course of the opening of the Berlin Wall on 9 November 1989, and at the European Council in Strasbourg, December 1989, where European solidarity for the Germans' genuine right of self-determination was demonstrated in a common text. See also *Declaration by the Twelve on German Unification*, 2 October 1990.
6   As for the twelve's understanding of these terms see the answer prepared by the British Presidency to several EP questions in 1986: Doc. 86/308 in: *European Political Cooperation Documentation Bulletin*, vol. 2 (1986), Luxemburg 1988, pp. 135–8.
7   See the Italian proposal to integrate WEU into EPC. Agence Europe, 6 October 1990.
8   During the German Presidency in 1988 Foreign Minister Genscher clearly indicated his intentions to enlarge the scope of security in EPC before the European Parliament. *Official Journal of the European Communities*, Proceedings of the European Parliament. Annexe 2–361.
9   As referred to in the Conclusions of the Rome European Council, 15–16 December 1990.
10   The value of convening Political Committee meetings in Brussels is no longer contested as the 1991 debate at the Intergovernmental Conference on Political Union demonstrates.
11   See the recent proposals tabled during the intergovernmental conference in 1990–1.
12   The uncoordinated nomination of UNESCO's new Secretary General after Mr M'Bow is but one example of recent EPC history.
13   As to concrete examples see pp. 277–79.
14   Another extension of the EPC instruments can be seen in the twelve's efforts to solve the Yugoslavian crisis particularly through the creation of 'monitors' in charge of supervising the agreements among the conflicting Yugoslav forces and the role of the twelve as key negotiator of the peace conference on Yugoslavia.
15   Text in: *European Political Cooperation Documentation Bulletin 1986*, 2(2), Luxemburg 1988, pp. 5, 7.

16 Since then, annual reports are submitted to the European Parliament by the presidency. The information available from there on the EPC demarches differs according to the reporting of the presidencies but also according to the political environment in which the twelve act, which more often than not forces them to act silently. The texts of the reports on the EPC human rights activities to the EP are published in the *European Political Cooperation Documentation Bulletins*.

17 E.g. already in the mid 1980s. See the *Declaration on the Guidelines for the Relations Europe–Latin America*, 22 June 1987 or the *Declaration on Human Rights*, 21 July 1986.

18 Which in 1991 suffered from the Soviet policy towards the Baltic states and had to be turned into a more restrictive course (interruption of aid programme).

19 E.g. British resistance towards the re-establishment of contacts with Syria after this country's involvement in terrorist activities in 1986, London's policy towards South Africa in 1985–6 and the British 'special relationship' with the US in the Libyan affair; Denmark's immediate recognition of the Baltic states before the twelve's common stance in 1991.

20 Proposals from both the European Parliament particularly in the Resolution to the Martin Report of November 1990 and the EC Commission go in this direction. See Com (90) 600 final, 23 October 1990. The proposals submitted by individual governments and fusioned by the Luxemburg Presidency in 1991 are far less progressive in this respect.

21 This is the official term used since 1990.

22 As suggested also by the EC Commission in its opinion Com (90) 600 final, 23 October 1990.

23 See article A on the principles and aims of a common foreign and security policy.

24 The CSCE process, disarmament and arms control in Europe including confidence-building measures, non-proliferation, control of arms exports and technology.

25 The European Council Conclusions of 14–15 December 1990 envisage the consideration of defence matters.

26 Including its integration, however not fusion, into the Council Secretariat. According to the IGC, the final proceedings would have to be settled at a later stage.

REFERENCES

de Bassompierre 1988: *Changing the Guard in Brussels: an Insider's View of the EC Presidency*. New York: Praeger.
de Schoutheete de Tervarent, Phillipe 1990: *La Cooperation Politique Européene et les Nations Unies*. Brussels: Institut d'Etudes Européenes, Université Libre de Bruxelles.
Edwards, Geoffrey and Regelsberger, Elfriede (eds) 1990: *Europe's Global Links: the European Community and Inter-Regional Cooperation*. London: Pinter.
Greilshammer, Ilan and Wriler, Joseph 1987: *Europe's Middle East Dilemma: the Quest for a Unified Stance*. Boulder: Westview Press.
Holland, Martin 1988: *The European Community and South Africa: EPC under Strain*. London: Pinter.
Nuttall, Simon 1988: Where the European Commission comes in. In Pijpers et al. 1988.
Pijpers, Alfred, Regelsberger, Elfriede and Wessels, Wolfgang (eds) 1988: *European Political Cooperation in the 1980s: a Common Foreign Policy for Western Europe?* Dordrecht: Martinus Nijhoff.
Sanchez da Costa Perrera, Pedro 1988: The use of a secretariat. In Pijpers et al. 1988.
Stadler, Klaus-Dieter 1988: Die Zusammenarbeit der Zwolf in der Generalversammlung der Vereinten Nationen in den achtziger Jahren. *Europa Archiv.*, 7, 181–90.
Stephanou, Constantin (ed.) 1985: *La Communauté Européene et les Etats-membres dans les enceintes internationales*. Athens: Presses Universitaires de France (PUF).
Tomkys, Roger 1987: European political cooperation and the Middle East: a personal perspective. *International Affairs*, 3, 425–37.

Wallace, William 1983: Political cooperation: integration through intergovernmentalism. In Helen Wallace, William Wallace and Carol Webb (eds) *Policy-making in the European Communities*. Chichester: John Wiley, 2nd edn, pp. 373–402.

Weidenfeld, Werner and Wessels, Wolfgang (eds): *Jahrbücher der Europäischen Integration*. Bonn: Institut für Europäische Politik. Europa Union Verlag (yearly publication).

12

Trade diplomacy and the European Community

Stephen Woolcock

Summary

This chapter discusses the EC's approach to trade diplomacy during the second half of the 1980s. A one chapter treatment of such a complex issue means that it is impossible to be comprehensive. The chapter therefore focuses on the EC's approach to the GATT Uruguay Round and considers the extent to which the EC was prepared to seek multilateral solutions to the current issues in trade diplomacy. The chapter describes the domestic factors which have influenced EC policy and the background of inter-dependence against which current trade diplomacy must operate. In its discussion of how this interdependence affects the EC it focuses on the US, which with the EC shares much of the work of establishing multilateral rules for trade and investment. It argues that trade diplomacy faces a grow-ing challenge of dealing not only with existing tariff and non-tariff barriers but new non-tariff barrier issues related to regulatory policies and wide ranging structural impediments to trade and investment.

The chapter considers two of the Uruguay Round negotiating groups in depth, agriculture and services, and a range of other issues more super-ficially. It finds that the EC's approach to the new issues in the shape of regulatory barriers and structural impediments meshes fairly well with multilateral efforts at liberalization. The EC's difficulties have been in areas, such as agriculture and safeguards, in established policies, and interests have been less affected by the dynamic changes in the domestic policy environment brought about by the 1992 programme.

Interdependence

EC trade diplomacy is carried out in an interdependent world. This inter-dependence has a major impact on the EC through visible and invisible trade, which accounts for 12 per cent of the EC's GDP, increased foreign investment and increased corporate interpenetration through the actions of multinational companies. Competition has become global and has resulted in an increase in cross border mergers and acquisitions, which, together with the growth of foreign direct investment in production and R&D, is resulting in a general dilution of the national identity of companies.

Economic interdependence goes hand in hand with a high degree of policy interdependence. Decisions taken by the EC will have an immediate effect on its trading partners, and vice versa. For example, measures taken by one major importer to restrict the flow of imports of cars or textiles will result in intense pressure for similar measures elsewhere in order to pre-empt trade diversion. Trade legislation also tends to be mimicked by others. For example, the US Section 301 provisions on 'unfair' trade, introduced in the 1973 Trade Act and subsequently developed in the 1980 and 1988 legislation, were the spur for the EC's New Commercial Instrument introduced in 1985. The US and EC have also learned from one another's legislation on anti-dumping. Policy interdependence between the major players also extends to the new challenges of trade diplomacy. Thus the US Congressional debate on 'reciprocity' which began in the early 1980s and ran up to, and beyond, the passage of the 1988 Omnibus Trade and Competitiveness Act, influenced the EC debate on the 'third country' provisions of its 1992 programme. The EC approach to reciprocity, such as in the Second Banking Coordination Directive (SBCD) was in turn seen as a model for Congressional bills on trade in financial services. In the past, such policy interdependence has tended to have a negative dynamic, with one country's protectionism mimicked by others. But, when the conditions are right, policy interdependence can have a liberalizing effect. This is, for example, the case within the EC, where high levels of interdependence combined with the principle of competition among rules, has generated a positive, i.e. liberalizing feedback from interdependence.

The challenge

During the 1970s the main focus of trade diplomacy shifted from tariffs to non-tariff barriers. This was reflected in the Tokyo Round of GATT negotiations from 1973 to 1979. Codes or agreements were negotiated on, for example, technical standards, subsidies and government purchasing. This did not, of course mean that tariffs disappeared from the trade agenda. There remained tariff peaks, and above all high and unbound tariffs in many developing and newly industrializing countries. The Tokyo Round made an initial, largely inadequate, attempt to deal with the non-tariff barriers and none of the GATT rounds have adequately dealt with agriculture. In addition to this list of issues, the 1980s threw up new challenges in the shape of barriers to trade caused by divergent national regulatory policies. The inclusion in the GATT Uruguay Round of trade negotiations from 1986 to 1990 of the so called new issues of services, investment and intellectual property was an attempt to address these on a multilateral level. Finally, there are the structural or non-statutory barriers to trade. Here the problems are even harder because their elimination generally requires positive action by governments or regulatory authorities. Multilateral rules prohibiting discriminatory measures or requiring national treatment have little effect on structural barriers to trade. In recent years the absence of such multilaterally agreed rules has resulted in bilateral trade liberalization initiatives such as the US–Japan Structural Impediments Initiative. Trade diplomacy therefore faces a formidable challenge. It must deal with the outstanding problems of tariff and non-tariff barriers, not to mention agriculture, while at the same time making enough progress on the new challenges of regulatory barriers and structural impediments to head off bilateral approaches inconsistent with a multilateral system. It must also accommodate countries at different levels of development. For the OECD countries, the central focus for the 1990s will be on such issues as the impact of competition policy on trade. For developing countries tariffs and non-tariff measures remain more important. Both will have to come to grips with the impact of environmental policies on trade and investment.

The domestic roots of EC policy

In order to understand the EC's policy it is important to understand its domestic roots. In the EC's *internal market programme* the Europeans have developed a distinctive approach to market integration based on the principle of competition among (national) rules. This has proved to be effective in tackling regulatory barriers to trade. Competition among rules, driven by mutual recognition of standards and home country control of regulatory policies, has also provided the dynamism for policy-led integration. Market pressures resulting from economic and industrial interdependence are thus augmented by pressure for policy convergence as firms seek to ensure that their national regulations do not put them at a disadvantage vis-à-vis firms operating in the same markets but under less restrictive rules. At the same time EC regulation provides a floor to deregulation to protect the European social market economy. Policy convergence resulting from competition among rules, augmented by EC legislation and an active EC competition policy and decisions of the European Court of Justice is also wearing down structural impediments within the EC.

The EC member states share *common interests* which tend to be accentuated in trade disputes with third countries. Compared to the US they play a greater role in their economies, whether in the form of public ownership or industrial or regional policies. The combined effects of the 1992 programme, a shift in national policies away from support for national champions and efforts by the Commission to reduce state subsidies have resulted in a general reduction in national intervention. Despite this Anglo-Saxon led trend towards deregulation during the 1980s, Europe as a whole retains more active structural/industrial policies than, for example, the US. At a Community level this is reflected in the desire for economic cohesion throughout the EC which finds expression in EC regional policy, the Social Charter and elements of industrial policy, especially in sectors such as information technology. This affects the EC's approach to multilateral rules on policy instruments such as subsidies, where it supports a policy of controlling trade distorting effects of such measures but defends their use per se as legitimate policy instruments. In this sense, the EC also shares a common interest with developing countries which wish to retain the option of pursuing national development policies.

Despite the moves towards integration and the desire for cohesion the EC remains *heterogeneous*. In any given sector, the interests of member states will differ depending on the structure of the sector concerned and its competitive position. For example, national positions on car imports from Japan and elsewhere are largely shaped by structural factors. Britain has large Japanese direct investment and therefore wishes to see output from Japanese plants excluded from any agreement to limit Japanese sales in Europe. In 1990 Germany had a trade surplus with Japan in cars and was therefore not interested in aggravating trade disputes. France and Italy on the other hand have industries which are highly dependent on their national markets and therefore determined to limit Japanese sales from whatever source. In general terms, the Netherlands, Britain, the Federal Republic of Germany and Denmark come towards the liberal end of the EC spectrum, Italy and France with support from Spain more often towards the protectionist end. But such generalizations are dangerous. Germany has always pursued more protectionist policies in agriculture. The place of any member states in the spectrum will also vary over time. Until the early 1980s Britain tended to be to the protectionist side of the spectrum. It is only in the last decade that it has claimed the extreme free trade end for itself. Divergences between the member states have clearly affected the EC's policies on issues such as agriculture and textiles in the Uruguay Round, and cars and electronics in the application of EC trade instruments.

The EC is also characterized by the way its *decision-making* processes operate. In multilateral trade negotiations the Commission negotiates on the basis of a mandate from the twelve, which closely monitor and advise through the so called 113 Committee. In the vast majority of cases the Commission is left with adequate room to manoeuvre in negotiations. The exception is the case of agriculture which, as shown below, has led to criticism that the Commission would not negotiate before it had a mandate from the Council and could not negotiate once it had obtained one because the mandate left no flexibility. It is argued below, however, that the EC's policy during the first four years of the Uruguay Round showed that the Commission has enough flexibility to negotiate complex trade packages. The problem in agriculture, was that the Council of agricultural ministers, was determined to prevent any concessions being made.

Decision-making in the EC is also relatively technocratic, in that it is primarily in the hands of national and EC civil servants. This has the disadvantage that politicians and business tend to leave trade policy, and in particular the details of GATT negotiations, to the experts. Only the sectoral interests opposing liberalization have consistently followed the intricacies of trade diplomacy. The advantage with the executive retaining control of trade policy is that it can be more consistent than when trade policy is determined by politicians seeking re-election. The officials can also conduct quiet trade diplomacy in which they assess what can be realistically achieved, given the positions of its negotiating partners. The EC has often been accused of foot-dragging when it comes to multilateral trade negotiations because of differences between the member states, its decision-making procedures, or both (Preeg, 1970). Indeed it has sometimes been seen as a threat to the multilateral system because its decision-making is slow, hard to predict and has a protectionist bias (Patterson, 1983). In contrast, the United States, from where most of these criticisms come, is seen as generally more active in trade policy and more likely to initiate new trade policies. The reality is inevitably more complicated. This chapter will show that the US has tended to blow hot and cold on multilateralism. Although it made much of the early running in the round, shifts in the domestic balance of interests reflected by the relative weight of lobbies, forced the US administration to back-peddle on a number of fronts. In comparison, the EC has pursued more modest objectives but done so in a more consistent manner.

The origins of the Uruguay Round

The origins of the Uruguay Round can be traced back to the end of the previous Tokyo Round, which ran from 1973 to 1979. This reduced tariffs, for the EC the average trade weighted tariff level fell by some 23 per cent from 9.8 per cent to 7.5 per cent, and concluded agreements on a range of technical issues such as customs valuation and technical barriers to trade. The Tokyo Round also introduced qualified most favoured nation codes into the GATT, such as in government procurement and subsidies and countervailing duties. These are agreements signed by only a limited number of contracting parties. The former consisted of fairly detailed provisions governing the placing of government contracts, but coverage was limited to central government purchasing of goods. State and local government was excluded because the US had no provisions for purchasing at these levels and utilities because the EC directives of the 1970s excluded such mixed ownership sectors. The latter reflected differences between the EC – supported by a range of other developed and developing countries – which argued subsidies were a legitimate instrument of public policy, and the US, which sought to limit their use. The EC made strenuous efforts to bring US trade law – that mandated the imposition of countervailing duties when foreign subsidies were provided – under full GATT control. But there was, in general, little desire among the EC member states for a significant increase in GATT powers.

The EC succeeded in resisting pressure, primarily from the US, for increased GATT discipline over agricultural trade and in particular the export subsidies used by the EC. Faced with a choice between no round or no agreement on agriculture, the US accepted an inconsequential agreement on agriculture which allowed the continued use of export subsidies provided these did not disrupt traditional markets. European farm lobbies and ministries of agriculture have long institutional memories and, as shown below, their experience of the Tokyo Round encouraged them to believe that the CAP could also survive the Uruguay Round unscathed.

The EC also blocked agreement on a revision of the GATT safeguard provisions (GATT art. XIX). From the outset it was recognized that countries would not liberalize unless there were some form of safeguard mechanism should liberalization result in or threaten substantial injury. But the art. XIX measures had proved to be ineffective and have for some time been undermined by other measures such as 'voluntary export restraint' agreements. Before it would accept discipline over such expedients as VERs the EC wanted the GATT safeguards clause to provide for selectivity, or the ability to take actions against one or a limited number of exporters. Such selectivity was strongly opposed, especially by Japan's and the newly industrialized countries' (NICs) exporters of manufactured products. The result was that no agreement could be reached on safeguards either during the Tokyo Round itself or during the specific efforts in 1982–3.

All in all, the Tokyo Round was a relatively modest affair compared to the Uruguay Round, but for most of the time it was negotiated under much less favourable economic conditions. All participants felt it was important to have a successful conclusion, so the result was 'sold' as a success in 1979. In reality, it resolved very little as was shown by the considerable increase in trade tensions following the conclusion of the round. Disputes held at bay during the negotiations resurfaced in the shape of trade frictions over the EC's agricultural policies, the US harassment of (subsidized) EC steel exports to the US, and differences over trade embargoes against the Soviet Union. There was also a sharp increase in the use of grey areas measures by the main importers such as VRAs aimed at restricting import competition from Japan, the newly industrialized countries and some developing countries. In the face of these pressures, the GATT consultative group of eighteen, meeting in June 1981, recommended that a ministerial level meeting be held to: reaffirm support for the GATT; seek to resolve outstanding issues, such as safeguards; and set out a GATT work programme for the 1980s (Golt, 1982). Some US commentators hoped that the ministerial meeting, which took place in November 1982, would be used to launch a new round, but the US administration's policy, and indeed that of the EC, was limited to these three objectives (European Commission, 1982). The 1982 ministerial meeting was a disappointment, especially for the US administration, but a work programme for GATT was agreed which included services, trade related investment measures and high technology trade. The EC supported this but without prejudice to any decision on their inclusion in a round of negotiations.

The absence of any major results from the ministerial meeting led the US trade representative to make a statement before Congress in which he gave the 'GATT, on that showing, a C minus', and in so doing encouraged a flurry of congressional trade bills aimed at a further enhancement of US domestic trade remedies and the ability to pursue bilateral trade liberalization on the basis of reciprocity (Hart, 1985). Paradoxically, this, in turn, led to the US administration pressing for a new trade round in order to contain such domestic pressures. In other words, the US desire for a new round stemmed as much from a desire to deal with domestic protectionist pressures as a desire to strengthen multilateralism. In many respects, the US oversold the round before it had even begun.

The domestic pressures in the EC were different. There was, and remains, no equivalent of Congress threatening to introduce protectionist trade legislation. The main concerns in the early 1980s were about high unemployment and the ever more advanced symptoms of Euro-sclerosis (Aho and Aronson, 1985, p. 77). The general economic climate in the EC therefore tended to militate against adventures in multilateral trade liberalization. The EC was also keen to achieve a balance between ensuring that developing countries were not left behind and promoting advances in the scope and effectiveness of trade rules. This was criticized by some observers as the EC hiding behind the LDCs but the EC moved progressively to accept a new round if only to contain protectionist pressures in the US Congress. As for the other countries in the GATT, Japan was very keen to see a new round and was probably the first country to come out formerly in favour. The objective, like that of the US administration, was to contain protectionist pressures in the US Congress. Other countries, and in particular developing countries, tended to be on the sceptical side. Many argued that what was needed was not a new round to extend the coverage of the GATT but serious efforts by the major trading countries, i.e. the EC and US, to stick within the existing rules. The developing and middle income countries were, however, interested enough to vote for the commencement of a new round in 1985. The round was formerly launched in Punta del Este, Uruguay, in September 1986.

The EC's objectives

The Commission's mandate for the round, adopted by the Council in the summer of 1986, reflected the cautious EC approach (European Commission, 1986). It stressed the need to be 'fully aware of what a trade negotiation can and cannot achieve' and, in reference to the US's maximalist tendencies, that 'the trading community is badly served by over-ambitious programmes accompanied by unrealistic expectations'. The EC argued, and argues, that a 'multipolar approach', including coordination of monetary policy and exchange rates as well as trade, is needed if protectionist pressures are to be properly addressed because these were largely the result of macroeconomic imbalances. The EC, encouraged by the French, would like to link trade with efforts to strengthen international coordination of fiscal and monetary policy, i.e. getting the US to address its budget deficit.

The EC saw one of the main objectives of the round to be the 'strengthening and reinvigoration (of the) open multilateral trading system' by demonstrating the continuing vitality and relevance of the general agreement as compared to bilateral or multilateral deals between interested parties to the exclusion of others'. In another veiled reference to the United States the EC sought a review of the special advantages of some contracting parties in the shape of waivers and grandfather provisions (a reference to the US waiver on agriculture). There should also be a review of the benefits accruing to federal states, by virtue of the non-application of certain GATT provisions at the sub-federal level (US, Canada and Australia). The Commission was mandated to find ways of dealing with the 'maintenance by certain contracting parties of national legislation, or even the enactment of new legislation which is in clear breach of GATT obligations'. Reading between the lines, therefore, one of the major targets of the EC was the United States.

Japan was another target. The mandate referred specifically to the imbalance in real advantages between Japan and her partners which had to be dealt with in the round. The EC recognized the case for continued special and differential treatment for developing countries, but also sought the graduation of newly industrialized countries to accepting greater rights and obligations in the GATT. Finally, the Council mandated the Commission to follow the GATT tradition and negotiate an overall package, i.e. not to agree on sections before it knew the overall shape of the package. This was conceived, in part, to exclude a separate deal on agriculture, but, in practice, the tables were turned on the EC with the US and Cairns group arguing that there can be no round without agriculture.

On the specifics, the mandate stressed that negotiations should not question the fundamental objectives and mechanisms of the policies of the contracting parties in agriculture, i.e. the CAP, and that all forms of agricultural support should be considered, not just export subsidies which are a characteristic of the EC system. A resolution of the safeguards issue by providing some form of selectivity figured high on the EC's priorities, in part, because this was one remaining issue from the Tokyo Round, which efforts at the 1982 ministerial and subsequently in 1983 and 1984, had failed to resolve. The mandate was non-committal on quantitative restrictions, or grey area measures as they came to be called. There was only a general reference to textiles and clothing, mainly due to Italian and Portuguese resistance to liberalization, but here, as on many other topics, the mandate left considerable flexibility by referring only to the need for the round to bring about a gradual liberalization of the sector and bring textiles and clothing trade back into the GATT.

Of the new issues the EC was most supportive of services, on which the Council envisaged a framework agreement which would be applied in stages to various services sectors. In each case, however, the legitimate expression of policy goals in regulatory policy was to be respected. There was a clear mandate to ensure the extension to the services field of the GATT article XXIV provision for customs unions. On intellectual property rights there was initially little to chose between the EC and the developing countries, which were broadly opposed to an extension of the GATT in this area. The EC mandate argued that GATT should only cover counterfeiting, and that the World Intellectual Property Organization (WIPO), should continue to retain competence for standards in intellectual property. The EC subsequently moved to support a comprehensive agreement on intellectual property rights. The EC's objectives were also modest in the investment field.

The mandate made a point of reiterating the EC's traditional opposition to quasi-legalistic methods of dispute settlement, arguing that such procedural mechanisms could not by themselves resolve problems resulting from substantive differences. In other words disputes were better resolved by negotiation than adjudication. Rather than a system in which rules would create a kind of case law, the EC's position was that 'rules and practices should relate to each other and evolve together'. The EC could not therefore be accused of 'over-selling' the round. The Council's mandate to the Commission was cautious if not defensive, such as on agriculture, but it left the Commission a good deal of flexibility by avoiding detailed policy objectives (Golt, 1986).

The impact of the 1992 programme

There is a long history of links between EC integration and multilateral negotiations. The work on the Spaak Committee, which formed the basis of the Treaty of Rome, was influenced by the earlier rounds of the GATT (Murphy, 1990). The US saw the Kennedy Round (1963–8) as a means of ensuring that the creation of a common market would not result in the EEC turning in upon itself (Hufbauer, 1990). There is clearly also a coincidence between the Uruguay Round and the creation of a single market in the EC. Although the GATT round was scheduled to end in 1990, two years before the EC's programme, key decisions on the shape of the EC regulatory regime post-1992 were in fact taken during the period 1987–90. There was therefore a genuine interaction between the EC and multilateral processes, particularly in services, such as financial services and telecommunications, and public purchasing.

The 1992 programme helped rather than hindered the multilateral negotiations. It engendered a more dynamic and positive climate in the EC, compared to the pessimistic and thus defensive climate of the early 1980s. The prospect of realizing a single market, which became credible during 1987, strengthened the EC's economic prospects and thus replaced Euro-sclerosis with a more positive outlook which enhanced the prospects for multilateral liberalization. The year 1992 brought with it an acceptance that change was necessary if economic performance and European industrial competitiveness were to improve. This, in turn, helped to overcome the opposition of vested interests to change and break some, though not all, of the chains of regulatory capture that existed within the various member states. For example, the Commission's determination to remove frontier controls loosened the grip of the protectionist lobbies built up in some sensitive sectors such as textiles and clothing. The year 1992 also provided an incentive for others to negotiate in the Uruguay Round. Rightly or wrongly, it was felt that the reformulation of EC legislation offered a window of opportunity for influencing the shape of the post-1992 regulatory regime. There was a consensus among the EC's major trading partners and those involved in the negotiations that 1992 had, on balance, a positive effect (*Financial Times*, 21 April 1989).

The efforts to achieve the 1992 objectives, however, also led to a certain 'crowding out' of GATT issues in the minds of business people and politicians, if not in the minds of trade officials. The impact of creating a single market in Europe and the removal of virtually all national trade policy instruments was simply much more immediate for business. Even at the level of the European Council of Ministers, GATT was also pushed off the agenda in 1989–90 by German unification and developments in central and eastern Europe.

The intensification of integration in Europe also means that the EC is internalizing more of the multilateral process. The GATT provides for customs unions, but article XXIV was initially devised more with the Benelux countries than an EC of twelve or a European Economic Area of eighteen in mind. The magnetic effect of 1992 on its EFTA neighbours, not to mention its eastern neighbours, means that these countries will, one way or the other, follow the EC model. This, in turn, means that decisions taken by the EC will determine a European regulatory system covering at least 45 per cent of world trade and significantly enhance the EC's negotiating weight. Japan, alarmed by the growth of trading 'blocs' has called for a review of GATT article XXIV, but with the US already planning to include Mexico as well as Canada in a US-based 'bloc', the issue never really surfaced in Geneva. The key question in the GATT round was therefore how this European regulatory regime meshed with the multilateral system and how it interacted with other regulatory systems.

It is also important to recall the areas little affected by the 1992 programme. Agriculture was only affected in the area of phytosanitary controls and standards. It might be argued that the internal market and the progress towards economic, monetary and political union reduced the significance of the CAP as a foundation of the EC and thus makes major reform easier, but this does not seem to have had much effect, at least during the first four years of the round.

The Cockfield white paper did not include EC legislation to reduce state subsidies, an issue in both the Tokyo and Uruguay rounds, but the Commission, with the grudging support of some member states, has become more aggressive against national state subsidies (Brittan, 1990). Nor did the 1992 programme per se have an immediate impact on instruments of commercial defence such as anti-dumping or quantitative restricts/safeguards, whose application by the EC is seen as 'protectionist'. The statistics do not show an increase in the use of anti-dumping actions by the EC. Indeed the Commission claims that the increase in attention paid to anti-dumping actions is the result of a shift in the kind of products (electronics) and countries (Japan, and south-east Asian countries) covered. There can, however, be little doubt that in the EC, as elsewhere, anti-dumping actions have grown in importance as a means of obtaining import relief. In so far as the 1992 programme is systematically removing other instruments of trade policy, industries seeking protection see anti-dumping as the only remedy left.[1]

1986 to the mid-term review

The first half of the round consisted mainly of refining the coverage of the negotiations and conceptual work on the possible structure of agreements in the new issues of services, intellectual property and investment. A mid-term review meeting was held in December 1988 in Montreal which was finally completed in Geneva in March 1989 (Kelly, 1989). In most of the fifteen negotiating groups this meant deciding on the scope and timetable for negotiations in the second half of the round. The US had originally wished to have an 'early harvest' but the EC argued for globality, i.e. that no one would agree on anything until they knew the shape of the final package. Substantive agreements were, however, reached on a number of important procedural issues, such as the establishment of a trade surveillance mechanism to enhance transparency, and the first stage of measures to strengthen GATT dispute settlement.

The first mid-term meeting in Montreal in December 1988 collapsed because the Latin Americans became frustrated with the lack of progress on agriculture. The US wanted a commitment from the EC that all support would be eliminated by the year 2000, which the EC could not accept as a serious proposition. There was also a failure to agree on how to proceed with intellectual property, textiles and safeguards because the newly industrializing countries such as Brazil, India and Argentina were not prepared to support inclusion of IPR unless there was a prospect for final agreement on textiles and clothing and agriculture.

After two months, with mediation by the GATT Director General, Arthur Dunkel, the MTR was finally concluded on 7 March 1989, when the new US and EC negotiators compromised on a 'substantial, progressive reduction of agriculture support over an agreed period of time'. The Cairns group, which had wanted short-term reductions of 10 per cent, had to accept a 'slushy freeze' of support levels. In Europe this was seen as the US finally giving up its 'unrealistic' objective of elimination. All that remained to be decided was the size of the substantial reduction, how it should be measured and over what period should it be made!

Once the agricultural issue was resolved, the other issues were fairly straightforward, except for textiles and clothing where Italy, supported by Portugal, held things up before finally accepting that the round would decide on the modalities for phasing out the multi-fibre arrangement. The hardline developing countries such as India and Brazil continued to hold out against the inclusion of intellectual property rights in the GATT. By the time of the MTR, however, the EC had swung around to support a comprehensive agreement, and this provided enough momentum to ensure the IPR talks continued. A compromise was reached with the hardliners which put the question of which body dealt with IPR standards – GATT or the World Intellectual Property Organization (WIPO) – on ice.

The EC and multilateralism

The Uruguay Round offers an opportunity of gauging how the evolving EC regime meshes with the multilateral system. But in a round of fifteen negotiating groups, including a whole set of negotiations on the extension of the GATT to services, it is not possible to deal in detail with each. This chapter therefore focuses on two: services and agriculture.

The *service sector* is important because trade in services already represents some 19 per cent of world trade and is expected to grow (GATT, 1989), and because efforts are under way to construct both EC-wide and multilateral rules. As noted above, these must find ways of dealing with regulatory barriers to trade. Within the EC this has been done by some harmonization, mutual recognition and, above all, home country control of regulation. The test case for the EC is the Second Banking Coordination Directive (SBCD), which establishes the principle of a single passport for banks established in the EC (Woolcock, 1991). The SBCD has also set a precedent for other directives in investment services and insurance.

Given the limitations of national treatment and non-discrimination in dealing with regulatory barriers to trade, the Commission's first draft of the SBCD included a general provision on reciprocity. This created a storm of protest from, in particular, a number of US-based financial services companies because of its vague wording. The US companies, with first hand experience of the efforts to introduce reciprocity provisions into US legislation, feared that the EC would likewise seek 'mirror image' reciprocity. As universal banking and inter-state branching of banks would be allowed in the EC and is either prohibited or severely constrained in the US, mirror image reciprocity could have meant the EC denying US financial services companies established in one member state of the EC the right to operate branches throughout the EC in the same way as European banks. The issue was defused when the EC made clear that its approach was based on reciprocal national treatment, not mirror image reciprocity, and that decisions on the interpretation of the reciprocity provisions would be taken by the Council rather than the Commission. Given the existence of a liberal blocking minority of Britain, Germany and the Netherlands, this gave greater assurance that the provision would not be interpreted in a protectionist manner.

In the GATT where the mid-term review meeting more or less coincided with the discussions on the reciprocity provisions of the SBCD, the EC sought a comprehensive multilateral agreement covering all services including financial services. The MTR meeting agreed that there would be a framework agreement based on the traditional GATT principles of national treatment, non-discrimination and most favoured nation (MFN) treatment. There would then be sectoral annotations to this agreement in order to see how the principles should be complemented or adapted to each sector. Some countries argued that it was necessary to know what the implications would be for each sector before agreeing on a framework agreement. The US and Japan, under pressure from the US Treasury and Japanese Ministry of Finance, opposed coverage of financial services in the general framework agreement and argued for a separate agreement. The main reason for this was that these national regulators of financial services did not wish to see their control over regulatory objectives jeopardized by trade policy or become a pawn in trade disputes. The EC argued for comprehensive coverage of all sectors, notwithstanding considerable hesitation from some member states. Opposition to loss of regulatory sovereignty from the European national regulators of financial markets was muted because they had already come to terms with it in the SBCD.

The other main issue at this stage of the negotiations was how to ensure that sufficient (developing) countries signed the agreement to make it a multilateral rather than a bilteral agreement (or qualified MFN code). In line with the Council's mandate, the Commission sought to keep the developing countries on board. This meant slower progress in the negotiations and was seen by some (the US) as the EC using the developing country participation issue as a cover for slowing the negotiations down, and helped create the general climate that the EC was dragging its feet. There were similar issues in the trade-related investment measures and trade-related intellectual property negotiating groups. With the executive branches firmly in control in Europe, the EC, unlike the US administration, did not need to constantly prove that concrete results were being achieved and could afford to be more patient and thus help to create the conditions for wide scale developing country participation. This was done, not by following the GATT part IV approach of granting special and differential treatment, but by using a concept of progressive liberalization. According to this, any countries that felt unable to accept coverage of a certain sector would be allowed temporary exemption. Future trade rounds would then progressively reduce the number of exemptions within the framework of overall reciprocity.

In April 1990 the EC and US confirmed the approach to the negotiations agreed at the mid-term review, which they saw as consisting of three parts:

the framework agreement; sectoral annotations applying the principles in the framework to each sector; and concrete liberalization. The last category was included because the US private sector lobbies wanted 'red meat', i.e. concrete results if they were to support adoption of the final package. The EC sought a framework agreement based on non-discrimination, national treatment and most favoured nation treatment and comprehensive coverage of all sectors, but was not willing to negotiate on concrete liberalization until the question of coverage had been resolved. At this stage, sectoral lobbies began asserting themselves. In the US the Treasury continue to oppose coverage of financial services. The shipping industry, which had succeeded in gaining an exemption from the US–Canada Free Trade Agreement (FTA) began its campaign for exclusion from the General Agreement on Trade in Services (GATS).

More seriously, there was a general disinclination, among a number of US service lobbies, to accept GATT constraints on their ability to initiate bilateral market opening liberalization. During 1988 and 1989 the threat of Section 301 had been successfully used to open markets for US companies. A GATS agreement including MFN and comprehensive coverage would severely constrain the ability of the US to use such measures in services. The US private sector services companies which had initially led the campaign for the inclusion of services in the round began to have second thoughts. By October 1990 these doubts had spread. The US administration announced that it would be seeking indefinite exemptions from the MFN provisions of the GATS for shipping, air transport and basic telecommunications. The EC held to its policy of comprehensive coverage and refused to accept indefinite MFN exemptions, but sought a compromise approach based on time-limited exemptions for certain sectors. Although the sectoral pressures for exemption had been largely contained within the EC, not least to strengthen its negotiating position, there was also pressure within the EC for temporary exemptions from MFN and national treatment for shipping, air and surface transport and motion pictures. At the Brussels ministerial meeting, which was intended to conclude the round, the US indicated that it would be prepared to modify its position but negotiations were broken off due to the collapse of the agricultural negotiations. Had negotiations continued, the basis of a GATS might have been agreed in Brussels, even if details, such as the concrete liberalization packages, would have had to be worked out subsequently.

Throughout the negotiations on services the EC pressed for a comprehensive multilateral agreement. There was no effort to retain the option of using bilateral market opening measures. In any case, the EC has only modest means to pursue such an approach. The EC was therefore supporting the establishment of multilateral rules which would constrain its use of the third country or reciprocity provisions in directives such as the SBCD. It recognized, however, the Uruguay Round would only be the first step towards creating such a multilateral agreement and therefore set realistic negotiating objectives and stuck to them. In contrast, the US initially raised expectations about what could be achieved, but could not sell the idea of multilateral coverage that would limit the sovereignty of US trade legislation. It was therefore obliged to back-peddle when it became clear that key sectoral lobbies were not prepared to support the agreement.

There are few similarities between *agriculture* and services. It accounts for some 11 per cent of world trade, compared to 59 per cent for manufactures, but has assumed an overriding political importance in the Uruguay Round. Unlike services, there is a long history of (failed) agricultural trade negotiations in the GATT. It was the US that originally insisted on a waiver from GATT discipline for its agricultural policies. Other countries followed suit, but used different means of gaining exemption, for the EC it was through multilateral negotiations. GATT article XI, paragraph 2, thus provides specific conditions for the maintenance of agricultural quantitative restrictions. In the Kennedy Round efforts were made to control agriculture subsidies by means of calculating the overall level of support and agreeing to progressively reduce this over a period of time, but the talks failed because the US did not feel the EC offer was sufficient. It has been argued that this was a missed opportunity and that acceptance of a less than fully satisfactory agreement during the Kennedy Round would have made it easier to contain the subsequent growth in levels of agricultural support. Talks also broke down in the Tokyo Round because of disagreements between the EC and the US, although there were modest agreements reached in certain sectors such as dairy products and beef. The equitable market share formula (see above), however, soon proved to be inoperable.

From the beginning, the US, this time supported by the Cairns group of agricultural exporting countries (including Australia, Argentina, Hungary and Canada), was determined to get satisfaction in the Uruguay Round. Indeed, by arguing that the round would resolve many of the problems facing US agriculture in the mid-1980s, the Reagan administration had staked a lot of political capital on getting concrete improvements in market access for US agricultural products. Up to the mid-term review, the US maintained its maximalist position, so there was little surprise that the first mid-term review meeting failed. The subsequent agreement on substantial and progressive reduction of support over a specified period, was interpreted in Europe as the new Bush administration finally adopting a realistic and sensible negotiating objective. However, in subsequent statements, Carla Hills and Clayton Yeutter repeated the call for elimination and its formal position on agriculture, submitted in October 1989, the US argued for the elimination of export subsidies over five years, domestic subsidies over ten years, and for the tariffication of existing import restrictions, with tariffs to be progressively reduced through negotiations.

For the EC this was seen as reneging on the MTR agreement and taking the agricultural talks back to square one. In its position paper submitted in December 1989, the EC called for all forms of support including export, domestic subsidies and deficit payments to be converted into an aggregate measure of support (AMS). There would then be an agreement to reduce the level of support, as measured by the AMS over a period of years. The EC insisted that there should be scope for rebalancing, or increases in border protection for specific products, provided the overall level continued to be reduced. The target here was oilseeds on which the EC had bound tariffs in the Kennedy Round and on which the agricultural lobbies and the Commission wished to impose levies in order to protect EC production. The EC opposed specific commitments on separate forms of support. It opposed bound tariffs, replacing other forms of import restriction because it wished to retain the variable levies without which the costs of the CAP price support system would spin out of control.

Faced with a large gap between the EC and the US and Cairns group positions, the EC negotiators opted to 'tough it out' in the expectation that the others would move. As a result, there were no serious negotiations on agriculture through the rest of 1989 and much of 1990. There was a strong belief among ministries of agriculture, despite statements to the contrary by US officials, that, as in the Kennedy and Tokyo rounds and the mid-term review, the US would ultimately be forced to move ground because Congress would not really buy elimination. Some ministries saw the fact that the EC was prepared to accept a progressive reduction in support as already too much of a concession.

During the first half of 1990 the pressure mounted for the EC to make some move and thus enable negotiations to begin. At the May OECD ministerial meeting the EC was attacked by the US, Canada, Australia and New Zealand for refusing to negotiate. The pressure continued in the run up to the Houston Summit. Again the EC was isolated as the US ensured that agricultural trade moved to the top of the agenda. The EC refused to move and complained that although agriculture was important it was wrong to focus on it to the exclusion of other negotiating groups, on which other contracting parties also had to make concessions. For example, the US was isolated on textiles and clothing and sought to keep it off the agenda while Congress was discussing a highly protectionist bill, which, if adopted, could have torpedoed the whole round. The EC argued that the round had to be seen as a package, and that it could not be expected to make early concessions until it knew what else was on offer.

The Houston Summit endorsed a text produced by the chairman of the negotiating group on agriculture for the July meeting of the trade negotiating committee (TNC), the de Zeeuw text, as a 'means of intensifying further negotiations'. The US had wished to have the de Zeeuw text accepted as *the basis* for negotiations, which would have been in line with the status of chairman's reports for the other fourteen negotiating groups. But the EC ensured that the wording of the communique differed, which enabled the Community to interpret the Houston text as not endorsing the de Zeeuw text but as relegating it to the level of all other means of intensifying negotiations.

The de Zeeuw text incorporated the principle of AMS and tariffication but also called for export subsidies to be reduced faster than other forms of subsidy. As de Zeeuw pointed out, everyone except the EC supported this. Like all the TNC texts it also set a timetable for the remainder of the negotiations. This fairly loose reference to the de Zeeuw text in the Houston communiqué was again interpreted in Brussels as a victory. The US had once again backed down from its maximalist position and the European agricultural lobbies took heart from the fact that the EC had avoided making any specific commitments.

For a brief period it seemed as if negotiations were finally beginning. At the TNC meeting in late July 1990, the US and Cairns group negotiators elected not to create yet another crisis. In return, the EC agreed to meet the de Zeeuw timetable and submit its list of support measures by 1 October and its specific negotiating position by 15 October. At the end of July the

EC agricultural commissioner McSharry proposed a 30 per cent reduction in support measured on an AMS basis. The US submitted its position on time and sought substantially greater reductions of 75 per cent over a ten-year period, but more importantly sought commitments to make reductions in each group of subsidies. At this stage, the EC could no longer avoid addressing the issues. Tensions began to grow within the Commission, between the external affairs commissioner, Andriessen, and the more hardline commissioner for agriculture, McSharry. There were also divisions between the member states with the British and Dutch, in particular, pressing for a compromise position and the Germans and French, strongly supported by the Irish, Spanish and Greeks, wanting to continue to tough it out.

Germany was initially the strongest opponent of the Commission's proposals. In a telephone call to Jacques Delors, President of the Commission, on 17 October, Chancellor Kohl is reported to have effectively blocked any early compromise agreement. The German position was widely attributed to the governing coalition's desire to avoid alienating key voters in advance of the first election in the new enlarged Federal Republic on 2 December. In the seven meetings of the agricultural and foreign affairs councils during October 1990, the Federal Republic of Germany blocked agreement on a negotiating position. When, at one stage, the FRG appeared ready to accept an internal EC compromise, France stepped in to prevent agreement and the FRG refused to allow France to be isolated.

The internal EC negotiations, and indeed those of the whole round, reached a critical point at the time of the special European summit (European Council meeting) in Rome at the end of October. The heads of state and government decided not to deal with the GATT agricultural issue but took decisions, on the two intergovernmental conferences on economic and political union, including one to set a 1994 deadline for the beginning of stage II of European economic and monetary union, which could potentially change the whole course of European integration.[2] This was interpreted outside the EC as the Community turning inwards and failing to face up to key issues in the GATT round (*Washington Post*, 8 November 1990). When the EC position finally emerged on 7 November after a thirty-three day deadlock it was not substantially different from the original Commission proposals, and thus far short of what the US was after. In the brief time left before the Brussels ministerial meeting no progress could be made because the Commission clearly had little flexibility in handling a mandate that had taken the Council of Ministers so long to agree.

Having held out for over two years the EC was unable to negotiate an agreement at the GATT ministerial meeting held in Brussels in December. During the course of what was often a confused meeting, the Commission sought to break the impasse by a verbal suggestion that it would, after all, be prepared to discuss reaching agreement on reductions in each category of support. But the US argued that the offer was too vague and did not believe the EC could in fact deliver this. As at the mid-term review it was the Latin American countries that finally got up from the table, and along with the GATT Secretariat brought the meeting to an end four days into the scheduled week long meeting. The EC wished to continue negotiating.

Following the Brussels meeting, the EC announced major plans to reform the CAP. The US administration decided that although the prospect of a reform of the CAP might be enough to get Congress to accept an extension of its 'fast track' negotiating authority, the EC was not offering enough on agriculture for the administration to be prepared to try to sell a concluding agreement to Congress. The administration, therefore, opted for an extension of the fast track authority. To extend fast track authority the administration must simply state its intention to extend authority. Within a specified period fast track authority will then be granted unless either the House of Representatives or the Senate vote by a simple majority to deny extension. Votes took place in May 1991 but neither side of Congress could find a majority against continuing to negotiate. In early 1991 there was much scepticism that enough progress would be made with the reform of the CAP to enable agreement in the GATT to be reached. Through 1991, however, efforts to 'decouple' CAP reform from the GATT agreement appeared to have succeeded. This means that although the EC will have to give ground on agriculture, the fate of the round will not hang on the pace of reform. Indeed, Germany and France in late 1991 emphasized the need to reform the CAP with a view to accommodating the agricultural exporting countries of central-eastern Europe.

Agriculture must be seen as an important diplomatic and tactical failure for EC trade diplomacy. Key decision-makers appear to have misinterpreted the position of its trading partners by believing that, as in previous rounds, the US, when faced with the choice between concluding the round and getting a satisfactory agreement on agriculture, would opt for the round. When this did not happen the EC was not in a position to recover in time. The failure to produce a credible negotiating position also meant that the US and other countries were able to shift the blame for the failure of the Brussels meeting onto the EC. In practice, as discussed below, the position was much less clear cut and one could equally make the case that the US was holding up progress more than the EC. The political groundwork had not been done that would enable painful decisions to be taken to reduce agricultural support. The only mitigating circumstance is that the EC was not entirely to blame for lost time. The initial US position of elimination of all support lacked credibility as anything but an opening gambit, but the US negotiators persisted with this until into the fourth year of the negotiations, despite appearing to have dropped it at the mid-term review.

The other issues

Consideration of services and agriculture only would give a very partial picture of the EC's performance in the round, after all they account together for about 29 per cent of world trade. What about the other negotiations which affect the rest of trade? If an agreement had been possible on agriculture the prospects for concluding the Uruguay Round on time were fairly good. Nor should it be forgotten that this was an ambitious round. Progress had been made on many of the negotiating groups. In the new issues the expected north–south confrontation did not materialize. Instead, the main lines of confrontation were between the EC and the US. The EC maintained consistent support for agreements on all three of the new issues. On services, as shown above, the EC maintained consistent support for a comprehensive agreement when the US began to waver. On IPR there was little to choose between the EC position and that of the rest of the OECD countries, once the EC had overcome its initial reservations. Detailed negotiations on the text of a TRIPs agreement continued for four days at the Brussels meeting, and the remaining political problems, such as opposition to the protection of pharmaceutical patents by some developing countries, would probably have been resolved. There were enough non-OECD countries expected to sign the agreement to make it a credible multilateral approach. A modest agreement on investment was also close on strengthening GATT discipline for a selected number of six or seven trade-related investment measures (TRIMs). Investment like all the new issues had been brought onto the agenda by the US, but as the dollar declined after the Plaza accord of 1985 and the US became a debtor country, concern about barriers to outward US investment in other countries declined, and with it the US taste for maximalist results on investment. Politically visible acquisitions, especially by Japanese companies, also created a degree of xenophobia against foreign investment in the US. In the future, the large capital requirements in the ex-centrally planned economies, a tightening of bank regulation in the US and even a demand for capital in the Gulf to rebuild after the war, are likely to mean that the 1990s will be a decade of capital scarcity. The trend towards avoiding TRIMs for fear of discouraging investment is therefore likely to continue in the 1990s. On these terms, the prohibition of seven TRIMs, including local content requirements, which was consistently supported by the EC and was close to being agreed in Brussels would be a satisfactory result.

On market access issues apart from agriculture the EC was not lagging. In textiles and clothing the EC was again able to contain protectionist pressures and support a policy of phasing out the MFA. Here it was the US that was isolated due to its difficulties in containing protectionist lobbies working through Congress. This pressure forced the administration to adopt a policy of moving from the MFA system of quotas on a country and product basis, to global quotas for all countries for each product. While this, at first glance, may appear less discriminatory, the low rates of liberalization proposed by Congress, 1 per cent a year growth in quotas, was far below the existing 8–10 per cent rate of growth of imports into the US and therefore represented an increase in protectionism rather than a reduction.[3] The US and Canada were isolated in its support of global quotas. The EC for its part was not giving much away either. It sought to link the phasing out of the MFA quotas to a set of conditions, including: reductions of tariff and non-tariff barriers in the exporting countries; respect of copyright and trademarks; and the introduction of effective defences against unfair trade practices in the shape of 'effective' anti-dumping and safeguard actions. These conditions could clearly be used as a means of stretching the transitionary period almost indefinitely. But the EC, nevertheless, supported an agreement in the round on phasing out the MFA rather than delay in order the get another renewal of the MFA in 1991.

Thanks to its experience with the 1992 programme the EC was in a position to initiate proposals for comprehensive liberalization of government purchasing. Although not formerly part of the Uruguay Round, this is an area in which structural barriers pose significant problems. The EC proposed extending GATT coverage to include sub-national government and sectors such as the utilities. In so doing, it was, in effect, proposing extending the EC regime to the multilateral level. Neither the US nor Japan were able to accept this, and a compromise had to be sought on the less rigorous, and ultimately less credible, idea of 'best endeavours'.

The EC's performance in the area of rule-making was patchy. On the revision of anti-dumping the EC was on the defensive, especially after the May 1990 GATT ruling against the EC's so called 'parts directive', which sought to prevent anti-circumvention of dumping duties. But industries facing increased import competition in other major importing countries also see anti-dumping actions as the best means of gaining relief and therefore fought hard to prevent any significant tightening of the GATT provisions. The EC was therefore able to allow the US to hold the line against the efforts by Japan to tighten GATT discipline.

On safeguards, however, it is the EC that has held out and the US which has tended to slip-stream behind the EC. In the face of strong opposition, the EC moderated its objectives and moved towards accepting a watered down form of selectivity based on temporary use of modulated quotas. These could provide some degree of selectivity by so structuring quotas that they affect the most 'disruptive' imports while maintaining established sources of supply. This, like all references to selectivity, remained in square brackets in the text tabled in Brussels. Another outstanding issue was whether grey area measures, should be phased out or brought into the GATT system. Towards the end of the round the EC was negotiating an EC 'voluntary' export restraint agreement with Japan in cars to replace the existing national VERs. Although this envisages a phased removal of the quota it will clearly be against the letter and spirit of the standstill agreement which formed part of the Punta del Este package. An EC acceptance of a revised GATT safeguards provision which does not provide selectivity could well mean that VERs and other grey area measures will continue to fall outside the GATT.

In the area of subsidies, the EC and US picked up where they had left off in the Tokyo Round, with the US seeking to extend a GATT prohibition to coverage to domestic subsidies as well as export subsidies. The EC sought to exempt certain categories of subsidy such as non-selective state aid altogether and a clearer definition of injury which would reduce the scope for the exercise of wide discretion by (US) national authorities.

Rules of origin was another area in which the EC came under strong criticism during the second half of the round. The EC's interpretation of the existing, vague, Customs Cooperation Council (CCC) provisions on origin were seen by exporters to the EC as protectionist. But after some initial prevarication, during which it argued that origin was essentially a technical issue and should not be included in the round, the EC agreed that origin should be included in the negotiations on non-tariff barriers. The EC then endorsed the approach proposed by Hong Kong, Japan and the US on how to move towards common rules of origin.

Last but not least, there was dispute settlement. As noted above, the EC, although traditionally opposed to quasi-legalistic approaches to dispute settlement and favoured negotiation over adjudication, had shifted significantly during the first half of the round. After the mid-term review agreement on improved procedures for the establishment of GATT panels, the EC supported improvements in procedures for the adoption of panel reports. GATT case law has not evolved because of the requirement for consensus in adopting panel reports by the GATT contracting parties in the GATT Council. This has meant that the 'guilty' contracting parties have been able to block adoption of panel findings. One problem with ending the consensus rule has been that precedents set by GATT panels can influence the structure of multilateral rules. The EC was concerned that a 'consensus minus two approach' which excluded the parties to a dispute, could mean that, in the event of a dispute affecting the EC, a panel decision affecting the interpretation of key GATT provisions could be taken without the EC having a say. To get around this, the EC supported the introduction of an appeals procedure to deal with such cases. Once this had been agreed, the EC supported replacing unanimity for adoption of a panel report with unanimity for rejection of a report. In other words, a panel report could only be rejected if all contracting parties, including the CB in whose favour the panel has ruled, oppose the decision. This represents an important shift in the EC's position and means that there is a convergence of views favouring stronger adjudication in GATT dispute settlement. Although brought about by concern about US unilateral actions, the support of the EC, added to that of the US and even a wide range of developing countries, which have also overcame their suspicion of GATT dispute settlement, meant an agreement was reached before the Brussels meeting. An improved dispute settlement procedure applied to all aspects of the GATT could have a significant effect in strengthening the multilateral system.

Taking the round as a whole, the EC's record in support of multilateralism was not too bad. Where it had problems these tended to be in areas such as agriculture or safeguards, in which there were entrenched positions. When it came to extending multilateral disciplines into new areas and areas in which regulatory and structural barriers were important the EC showed a willingness to mesh its approach with the multilateral regime and did not seek to retain scope for the use of EC legislation as a means of pursuing bilateral trade liberalization. The EC did not move quickly but it showed real movement towards supporting multilateral agreements during the course of the round. This is not to claim that there are not areas, such as anti-dumping, subsidies and, above all, agriculture, in which the EC has resisted greater multilateral discipline. But one cannot say that the EC has done so any more than any other contracting party.

The relative lack of domestic pressure for concrete results has also meant that the EC has been prepared to go the extra kilometre for a multilateral agreement which kept the developing countries on board rather than go for the easier route of a code or multilateral agreement between like-minded countries.

Future issues in EC commercial policy

A key issue for EC trade diplomacy as for other participants in the Uruguay Round is how to maintain momentum in the negotiations. During the first four years of the negotiations much of the momentum came from the US.

This stemmed from the US administration's need to satisfy Congress. Following the two year extension of fast track by the US Congress, this pressure has eased. The extension was also intended to enable the US administration to negotiate a free trade agreement with Mexico, which seems likely to take the full two years. Domestic difficulties over a range of issues in the round also mean that it was convenient for the US that the EC was bogged down in agriculture. In the run-up to the London CV Summit the EC, led by the British as chairman for the summit, sought to use the summit as a means of giving the round enough momentum for it to be completed at or around the turn of the year in order to avoid the complications of a US presidential campaign.

Another important issue is the status of the near agreements reached in Brussels in most negotiating groups. It is important that progress, which in some cases goes beyond the consolidated text of 376 pages submitted to the Brussels meeting, is not lost. The EC must therefore seek ways of retaining what has already been achieved. This is difficult because separate parts of the package cannot be agreed and implemented without an agreement on agriculture which, even if successful, could take the EC twelve months or longer to agree on CAP reform.

The failure to agree on the round would undoubtedly contribute to an increase in disputes. Bilateral problems put off so as not to pollute the atmosphere in Geneva will be brought back to the table. Indeed, some agricultural disputes were reopened almost before the delegates had returned from Brussels in December 1990. The US also reopened the CAP dispute with the EC in February 1991. These disputes, many of which – but not all – affect US–EC bilateral relations will have to be managed. The way this is done will have a direct bearing on the future of multilateralism. There was a moderate measure of success in managing disputes during 1991, which helped to defuse some of the rhetoric. For example, the bilateral issue with Japan on car imports, which had been seen as a litmus test of EC policy in Japan and beyond, was resolved fairly quietly, at least for the short term, in August 1991.

A delay in multilateral talks is likely to increase pressure in the US for greater use of bilateral market opening measures. This will raise fundamental questions for the GATT system as a whole, and for the EC. To date the US administration has managed to avoid extensive use of Section 301 actions against the EC. But a significant 301 action could easily escalate as the EC is unlikely to accept any negotiation under the threat of bilateral action. If this happens one could well see a kind of transatlantic strategic impediments initiative. The prospect of such a development has led to suggestions that talks on regulatory and structural barriers to trade should be initiated in the OECD.

There is likely to be general pressure for more multilateral approaches to trade issues, especially from the US. The EC should not resist such approaches, but should seek to ensure that the OECD is not burdened with the same kind of false expectations that have weighed heavily on the GATT Round. The case is still to be proven that bilateral approaches will be any more successful than multilateral approaches. They weaken the multilateral system, but as the Uruguay Round has shown, the lines of confrontation in current trade policy are as much transatlantic or transpacific as north–south.

OECD agreements are therefore unlikely to result in any substantive advance unless the major players are prepared to cede more sovereignty. The OECD will, however, continue to be an important forum for consultation and debate as in the past, and an intensification may help to defuse the political pressures for bilateral action.

In conclusion, whatever the outcome of the Uruguay Round, the EC will face major challenges in the field of trade diplomacy in both multilateral and bilateral relations. If it is to meet these and fulfil its growing responsibilities for the international trading system, ways must be found of moving extra-EC trade issues up the EC's internal agenda. This means, in the first instance, moving it up the agenda in each of the member states. External trade policy, and the GATT in particular, is too often left to the experts.

NOTES

1 This is particularly the case in the EC where there are no alternatives in the shape of countervailing duty or unfair trade provisions. These are relatively underdeveloped in the EC compared to the US.
2 The British lobbied hard to get the GATT agricultural issue on the agenda, some would argue, in order to keep the IGC issues off it, but failed.
3 Had an agreement been reached in Brussels the US would probably have conceded on global quotas, but in the absence of a conclusion to the Uruguay Round the MFA was extended.

REFERENCES

Aho, Michael and Aronson, Jonathan 1985: *Trade Talks: America Better Listen!* New York: Council on Foreign Relations.
Brittan, Leon 1990: Speech at the Confindustria, Rome, November.
European Commission 1982: Communication to the Council: general policy orientation for the GATT ministerial meeting, November. In Golt 1982, appendix II.
European Commission 1986: *Mandate for the Uruguay Round trade negotiations*, unpublished, June.
GATT 1989: *International Trade*, Geneva 1989.
Golt, Sidney 1982: *Trade Issues in the 1980s*. London: British North American Committee, October.
Golt, Sidney 1986: *The GATT Negotiations 1986–90: Origins, Issues and Prospects*. London: British North America Committee.
Hart, Jeffrey, Woolcock, S. and van der Venn, N. 1985: *Interdependence in the Post Multilateral Era*. Boston: University Press of America.
Hufbauer, G. C. (ed.) 1990: *Europe 1992 and American Perspective*. Washington DC: The Brooking Institution.
Kelly, Jilyan and Woolcock, Stephen 1989: GATT: A midterm agreement. *World Today*, June, 92–3.
Murphy, Anna 1990: *The European Community and the International Trading System*. vol. II. Brussels: Centre for European Policy Studies.
Patterson, Gardner 1983: The European Community as a threat to the system. In William Cline (ed.), *Trade Policy in the 1980s*. Washington: Institute for International Economics.
Preeg, Ernest 1970: *Traders and Diplomats*. Washington DC: The Brookings Institution.
Woolcock, S., Hodges, M. and Schreiber, K. 1991: *Britain, Germany and 1992: the Limits of Deregulation*. London: RIIA.

13

The 1992 breakthrough and the global economic integration agenda

Albert Bressand

At first, the 1992 programme did look like a mere restatement of the 'common market' objective set up in the 1957 Treaty of Rome which was thought to have been achieved in 1968. Yet, in addition to dealing with its traditional trade agenda, Europe has unleashed, almost unknowingly, a new economic dynamics centred on services, regulatory convergence, advanced and integrated public infrastructures and corporate cross-border networking strategies.

The present chapter therefore begins by looking at the corporate strategies behind the 1992 momentum. A second section briefly renews the type of policies, notably with respect to infrastructures behind this post-interdependence dynamics in which trade is only one of the dimensions of a far more complex set of cross-border interactions. Looking at the external implications, the third section then suggests that, rather than a 'fortress', Europe needs to be seen as an outpost in changing globalization trends to which other regions of the world will also have to react.

On the whole, and with many caveats, the point is made in this chapter that Europeans have initiated the first large-scale rethinking of international economic cooperation since the US-sponsored initiatives of the late 1940s and early 1950s that laid the ground for the postwar reconstruction and prosperity. The fact that this has come as the result not of political acumen but of unexpected synergies between the broad integration objectives laid in the 1957 Treaty of Rome and the present global economic dynamics should not distract from further conscious efforts to develop this new mode of international cooperation. Hence the chapter concludes with recommendations as to an OECD centred process and treaty that could provide an outward looking solution to the present tensions.

Corporations as architects

Unlike the 'common market' of the 1960s which, in many countries, was often imposed upon reluctant corporations, the 1992 process has been initiated by large European firms acutely aware of the decreasing – and often counter-productive – role of protected national markets in today's global competition. Not that such companies are especially enlightened: many of them had been instrumental in setting up or preserving the barriers now being dismantled. But they realized that the numbers simply no longer added up.

While this had been the case a long time ago for the smaller European countries, the early 1980s marked the limits of the national consolidation process in the larger countries in sectors such as telecommunications, electronics, automobiles etc. Having nationalized and merged almost all important national telecommunication companies, France was left in 1986 with one national champion, Alcatel, the offspring of the 1983 merging of the telephone subsidiaries of its two leading information technology companies, Compagnie Générale d'Electricité (CGE) and Thomson. Yet, even the sizeable French PTT procurement programme could no longer provide support and subsidies commensurate with the 1 billion dollars R&D effort called for by the new generation of public telephone switches: the national champion policy was becoming too costly and too ineffective for both governments and their champions. Hence the role of the European Business Roundtable in shaping what was to become the 1985 White Paper internal market agenda.

Similarly, small and medium companies are increasingly aware of the potential of tighter European integration in relaxing the grips of national authorities and of their favourite large corporate champions. In France, mavericks such as the Leclerc distribution group and the UTA airline – a company now absorbed by Air France – have been systematically challenging restrictive national laws, state monopolies and de facto oligopolies before the European Court on subjects ranging from the pharmacists' monopoly over the sales of baby milk formulas to transportation policies.

Last but not least, a major influence has come from individuals. Tired of waiting behind lorries at the borders, and tired of being denied access to benefits available next door – such as those associated with lower taxes and deregulation – they have began to vote with their feet, their purse and in court. The European Court is the least mentioned, yet indeed a key actor, in the overall liberalization process. Its 1979 'Cassis de Dijon' decision was a major blow to non-tariff barriers of all types. 'Cassis de Dijon' refers to a ruling by the European Court of Justice adopted in 1979 which dealt with the case of a small German importer of liqueur de Cassis produced in Dijon, France; import was being prohibited on the pretext that the alcohol content was too low to qualify as a liqueur but too high to qualify as wine. The Court decided that free access onto the territory of any other member state implied that national norms could not be used to discriminate against imports. This ruling was followed by a number of others related to the import/export of meat, wheat and pasta within the Community. 'Cassis de Dijon' has remained the judicial reference for the enforcement of mutual recognition. The Court's 4 December 1986 insurance decision established cross-border service delivery as legitimate under the Treaty of Rome for all services. As individual actors turn to the European Court to enforce an increasing array of rights to interact across borders, policy makers have decreasing confidence in their capacity to enforce policies that would depart too much from those of the more open European countries.

The new dynamics of corporate interconnection

Rather than simply seeking exports and economies of scale, European-based companies are now focusing on developing Europe-wide delivery systems, corporate alliances, production networks and electronic marketplaces. Rather than just shipping goods across borders, they are seeking customized, in-depth interactions with clients, suppliers and partners, through an expanding gamut of networking strategies, many of which have a strong information and advanced communication content. In this sense, this physical elimination of custom, houses an almost narrow symbol of the deeper and more complex ways in which corporate strategies are reshaping the new phase of economic integration (*Perspectives*, no. 8, 1989).

When Allianz, the leading German insurance company seeks to develop its business in Spain, it does so neither through 'exports' (i.e. cross-border delivery) nor through the traditional 'foreign investment' in their insurance sector but through a networking arrangement with two Spanish *banks* interested in innovative and cost effective use of their distribution networks and in which Allianz takes a significant yet far from dominant 5 per cent equity stake. Our work at PROMETHEE (Bressand, Distler and Nicolaidis, 1989) has focused on the role of these and similar strategies whereby corporations seek productivity gains not just through economies of scale but through higher levels of efficiency in the management of the web and external relations on which their production and profits depend (e.g. a more efficient management of value creating relationships with customers, suppliers and partners). To achieve the economies of scale in customized products that we label mass-customization, corporations need a depth and quality of interactions that go beyond the arm's-length relationship associated with markets, even when market forces are actually shaping such relationships. A concrete example is the move of US and European car manufacturers from piecemeal sub-contracting aimed at short-term cost optimization to the development of long-term strategic relationship with suppliers.

Such depth and quality of relations is made possible by two types of factors, namely *access to infrastructures* through which interactions can be conducted, and definition of – and adherence to – common sets of rules to which we refer as *infostructures*. Without going into detail here, this combination of infrastructures and infostructures is what we call 'networks', thereby giving to this term a broader sense than is usually implied. A lot of the restructuring at work in Europe falls within this type of interaction rather than under the traditional trade specialization and economies of scale paradigm. While high technology and services (finance, transport, communications, advertising etc.) are presently the key fields of applications, such strategies and the policies explicitly or implicitly supporting them are at the heart of the 1992 dynamics, and go a long way in accounting for the discrepancy between traditional political visions of Europe and the unexpected renaissance of regional integration.

Seen at the level of individual actors, this new type of interactions appears to rest on four types of 'networks'.

Two of them are *data* networks: depending on whether they are internal to one corporation or shared among several, we refer to them as *intracorporate* networks and *transcorporate* networks. Computer–Aided Design and Manufacturing (CAD–CAM) networks and Computer Integrated Manufacturing Networks (CIM) are well known examples of intra-corporate networks. Meanwhile, Electronic Data Interchange (EDI) is the fastest growing type of transcorporate networks: linking manufacturers, suppliers and dealers, it makes possible new types of production integration.

Two other types of networks are of a *strategic nature*: *intercorporate* networks include strategic alliances and joint ventures of all types, while *meta-corporate* networks are intended to influence the corporate environment through lobbying, standard setting, etc.

The politics of mass customization and networking

A critical question has to do with the relationship between this private sector dynamic and the more traditional government-led process of formal integration. European politicians of all creeds have been taken by surprise by the process they had themselves put in motion. It is ironic to remember the sober and less than enthusiastic atmosphere that had presided over the launching of the 1992 programme. President Mitterrand, for instance, remarked at the end of the Luxembourg Summit that this agreement (the Single Act) 'goes in the right direction' but that 'France has a more ambitious view of what Europe could do'. Margaret Thatcher referred to the Single Act as a 'modest decision' (*Le Monde*, 4 December 1985; *La Tribune de l'Economie*, 5 December 1985). Editorials referred to the signing of the Single Act as just another of those face-saving diplomatic gimmicks used to give the appearance of progress. By contrast, two and a half years later Margaret Thatcher's July 1988 BBC interview and her Bruges speech of 20 September 1988 illustrate a British awakening to the fact that the 1992 *process* goes well beyond what it seemed to imply initially.

One should indeed remember that the Single Act was the outcome of a merciless watering down process whereby European governments of all opinions had tamed and, in their view, reduced to a set of technical and symbolic decisions, the federalist proposals put forward by European Parliament's Vice-President, Altiero Spinelli. Indeed, the true believers in European integration were less than thrilled by the launching of 1992 which they assessed in terms of what was *not* undertaken rather than of the process of change around which many are now rallying. In a speech before the Institutional Affairs Committee of the European Parliament on 4 February 1986, Altiero Spinelli was quoted as saying 'the Single Act contains a few modest novelties . . . and will almost certainly have proven its ineffectiveness within two years'.

The present changes in government role now apparent throughout the western societies make it increasingly difficult, however, to define what formal integration is or should be. Are, for instance, common tax rates a sign of greater 'integration' than dissimilar tax rates all moving in the same direction? Is a Brussels-centred European fiscal process a step towards 'integration' or a choice among possible integration concepts?

From harmonization to mass customization

In the mass-production, mass-consumption societies of the 1960s and 1970s, moves towards greater uniformity were likely to translate into economies of scale and additional growth. Today, production, marketing and consumption processes however reflect new technological and strategic opportunities based on far more customized interactions and putting a premium on diversity, flexibility and experimentation. Hence, harmonization of the national approaches is unlikely to play the same role in economic integration today as it did when the Common Market was being built.

A critical field in which to test this changing relationship between economic and political integration is the fiscal one. While the Commission initially assumed that similar VAT taxes were a natural part of an open internal market, one may wonder whether a more fundamental analysis would put as much emphasis on the need for fiscal harmonization. Uniformity on tax matters would imply such massive changes in the levels and structures of national tax receipts that the problems created would exceed not only the absorptive capacity of many national political systems but also the measurable economic benefits. Yet, diversity and the free competition among differing national approaches – in principle a very fruitful process – is fundamentally skewed by the fact that cross-border purchases would respond to differentials among national VAT rates irrespective of the different role VAT taxes plays in the various national tax structures.

Only in a longer term perspective, when private interlinkages have achieved some sort of no-return point, will it become advisable to take the political risk of using European economic integration as a deliberate engine for comprehensive national fiscal reform.

The commission as a catalyst of networking

Obviously, many obstacles may come in the way of interlinking and of corporate networking across Europe. But a number of policies in place, within the 1992 White paper framework as well as outside of it, are actually facilitating or fostering as never before the various levels of networking behind information age dynamism:

Seen in the US as a timid step towards deregulation of telecommunications, the July 1987 *Green Book* sets the stage for the development of Europe-wide intracorporate and transcorporate networks as well as of value added networks in general. The 1991 *Green Book* on satellites, the still in the making *Green Book* on mobile telecommunications and the RACE programme (seeking to foster Europe-wide broad band integrated services digital networks) will further accelerate the shift from national systems centred on public monopolies towards open network architectures in which customized private networks can flourish.

The European Commission is giving its blessing to the development of Europe-wide electronic networks – which we refer to as networked markets – bringing together market participants in sectors such as travel services, chemicals, electronic banking services, etc. To take just two examples, the

Commission has given the green light to the effort of European banks to interconnect all networks of automated cash dispensers. Meanwhile, the Amadeus and Galileo Computer Reservation Systems are now at the centre of the restructuring and strategic alliance process reshaping the European airlines industry. Alliances entered into by European airlines with US partners also give prominence to electronic interconnection (Bressand, 1989, pp. 51–64).

Launched in 1984, the pace setting ESPRIT program has been followed by a number of more specialized programs such as BRITE, SCIENCE, that facilitate cross-borders intercorporate networks (joint ventures, common projects, precompetitive R&D, etc.). At the French urging, governments have followed suit with the more flexible, closer to market, EUREKA program in which the EFTA countries and even Canada are also involved. More than three thousand companies or research institutions are now involved in the 470 EUREKA programs, first among which the JESSI semi-conductor joint venture and the high definition television program. Total budget involved is now above 10 billion ECUs.

The creation of new standards-setting fora bringing together public and private actors, such as the CEPT sponsored European Telecommunications Standardization Institute (ETSI) in which PTTs, manufacturers and users come together to develop standards, reinforces the developments of European meta-networks. European companies that did not talk to one another ten years ago are now routinely involved in setting Europe-wide standards in fields ranging from computer assisted driving to digital cellular phone and credit cards.

In the meanwhile, the encouragement of cross-border, multilingual studies and research by students, teachers and scientists (Erasmus and Comet programmes) contribute to breaking the barriers between the national education system by requiring graduate students and researchers to expose themselves to at least one other European higher education system.

Federalism, deregulation and the search for a political doctrine of interconnection

This networking dimension of EC and national policies, however, have tended to develop piecemeal, do not cover the whole gamut of cross-border dynamics and still lack a unified strategic concept. Yet, a group has been convened in Brussels on European networks, and an integrated approach spanning the electric utility, railways and other networks is gradually taking shape.

European interconnection however is still far from being embodied in a fully fledged political doctrine. As in the previous decades, the conflicting political visions of European integration at the centre of the present debate are the federalist vision and the European 'deregulationist' vision. The federalist vision is the one to which Jacques Delors alluded in the summer of 1988 when he mentioned the prospect of 80 per cent of the key decisions being taken in Brussels against 20 per cent in the national capital. Commenting on the choices to be made at the intergovernmental conference on EMU, Jacques Delors stressed the point again in September 1991, expressing his worries at the prospect of 'economic policy being narrowly equated with fiscal and monetary policy'. In his view, a genuine EMU should recognize 'the leading role of politics, without which Europe would gradually restrict itself to being a free trade zone deprived of internal consistency – and therefore a highly vulnerable region – and deprived also of the social objectives that give its ultimate meaning to political action' (*Liberation*, 6 September 1991).

Hence the ambiguity of the scope and implications of the transfer of sovereignty involved in monetary union. In a federalist perspective, this is an integral part of a broader transfer of power in the economic and political field. In the narrow free trade perspective which Delors opposes, the same decisions in the monetary field would simply be the roof over the free trade building: sovereignty would not be really transferred, in the sense that it would be acknowledged simply to have dissolved anyway in a complex web of macroeconomic and trade interdependences. The intergovernmental conference on political union had to deal in one way or another with this ambiguity stemming from the overlap between the politics of federalism and the economics of monetary interdependence.

The 'deregulationist' vision, by contrast, is the re-expression of the 'free trade zone' approach, according to which what matters is to eliminate trade barriers and to deregulate within each national country.

While 'deregulation' is a fundamental source of economic dynamism, it is also a far more complex – and regulation intensive – process than commonly realized. Having 'rolled back the state' from the United Kingdom, the now retired Mrs Thatcher need not board a deregulated flight to Brussels to watch regulation creeping back: a tube ride to Bank Station would suffice. Anyone who thinks the City and the British authorities are attempting to lure in foreign investors and banks through more financial deregulation has probably not perused the Financial Services Act: if there is any logic behind it, it would rather be that what deregulation allowed to gain, re-regulation will aim to keep! Similarly, in the field of telecommunications, the successful British experience shares with the more chaotic American one a high level of government interventions in favour of new entrants like Mercury and MCI that could not yet withstand full competition with the dominant provider.

In this sense, the challenge for post–1992 Europe will be to spell out the political doctrine called for by its actual integration process, the success of which may rest largely on departing from what political leaders pronounce it to be.

The new citizenship of mutual recognition

A source of inspiration for this political *aggiornamento* can be found in the watershed decision by the twelve European Community countries to break away from previous, and increasingly futile, efforts to harmonize regulations and technical norms in favour of an amazingly speedier process based on a limited number of core principles and on mutual recognition. The ensuing approach, now referred to as 'mutual recognition' happens to be in strong synergy with the dynamics of corporate cross-border networking behind the 1992 momentum.

The implications of mutual recognition are quite fundamental, as national authorities will now accept that other governments grant establishment rights to their own national firms as well as to third country firms, taking into account their own regulatory criteria rather than that of the host country. To the extent that some core principles are adhered to, the Second Banking Directive allows banks, financial services providers to carry a number of activities on a European scale under their *home country regulations* (Schwartz, 1989). By the same token, following the 1979 'Cassis de Dijon' European Court of Justice landmark decision, standards and norms considered acceptable in one of the EC countries and confirming to a few general EC guidelines will have to be accepted in all countries.

As remarked by Michel Albert – chairman and CEO of the AGF insurance group – mutual recognition as will be practised in Europe has no equivalent in the world and goes beyond the federalist vision borrowed from the US experience (Albert, 1988). As he likes to stress, Europeans have accepted a direct interaction and competition among national regulations and tax structures without creating the political institutions with which a transfer of sovereignty of that order had always been associated.

Fortress Europe . . . or the European challenge?

The 'Fortress Europe' motto has come to be accepted as a central reference in the US and in some European countries – most notably the UK – in thinking about the external implications of the 'Europe 1992' process. Interestingly, the term itself is quite ambiguous as it can suggest not just protectionism but also a strengthening of European competitiveness. More importantly, the term does fail to capture the real nature of the 'European challenge' that '1992' might indeed represent.

Obviously, protectionist trends exist in Europe as in most other parts of the world. With the exception of UK–Netherlands–Belgium–Ireland mini common markets, European airlines for instance have dragged their feet to abandon the cosy world of bilateral quotas where allowing 40–60 rather than 50–50 revenues sharing arrangements is seen as deregulation. Patterned after the US measures that had kept Japanese exporters to a (hefty) quarter of the US car market, the quotas and national sub-quotas imposed on direct exports of Japanese cars in July 1991 are a far cry from the constructive cooperative approach that should preside over EC–Japan relations (Bressand, 1991).

Yet, it is worth emphasizing that foreigners – mostly Americans – cried wolf before the EC had even a clear sense that there was such a thing as an external dimension to 1992. For weeks, the only hard information that the first burst of press articles on Fortress Europe of the summer of 1988 could mention were the statements by Jacques Calvet, Peugeot's Chairman, that the EC should provide some substitute for the national quotas on Japanese cars: one would indeed expect the protected to become vocal as protections come closer to being removed. Then came the Nissan made-in-the-UK cars for which the French, following an informal car manufacturers' agreement, boldly required an 80 per cent European content as opposed to the amazing 70 per cent already achieved by Nissan (one should note that when Spain was not a member of the EC, a number of Renault cars would not have passed the test!). But it was not really until discussions heated up around the January 1988 Second Banking Draft Directive that the Fortress Europe leitmotif met some issue of substance with which to be identified. The *reciprocity* issue raised by this market opening directive is of fundamental importance for the redefinition of trade liberalization concept in the 1990s. It calls, however, for very careful, high-level discussions, and possibly initiatives, that only the superficial mind would address in the metaphorical 'fortress' context.

Indeed, even if one were to discount every single word uttered in Europe in favour of free trade, there are fundamental reasons why European integration in general, and the 1992 process in particular, are bound to reduce the *capacity*, if not the will, of Europeans to implement protection.

A first reason is the greater diversity of interests in any given sector among the different countries, and therefore the more elusive nature of a consensus for protection. Germany, for instance, has little consumer electronics industry left and will not be sympathetic to French efforts to keep the Japanese at bay. Vice versa, foreign companies' pressures for a level playing field with respect to cross-border acquisitions are beginning to challenge the dominant role played by German banks in the German 'market for corporate control'. An interesting precedent was set in a country of similar banking and corporate culture when Nestlé found that it could not go on for ever acquiring non-Swiss companies such as Rowntree while forbidding its own foreign shareholders the right to own voting shares. More generally, the EC provides a framework superior to any existing one – including the GATT – to bring attention to, and deal with, restrictive practices outside of the field of 'trade' as defined after the war.

Another reason why 1992 will mean, on the whole, greater rather than more restricted openness – a reason many non-Europeans do not fully appreciate – is the element of due process that Europeanization introduces. Protectionism is more easily implemented as an implicit, discretionary state of affairs than as an explicit collective strategy. True, the Multi Fibre Agreement (MFA) and a few other similar undertakings illustrate a collective capacity at protectionism. But, in general, the type of cosy arrangement national bureaucracies can provide are made more difficult by the existence of a discussion process involving twelve countries under the scrutiny of a multinational Commission and with the possibility to turn to an independent and highly respected European Court of Justice for redress.

All these factors suggest that 'Fortress Europe' metaphor has its roots less in actual European policies (with due exceptions in limited subjects) than in the fortress fighters' own worries, inhibitions and unspoken agenda. What is, after all, a 'fortress'? Is it a region which is more *protected* – something 1992 Europe, with no internal border control, free flow of capital and limits to governments' discretionary power is unlikely to be? Or is it a region that is more difficult to conquer, which many of the more dynamic European markets may indeed turn out to be? Rather than a dungeon around which to gather the usual lame ducks, the fortress that Europe can end up building could be an outpost overlooking the new global economic opportunities. In other words, a 'European model' and a 'European challenge' rather than a 'Fortress Europe' may well be taking shape.

As suggested above, this European challenge has little to do with an exceptional foresight on the part of European leaders, and much more to do with unanticipated synergies between the broad policy framework available in the European context and a new global economic dynamics that can no longer be understood and managed in the traditional narrow trade framework.

1992, GATT and the state of US deregulation

Beyond the 'fortress' syndrome discussed above, the 1992 process has far-reaching implications outside Europe. At the risk of shocking the American reader, I will suggest that a first type of implications has to do with the need for an updated, broader perspective on a set of American domestic policies loosely referred to as deregulation (Distler, 1988). While these innovative policies had set the pace for international economic restructuring in key services in the 1980s, they are now more or less stale and may well be leap-frogged by more coherent European and Japanese initiatives. Conducting banking activities under quasi-universal banking rules and across borders is clearly bound to be more efficient than the state-by-state way in which the US still regulates a fragmented financial industry.

The 1992 programme can be seen in part as an acknowledgement – an explicit one in the UK, a tacit and sometimes reluctant one in some continental countries – of the effectiveness of the deregulation approach pioneered by the US since the late 1970s. As often the case, late starters have the benefit of their predecessors' experience and, in this sense, the 1992 programme sheds some cruder light on the unfinished state of the great American deregulation.

It will, however, take a while before Americans accept to look at such delicate domestic policies in the fields of finance, telecommunications and transportations in the international context in which they increasingly belong. Indeed, many American readers will probably be uncomfortable with the notion that a European initiative could have any impact on the definition of US priorities. The fact that Europeans already live in a world where not just policies but regulations and judicial processes are open to international influence will take a long time to be incorporated in US thinking. Hence, one can expect the Euro-American debate to revolve in large part around the more familiar trade arena, and most specifically around the mutual implications of 1992 and the Uruguay Round of multilateral trade negotiations.

A second type of global implications has to do with multilateral trade negotiations. The impact of '1992' on GATT is not limited to the US concern of seeing twelve key nations – and many of their EFTA associates – come to the multilateral negotiating table with a pre-agreed and rigidified common negotiating stance. The real challenge for the US is that the European process has a depth and scope that multilateral negotiations as well as American bilateral strategies simply do not match. Far from being incidental, this discrepancy reflects the qualitative difference between the objective of *integration* pursued by the European and the more narrow *trade* agenda embedded in the multilateral system.

Uruguay Round negotiators have struggled, for instance, with 'narrow' versus 'broad' definitions of services and consider as a key principle that national regulatory objectives be left untouched. Europeans, by contrast, have come to accept as natural that their tax structure become the subject of intra-EC negotiations, that other EC authorities be responsible for the regulation of important aspects of foreign firms' activities on domestic soil, that EC nationals be entitled not just to free movement and right of work but to have their national diplomas recognized as equivalents to national diplomas, including access to the professions and to highly regulated activities. In the past, free movement of people, regulatory harmonization etc. were seen as political objectives that Europeans were pursuing in addition to, and quite separately from, the core of economic objectives common to the western nations. In today's information and services-intensive world economy, however, such a distinction no longer applies, and Europeans are clearly at an advantage to deal with the critical issues related to trade in services.

It is clear that the international trade agenda needs to be substantially expanded to cover the increasingly central services activities, and to reach into critical dimensions of economic organization, such as telecommunications, that were until then considered as purely domestic. In the aftermath of the Tokyo Round and of the GATT ministerial meeting of 1982, Europe was clearly lagging behind in this international rethinking effort. The paradox is that Europe has now arrived, in part in reaction to Americans' initiatives and in larger part as a result of its 1992 objectives, at an agenda of its own that goes further towards addressing those key issues.

To put it in a nutshell, and with due caveat, Europe is now poised to implement changes that Americans have painstakingly advocated, and to do so with a more powerful set of tools than the US has ever considered appropriate or even thinkable at the international level.

Towards an OECD-wide '1992'?

A fundamental lesson from the 1992 process is that the discrepancy is growing between what has become possible – in terms of market effectiveness, technological capacities, corporate strategies, financing techniques, individual mobility, cultural cross-fertilizing etc. – and the long-term goals that the advanced nations are setting up for themselves in the various international fora. Dreams and visions are already lagging behind reality. With the 1992 process and the set of policies put in place on its side, Europe has almost unwittingly bridged part of the gap. In many ways, however, this rethinking remains partial within Europe and even more so in other fora. The risk therefore exists that major international economic opportunities will remain untapped.

To extract the full benefit possible from the global economy, governments, companies and individuals now require much more than used to be implied by the concept of 'free trade'. In this sense, the great unforeseen merit of 1992 is to confront the international economic community with actual examples of economic integration beyond what we are used to considering as an ideal. As pointed out by Michel Albert, the Single Act once seen as a 'modest document' has been the catalyst of a change going beyond federalism and yet unaccompanied by the creation of the institutional framework that federalists see as the fundamental goal. Hence his view that the process has been somehow turned on its head, even if for Europe's good.

In this respect, the debate on the external implications of mutual recognition is a pivotal issue. Understanding its true implications calls for an explicit discussion of the rule-setting processes in the background of the economic interactions at stake, as well as of the political mechanisms from which these rule-setting processes derive their legitimacy. The catch–22 situation resulting from the conjunction of national treatment and mutual recognition presents European regulators with a loss of sovereignty *erga omnes* that is not legitimized by the political decisions that have made it acceptable within the European framework.

The actual 'reciprocity' that Europeans are trying to define – and have so far more or less failed to articulate – could probably be derived from the political fact that a number of countries have now opened their domestic regulations – including, directly and indirectly, on tax matters – to each other's in-depth influence. Obviously, interactions among countries with such an influence over one another can go well beyond what is politically acceptable between countries whose regulatory systems are closed to one another.

This dilemma should be seen as an opportunity to promote a broader international discussion of what goals the community of nations should set for themselves in a long-term economic perspective. The confusion surrounding the debate on national treatment reflects a definition of free trade designed for a world in which countries were neatly separated from one another, and in which value was exchanged through the arm's-length trade in goods channel rather than through regulation intensive cross-border processes. 'Free trade' has been – and still remains – a fundamental guiding objective, yet today's technologically advanced and interconnected world needs an upgraded concept of multilateral economic openness.

The 'Europe 1992' experience holds some lessons for the US: while Europeans accept that a European Court of Justice can challenge national laws and regulations, the US has resisted even the relatively limited Canadian proposal for a binational tribunal with authority over national anti-dumping processes. The US, nevertheless, could take note that a stronger EC is already in a position to put forward some of its legal approaches in the extra-territorial fashion that Americans have been fond of (witness the recent application to Nordic pulp and paper companies of EC competition rules). More importantly, joint approaches to global regulatory issues are anyway creeping onto the agenda – in fields such as global security trading, foreign direct investments and certification. It would be better to anticipate this evolution in an open and forward-looking manner rather than to react defensively to issues and tensions as they will arise.

Hence, rather than debating *ad aeternam* how the new European approach could fit within the narrower traditional concepts, we strongly suggest that the time has come for a major international initiative that could carry, with due adaptation, the 1992 momentum into a broader community of nations.

Based on its – still not fully clarified – experience with new dimensions of international economic openness, the European Community would have a major responsibility in promoting a 'free trade plus' initiative. In our view, the EC should explicitly initiate a debate, even if of a purely analytical nature, in all international fora in which it participates. Two such fora stand out, namely the GATT and the OECD.

At GATT, the EC should not shy away from putting forward new and complex issues in a manner comparable to what the US did for services issues during the years leading to the launch of the Uruguay Round. Rather than being seen as the eighth round of multilateral trade negotiations, the Uruguay Round can better be compared to the Havana Conference in the sense of being the initial step in a long and complex process in a number of new fields. Hence the importance of seizing the opportunity it provides to re-express and upgrade free trade objectives in the information age economic, corporate and technological environment.

At OECD, one could probably think in terms of a more ambitious initiative – if possible a joint EC–US proposal – patterned after the pioneering experience that the US and Europe now share with respect to economic interactions beyond and above trade as traditionally defined. The headlines of such a post-interdependence initiative could entail free movements of persons, common approaches in competition law, freedom to build, operate and use networks across borders, and regulatory convergence – including mutual recognition – in certain important fields. Such objectives would challenge both those in Europe who think of the internal market as stopping at the water's edge and those in the US who think of global openness as the extra-territorial application of US statutes as they now stand.

Such an initiative would propel the OECD in a role going beyond technical cooperation and non-binding agreements. One might think in terms of an equivalent of the European Single Act that would create a 'second floor' in the OECD mechanisms. Based on optional participation by each member country in a number of sub-initiatives (e.g. mutual recognition in given regulatory fields, high-tech programmes, electronic networks, telecommunications etc.), this treaty would give the OECD a role in promoting not just cooperation but elements of economic integration.

The *ThinkNet Commission* (a high level group of corporate, academic and international organizations leaders, who have met regularly since 1987) has put forward, in its 'Tokyo Declaration' (June 1990) a proposal for such an OECD initiative. Seven issues have been identified, with a special emphasis on regulatory convergence and on a reconciliation of diverging national approaches in the field of competition law. The PROMETHEE Institute is presently conducting a detailed analytical and scenario work on each of these subjects.

Regional integration thus appears as only one economic and political aspect of a broader globalization process. The division of labour between these two levels is, however, not straightforward, and can even be the source of major tensions. While the momentum of economic integration is more global in nature, political will and the readiness to challenge well-entrenched national frameworks tends to manifest itself in the regional or even bilateral arena.

In the past, Americans were the only ones to advocate the global approach. This American exceptionalism had its drawbacks in the sense that the need to change well-established American practices in the process was not easily recognized. As I have tried to show, what has already been achieved in the 'Europe 1992' framework does create a more symmetrical situation in which Japan, the US and the EC are each leaders in differing areas. The regulatory structure now in place in Europe in the area of financial services is one example of successful European leap-frogging and should be an incentive for bolder, more imaginative, deregulation of an American financial scene that is only slowly breaking away from the various barriers inherited from the 1930s. In other fields, the US or Japan are the source from which to seek this type of cross-fertilizing. Hence our recommendation for an 'OECD 1992': globalization would develop more rapidly and with more broadly-shared benefits if the type of mutual influence accepted in the EC became an additional benchmark for integration.

On the whole, the more lasting lesson behind the '1992 process' may well be that the reality of today's international economic interactions is calling for a broadening of the concepts of international economic openness. What can be achieved over the next forty years goes far beyond what was thinkable forty years ago. Post-communist, post-Europessimism Europe can play a central role in the coming to life of this new generation of historic opportunities.

REFERENCES

Albert, Michel 1988: *Crise, Crack, Boom*. Paris: Le Seuil.
Bressand, Alfred 1989: Computer reservation systems: networks shaping markets. In Bressand and Nicolaidis (eds), *Strategic Trends in Services*, New York: Harper & Row.
Bressand, Albert 1991: Defi Japonais: la fourmi, l'autruche et l'abeille. *Politique Internationale*, 53, 393–406.
Bressand, Alfred, Distler, Catherine and Nicolaidis, Kalypso 1989: Networks at the heart of the service economy. In Bressand and Nicolaidis (eds), *Strategic Trends in Services*. New York: Harper & Row.
Distler, Catherine 1988: *La Dereglementation dans les Années 1990*. Paris: Prométhée.
Project Prométhée, *Perspectives 1989: Beyond Free Trade*. no. 8, Paris.
Schwartz, Marc 1989: L'Europe financière. *Prométhée Report*, 47, Paris.

14

The politics and diplomacy of monetary union: 1985–1991

Jonathan Story and Marcello de Cecco

Europe's latest attempt at monetary union came after the dynamics leading to German unity were already underway. A revival of the debates swirling around European Monetary Union (EMU) may therefore be divided into before and after 9 November 1989. Up to the time of Gorbachev's visit to East Berlin on 6 October, the departure of Secretary General Honecker and the breaching of the Wall, monetary union turned around the role of the Bundesbank in European monetary policy. As Germany moved to unity, monetary union discussions merged into the wider debates on the future shape of Europe. Allies in western Europe, and prospective partners in eastern Europe, had to adapt and innovate as best they could to the Federal Republic's self-assertion of its right to enlargement and state unity. Domestic *and* external policies of the key country, Germany, became the central consideration for European neighbours. The Delors plan, presented in April 1989 – which proposed that member states move to full monetary union in three stages – was inevitably modified as events unfolded and negotiations proceeded.

The argument here is that Germany had been gearing up to act as the federator of the EC, at least in the monetary dimension, since early 1988. The German government, including the Bundesbank, presented a choice for its prospective partners in monetary marriage between acceptance of Germany's unilateral decisions, or multilateralizing them on Frankfurt's conditions. France led a disparate camp of EC member states aiming to moderate the Bundesbank's hegemony, while drawing on its authority to contain inflationary pressures in their own economies. Great Britain came to accept the deutschmark's role as an 'anchor of stability' in a European hard currency zone, but refused to subscribe to the French and Commission goal of a European central bank, requiring the consolidation of a European federal government. Changing conditions on markets, domestic politics, international relations and the relevant ideas in circulation were woven into the complex negotiations to move to monetary union (Odell, 1982; Story, 1988). They shed light on the background to the relaunch; the timing of its introduction; the factors influencing its possible or proposed content; and the manner of its negotiation as tied into the wider discussions on Europe's future shape.

Towards regional markets

A market perspective on the latest efforts to launch European monetary union in the second half of the 1980s would have to start with the consolidation of the Federal Republic's position as Europe's industrial workshop and prime exporting country, with 80 per cent of exports going to western Europe. France was the Federal Republic's main trade partner. The launching in March 1979 of the European Monetary System (EMS) had been a Franco-German initiative. France was assured stable exchange rates, without which the yearly setting of farm prices in the CAP would have been impossible to sustain. German industrialists won on price competitiveness in world markets, as the deutschmark was tied to weaker currency countries and less prone to revaluation against the dollar. The EMS' formal aim was to achieve 'a zone of monetary stability' in Europe. It encompassed three features: a European Currency Unit (ECU), operating as a basket of currencies, and created as a counterpart to a portion of member states, total reserves; an Exchange Rate Mechanism (ERM) in which participating currencies would be allowed to float against one another within narrow bands – 2.25 per cent for all currencies except the Italian lira, which would float 6 per cent. Of the member states, Britain participated in the EMS and the ECU, but not in the ERM. The third feature had been the initial idea to create a European Monetary Fund of which the ecu would be the full reserve instrument. But its creation was indefinitely delayed for a 'more opportune moment' at the European Council meeting of Brussels in December 1980.

The heart of the matter was the Bundesbank's dual status as de jure central bank for the Federal Republic, while operating as Europe's de facto financial manager. As such, the Bundesbank had a special relation with the United States and Japan. The Bundesbank could opt for stabilization or expansion, either in concordance with the United States as the world's central banker, or in non-concordance with the United States. These two sets of policies (stabilization/expansion) and relations (concordance/non-concordance) postulate four situations for the Bundesbank on monetary and exchange rate policy.

In the first situation during the period of stabilization between 1981 and 1985, the Bundesbank became Europe's de facto central bank, and the Federal Reserve Bank's principal counterpart in managing the $–DM rate. Germany's European trade partners – whether in or out of the ERM – were left to gauge their exchange rate or monetary policies on the deutschmark (Guerreri and Padoan, 1989). The Bundesbank opposed development of the ECU on the grounds of its composition as an index of currencies, softer than the deutschmark. Most notably, the Bundesbank's abrupt shift to tight monetary policy in February 1981 – in response to high interest rates in the United States – condemned President Mitterrand's moderate reflation of 1981–3 to failure. The French current account deficit tripled. In March 1983, after prolonged negotiations with Bonn and Frankfurt, France decided to keep the franc within the ERM. The franc was devalued, and a stabilization policy introduced. The Christian Democrat–Liberal coalition, displacing the Social Democrats from government in Bonn in 1982–3, made a virtue of restricting budgetary outlays. In this climate, European savings flowed to the United States, fuelling the solitary US boom of 1982–5. Furthermore, the high dollar raised the oil bill for energy-dependent countries, while interest rates increased debt charges of developing countries.

In the second case of non-convergence between Bundesbank priorities and an OECD alliance pushing for Germany to act as a locomotive, the catalyst for action had been frustration in Paris, Rome and Madrid at the stabilization policy imposed on Europe by the German Bundesbank. Resistance in Bonn and Frankfurt to expansionary measures could only be overcome in alliance with the United States. The alliance was forged at the meeting of the G5 Finance Ministers in the Plaza Hotel, New York, in September 1985, and again at a meeting in the Louvre in February 1987. There ensued a general lowering of interest rates, a surge in the yen and a lowering of the dollar against the deutschmark. Subsequent interventions by the major central banks to sustain parities prompted a renewed expansion of international liquidities.[1] At Nyborg, in September 1987, EC Finance Ministers sought to force the Bundesbank's hand to intervene on foreign exchange markets to sustain weaker ERM currencies. The Bundesbank initially denied any obligation. But the financial crash of October 1987, accompanied by angry exchanges between Bonn and Washington, exposed the Federal Republic's isolation, counselling closer cooperation with ERM partners. Fiscal restrictions were slightly eased, and Germany's monetary targets were exceeded. Bonn and Paris cooperated through the financial disorders of November. At the Franco-German summit that month, it was agreed to introduce an Economic and Financial Policy Council, within the bounds of the 1963 Franco-German Treaty. The Council was initiated against Bundesbank opposition in January 1988 (*L'Année politique, économique et sociale en France*, 1987, pp. 464–70).

In the third case of convergence *and* expansion, conditions in the world market oiled relations between the Bundesbank and its OECD Europe partners and the United States. A number of factors militated in favour of the European boom of 1988–90. A growth rate of 4–5 per cent for the two years had been helped by the fall in oil prices in 1986 and the abundance of international liquidities. Spain's entry to the EC opened a protected market to EC suppliers. After the eleventh realignment in the ERM in January 1987, France refused to agree to the deutschmark's revaluation. Germany's competitively priced capital goods exports irrigated the EC markets at ever more advantageous prices to customers. Business self-financing reached an all-time high in Germany, reducing the impact of higher real interest rates on corporate financing. The partial liberalization measures of the mid 1980s paid off in France, with a boom on stock markets and corporate profits. Monetary conditions stabilized, narrowing the interest rate differential with the Federal Republic. The British government, meanwhile, had introduced a series of tax-cutting budgets, and moved to financial market deregulation, thereby undercutting government control over the monetary aggregates. House ownership was encouraged on liberal finance. The result was a consumer boom, and a growing trade deficit with continental Europe. Corporate investment in Europe surged, encouraged by the optimism surrounding the launching of the '1992' programme. World financial markets recovered quickly from the fright of the October 1987 crash (*BIS, 60th Annual Report*, pp. 208–9).

The European boom of 1988–90 created the conditions for the fourth situation, where western Europe had an option between creating a Eurocentric economic and financial system, incorporating the Bundesbank into a wider European System of Central Banks (ESCB, henceforth ECB), or accepting Bundesbank priorities in shaping European monetary and exchange rate conditions in the light of domestic circumstances in a united Germany. The European economies, on which the German economy relied for exports, would have to submit to the diktat of Frankfurt. This highly conflictual prospect could be postponed to the extent that the urgency of reconstruction in the eastern regions would drive the German economy forward as Europe's locomotive well into the mid 1990s. But a German boom, financed by high interest rates and modest tax hikes, would increase the debt charges on European governments facing high levels of debt, while exerting a deflationary pressure on business activity across the continent. High interest rates also brought Germany into competition with the United States to capture a share of world savings.

The German government thus faced a choice between four policy directions. *One* was to allow the deutschmark to revalue in the ERM and against the dollar. Realignment in the ERM would help keep inflationary pressures down in Germany through cheaper imports. But this would tend to postpone convergence of inflation rates among ERM members, as the deutschmark-denominated price for German goods rose for European purchases. Allowing the deutschmark to rise against the dollar would pull up the currencies in the ERM, thereby increasing their competitive disadvantage on dollar markets.

A *second* option was to allow German inflation rates to rise with a view to easing the costs of reconstruction. During 1990, German monetary policy remained supportive of growth. But higher taxes in 1991, coupled with a surge in pay demands by trade unions, brought price increases to an annual rate of over 4 per cent. The development challenged the Bundesbank to defend its cherished reputation at home and abroad as a guardian of currency stability.

A *third* option was therefore to impose a dose of European stabilization as the Bundesbank drove up interest rates to keep domestic inflationary pressures under control. There could have been no surprise, therefore, when the Bundesbank decided on 21 December 1991, to raise its lead rates to the highest real level since the Great Depression of 1931 (*Financial Times*, 21–22 December 1991).

A *fourth* option was for the Bundesbank to endorse an ECB, thereby ending the permanent struggle to reconcile domestic priorities with pressures from other European governments to determine monetary and exchange rate policies for Europe as a whole. But such a sacrifice could only be contemplated if the German guardians of currency stability could be assured that the ECB's record would be as good – and preferably much better – than their own.

Realignment or stabilization were the two policy options marking continuous Bundesbank autonomy. A more accommodating stance on inflation, and/or an endorsement of an ECB, entailed a risk of subordinating the Bundesbank to political considerations in the EC and in Germany.

Political considerations were to the fore in the general trend towards a fixed exchange rate regime across Europe, as governments hitched their currencies to the deutschmark to ensure their import of price stability. Domestic inflationary pressures derived from a variety of sources. In Great Britain, control over domestic monetary aggregates had been abandoned by a Tory government bent on financial deregulation to sustain the City of London's standing as Europe's premier trading market. The policy of pegging sterling to the deutschmark at a rate of 1:3 led to a surge in the money supply, as the Bank of England in 1988–9 bought up deutschmarks and dollars to maintain the exchange rate, with the result that inflation rose to double digits again.

After much internal strife, the Tory government opted to borrow the deutschmark's external discipline by bringing the pound into the wider ERM band in October 1990. In Spain, unit labour costs continued to rise at over 6 per cent annually, contributing to the PSOE government's decision to enter the ERM's narrow band in June 1989. Sweden attached the krone to the ERM in the course of 1991, for similar motives and in preparation for its bid to join the EC. Fiscal imbalances in Belgium, Italy, the Netherlands, Denmark, Greece, Portugal and Ireland were rooted in party politics and political culture, only marginally susceptible to discipline through a hard currency zone hinging on the deutschmark. Nonetheless, the lira entered the ERM's narrow band in January 1990. In France, the counterpart in not agreeing to any realignment of the deutschmark in the ERM since 1987 had been the hard franc policy. The two casualties were wage earners and the trade balance. Unemployment remained stubbornly over 9 per cent, while the manufacturing trade balance deteriorated.

Political considerations also won out in Kohl's rush to German unity in the course of 1990. In marked contrast to the past twenty years of Bonn's insistence in the EC on the prior need for 'convergence' of policy and performances among economies entering a monetary union, German monetary union came fast. Immigrants were pouring into the Federal Republic from East Germany at the rate of three thousand a day; East Germans were clamouring for full access to the deutschmark. On 6 February, Kohl overrode the Bundesbank, and announced a deutschmark–ostmark convertibility at 1:1. General elections in East Germany were brought forward from May to 18 March. The negotiations for the Union Treaty were completed by 18 May (*Die Welt*, 16 May 1990; Siebert, 1990). German monetary union came into force on 2 July. The treaty preamble referred to economic union as a step towards political union, and affirmed that EC law would apply after state unity had been achieved. The Bundesbank was to take over full power in the monetary union. A German unity fund, initially capitalized at DM 115 billion, would issue Bund-backed bonds.[2] Three mini-budgets in March, May and October raised Federal government financing requirements, which the OECD reckoned would be over 4–5 per cent GNP for 1991 through to 1995.

Unity without taxation promised to keep growth rates up, and pull in imports, reducing the trade surplus. Funds moved into the deutschmark from October 1989, attracted by rising German interest rates, and after two years of weakness in the markets in anticipation of the government's defeat in the December 1990 elections. The Bundesbank welcomed a stronger deutschmark to contain the rise of prices in imported goods. The inflow would help finance unity, but would also attract funds away from the US Treasury bond markets. From April 1990 on, exchange rate coordination, inherited from the Louvre accords, weakened. The dollar floated down, as the Federal Reserve moved to lower interest rates in response to lower domestic growth and fears of financial fragility. Over the year, the dollar lost 13 per cent against the deutschmark, and 9 per cent against the yen. Weaker currency countries in the ERM therefore were squeezed between higher interest rates, and more US competition on product markets.

Through 1991, as the intergovernmental conference on monetary union proceeded, the Bundesbank became increasingly obsessed with the inflationary consequences of unification. In addition, the international markets voted in the early part of the year against the deutschmark, in view of Germany's exposure to unstable conditions in central–eastern Europe, the costs of unity, and the consolidation of the US position in the Gulf, following Iraq's defeat. By the summer, German interest rates were three points over US rates, fostering slower growth in the European economy. Then, from October on, international investors moved into the deutschmark as it became evident where the Bundesbank's priorities lay, and the US administration once again gave priority to domestic growth over the dollar's external value. With national elections in late 1992, the US authorities became obsessed with the deflationary consequences of debt. In December 1991, the German discount rate stood at 8 per cent, and the US rate at 3.5 per cent. The yield differential of 4.5 per cent in favour of the deutschmark had moved from a yield differential in early 1988 – when negotiations on the ECB were initiated – of 3.5 percentage points in favour of the dollar.

From a market perspective, this swing of 8 percentage points marked one simple conclusion: despite all the attempts by neighbours to control the Bundesbank, the Federal Republic was more than ever dictating monetary and exchange rate conditions. Europe was locked into high interest rates, in a hard currency zone hinging on the deutschmark. The Bundesbank's decision of December 1991 to tighten monetary conditions to the highest levels since 1931 left the other European countries no option – short of a spate of currency realignments – than to give absolute priority to policy convergence on price stability.

European intermestic politics

A domestic politics perspective on Europe's interdependent polities provided no clear support for a move to a federal government for Europe, as the pendant to the creation of an independent ECB. Political activity remained embedded in national conditions, with electoral timetables stretching into the mid 1990s. The speed with which German union was accomplished contrasted with the slow movement on European union, encumbered by the tensions between the EC's internal cohesion and the prospect of the EC's further enlargement. The debates on Europe's future shape revealed the perennial differences between the member states over the balance of institutions in the EC.

The interactions between EC policy and national politics had moved closer than ever. On the one hand, there was the political process in Brussels surrounding '1992', that affected an ever wider range of policies and people. The states brought their own broader concerns and afterthoughts to play in the EC policy process. When facing changes in taxation, standards, or rules on market access under the '1992' programme, national constituencies mobilized to promote or defend their causes. Lobbying activity in Brussels grew. The states sought to shine in the EC firmament, for the benefits reaped at home; but their pursuit of particular concerns pulled the Community into ever wider areas of policy, requiring the deployment of Community powers, and further amendments to the 1957 Rome treaties. On the other hand, support for the internal market programme fell off in Germany and France as the implications of more competitive markets reached a wider audience. In France, abstention rates in the June 1989 EC Parliament elections totalled 51 per cent of the electorate. The British public was thus not alone in its lack of enthusiasm for European unity as conceived by the Commission: one opinion poll showed that 40 per cent of Germans saw their model state as Switzerland, with the United States, France and Britain attracting 6, 8, and 2 per cent of the respondents respectively (*Suddeutsche Zeitung*, 4 January 1990).

The country most sensitive to the changing European context was Germany. The Christian Democrat–Liberal coalition government in Bonn had been re-elected in January 1987, but the Christian Democrats had dropped 4 points over 1983, leaving them more dependent on their coalition partner. There was to be no respite on the electoral front, as the political parties contested the regular schedule of Land elections. In April 1989, Kohl created a new cabinet in Bonn, marking a sharp swing to the right, and a more assertive stance in EC and European affairs. As German union gathered pace, Kohl wooed the nationalist vote and won over the 'East' German voters in the regional elections of 18 March 1990 by granting them a 1:1 conversion rate for ostmarks to deutschmarks. Following the monetary union of July, the GDR was merged into the Federal Republic through the use of article 23 of the Basic Law – the fastest ever EC enlargement. The result was victory in December of the CDU–FDP coalition in the first all-German elections since November 1932. But Kohl's popularity slumped in 1991, as the electorate awoke to the cost of unity. Nonetheless, he could anticipate remaining Chancellor through to general elections in late 1994.

Meanwhile, the Bundesbank's cherished discretionary powers were under attack. The February 1987 Louvre accords had obliged the Bundesbank to intervene heavily on exchange markets, while Paris refused to agree to any further revaluations of the deutschmark in the ERM. The Bundesbank was informed at the last moment about the creation of the Franco-German Finance Council. There followed the difficulties of monetary control under conditions of near-fixed exchange rates in the ERM; the battles between the Bundesbank and the Finance Ministry, backed by Paris and Rome, over the introduction of withholding tax on bank deposits in the EC in the winter of 1988–9; and the threat from French plans to have the Finance Ministers play a greater role in EC economic policy coordination. Then, Kohl repeatedly overrode the Bundesbank in the first half of 1990 over German unity, ignoring the governor's warning that German unity would have to be paid either by a rise in taxation or a rise in interest rates. The new Land governments insisted on full representation on the Bundesbank board, against the governor's preference. The struggle indicated the significance attached in Germany to preserving influence over monetary policy and the scale of political misgivings in the new Germany about abandoning powers to an ECB. Governor Pöhl took early leave of his post in October 1991.

With electoral timetables stretching between 1991, in the case of Belgium or Italy, to 1995 for the presidential elections in France, Germany's neighbours would have a permanent interest in keeping Europe's main economy on the growth path. This was particularly the case for France. In the presidential elections of May 1988, Mitterrand nailed his flag to the mast of an ECB, which would – it was hoped – dilute the powers of the Bundesbank to set policy for France.

But the domestic position of central banks in national economic policies varied considerably between the member states. The statute of 1957 bound the Bundesbank to defend the value of the currency, but to cooperate with the government in economic policy. The Bundesbank was more than ready to draw on public support for the deutschmark, against an untried European currency. The Bank of France fell under the tutelage of the Ministry of Finance, whose adoption of a hard currency policy was recent. With general elections approaching in 1993, and unemployment rates near 10 per cent, France faced a choice between subordination to the Bundesbank, or moving forward as rapidly as possible to an ECB. The Bank of Italy, too, depended on the Bundesbank, hitching the lira to the deutschmark in the ERM, in order to place a ceiling on wage demands, and on the expansionary thrust of party political competition for fiscal resources. The competition was likely to intensify, as the end of the cold war opened the prospect of alternative government to the Christian Democrat hegemony of the past forty-five years.

The champion of limiting the EC agenda to achieving the internal market was Britain. As the location for Europe's main financial and foreign exchange mart, London's interest was in promoting freer financial services in the EC, as well as the liberalization of capital movements. Global foreign exchange trading was located 60 per cent in London, New York and Tokyo (with Switzerland, Hong Kong and Singapore accounting for another 20 per cent), and amounted to over forty times the daily average of world exports of goods and services (*Bank of International Settlements*, 60th Annual Report, pp. 208–9). Both Germany and Britain had liberalized capital movements, but the prospect posed serious difficulties for Paris and Rome. France had reintroduced controls on capital movements after the events of May 1968, engendering a flight out of the franc; Italy had used capital controls to regulate the balance of payments, and in response to flights out of lira prompted by the shifts in party political fortunes in Rome. Both Paris and Rome, therefore, linked demands for monetary union to a harmonization of indirect taxation in order to dilute incentives to move capital to tax havens within the EC. But as freer factor markets within the EC threatened established interests in labour markets, Bonn joined Paris in demanding a 'social charter' to protect worker rights, pitting the continent against Tory Britain.

The Labour party espoused the EC's social policy, as the best means to reintroduce social democracy to the country. Prime Minister Thatcher resigned in November 1990, as Tory party leaders took fright at the plunge in the party's popularity at home, and the Prime Minister's isolation in European discussions on union.

The impetus to European union was accentuated by the combined effect of '1992' and German unity. The German EC Presidency of early 1988 achieved agreement in June on liberalization of capital movements by July 1990. But in April 1989, Bonn unilaterally decided to withdraw the withholding tax on bank deposits, previously agreed with Paris and Rome, while the Bundesbank raised interest rates. Then, in October, European Commission President Delors and EC member states demanded a 'qualitative leap' forward to political union as the only means of binding Germany in (*La Semaine Européene*, 20 October 1989; *Europolitique*, 28 October 1989). Despite serious differences between Paris and Bonn, the two reached agreement at the EC summits of Strasbourg on 8–9 December, and of Dublin on 28 April 1990. The EC pledged support for the German people to 'refind unity through self-determination', and Kohl agreed to an intergovernmental conference on monetary union in December 1990 under the Italian presidency. At the Dublin European Council of 28 April, the signal was given for a second intergovernmental conference to work in parallel with that on monetary union, 'with a view to ratification by member states in the same time frame', 'beyond the end of 1992'. The Dublin Summit of 27–28 June merely recorded that the two intergovernmental conferences on monetary and political union be launched in December 1990.

The events of 1989–90 opened the prospect of the EC's enlargement. Kohl stated in Paris that 'our common aim must be to build up the EC as the kernel of a future European peace order' (*Le Monde*, 19 January 1990). But he also pointed out, 'Europe is much more than the economic Community' (Kohl, 1990). Implicitly, a western-anchored Europe would be centred on Paris, while a wider Europe could be centred eventually on Berlin. The development was inherent to the transformation in European security, raising Moscow's previous veto on the neutral states from joining the EC. But it raised the prospect of the EC's early enlargement. In January 1989, Delors therefore proposed the creation of a European Economic Area (EEA) to the EFTA countries as an alternative to membership in the EC. But the EFTANs were determined to participate directly in the making of future EC legislation affecting them. Austria lodged its candidacy for membership in June 1989, followed by Sweden in July 1991. The EEA talks were concluded in October 1991, and would have to be ratified by all EC and EFTA country parliaments, as well as by the European Parliament. The accords meant that the EFTANs would be taking on board the ten thousand pages of existing legislation, and accelerating the changes already underway in their economies and societies. Switzerland announced its bid to enter the EC in the same month.

The newly liberated countries of eastern European also proclaimed their interest in as early an entry to the EC as possible. The EC hastily negotiated association agreements, facilitating improved central–eastern European access to EC markets. Funds were made available through a variety of channels, such as the western aid programme; or the European Bank for

Reconstruction and Development (EBRD), with its $10 billion capital of which 51 per cent was held by the Community.[3] But the contradiction was blatant between the EC's proclaimed objectives of promoting stable political and market transitions in the former party-states, and Bonn and Paris's insistence on protecting markets, notably in agricultural trade and the lower value added manufacturing sectors.

The prospect for a Community of eighteen or even twenty-four within a coming decade or more pointed to a renewed battle of the EC budget. German unity jeopardized the EC's farm policy, and ended Germany's capacity as the EC's paymaster. In February 1988, Kohl had volunteered a 50 per cent increase in German contributions to a five-year EC budget, freeing the agenda to focus on the '1992' programme. By 1990–1, EC farm budget limits were once again breached, and poorer member states, led by Spain, were preparing to ask for more. As Vice-President of the Bundesbank Schlesinger stated, Germany could not make transfers to the EC similar to those going to 'East' Germany (*El Pais*, 11 June 1991). The treaty renewal agreed on by the heads of state and government at Maastricht on 9–10 December 1991, nonetheless, specified that a 'cohesion fund' would be set up in 1994 in order to meet some of the poorer states' demands. The Maastricht accord heralded a renewed battle of the EC budget, but with Germany either less willing or less able to act as European paymaster.

The United States was determined to play a central part in the new Europe. Germany, President Bush declared in May 1989, was a 'partner in leadership', and he expressed support for the right of the German people to self-determination. Washington's new vision of Atlantic relations was spelt out by Secretary of State Baker in Berlin in December 1989. It was predicated on a redefinition of NATO's tasks; an EC, reinforced through the signing of a treaty with the US; and new ties between east and west to be built on the institutional foundations provided by NATO, the CSCE and the EC. The US objective, Baker repeated in June 1991, was a Europe 'whole and free', and a Euro-Atlantic community stretching eastwards 'from Vancouver to Vladivostok' (*Financial Times*, 19 June 1991). Along with this came a renewed round of discussions in the EC on agricultural reform, accompanied by pressures from the United States, eastern European producers, and the food exporting countries for improved access to EC markets. The breakdown of trade negotiations in Geneva in 1990–1 over agriculture heralded tougher transatlantic trade negotiations (see chapter 12 on trade diplomacy).

The United States vision of Euro-Atlantic relations was based on preserving NATO as an alliance of sovereign states. The EC's intergovernmental talks, launched in 1991, saw France propose a strengthening of the EC Presidency, of the European Council and a Senate made up of national parliamentarians. The federalist camp was led by the Belgians and Germans, both with their own federal states. Their ambition was to strengthen Commission, Parliament and Court of Justice. The European Parliament won Kohl's backing for an increase in its powers by the June 1994 elections. 'We Germans', said Kohl, 'will only sign and ratify the documents of the two intergovernmental conferences together' (*Financial Times*, 14 March 1991). The EC was to be founded on three pillars: a reinforced EC, including monetary union; a foreign and security policy, on which Britain, the Netherlands, Denmark, Portugal and Eire had reservations; and a judicial and internal security space. France agreed to, but Britain successfully opposed the suggestion that the preamble refer to the 'federal vocation' of the union. At the Maastricht Summit, the three pillars were incorporated in a new edifice, the European Union. Monetary union was to be achieved by 1999 at the latest; the member states agreed on a separate foreign policy arrangement (see chapter 11 on European political cooperation); new competences were granted to the Community institutions, while the European Parliament's powers to veto legislation were enhanced. The texts were littered with provisions for treaty changes at a further intergovernmental conference, earmarked for 1996. Great Britain won the right to opt in to full currency union, and opted out of joining its eleven partners in implementing a common social policy.

The internal political perspective on western Europe, in short, would have pointed to the immense complexity in adapting EC institutions and policies to the conditions of the post-1989 Europe. It would suggest the common urge to postpone major decisions, tinged by fears that time was counted as Germany became absorbed in digesting its eastern part. The novelty was that Germany was pulling France to accept a more federalist interpretation of the EC, as part of Kohl's vision for 'a kind of United States of Europe'. That vision was endorsed by the Bush administration, on the condition that the new Europe would not be built at the expense of traditional transatlantic ties.

The transformation in European security

German–American relations have been at the centre of European affairs since World War II. The Federal Republic, as a net importer of security within NATO, consistently gave priority to relations with the United States over French aspirations to create a 'European' Europe. The one exception to this general rule lay in Germany's support for a high-priced agricultural policy in the EC, and in European co-production programmes, such as the Airbus, in competition with Boeing. The Bundesbank emerged as the Federal Reserve's main counterpart in international financial relations. The Bank held dollars in reserves, but remained opposed to buying up the currencies of its European partners. As the ECU was composed of a basket of European currencies, the same ban applied to its full development as European reserve currency. Germany's special financial relationship with the United States thus stood as a metaphor for its special relation with the United States on defence.

In the course of the 1980s, this special relation in defence was challenged by the reorientation of the postwar foreign policies of the United States and the Soviet Union, and the parallel attempts in western Europe to develop a more autonomous security policy. The impetus to forge closer defence ties between Paris, London and Bonn was reinforced in 1986–7, when the two powers edged towards agreement on partial nuclear disarmament. Gorbachev's proposals in February 1987 to dismantle intermediary range missiles in Europe, as separate items from discussions on the US and Soviet central arsenals, were listened to attentively in Washington. Pressure was brought to bear on the NATO allies, particularly Bonn, to agree. Kohl, reluctantly, conceded. Washington then had Bonn renounce part possession of short range nuclear weapons based in Germany. The way was cleared for the Washington Treaty of 8 December 1987, between Gorbachev and Reagan. The treaty meant the removal of nuclear weapons that the Soviet Union feared, while leaving 'battlefield' nuclear weapons, whose use spelt the devastation of Germany.[4]

The treaty, and the parallel changes in eastern Europe, transformed Germany's international context. France was particularly sensitive to these developments. Diplomatic activity was limited to the domain of institutional engineering. The West European Union (WEU) was revived in October 1987, when its member states reiterated the principles of NATO strategy, predicated on nuclear deterrence. These were promptly undermined by the Washington Treaty. Prime Minister Chirac's government then revived the military provisions in the 1963 Franco-German Treaty with the setting up in January 1988 of the Franco-German Security Council. A 4,200 man Franco-German brigade was constituted. But Mitterrand won the presidential election against Chirac in May 1988.

France's new government, formed in June and based on centrist support in the National Assembly, would follow a dual track policy on Europe: a federalist dimension for EC policy, and national defence to preserve the consensus on security policy. 'The mission of France', Mitterrand declared in October 1988, 'is not to assure the protection of other European countries' (Fondation pour les Etudes de Defense Nationale, 1989, pp. 316–26). The creation of a European pillar within the Atlantic alliance would have to wait until 1992–3, and the completion of the internal market. France's nuclear doctrine of massive retaliation was confirmed in the defence programme presented to the National Assembly in September 1989. Nine regiments, posted on France's eastern frontier, were to be equipped from 1992 on with the Hades nuclear missile system, with a range of 450 kilometres. The Germans had not been consulted through the Franco-German Security Council (Die Welt, 15 September 1989).

The more assertive Germany, evidenced in the April 1989 cabinet reshuffle, had been maturing for some time. As NATO's front line state, the Federal Republic felt the presence of foreign troops on its soil most keenly. The struggle in the alliance over intermediary and short range weapons left Bonn more determined to defend its particular national interests. Public opinion polls showed active support for Gorbachev's policies. The new US administration proved accommodating. The Bush administration redefined policy to favour 'the integration of the Soviet Union into the Community of nations',[5] and to encourage Bonn 'to stand for its own positions and policies' (Financial Times, 1 June 1990). At the May 1989 NATO Summit, President Bush opted for progress in the conventional arms talks being held in Vienna and joined NATO allies[6] in expressing support for the right of the German people to self-determination. Paris shared London's concern at Germany's de-nuclearization, but at the Franco-German Summit of May 1989, picked up on Bonn's initiative to reassert their common objectives of a 'social Europe' and a European monetary union in reaction to Prime Minister Thatcher's known hostility to the projects (Financial Times, Le Monde, 20 May 1990). European 'union', in other words, was a temporary substitute for a common security policy.

Meanwhile, the communist party-states' hold in central–eastern Europe was crumbling, leading to the collapse of the regime in East Germany. The breaching of the Berlin Wall on 9 November 1989 precipitated events. Suspicious that Moscow on the one hand, and his western partners on the other, might seek to perpetuate Germany's division, Kohl unilaterally announced his ten-point plan for German unity in the Bundestag on 28 November 1989 (*Die Welt*, 29 November 1989). The aim was for a gradual transformation in relations between the two states towards a confederation.

Bonn, however, opted for a fast track to German unity. With three thousand immigrants pouring into the Federal Republic daily and East Germans clamouring for access to the deutschmark, Kohl could calculate that his offer of a 1:1 exchange rate would benefit the Christian Democrats in the forthcoming 18 March elections. Haste, said Chancellor Kohl, was justified by the 'globally dramatic situation'. On 1 February 1990, Moscow offered German unity in return for neutrality. Bonn and Washington promptly reached broad agreement on the timetable for German unity within NATO. The argument was also deployed that a deal with Moscow had to be struck quickly, before Gorbachev's internal position weakened.

German unity, negotiated between Bonn, Washington and Moscow, while keeping the Poles, Italians, French and British at arms length, scarcely augured well for cooperative relations within the EC. During Kohl's visit to Camp David on 24–5 February 1990, Bush concurred that the two German governments should meet with the four wartime allies for discussions 'on the external aspects of the realization of German unity, including the questions of the security of their neighbouring states' (*Le Monde*, 16 February 1990). This bilateral management of Germany's race to unity limited the significance of the 'two plus four' talks. Bush bluntly announced that the United States had no intention of giving France the supreme command of Allied forces – the preserve of a US officer – as a way of bringing France back into NATO (*Le Monde*, 4 April 1990). But the President agreed with Bonn's urging to alter NATO's nuclear strategy, in order to secure Moscow's blessing for German unity. At the NATO summit in London on 6–7 July 1990, the Alliance leaders interred the nuclear doctrine of flexible response, introduced in 1967, in favour of the use of nuclear weapons only as a last resort.

NATO subsequently further redefined its strategy for the new Europe. At the May 1991 meeting of Defence Ministers in Brussels, NATO approved the creation of five multinational corps, and a rapid reaction force, composed of multinational units, including US troops, and coming under a UK command. Air support was to be provided by the United States. The deal allowed for a reduction of the US troop presence in Europe, while binding the United States into Europe's future security arrangements. It helped resolve the problem for German sovereignty created by the presence of occupation forces. The force would be polyvalent, capable of being operated under NATO or WEU auspices. At the NATO Foreign Ministers meeting in Copenhagen in June, a framework of relations was offered to the Soviet Union and the countries of central–eastern Europe, with a view to dissipating the fears of the former that NATO strategy would be directed against it while reassuring the latter that NATO's concern was for security in all Europe. Following the events of 19–22 August in Moscow, Foreign Minister Genscher and

Secretary of State Baker proposed a North Atlantic Cooperation Council that would institutionalize eastern Europe and Moscow's participation in NATO's non-military activity. Paris disapproved on the grounds that the Council would duplicate the CSCE's role. But when Bush confronted the Europeans at the NATO Summit in Rome in early November 1991, with the question of whether the US assumption that the Europeans wished the US to maintain forces in Europe was correct, the answer was clearly in the affirmative.

Meanwhile, the Paris Summit of leaders from the thirty-four signatory states to the 1975 Helsinki accords was held on 19–21 November 1990. The Charter of Paris proclaimed democracy as the sole legitimate system of government in Europe. The twenty-three nation Council of Europe would provide the parliamentary amenities and jurisprudence on human rights as the underpinning to the CSCE. The new pan-European order would be lightly endowed with a permanent secretariat based in Prague; a Vienna Centre for Conflict Prevention; yearly meetings of foreign ministers, and biennial meetings of heads of government and state.

Kohl's understanding with the United States laid the ground for his diplomatic triumph in relations with the Soviet Union. Moscow's initial aims were multiple. The transition to unity was to be consecrated by a de facto neutrality status for Germany. The Soviet Union was to secure German economic aid for reconstruction, and be introduced as a full partner in Europe's new economy and security system. This would hinge multilaterally on the CSCE (*Le Monde*, 2 December 1989), and bilaterally on privileged relations with a united Germany as the key state in the EC.

The momentous meeting in the Caucasus between Kohl and Gorbachev, laying the ground for a new special relationship, took place on 17 July 1990. The two leaders agreed that a reunited Germany 'exercising its unlimited sovereignty, may freely decide to which alliances or blocs it wants to belong'. Soviet troops were to remain in Germany for the next three to four years, with Germany offering financial assistance for their withdrawal. The 'Final Settlement for Germany' between the 'two plus four' was signed in Moscow on 12 September. On the 13th, Gorbachev and Genscher signed a twenty-year Soviet-German Treaty of Friendship and Cooperation.

The Kohl–Genscher unity policy was predicated on successful transition in the Soviet Union towards a democratic state, under the rule of law, and based on market economics. But as conditions deteriorated, the Soviet Union lurched towards autocracy, in a determined conservative bid to crush demands for national independence within the union. Economic reforms failed to materialize. The dynamics of German unity, though, spelt a withdrawal of foreign troops from Germany, and Europe. This was recorded with the signing on 19 November 1990 at the Elysée Palace of the accord on Conventional Forces in Europe (CFE). Doubts over the Soviet Union's commitment to disarmament, as troops and equipment were reportedly not destroyed, but moved eastward, were only allayed in June 1991, after Gorbachev had swung back to a more accommodating position on the nationality question within the Soviet Union. The 19–22 August putsch in Moscow then signalled the collapse of the USSR, and the urgency of a combined policy to deal with impending dangers of nuclear proliferation and economic collapse, as the Soviet empire disintegrated.

The manner of Germany's move to unity prompted a sharp deterioration in Franco-German relations. Paris, with London and Rome, had been by-passed in Bonn's dealings with Washington and Moscow. So Kohl and Mitterrand – in a bid to repair relations – launched the Franco-German proposal of 19 April 1990 to accelerate the EC's political construction. The differences between Kohl and Mitterrand on security policy were papered over at the Franco-German Summit, prior to the Dublin 28 April EC Summit. At Dublin, the member states agreed to hold a second intergovernmental conference on political union. But Mitterrand disassociated France from the July NATO Summit statement on 'last resort' use of nuclear weapons; and the French Council of Ministers agreed to Strasbourg as the seat for a new command, tied into the tactical nuclear strike force located at Metz, and stretching from Belgium to Switzerland. French concerns over Germany were compounded by Kohl's 17 July visit to the Caucasus, leading to the 13 September German–Soviet Friendship and Cooperation Treaty. The Franco-German Munich Summit of 17–18 September was reported as a disaster (*Le Monde*, 9 October 1990). On 22 September the French Council of Ministers decided to start withdrawal of the French army corps in Germany from 1991. The Franco-German brigade would stay in Germany at the request of Bonn.

The Gulf war, the USSR's disintegration and the collapse of Yugoslavia subsequently revealed Germany's domestic sensitivity and geopolitical vulnerability to the momentous changes in world politics. A poll on German public opinion showed 75 per cent of respondents opposed to Germany's engagement in international conflicts, and wanting good relations primarily with the Soviet Union (59 per cent), the United States (44 per cent) and France in third place (38 per cent) (*Suddeutsche Zeitung*, 4 January 1990). A constitutional amendment would be required to allow for the eventual use of German troops under United Nations or WEU auspices. The SPD, gaining in the polls in 1991, opposed the deployment of German troops outside the NATO area, other than in UN peacekeeping operations. Both France and Britain, meanwhile, sent their own forces to operate under de facto US command in the Gulf war of early 1991, demonstrating that as permanent members of the UN Security Council, they were great powers only in name. The Dutch and British, with US backing, then won the diplomatic victory in May–June 1991, confirming NATO as the pillar for European security. But the utility of the rapid reaction force was questionable, as it could only be deployed within the NATO area, and therefore not in the Gulf or central and south-eastern Europe where future threats to European security were likely to emerge.

This left the way open for Mitterrand to bring forward his aspiration to create a European pillar in the Atlantic alliance. In early February, the French and German Foreign Ministers launched a plan for 'a progressive development of an organic relationship' between the EC and the WEU, leading to their merger by 1996. The plan was backed by their colleagues from Spain, Italy, Belgium, Greece and Luxemburg. At the NATO Foreign Ministers meeting in Copenhagen in June, there was general agreement that the EC develop a security 'identity' but only in conformity and not separate from the Alliance. It was the attempted coup in Moscow in August 1991 and Yugoslavia's slide to war that gave renewed life to the project. France seized the opportunity provided by the subsequent Moscow–Washington accords on nuclear arms reductions to reduce the number of Hades nuclear weapons to be introduced in 1992, and capable only of hitting Germany. Bonn urged a joint European and security policy as the best means to contain present or future domestic pressures for unilateral initiatives in response to the revolutionary changes in the former Soviet Union and the Balkans.

In October, an Italo-British proposal to strengthen the WEU finally prompted Paris to launch an ambitious plan for a European army in the service of a common European foreign policy. The Mitterrand–Kohl plan of 14 October 1991, proposed that the EC member states move to a joint foreign policy of relations to the former USSR, the United States, the Middle East and the Mediterranean, as well as in the United Nations, on arms control and in peacekeeping. The plan called for the Franco-German brigade to serve as a kernel for a future European corps. The EC would deal with defence 'wholly or partially' under the WEU. The WEU would move to Brussels, with its own permanent staff, arms agency and troops assigned to it. Its development would be reviewed in 1996, with the calling of a further intergovernmental conference. The proposal was incorporated into the new treaty, defined at Maastricht. The WEU was to be an 'integral part of the development of the European Union'. But the British and Dutch won acceptance that these arrangements would be compatible with NATO. In supporting them, did Kohl want to pull the French into the ongoing reforms in NATO, or did he want to go ahead with the French in creating the kernel of a European military power, in anticipation of a much reduced US military presence in Europe? The choice would be postponed until the intergovernmental conference of 1996, in anticipation of 1998 when the WEU Treaty runs out. It would be possible then for the EC to take over its role.

Germany, in short, achieved unity primarily through negotiations with Washington and Moscow. Paris, London and Rome played at best supporting roles. Diverse perspectives on Europe's future barely concealed the persistence of divergent, but overlapping security policy interests. The end of the cold war opened the prospect for Germany of a European peace system, hinging on a continued US presence and a network of institutions, including the EC, while French defence policy appeared geared to achieving security both with, and eventually against a united Germany. For France, the new order in Europe meant preserving the Atlantic alliance, but upgrading the WEU as an eventual instrument of the European Council, but not at the expense of NATO, and Germany's central relationship with the United States.

In the meantime, neither NATO nor the WEU provided a readily available military instrument for use in the event of crisis. Defence policy would remain firmly within the domain of the sovereign states, and therefore NATO, until 1996 when the EC's intergovernmental conference would review the organizational aspects of a still undefined EC security 'identity'. One inference was that Germany's special financial relationship with the United States would continue to stand as a metaphor for its special relation with the United States on defence. The other was that the United States' world role after the cold war, and its centrality in any future foreign policy for Germany, set undefined limits around Bonn's readiness to base security on prior alliance with Paris.

Diplomacy and ideas

The Single European Act – the vehicle for relaunching the EC in the mid 1980s – had been drawn up in a divided Europe, where the Federal Republic was primus inter pares, but not a prospective dominant power, overshadowing its neighbours or major EC partners. The SEA's main objective was the completion of the internal market, making only brief reference to economic and monetary union. The reference was the result of an understanding between Kohl and Mitterrand in December 1985 at Luxemburg, that France would agree to liberalize foreign exchange controls if Germany would renew its recognition of monetary union as a goal. The Act noted that the Paris Summit of October 1972 had approved 'the objective of the progressive realization of economic and monetary union', and it alluded to the Rome Treaty's art. 102a, referring to 'further development in the field of economic and monetary policy'. Only with union would the Community benefit fully by the internal market.

Public discussion on European monetary union was renewed in 1987, in the light of the financial events of that year. Two key ideas were in circulation, indicating fears in Paris and Rome of an Anglo-German alliance cementing the Bundesbank's position and the City of London's primacy in international finance. One, mooted in a memorandum by French Finance Minister Balladur, focused on the inequity of Germany setting monetary policy for others. It provided the thrust for the creation in January 1988 of the Franco-German Economic and Financial Council – in parallel to the Defence and Security Council – modifying the Elysée Treaty of 1963. The Council was to meet three times a year, and be attended by the Economics and Finance Ministers, as well as the two central bank governors. A second proposal, advanced in Rome, was for all currencies to join the ERM, and for an ECB to be set up as the central coordinator for a European currency policy.[7] In this way, the German economy would not continue to make 'structural gains' through the deutschmark's undervaluation, while Britain would not be able to gain from capital liberalization, 'without being subject to the restrictions [membership in the ERM] places on domestic economic policies' (*Financial Times*, 25 February 1988).

During Germany's EC Presidency in early 1988, complex alliances were formed on the monetary union and the financial services programme in the EC's '1992' policy. Chancellor of the Exchequer Lawson sided with Bonn, Rome and Paris against Prime Minister Thatcher in favour of the pound sterling's early entry to the ERM, but fully supported the German EC Presidency's move to liberalization of capital movements, decided that June by the EC Finance Ministers, for 1 July 1990. London was sympathetic to the Italian view on the need to build adequate flexibility into the ERM, and shared Rome and Paris's reticence about Frankfurt's interest to intensify the use of the deutschmark in central bank settlements. The three wanted the official use of the ECU to be developed alongside its private use. The UK Treasury then floated an ecu-denominated bond issue. Chancellor Kohl and especially Foreign Minister Genscher favoured monetary union as essential for the success of '1992'. Genscher proposed that the Hanover European Council of June appoint a panel of experts, to draw up the principles upon which a currency area would function; to draft a statute for an ECB; and work out what should be done about the crucial transition phase (*Financial Times*, 27 February 1988). The heads of government concurred at the European Council of Hanover on 27 June 1988.

Commission President Delors presented the committee's report in April 1989 (Comité pour l'Etude de l'Union Économique et Monetaire, 1989). The conditions for union were spelt out as entailing fixed exchange rates, complete freedom of capital movements, a single financial services market and a common monetary policy. The ecu was seen as having 'potential' as a common currency. The process of moving to monetary union was to involve three stages. Article 236 of the Rome Treaty required ratification procedures for any major institutional changes.

The first stage would come into effect on 1 July 1990, and involve central bank governors in presenting finance ministries with recommendations for a closer convergence of macroeconomic policies and performances. This meant a strengthening of the 1964 Central Bank Governors' Committee, the Monetary Committee, and of the 1974 economic policy 'convergence' procedures in the EC. The Central Bank Governors' Committee had acted as a discussion forum. The Monetary Committee, established under the treaty, and composed of member states' monetary experts from central banks and finance ministries, exerted a purely advisory role. The 1974 procedures for convergence of EC macroeconomic policies had been largely dormant.

The second stage would start at an unspecified date with the entry into force of a new treaty establishing the European System of Central Banks. The bank would have a president and a directorate, nominated for periods of five to seven years, and responsible for exchange rate, monetary and macroeconomic supervision. There would be precise, but not binding rules relating to the size of budget deficits. A start thus would be made on a common monetary policy, and to reduce the margins of fluctuation in the EMS.

The third stage, also starting at an unspecified date, would lead to 'irrevocably fixed' parities and would be sealed by the transfer of most economic and monetary policy powers to the union. National currencies would be replaced by a single currency. The stage would only be embarked upon once all the instruments had been tried and tested. The instruments for the internal market would be an efficient competition policy; regulation of take-over bids; a set of common policies; and very close macroeconomic policy coordination.

At the June 1989 Madrid European Council, Prime Minister Gonzalez used the Presidency to find a compromise: the Delors report was to provide the basis for future discussions on monetary union. The first stage was to start on 1 July 1990, and EC institutions were to make 'complete and adequate' preparation for an intergovernmental conference that would establish the proceedings for the later stages. The conference would meet once the first stage had begun. The baton of the EC Presidency thus passed to France. On monetary union, it was generally agreed that the matter was inseparable from political union. As indicated, German support for an intergovernmental conference on monetary union was won at the European Council at Strasbourg, in December 1989; at the Dublin Summits of April and June 1990, the political and monetary union talks were set to begin in December, and to end one year later under the Dutch Presidency in December 1991.

The tone of Bonn's position on monetary union had been set by a February 1988 resolution of the German cabinet. 'The longer term goal is economic and monetary union in Europe, in which an independent European Central Bank, committed to maintaining price stability, will be able to lend effective support to a common economic and monetary policy' (*Financial Times*, 23 June 1988). But the ECB had to be along Bundesbank lines. The Delors report subsequently bore the Bundesbank's firm imprint, and was defended by Foreign Minister Genscher on the grounds that the proposal met German criteria for priority to price stability; political independence; no inflationary financing of government deficits; and a federal structure, in the manner of the institutions of the Federal Republic or the United States (Genscher, 1989, pp. 13–20). A terrain was duly reserved in Frankfurt to locate the future ECB (*Le Monde*, 10 February 1989). The Bundesbank set about strengthening its European network alongside its established representations in New York, London and Tokyo (*Financial Times*, 6 June 1989). One proposal had the Bundesbank take over the role of open market manager, with a permanent place on the ECB committee and rotation for the rest, as in the United States' Federal Open Market Committee, based in New York (*Financial Times*, 9 January 1989; Thygessen, 1988, pp. 6–13; 1989, pp. 91–114).

Within the German government's consensus on the requirements for an ECB, there were shades rather than differences of opinion. Genscher had no ministerial responsibility for financial policy, so could clothe his discourse in federalist language. The Bundesbank sceptics could follow suit, with more of an emphasis on the long term. The favoured analogy was that the creation of an ECB should 'crown' a long process, and that Paris's and Rome's demands for an end to asymmetry meant first building the 'roof' through a move to common policy making. Bundesbank and Finance Ministry sang in unison on the vexed question of the transition out of the status quo: an ECB had to 'succeed at the first attempt' (*Financial Times*, 13 May 1988). The Delors report was too vague about the conditions of the second and third stage, placing too much emphasis on policy coordination (Kloten, 1989a, pp. 251–60). There was unanimity that the ECU, as a basket of currencies, and softer than the deutschmark, could not serve as a satisfactory reserve asset. As Pöhl admitted, the passage that he found most attractive in the report referred to 'the role played by the DM as anchorage point for monetary and intervention policies of the participants' (*Le Monde*, 23 May 1989). If a political decision was taken to end deutschmark hegemony, the only way was the creation of an authentic currency by an ECB (*Europe*, 4 November 1989).

The main battle lines were clarified at the Finance Ministers' meeting at Antibes in September 1989, held to prepare the intergovernmental conference. Lawson opposed monetary union but feared the City of London being marginalized, as the continental member states went their own way together. The German Finance Minister insisted on the autonomy of the strengthened Central Bank Governors' Committee. The French led with demands for an equal say for national governments in the determination of economic policy. Conflict over the division of powers between central banks and finance ministries, reflecting the distinct traditions of the member states, ran like a silver thread through the discussions for an ECB. Belgium, the Netherlands and Luxemburg supported a federal development of EC institutions as the surest way to secure the influence of the smaller member states. The Commission played a central part in the fiscal policies of Dublin, Lisbon and Athens: they could be counted on not to appear 'anti-communautaire'.

On 13 November the Finance Ministers agreed on the revision of the 1964 measure creating the Central Bank Governors' Committee, and the 1974 procedures to facilitate 'convergence'. The new measures to improve the coordination of economic and monetary policy among the twelve were to come into effect on 1 July 1990. The Finance Ministers were to meet twice a year, with the President of the Central Bank Committee in attendance, to analyse the EC's economic condition. The Monetary Committee, attended by member states' delegates from central banks and Finance Ministries, would discuss multilateral surveillance of each others' policies – an idea borrowed from the G7. On 13 February 1990, the Central Bank governors at Basle agreed to 'intensify' their work on monetary union (*Le Monde*, 15 February 1990). With European parliamentary assent assured, the Council of Ministers modified the procedures of 1964 and 1974 to assure closer cooperation during the first stage (*Official Journal of the European Communities*, 24 March 1990). The governors committee would be informed ex ante of national decisions on the direction of monetary policy. The governor would be empowered to speak out on specific measures adopted by member states.

In fact, this emphasis on 'convergence' reflected Bundesbank priorities. With his European dimension as the President of the EC Central Bankers Committee confirmed in March 1990, Pöhl could address the national interest more clearly. Germany's interest could become Europe's cause. Once monetary stability had been achieved, Pöhl stated (*Le Monde*, 18 January 1990), the conditions for an ECB would be strict: the ECB would have to be assured policy independence; Council members would have to enjoy long-term appointments; the ECB would have to make monetary policy for the EC as a whole, have all modern monetary instruments and have the monopoly of money creation. German monetary union served as a cautionary tale against too hasty a move in European monetary union. Tying two economies with different productivity rates together in one currency, or on permanently fixed rates, required a considerable growth in transfers (*Zurcher Zeitung*, 8 September 1990). A substitute for the deutschmark was not acceptable. The German people would be 'sacrificing a hard currency on the European altar without knowing what we would get in return' (*Die Welt*, 4 September 1990). If public support was to be assured for such a bold step, a number of conditions would have to be fulfilled. The ECB would have to: be based in Frankfurt (*Financial Times*, 8 September 1990); have undivided power over monetary and exchange rate policy, binding on all members (*Frankfurter Rundschau*, 4 July 1990); have price stability as a priority, requiring political independence as well as binding rules on government spending. The intermediary stage two of the Delors Report would have to go, and an immediate jump be made into stage three.

The difficulties facing the Commission in promoting its plan for union became evident at the Finance Ministers meeting at Ashford Castle, Ireland on 31 March–1 April, 1990. The Commission presented a document analysing the costs and benefits of monetary union (*Agence Europe*, 24 March 1990). The Monetary Committee also chipped in with a report, notably dealing with the vexed matter of budgetary financing (*Europolitique*, 31 March 1990). Discussions revealed the complexity of the task undertaken. There was opposition to centralized controls over national budgets, while the Finance Ministers cited the principle of subsidiarity to restrict the Commission's budget to its present size. The Portuguese won the support of the Greeks, Spanish and Irish for an extension of the EC's structural funds from 1993 on. Paris and Bonn disagreed about whether the ECB or the Finance Ministers should have responsibility for external relations, while the German concerns about the vague terms of the second stage were not allayed. There were also differences over the distribution of competences between the ECB board, composed of the governors, and the directory, which would include the six members nominated by the European Council. The Commission President consequently promised a subsequent avalanche of reports with a view to including the Foreign Ministers in the discussions (*Europolitique*, 4 April 1990).

Bonn and Paris glossed over the fundamental problems that had surfaced at Ashford Castle (*Le Monde*, 8–9 April 1990), and swept forward on the tide of agreement to hold a political union conference. The first stage of European monetary union entered into effect on 1 July, followed by German monetary union. Further European Commission proposals were discussed at the Council of Finance Ministers in June and July. The ECB directory would be made up of twelve governors, and four members nominated by the European Council, forming the full-time board. The European Council would consult the European Parliament before appointing a board member for a five-year term. The ECB would have sole rights to issue the currency, and define monetary policy. Decisions would be taken by qualified majority. The President of the Council of Finance Ministers and one commissioner would attend, but not vote at ECB deliberations. The Commission would make 'observations' on consistency of policy, and the European Parliament would receive a yearly report. On economic policy, stage one would see closer 'coordination' of policies, based on Commission recommendations to the Finance Ministers and European Councils. By stage three, the Council should adopt three-year policy guidelines for the EC and the national governments.

With many points unresolved, the discussions entered autumn 1990. Doubts emerged in all member states about the project. Britain refused to agree to the ultimate objective being the creation of a single currency. Spain led the poorer states in insisting that monetary union be accompanied by a further large transfer of resources from rich to poorer states. France did not want to get trapped in a two-speed monetary union with Germany. The opportunity was therefore offered for Britain to suggest gradualism, with its proposal for a 'hard ecu', managed by a monetary fund. The original proposal had satisfied none, but its virtue was to bring Britain back into the debate as an ally of the ECU against the deutschmark, and of the Bundesbank for convergence first (*Financial Times*, 22 June 1990).

At the Finance Council of 8 September, held in Rome under the Italian Presidency, Spain's Finance Minister, Solchaga, picked up the British idea, calling for a European Monetary Fund to issue ecus from 1994 on, and not 1 January 1993 as Delors wanted. The extra year, Solchaga said, could be used assessing the results of the internal market programme. Stage three could then follow in five to six years' time. Germany and the Netherlands expressed sympathy with Chancellor of the Exchequer Major that no date be set without much greater convergence among the member states' budget deficits, inflation rates and labour markets. Content was preferable to speed.

The pound sterling entered the EMS three days after German unity, strengthening British diplomacy in the negotiations on monetary union. Thereupon, an unofficial Bundesbank paper, 'Compromise Proposal for the Second Stage of EMU', circulated among other central banks, proposing a tough set of preconditions before any move to the second stage.[8] 'It is in the interest of Germany, but also of its partners, that the German currency remains a haven of stability', the President stated (*Le Monde*, 17 December 1990). Both Bundesbank and Finance Ministry in Bonn opposed a firm date for stage two.

The French Finance Minister, Bérégovoy, suggested that discussions now proceed. The new mood was apparent at the EC Finance Ministers meeting at Luxemburg on October 8. A consensus was emerging, linking the Netherlands' support for Spain's date of January 1994 to Germany's demands for tough preconditions. Solchaga backed the British hard ecu, which Major described as the EC's common currency 'at the end of the process'. Kohl then overrode the reticence of Finance Ministry and Bundesbank, by announcing on French TV his accord with the Spanish proposal of January 1994 as the beginning of stage two. 'We need a European Central Bank', the Chancellor said, 'which is completely independent and whose sole concern is the quality of the currency' (*Die Welt*, 19 October 1990).

At the European Council in Rome on 27–8 October, the Italian Presidency decided – without any binding commitment – on January 1994 as the starting date for the second phase. The Bundesbank won acceptance of its preconditions. The new institution would coordinate monetary and exchange rate policy; develop the necessary instruments; and supervise the development of the ecu. But another interpretation of the text would confirm a prolonged second stage, where the ECB's task would be the coordination and not the conduct of monetary policy. Its independence would result from 'a process [that] has been set in train designed to ensure the independence of the members of the new monetary institution at the latest when monetary powers have been transferred'. In 1997, Commission and Council would report on the progress achieved, and advise on the move to the third phase. Britain expressed reservations, but agreed to work towards the creation of a common institution and a common, as opposed to a single currency. The French position was later spelled out in a government communiqué, rejecting 'the delegation of sovereignty to a technocratic institution' (*Neue Zurcher Zeitung*, 10–11 December 1990). The economic governance of a united Europe would have to be predicated on the Council of Ministers, and answerable to the European Parliament. The draft treaty, drawn up by the Central Bank Governors' Committee, was presented to the intergovernmental conference, held in Rome on 15 December.

The first multilateral surveillance exercise by EC Finance Ministers was held in January 1991. The Council of Ministers would make recommendations every six months, with responsibility for implementing these 'convergence' programmes in the hands of each government. The declared aim was to bring policy and performances into line, in preparation for the beginning of the second stage. Two basic rules had been agreed on: there should be no monetary financing of government deficits; errant governments should not be bailed out, but be held liable for their debts. Five countries were signalled out for comment: the Federal Republic was invited to finance unity through raising taxes; Italy's government deficit was described as 'preoccupying'; Spain and Britain were signalled out for having too high inflation rates; Greece was in any event implementing a restructuring programme under EC guidance.

The intergovernmental conference on monetary union was launched simultaneously. All agreed to accentuate the drive to price stability, while Britain, Spain, Italy and France advanced ideas on promoting the ECU. Germany, with Dutch and Danish backing, proposed to make the move to stage two, starting in January 1994, dependent on 'lasting progress towards convergence, especially in price stability and improvement in public finances' (*Agence Europe*, 20 March 1991). In January 1994, the present Committee of Central Bank Governors would be upgraded as a 'Council', leaving the decision to move to an ECB until 1997. This would be conditional in turn on stringent criteria of stability. The French proposal suggested 'heightened growth without inflation' through the creation of an 'economic government of Europe', based on the European Council and Finance Ministers (*Agence Europe*, 31 January 1991). In stage two, starting in January 1994, the ECB would give priority to price stability, and support the Community's economic policy. This would be shaped by the Council of Ministers, voting on a qualified majority. The Ministers would determine foreign exchange policy, while the ECB would execute. The Luxembourg Presidency advanced a compromise, whereby the governors would cooperate to promote convergence, but that the Council of Ministers, voting on a qualified majority, define the broad lines of policy. The move to stage three would be by unanimity, with Britain's acquiescence still undecided.

Further concessions were made by the Finance Ministers at their meeting on 21–2 September at Apeldoorn, and at Schevenningen on 1–4 December, during the Dutch EC Presidency. Contention focused on the transition to stage three. Stage two would begin in 1994, with the creation of a 'European Monetary Institute', with responsibility 'to coordinate monetary policies'. The Institute's powers would be greater than the Central Bank Governors' Committee, but it would be less than the ECB which the French and Italians wanted. Member states would be free to hand over their foreign exchange reserves, but their central banks would not have to alter their relations with their governments until the end of stage two. This hybrid EMI, with the EC Commission, were to report in 1996 on the degree of 'convergence' achieved. If seven member states met the criteria (low inflation, interest rates, stable currencies in the ERM, and not excessive government deficits), the Finance Ministers would advise when stage three was to start. The decision was to be taken by unanimous vote in the European Council. The Finance Ministers would then decide by majority vote who was qualified to join.

Would this not offer Britain or Germany ample occasion to exercise their right to veto? At Maastricht, a complex package was negotiated to pre-empt any blockage. Kohl acknowledged the 'irreversibility' of the process of monetary union. Major won a protocol allowing Britain alone the right not to join the single currency. Mitterrand extracted a concession that if the European Council decided against a move to stage three in 1996–7, the passage would be automatic in 1998 for those member states which met the convergence criteria. Those member states not able or willing to join would be excluded from the ECB's 'Governing Council', with full powers over the union's monetary policy, but all would have a seat on the 'general Council'. The member states, it was agreed, would keep control of fiscal policy, but the German negotiators won their point that governments running 'excessive government deficits' would be subject to sanctions.

The monetary union treaty, agreed by the heads of state and government at Maastricht in December 1991, was ninety pages long. It spelt out a programme leading to a single currency starting on January 1997 at the earliest or January 1999 at the latest. All participants could claim victories. The French won Germany's commitment to a single currency. The Germans won agreement for an ECB based on their own design. Britain won an escape clause that would allow it to opt in. Italy won some time to align its public finances on the EC's tough convergence criteria. Spain won a promise to increase the 'structural' funds flowing to the poorer states. But there could be no concealing the fact that the complex terms of the treaty pointed to the prospect of a two-tier EC, composed of leaders and laggards.

Conclusion

What do the varied perspectives bring to a comprehension of the discussions on monetary union? All point to the pivotal role of Germany. The key country's domestic and external policies were a central consideration for all European states. The Bundesbank was determined to preserve price stability in a hard currency zone covering western Europe. All states continued to give priority to domestic considerations, offset by their fears that failure to negotiate major revisions of the Rome treaties would enable Germany to consolidate leadership in a Europe of the states. The security dimension highlighted the perennial divergences in state interests, with the year 1996 heaving into sight as the new watershed year, substituting for '1992'. An intergovernmental conference would be held thereabouts to review progress on the internal market, on monetary union, and to hold a further round of discussions on the conundrums posed for European security policy, in anticipation of 1998 when the WEU Treaty runs out.

Chancellor Kohl's agreement on January 1994 for the opening of stage two left the content of monetary union still undecided. France championed a stage two where budgetary, monetary and exchange rate policy were to be 'coordinated' through a strengthening of the role of the Council of Ministers. The Bundesbank and the German Finance Ministry had won entry to stage one on their own terms of convergence of policy and performances on price stability and budgetary discipline. France had had to follow suit. In theory, a stage two which incorporated all the elements of Germany's stage three could start on 1 January 1994. But the EC lacked an adequate fiscal basis for a budget to be manipulated in counter-cyclical fashion, or to allow for an acceptable flow of funds from the richer to the poorer regions. So Spain led the field in autumn 1990, proposing a prolonged stage two, that would come into force on January 1994 – allowing Kohl to meet his promise that the European electorate would have something to vote about in the elections for the European Parliament that June. The review in 1996 would allow for a move to stage three in 1997–9.

One interpretation of these developments would be that the option for delay was a means of disguising opposing state interests, while reaching agreement on a minimum (stage one), and leaving the future open for negotiations. These turned around the timing and content of measures, and whether they should be introduced in stages two or three. There was little way of reconciling France's demands for empowering the Finance Ministers' Council as at least a co-equal of the ECB, and the German demand for an autonomous ECB, minimally accountable on monetary, exchange rate and even budgetary policy to the Council or to the European Parliament. Nor was there a readily available formula to reconcile divergent French and German views over the future institutional form of the EC. German unity from April 1989 on was accomplished in intimate liaison with the United States. Not surprisingly, relations between Paris and Bonn were strained. As far as monetary union was concerned, Germany offered monetary and political union on its own terms. It could thereby proclaim its European credentials, while preserving cherished national institutions for the future.

Another interpretation, though, is permitted. As the cost of German re-unification rose, the rift within the country deepened between those favouring priority to reconstruction in the immediate future, and those – like Kohl – who anticipated the costs to Germany and Europe of a German 'Alleingang'. The central issue in domestic politics for the 1990s would be the absorption of 'East' Germany, with unemployment rates there expected to rise to over 50 per cent of the six and a half million labour force. Bouyant revenues would be required to fund transfers amounting to 6 to 8 per cent GDP per annum, with the prospect of their remaining high over the decade.

Yet the Bundesbank's determination to protect its reputation as a guardian of price stability ran counter to the dispersed coalition in Germany and Europe in favour of expansion, at the cost of some inflation. If the other member states were determined to have Germany abandon the deutschmark, their only course of action was to walk the path of price stability, according to the tablets of the Bundesbank. Their moment to call in the political credits accumulated in the Bundesbank's metaphorical vaults would come in 1996. Any backsliding then would be tantamount to the Federal Republic breaking a treaty commitment.

There was another hidden incentive built into the terms of the treaty. A united Germany in a Europe of the states could expect to be the object of multiple demands, requiring decisions to be taken for or against the urgent petitions of neighbours. By contrast, Germany's incorporation in the new European union would spread the burden across the member states. The focus of attention would no longer fall on one country, but on a European union, armed with its own currency, fiscal resources, commercial law and common foreign policy.

Germany, then, stands ready to sacrifice the deutschmark for European political union. This implies a Europeanization of the Bundesbank, parallel to the Europeanization of Germany's trade dependency. It would mean that German unity proceeds apace with European unity, as Chancellor Kohl so frequently reiterated as his objective and intent. And it would mean the assertion of a European currency identity rivalling, possibly displacing, that of the dollar in the world economy.

But the process is not 'irreversible', whatever the treaty states. Exchange rates within the ERM, and between the deutschmark, dollar and yen, are subject to conditions on world financial markets. Public opinions across the European union have yet to sanction the Maastricht accords through their parliaments or by referendum. The United States could switch from benevolent support of European 'integration' to hostility, as the implications of the ECU's emergence as a competitor to the dollar become clearer. Contrariwise, the continued differences between the European states over defence and security perpetuate their preferences to preserve the Atlantic alliance, and US leadership in NATO. Not least, the Maastricht accords in their monetary dimension sanction the deutschmark's supremacy in Europe, at least until 1996. In other words, French attempts to mitigate the Bundesbank's autonomy through active diplomacy will bear no fruit until the late 1990s. A decade in politics is a *very* long time, especially in the light of developments in world affairs after the end of the cold war.

NOTES

1 The value of official reserves in current dollars had risen in 1987 by 40 per cent, the highest increase recorded since 1971–3. *BIS, 59th Annual Report*, Basle, June 1989 p. 216. The central banks then reconverted these into US Treasury bonds.

2 In a 15 May 1990, communiqué, the Bonn Finance Ministry put German savings deposits at DM 280 billion, and DM 120 billion capital exports. On average, Länder governments raised DM 80 billion per annum. The fund would need DM 20 billion in the first year. This communiqué was preceded by rumours that the issues could attract Japanese savings, drawing on the world's limited pool.

3 BERD, proposed by President Mitterrand in October 1989, was placed in London after a prolonged squabble over its location; the Soviet Union was given limited access to its services; France was given the chair.

4 Franz Josef Strauss characterized Kohl's August 1987 decision to abandon the Pershing IA missiles as reducing the Bundeswehr to the status of a colonial army. Franz-Josef Strauss: *Die Errinerungen*, Siedler Verlag, 1990, p. 435. See also Joseph Rovan's introduction to Kohl, *L'Europe est notre destin*, p. 32.

5 President Bush's five key speeches laying down the guidelines for a redefined US foreign policy are: 17 April 1989 on Poland; 2 May, on the Americas; 12 May, on welcoming back a reformed USSR into the world order; 21 May, on the emergence of a united Europe; 24 May, on the eclipse of communism. *Wireless File, United States Information Service*.

6 'The wall which divides Berlin', the communiqué read, 'is an unacceptable symbol of the division of Europe. We wish for the establishment of a situation of peace in Europe in which the German people recovers its unity through free self-determination'. *Le Monde*, 31 May 1989.

7 Italian financial circles were generally sceptical at the efficacy of supposedly 'spontaneous' mechanisms leading to monetary union. Free capital movements would disrupt the EMS, in view of different inflation rates between European currencies. See Marcello de Cecco and Alberto Giovannini, *A European Central Bank?*, Cambridge University Press, 1989. The book was based on a conference at Castel Gandolfo, June 1988.

8   These were: the EC must have completed the internal market; all member states would have to be in the narrow band; the treaties in monetary union would have to be ratified by all; monetary and compulsory financing of deficits would have to be banned in all member states; laws would have to be changed to ensure that central bank governors would not be subject to instructions or to recall; anti-inflationary policies would have to have 'progressed substantially'. *Financial Times*, 8 October 1990.

REFERENCES

Bank of International Settlements, *Annual Reports*.

Comité pour l'Etude de l'Union Economique et Monetaire 1989: Rapport sur l'union economique et monetaire dans la Communauté Européenne. Brussels.

Deutsche Bundesbank, *Auszuge aus Presseartikeln*, 27 April 1989.

ECU Banking Association, Newsletter no. 5, November 1988.

Fondation pour les Etudes de Defense Nationale 1989: *La Politique de Defense: Textes et Documents*. Paris.

Genscher, Hans-Dietrich 1989: Die Rolle der Bundesrepublik Deutschland bei der Vollendung des Europaischen Wahrungssystem. *Ergebnisse einer Fachtagung, Strategien und Ergebnisse fur die Zukunft Europas*. Gütersloh: Bertelsmann Stiftung.

Guerreri, P. and Padoan, P. 1989: *The Political Economy of European Integration*. London: Harvester Wheatsheaf.

Kloten, Norbert 1989: Der Delors Bericht. *Europa Archiv*, 9, 251–60.

Kohl, Helmut 1990: *L'Europe est Notre Destin*. Paris: Editions des Fallois.

Odell, John S. 1982: *US International Monetary Policy: Markets, Power and Ideas as Sources of Change*. Princeton: Princeton University Press.

Official Journal of the European Communities, 24 March 1990: no. L 78/25 and no. 78/23.

Siebert, Horst 1990: The economic integration of Germany. *Kieler Diskussionsbeitrage*. Kiel: Institut fur Weltwirtschaft.

Story, Jonathan 1988: The launching of the EMS: an analysis of change in foreign economic policy. *Political Studies*, 36, 397–412.

Thygessen, Niels 1988: A European central banking system – why and when? *Association Bancaire pour l'ecu*, 4, 6–13.

Thygessen, Niels 1989: Decentralization and accountability within the Central Bank: any lessons from the US experience for the potential organization of a European central banking institution? In Paul de Grauwe and Theo Peters (eds), *The ECU and European Monetary Integration*, London: Macmillan.

PART V

Regime and System Change

Editor's introduction

The focus of the fifth section is on the regime and system change underway in the former communist party-states, and Soviet Union, from either political or market perspectives. However the forces driving the transitions may be identified, the failure of the August 1991 coup in Moscow and the two revolutionary years in its former satellite states are irreversible. There can be no turning back to monopoly rule by communist parties and to command economies.

The revolutions in central and south-eastern Europe would not have taken place but for Gorbachev's *perestroika*, and new thinking in foreign policy. Changes in policy in the Soviet Union between March 1985 and August 1991 brought expanding cooperation with the United States, at the same time as a slackening of tensions in the cold war. For Poland, whose party-state had lacked legitimacy as an imposition by Moscow, the loosening of communist control in the late 1980s opened the prospect of a 'return to Europe', despite the arduous domestic and foreign tasks confronting the country. But for the Balkans, the end of the cold war and the retreat of communist control undermined the political settlement of the post–1945 years. Ethnic conflicts and border disputes were revived, at the same time as the rival powers withdrew their subsidies to client Balkan states.

There was no predestined path out of communism. The market came to be accepted as a last resort, after all other paths to reform of the command economy had failed. The cracks in the communist economic edifice opened into chasms in the 'crash of 1988', challenging Gorbachev to choose between his role as renovator of socialism, or as the country's saviour. Once embarked on reform, the party-states confronted the challenge of a return to market relations, which they had abolished. Changes in economic system could not be disentangled from changes in regime.

15

Poland and the other Europe

Paul G. Lewis

Introduction

The return to Europe has been a prime policy emphasis in post-communist Poland. The movement towards European integration was described in November 1990 by Prime Minister Mazowiecki as the 'fundamental direction of our policy'. In distinction to the outlook of the pre-war Polish state, stated Foreign Minister Skubiszewski (1990, pp. 8–9), 'our aim is European cooperation and European unity'. In September two-thirds of those polled were acquainted with the term 'return to Europe', and 80 per cent of them understood it in terms of the observation of human rights, freedom and civil liberty, the convertibility of the currency, free elections and the democratic exercise of power (*Rzeczpospolita*, 13 September 1990). Forty per cent of Poles opted for the European strategy, while one-quarter plumped for a national orientation in social development. National solutions to the problems of Polish development, however, had already contributed to the prominence of Europe on the country's agenda, while the idea of Europe had underlaid recent ideas of Polish nationhood.

Poland, more than any other of the countries that came to be classified after 1945 as part of eastern Europe, retained throughout the postwar period a strong sense of overall European identity and had striven to preserve a major part of its historical legacy. Powerful sentiments of national identity, high levels of religious commitment and the retention by the church of considerable autonomy, the strength of links with sizeable groups of Poles living in western Europe and countries throughout the world, and recurring attempts to develop and sustain policies which reflected national needs and capacities all helped Poland to preserve a somewhat higher level of independence than that seen in most countries of Soviet-dominated Europe. Eurocentrism had been a major characteristic of the opposition in communist Poland, while Pope John Paul II in the 1979 visit to his homeland had also stressed that Europe 'despite its current, still continuing divisions of regimes, ideologies and economic-political systems cannot cease to seek its fundamental unity'.

In combination with the fact that it was also the most populous country in the Soviet bloc (38.2 million inhabitants in 1990 in contrast to 22.9 million Romanians in the late 1980s, the next largest nationality – although it should be noted that there were 51.4 million in the Soviet Ukraine) this position gave it considerable importance in the postwar European order. This status was further reflected in the decision to hold in June 1989 the semi-free elections that led in September to the installation of the first non-communist prime minister in eastern Europe for over forty years. This was one of the first formal breaches in the hitherto monolithic system of communist rule and was accompanied by the development of further pressures for reform in Hungary. In November the Berlin Wall was opened and senior communist leader Todor Zhivkov removed in Bulgaria. Czechoslovakia's 'velvet revolution' soon followed and the overthrow of the Ceausescu tyranny in Romania was also achieved before the year was out.

The Polish breach in the wall of communist rule was, therefore, soon followed by a wave of change that swept away the Sovietized structures and, indeed, much of the postwar conception of eastern Europe as well. Poland also led the way in adopting a rigorous programme of economic stabilization in 1990, curbing inflation and achieving the convertibility of its currency. Poland, even more than the other post-communist countries of east-central Europe, is a society in transition and this fact will mark the account given here of its place in Europe. Its institutional structures, economic situation and policies have been subject to rapid and fundamental change and this description of Poland in the new Europe will outline the process of transition and the contemporary situation within the context of an historic transformation. The prominence of Poland's status in Europe and the general achievements it has secured, moreover, have not been without serious cost to Polish society and its own population.

Wladyslaw Gomulka's stand for greater Polish independence in 1956 was followed by the pursuit of a highly conservative domestic policy which steered clear of economic reform, leaving the economy in a weak and moribund state and culminating in the workers' demonstrations of 1970 in Gdansk and other northern areas. Edward Gierek conducted an economic policy more open to foreign influence but left the country with enormous debts and the economy, towards the end of the 1970s, in a state of major imbalance. This again provided the conditions for major strikes, leading to the formation of the free trade union 'Solidarity' and its public operation for nearly sixteen months until the proclamation of military rule in December 1981. The conditions for economic recovery and growth were no better during the 1980s. Poland thus entered the post-communist period soon after further rounds of strikes in 1988 in a state of considerable economic debility, still highly indebted, with public services disorganized and impoverished, and now suffering major ecological damage.

The political elan and qualified optimism that accompanied the establishment of Solidarity in 1980 was dispersed during the conflicts that followed and amidst the rigours of martial law. The formation of a non-communist government in 1989 was greeted with restrained enthusiasm and with few hopes of immediate improvement. Even fewer, however, envisaged the severe consequences that would follow from the adoption of Finance Minister Balcerowicz's stabilization programme. Inflation fell dramatically in 1990, but industrial output also declined by 30 per cent, wage levels dropped by 40 per cent and unemployment rose to over 0.5 million by mid-year. Expenditure on food rose to account for more than 55 per cent of household outgoings, a level it had not stood at for over thirty years. Discontent grew and disillusion became more widespread, contributing to the low level of support received by Prime Minister Tadeusz Mazowiecki in the presidential vote of November 1990. Poland's return to Europe, then, while undoubtedly welcome was hardly the occasion for mass rejoicing.

The international environment

While there were strong domestic pressures behind the loosening of the communist hold on Poland and the withdrawal of Soviet rule from east-central Europe, the decisive factors lay in the changing nature of the super-power relationship and the slackening tensions of the cold war. The security function of the Soviet Union's empire in Europe as a *cordon sanitaire* had declined with the build-up of nuclear arsenals and the development of new missile systems. The ideological value of the socialist commonwealth also diminished with the spread of economic stagnation and growing crisis tendencies within and beyond the Soviet Union, and as Gorbachev himself attacked the political shortcomings of the Soviet system. The idea of less dependent but more stable and economically viable European neighbours was obviously attractive to Mikhail Gorbachev, although it is by no means clear that he initially envisaged the total collapse of communist rule and the dissolution of the region's military and economic organizations.

As also became clear within the Soviet Union, though, once a programme of even limited reform was put into operation the process of change within communist systems gathered considerable momentum – both because of the close interdependence of the structures that made up the Soviet-type system and because of the need to press hard for change if anything was actually to be achieved. Major reform was also clearly necessary for Poland if a solution to deep-rooted domestic problems was to be found, political stability enhanced and any real possibility of economic development placed on the agenda. Meaningful economic reform, involving greater use of market forces and the breakup of centralized administrative authority, was hardly conceivable under conditions of military rule or even the qualified author-itarian system that succeeded it. Solidarity forces were neutralized with some success for much of the 1980s and a measure of political stability achieved. But the balance was a tenuous one, as the outbreak of further industrial unrest demonstrated in 1988.

The communist leadership under General Jaruzelski was, then, already inclined to make use of the more flexible atmosphere promoted throughout the region by Gorbachev and agreed to enter into round-table talks with representatives of Solidarity and members of the opposition before the end of 1988. It was the combination of domestic readiness to contemplate change and the more permissive conditions established by the Soviet leadership that facilitated the rapid development of events in Poland during 1989. But other forms of international influence were also significant. The high level of foreign debt that became established during the 1970s under Gierek was carried forward and continued to grow in the 1980s as interest arrears mounted. The prospect of any real economic recovery meant that new financial arrangements would need to be worked out with creditor nations and organizations. Meanwhile, Solidarity, although having reduced powers inside Poland, continued to enjoy great prestige externally.

There was considerable international support for Lech Walesa (winner of the Nobel Peace Prize in 1983), his entourage and the ideals they represented. As Poland emerged from the lengthy period of the communist power monopoly an immediate focus of attention was the developed western nations and, particularly, those whose assistance promised some relief from the debt burden and support for a programme of economic recovery. Indeed, one of Jaruzelski's actions immediately after the elections of June 1989 was to visit British Prime Minister Margaret Thatcher, who had earlier drawn explicit links between the spread of democratic practices in eastern Europe and economic assistance for Poland. There were, indeed, suggestions that the negotiations with Solidarity and opposition representatives which led to agreement on a number of political reforms (including the opportunity to compete for a minority of seats in the Sejm, Poland's legislative chamber) reflected an attempt by the leadership to strengthen its position in international and domestic terms by co-opting the opposition.

If that was the intention, however, matters soon got out of hand with the overwhelming defeat of communist candidates in the seats they contested, the problems experienced by the communist leadership in forming a government and the defection of some members of the former ruling coalition that opened the way to the formation of a non-communist government. The attention of the Mazowiecki government was even more firmly fixed on the improvement of economic relations with the western powers, and one of the first acts of the leading economic appointees in the new team was to attend in September 1989 the annual conference of the International Monetary Fund (of which Poland had been a member since 1986) and World Bank. While the western response to the recent changes was undoubtedly positive, it was also guarded and circumspect in economic terms, at least in the early stages and particularly on the part of the United States. It was made clear by the IMF that any eventual agreement would be dependent on the nature of the economic programme finally adopted by the Polish government.

Poland's letter of intent on the economic reforms was finalized in Warsaw on 19 December 1989 and an agreement signed on 23 December. Despite considerable success in achieving economic stabilization and reducing inflation, though, Polish debt levels continued to rise (by at least $4.5 billion) to reach a total of more than $46.1 billion, or thousand million, by the end of 1990. It was this prospect that underlay Balcerowicz's request in the spring of 1990 to reduce debt levels by 80 per cent in order to facilitate the inflow of credits and foreign investment needed to restructure the economy and facilitate the privatization of state assets. Only if measures were taken to prevent the continuing growth of old debts, it was understood, would Poland gain normal access to international finance markets, compile a long-term projection of the balance-of-payments situation and be able to reach agreement with the IMF on more extended support for economic reforms.

The operational structure

The role played by Poland in leading the east European reform movement under communist rule meant that the political outcome of 1989 represented only a partial solution to the nation's conflicts and that it was soon overcome in terms of political innovation by its neighbours once Soviet influence was finally withdrawn. It also meant that significant elements of the tensions characteristic of the communist period were carried over into the post–1989 period and that some of the victors of the summer of 1989 soon lost their popularity. This was particularly the case with Prime Minister Mazowiecki, whose support waned rapidly during the presidential campaign of late 1990. The institutional framework within which the initial part of Poland's post-communist political life was conducted was shaped by the agreements reached at the round-table discussions held in the spring of 1989. These followed the industrial conflicts of 1988 and were conducted by members of the party leadership and government with representatives of Solidarity and the political opposition.

As a result of the round-table agreement, the trade union Solidarity was again legalized in April 1989, and joint decisions reached about the reform of central political institutions. In the first round of elections held in June 1989 Solidarity-sponsored candidates won 160 of the 161 seats available to them in the main legislative chamber (Sejm) and 92 of the 100 Senate seats. A devastatingly low level of support for the ruling coalition was thus evident. When formed in September 1989, Mazowiecki's government was made up of twenty-three ministers, twelve of whom were nominated by the Solidarity side and four of whom represented the communist Polish United Workers' Party (PUWP). Two other official groups, the Peasant and Democratic Parties, were also represented. This was, broadly speaking, the parliament and government that steered Poland through the first phase of post-communism. In view of the rate of political change during the first months of non-communist rule it was hardly surprising that the 1989 Sejm and Mazowiecki government found themselves somewhat outpaced by the course of events and often out of touch with the public mood.

As the PUWP dissolved itself in early 1990, being succeeded by two much smaller parties with greatly reduced membership, the 65 per cent of Sejm deputies who received their seats through allegiance to the former communist coalition now found themselves neither representative of any public constituency nor the proteges of any real political establishment. Matters also became increasingly complex within the Solidarity camp. There were signs during the spring and early summer of 1990 of growing dissatisfaction with the Solidarity-sponsored government and its economic policies. Railway workers and peasant farmers were the first groups actively to demonstrate their resistance and both the established communist trade union organization (OPZZ) and a more militant offshoot of Solidarity joined in to support the workers. Lech Walesa intervened to defuse the situation and the strike was called off, but such events showed the growth of new tensions and sources of conflict in post-communist Poland.

The critical factor here was the situation of Solidarity, the status of its parliamentary group and citizens' committees, and its multiple role as political force, main support and constituent of the Mazowiecki government and trade union. The movement for a more decisive confrontation between the different political currents was clearly growing stronger and the occasion finally arrived with Jaruzelski's decision to resign the presidency. The conflict between Walesa and Mazowiecki and their supporters understandably emerged as the immediate focus of the presidential campaign, but in the first round of elections Mazowiecki was defeated both by Walesa and a somewhat mysterious Polish emigré, Stanislaw Tyminski, who appeared to have some support from former communists and the security forces. In December 1990, though, Lech Walesa was elected to the presidency by a decisive majority. In the new year he nominated as Prime Minister Jan Bielecki, a thirty-nine-year old economist with a firm commitment to privatization and free enterprise.

Jaroslaw Kaczynski, leader of the Centre Accord which had launched Walesa in his bid for the presidency and coordinated efforts to accelerate the pace of political developments, was named as head of the presidential chancellery. In January 1991 Bielecki presented his cabinet to the Sejm, where it was accepted by a decisive majority. Despite President Walesa's call for a significant acceleration of the pace of political change, the new government did not signal a radical departure from the orientation of Mazowiecki. A number of members of the former cabinet were retained, including Foreign Minister Skubiszewski and Finance Minister Balcerowicz. The position of the latter was, indeed, enhanced as Balcerowicz was now the only deputy premier and clearly held prime responsibility for the development of the Polish economy. Despite Walesa's earlier suggestions that workers needed protection from the rigours of economic transformation the liberal, free-market wing of the government emerged stronger than before and it was in this direction that the mooted acceleration seemed most likely to occur.

The sources of political conflict had by no means disappeared, though. There were significant tensions between president and parliament. Having argued the need to hold parliamentary elections at the earliest opportunity President Walesa in June 1991 vetoed the electoral regulations proposed by the Sejm, although his veto was subsequently overridden by the requisite parliamentary majority. Pressures to extend religious instruction in state schools and criminalize abortion raised issues not only of public policy but also those of Church–state relations and the nature of the new constitution which was being prepared. Moves were made in April 1991 within parliament to remove Bronislaw Geremek from the chair of the Sejm Constitutional Committee. All in all, it did not seem likely that Poland would see the degree of consensus achieved in Spain (see chapter 10) for the process of constitution-making which had been so instrumental in securing the transition to democracy there.

The economy

Economic policy in postwar Poland followed a pattern common to the other countries of eastern Europe. After a relatively successful programme of postwar recovery the consolidation of communist rule was accompanied by the imposition of Soviet-style planning with excessive weight placed on high investment levels, heavy industrial development and military production. After Stalin's death in 1953 this emphasis was relaxed and wages began to rise again (averaging an annual increase of 5.1 per cent between 1956 and 1960), having fallen by 8 per cent in the early 1950s. But while peasant farmers were allowed to retain the land they had withdrawn from the collective farms and the emphasis placed on armaments and heavy industry was reduced, no programme of full-scale reform was adopted and the basic principles of central planning and administration of the economy remained in place. The consequences of this were rather more severe in Poland than elsewhere in eastern Europe.

By the late 1980s, signs of severe crisis were clearly evident. Foreign debt had become an established sign of weakness which became progressively worse as the decade progressed. The level of hard-currency debt reached $39 billion in 1987, with most of the increase since 1981 arising from Poland's inability to make interest repayments although hard-currency exports had exceeded imports every year from 1982 to 1987. A further symptom linked with this was the progressive decapitalization of Polish industry, partly because of the difficulty experienced in obtaining spare parts for the equipment imported from the west in the 1970s and partly because of the diversion of available funds to the consumer sector to avoid further decline in living standards. A third symptom of crisis was the growing deterioration of Poland's infrastructure and continuing under-investment in transport, energy, water services, housing, health and education. By the late 1980s environmental damage was calculated to cost 10 per cent of national income, matters not being helped by the increasing use of brown coal in Czechoslovakia and the German Democratic Republic as well as Poland, which made a significant contribution to the atmospheric presence of sulphur dioxide. Unusually for Europe, in 1989 Poland still obtained 80 per cent of its energy from coal, of which 82 per cent went for industrial use.

During 1989 it became apparent that persistent crisis was threatening the collapse of the economic system as a whole, a factor which played a major part in the steps taken towards reform in the spring and early summer and the acceptance of their negative outcome for the communist regime. The plan drawn up by finance minister Balcerowicz and implemented from the beginning of 1990 had considerable success in restraining inflation, achieving a surplus in foreign trade and significantly raising the level of currency reserves. But the economic cost was severe as the average real wage fell and unemployment rose. The decline in production and the consequences for family budgets, moreover, were greater than envisaged and the reduction in inflation (still 4.5 per cent during September 1990) somewhat less dramatic than originally hoped for. In December 1990 industrial production (with the exception of the still relatively small private sector) was 24 per cent lower than the level of a year earlier.

Growing unemployment (to a level of 1.089 million by the end of November 1990 and 1.370 in April 1991) and a drop in real income produced major hardship for those affected and gave rise to dissatisfaction and sentiments of frustration that become more prominent in the political arena as the year progressed. Yet, while dissatisfaction and political discontent did grow, the population as a whole seemed to bear a major reduction of the real wage

(30 per cent over 1990 as a whole) with remarkable fortitude. Attention was drawn by the American co-authors of Balcerowicz's plan to the base-line inherited from 1988 and 1989 when, as demonstrated, the Polish economy was showing signs of severe crisis – but an official rise of 28 per cent in the real wage was recorded (*Financial Times*, 29 January 1991). While 1987 was indeed a bad year (national income fell for the first time since 1982) it was unlikely that there was much effective recovery from this situation or that the situation of working people improved to the extent suggested by the real-wage index.

Even according to the official record, the decline in income during 1990 was considerably less dramatic when compared with 1987. Neither did the publicized statistics take account of developments in the private sector, partly because an accurate picture of what was happening in largely uncontrolled sectors was impossible to obtain. Government estimates of the size of the private sector in fact suggested that it had grown by one half during 1990 and accounted for 18 per cent of the national income by the end of the year. Private employment was estimated to have grown to between 1.8 and 2 million by this stage. Current unemployment levels, too, might have been exaggerated in a situation where previously, under the communist regime, no facilities for registering people as unemployed existed. Ministry estimates suggested that only half of those registered unemployed at the end of 1990 had actually been laid off as casualties of the economic transformation.

The capacity of heavy industry to survive virtually intact under the new conditions raised serious doubts in this respect and it was noted in October 1990 that, while employment in state industry had fallen by several per cent, labour productivity had dropped by over 20 per cent despite better supplies of energy and raw materials. There was a strong current of opinion that the initial phase of economic stabilization had not been followed through with policies of sufficient economic rigour directed to the pursuit of effective structural change. It was important not to underestimate the fundamental nature of the transformation that was necessary and the amount of time and effort that would be required to achieve it. The full-scale restructuring of the economy was unlikely to be viable before the second half of the 1990s.

External policies

Prior to 1989 Poland's firm location within the Soviet sphere of influence and membership of the Warsaw Treaty Organization (Warsaw Pact) and the Council for Mutual Economic Assistance (CMEA, or COMECON) gave little opportunity for the development and articulation of an independent or authentically Polish foreign policy. Poles' awareness of their European identity and strong sympathies with the western powers led Poland, however, to explore the limits imposed by Soviet domination and to develop more original conceptions of international relations than most other members of the alliance (see Kolankiewicz and Lewis, 1988, pp. 178–82). But conditions were not favourable for developments in this direction in the face of growing economic problems during the 1970s, and the onset of military rule in

December 1981 and imposition of western sanctions in response to it contributed to a further weakening of Polish ties with the west.

The volume of Polish imports as a whole fell during the early 1980s,
standing in 1985 at 88 per cent of the 1980 level and rising to a level only
6 per cent higher in 1988. Relations with western countries accounted for
most of this decline and in 1988 imports from non-socialist countries
represented only 90 per cent of the 1980 total, while those from the socialist
community were already 16 per cent higher. Exports, however, were maintained and in 1988 stood at 29 per cent above the level of 1980. Most of this,
again, reflected closer integration with socialist countries and exports to this
area rose by 46 per cent between 1980 and 1988, in contrast to only 12 per
cent to other parts of the world. The 1980s, therefore, saw an economic
reorientation from the west and the trend Poland had followed in the early
1970s, a shift that was particularly marked in the first half of the decade.
By 1985 the Soviet Union, by far Poland's largest trading partner, accounted
for 34 per cent of imports and 28 per cent of exports.

The strengthening of economic links accompanied the reinforcement of
the military component in communist rule, which had been a major feature
underlying Soviet control of the region since the Red Army's defeat of Nazi
forces and the creation of conditions for the installation of communist
governments. On occasion the role of Soviet military forces had become
particularly prominent and they had been used directly to maintain the
integration of the bloc (Berlin 1953, Hungary 1956, Czechoslovakia 1968).
During December 1981 in Poland, though, it was the Polish army (or, more
accurately, its political wing in association with security forces) which took
power and suppressed organizations and groups (especially those linked
with Solidarity) that had escaped central party control. The 1981 operation
to reimpose orthodox Soviet-style communist rule performed, however, a
role similar to that played by previous Soviet or WTO invasions of east
European allies.

The tight integration of the east European military within the Warsaw
Treaty Organization and the strength of the Soviet chain of command,
moreover, meant that the Polish operation could not have been mounted
without full Soviet cooperation and encouragement. But the number of
Soviet military personnel stationed in Poland, which stood at approximately
50,000 in the late 1980s, was in fact quite low and represented a smaller
force than that stationed in Hungary (65,000) or Czechoslovakia (70,000),
let alone the Soviet military presence of some 350,000 troops in East
Germany. The Mazowiecki government proceeded cautiously in its initial
dealings with the Soviet government and provided early reassurances that
Poland would not withdraw from its alliance obligations to the WTO. Matters
soon proceeded further, though, and in February 1990 agreement was reached
with the Kremlin on talks about the withdrawal of Soviet forces stationed
in Poland.

While some countries, especially Poland, saw advantages in staying within
a modified Warsaw Treaty Organization, Soviet resignation from territorial,
political and military claims over east-central Europe soon undermined the
entire basis for its existence. By the end of 1990 the demise of the regional
military organization as a whole was coming into sight. In December it was
reported that 90 per cent of the text on the withdrawal of Soviet troops from

Poland existed in draft form, although further tensions developed over the conditions of the Soviet departure and the transit arrangements to be made concerning the retreat from East Germany. After the Soviet use of force during January 1991 in Lithuania and Latvia the central European members became more active in seeking termination and the WTO was wound up as a military alliance at the end of March 1991, its residual political functions being ended in July.

The course of events ran on similar lines within the economic organization. CMEA had never provided a framework for the effective economic integration of the socialist community. It had, rather, served as an organizational mechanism for the politically mediated exchange of nationally-produced goods and the administration of barter relations between the individual countries. There were, not surprisingly, no economic relations of a market character involved nor was there much notion of specialization in terms of complex regional organization and forward planning. CMEA served to buttress and enhance Soviet control over eastern Europe as much as to further economic growth and the common development of the region. As the special relationship (as it might euphemistically be termed) of the Soviet Union with Poland and other east European neighbours was drawing to a close it nevertheless appeared that the legacy of former links (particularly with regard to trade and energy supplies) would continue to be of major significance.

But even these were subject to considerable reduction as Polish–Soviet trade switched to a hard-currency basis and the collapse of the Soviet economy continued. Soviet oil deliveries were forecast at a level of 4.5 million tons for 1991 compared with former supplies of 13 million tons, but this was also unlikely to be achieved. Such developments had direct implications for CMEA. Its executive committee announced in January 1991 that it would henceforth act on a different basis as an organization for 'economic cooperation', but its complete dismemberment was announced the following month. Poland did not find itself in a strong position as the conditions imposed on CMEA members were lifted and it became exposed to the full pressure of global economic pressures. It was apparent that of greatest importance was the continuing debt burden (whose role in producing serious imbalance in the economy could be traced back as far as 1974) and the need to stabilize and restructure Poland's economy in order to secure the conditions for growth and profitable participation in world economic processes.

Considerable progress was achieved in March 1991 with the decision of the Paris Club of western governments to cut Poland's $33 billion debt to them by half. Further steps in this direction were made when President Bush announced the intention to cut the American portion of the debt by 70 per cent and subsequent declarations were made by France and Britain. Accompanying these aspects of Poland's new international situation were more traditional security concerns and the need to establish and develop relations with neighbours who were undergoing similar processes of regime transition. Relations with the superpowers were still of considerable significance, but it was the European dimension and processes of regional integration that now came to occupy the position of prime importance. US economic influence was, of course, significant but much of it was exercised through international or transnational organizations rather than being transmitted direct from Washington.

On his return in November 1990 from the Conference on Security and Cooperation in Europe, Mazowiecki reaffirmed the movement towards European integration as the fundamental direction of his government's policy. An official invitation to join the Council of Europe was issued in October 1990 by its ministerial committee, the process to take effect after the holding of free parliamentary elections, a development later anticipated for autumn 1991. Poland was also instrumental in promoting the extension of the CSCE process and secured agreement to locate an Office for Free Elections in Warsaw and an International Centre for Culture in Cracow. The immediate concern, however, was the process of gaining associate status for Poland with regard to the European Community and Polish signature of the Treaty of Association was declared to be imminent.

The process of integration promised, however, to be a lengthy one. The initial accord between Poland and the EEC made in November 1989 explicitly affirmed existing agreements concerning textiles and agricultural products and left the provisions of the Treaty of the European Coal and Steel Community untouched.[1] This form of EC protection was particularly critical for Poland, as these products comprised over half the total value of its exports to the Community. Poland's 'return to Europe' was as much, if not more, dependent on EC willingness to shift from this position as it was on Poland's will and capacity to create a market economy. It was, as Pinder (1991, pp. 65, 69) delicately points out, hardly 'seemly for the Community to insist that eastern countries abandon price controls and a system of import levies and export subsidies which have insulated their industries from international market forces, while at the same time insisting that it retain just such a system for its own agriculture'.

National orientations

Apart from relations with pan-European institutions, links with individual nations or groups of countries were also of particular significance for Poland. Three different orientations may be identified, the first of which for a variety of political, historical and economic reasons had a special significance.

(1)   This concerned Poland's relations with its increasingly powerful western neighbour, first divided between two states but since October 1990 unified as a single Germany. In the absence of a formal peace treaty after World War II and the placing under Polish administration of an area of the former East Prussia and territories to the east of the Oder and Neisse rivers, Poland's claim to large parts of the lands that made up its post-1945 territory remained for some time subject to question and a source of continuing international tension. It was one of Gomulka's achievements, though one too easily neglected and overshadowed by the grave events that followed soon afterwards, to reach agreement with the Federal Republic of Germany on Poland's western borders in 1970 only a few weeks before his removal from office after the worker demonstrations and deaths in northern Poland. The agreement was ratified by the Polish and West German parliaments in May 1972.

The effect of this accord, in association with the successful economic and political outcome of joint European endeavours, was to defuse much of the well-established Polish phobia concerning the German state and nation. By 1980 an opinion poll showed that only 4 per cent of Poles feared the Germans while nearly 50 per cent expressed such sentiments in relation to the Soviet Union (Zielonka, 1989, p. 168). The collapse in 1989 of the communist order imposed by the Soviet Union on eastern Europe and the threat to the stability that followed on the division of Germany into two states nevertheless raised some anxiety in Poland. It soon became clear that existing agreements with West and East Germany on Poland's western border would be open to reconsideration in the process of reforming a unified German state. The situation was not eased by Chancellor Kohl's evident willingness to make use of his achievements in East Germany during the course of his electoral campaign in the west, where former inhabitants and others associated with the territories that formed part of post-1945 Poland as well as some right-wing political groupings were eager to reassert traditional German territorial claims.

Polish–German relations were, however, stabilized and set on an even course of post-communist development. In November 1990 the foreign ministers of Poland and Germany signed a treaty confirming the border between the two countries along the Oder and Neisse. Talks were also held by defence ministers on security issues, and shared concerns about developments in the Soviet Union and its growing instability were explored. Not all developments were so positive and the evident imbalance between the two countries in terms of economic development and capacity produced friction. The differing treatment by Germany of relations with Czechoslovakia and Hungary was also a source of Polish dissatisfaction. Czechs, Slovaks and Hungarians could travel throughout Germany without a visa, a right which Poles were denied and which was described by the Polish Foreign Minister as being perceived as a form of discrimination in the eyes of Polish public opinion (*Rzeczpospolita*, 20–1 October 1990).

Poland lifted all border restrictions for German citizens on 1 January 1991 although Germany, in common with west European partners, hung back from making changes in the existing situation. Poles who took on casual work in Germany and the individual economic initiatives undertaken by increasing numbers of visitors provoked not a little resentment. But progress was soon made and visa-free travel introduced in April 1991 to France, Italy, Luxemburg, Holland and Belgium as well as Germany. Nor was the view towards Germany taken within Poland wholly positive. It was argued that Polish government policy had been passive and conservative in relation to its immediate western neighbour and generally unimaginative in terms of European developments. Complaints were expressed in an emigré Polish journal of a 'national tumult of anti-German hysteria' and fears of a 'crusade of German capital' into the lands of the former Reich (Kaczmarek, 1990). Polish economic weakness combined with fears of political insecurity could produce dangerous tensions and anxiety about the consequences of strengthened foreign influence. It was probably the case that some misjudgements were made by the Polish government in dealing with the German question or, rather, series of questions.

Negotiations about the withdrawal of Soviet troops were delayed as Poland tried to maximize its freedom of manoeuvre in dealings over the border and treaty issues. This did not help in relations with other central European partners, although the tactic was an understandable one in view of Polish experience of the western power, certain instabilities in West German behaviour itself, and the small size of the Soviet forces involved. The changing situation in east-central Europe also brought into prominence the position of the German minority in Poland, its claims for better treatment and recognition of former injustices – including the treatment of Germans inhabiting the areas taken into Polish jurisdiction in 1945. The number of Polish citizens registered as being of German nationality rose markedly as new political and international conditions became established following the withdrawal of Soviet control. Some 250,000 Germans were registered in Oppeln Silesia (Opole) and it was claimed that the whole minority might well number over 300,000 in that area alone. The appeals of the German minority were strengthened by Chancellor Kohl's reference during his visit to Poland in 1990 to the events of 1945 and the movement of the indigenous population to the west.

(2)   A second dimension of Poland's place in Europe concerned relations with its southern neighbours. Tensions and conflicts between the different nations and ethnic groups of east-central Europe had a long history, but were submerged first by Nazi conquest and then by the period of Soviet domination and communist rule. Existing sympathies between Poles and Hungarians, on the other hand, were strengthened by similarities in their experience of 1956 and their common stand against Soviet dictatorship. Cordial relations were established between the activists of Charter 77 in Czechoslovakia and the Polish opposition, tendencies that President Havel and members of the post-communist leadership in Poland tried to build on. In his first official visit to Poland Havel emphasized the opportunities for cooperation now open to Poland, Czechoslovakia and Hungary. But the fact that he had visited Germany before his trip to Warsaw had already offended some Poles and there was also criticism of Czechoslovak efforts to establish relations of mutual understanding and forgiveness with the Germans.

Matters did not greatly improve during 1990. The border with Poland was the only one that Czechoslovakia refused to open for unrestricted traffic, and relations remained strained. This was particularly the case with Slovakia, where up to half a million Poles were said to be involved in economic activities. Talks on the border situation were held in October, and the Polish government, in the face of persistent lack of progress, accused Prague of breaching human rights. Travel restrictions were in fact lifted in May 1991. Relations with Hungary, which does not have a common border with Poland, were less critical, but a joint committee was set up in June by the Polish and Hungarian Prime Ministers to review obstacles to the development of bilateral relations. Affairs looked more negative from the Polish point of view in view of the progress made towards stronger regional integration by other countries.

Developments had begun earlier to strengthen cross-border cooperation in a region centring on the Alps and Adriatic, an Alpe–Adria organization having been founded in 1978. This progressed further with a meeting in

December 1989 of the foreign ministers of Hungary, Yugoslavia, Austria and Italy. In May 1990 Czechoslovakia joined the group, which was then reconstituted and became known as the Pentagonale. It undertook efforts to strengthen concrete cooperation and coordinate the activities of the relevant members of the group to join the European Community. Poland later made an unsuccessful application to join the group. Progress was made towards Polish involvement in December 1990 as Hungary and Italy expressed their willingness to assist the Polish application, and the imminent prospect of full membership was announced in May 1991. Poland's international position had not been enhanced by the fact that Hungary had already succeeded in joining the Council of Europe.

There were, indeed, growing fears during 1990 that Poland was losing out in the new geopolitical arrangements in relation to some of its neighbours in the region (*East European Report*, 1990). The concept of central Europe had gained considerable support and momentum since the mid 1980s and flourished as a symbolicimage of the new Europe when Soviet influence receded and cold war divisions lost their sharpness. The meaning of the term central Europe had never been very clear, though, and it had not gained much currency in Poland itself. While it had attracted the more theoretically inclined former activists of KSS–KOR (the workers' defence and civil rights organization), the idea of central Europe was more marginal to the interests and concerns of Solidarity trade union militants. One reason for Poland's relative isolation in its own part of Europe undoubtedly lay in the strength of the Polish national identity and suspicion of neighbouring national communities.

Long-standing disagreements with Czechoslovakia over the ethnically mixed Cieszyn (Teschen) region were a backdrop to the tensions of the post-communist period. The Polish nation, numbering over 38 million within the borders of the contemporary state, is also considerably larger than potential small or medium-sized partners in a regional association and could easily be seen as a destabilizing force. Poland's central position between Germany and Russia had, of course, been a source of conflict for centuries and its continuing significance in this respect could well be a cause of further security problems. Another reason rested on the nostalgic association of the central European idea with the former Austro-Hungarian empire and the tendency of Czechs, Slovaks and Hungarians to exclude Poles from this portion of their heritage. Political identity in east-central Europe had, too, been closely associated with nationality and the idea of independence intimately linked with that of nationalism.

This militated against a strong regional identity and, curiously enough, was affirmed and strengthened by the communist experience in which internationalist rhetoric contrasted with the practice of isolating individual states and minimizing possibilities of free communication. But too much weight should not be placed on historical determinism. Growing awareness of the common problems faced by the post-communist regimes and the experience of the radical measures taken to secure effective economic and political change soon tended to strengthen tendencies of regional coordination and enhance the identity of Poland as part of a modern central Europe. Meeting at the Visegrad Summit in February 1991, Polish, Hungarian and Czechoslovak leaders showed that the problems deriving from early over-optimism had largely been overcome and that the course was set for more regional cooperation and the undertaking of common efforts in the search for solutions to shared problems.

(3)   In the light of certain questions surrounding Poland's position in central Europe attitudes towards and relations with a third group of nations, those lying more to the east and south, take on particular significance. The potential importance of this orientation had been noted by Zbigniew Brzezinski some time earlier when he alluded to the threat of a geopolitical vacuum in east-central Europe and emphasized the prime importance of constructive Polish relations with Russia as well as those with Czechoslovakia (*Polityka*, 10 June 1989). The largest neighbour to the east, of course, was Russia itself, although not too much could be expected in terms of future intimacy (concrete trade relations were something else) in view of historic tensions, the more recent Soviet heritage of communist rule and contemporary disturbances. Earlier surveys had suggested that Russians had replaced Germans as the prime object of Polish fears and anxiety.

More recently, however, surveys suggested that Poles were largely indifferent to the Russians (62 per cent expressed this sentiment), while 44 per cent held that Poles were not well disposed towards them. Only 21 per cent expressed any degree of sympathy (*Rzeczpospolita*, 11–12 August 1990). The issue was somewhat different with Lithuania and the Baltic states, Bielorussia and the Ukraine, yet the situation here was not uncomplicated either. The area that has formed the west Ukraine since 1939 (with the interruption of Nazi occupation) was part of Poland in the interwar period and the division between the two halves of the Ukraine has retained considerable significance. Following the German invasion of the Soviet Union in 1941 some Ukrainians sided with the occupying forces. After their expulsion there were also independent Ukrainian groups who resisted the authority both of the restored Soviet and newly installed Polish rulers by force of arms.

The crushing by the government of insurrectionary Ukrainian forces over several years after 1945 in combination with the compulsory resettlement of the indigenous Ukrainian population of south-east Poland was a matter of some ambiguity and caused considerable resentment. Action against the local population was widely interpreted as the repression of a minority ethnic group, although officially the local Ukrainian population was seen to be, if not generally a source of active support, at least a form of cover for the guerrillas. Much of the south-eastern corner of Poland was cleared by force and many inhabitants resettled elsewhere in Poland. As many as 1.385 million people were recorded as having been resettled in all. Like the German minority, the Ukrainians (estimated to number some 2–300,000) now demand historical clarification of the postwar record as well as greater cultural and religious freedom. These antagonisms reflect on contemporary relations between Poland and the Soviet Ukraine and on the position of the Polish minority in the Ukraine itself.

Concerted efforts, however, were made by representatives of the post-communist leadership and the Polish reform movement to strengthen relations with like-minded forces in the Ukraine and to neutralize the effects of historic tensions. This included links with the potentially powerful workers' movement like that which first made itself evident during the coal-miners' strikes in the summer of 1989. Relations with eastern neighbours have been treated carefully by the post-communist government. Pope John Paul II also played a part in making a specific appeal for reconciliation between Ukrainians and Poles on his visit to Poland in June 1991. The first official visit of Foreign Minister Skubiszewski to the Ukraine in October 1990 was conducted in a favourable atmosphere and ended in the signing of a bilateral agreement on cooperation, as did the Russian part of the journey which concluded with a similar declaration (the first international agreement, in fact, since Russia declared its sovereignty within the Soviet Union). In Bielorussia, however, *perestroika* had made less progress and no agreement was signed, local leaders dwelling on continuing problems in Polish–Bielorussian relations.

To the north east, relations with Lithuania carry a related historical burden, the origins of the Polish Commonwealth lying in an initial union of the Polish and Lithuanian crowns during the fourteenth century. With the re-emergence of independence prospects for both nations after World War I ethnic Poles and Lithuanians contested areas like that around Vilnius (Wilno), the historic capital of Lithuania, with a lengthy record also as a Polish cultural centre. Relations with Lithuania have not been smooth since 1989 with Prime Minister Prunskiene complaining during her visit to Poland in December 1990 about the Mazowiecki government's failure to render proper assistance to Lithuania. Polish policy had in fact been carefully modulated to take account of the threats and tensions embedded in the difficult international situation and the complex domestic pressures that bore on it. The policy had been defined as multilateral and non-interventionist, with Poland attempting to maintain constructive relations with all involved.

The status of Lithuania within the Soviet Union was therefore regarded as a matter for prior settlement between Vilnius and Moscow. The Soviet use of force in January 1991 introduced a new element, though. The Soviet attack on the Vilnius television building was not regarded as a purely Soviet affair as it put into question the overall status of the Soviet Union, the position of Lithuania, Russia, the Ukraine and Bielorussia within and to it, and the relations of Poland with all concerned. The use of force within the Soviet Union had major implications for the future tenor of regional and international relations. The Polish parliament thus took a strong stand on developments in Lithuania and decisively reaffirmed its support for their right to freedom as well as that of other nations. Throughout 1990, meanwhile, Warsaw had continued to make representations about the treatment of the Polish minority in Lithuania. Questions surrounding the status of Poles within neighbouring states, notably Lithuania, Czechoslovakia and the Ukraine have therefore continued to play a significant role in Poland's external relations. These, however, form only one part of Poland's diaspora which has been important in foreign policy issues.

Some 13 million people of Polish origin were estimated to live outside Poland, 8.4 million of them in the United States. In October 1990 a meeting of their representatives opened in Rome, involving for the first time members of such communities in the east as well as western emigres and the well-established Polonia organization (the eastern communities rejected association with Polonia and emphasized that they were not emigres but found themselves on the other side of the Polish border for other reasons).

A total of 1.2 million Poles had been estimated to live in the Soviet Union in the late 1980s, although the official figure was revised to 1.5 million in 1990. Unofficially, it was accepted that there were around three million. A main theme of discussion was the establishment of institutionalized links with the Polish homeland, and a permanent secretariat was established to facilitate the process. The external community was also targeted to take on major tasks in Poland's economic recovery, and a Polonian economic forum proposed the establishment of a Polish–Polonian fund that would later be transformed into an investment bank.

Conclusion: Poland in the new Europe

The post-communist Polish government has had as a firm priority the 're-turn to Europe', extrication of Poland from the unwelcome embrace of the Soviet Union and the cumbersome regional institutions it had imposed, and the integration of the Polish Republic with the Europe of the EC and the broader continental association that promised to develop on the base it had constructed. It was certainly a principle held firmly by Mazowiecki and his government during the fourteen months of its effective life (Mazowiecki having announced the day after his defeat in the election of November 1990 the intention of his government to resign), but it was not so clear that the rest of society shared this conviction with quite the same degree of enthusiasm. National sentiments remained strong and nationalism grew as political diversification progressed with growing divisions within the Solidarity movement. External obstacles to the firmer integration of Poland with Europe also proved to be stronger than anticipated.

The promise of stronger ties within central Europe was more difficult to fulfil than originally thought: echoes of historic conflicts with former antagonists like Lithuania continued to make themselves heard, and the establishment of a unified Germany could not fail to prompt some qualms about future developments. The problems with a united Germany, as well as with other partners in the new Europe, were likely to lie not so much in the conduct of immediate diplomatic relations and the way in which more freely expressed national sentiments were handled as in the more entrenched inequalities and divergent structures that were becoming increasingly evident. The emergence of a unified Germany with a GNP equal to that of France and the United Kingdom combined could hardly fail to pose problems and prompt feelings of anxiety on the part of its impoverished eastern neighbour. These were all the more significant in view of the fact that established global and regional structures were undergoing rapid change.

The dominant tendencies in western and eastern Europe had run in different directions in this respect over recent years. The slowly advancing integration of the EC gained momentum in the 1980s while tendencies towards the disintegration of regional associations and enhanced national sovereignty grew stronger in the east. Poland's response to this situation was to work patiently on the improvement of relations with all potential European partners and to lay particular emphasis on approaches to established regional organizations. It was often difficult to make headway towards this goal in the face of established interests, entrenched inequalities and historical associations. This aspect of the European situation was by no means changed with the dissolution of CMEA and the Warsaw Pact, both placed on the agenda once basic views changed in the Kremlin. Rather, the collapse of the eastern bloc organizations enhanced the tendency towards selective organization and strengthened relations between different sets of European partners.

One basic problem was that the new Europe just did not dispose of structures that could guarantee democracy, disarmament and prosperity, while the established hegemonic alliances dominated by the superpowers could afford less effective guarantees of security in an increasingly independent Europe (Nelson, 1990, pp. 150–1). The reversion to a multiplicity of bilateral arrangements as the bedrock of European peace, it was not difficult to argue, entailed an illusory security. Envisioned patterns of new security arrangements, even those drawn up after the cataclysmic events of 1989, could be soon overtaken by events like the unexpectedly rapid unification of Germany (Snyder, 1990, p. 33). While there was widespread agreement on the advisability and wisdom of integrating central and eastern Europe into Europe as a whole there was little consensus on the appropriate method or framework for achieving it.

The Conference on Security and Cooperation in Europe, it might be agreed, had performed a valuable role in the recent past but did not really have the appropriate powers to take integration much further (Mroz, 1990, p. vii). Foreign Minister Skubiszewski directed attention to the revival of the Helsinki Process and the establishment of new treaties on the basis of some of its provisions. The idea of a Council for European Cooperation was another Polish proposal. Suggestions for broad, inclusive organizations certainly served to focus attention on possible developments and creative solutions to the problems facing a politically enlarged Europe. But the strengthening of more specialized regional links was also necessary and emerged as a tendency increasingly prevalent in the post-cold war situation. This was certainly the view reflected both in the actions of post-communist states other than Poland and in developments within western Europe. It was, however, a strategy that Poland encountered a number of problems in pursuing within the context of the new Europe.

This became evident from the complexity of the processes encountered by Poland in exploring methods of access to existing European organizations based on the western powers and in establishing new relations with neighbouring post-communist states. In one view, such obstacles could only grow in consequence of EC responses to the rapidly moving developments in eastern Europe. Two shocks had been significant here: firstly, discovery of the magnitude of the economic task facing a more integrated Europe and growing recognition of the costs of German unification and, second, increasing fears of political and economic collapse and disorder in the Soviet Union. One consequence detected towards the end of 1990 was the emergence of a different conception of regionalization within eastern Europe whereby, on the one hand, relations of trade and production cooperation might strengthen between the more reform-oriented countries and the Soviet Union – with the former developing a greater managerial role vis-à-vis the afflicted superpower.

On the other hand, east-central Europe might be used to absorb and contain the movement of migrant labour that might be expected to grow with the weakening of central Soviet power (*Polityka*, 12 January 1991). The future of east-central Europe, and above all Poland in this context, would lie less in its integration within a broader association patterned on recent west European developments and more in its capacity to contain the impact of the developing east European crisis on the west. The idea of a *cordon sanitaire* that had been a major current in the lengthy ramifications of the Yalta settlement was set, in this view, to make a speedy return to east-central Europe under the radically transformed conditions of the closing years of the twentieth century. This conception, however, neither accorded with existing aspirations nor with existing trends to openness and freer exchange. Such an idea of regionalization was unlikely to have much attraction for most Poles or make much headway against the increasingly influential conception of a specifically European society of states characterized, as Jonathan Story suggests in chapter 1, by a density of complex political and economic interdependence that marks it off from the rest of the world.

Related problems developed in the parliamentary sphere. The low turnout of 43 per cent in the general election of October 1991 and its inconclusive outcome suggested that the volatility and uncertain mood of the Polish electorate that had surfaced during the presidential elections the previous year had taken firmer hold – exacerbated by the complicated voting mechanism adopted, the extended wrangle that had attended its production, increasing disillusion with the course and tenor of national political life and (by no means least) the continuing burdens of everyday life in post-communist Poland. The low turnout favoured parties with firmer support and stronger organization – and helped explain the success of the ex-communist Democratic Left Alliance, which gained sixty parliamentary seats, only two behind the Democratic Union, which included Mazowiecki and former members of his government.

Five other groups, representing the post-communist Peasant Party, Catholic Election Action, the nationalist Confederation for Independent Poland, Centre Alliance and the Congress of Liberal Democrats, each obtained 37 or more seats in the 460–place parliament. The proportional emphasis in the electoral system finally applied had indeed borne out predictions of a fragmented parliament – but this also reflected the nature of an increasingly diverse society and its fragmented political culture. An artificially contrived majority might have made the process of government formation easier, but it would also have reduced the Sejm's capacity to establish its legitimacy as a representative body, and created further problems in the sphere of government capacity and its authority in terms of policy implementation. As many as ten groups gained a significant parliamentary presence (sixteen seats or more, a further nineteen parties receiving lower levels of representation).

It was not at all clear how a single-party majority or one constructed by a small number of parties could have been realistically achieved, however, (at any rate, through a single ballot), as it already took five parties to reach a parliamentary majority (the four leading parties occupying only 219 of the 460 seats). Six parties had taken 375 (97.2 per cent) of the 386 seats in the Hungarian parliament, while Civic Forum gained as many as 53.15 per cent of votes in the Czech Republic and Public Against Violence 32.5 per cent of votes (with Christian Democrats a further 15 per cent) in Slovakia. But it was difficult to see how such forms of representation and majorities were available in Poland without doing considerable violence to the principle of democratic representation and leaving large parts of Polish society without any sentiments of democratic efficacy.

NOTE

1   I am grateful to Jonathan Story for bringing the relevant documents to my attention.

REFERENCES

East European Reporter (London).
Financial Times (London).
Kaczmarek, R. 1990: Miedzynarodowe czynniki rozwoju gospodarczego. *Kultura*, (Paris), December.
Kolankiewicz, G. and Lewis, P. G. 1988: *Poland: Politics, Economics and Society*. London: Pinter.
Mroz, J. E. 1990: Foreword to *Eastern Europe and Democracy: the Case of Poland* (Institute for East–West Security Studies). Boulder: Westview Press.
Nelson, D. N. 1990: The Soviet Union and Europe. *Telos*, 84, 142–54.
Pinder, J. 1991: *The European Community and Eastern Europe*. London: Pinter/Royal Institute for International Affairs.
Polityka (Warsaw).
Rzeczpospolita (Warsaw).
Skubiszewski, K. 1990: Change versus stability in Europe: a Polish view. *World Today*, 46, 148–51.
Snyder, J. 1990: Averting anarchy in the new Europe. *International Security*, 14, 4.
Zielonka, J. 1989: *Political Ideas in Contemporary Poland*. Aldershot: Avebury.

16

The marketization of eastern Europe

Michael Kaser

The sequence of revolution

If there is one seminal difference between the Europe of late 1991 and that of late 1988 it is the disappearance of lip service to Marx. Adherents to his propositions may be found, just as to any of the world's great thinkers, but no government of the Continent now cites the historical inevitability of socialism in defence of a one-party monopoly nor abjures capitalism for its exploitation of the proletariat. Political monopolies persist on other continents but a more rational use of resources has almost everywhere displaced the executive rule of the state over the economy.

The analysis of time and sequence which is the core of Marx's economics is nevertheless relevant to the newly democratized and currently marketizing states to the east of the old 'Iron Curtain'. This chapter hence begins with the political conditions which invoked two revolutions in central and eastern Europe in the forty-five years to 1990 – from imperfect markets into imperfect planning at the start, and from somewhat better planning to a hopefully better market system now. Never has so purposive a transition to the use of market forces been undertaken on so vast a scale – more than a hundred million population are affected in the countries considered here – and it would be difficult enough at the best of times. But, as the chapter goes on to show, the industrial structure inherited from the 'socialist' period, the loss of incentives among the workforce, the neglect of environmental protection and uncompetitiveness in international trade add to the problems of change. Moreover, the five members of the Council for Mutual Economic Assistance (COMECON) at the start of 1991 dismantled their preferential bloc with the USSR just as domestic economic crisis hit Soviet trade. The year ended with the disintegration of the USSR. The contemporary western recession and the disappearance of the German export surplus rendered the rest of the world less of a shock absorber to east Europe than otherwise it might have been.

The chapter then examines in detail the nature of the changes being effected to transform the economic systems and describes the differences in emphasis and sequence among the six countries in transition – the 'COMECON five' and Albania. The violently disturbed state of the territory that was once a paradigm for east European reformers – Yugoslavia – precludes a reasoned view of its place here. The economic transition in the other six involves and is partly determined by social and political factors, with which the chapter goes on to deal. A mishandling of economic, social or political forces could distort the process of assimilation into the west European system and it is incumbent on governments in the latter to promote an orderly and successful transformation. The chapter therefore concludes with an assessment of the ways in which governments and business in the developed world can help the peoples of central and eastern Europe achieve the economic objectives which they have now politically chosen.

The politics of marketization

Most political revolutions take place without a change in economic institutions, but where a different economic system does emerge it is an outcome of a political act. The overturn of property rights after Lenin's revolution of 1917 by the regimes installed as Soviet satellites in east Europe after World War II followed and consolidated a set of political actions. The Bolsheviks overthrew private ownership of the means of production in the name of Marx, and it is indeed true that Marxian dynamics justify a socialist society. His theory of expanded reproduction demonstrated that the role of material growth was a function of the rate of investment (accumulation) formed from 'surplus value'; a socialist state could appropriate that surplus for capital formation. His theory of dialectical materialism postulated a change of 'productive relations', that is, of ownership, when they failed to respond to the potential of 'productive forces', that is, of technical progress and resource availability. The political 'superstructure' conforms to the new productive relations. Such was not the sequence of 1917–30: it was the new political regime which imposed its own set of property rights; Stalin recognized this by designating his policy 'Marxism–Leninism'.

The withdrawal from a regime of socialist property rights in east Europe and the USSR in 1989–91 can paradoxically vindicate the Marxian dynamic. The ruling communist parties demonstrably could not ensure that their 'productive relations' exploit the 'productive forces' at their entire disposition with the same efficiency and welfare as did the developed market economies. On this line of argument the inefficiency of central planning was the principal factor which initiated the dissolution of the USSR. In 1985 Mikhail Gorbachev's *perestroika* was economic – avowedly to reverse the production decline of the 'period of stagnation' under Leonid Brezhnev. His 'new thinking' to scale down east–west political confrontation had two economic motives – to permit the reduction of the excessive burden of military expenditures on civilian potential and to obtain some of the gains derivable from trade and technology transfer with the west. The east European revolutions would not have taken place in 1989 but for *perestroika* and 'new thinking', and the August coup would not have been attempted in Moscow had the plotters not believed that economic collapse could be averted and military power regained by resocialization. The coup, of course, failed for more reasons than popular and nationalist opposition to economic recentralization, but a consequence is that marketization is now adopted by all the states bordering those to which this chapter is devoted. The Baltic states, Belorussia, the Ukraine and Russia itself, all had plans for economic transformation when the USSR was dissolved at the end of 1991.

A second nexus in the politics of economic system change, which may be found in the history of early capitalism, is the abnegation of political rights for those adversely affected, wage labourers or peasants becoming wage-earners. The first industrial and agrarian revolution in Britain took place while the workers were disenfranchised – they gained the vote only in 1867. The same is true of France under Louis Philippe, of Germany under Bismarck, of Russia under Witte, the USSR under Stalin, of Japan under Tojo, or of Chile under Pinochet. There are exceptions – in North America and Scandinavia an 'open frontier' of extensive agriculture cushioned the impact on labour use, real wages and the food supply – whereby the industrialization could take place under democratic constitutions. There are, however, no freely disposable resources available for eastern Europe today. A transition from a regulated, fully employed but inefficient economy is taking place under conditions of rediscovering democracy. Revolutions which come politically 'from below' generate welfare expectations which marketization cannot, in the short or medium term, assure.

The paradox has another dimension, for the monopoly of political power previously exercised by communist parties had been dissipated before the deconcentration of economic authority had begun. The complement to the diffusion of the political base is the broadening of access to property rights. Ownership was previously nationalized to consolidate a political monopoly; its dispersion helps to preclude a return to 'mono-archy' (as formulated by Brus and Laski, 1989, p. 39). The political paradigm for eastern Europe after World War II was the USSR: Lenin in 1917–18 prohibited the private ownership of land and nationalized virtually all non-farm productive assets; after the respite of the new economic policy (1921–8) the central planning of Stalin and his successors re-nationalized those assets and collectivized agriculture; the collective farms were cooperative only in name, being subordinate to the local, and thence to central, economic authorities; even handicraft cooperatives were nationalized (in 1962). A sweeping nationalization after World War II and collectivization in the 1950s and early 1960s brought the east European economies under a similar mono-archy. Private agriculture persisted throughout in Poland and Yugoslavia, but in all other countries was restricted to the household plot; very few non-farm assets were in private hands, but some latitude was afforded in cooperatives and the small-scale leasing of state-owned equipment and premises. Permission for minority foreign participation in state enterprises had been initiated in 1972 (in Hungary and Romania) but even in the ensuing decade was not available in Albania and East Germany until 1990 – in the latter only on the very eve of economic unification with the Federal Republic.

Some relaxation of monopoly ownership in the non-farm sector occurred before the revolutions of the second half of 1989 in east Europe – the limit on employment in private firms was abolished in Poland and raised to 500 employees in Hungary – and majority, even 100 per cent, ownership was allowed to foreigners there and in Bulgaria and the Czech and Slovak Federal Republic (CSFR).

A general accessibility to property rights is a fundament of the economic transformation; no external circumstances are likely which would compel reversal in east Europe (in the way that the Soviet armed forces quashed reform in 1945, 1956 and 1968); privatization is vigorously under way in Hungary, Poland and the CSFR, and is in process in Albania, Romania, and Bulgaria. The political significance of industrial deconcentration is no longer a guarantee of systematic irreversibility but to 'level the playing field'. Citizens of the newly democratized states entertain a certain fear of subordination to foreign capital which could buy up ready-made monopolies. On the other hand, large firms will better withstand, or engage in, foreign competition. Vertical disintegration and the fostering of new businesses is advantageous in bringing eastern manufacturing closer to the size distribution of western firms, among whom a network of small enterprises (under 500 employees) has proved to be more efficient than fewer large ones.

The inheritance

It was not only in the east of the continent that peoples and governments saw central planning as the principal instrument of postwar reconstruction. A Soviet economist of the day wrote of the British Labour administration of 1945–51 running a 'sort of Gosplan'; Wilson, like Attlee, as well as Monnet, freely applied the term 'national plan' to their policy making. Non-communist parties in the postwar coalitions of eastern Europe were ready to do the same, although the content of their draft plans differed significantly from those propounded under Soviet direction by the communists in those governments. The depression of the 1930s had been particularly severe in those states – Romania and Albania excepted (largely by virtue of a capital inflow justified by their growing oil exports) – and the coalitions of the mid 1940s saw planning as a protection against cyclical fluctuation and as an instrument of industrialization (for only the Czech Lands were on a par with western Europe). When those coalitions had been repressed into vassals of a ruling communist party, and those parties themselves repressed into vassals of Stalin, five-year plans adhered to the Soviet model in form and in content.

Their content and their outcome in the 1950s and 1960s created a production profile which, for lack of new capital and alternative trade opportunities, was little changed during the 1970s and 1980s. The production of military goods was substantial, though never as proportionally large as in the USSR, and producers' goods (absorbing inordinate inputs of raw materials and energy) were re-invested into virtually the same lines. Consumers' goods and services were not promoted by innovation, competition and household demand; Hungary alone achieved an efficient agriculture, and the Soviet dominance in COMECON oriented members' trade towards the USSR and among the east European partners.

Most of those partners sought a way out during the 1970s with policies of 'import-led growth'; that is, borrowing from western banks rendered especially liquid by the deposit of OPEC-member surpluses, ostensibly to re-equip industry for the production of exportables for convertible currency. But the funds were misdirected, the exports were not generated and debts reached crisis proportions in the GDR, Hungary, Poland, and Romania. The latter two were compelled to reschedule their debt. Negotiations with Poland were frozen (and the unpaid interest accumulated to the principal) while its government of martial law was ostracized by the west, but Ceausescu ferociously seized exportables and axed imports to pay back Romanian debt – achieved, as it happened, just nine months before he was executed for these and many other extortions. Even the much more consumer-oriented regime in Hungary failed to generate the incentives and competitiveness characteristic of contemporary western Europe.

But the deficiencies of the 'Soviet bloc' were more than systemic. Politically-dictated priorities had neglected the production of foodstuffs, of consumer manufactures, of adequate housing, of financial and other business services. Capital and training had been devoted to health care and education, but current inputs to those sectors were far outpaced by demand (little of which had to be paid for – at least officially – by the beneficiary). Serious health hazards had been created by neglect of environmental protection and the regulation of worker safety. The Chernobyl disaster alerted eastern Europe, as the rest of the world, to the need for much higher standards. Consumer services of all kinds lagged behind the provisions that had become the norm in western Europe. The suppression of inflation by price control and of unemployment by enterprise subsidies generated monetary disequilibrium, the extent of which differed by country, frustrating consumers by shortages and queues. Limitations on travel to the west – least in Hungary, worst in Albania – added to citizens' frustration.

The political situation was transformed between September and December 1989, starting with the appointment of the region's first non-communist government for four decades, that of Poland, and ending with the downfall of the Romanian tyrant. Albania alone remained outside the stream, until its first ever free elections of 1991 brought opposition parties into a coalition government between June and December. They failed to secure an economic transformation in advance of new elections in 1992.

The political inheritance of forty years of communist rule is less easy to define. Nationalisms made silent by central authority are being given expression. Poland is at odds with newly independent Lithuania over the Polish minority there; Czechs and Slovaks have difficulties within their federal republic; Hungarians are deeply concerned over fellow-Magyars in Romania and Yugoslavia; the Albanian government is justifiably shocked by the withdrawal of all political rights from the Kosovars and tolerates agitation over the rights of Albanians in Greek 'Cameria'; the Macedonian dispute between Yugoslavia and Bulgaria could re-erupt, as could Bulgarian relations with its Turkish minority. The independence declared by Belorussia and by Moldova will not leave Poland or Romania unaffected.

Nor does political maturity come with the first parliamentary elections. The broad fronts of opposition in Poland and in the Czech and Slovak Federal Republic broke up within months of their electoral victories, Hungary started its new parliament with a range of differing parties, and the post-Ceausescu Romanian government dealt harshly with its opponents. The freely elected assemblies of Albania and Bulgaria began with majorities for the former communist parties. Except in Romania, western standards apply to freedom of the media; everywhere restrictions in foreign travel are purely financial.

The international environment for marketization

Neither politically nor economically is there even a residual of the 'Soviet bloc', epitomized by the Warsaw Treaty and COMECON's 'socialist economic integration'. In the space of a weekend both organizations disappeared. The dissolution of COMECON was signed in Budapest on Friday 28 June 1991 and the Warsaw Treaty terminated in Prague on Monday 1 July. No continuing formal links were introduced, but in October 1991 a conference was held in Moscow of six ex-members on the creation of an advisory 'Organization for East European Cooperation and Trade'. The two banks established by COMECON members, IBEC and IIB, paid off their capital in transferable roubles and reconstituted their capital in terms of ECU (400 million ECU for IBEC and 1,300 million ECU for IIB). The protocol ending the Warsaw Treaty declared an intention of the signatories 'energetically to develop relations among themselves on a bilateral and, depending on the degree of interest, a multilateral basis'. Deprived of their most industrialized member when the GDR became five Länder of the Federal Republic, central and eastern Europe is now confronted by the scission of the Soviet Union, which generated 40 per cent of their total foreign trade in 1988. It is an advantage to be free of a bloc using preferential mutual prices in lieu of a common external tariff, investing in multilateral projects without a capital market and coordinating plans without meaningful prices, but the loss of a dependable Soviet market undermines much of east European manufacturing. The east European heritage is a wasteful use of Soviet energy and materials and a capacity to produce manufactures, few of which met the competitive standards of western markets.

Already before the radical policy shifts following August 1991 the USSR had fallen into overall deficit in visible trade. Beginning with the collapse of the oil price in 1986, its terms of trade with the west had fallen precipitously. Eastern Europe, too, had not been faring well in its western trade, its share partly eroded by competition from east Asian and Latin American exporters.

The political changes which primed those in COMECON had already disrupted east European industry by terminating defence orders. The Warsaw Treaty network would no longer procure material in other member states; armies and security forces were to be smaller; and there would be fewer overseas armaments contracts. Czechoslovakia's long-standing and much-enlarged armaments industry was especially hard hit. Conversion in Russia and the Ukraine is so far generating unemployment, rather than consumer goods.

Partial trade returns for 1991 indicated a halving of east Europe's trade with its previously protected Soviet partner. On 1 January 1991, the Soviet Union had placed the mutual trade of the five east European states, like the non-European COMECON members, onto world prices (instead of a moving average of five previous years and subject to further divergence from current relativities) and onto convertible currency payment (instead of bilateral clearing in transferable roubles). Taken together with the shrinkage of what was the Soviet market and a cut in credit deliveries to Cuba and the Asian 'socialist countries', the changeover required fundamental orientation of the five countries' exports away from 'socialist' partners to the market economies. The association agreements of the European Commission with three of them (Czechoslovakia, Poland and Hungary) in December 1991 and their own free trade zone, initialled in September, signed in December, fosters commerce within western and central Europe in the future. Meanwhile, there was little western demand to take up east European slack. Overall, OECD members are only slowly emerging from recession, and expect a growth of only 2 per cent in 1992. The German trade surplus was being sunk in the eastern Länder and the Tokyo stock-market shock had cut the capital outflow from Japan. Generally, there would remain a high demand for international capital funds and consequentially high interest rates. German borrowing for the cost of unification, the retention of previously outflowing capital in Japan and the borrowing on which the Gulf states had embarked after the Gulf war were all disadvantageous to capital-hungry east and central Europe. A study by Morgan Stanley, the US merchant bank, of December 1991 estimated that every $100 billion west-to-east capital transfer would add 0.5 per cent to interest rates. Adding 3.5 per cent to the already astronomical interest rates prevailing at the end of 1991 (implicit in the maximum flows listed below) would drive the west into deep depression.

A variety of ways have been tried to estimate the size of those capital needs, of which three may be listed:

Annual foreign capital inflow needed ($ billion) to:

- Achieve current account balance and to repay debt over five years: 47.5
- Double GNP over ten years: 327.5
- Bring labour productivity to western levels over ten years: 420.7

For comparison the Marshall Plan was equivalent to 2 per cent of the recipient countries' GNP over its four years: at present prices and for the east European states, only $14 billion annually would be needed. The total worldwide flow of foreign direct investment in 1989 – incidentally, a record level – was $196 billion and the aggregate stock of such investment in east Europe and the then USSR was a mere $9.6 billion by October 1991 (Economic Commission for Europe, 1991, p. 5). A corresponding estimate for inflow to the former Soviet republics for structural adjustment is $100 billion annually for the foreseeable future. The same could be reached in the eastern Länder of Germany with $65 billion over just four years. A smaller issue also affecting interest rates confronts the ex-COMECON partners of the former GDR. In the second half of 1990 the Federal Government sought to avoid a sudden collapse of the exports of GDR firms between monetary union in July and political unification (and the end of the COMECON settlement system) in the following December. It allowed east German exporters to value exports to COMECON partners at the 2 M to 1 DM rate and at the official rate to the rouble, that is 2.34 DM to the transferable rouble.

Exports rose 26 per cent and imports plunged 34 per cent in that short period, pushing Germany's surplus from 2 billion to nearly 11 billion transferable roubles. As Germany had withdrawn from both IBEC and IIB before the transferable rouble was withdrawn and the two banks – as already noted – settled their capital status (though leaving current balances for bilateral settlement), the Federal Republic is now owed 25.8 billion DM, which it has already paid out to domestic firms (including, it is said, some 3 billion DM fraudulently claimed). A solution being explored with the east European debtors is to revalue the rate to 1.60 DM per transferable rouble (the rate at which Czechoslovakia cleared its transferable rouble surplus with the USSR) and leave the DM balance to be borne (8.2 billion DM under such circumstances) by the German tax-payer.

The two Balkan communist states which were not COMECON members are in a most perilous state. Productive assets in Yugoslavia have greatly suffered from war damage, sanctions on imports and non-execution of repair work. On current account tourist revenue has been annihilated, and civilian production lost by army mobilization and physical damage. The gains of the January 1990 economic reform have been nullified. Current account convertibility pegging the dinar to the deutschmark introduced on 1 January 1990 was abandoned the same November and the privatization of worker-managed enterprises has turned into their nationalization and their subordination to separate republican sovereignties. Albania, where a coalition government of the Socialist (ex-communist) and Democratic Parties succeeded a rigid and isolationist authoritarian regime only in June 1991, had the worst starting-line of any country in systemic transition. The withdrawal of the Democratic Party in December 1991 put the entire reform into doubt. Albania has been left so poor by forty-five years of autarky or ties with inappropriate partners (successively between 1945 and 1978 Yugoslavia, the USSR, and China) that its standards are those of the poorest countries of Asia rather than Europe: the most optimistic estimate of GDP per capita is $600, about the same as Mongolia, but it was down to $400 in 1991. All east European states were confronted by worsening terms of trade and, save Romania, entered the post-cold war world encumbered by heavy debts, so that trade deficits could be little offset by borrowing. The new Poland had by 'shock therapy' transformed a 1989 deficit to a 1990 surplus, but showed a deficit in 1991; it gained the benefit of a 20 per cent reduction of its $33 billion of official debt subject to the successful implementation of a three-year adjustment programme simultaneously agreed with the IMF. Bulgaria and Hungary carried a per capita indebtedness which was even higher than the Polish. Estimated for 1991 gross debt as a multiple of foreign earnings (visible and invisible) was highest in Bulgaria (4.2) and Poland (3.6) and lowest in Romania (0.4) and Czechoslovakia (1.1) with Hungary in between (1.9).

It was in such unpropitious international economic circumstances that these countries undertook to initiate a radical transformation of their systems. The political swing brought problems enough, but the new governments recognized that the transition would bring such serious consequences as higher unemployment and lower real wages. They could not ease the trauma by printing money, because they were just as determined on equilibrium markets, and they could not repress dissent or stifle the media because they were just as determined on democracy.

The economic transition

These six countries are not unique in systemic change – modern economic mechanisms are of their nature dynamic, and what is meant by a market economy today greatly differs from the mechanism they shared with the west in 1913 or in 1929. There is no clear division between the 'state centralized' and the 'free market' mechanism. The degree of regulation which had proved to be necessary in today's market economies is something of a model for east European governments intent on privatization. No government, for example, would leave monopolies unrestrained or withdraw from the provision of information – both state functions are needed for the operation of an efficient market. Agencies in both the public and the private sectors have to collaborate in establishing the rules and parameters for a market. It was soon evident in central and east Europe that deficient accountancy practices were inhibiting transactions between market-driven firms; publicity and education are needed to habituate people to the use of commercial banks and to promote and channel personal savings into corporate capital formation.

Western parliaments and governments are continuously engaged, not always successfully, in retooling their economic mechanisms. During the 1980s most had moved in the same direction as Mrs Thatcher's administration – 'rolling back the state'. Gorbachev's *perestroika* and the new east European governments had embraced the same policy. In the case of east Europe never has the process of denationalization been so comprehensive; the very magnitude of the change constitutes its novelty. In Chile under Pinochet privatization was sweeping, but in 1973–89 it covered just 470 enterprises and organizations. In Hungary there are 2,300 listed for privatization and 6,000 in Romania, but in Poland initially only 200 are on offer of the 7,500 that will eventually be put up. It remains to be seen whether western investors will find any more tempting purchases among the 47,000 likely to be offered in the republics of the former USSR. Throughout the countries in transition foreign equity purchases will bring capital inflow (if, of course, capital flight is prevented), and privatization in general will contribute to political pluralism by divestiture by the state and to economic efficiency by competitive profit seeking. Nor, in the model being sought, is the state to be purely regulatory (still less the 'night-watchman' of the nineteenth century); Austria, Japan and the Republic of South Korea offer contemporary examples of significant government guidance over dynamic capitalist economies.

Government support is needed for the reshaping by private enterprise of industrial structure. Firstly, growth strategy under communist regimes accorded priority to certain industrial manufactures, including armaments, to the detriment of other productive branches and of the environment. Secondly, east European input needs of energy and raw materials far outstripped production and were supplied largely by the USSR. The abandonment of a Soviet 'empire' left east Europe without a supplier willing to weigh its economic subsidy against political thrall, but it also left east Europe a highly inefficient user of the energy and materials it purchased cheaply. Russia itself, also distorted by over-cheap energy, saw its energy supplies in actual decline. Thirdly, private equity is needed for meaningful property rights over capital: state-run enterprises were not conduced to maximize the value of their assets and many (by reason of obsolescence or the need for investment to check environmental damage) now have a negative net value. Nevertheless, the staff of a state enterprise inherit a psychology of entitlement to employment in it: the workers expect job security and the managers the protection (in effect, subsidization) of its continued existence. Social protest is inevitable if, as forecast for the end of 1992, average unemployment in the five ex-COMECON states is 19 per cent (against 3.4 per cent in 1989 when structural changes began). It is the more likely because the rectification of these three wayward policies has to be undertaken simultaneously. Reactions from the many interests affected could throw out the interlocking of the measures. Pressures could be eased if the pace of change were slower, as in the case of the Spanish transition. The period to Spain's full entry to the EC was eleven years (1975 to 1986) but the inception was much slower than east Europe is currently effecting. After the elections of June 1977, Spanish economic policy evolved little for some six years. Spain, moreover, had never renounced or anathematized market relationships as had east European states in the worst phases of communist rule.

That rule overturned so many institutions underpinning a market system that time measured in years is required for new structures to be built and for agents habituated to their use. The changes may usefully be considered in relation to the factors of production – capital, labour, land and entrepreneurship.

Capital

The east European states, while experiencing certain investment cycles, did not under-invest. They were high-savings economies, guided by Marx's model of expanded reproduction and injunction to accumulate. Household savings propensities were low because of the lack of many of the incentives to save (for retirement, for ill-health, for inter-generational transfer and for owner-occupied housing), and because there were no institutions to mobilize personal saving other than a low-interest deposit in the state savings bank. A high rate of government saving was imposed by indirect taxation, levies on state-enterprise profits and by printing money. Much of the investment had been to no or little purpose, some even induced subtracted value (the negative of value-added) because the capacity installed used a mix of imports which at world prices would have cost more than the world-priced value of output. Environmental damage which the new governments wish to minimize requires the closure of industrial facilities previously tolerated. Since there was no competition in product markets, the capital installed did not generate the assortment of outputs which market-clearing prices would have evoked. Policy reforms after the events of 1989 dealt with the resultant 'chronic shortage economy' by changing the supply-side by product mix, by imports and of course by new capital formation, both home and foreign-funded.

Labour

The domestic adaptations should not be hindered by an insufficiency of labour. Over-full employment, job security, labour-hoarding, zero migration and in some countries a decline in numbers of school leavers had induced an apparent labour shortage. Once restructuring started, unemployment has, as just noted, become the norm. For those countries as a group there was some, but not yet definitive evidence that the 'shake-out' effects – higher productivity of capital and labour combined – were beginning to be beneficial. The broadly-based educational systems provide many in the thirty to forty age group who can take over from existing managers once they are inducted into the newly needed techniques. The experience of working with markets has not been as submerged in east Europe (least of all in Poland and Hungary) as it was in the USSR and has been reinforced by partial reform since the 1960s. But it is by no means certain that the region's present comparative advantage in prime cost can be maintained. Labour charges are certainly low with respect to west European levels, but they are being pushed up by wage demands, which employers find hard to resist. The balance of wage-bargaining has been tilted in favour of the employee: the compliant 'state-company unions' under the party *nomenklatura* have been replaced by protagonists of the workers; governments have to be attentive to their mass urban electorates; new owners can be pricked into pay concessions by accusations of capitalist or alien exploitation. Non-wage labour costs are heavier because social security premiums have to keep up with the governments' need to pay unemployment and other benefits and to reduce budget deficits, and because mines and factories must spend more on worker health and safety.

Land

Property rights to land and sub-soil material are essential to marketization, but only Albania (like the USSR) prohibited the private ownership of land. The denationalization of state mining enterprises opens the way to private mineral extraction. The institution of markets for both these types of asset requires, however, processes of valuation, conveyancing, rents, leases and royalties which are being adapted from western practice.

Sales of state-held fixed assets have been complicated by the claims of previous owners: in the CSFR and Hungary (as in the eastern Länder of Germany) legislation provides for restitution and/or compensation, and elsewhere proprietors dispossessed by the earlier regimes have entered claims; in Albania and Romania farmland has been taken back by force.

Energy and materials imported from the USSR were cheap until the end of 1990, at which point their prices were adjusted to world levels; the supply of Russian oil and gas and of Ukrainian hard coal is already declining and is further threatened by production difficulties. Bulk transport from the USSR has been cheap, but at the expense of inadequate maintenance. Without repairs, the Russian oil pipeline serving east European refineries would soon be useless. There were 40,000 leak incidents in Soviet gas lines during

1989. Soviet railways were over-loaded and were rent in dispute between regional administrations even before the republican divisions of late 1991. Lorry transport is scarcely utilized for lack of roads and appropriate vehicles. What was once the Warsaw Treaty interest in logistic transportation to its east European forward bases has dissipated.

Entrepreneurship

Entrepreneurship is in singularly short supply for the scale of operations involved in pulling large enterprises out of the state sector and providing the services to support and facilitate markets for goods, capital, land and labour. Poland and Hungary in the 1970s and 1980s had a substantial private sector in small enterprise and in farming, and have benefited from the return of emigrants with managerial and entrepreneurial experience. Poland had harnessed some of these from the mid 1980s in 'Polonia' enterprises; also, business success abroad – now devoted to developing Hungary and elsewhere in the countries of change – is epitomized in George Soros, the highly successful Hungarian-American investment manager who has laid down millions of dollars 'to open closed societies' (Soros, 1990, p. 7). The 'new' men and women may have to displace in management and ownership officials, managers, and party staffs of the old regimes who have been able to obtain possession of privatized state assets.

Markets in goods, services and assets are, of course, not only made by enterprise and by its exercise, but need underwriting by legislation, of which four categories may be distinguished: *facilitating laws* (such as on contract) which allow markets to function; *prudential laws* (e.g. bank supervision) which regulate the behaviour of financial institutions and transactions in assets; *consumer protection laws* (e.g. against fraud or misrepresentation) which define standards and establish liability for deviance; and *economic regulation* (e.g. on public-utility tariffs) which directly control markets in products and factors of production. It is the first two categories which are the priorities for east Europe today. As state enterprises are transferred to corporations, cooperatives or individual proprietors, the new owners have to have secure title and to be able to profit from the increment they may foster in the value of their assets. The manager of an east European state enterprise or the workers under Yugoslav self-management could not, on leaving the firm, encash the added value of the enterprise attributable to ploughed-back profit or to risks and investment decisions undertaken. The most deep-set lacuna of the Soviet-type system is motivation at the level of the firm to augment (or to avoid reducing) asset value: Lenin's principle of 'cost accounting' for the state enterprise was flawed in being limited to the coverage of current outlay from sales revenue, but even this rule was flouted by massive subsidization in all the planned economies. It was in effect the case (particularly evident in post-1968 Hungary where state enterprises were supposed to be in competition with each other and with foreign markets) that profit taxation of the most successful enterprises supplied part of the revenue to subsidize the least viable. This funding inverted the rational relationship of funding the efficient and bankrupting the loss-maker.

Although a thorough overhaul of fiscal practice is essential, this is not to say that governments should import the west's panoply of consumer protection and economic regulation. Such laws should evolve gradually, while facilitating and prudential measures should be applied quickly. Because all six countries expect eventual membership of the European Communities it is desirable that the process contribute to harmonizing legal structures with those of the EC.

Implementation

An early essential, but not necessarily the first phase is the achievement of equilibrium between household money balances and the availability of consumer goods and services plus personal taxes and savings. No east European country has demonetized some of the inflationary overhang as occurred after the war and in the early 1950s. The differential rate of exchange of GDR marks for deutschmarks in July 1990 could be construed as a demonetization for funds converted at 2 M to 1 DM, but with equal justice the 1 to 1 exchange could be interpreted as a preferential rate made for political reasons. The demonetization of higher denomination rouble rates in January 1991 was so ineffective in the then USSR that no east European government was tempted to follow suit. Governments have preferred to liberalize retail prices and allow inflation to soak up the monetary overhang. Poland in January 1990, and the CSFR, exactly a year later, effected a simultaneous decontrol of domestic prices and external transactions on current account. Leszek Balcerowicz, the principal author of the Polish programme, was however dropped from the government in December 1991, and the minister who directed the corresponding Czechoslovak programme was by then under threat, despite having become the leader of his parliamentary party. Romania and Bulgaria partially decontrolled prices (in November 1990 and February 1991 respectively), but the fall of the Petru Roman government in September 1991 when the Jui miners stormed into Bucharest halted radical reform save for farm and enterprise privatization. Bulgaria, on the other hand, continued to free retail prices. Albanian communists under Ramiz Alia held out against all manifestations of a market until early 1991, but the programme of transition launched by the Democratic Party Deputy Premier, Gramoz Pashko in August 1991, weeks only after taking office, comprised a commitment to transition. Some price freedom took place in November, but the party had to withdraw from government in December as Albania lapsed into deeper political and economic crisis. Hungary, having undergone steady inflation during the 1980s and with many prices already flexible had no need for a sudden decontrol; like Poland de jure, it and Czechoslovakia have come close de facto to current-account convertibility, which allows wholesalers the unrestricted option of buying consumer goods abroad. State-run monopolies at home were forthwith subjected to competitive pressure from foreign firms.

Without a supply-side response, freedom for prices and incomes would spell a surge in inflation. Such an abrupt rise in the level of prices promised to be all the more devastating in relation to the size of involuntary savings held by households, and/or to the tightness of constraints on imports. All three of the domestic institutional changes were everywhere being made in order to effect supply responses, not only for consumer goods but for producers' goods and the direction of capital formation. Except in Albania, all state enterprises could adjust their production as demand requires. Restrictions on the establishment of private businesses, domestic or foreign, have mostly been lifted (Albania was the last to conform, but Romania under its law of March 1991 retains significant obstacles to foreign entry). Any expansion or change of demand can now, in principle, be met by new entry into the private sector.

Unless limited by monopoly – the scope for which remains large – sensitivity to price and profit mechanisms is enhanced by privatization. As already noted, governments of all six countries provided in their reform legislation that some part of their equity in productive assets will be sold off. Foreign direct investment, domestic purchases, the allotment of shares to financial institutions (pension funds and state banks), which would themselves be privatized, and share auctions were all envisaged or introduced. Some restrictions – also as in western privatization – have been placed on foreign purchases. Three governments – of Bulgaria, the CSFR and Poland – offer preferential terms to staff of the enterprise being privatized, as has also been offered in western cases. But four governments offer the population at large an incentive to become shareholders. The adult citizens of Poland and Romania are to receive vouchers gratis, which can be used to buy shares (but not encashed) and those of Albania and the CSFR will be able to buy vouchers with a face value for equity purchase well above the voucher price.

If not already effected, the final phase must be to eliminate further inflationary pressure. The macroeconomic desirability is obvious – to stop a wage-push spiralling after price liberalization, and to stabilize expectations with respect to market-clearing prices and the exchange rate – but tight money puts a brake on subsidization. The keystone is constraint of public expenditure to revenue and an appropriate borrowing requirement. The canon of sound finance is being imposed, however, at a time when calls for social expenditure are politically difficult to resist.

Political and social adjustment

A market system is the objective of all east European states. Enterprises – private or residually in state hands – should, given market-clearing prices in open economies, be profitable. Any government decision, central or local, to offset losses would thereupon become explicit, whereas when production has been run by industrial ministries such finance has been hidden. 'Transparency' is a gain in itself and facilitates informed judgement on public expenditure. Nevertheless, four considerations may weigh in favour of subsidies to individual enterprises.

The *first* factor is external to the economies concerned. The prices payable for deliveries to other ex-COMECON countries from 1 January 1991 rendered many exports – particularly manufactures sold to the USSR – unviable. East Europe in consequence turned to trade with the west, but adjustment takes time and capital. The time element is not only that of the turnaround in shifting to new processes, products, markets and agents, but of access to markets which must await others' decisions. Membership of the European

Communities is a mutually acceptable, as yet not guaranteed, objective of the CSFR, Hungary and Poland, all of which since December 1991 have an Association Agreement; Albania, Bulgaria and Romania have set their sights on the same target. All anticipate some weakening of barriers to their agricultural exports with modification of the Common Agricultural Policy. Under all such conditions, home producers merit transitional subsidies.

A *second* factor has mainly domestic but some international elements: capital allocations to state enterprises in the past put scandalously little to environmental protection and to worker safety. Pollution is no respecter of frontiers and the cost of control should quite properly be borne by governments of the offending territory; the deliberate deficiency of past state investment should not have to be met by a newly-established corporate owner. Western assistance towards the costs involved under these two considerations would not be misplaced and would foster the inflow of foreign capital into joint and wholly-owned enterprises.

The two domestic factors – one economic, and the other political – are emerging with the output decline of the transitional period, into a *third* consideration. Plant or product-line closures under 'hard budget constraints' has already brought unemployment, and the standard multiplier effect has spiralled economic activity downward, albeit with gains in productivity per worker. Without resuming the perverse effects of past fiscal practice – taxing the most profitable firms to keep the least efficient going – a case can be made out for subsidies which aggregate to less than the unemployment benefit that redundancy would occasion. The decision merges into the more general political issue of maintaining the new governments in face of a populist opposition fuelled by resentment at the loss of job security.

A *fourth* factor is that politically motivated subsidies, including foreign assistance, can be defended as keeping recession at bay until world demand turns upward again. The new governments, fired by zeal for a free market, might allow small and medium enterprises to fail while funding the large employers for fear of the social and political consequences of closure. They would be influenced by the new or reinvigorated trade unions, which are strong in the big plants and almost non-existent in small private business. This discrimination should be resisted: big enterprises can make big losses and nurturing an array of small enterprises may well prove a better use for public funds.

The former GDR, although not the subject of this chapter, may be cited as a contrast to the other ex-communist states. One estimate (already cited) puts the annual capital subsidy at DM 100 billion for their enterprises to reach the western Länder productivity level in six years. Whether such an enormous sum can be provided depends on private investment and public funding, from taxation, borrowing and defence cuts, but the social security cover of unemployment (possibly rising from 22 per cent in late 1991 to 45 per cent at end of 1992) could assuredly be met, and labour made redundant in those Länder can freely seek employment anywhere in the EC.

As already discussed, none of the other reforming economies has that access to the EC. The present proportion of Poles and Yugoslavs in west European labour forces is very small in relation to the potential flood of economic migrants, especially as the former Soviet Republics relax their constraints on emigration. All the OECD countries have strict control over the employment of foreigners, but the issue has to be faced. The prospect of large-scale migration in itself makes the provision of western aid and capital inflow still more urgent, so that populations may be gainfully employed at home.

Western involvement

The transition to market economies in central and eastern Europe, now actively in progress, is bound to be difficult and protracted. But adjustments in western Europe – indeed among OECD countries as a group and individually – are consequential and inevitable. Political parties sensitive to their electoral chances and public opinion at large may be averse to those adjustments. In the case of aid or preferences, the claims of countries much poorer than European beneficiaries can be pressed with as much justice as ever.

Pragmatic western governments and legislatures may accord little weight to international justice in a political or idealistic sense, but public opinion, expressing itself anew in east and central Europe, claims some compensation for the abandonment of their countries, as it seems to them, by the Yalta agreement and by NATO's neglect, again on their view, of previous opportunities to roll back Soviet influence and force. They may also claim that policies against a potentially inimical superpower harmed the east European subordinates more than the USSR itself, or could at least have been modified to reduce the impact on those subordinates. The strategic and military embargo supervised by CoCom affected east Europe more than the USSR: the smaller states were more trade dependent than the USSR; they would normally have drawn on western institutions and firms for their research and development of new technologies and products, whereas the USSR had mobilized vast technological resources (but directed them to military rather than civilian ends); and their infrastructure (such as telecommunications) could not be modernized, with severe effects on their efficiency and competitiveness.

The Commission of the European Communities was cautious in offering access to the European COMECON states as distinct from the USSR even though claiming, as did most western governments, that they practised a 'differentiated approach'. The first round of negotiations between the EC and COMECON members (1974–80) was broken off as a rebuke to the USSR for invading Afghanistan, not because of anything east European governments had done.

Since the 1989 revolutions, western governments have offered east Europe institutional and material support. To fill the security vacuum, they provided a newly permanent CSCE. To monitor and help underwrite the economic transformation they have brought all the six states into the World Bank, the IMF and the EBRD.

Two sets of west-to-east flows are being generated to compensate the deficiencies of the six countries in capital stock and technology – private direct investment and technical assistance. In the case of the first, private investment in eastern Europe would be deterred by political risk. Among the factors cited are the entrenchment of discredited political groups in new managements ('privatization for the nomenclature'), popular resentment at foreign ownership, the slow pace of economic reward for political revolution, and the temptation unilaterally to renounce debt when the overhang becomes oppressive. Primarily, of course, the political protection of transition to a market system is the responsibility of the east European governments and peoples.

Western governments and the international agencies should, nevertheless, do all they can to facilitate private portfolio and direct investment. The chief vehicles for direct investment (by new implantation, in joint ventures or through purchase of privatized shares), are transnational corporations. This is as true for east and central Europe's prospects as it is within the developed world to date. Not only do they bring in capital, but managerial services, technology and markets. It is too early to analyse their effects on the six economies, for the latter have only just assured the conditions to make them welcome, and, because only a start has been made, magnitudes are still modest. So far, it is Hungary which has most successfully attracted private capital inflows; it more than doubled in 1990 and in that and the following year was more than half of all such investment into the six countries. It had accepted joint ventures since 1972 and by 1990 the value of foreign direct investment in Hungary bore the same share to GDP as such capital did in the United States (about 5 per cent). That Hungarian share exceeded by a factor of ten or more the corresponding shares in other east-central European states.

A third important desideratum is improved access to western markets. 'Trade not aid' has long been the west's watchword for third world policies, and the end of the cold war rendered otiose all but strictly military restrictions on east–west trade. It is only a matter of time before all the east European countries are within GATT, but the obstacles raised during the Uruguay Round suggest that east Europe must be far more interested in a European economic area and in a Community with its single market solidly in place by the end of 1992; the United States, Canada and Mexico are creating a counterpart; and Japan remains a net seller, not a buyer. Trade concessions to countries with the relative affluence of eastern Europe are, nevertheless, hard to defend in face of African poverty. Within the EC, the claims on Community resources of the least-developed regions or of communities in industrial or mining decline must be set against the encouragement of imports which could worsen their plight.

Western governments cannot close their eyes to such realities, but know that a special case must be argued for east–west trade on grounds of political exigency. The EC, having bilateral treaties with all the states concerned, except Albania (to which a Commission delegation went in July 1991), intends to complete its 'second generation' of association agreements when conditions are appropriate in Albania, Bulgaria and Romania (Pinder, 1991). The equivalent agreement of 1980 with Yugoslavia was suspended during the 1991 hostilities. Western industrial economies in general could still do more to enlarge access for east European products – in food, textiles and clothing, in particular.

The same advocacy of third world needs arises about the fourth line of western help, the alleviation of the burden of east European debt. Many poorer countries have bigger debts than Poland, Hungary and Bulgaria, and bankers are justifiably unwilling to slide into worldwide debt forgiveness. While there is no global solution through debt-for-equity and debt-for-nature swaps, a sound case can be made for reduction both of principal and of the interest component of debt service, and for the public provision of new money. The reduction of the Polish debt was a start, and international financial agencies, the World Bank, the EBRD and the European Investment Bank, are active in providing inflows which afforce those from the private sector.

In the 1970s technology transfer from west to east was financed by bank lending – but the principal channel is now an equity stake. It is accompanied by 'disembodied technology' to satisfy east Europe's need for professional consultancy in financial, fiscal and accounting reform and for the improvement of management education. Such transfer is partly assured by programmes administered by the EC and by national governments – notably the 'know-how funds' of the UK government.

Consumer policy

Marketization has some specifically monetary parameters – currency convertibility, a meaningful definition of property rights in financial assets, credit restriction and budget restraint. The 'social safety net' is costly, for unemployment benefit had not previously been widely needed and many social provisions (such as creches, sanatoria and holiday hostels) had been incorporated into production costs. The closure of loss-making enterprises not only involves mass redundancy but reduces the tax base (insofar as the products were not previously subsidized).

The objective of a balanced budget contributes to the relaxation of inflationary pressure, but, as already discussed, must be accompanied by a market-clearing price mechanism. Thoroughgoing price restructuring is essential because east Europe, except for Hungary, endured both a chronic shortage economy (individual prices were wrong in relation to each other and to buyers' preferences) and chronic excess supply (overall there was 'too much money chasing too few goods'). But public opinion is already volatile on the price issue. The Romanian riot of September 1991 over price rises has already been mentioned, but a miners' rampage is part of the political scene. In more stable Hungary a relatively modest rise in the prices of oil products in 1990 triggered a protest by drivers of taxis and lorries that forced the government to change tack. Imports are crucial to furnish the competition to dampen the price rise after liberalization. Poland, Czechoslovakia and Hungary have effectively facilitated consumer-good imports by relaxing exchange control on the current account. Bulgaria is contemplating the step and in February 1991 abolished the customs tariff, with only a few exceptions, in order to attract imports.

The effect on real incomes is deliberately negative, especially where, as in Poland, the CSFR and Bulgaria, wage constraints have been fairly effective (penal taxation in Poland and the CSFR on wage increments exceeding a pre-set maximum, and in Bulgaria prohibition of wage increments exceeding 70 per cent of the price rise). At the same time the fostering of private entrepreneurship accords higher money incomes to some, while wage-earners suffer a real decline in purchasing power. Against this decline must be set the greater utility undoubtedly derived from the exercise of choice among goods and services available and the time saved (not to say the psychic gain) from queuing and frustration at informal rationing.

Policy towards the consumer is the key to east Europe's integration with the west. Citizens have had their expectations aroused by the free exercise of the vote and by the higher standards of countries they can now freely visit. Czechoslovakia apart, the pre-war history of east Europe was not strongly democratic; authoritarian preferences persist among ex-communist party members and officials, as well as among those, such as President Walesa, who were their most strenuous opponents. On the positive side, adjustments can more acceptably be made when economic activity is rising than when it is falling.

The responsibility of western governments and of international agencies is to facilitate economic transition without weakening the political will to make those changes. The London Summit of the Group of Seven in July 1991 explicitly promised better access for east Europe to their markets for their exports in which they have a comparative advantage. In the midst of the struggle to complete the Uruguay Round it was a paradox that liberalization was being advocated by the countries in transition and by the developing world, most of whom had suffered illiberal regimes, against the two areas, the EC and the USA–Canada nexus, keen to maintain their protective barriers. In these different ways the 'new Europe', like charity, 'begins at home'.

REFERENCES

Brus, Wlodzimierz and Laski, Kazimierz 1989: *From Marx to the Market*. Oxford: Oxford University Press.
Economic Commission for Europe 1990: *Promoting Foreign Direct Investment in the ECE Region* (Document TRADE/R.572, 10 November 1991). New York: United Nations.
Oxford Review of Economic Policy 1991: Microeconomics of transition in eastern Europe, 7(4).
Oxford Review of Economic Policy 1992: Macroeconomics of transition in eastern Europe, 8(1).
Pinder, John 1991: *The European Community and Eastern Europe*. London: Pinter/Royal Institute for International Affairs.
Soros, George 1991: *Opening the Soviet System*. London: Weidenfeld & Nicholson.

17

Reforms in the Soviet economy: the tribulations of *perestroika*

Georges Sokoloff

In the winter of 1990, as conservative forces gained ground in the Kremlin, aiming to stem the tide of changes sweeping through the crumbling Soviet empire, renewed rumours circulated that *perestroika* might be but one more Soviet stratagem to disarm the west. Gorbachev's undaunted followers saw *perestroika* as a plot by Gorbachev, the Great Liberator, to mystify his conservative opponents at home. According to both viewpoints, the social and economic pains involved were to be part of a master plan.

The old Kremlin's inclination for political montage should never be under-estimated, any less than the ideological rigidity which fuels it. As any honest observer of the Soviet economic scene undoubtedly recalls, shifts in interpretation tended to swing with the events of the last decade. The dominant mood until the mid 1980s was the overwhelming triumph of conservatism, followed by scepticism over Gorbachev's early initiatives, hope about the 1987 reforms, worry over the crisis which began to unfold by the end of 1988, hope again when Gorbachev opted for the market economy, fear again when, on 20 December 1990, Edward Shevardnadze denounced the danger of dictatorship, despair during the days of the 19–22 August 1991 putsch, and incredulity at Boris Yeltsin's 28 October speech announcing price liberalization, but with little reference to the necessary accompanying structural reforms.

To the extent that swings in mood may be trusted, they also suggest that *perestroika* was anything but a ploy. Much to the contrary, 'restructuring' resembled a sequence of acrobatic acts performed by an unskilled circus, moving rapidly in one direction, then retreating, precariously off balance most of the time. The whole episode points to the fact that, initially, there was no such thing as a coherent reform policy, hence the difficulty of conceiving one, let alone the difficulty of its implementation.

Despite its tribulations, *perestroika* assumed major historical significance. Through its successive upheavals up to the disintegration of the Soviet Union in late 1991, it fully earned its revolutionary credentials. In the process, the economic situation deteriorated. Disillusion set in, adding to the political confusion, to the pangs of regret over the loss of empire and the social vacuum that it left behind. In its last year, a sense of continual vertigo, led first to a feeling of nostalgia for the old 'socialist order', and then to a scramble to escape an uncertain future.

The old system

As good a starting point as any is the old system and its main characteristics. In the Marxist–Leninist tradition, the economy was handled and owned directly by the party-state. The central bureaucratic apparatus pulled the strings of the economy as if it were a puppet which, despite the artificiality of its many parts, was assumed to have the energy and grace of a living organism, but without being quite so whimsical.

To make things work, the central apparatus and its partners (mostly the branches of industry) wielded the double-edged axe of the plan and of 'funding'. Each company was told what to produce and thus obtained the labour, equipment and materials required. Those resources that could only be obtained from abroad (and those which in return had to be exported) fell under the control of the centre. The Ministry of Foreign Trade monopolized the right to buy and sell abroad. The Bank of Commerce dealt with the financial transactions.

Alongside the blunt manipulation of the production cycle, a price mechanism of sorts had to be provided for. Since evidently prices were not meant to ensure market equilibrium, their role amounted to mere accountancy. And since the companies' profits and losses had no influence on their financial resources, the rouble duplicated the same trick. By means of accountancy, corporate sales and purchases appeared as financial transactions. But the resulting financial situation hardly affected the companies' routine. When they showed good results, it was impossible for them to obtain better funding to increase production. When they showed bad results, they still received the funding, as laid down in the plan. Either way, the practice of administered prices was at fault. Indeed, although administered prices were periodically – and solemnly – revised by the relevant state committee, they remained hopelessly arbitrary.

The slow turnover of capital was in itself an indication of how primitive the banking system remained. Only two banks dealt with overall domestic operations. Stroïbank handled investments while Gosbank centralized regular banking accounts. The latter also issued currency for private usage. Before such an issue, Gosbank would try to evaluate how people's incomes would balance out its own expenses. Theoretically, such projections should have been easy to make. After all, the state was in command of people's income; indeed, the state presided over whatever income the workers earned, while also setting the price of commodities. Unfortunately, such projections were most often erroneous. The plan had a compulsive tendency to promise consumers a lot more than the economy could provide. Furthermore, unlike the rouble used in wholesale dealing, the rouble used for current outlays did not affect the commodity market: buyers could decide, hesitate, or refuse to buy. The result was a constant over-estimation of spending projections. Citizens placed their savings in the bank, all the more as they knew, among other things, that their retirement pensions would be too meagre to support them. So, not all savings ended up under the mattress. The savings banks, controlled by Gosbank, were there to take care of that. But, the mass of liquid assets held by this state 'reservoir' continued to accumulate and became a major subject of concern. The planners' nightmare was that a panic would set in, with the monetary overhang flooding an impoverished market.

The other weak point in the system was, unhappily, located quite close to its heart, in the various bodies which received their 'funding' in kind as part of 'planned production'. Indeed, more often than not, the haggling that went on in this kind of barter would be done at a profit for the enterprise negotiators, who would use technical arguments and their know-how so as to ask for more funding than was actually needed. The negotiators' rule of thumb was straightforward enough: hoard now, because one never knows what the future might have in store. This compulsive stockpiling placed even more pressure on a production system which already had problems enough of its own. It made the company supply system based on coupons even more incoherent, and was denounced as early as 1964 in the following terms: 'Like all rationing cards, those coupons do not guarantee access to the quantity of supplies actually needed at the right place and time, but provide only access to what funds and coupons will allow' (Nemcinov, 1964).

Aborted reforms and the system's decay

The leadership was quite aware that Soviet management suffered from severe circulatory problems requiring treatment. But their grasp of the difficulties weighed less than their visceral attachment to the system. Centralization of the economy gave them prominence and status, and was immune to change for several reasons: its internal cohesion, the privileges it bestowed on the *nomenklatura*, and the habits it had steadily developed in all layers of society.

Under Stalin, central economic management was periodically submitted to a *perestroika* of sorts (in fact a current term in technocratic Russian). In the midst of the 'Great Patriotic War' of 1941–5, Nicolaï Voznessenski orchestrated a debate on 'price value', in an attempt to bring some coherence into the wholesale price system, but to no avail. Shortly after the despot's demise, in August 1954, a decree harshly criticized Gosbank for its failure to impose genuine budget stringency on enterprises (Gosbank, of course, had no business playing that role). In May 1957, Khrushchev by-passed the central chain of command by entrusting the management of industrial supplies to *sovnakhozes* (regional bodies) as opposed to the technical ministries. This ran contrary to the whole logic of central planning. The utter disorder which ensued paralysed bureaucracy and fostered the idea that enterprises could assume responsibility for their own management. And indeed, the reform of September 1965 enabled enterprises to come up with their own autonomous results. But that reform was far from signalling the advent of a market economy; rather, the backlash against it gave new legitimacy to the entire Stalinist apparatus of central economic management.

The system, in short, tolerated only perfunctory changes. A few examples suffice to make the point: the decree of July 1955 granted managers a semblance of power (mainly to give fringe benefits to their employees); the

1973 law had companies reorganized in conglomerates (fewer conglomer-ates being easier to handle); and the pseudo-reform of July 1979, which introduced a new collection of planning gadgets.

Conditions, then, continued to deteriorate. At a time when the USSR was the stronghold of economic conservatism, the Hungarians began their slow immersion in 1968 into the cold waters of a market economy. The Chinese took even bolder steps, 'decollectivizing' their agriculture and in 1980 opening their first 'free-zones' to foreign investors and Chinese entrepreneurs. This was followed by the industrial reform of 1984, reducing state control over industrial enterprises, and extending regional responsibilities for foreign trade. Compared to other socialist countries, the Kremlin's immobility was shocking; even more so in view of the evident deficiencies. The system stumbled along, as industrial growth slackened, and finally came to a halt.

On his 1984 visit to Paris, Nicolaï Pavlovitch Lebedinski, Gosplan vice-president, jolted his interlocutors when he said: 'Gosplan is no longer cap-able of controlling economic activity'. By then, the number of civil servants in Gosplan was the same as the number of products they were handling, approximately 6,000. With the help of Gossnab and the ministries, the Soviet administration could at best handle 30,000 products. The enterprises needed over 20 million products to be dispatched to 44,000 industrial organiza-tions, 32,000 construction companies, 47,000 farming units and about 1 million sales outlets. Central planning was left to choose between cutting down on the number of products it could actually handle – a nonsensical solution – or leaving the enterprises to their own devices.

To this effect, the state was prompted to allow a few pockets of freedom into the system and, short of upsetting the entire supply distribution system, Gossnab established a number of direct connections between companies. Of course, in the realm of arbitrary central planning such 'marriage contracts' did not go very far. Yet, partnership did enable the companies to define their own needs and specific requirements. Besides, local 'wholesale' outlets were starting to operate, and their transactions entailed cash operations; in other words, the company rouble was not as passive in actual fact as it was supposed to be in principle. It was not at all passive in those more obscure areas of the system where it was illegally converted into cash and used by enterprises as under-the-counter payment for those items which the plan could neither control nor provide.

Thus, one of the flaws in central planning rapidly became a rift. Managers beat the plan as they bargained for supplies independently. Indeed, they dispensed with the plan altogether by finding their own means to keep their production going. That way, they generated funds, which meant another dent in the system. Excess of liquid assets among the citizens was not to be blamed solely on Gosbank mismanagement. The productive system oozed money so as to oil the cogs of its own machinery, with most of the cash ending up in workers' nest eggs, in the form of various fringe benefits.

In the spring of 1983, *Eko* magazine assembled a number of enterprise directors, planners, economists and workers' representatives around Abel Aganbegjan – the Armenian economist, who had long seen fundamental flaws in the Soviet economy, and who was soon to become adviser to Gorbachev. The meeting took place in Novossibirsk. The atmosphere at the round table was tense, as participants blamed the crippling shortages on each other. All of them were critical of the system but none of them really wanted to change it. They had all become quite familiar with it and had learnt to exploit it to their own advantage. In other words, the prevailing conservatism could not be blamed solely on the leadership. The diagnosis that the economy needed 'a thorough restructuring' was shared by Yuri Andropov, who had just come to power as Brezhnev's successor. Unfortunately, things got no further than the already existing direct contracts between companies and Andropov had to make do with the ever widening discrepancy between the amount of money stashed away by the population and the scarcity of available consumer goods. As for poor old Konstantin Chernenko, Andropov's successor, neither his convictions nor his strength could possibly bring him to tackle the economic problems of the USSR.

The pale dawn of revival

During the first year of his mandate, Mikhail Gorbachev did not elicit much enthusiasm (Sokoloff, 1985). Like Andropov (though with more vigour and less discretion), his political inspiration was a kind of patched up Leninism adapted to modern times. He could be called a 'socialophile': a renovator or a 'reconstructor', but not a reformer. This judgement is confirmed by the economic orientations he first introduced.

His stainless-steel faith in bureaucratico-industrial solutions led him to create the monstrous Gosagroprom on 21 November 1985 to try to solve the Soviet agricultural problem. His conviction that economic police work would check on product quality better than would the law of the market led him to the creation of the Gospriemka on 13 March 1986. In line with this disciplinary approach – and a moralizing one at that – he imposed the prohibition of vodka, a measure which may have been called for by the declining health of the Soviet people but not by the ailing budget.

Another source of income for the state was the hard currency earned by oil sales on world markets. But prices fell away in early 1986, severely curtailing earnings. With what was left, the government preferred buying equipment with a view to stimulating investment. Investment was to help implement Gorbachev's great ambition – equally typical of his taste for drastic measures – i.e. 'acceleration' of development in order to do away with the previous 'stagnation'. Gorbachev failed to identify the essential cause of prior difficulties, namely the long-standing sacrifice of growth in favour of overarmament. The military expenses written into the twelfth plan (1986–90) were congruent with 'tradition' (the phrase is Nicolaï Ryzkov's, of 7 June 1988, illustrating the inspiration of early *perestroika*), that is to say, that military expenses would grow faster than the state's income.

The budget deficit increased sharply as income wavered and charges went up ostensibly. By the end of 1985, the deficit was only 18 billion roubles, i.e. 2.3 per cent of GNP. By the end of 1986, it came close to 48 billion roubles, i.e. 6 per cent of GNP (GOSKOMSTAT, 1989). Gosbank, which had no autonomy from the Treasury, started printing money, causing inflation to rise. Andropov had been more concerned with that imbalance between goods and money than was his spiritual successor.

On the other hand, despite his blindness, which made him lose precious time, Gorbachev quickly gained in stature. He owed it to the dark warnings in his speeches about the threats weighing on the country's destiny, about the country's incapacity to remain a superpower unless it salvaged its economy. His warnings recalled the great shake-ups which had punctuated the past. They occurred after conservative periods had made the situation ripe for change, when some 'external challenge' had pointed to the internal limitations to international expansion, or when a political saviour aptly made his appearance on the stage. His was the voice of dreams. In retrieving its ancestral reflexes, the country would perhaps recover its identity and cast off the mask of ideology, which made it unrecognizable and unable to breathe. In short, Gorbachev edged towards having to choose between acting as a renovator of socialism, and his role as the country's saviour.

As in most matters, counter-arguments may be advanced. Certainly, a Secretary General did not exercise as much power on his party as the Czar used to have over his nobility. 'External challenges' such as Reagan's 'star wars', and the Afghanistan venture were harsh enough. Given the critical state of the country left by the preceding gerontocracy, the adverse international situation only compounded internal difficulties. Gorbachev's predicament barely bore a solution: he had to change an economic system which was untouchable according to the ideology still represented by Gorbachev at the time. Besides, switching from communism to 'the Russian idea' would only threaten the empire (an item that was not even on the agenda yet). The ambiguity of Gorbachev's project is well expressed in the Stalinist formula: 'the historical destiny of the country and the position of socialism in the world today'.

Perestroika in progress

In his early years as Secretary General, Gorbachev still cut the figure of a communist with a difference, one who was open to new ideas; he looked like a man who would take risks. The return from their exile in Novossibirsk of reformist sociologists and economists like Tatyana Zaslavskaïa or Abel Aganbegjan may have led Gorbachev to give up his impossible economic policy of 'acceleration' in favour of *perestroika*. Protest, of course, also held the promise of liberation for the true faith from the shackles and tinkering of long-standing orthodoxies.

Short of a more reliable explanation, the facts still stand. Gorbachev had been noted for his openness to new ideas for some time. Once in office, his record was strewn with innovative formulae, initially dismissed by the sceptics as all talk and no show. At the Thirty-seventh Party Congress in February 1986, a revised version of the Third Programme was adopted, whose terms both lacked the audacity of Krushchev's formulations, and remained demagogic. The decree of 23 May 1986 concerning the punishment of illegally earned income (i.e. not acquired by 'labour') confirmed the fears of the more pessimistic.

But the mood changed quickly. On 19 August the decree on 'foreign trade' came out. This decree and the complementary measures taken in its wake make it possible for foreign companies to invest directly in the Soviet Union; even more important, they allow Soviet enterprises to conduct exchange deals with foreign partners of their choosing and to supply them – although minimally – with the required currencies. In the autumn of 1986, the Industrial State Committee welcomed a delegation of Russian economists from the Institute of World Economy (a body of the Russian Academy of Sciences) who had come to announce that the nascent economic freedom in the realm of foreign trade was in fact part of a larger train of reforms soon to include all sectors of Soviet activity. This was confirmed the following summer when major decisions were made by the party and the government in June–July 1987. The best known of these measures was the law concerning the public sector. The text reads like the reformists' revenge over the party apparatus after their aborted attempt of September 1965, associated with the name of Kosygin. In fact, the novelty lies elsewhere. The decree stipulated that the driving force of the Stalinist economy, i.e. the plan/funding duo, was to be jettisoned. By 1992 (a deadline laden with symbolic meaning), the enterprises would have leeway to buy wholesale supplies from one another. Buying would be left to their own discretion, according to their order books. By 1992, however, one-third of their orders would still be orders from the state. But the latter was to lose much of its influence. The state's great agencies were to have redefined their current functions to strategic ones for Gosplan, or logistic ones for Gossnab.

This new direction in policy was fundamental for three reasons. First, it meant a time break with the old system and the end of the rouble's arbitrariness. Second, it held out the promise of improving the circulation of supplies and the distribution of goods. Third, it made joint ventures with foreign companies possible. The activities of independent workers, legalized in November 1986, were to contribute to the renaissance of the private sector. The already-developed cooperative sector was regulated by a new decree in May 1988. The workers could lease productive assets from state enterprise to improve their gains.

Did all this mean the victory of a market economy introduced by a modern state in the interest of the country, and to the detriment of the party-state? (Nujkin, 1988). No. The 'commercial socialism' that was being sketched in 1987 was a far cry from all that.

Overcoming opposition

The principles adopted by the end of June 1987, along with the subsequent enforcement decrees were teeming with conceptual errors. For companies, free choice of suppliers and clients obviously should have implied price deregulation, but official considerations on that subject remained timid, to say the least (Pavlov, 1987).

Reactivating the role of money in enterprise was inconceivable, if it was not sustained by the restoration of a true banking system (Brainard, 1990). But the central government created only two new credit institutions, the Agro-industrial Bank or Agroprom and the Bank for Housing and Social Equipment or Zilsocbank, and gave two existing banks new names (Strojbank was renamed Promstrojbank, literally 'the bank for industry and building'; Vnestrojbank, the bank for foreign trade', was renamed Vnesekonombank, literally 'the bank for foreign economic relations'). The government took the handling of savings away from Gosbank and trusted it to Sberbank. Notwithstanding, Gosbank did not really obtain the status of central bank (de Boissieu and Renversez, 1990). In part, because this banking reform was inadequate, capital flow between companies was still trapped in the old system. Simply, the former 'plan' became 'state orders' (Valovoj, 1988).

These new measures on private enterprise said nothing about the possibility of 'privatization' and nothing about the possibility of joint-stock companies. The long maturation of the Hungarian reform had by then already shown that responsible company management implied modifying the status of ownership. Finally, and for the same ideological bias vis-à-vis private ownership, the vast problem of agriculture was not even addressed. The topic was in fact discussed later, during the party plenum of March 1989, but with no conclusive results (Giroux, 1989).

Despite its insufficiencies, the 1987 reform met with the resistance of those who found it was going too far. The very authors of the reform were reluctant to use the abhorrent word 'market'. Opposition near the top of the hierarchy forced Gorbachev to drop Boris Yeltsin on 21 October 1987, which started up a deep crisis in *perestroika* the following spring, one of the episodes being the publication by Nina Andreeva in 13 March 1988 issue of *Sovetskaya Rossia* of her famous reactionary diatribe 'I can't compromise on principles', a bureaucratic sabotage, passionately denounced by Gavril Popov (Pravda, 1987). The reaction denounced the incompetence, misplaced arrogance, and other forms of infra-cultural attitudes from the very officials who were expected to carry out the reforms. Disarray spread among the citizens who had for decades managed to protect themselves from the plan (in the sense that an umbrella protects from rain or a lightning-rod protects from lightning) and who obviously did not wish to be exposed to new types of restrictions and who, faced with the hubbub of reforms and the growing difficulties of daily life kept grumbling 'A lot of steam, but what have we got in the soup?'

Nonetheless, *perestroika* did not seem to run out of steam; in fact, it was making breakthroughs on other fronts. *Glasnost*, launched by the party plenum on 'cadre-policy' in January 1987 came into full swing when Andrei Sakharov returned from exile and exposed the crimes and misdemeanours of the 'ancien regime'.

The 'new way of thinking' had not yet yielded its full harvest. But, as early as May 1986, Gorbachev – says Eduard Shevardnadze – questioned the conception held by his predecessors concerning the international balance of forces. In December 1987, the Treaty of Washington brought 'the Euro-missile battle' to a peaceful close. Early in 1988, the USSR clearly showed its intention to leave Afghanistan and to put a stop to a series of regional conflicts inherited from Brezhnev's expansionist policy (Amalric, 1988). The Kremlin was heading for a new foreign policy that would relieve the economy of the crushing burden of military expenses and the 'cost of the empire'.

As for internal policy, Gorbachev patiently weakened his immediate rivals and replaced four-fifths of the governmental administrators. He did not manage to charm his fellow citizens as much as he enthralled or 'electrified' personalities and public opinion abroad. But even his declining popularity at home was a point in his favour, to the extent that it encouraged more democracy in political life. An important step was taken in the summer of

1988 by the Nineteenth Party Conference, which considered it was necessary for the state to protect itself from its own interfering.

There were countless signs that Gorbachev had chosen to fight adversity
from the vantage point of political institutions rather than by surrendering
his own power. Likewise, he did not follow up on the statements (more
'russotrope' than 'socialophile') he had made in his speech commemorating
the seventieth anniversary of the Russian revolution. He must have thought
that, in order to counteract the rise of 'nationalisms' and save the empire,
he had to kindle some cosmopolitan ideology (a strange mixture of communist, humanistic and democratic values) which might ease integration.
That was a severe blow to the Russian tradition of reform through dictatorship, and some of Gorbachev's close collaborators were soon to criticize
him for not ruling with a firmer hand (Arbatov, 1988).

On the whole, however, the movement was rather dynamic. As for the
many road-blocks in its way, their absence would have been disturbing. The
picture of the battle for change remained a heroic one. And we might agree
with nineteenth-century poet-diplomat Tiuchev when he said 'One can only
believe in Russia.'

Disjunctions

No one had really expected the crisis which developed in the winter of 1988.
Glasnost was making progress. Democratization was moving ahead. For the
Soviets, the first meeting of the People's Representative Congress, from 25
May to 10 June 1989 actually meant a first step towards democracy. The
second Congress established a presidential regime in March 1990, after the
party renounced its leading role in February. The Soviet moves in international politics were just as striking. As announced, the last Russian soldiers
left Afghanistan on 15 February 1989. In July, Gorbachev made a speech in
Strasbourg in which he hinted that eastern European countries were free
to opt out of the empire. By the end of that year, that possibility became reality. On 2 December the Bush–Gorbachev Summit in Malta allowed
the USSR into the circle of 'civilized' states. Normalization was reinforced
the following year when the Kremlin aligned its position on Washington's
in the Gulf crisis.

And yet, political advances stopped playing the same role in *perestroika* as
a whole. Previously, its dynamics had apparently been able to remove all the
obstacles to economic change. Now, they rather made economic paralysis
more evident.

Indeed, some of the reforms were wavering and others looked like they
would not make it through the winter. The new liberalization of foreign
trade, made public on 2 December 1988, was emptied of its substance by
the decree of 7 March 1989 (Bondarev, 1989). The cooperatives, which were
doing quite well by the end of 1988, aroused fury and envy on the part of
the population and started to seek refuge with state enterprise, often enough
leaning on them like parasites. The co-ops which developed in the fields of
banking and insurance opened new training ground to experiment with new
financial techniques. And that was even more true of the new commercial
banks. So, some aspects of reform were still making progress (Crosnier,

1990). Thus, in accordance with the 'legislation on leases' of 1 January 1990, the leasing of company productive assets became widespread and institutionalized. Besides, the reform offered farmers the possibility to be 'their own masters', even though that entailed risks many were reluctant to take. In August 1989, after the People's Representatives voted the necessary amendments, the issue of shares and bonds became legal. These measures were written into most legislative texts, including the Property Act of March 1990 and the Company Act of June 1990.

By then, news from the reform front, good or bad, was no longer a reliable criterion on which to evaluate the chances of the Soviet economy. The dominant feature was the extreme deterioration in people's living conditions, a crisis which calls for analysis.

Crash, Soviet style

Early in 1989, the shortage of consumer goods – including food and durable commodities – became considerably worse. Rationing had to be enforced on a larger scale and brought a wave of panic with people buying just about everything they could find.

Some Soviet economists were right when they blamed the situation on the structural deformities which had plagued their country's economy for decades (Nikitin and Gel'vanovskij, 1990). The cause, of course, is the systematic priority previously given the military, and investments to spur consumption. If Soviet purchasing power is compared to that of other countries, the figures (those by Soviet researchers vary only slightly from western figures) show that in 1985, compared to the US, the GNP per capita was about 40 per cent, whereas consumption per capita was only a quarter (Illarionov, 1990). Gorbachev was so enthused by 'acceleration' that he was not clairvoyant enough to see that past trends ought to be reversed. The poor results of growth (not any better from 1985 to 1988 than in the worst 'stagnation' years, 1981–4; in both cases an average growth of about 1.8 per cent a year) did not leave much room for manoeuvre. The disastrous projections for the budget deficit made public at the end of 1988 by Finance Minister Gostev – more than 11 per cent of the GNP – can in part be explained by traditional spending priorities.

The Soviet citizen would be lucky if he found enough goods on sale to even spend a quarter or a fifth of what a western citizen spends. And Soviet commentators were quite right when they saw in Gostev's forecast a cause of even more serious concern than the weight of old spending habits, namely the risk of a total crash of the monetary and financial structure of the USSR (Gajdar and Lacis, 1988). In fact, the crack that had always existed in the Soviet system had become a chasm.

That situation can be attributed to the conceptual errors of *perestroika*. While it loosened the shackles that kept enterprise in harness, it did not impose any new budget limitations on enterprise. Entrepreneurs took advantage of the June 1987 Act to lavishly increase workers' salaries and were all the more generous as they were to be elected by those same workers. Moreover, company directors converted their hitherto frozen accounts into liquid assets so as to pay the workers fringe benefits. Gosbank backed their largesse by issuing more credit and printing more money, and did it without any qualms since the Treasury was urging them to print money to sponge up the budget deficit.

Citizens' incomes exceeded their ordinary spending (by 28 billion roubles in 1986 and by 62 billion roubles in 1989) (GOSKOMSTAT, 1989). Shortages started to plague the country, caused by the imbalance between excessive income and scarcity of commodities offered and still largely sold at regulated prices. With the pressure of demand and the development of distribution channels, prices started to go up (the most reliable estimations put inflation at 7.5 per cent for 1988). Price increases fuelled wage claims, thereby creating yet another problem.

Since Soviet citizens were unable to buy as much as their income allowed, family savings piled up. By the end of 1990, savings neared 500 billion roubles, i.e. half of the GNP. As long as inflation remained minimal, savings stayed put, even though the interest rate on deposits was low. Price mobility made the savings unstable. As of May 1990, the worst possible scenario started to happen (Abalkine, 1990)[1]: citizens started to withdraw their savings massively, thus threatening the market with total explosion.

The market as last recourse

The Ryzkov government did not wait on the collapse to try to react. During a Luxemburg colloquium of December 1988 (Clesse and Schelling, 1989), Leonid Abalkine – the leading figure of that period in much the same way Aganbegjan had been the leading figure of the previous period – announced that a 'rehabilitation plan' was on its way. Such plans also referred to as 'stabilization' or 'consolidation' plans were very much in the limelight all through 1989 and until the spring of 1990.

Theoretically, such plans were meant to restore balance between supply and demand by tipping both scales. To act on demand, the authorities – if that is an appropriate title – tried to reduce the budget deficit, taxed income to prevent inflating salaries, or sold public assets (financial or other) to the population. Ultimately, on 24 May 1990, a price increase on consumer goods was decided. Other actions taken included the stimulation of consumer goods imports (a compromise vis-à-vis Nicolaï Cheliev's 'rublovorous' recommendations) converting military industries, and above all, investing in consumer goods industries to increase turnover.

Unfortunately, the government decided on that last course of action and favoured stimulating supply over reducing demand. In short, this type of solution intended to fight excess of income by increasing production, that is to say by producing more income.

To saturate demand by supplying more is an idea which reflects the 'engineering' mentality which still prevailed in the main economic bodies of the USSR. On the other hand, new literature provided insights and constructive ideas as to which instruments to use to regulate macroeconomics for good (Bogacev, 1989). Early in 1990, (17–22 February), a delegation of French experts, led by Lionel Stoleru met with high-ranking Soviet personalities (Yuri Maslinkov, member of the Politburo and Gosplan President; Lev Voronin, first Vice-President of the Board of Ministers; Leonid Abalkin,

Vice-President of the Board of Ministers and President of the Committee for Economic Reform; Stepan Sitarian, President of the State Commission for Foreign Trade; Nicolaï Petrakov, Gorbachev's economic consultant; and Academy member Shatalin). Their message was: 'The USSR is standing at a parting of the ways. Either it retreats, Chinese style (after the Tiananmen Square massacre of June 1989), and screws down the loose nuts and bolts of the old Stalinist machine, or it breaks away from the past and opts for the market economy'. Our Soviet interlocutors would rather have the market economy option, provided it were sugared by important measures of social protection and substantial aid from the west. They remained cautious as to the terms used for the new market, calling it 'planned', 'regulated' or 'socialist', at least at the beginning. But that was a radical change of course, which, some say, was agreed upon by Gorbachev on the fifth anniversary of his coming to power.

The prospect of a market economy in the USSR was sensational enough to deserve explanation.

- It came as the result of a long evolution. All prior attempts at reform since Stalin's death were pointing in the right direction, including when they failed.
- Shortly before it was abandoned, the 'socialist economic order' had shown its obvious incapacity to grant enterprises the status needed to play their role; it had also demonstrated its incompetence to ward off monetary collapse.
- As opposed to the many problems of Soviet economy, the crash of 1988 raised a true economic issue, whose logic pertained to macroeconomics.
- Opportunely, *perestroika* was evolving towards a system where the dominant ideology, while remaining socialist, no longer determined social activity. If the 'normal' world could function with freedom of expression, democracy, legal rights, a 'civilized' foreign policy and a market economy, then, the USSR could probably follow the recipe without losing its soul.
- An explanation of lesser importance, though not a negligible one, is that Gorbachev had until then tried everything but the market. The private lectures he received from economist Nicolaï Petrakov might have helped him decide in favour of the market.

Given the economic deterioration, both internal and external, introducing the market was proved a terribly complex matter. Soviet economists began to elaborate transitional programmes. Some of their contents were already listed in the previous 'stabilization programmes' as long-term objectives. The most important and the most well-known document is the '500 Days Plan', the result of team work directed by Academy member Shatalin (Changing for the market, 1990), and 'Basic Orientations' elaborated under Aganbegjan's supervision, signed by Gorbachev and ratified by the Supreme Soviet (Pravda, 1990). 'Basic Orientations' allowed Gorbachev to issue enforcement edicts, in accordance with the special powers conferred on the President by the vote of 24 September 1990.

Compared to Gorbachev's first texts, 'Basic Orientations' marked considerable conceptual headway. Economic reasoning finally prevailed and with it the progressive release of market forces over central management. The presidential programme included all essential aspects of transition:

- stabilization by means of monetary and financial stringency;
- free prices;
- radical change in the status of economic agents;
- distribution of responsibilities between the republics and central power.

The contents of 'Basic Orientations' and alternative programmes were scrupulously examined by the EC Commission (EC Commission, 1990) and by other international economic bodies at the Houston Summit in July 1990.[2] Experts expressed relevant criticism, mainly regarding the first – crucial – phase of transition and more specifically the mixture of financial rigour and administrative coercion. In fact, Soviet officials believed that if they no longer controlled cash flow and industrial prices, wholesale prices would go sky-rocketing. In addition to that, containing retail price increases would entail state funding, which would be incompatible with the reduction of the budget deficit. Watching the Soviet economic scape, and even more its successors, one gets the impression that, for all its faults, any programme would help as long as it could be implemented. But that condition, fundamentally political, is far from being fulfilled.

Denial of competence, the temptation of dictatorship, and disintegration

By 1990–1, the prevailing climate in the USSR was one of widespread disillusion. And the economic agents' only rule was a cross between 'every man for himself' and 'run for dear life'.

This could be said of all the echelons of the social pyramid. At the top, Boris Yeltsin, now President of the Republic of Russia, swore by the '500 Days Plan' (in that it differed from Gorbachev's) and by the same token, Gorbachev, President of the USSR, swore by his own programme. Traditional exchanges between the republics were reduced, as demands for national independence multiplied, and their contributions to the central budget were cut. Whatever the reason, regions and cities moved towards autarchy; and as they closed in on their own affairs, the economic unity of the USSR began to unravel.

Administrative bodies sought to cling to the illusion of their past prerogatives by denying the competence of others. Enterprises now faced the dismantling of the guaranteed supply system, which had been nourished by state orders. They could buy supplies directly, at least in part, with roubles, and pay high prices since they had reserve assets which they disposed of freely. But mainly, they bartered or paid with foreign currency. To prevent the state from having access to their assets, enterprises had them partly transferred to overseas accounts. In self-defence, they also developed general stores for their workers, which solved the daily problem of shopping but short circuited the normal distribution channels. The privately owned 'cooperatives' indicated that the spirit of free enterprise was still alive in the Soviet Union. Functioning on the margins of law, this renascent capitalism revealed the characteristics which Marxist leaderships had long insisted on. This 'lumpen capitalism' only fostered the latent panic and indiscipline among the population. On the fringes of society, a growing number of people felt they were justified in stealing what was not available to them. The crime statistics provided damning evidence of a rising trend (GOSKOMSTAT, 1989).

The ongoing disintegration (reinforced by the strikes in the transport and coal industries and the 1990–1 recession) also affected international economic relations, whether with third world countries – the 'ex-conquests of socialism' (Sergeev, 1990) – or the widespread payments in dollars of commercial exchanges, or the outstanding payments to western banks. Output statistics showed sharply negative trends; imports fell in 1991 by 45 per cent, and the estimated foreign debt of the USSR was edged up from $57 billion at the time of the G7 London Summit, to about $100 billion by the end of the year. Indeed, payments on the USSR's foreign debts for 1992–4 were far in excess of estimated earnings from hard currency exports. Not least, reports on the deterioration in the state of the Siberian oil and gas fields and the low investment devoted to maintaining the pipelines suggested that the Soviet Union, or its successors, would become net gas importers by 1994.

From autumn 1990 to April 1991, things took a reactionary turn as calls were heard for a return to the old ways. The central authorities, and what was left of its apparatus – the party, the militaro-industrial complex, Gosplan, police forces, state farms, managers – all demanded a return to the 'socialist economic order', in parallel to popular yearning for *poriadok* (order). Even the liberal intellectuals were ready to sacrifice part of their political preferences on the altar of the common good. Also calling for order were 'private' companies and local authorities intent on protecting the workers and their families. Even the West pleaded for more order, fearing a financial breakdown in the USSR. For a brief moment, people were almost ready to trust the country to some liberal dictatorship that would come and save it. Indeed, Gorbachev, despite his unpopularity at home, disposed of full powers.

Imperceptibly, power and events began to slip from Gorbachev's grasp. His aura of international incontrovertibility faded as the United States took the lead in the UN sponsored coalition during the Gulf war of winter 1990–1, while his 'Basic Orientations' met with muted reception at home and abroad. His contradictory attempts to preserve the old party establishment, in the hope of making it simultaneously an instrument of reform proved a flawed strategy. In the winter of 1990–1, the reactionary turn of events in the Soviet Union frittered away the political capital arduously accumulated in previous years. The armed repression of the Baltic republics froze relations with the EC and the United States; the exclusion of leading reformers from his entourage rebounded to the benefit of Yeltsin, his rival–partner; and the comeback of communist organs in favour of tradition seemed momentarily to endanger *glasnost*. The presidential decrees went way beyond the guidelines of 'Basic Orientations'. Soviet economists proposed more than once the possibility of a monetary reform aiming at the elimination of surplus demand (Krasin and Galkin, 1989) – a strong medicine, which Stalin used brutally in December 1947, but a possible recourse if coupled with price deregulation. Government initiative, predicated on 'Basic Orientations', came haltingly, in three tranches. First, the decree of 22 January 1991, introduced by the reactionary Pavlov, who had replaced Ryzkov as Prime Minister, ordered the withdrawal of all 50 and 100 rouble notes. This measure hit both profiteers and pensioners, and turned out to be economically inefficient, as well as blatantly inequitable.

A second tranche was introduced in early April 1991, partially easing price controls. Wages and pensions were raised to 85 per cent of the expected 'average' price level. The resulting inequities only stirred popular discontent, and brought the party apparatus into further discredit. Matters were made worse by the republics' refusal to hand over revenues to the centre. As enterprise financing was meshed into the flow of state resources, the government took recourse to the printing presses in order to compensate for the shortfall.

A third initiative came in late April, dubbed Pavlov's 'anti-crisis programme'. The intention was to make good the deficiencies in the previous measures. Autumn 1992 was set as a target horizon for the freeing of all prices, along with extensive moves towards creating a private farm and services sector for small and medium size business. A federal reserve system of republican central banks was to be set up, with strict instructions not to lend to the government. But numerous powers were reserved for Moscow. As powers were devolving de facto from the centre, the republican leaders were unimpressed and looked to their own, more radical measures.

Perhaps Gorbachev's calculation was that he could somehow remain President of the socialist empire, while escaping the embrace of the reactionary forces which still sustained it. The 17 March referendum on a new Union Treaty between the fifteen republics no doubt comforted such optimism. The electorate voted 75 per cent in favour. The result provided Gorbachev with a mandate comparable to that of Yeltsin as leader of the Russian parliament. On 23 April nine republican leaders and Gorbachev met to thrash out a new Union Treaty, envisaging a federation between 'sovereign states' with extensive rights and privileges. It was the prospect of an irrevocable loss of power to the decaying centre that prompted the reactionaries into their desperate bid in the putsch of 19–22 August, to rescue the union from disintegration.

Their action precipitated the USSR's demise, and fuelled the republics' move to independence. Yeltsin, recently elected in June as Russia's President, emerged as the champion of national rights. The Ukraine declared independence on 24 August a measure confirmed in the 1 December referendum by a massive 90 per cent vote for. The most that could be hoped for now was a loose confederation. The practical arguments in favour of preserving a single currency and product markets across the old union were convincing enough. Trade between the republics amounted to 40–60 per cent of their output, with Russia the main exception at 15 per cent. Russia accounted for four-fifths of the old union's exports, and would have to assume the main burden of the USSR's debts. Indeed, the Commonwealth of Independent States established on 8 December by the leaders of Russia, Belorussia, and Ukraine – later joined by Kazakhstan – would serve perhaps as a vehicle for implementing a coherent set of policy reforms across the old union.

Yet political ambitions and inter-republican jealousies weighed heavier than the sober realities of economic interdependence. In his first major address to the Russian Parliament on 28 October, Yeltsin spoke of his programme of reform, much along the lines of the '500 Days Programme'. Prices were to be freed; there was to be a faster move to the sale of state assets; land reforms were to be introduced; and perhaps an independent currency for Russia. Price liberalization was one key of the programme: it was introduced on 2 January 1992, prompting a huge rise in prices. But hoarded goods returned quickly to circulation. Privatization was the other key: an 'accelerated' programme was introduced the same month. In other words, Russia went its own way. The others would follow as best they could. Given their inherited interdependence, they had little choice. Gorbachev resigned on 25 December 1991, signifying the final demise of the USSR.

Gorbachev had shrunk from applying shock therapy to the fabric of Soviet society. He had tailored political considerations into the series of economic plans from 1990, seeking to balance out the urging of reformers and the inhibitions of conservatives. Some of the more radical elements of the '500 Days Programme' found their way into 'Basic Orientations', just as some of Pavlov's reservations were folded into the economic plan presented by Gorbachev to the G7 leaders at their London Summit in June 1991. Gorbachev sought western economic aid and support for implementing reform at home; the G7 asked for reform first – a freeing of prices, privatization, and fiscal and monetary control – with aid as an incentive later. Would a more generous policy have stalled the August coup, providing a role for the centre while introducing reforms throughout the republics? Yeltsin, as the elected President of Russia and heir to the status of the USSR as a permanent member of the Security Council, chose the western sequence. Russia, in short, was preparing to join the world economy, fast.

A few points to conclude

To the extent that *perestroika* has been a haphazard piecemeal reform, *ex post* it is difficult to deny that its path could have been anything other than sinuous. *Ex ante* there was no knowing which way it would end. Only after the bungled coup of August 1991 was it possible to start writing perestroika's epitaph as a series of pragmatic measures whose compounded effect was the disintegration of the USSR. It was this momentous event which would pose one of the west's principal challenges for the 1990s.

(1)   There was nothing inevitable in the USSR's economic collapse. The Soviet economy went on supplying basic services. Its disorganization may have been endlessly deplored, but there was also the fact of its capacity to maintain basic production, exchange and consumption. It was blatantly untrue that people suffered from cold and hunger, even in the large cities that were hit hardest. Besides, measuring the rouble's parity by using its rate on the black market is simply dishonest. The Soviet economy was able to withstand collapse: it was fairly robust and able to produce a decent variety of products and services. Company managers proved very resourceful people too. The economy had ensured its own survival by retaining a certain morality which, despite negligence and dubious transactions, had maintained a level of activity. If the economy could be cured of its monetary overhang, with its military burden alleviated by the de facto winding down of the cold war, and if the economy were to make better use of people's intelligence through an overall improvement in its organization, things could look a lot brighter.

The problem of reform was one of seizing opportunities. The 'socialist economic order' had clearly showed its inadequacy. Since the mid 1980s, much progress had been made to think up a less primitive approach. Most economic actors – and not only profiteers – wished for a more stimulating economic environment. No matter how anarchically it was done, territorial decentralization was an objective necessity. This was all the more true of the market option. The necessary adjustments will undoubtedly require more time, more money and more pain than if they had been decided upon by a courageous, strong, competent government from the very start. But that those adjustments would be made was admitted by even the most pessimistic of Soviet economists.

(2)   The trading practices that spontaneously developed between enterprises were open to rationalization by the proper authorities so as to endow the Soviet Union or its successor states with a network that would include most of the mechanisms of a market economy. On the other hand, the status of economic agents was likely to lag for quite some time. In the short run, reforms had to be directed at facilitating the activities of small to medium-sized private companies, directly servicing consumer needs. As for agriculture, no ready solution was at hand. The peasants could not be evicted by force from the *kholhoz*, as Leonid Abalkin has pointed out, in the same manner as they had been drafted in.

Most of all, large industrial enterprises and financial institutions would remain part of the public sector for a long time. The citizens' savings, though important enough to destabilize the economy, were not abundant enough to sustain major privatizations. The development of a share-holding system, of joint-stock companies with the state participation, allied to a stricter surveillance of the banks' credit policy might update management responsibility. However, it was likely that agreements of all sorts between managers of the public sector, and across republican boundaries, would pervert the market working order for a long time to come.

(3)   The robust constitution of the inherited Soviet productive apparatus was, nonetheless, worn and obsolete. To bring it up to date would require time and money. And that stumbling block on the road to liberalization should not be overlooked. Just as the young nations of the nineteenth century had to fend for their 'infant industries' and had to curb foreign competition, the eastern countries (excluding the late East Germany but including the former USSR) would have to maintain protectionist barriers to shelter their 'dying industries', particularly in the light of the current debt and of the balance of payments. When he was in power, Finance Minister Witte was able to combine drastic protectionism while opening the Soviet economy to foreign investment. In order to achieve this, and thus aptly accelerate privatization and sharpen entrepreneurial spirit, Witte played a master card: the perfect gold convertibility of the rouble. His successors, whoever they may be, would confront a paradox. On the one hand, there were high risks associated with introducing convertibility in order to hasten the advent of the market and attract foreign investors, but on the other hand, there were equally high risks in waiting for the full advent of the market as a precondition to establishing convertibility (Aglietta, 1990). Only after significant steps have been taken towards the market would it be advisable to move the

rouble gradually towards convertibility. It follows that foreign investors would remain cautious in venturing into the former USSR.

(4)   Even though reforms would not immediately generate growth, the assumption that, once better regulated and more buoyant, the successor economies to the Soviet Union would forge ahead, requires some amendment. The assumption holds on a number of restrictive conditions. Around the middle of the nineteenth century, the Russian GNP per capita was roughly a third of the American. By 1975, after enormous exertions, it had gained a few points, representing slightly over 40 per cent of the US figure. Since then, it has lost ground. Seen in this light, one can understand the attraction of officials of the republics to the 'leap-frog' strategies deployed by the Asian 'dragons'; (indeed, Lee Kuan Yan, former Prime Minister of Singapore, advised in the drawing up of Kazakhstan's economic policy for the transition to a market economy). But the best that could be hoped for, in fact, was continuous arduous efforts to catch up with the developed economies.

This marathon prospect could be reasonably expected to generate a 'transitional ideology' that would offer symbolic compensations for lack of dynamism, and that would integrate elements of continuity and change, in the form of a mixed economy system, a redefined political legitimacy and a remodelled empire. The 8 December accord at Minsk for the Confederation of Independent States (CIS), precarious as it was, increased the forces at work to remodel the inheritance, while recognizing its inevitability.

(5)   Whatever the pace of events, foreign aid would be required as an adjunct to reforms. This aid could not realistically expect immediate rewards, such as a speedy transition to a free economy, access to a dynamic market, the discovery of an Eldorado for investors or the promise of a submissive foreign policy on the part of the successor states of the USSR. Nor could any one country play a paramount part in guiding the transition. More explicitly, it is unlikely that Germany would sacrifice its European engagements in order to launch an economic offensive in the east. Financial support to transformation of the new republics would stand a better chance if it were given by the European Union, in combination with the USA and Japan. The EBRD (European Bank for Research and Development) is well suited to the task, as it is essentially designed for gradual, patient, circumspect action and devoted to long-term strategic task.

(6)   Aid for the new republics is not enough on its own. Inevitably, the transition from a command economy to a mixed market economy depends also on ready access to western markets. For a long time ahead, manufactured goods' sales from the successor states on the world markets could be expected to be limited in scale and scope. The main foreign exchange earners for Russia are oil and gas, gold and raw materials – driving down world prices for other producers, from Africa, Australasia, or the Americas. The political transition in the republics, furthermore, fundamentally address the geopolitics of the world energy industry: oil supplies from the Middle East and the Gulf were developed during the cold war as alternatives to politically tainted resources in Siberia. After the second Russian revolution those inhibitions in western investment for the development of Russian reserves

no longer hold. The same applies to the Ukraine, Europe's granary prior to 1914. In 1990, the Ukraine, with its primitive agricultural system, produced 51 million tons of corn, compared to France's 55 million tons. Over time, and with due care, the full potential of Ukrainian comparative advantages in agriculture stand to be developed. That development inevitably implies profound changes in the structure of western European agriculture. Indeed, the economic transitions underway in the former USSR point towards truly pan-European markets, with extensive implications for the structure of world markets and exchanges, inherited from the old empire's autarchy.

NOTES

1   This is Abalkine's report during the Supreme Soviet session of 26 November 1990: in fact, the last major public speech made by the Vice-President of the Soviet Board of Ministers, in charge of economic reforms, before his disappearance from the government scene.
2   International Monetary Fund; International Bank for Reconstruction and Development; Organization for Economic Cooperation and Development, *The Economy of the USSR, a Study Undertaken in Response to a Request by the Houston Summit, Summary and Recommendations*, OECD, 19 December 1990.

REFERENCES

Abalkine, L. 1990: O prakticeskih sagah po per hodu k rynocnoj ekonomike (The concrete steps towards the market economy). *Ekonomika i zizn*, 49, December.
Aglietta, M. 1990: La convertibilité du rouble. *Economie Prospective Internationale*, 44, 7–33.
Amalric, J. 1988: Aggiornamento soviétique. *Le Monde*, 13 April.
Arbatov, G. 1988: Razmysleniâ neekonomista ob ekonomike (The reflections of a non-economist on economy). *Izvestiâ*, 13 September.
Bogacev, V. 1989: Ese ne pozdno (It is not too late). *Kommunist*, 3, 31–41.
Bondarev, A. 1989: Vnesneekonomiceskij mehanizm – neresennye problemy (The mechanism of foreign trade: the unsolved problems). *Kommunist*, 12, 16–24.
Brainard, L. 1990: Strategies for economic transformation in eastern Europe, the role of financial market reform. OECD seminar on Economic Transformation in Planned Economies, 21 June (revised 20 August). Paris.
Changing for the Market 1990: Perehod k rynku, Koncepciâ i Programma, Cast'l (*Changing for the Market, Conception and Programme, Part I*). Moscow.
Clesse, A. and Schelling, T. C. (eds) 1989: *The Western Community and the Gorbachev Challenge*. Baden-Baden: Nomos Publishing Company.
Crosnier, M.-A. 1990: Désarroi et crise d'autorité en USSR. *Le Courrier des Pays de l'Est*, 349, April.
de Boissieu, C. and Renversez, F. 1990: La question monétaire et bancaire en URSS. *Economie Prospective Internationale*, 44, 35–45.
EC Commission 1990: Stabilisation, libéralisation et dévolution de compétences, évaluation de la situation économique et du processus de réforme en Union Soviétique. *Economie Européene*, 45, December.
Gajdar, E. and Lacis, O. 1988: Po karmanu li traty? (Can we afford to spend?). *Kommunist*, 17, 26–9.
Giroux, A. 1989: Le plenum de mars 1989 sur l'agriculture soviétique: un compromis. *Le Courrier des Pays de l'Est*, 338, March.
GOSKOMSTAT SSR 1989: *Narodnoe Hozâjstro SSR v 1989 g., Statisticeskij ezegodnik (National Economy in the USSR in 1989, Yearly Statistics)*, 11 and 612.

Illarionov, A. 1990: Paradoksy statistiki (The paradoxes of statistics). *Argumenty i fakty*, 3.

Krasin, U. and Galkin, A. 1989: Dengi dozny byt' den 'gami (Money must be money). *Ekonomiceskaâ gazeta*, 38, September.

Nemcinov, V. 1964: Socialisticeskoe hozâjstvovanie i planirovanie proizvodstva (Socialist management and production planification). *Kommunist*, 5, 74–87.

Nikitin, S. and Gel 'vanovskij, M. 1990: Gde ze my? (Where are we now?). *Memo*, 1, 20–34.

Nujkin, A. 1988: Idealy ili interesy? (Ideals or interests?). *Novyj Mir*, 1, 190–211, 205–28.

Pavlov, V. 1987: Radikal'naja reforma cenoobrazovaniâ (The radical reform of price formation). *Pravda*, 25 September.

Popov, G. 1987: Perestrojka v ekonomike (The economy of perestroika). *Pravda*, 20–1 January.

Pravda 1990: Osnovnye napravleniâ po stabilizacii narodnogo hozâjstva i perehodu k rynocnoj ekonomike (Basic orientations concerning the stabilization of national economy and changing for the market economy). *Pravda*, 18 October.

Sergeev, B. 1990: Sedra ruka daûsego (The giver's generous hand). *Ekonomika i zizn'*, 12 March.

Sokoloff, G. 1985: Le dynamique Gorbachev. *Politique étrangère*, 3, 611–24.

Valovoj, D. 1988: Gosudarstvennyj zakaz (State orders). *Pravda*, 30 May.

PART VI

Redefining Europe

Editor's introduction

An end to the cold war in Europe prompts a process and questions about the new configuration required to preserve the peace. Three security systems have been tried in Europe in the past. The most successful was that which existed between 1949 and 1989, with Europe and Germany divided between the United States and the Soviet Union as the leading powers in their respective alliances. All existing European institutions, such as the Council of Europe, the European Communities and the Conference on Security and Cooperation in Europe were created in the context of the cold war. The peace was unjust, but it achieved its essential purpose of preventing war. And it facilitated the creation of the western European society of states, based on the same principles and adhering to the same values.

The older European system was the balance of power between the European great powers, involving a close association between diplomacy and military–industrial capabilities. It served to reduce the number of smaller states in the system, but was prone to the use of war as an instrument of policy. Over time, its costs rose along with the technology of warfare, ending in the terrible wars of the first half of the century, as sketched in Part I of this book. The privileges accruing to the permanent members of the United Nations Security Council bore token to the continued salience of great powers in the international system. In fact, Great Britain and France were dwarfed by the United States and the Soviet Union as the pillars of a global and competitive state and market system.

A third security arrangement is the unit-veto system, where all states, great or small, are assumed to be equal in law if not in fact. Modern manifestations are the United Nations General Assembly and the Conference on European Cooperation Security (CSCE). The CSCE in particular has been successful in creating a climate of international relations, vindicating the strategy of the gradual erosion of Europe's division. But it is better equipped for talk than for action. And like other institutions created in the context of the cold war, its proceedings confront a decline in the sense of a collective interest over the particular concerns of states.

The conditions for a prosperous and secure Europe are no doubt easier to enumerate than to implement. A reconciled pan-Europe would require shared political and market institutions and values, allowing for the peaceful settlement of conflicts over frontiers, the rights of minorities or market access.

Where is the authority able and willing to enforce the law of Europe on a recalcitrant state? None may arbitrate alone for others without engendering resentment. The surrender of sovereign powers to joint institutions remains voluntary, and prone to recision. Europe's society, inherited from the past forty-five years, will continue to prosper to the extent that the collectivity continues to serve the interests of its diverse members.

18

The Helsinki process and a new framework of European security

Vojtech Mastny

More than anything else on the international scene, the Conference on Security and Cooperation in Europe (CSCE) has been the measure of the hopes and disappointments underlying the continent's transformation during the fifteen years since the landmark Helsinki agreement was signed in 1975. Originally Moscow's design for making Europe stable under Soviet auspices, the conference unexpectedly turned the tables by helping to foster destabilization in Moscow's own part of the continent. Yet for many years, the slow pace of change nourished doubts among western critics about the adequacy and, indeed, desirability of the whole 'Helsinki process'.

Only the pluralization of the Soviet Union under Gorbachev and the collapse of Moscow's hegemony in eastern Europe that ended the continent's division laid those doubts to rest. In turn, however, the demise of the familiar order on which, for better or for worse, Europe's stability had been resting for forty years, began to generate new expectations about what, if anything, the CSCE could do to provide a new framework for international security.

The innovations of Helsinki

Launched after three years of intensive negotiations, involving all European states except Albania, as well as the United States and Canada, the CSCE during its first ten years established itself as a novelty in the history of international relations. Not all of its innovations could be immediately seen as constructive or productive. Yet they all proved peculiarly suited to address some of the key ingredients of the European security environment that did not seem crucial at first but proved increasingly so with the passage of time.

Distinct from the assorted arms control negotiations that made headlines but during many years produced precious little, the CSCE addressed primarily the non-military aspects of security – that array of intangibles that make nations and their leaders feel secure or less so for political, economic, cultural, and a host of other reasons. Of the military dimensions of security, the conference originally concerned itself only with those liable to influence the degree of international confidence because of their bearing on the intentions rather than the capabilities of potential belligerents.

The most spectacular innovation of the Helsinki process was the inclusion in its 'Basket Three' of a growing number of items under the general rubric of 'human rights' – in effect those diverse dimensions of security, or insecurity, that impel governments to repress their citizens. The universal acceptance by the thirty-five CSCE members of the principle that the manner in which sovereign states treat their own citizens is a legitimate concern of other sovereign states because of its implications for international security was nothing short of revolutionary.

The practical effects of this innovation were initially underestimated because of the nature of the Helsinki accords as a statement of intentions rather than a treaty under international law. Yet this apparent weakness was more a strength because it made adherence to the stated intentions a test of political credibility rather than an invitation to a search for legal loopholes. Nor was the principle of consensus, which required all the participating states to make all their decisions unanimously, the prescription for impotence that it seemed to critics. In a Europe divided against its will, this was a device through which a common will to overcome the division could gradually be built. Aided by the practice of proceeding by stages, which made agreement on one set of issues a precondition for tackling the next, the consensus principle produced results. Its often cumbersome and convoluted workings were, after all, only too true a reflection of the state of Europe at the time.

Vast enough at its beginning, the CSCE's mandate kept expanding. That, too, proved more of an asset than a liability because it allowed the CSCE to address almost anything as a security issue. The expansion gave justice to security as a changeable rather than fixed notion, whose different dimensions were interrelated. The ensuing linkages could then facilitate agreements by connecting seemingly disconnected issues. Helsinki made a virtue of the alleged sin of 'mixing apples and oranges'.

The first ten years

Born of the hopes and illusions that shaped the cramped détente of the Brezhnev–Nixon era, the Helsinki process reflected faithfully its ambivalences. To different people, détente meant different things. For Brezhnev and his acolytes, it meant a temporary state of affairs conducive to producing, amid reduced international tension despite the persisting arms race, a gradual but irreversible shift in the global 'correlation of forces' in Soviet favour. It promised access to the bounties of western trade and technology on Soviet terms, without a political price to pay.

For the United States, which held much of the bounties, détente was a more lasting condition, promising to enmesh Moscow in a web of economic interdependence that would, also gradually and irreversibly, end the arms race and turn the superpowers from adversaries into partners. For most Europeans détente meant above all the prospect of ending the division of their continent by de-emphasizing the military ingredients of the east–west confrontation. This was the key concept that animated their dedication to the Helsinki process.

The respective Soviet and west European, rather than American, expectations about détente were at the heart of the controversial trade-off that launched the process in 1975. Linking *political security with human rights*, the deal satisfied Moscow's yearning for international recognition of the political status quo it had imposed in eastern Europe as a result of World War II, in return for its acceptance of the 'Basket Three' principles designed to protect the human rights the Soviet Union considered necessary to suppress for the sake of its security. The Soviet gain concerned the past – confirmation of something Moscow already had; the western gain concerned the future – something that might be achieved by giving the paper undertaking a political substance.

The Helsinki process evolved at a time when, for reasons extraneous to it, the peak of détente had already passed. During the latter parts of the 1970s, the two superpowers resumed their confrontational course. In resisting western pressure for an improvement of its human rights record, the Soviet Union invoked the clause in the Helsinki Final Act that prohibited interference in the internal affairs of the member states. At the same time, it signalled that it might make change in practices if the west treated favourably its economic demands. This suggested a second Helsinki linkage – that between *trade and human rights*.

Trying to exploit the linkage, the United States enacted legislation that made trade with the Soviet Union and other countries contingent on their human rights practices, particularly the free emigration of their citizens. Moscow proved not totally impervious to this pressure, allowing substantial Jewish emigration to continue for a while even after the enactment of the American legislation. However, as the paucity of Soviet concessions failed to satisfy Washington and détente received a *coup de grâce* with the Soviet invasion of Afghanistan in 1979, nothing more could be expected from the second Helsinki linkage.

Indeed, the CSCE's very survival was uncertain when the linkage between *military security and human rights* superseded the previous two linkages during the apparent relapse into the cold war in the early 1980s. Insisting that there could be no 'political détente' without 'military détente', the Soviet Union pressed for a conference on disarmament in Europe within the framework of the CSCE, hinting that its being more forthcoming in matters of human rights depended on the acceptance of the proposal. This was out of the question at a time when the United States presided over NATO's massive rearmament programme.

Yet while the United States resisted any 'militarization' of the Helsinki process at the expense of human rights, a consensus was eventually reached at the end of the acrimonious second CSCE follow-up meeting in Madrid. The compromise entailed modest improvements in the human rights provisions of the Helsinki Final Act in return for western acceptance of a 'disarmament' conference to be held in Stockholm, which would concentrate on confidence-building measures. The outcome proved common interest in preserving the Helsinki process even during high east–west tension – or precisely then.

The Soviet approval of the Madrid document in September 1983 promised to strengthen the hand of the western opponents of the NATO 'Euromissile' deployment. Yet the next month a favourable vote in the west German parliament opened the way for the deployment, thus frustrating high Soviet hopes in the opposite outcome and compelling Moscow to honour its threat to break off the arms control negotiations then under way in Geneva. Indeed, by the time Mikhail Gorbachev became the top Soviet leader in early 1985, the only east–west military negotiations were those under way in Stockholm under the CSCE's auspices.

Security and human rights

The initial Soviet conduct at Stockholm hardly suggested that Moscow regarded the conference as anything but an additional forum in its public campaign against NATO rearmament. With scant regard for the mandate of the conference, which concerned confidence-building measures, Soviet representatives tried to put on its agenda totally unpromising proposals, including the prohibition against the first use of nuclear weapons that NATO was certain to veto, or such catchy but meaningless items as a mutual non-aggression pledge. For their part, western delegates harped on how Soviet observance of the Helsinki human rights provisions would foster an atmosphere of mutual trust. There was little reason to expect a meeting of minds when east–west negotiations had been failing everywhere else.

At CSCE meetings, US representatives sought to impress upon their Soviet counterparts the linkage between the arms control agreements Moscow wanted and the human rights commitments it failed to honour. Did the Soviets understand the message? They had always been acutely sensitive to the security implications of their human rights practices but exceedingly reluctant to act. While under fire at the CSCE, they usually preferred to take shelter behind the non-interference clause of the Helsinki Final Act. As the missile build-up proceeded, they advanced the outrageous notion that the only human right that mattered was the 'right' to survive.

Shortly before the CSCE experts meeting in Ottawa, the Soviet Union had returned to the Geneva strategic arms talks, despite NATO's having ignored its precondition that all the Euromissiles must be removed first. But this signal reversal in arms control policy did not seem to influence the human rights practices. Indeed, as the new Gorbachev leadership called for discarding the Brezhnev legacy, there were reasons to wonder whether the CSCE might be included. Nor was there a shortage of influential supporters of the Reagan administration who insisted that the Helsinki 'charade' should stop.

The failure at Bern

Accordingly, the United States anticipated without illusions the experts' meeting on human contacts convened in Bern in April 1986. Rather than to aim at negotiating a concluding document, which had eluded the preceding two CSCE meetings, the administration instructed its ambassador, Michael Novak, to use the occasion mainly for pressing the Soviet Union and its allies to expedite the resolution of specific human rights cases on the American agenda.

Novak, a noted Catholic theologian and philosopher of east European descent, spoke eloquently about the pathetic predicament of a superpower whose security required putting priests and poets behind bars while keeping children of defectors as hostages for the transgressions of their parents. He looked forward to a time when the Soviet Union would be ready to open itself to the rest of the world, although he hardly believed the time to be coming soon. In this, he found himself out of step with many of the western European delegates, who sensed that the Soviets might actually be trying to get out of their predicament and deserved to be tested.

The Soviet representatives at Bern, however, offered little encouragement. They kept delivering speeches that their western counterparts, wondering whom they tried to impress, considered 'worn-out propaganda' (*Radio Free Europe/Radio Liberty*, 12 May 1986). Yet in the end they accepted tangible, if modest, improvements of human contacts, while ensuring that loopholes would remain open as well. Moscow unexpectedly agreed to give exit visas to an unprecedented number of emigration applicants who figured on the American list. The gesture came too late to prevent the United States from casting the lonely veto against the final document, shocking nearly everyone present. Yet even prompter Soviet action would have hardly made a difference, for Novak and his Washington superiors had in any case been set to cast the veto. They acted on the premise that the Gorbachev regime intended to continue the policy of human rights violations.

The subsequent course of events proved the premise false. Although Soviet Ambassador at Bern, Iuri Kashlev, exploited to the utmost the god-sent opportunity to berate 'people from far away overseas' who arrogate to themselves the role of 'world policemen' (27 May 1986), Gorbachev on 8 July proclaimed his country's readiness to abide by the provisions of the vetoed Bern document anyway. More importantly, his policies brought effective and substantive improvements in the very areas where Novak suspected Soviet loophole-building – family reunification, short-term travel for urgent family matters, publication of laws and regulations.

Thus, apart from the set-back that the United States suffered because of the timidity of its diplomacy, Bern was not the 'meeting of lost opportunities' that the Polish representative pronounced it to be (*Nowak*, 27 May 1986). Indeed, the conference had been well suited to impress on the Soviets the necessity of adapting to the Helsinki standards if, as Gorbachev so obviously wished, they were to be accepted as bona fide inhabitants of the 'common European house'. In this light, their seemingly sinister manoeuvres at Bern appear in retrospect more like desperate and clumsy attempts to convince the incredulous that the intention to adapt was at last serious – but do so without losing too much face.

The success at Stockholm

Rather than at Bern, the watershed was reached at Stockholm. On 12 November 1985, Reagan and Gorbachev affirmed at their first summit in Geneva their intention to conclude the negotiations on confidence- and security-building measures (CSBM), conducted in the Swedish capital since 1984, in time for the opening in November 1986 of the third CSCE follow-up meeting in Vienna. Other western leaders perceived further opportunities in the Stockholm talks. In a dramatic joint appearance before the participants, French Foreign Minister Roland Dumas and his West German colleague Hans-Dietrich Genscher hailed the talks, predicting correctly that they could eventually lead to negotiations resulting in reductions of conventional armaments.

Given the fundamental importance of secrecy in the Soviet system, the key issue was that of inspection and verification on the spot. On 15 January 1986, Gorbachev declared for the first time Moscow's readiness to allow on-site inspection of its nuclear test facilities. However, in Stockholm the Soviet delegation showed no willingness to extend this also to conventional forces. Perhaps its superiors were awaiting the outcome of the Bern conference, where the seriousness of Soviet intentions was also being tested. If so, then the American diplomatic fiasco at Bern may have reduced Moscow's incentive to make reassuring concessions elsewhere. Most probably, the whole idea of making concessions to reassure the west was intensely controversial in the Kremlin councils.

By August in Stockholm, Moscow unmistakably showed the will to an agreement. Not only did it agree in principle to on-site inspections of military exercises but it did so without even reserving the right of refusal envisaged in the proposal drafted by the neutral and non-aligned states. On 29 August, the appearance at Stockholm of no lesser a figure than Soviet Chief of Staff Marshal Sergei Akhromeev, calmly announcing to the assembled diplomats the historic turnabout, was an event of dramatic proportions. The sense of triumph felt by most of the western delegates at the signing of the Stockholm final document on 30 September was amply justified by Moscow's acceptance of specific measures that for the first time materially reduced the threat posed by Soviet conventional forces in Europe.

Nor were the verbal statements in the document mere empty words. Those statements included, in particular, the prohibition of the use of force even against allies – a thinly veiled allusion to the 'Brezhnev doctrine' that had sought to justify the 1968 Soviet invasion of Czechoslovakia. Furthermore, the affirmation of a search for methods of peaceful solution of disputes that would be compulsory rather than optional marked a reversal of the Soviet position that frustrated two previous CSCE conferences on this subject. Finally, the specific reference to human rights as one of the indispensable ingredients of security indicated how much closer the east had come to the west at least in theory, if not yet in practice.

Vienna between new thinking and old

The persisting obstacles to east–west convergence re-emerged at the Vienna follow-up meeting, which opened on 4 November under the shadow of the abortive Reykjavik Summit between Reagan and Gorbachev. That Summit had concerned weaponry but also trust, which Gorbachev put in jeopardy by overplaying his hand with his bid for complete nuclear disarmament –

a prescription for western military inferiority. Nor did Reagan's clumsy acceptance and subsequent rejection of the idea exactly breed trust, not to speak of confidence in his judgement. Under such circumstances, it became more difficult again to believe in the novelty of Soviet thinking or in Washington's readiness to give Moscow the benefit of the doubt.

These were the two central issues in Vienna amid further interplay between security and human rights. This permeated already the opening speech by Soviet Foreign Minister Eduard Shevardnadze on 5 November. After bitter charges of alleged American responsibility for letting pass a great opportunity at Reykjavik, Gorbachev's chief collaborator turned more pertinently to the meaning of security. He properly noted that the concept of security is acquiring new dimensions. It is increasingly seen as a task of creating, through joint efforts, political, material, institutional, and other safeguards for preserving peace that would preclude the very possibility of war breaking out (Shevardnadze, 5 November 1986).

But Shevardnadze's *tour de force* was his proposal to hold the next CSCE meeting on human rights in – of all places – Moscow. The proposal caught his audience by surprise; it was as if a meeting about chicken were to be held in a fox den, *Die Presse* of Vienna later commented wryly.

The actual human rights situation in the Soviet Union, and even more in eastern Europe, presented a similarly mixed picture. This conformed with the later explanations by Soviet diplomats in Vienna that Shevardnadze's proposal for the human rights conference in Moscow and the whole notion of make Soviet human rights policies conform with the Helsinki standards encountered strong opposition in some quarters of the increasingly divided Soviet establishment. In any case, the Foreign Minister's initiative was not actively pursued.

Nor was the persistence of old thinking limited to the Soviets and their allies. The United States came to Vienna determined to apply much the same strategy as before, and for a good reason: the old American strategy, unlike the old Soviet strategy was showing results. Washington therefore continued to press Moscow and its allies to resolve specific human rights cases in accordance with their Helsinki obligations, while resisting their efforts to shift the CSCE's weight from human rights to military security.

There was an air of *déjà vu* at the conference on 12 December, when chief US representative Warren Zimmermann called for a minute of silence in memory of the recent death in a labour camp of Ukrainian dissident Anabolic Marchenko, whereupon the Soviet delegates, duly followed by the Czechoslovak and Bulgarian ones, stormed out of the hall. What had not been seen before was the follow-up, indicative of a Soviet desire to overcome by deeds not only the effects but also the causes of the shameful episode.

On 19 December, eleven days after Marchenko's death, the Soviet Union announced that its most famous dissident, the Nobel Prize winner Andrei Sakharov, had been freed from internal exile. This was followed by news of other political offenders released from prisons and additional emigration applicants from the prison-state. Important for the future was the readiness of the Gorbachev government to move forward in ways it had not contemplated previously. This did not preclude, but may have rather made more necessary, efforts by Soviet diplomats in Vienna to cover up, by aggressive posturing, concessions and retreats that their government had earlier been trying to avoid but now considered inevitable and even desirable.

The emerging linkages

On the American side, the new thinking proceeded more slowly than on the Soviet side, where it had been more overdue. But once the change came, it had greater effect on the Helsinki process. It took the United States seven months – and pressure from their allies disappointed by the outcome of Reykjavik – to act on the April 1986 Warsaw Pact proposal to incorporate in the Helsinki process negotiations for a reduction of conventional forces in Europe. However, given the remarkable Soviet eagerness to get the talks started, it made tactical sense for the west to hold out and exact a price.

In mid December, NATO agreed to the talks in principle. Yet the United States insisted that these must be different from the ghastly talks on mutual and balanced reduction of conventional forces in Europe (MBFR) that were still marking time in the Austrian capital after more than a decade of sterile debate. At the same time, Washington wanted the new negotiation to remain separate from the Helsinki process, lest the CSCE's primary content of human rights be diluted and an agreement on conventional arms be held hostage to consensus by all of the conference's thirty-five members.

In contrast, the Soviet Union wanted the conventional arms talks to take place within the Helsinki process, and so did France, though for different reasons. Moscow may have been ready for a significant reduction of its forces – but at the lowest possible political price. That goal could better be achieved in the overwhelmingly political CSCE than at a specialized gathering of disarmament experts. For their part, the French favoured the CSCE framework as being more conducive to preventing the superpowers from dominating the talks. Unlike Moscow, however, Paris was in no hurry to start the conference any time soon, thus allowing for extensive bargaining beforehand.

The ingenious solution finally adopted to get discussion about conventional arms started was NATO's initiative. It provided for representatives of the two alliances to confer in Vienna but in places separate from the CSCE premises.

Western diplomats believed that, since 'the Soviet Union is anxious to have a conference on military security [it] should be made to pay for it by concessions on human rights' (*Radio Free Europe/Radio Liberty*, 1 April 1987). The Soviets, aware only too well of the linkage they had themselves helped to establish, sought to limit the necessary concessions. They and their allies flooded the Vienna conference with propagandistic proposals that could be painlessly withdrawn while demanding real western concession in return. Yet the west also prepared proposals, which required from the Soviet bloc real – rather than fake – concessions in matters of human rights.

In particular, the states of the European Community proposed in February 1987 to introduce into the Helsinki process a new 'human dimension' mechanism that would make the enforcement of human rights easier. Envisaged were several stages. First, governments suspected of violations would be required to supply information. If this proved unsatisfactory, any member state could then ask for bilateral consultation. Finally, a CSCE meeting could be called to address the situation. So far-reaching was the proposal that its authors did not expect it to ever obtain the necessary consensus. Yet the Soviet delegation did not reject it out of hand. In the process, weaponry and human rights were to be traded as they had never been before.

Trading apples and oranges

Connecting the seemingly disconnected had always been a Helsinki tradition. The wider and more complex grew the ramifications of security, the greater also became the possibilities of agreement – provided, there was a will to agree. That depended not only on what was happening in Vienna but also on the changing course of east–west relations around it and, above all, the momentous changes in the Soviet Union and eastern Europe. Their relentless but difficult progress was the main reason why the conference eventually lasted well over two years, much longer than originally anticipated.

The signing at the December 1987 Washington Summit of the intermediate-range nuclear forces (INF) agreement clarified the three main principles of further arms control negotiations. These were asymmetrical cuts, reductions of substance rather than of merely the rate of growth and, most importantly, intrusive verification – the principle that cut into the very heart of the Soviet concept of closed society.

Just how distasteful its opening must have been to those vast segments of the Soviet establishment that functioned by habitual disregard for human rights could only be guessed from the stop-and-go progress of Shevardnadze's dormant project of the CSCE conference in Moscow in 1992 – by which time the country's record would presumably have to meet the Helsinki standards. Soviet representatives in Vienna revived the project in April 1988. Yet its revival proved at first short lived, despite the upsurge of good feelings between east and west after the ratification of the INF treaty. Only at the beginning of July did the Soviet delegation at the CSCE reaffirm its interest in the Moscow conference, and began to press for its acceptance.

Sensing a new bargaining lever, the United States responded by presenting a set of conditions that would have to be fulfilled before its consent could be forthcoming. These amounted to measures conducive to the further opening of Soviet society – something that Moscow's diplomats had been but grudgingly conceding during the drafting of the Vienna final document. Now they not only indignantly rejected the American demands but, together with four of their Warsaw Pact allies, also introduced amendments backtracking on the already agreed draft. Yet two other of their allies, Poland and Hungary, accepted the text as it was – a breach of bloc solidarity the CSCE had never seen before.

Beyond the CSCE, the Soviet Union was at that time still refusing to take sides in squabbles among its east European allies. In Vienna, it finally did so, and the change was dramatic. As late as 19 September, a Soviet representative vowed that his government would never end the jamming of foreign broadcasts it considered hostile. Eight days later, Moscow announced the end of all jamming, except that of the allegedly subversive programmes by the Munich-based *Radio Free Europe/Radio Liberty*. In another three months, all jamming of western broadcasts ended – by the Soviet Union and, under its strong pressure, by its reluctant allies as well. This was the largest opening of their closed societies so far.

By then, Moscow had been pressing hard to get the approval of its controversial human rights conference, hinting at first that its consent to the Vienna final document might depend on this. It added the telling argument that the conference was needed to strengthen the hand of the advocates of democratization inside the Soviet Union; rejection of the project would thus presumably amount to their betrayal by the west. In the end, however, Soviet diplomats in the Austrian capital made it clear that the rejection would not jeopardize consensus on the final document. In Vienna, the way to a successful finale was open.

An unexpected achievement

On 3 January 1989, the United States government announced its approval of the Moscow conference despite considerable opposition by both conservatives and human rights groups. The decision was based on the recognition of partial improvements and promises of more to come – promises whose fulfilment the prospect of the conference would encourage by allowing the west to threaten cancelling participation any time.

Soviet assurances that improvements would continue included not only the termination of the jamming and a wholesale release of political prisoners but also allowing western journalists to visit a notorious labour camp. On 10 December 1988, Gorbachev made at the United Nations the sensational announcement that Soviet conventional forces in Europe would be cut drastically. As a down payment for the forthcoming talks about the mutual reduction of those forces – the talks that Moscow wanted so badly – a unilateral withdrawal of the Soviet ones actually began even before the Vienna Conference ended.

It was not the Soviet Union but the repressive Romania of President Nicolae Ceausescu that delayed, at the last moment, the conclusion of the Vienna Conference. The Romanians raised as many as seventeen objections to the already agreed text of the final document. After all of these were predictably rejected, they outraged the assembly by signing the document while declaring that their government did not feel bound by those of its provisions it deemed objectionable. Far from suggesting the ineffectiveness of the Helsinki process, the prospective violator's desperate manoeuvres testified to its growing influence.

The two conferences on military matters were to follow closely after Vienna. One was a continuation of the Stockholm talks on security- and confidence-building measures (CSBM), which involved the CSCE's all thirty-five participants. The other was a new negotiation on the reduction of conventional forces in Europe (CFE) which, though declared part of the Helsinki process, included only the twenty-three members of NATO and the Warsaw Pact. It was at this conference that the removal of the military, apart from the mental, barriers to Europe's unification was to be decided, and those who judged the former more formidable than the latter braced themselves for 'most complicated negotiations' (*Los Angeles Times*, 4 March 1989).

Confidence-building and conventional disarmament

The reason negotiations eventually turned out to be not as difficult as the west anticipated could be detected in the initial Soviet optimism about their outcome. It became evident later that the Soviet Union, unlike NATO, went into the conference aware of the concessions that needed to be made to ensure its success and was determined to make them. Although this did not necessarily mean that it was not going to bargain hard, already its opening positions differed diametrically from those that had previously blocked the MBFR talks. Not only did Shevardnadze amplify on Gorbachev's UN speech by announcing in January 1989 further, albeit unspecified, unilateral cuts of Soviet conventional forces. He also submitted at the CFE a proposal which could form the basis of agreement, provided Moscow was indeed reconciled to give up its military advantage in Europe.

As Shevardnadze candidly admitted, the viability of the plan depended on trust. It stood to reason that any ingenious stratagem or undisguised attempt to retain an advantage in a particular kind of arms could torpedo the negotiations. This is not a matter of arithmetic but more properly of morality. Honesty and fair play are indispensable components of the process of negotiations (Shevardnadze, 6 March 1989).

This gave authority to the other set of talks – that on confidence-building measures. Yet precisely there the western negotiators discovered more than just a few remnants of 'old thinking' in Soviet manoeuvring for special advantages. Moscow resumed its former demand for compulsory notification of naval and air activities, although these were outside the mandate of the conference. It further blocked progress by trying to link conventional arms reductions to cuts in NATO's tactical nuclear weapons, which were also beyond the mandate.

Yet regardless of these less than 'ingenious stratagems', the announced unilateral reductions continued, thus reducing Soviet capability to wage war and consequently also altering the western perceptions of Soviet threat. An arms race in reverse was now being waged when President George Bush on 29 May turned the tables by announcing NATO's readiness to negotiate about combat aircraft and further reduce the proposed troop ceilings. He challenged Moscow to conclude the CFE in six months.

The London information forum

Not only was the CSCE changing because the world around it was changing but it also influenced in important ways the form and pace of this wider change. At the London 'Information Forum', which met in April 1989, the division between the reformist and anti-reformist states in eastern Europe became ever more pronounced. The conference induced them to sharpen their contrasting views on the one human right that defined the difference between closed and open societies – the right to receive and impart information. While Romania harped on the need for 'responsibility' in spreading information, the Hungarian delegation included for the first time persons who dared publicly to criticize their government.

The Soviet Union preferred to distance itself in London from both its reformist and its anti-reformist allies, thus suggesting a reluctance to interfere with the direction reform might take in different parts of eastern Europe. Its representatives evidently relished the situation when some western delegates, trying to prod the conservative east European regimes to improve their observance of human rights, alluded to the Soviet Union as an example to follow. But Moscow pointedly rejected the liberal western notion of freedom of the media, referring to them as an instrument of *glasnost*, rather than its beneficiary.

The London Forum further encouraged a split among the conservative regimes themselves – between those trying to gain time by appeasing criticism and the aggressively unrepentant Romania. On the one hand Czechoslovakia, dwelling on its supposed reform efforts, pleaded for their better appreciation abroad. On the other hand, the Ceausescu regime proclaimed its contempt for the Helsinki principles by vetoing the conference's final document because of a paragraph that reminded CSCE members of their obligation to honour those principles, and another passage alluding to criticism of Romania. Bucharest thus set a record for having blocked final consensus at CSCE meetings for the third time – not counting its repudiation of the inconvenient portions of the Vienna document.

The Paris meeting on human dimension

Rather than hampering the Helsinki process, Romania's self-imposed isolation facilitated its progress. At the subsequent Paris meeting on 'human dimension', the focus was less on the rectification of the remaining human rights abuses than on the nurturing of political structures that would help prevent them.

At issue were such practical matters as the presence of observers during political trials, guarantees of the right to leave one's country and return, besides the panoply of individual rights that had been the traditional mainstay of western liberalism. The many western proposals submitted at Paris sought to safeguard the rights under the rule of law – something that Gorbachev insisted must become the foundation of the Soviet state as well. Unlike its anti-reformist allies, Moscow proved receptive. Together with France and Germany, it proposed the creation of a European 'legal space', which gave expression to the belief that everywhere the rule of law ought to rest on the same basic values.

The Paris meeting was the first where clashes about eastern Europe's ethnic minorities erupted into the open. Although veiled polemics had occurred at the CSCE before, now Hungary accused Romania forcefully and by name of denying the Magyar population in Transylvania its rights, whereupon Romania responded in kind. By now, the increasingly rigid Ceausescu regime remained the only one to seem totally impervious to criticism; other violators tried in their own ways to pre-empt or divert it.

On the eve of the Paris meeting, the Czechoslovak regime (which was remembered for having had its police beat up demonstrators on the very day it appended its signature to the Vienna document) released from prison the country's leading dissident, Václav Havel. It proceeded answering, though not satisfying, the numerous inquiries about its misdeeds that it had been receiving from other CSCE governments under the recently created human dimension mechanism. It did gradually loosen press and travel restrictions though, as western critics pointedly observed, not as much as the Soviet Union – its persistently invoked model.

Also on the eve of the conference, the Sofia government announced a sudden reversal of its policy of forcible assimilation by opening its border with Turkey to those 'Bulgarian Moslems' who wished to emigrate. It proceeded expelling tens of thousands of members of a minority whose existence the regime pretended to deny. The sudden turnabout, which created in Paris outrage and consternation, was as puzzling as had been the sudden launching of the assimilation campaign five years before in the first place. Neither added stability or respect to the regime; indeed, the subsequent stopping of the expulsions under pressure from abroad may have been the beginning of its end.

The CSCE and revolution in eastern Europe

In October 1989, the CSCE contributed more directly to putting the Bulgarian regime of Todor Zhivkov on a slide by convening in Sofia a meeting of experts on environmental matters – something that the regime had long desired for prestige reasons. After the Budapest Cultural Forum in 1985, this was the second time the CSCE met inside the Soviet bloc, and the results indicated how much had changed there.

In the Hungary of 1985 – at that time the bloc's most liberal country – the Budapest dissidents had barely managed to hold as a political gesture a parallel forum in their own apartments; in the repressive Bulgaria of 1989, the Ecoglasnost opposition group went into the streets and eventually gained official recognition. In both cases, pressure from the CSCE delegates present in town helped to persuade the reluctant governments to yield. After 1985, Hungary's further liberalization had then followed gradually; what occurred in Bulgaria in 1989 precipitously was nothing less than the downfall of the Zhivkov regime.

By that time, the CSCE had already made its major contribution to eastern Europe's revolutionary upheaval. On 10 September, the Hungarian government, invoking its recent adherence to the UN Convention on Refugees and its Helsinki obligations, invalidated its twenty-year agreement with East Germany that provided for collaboration in returning defectors. It was this decision that made possible the mass exodus of East German citizens across the open Hungarian border into Austria, thus starting the chain of events that led to the collapse of communism in East Germany and eventually German unification.

In Czechoslovakia, the downfall in November of its communist government brought into power without violence some of the leading human rights activists whose endeavours the CSCE had vigorously publicized. What happened the next month in Romania – the bloody downfall of the Ceausescu dictatorship – could not be credited to the Helsinki process. Yet one of the first acts of the successor government was to end the country's alienation from the CSCE by revoking the Romanian reservation to the Vienna concluding document.

In a deeper sense, eastern Europe's largely peaceful revolution, despite the presence there of thousands of armed men capable of preventing it, vindicated the strategy of gradually eroding Europe's divisions, a strategy that had been the hallmark of the Helsinki process initiated fifteen years earlier. The outcome finally laid to rest the criticism of the CSCE as a sinister tool of Moscow's permanent domination of the area or, at best, an ineffectual forum for academic discussions about the plight of its citizens.

Now the all-inclusive conference began to appear to many people as a panacea, better suited to deal with Europe's future problems than either its obsolescent military alliances or its economically exclusive communities. The demand for an institutionalization of the Helsinki process gained momentum. Not surprisingly, in trying to sort out the debris of its empire, the Soviet Union was the first to embrace the idea even before the empire's last rotten pillar fell in Romania.

Europe's new architecture

On 30 November, Gorbachev, during his visit to Italy, proposed to convene the following year another Helsinki Summit to address the new European situation. The proposal was not entirely new, but its meaning in the new situation was. Earlier, the idea had had little attraction to the west because of the Soviet desire for an agenda dominated by security and economic issues, leaving human rights in abeyance. Now Gorbachev's overriding priority was damage limitation. Still determined that 'no harm must come to our East German ally' (9 December 1989), he tried to slow down what suddenly seemed an irresistible movement towards German unification. Musing that one cannot build the common European home if 'the walls keep moving' (30 November 1989), he implied that the possible removal of the border between the two German states could be a breach of the Helsinki accords providing for the inviolability of frontiers. However, the accords did not rule out peaceful changes mutually agreed upon, and the Soviet leader abstained from pursuing his proposition.

The Americans were slower than Europeans in adapting to the sudden disappearance of the east–west cleavage that had been the familiar hallmark of the Helsinki process for so long. But once adapted, they were more practical in presenting specific proposals. In a keynote speech about the 'architecture for a new era', delivered in Berlin on 12 December, Secretary of State James A. Baker admitted that the CSCE 'could become the most important forum of east–west cooperation'. With an eye on the continued importance of military security, however, he made his immediate priority an early conclusion of the Vienna negotiations on confidence building and conventional arms reductions.

In deference to the former Soviet bloc's economic plight, Baker elaborated on Bush's suggestion to give more substance to the Helsinki Basket Two. He still put the greatest weight on the need to make the recent political changes in eastern Europe irreversible by having the CSCE ensure there the system of free elections. He went so far as to describe such elections as 'the ultimate human right ... that secures all others' – as far-fetched a proposition as the now discarded Soviet one which equalled this ultimate right to man's survival.

Endorsed by the NATO Ministerial Council three days later, Baker's blue-print conveyed different expectations and priorities from the evolving Soviet design. Shevardnadze, speaking in Brussels soon after the removal of the Ceausescu tyranny in Romania, suggested that Europe had now become politically the most integrated part of the world. He judged the CSCE agreements as so successful as to be, in effect, binding part of Europe's emerging 'legal space'. From there he believed it was just a short step to creating CSCE institutions that would serve as the new framework of European security. He thought the unification of Germany, as of the whole continent, could best be managed within that framework.

Between these different, though not necessarily incompatible visions of the two superpowers, there was room for Europeans in east and west to give free rein to their imagination about the continent's future architecture. French President François Mitterrand greeted the new year by a radio address which exalted the CSCE as the core of a future confederation of European states, although he remained vague about specifics. This absence of specifics helped east Europeans to build on the idea: Polish Prime Minister Tadeusz Mazowiecki by linking it with the creation of a European Security Council; Czechoslovak President Václav Havel with the still more ambitious European Security Commission that would consist of two chambers and eventually lead to a United States of Europe. But even the most daring of these visions risked becoming quickly obsolete because of the continued rush of events, as had already happened to the pending disarmament talks in Vienna.

Demilitarization of security

As the content of European security became progressively demilitarized, at issue was assigning more security functions to the CSCE without necessarily interfering with the atrophy of the two military alliances. Italian Foreign Minister Gianni de Michelis saw a stronger CSCE necessary because of the collapse of the Warsaw Pact and the possible withdrawal of the Soviet Union, beset by internal crises, from European affairs. But there was no inherent contradiction between a stronger CSCE and the continued existence of NATO. Hence even staunch opponents of the institutionalization of the Helsinki process, notably the United States, Great Britain, Canada, and the Netherlands, gradually came around to the conclusion that some institutions had become both inevitable and desirable.

Already the interaction between the CSCE's non-military and military components gave impetus to its institutionalization. The three-stage 'human dimension' mechanism, devised at the Vienna follow-up meeting to pinpoint and rectify human rights violations, served as the model for the procedure which the conference on confidence-building measures designed to handle suspicious military movements. Conversely, the emerging consensus at the conference that high officials should meet annually to review compliance and that a permanent communications network be established to assist them set an example to the CSCE as a whole.

After Gorbachev at the Washington Summit in June had accepted the US condition that the CFE treaty must be completed before the Helsinki Summit could be held, NATO in its 6 July communiqué took a decisive step ahead. The statement was conspicuously vague about the alliance's own future but all the more definite in its recommending an extensive build-up of the CSCE. Declaring in solemn language NATO's original mission fulfilled and its adversarial relationship with the Warsaw Pact ended, the statement enumerated more precisely the different components of a new CSCE. These also included, besides most of those proposed by Genscher and others, a centre for the monitoring of elections and even a parliamentary assembly of all Helsinki states.

This ambitious programme was advanced after encouraging developments, including the successful CSCE conferences in Bonn and Copenhagen, had brought the convergence of values between east and west farther than could have been possibly expected before. The conviction took root that the democratization of the former communist states had become irreversible, thus making it possible to proceed with erecting a roof over the common European house. Rare were those who wondered why the roof was needed at all if everyone believed that the sun was shining.

The triumph at Bonn

Of the two successful conferences, the April 1990 meeting on Basket Two in Bonn targeted the economic and social foundations of the Soviet system that were indispensable to its very survival. Its representatives' willingness to cooperate in dismantling them could therefore be seen as the acid test of communism's self-demise. Hence also the United States, having at first been lukewarm to a conference, rightly perceived the issue at stake, and prepared its strategy for Bonn carefully.

Washington sensed that not only had the promise of western economic aid become a much stronger lever in dealing with the Soviet Union. It was now also true that the Soviets themselves – let alone the new east European democracies – had come to regard a shift from command to market economy indispensable for their countries. Thus nothing less than the victory of capitalism over communism in the final battle that Marx had once predicted was being consummated in Bonn.

It was indicative of the extent of the victory that the United States and the countries of the European Community were the ones that drafted most of the elaborate final document and that this was approved after hardly any discussion. The Soviet delegates demurred at too many enthusiastic references to 'private enterprise' and 'free market', but they seemed to lack the inner conviction and will to alter the text substantially. The result came closer to what might be called a Magna Carta of private enterprise than anything the twentieth century had produced.

Far from being limited to a ringing affirmation of principles, the document went to minute details about the ways and means by which the Soviet-style socialist system needed to be subverted, destroyed, dismantled, and buried beyond resurrection. The operational provisions ranged from the provision of accurate economic data to the creation of institutions that would protect entrepreneurs from state interference.

The lights and shadows of Copenhagen

Resuming under more propitious circumstances the unfinished business left from the Paris meeting the year before, the second conference on the 'human dimension' met in Copenhagen in July 1990. It set itself the ambitious task to move beyond Helsinki and Madrid – from the protection of individual human rights to the creation of safeguards that would protect minorities from the tyranny of majorities, the safeguards that constitute the essence of democracy.

The creation of safeguards for political pluralism under the rule of law was the leitmotif of Copenhagen. At issue was breaking the political backbone of communism after the Bonn principles had broken its economic backbone. Again the Soviet Union, along with the east European countries farther on the road from one-party rule to democracy, was ready to collaborate on dismantling their old system of power. Principles apart, there were pragmatic reasons for doing so. It was the price to be paid for ending the cold war and obtaining the western assistance needed to overcome the economic catastrophe the system created. As a result, the unanimously approved Copenhagen final document was an exuberant affirmation of the fundamental principles of western democracy, echoing themes from the US Declaration of Independence, the *Federalist Papers*, and the Bill of Rights.

Yet the triumph of democracy at Copenhagen was more illusionary than real. This was not necessarily because some of the participants' commitment to democracy was doubtful, although subsequent developments in such countries as the Soviet Union, Yugoslavia, and Romania proved that this was, indeed, the case. More pertinent were the emerging shortcomings of the Helsinki process itself. Approaching the limits of useful textual improvements, the CSCE, having been so successful in fulfilling its original mandate of helping to overcome Europe's division, was now beginning to navigate in uncharted waters, for which its instruments were untested. The Helsinki process reached the stage where it was no longer differences between east and west but the varieties of western democracy that created disagreements because of the legal and constitutional problems involved.

Minorities and European security

At Copenhagen, disputes about ethnic minorities were suggestive of the most vexing of the new Europe's security problems that the CSCE was ill equipped to handle. Some of these could be gleaned from the now more civil though no less sharp argument between post-communist Hungary and post-Ceausescu Romania about the collective rights of the Magyar minority in Transylvania. Did the recognition of such rights, in addition to the civil and human rights of its individual members, entitle the minority to special protection by the Hungarian government – as this government claimed on behalf of compatriots in not only Romania but also Czechoslovakia? And if so, where was the line to be drawn between a minority's allegiance to its state of residence and to its national state?

Nor was the Hungarian–Romanian dispute the most vexing; that distinction always belonged to the Macedonian question. At Copenhagen, Yugoslavia accused Bulgaria of denying minority rights to Macedonians, whose existence Bulgaria denied, reminding the Yugoslavs of their own plethora of ethnic problems. It asked rhetorically what happened to their Bulgarians – whom the Yugoslavs considered Macedonians. On behalf of these Macedonians, Yugoslavia then raised a voice in support of their alleged compatriots in Greece. Tongue in cheek, the Greeks proposed convening a special conference to define what a minority really is – something that had always eluded experts. In any case, as the delegate from Cyprus reminded the conference, there was an oppressed Greek minority in the Turkish-occupied part of the island.

As if the resurgence of these ancient disputes were not enough, new minorities asked for recognition. Turkey and Yugoslavia spoke up on behalf of Europe's growing population of migrant workers, asking the CSCE to confer on them the rights and protection due to minorities. And outside of the conference hall, a spokesman for European Gypsies, himself a member of the Romanian parliament, called attention to their particular plight, demanding their recognition as a 'non-territorial minority'.

Not surprisingly, the section on minorities in the Copenhagen document, though verbally extensive, in effect hardly advanced beyond Helsinki, Madrid, and Vienna. It was further restricted by Bulgaria's 'interpretive statement', sadly reminiscent of the earlier Romanian antics. According to the statement, each participating state was free to decide whether to apply the 'political provisions' to its own national minorities. Most important, the document failed to address what was rapidly becoming Europe's pre-eminent security issue – the possible separation or secession of a growing number of its nationalities from existing multi-ethnic states.

Already the mounting crisis in the Soviet Union's Baltic republics, which raised the spectre of Moscow's use of force while the Copenhagen conference was in session, revealed the new security threat and the scant relevance to it of the CSCE as a creation designed to preserve Europe's territorial status quo. The Baltic states themselves, alert to the importance that international recognition could have for their struggle for independence, pressed for admission to the CSCE at least as observers, the status recently granted even Albania. They could not count on the admission because of Soviet veto; what they could count on were the CSCE's well-tested powers of persuasion, provided there were enough willingness to apply these. That willingness, however, was lacking, at least for the moment.

Critics argued that under the new circumstances the use of the Helsinki process could actually more hamper than advance human rights. Encouraged by the activist president of the Council of Europe Catherine Lalumière, they saw the Council better equipped to foster the reintegration of the continent. Not only was it well-established and respected, notably by those east European states that were eager to 'return to Europe'. It also provided an efficient mechanism for the enforcement of human rights by enabling individual citizens to sue any member government in the European Court of Human Rights, whose decisions were accepted and enforced. Supporters of the Council of Europe campaigned for its being given the function of the CSCE's representative assembly.

The elusive peaceful order

In August, the Iraqi invasion of Kuwait and the ensuing Gulf crisis destroyed the illusion of an incipient peaceful international order extending beyond Europe. Next month, at the CSCE meeting of experts at Palma de Mallorca, originally intended to deal mainly with environmental issues, Italy and Spain promoted the possible extension of the Helsinki process to the non-European parts of Mediterranean, the Middle East, and even the Persian Gulf. They hoped to prevent Europe and the Islamic world from getting on a collision course; with war looming in the troubled region, however, the extension risked making discord rather than peace contagious. Besides modest progress in environmental cooperation, the conference at least achieved an agreement to convene the year after a conference on security in the Mediterranean – but outside the CSCE.

In Europe, too, the most drastic change of its established state system was rushing onwards outside of the Helsinki process: the unification of Germany which entailed the extinction of one of the CSCE's founding members, the German Democratic Republic. Although the planned CSCE Summit was originally expected to give the unification the necessary authorization, this became obsolete as the process was already being implemented by the Germans themselves, assisted by the four occupation powers formally responsible for the settlement.

The conference of CSCE foreign ministers in New York at the beginning of October – the first Helsinki meeting to be held in the United States – therefore merely conferred its blessing on the absorption of East Germany by West Germany, made effective a few days later. It was not the CSCE but rather a bilateral deal between Bonn and Moscow that made this remarkable denouement of a seemingly intractable problem so easy.

In addition to the disintegration of the Warsaw Pact and its economic counterpart, COMECON, the break-up of Europe's two remaining communist multi-ethnic states – the Soviet Union and Yugoslavia – also loomed increasingly, making the long-awaited CSCE summit anticlimactic. Whatever of substance the meeting was expected to achieve had already been achieved before its opening in Paris on 19 November. And the CSCE's limitations in achieving more of what needed to be achieved was bound to breed further disappointment.

One anticlimactic accomplishment was, besides the retroactive sanctioning of Germany's unification, the conclusion of the CFE treaty which Washington had made a precondition of the summit. Though impressive in its 200-page enumeration of the assorted arms control and disarmament measures that would ensure the end of east–west armed confrontation in Europe, the treaty itself merely confirmed and tidied up the inevitable military consequences of the collapse of Soviet political power in eastern Europe.

In contrast to the down-to-earth minutiae of the CFE treaty, supplemented by an equally tight agreement strengthening confidence-building measures, there was an air of unreality about the pompous 'Charter of Paris', with its encomiums about the millennium of peace, friendship, democracy, and human rights. It seemed the useful textual improvements of the Helsinki process may have already exceeded their limits. More substantive, though as yet untested, was the annexe, which described the several new institutions the conference established: the council of foreign ministers meeting annually, the committee of senior officials to assist it, the small permanent secretariat in Prague, the conflict prevention centre in Vienna, and the office for free elections in Warsaw.

The new CSCE and its institutions

The institutions marked the beginning of a different CSCE in a different Europe. The provisions for regular meetings of high officials conveyed a readiness to communicate and consult if not necessarily decide in concert, thus acknowledging that the previous east–west conflict had been partly, though not entirely, a failure of communication. The creation of the secretariat reflected the conviction that the Helsinki process, having helped to successfully erode Europe's division by its advocacy of principles and persuasive debate, should now move on to the formulation and execution of policies, albeit on a modest scale. The field office in Vienna for dealing with the implementation of confidence-building measures and the one in Warsaw for monitoring free elections suitably embodied that modesty of purpose.

No less important than the institutions, the Paris Summit created was what it did not create. Besides its failure to provide a mechanism for mitigating ethnic conflict, the Summit also left open the question of whether the Council of Europe should assume the function of the CSCE's quasi-parliamentary representation, and if so, how. Meanwhile it called upon the Council to share some of its expertise at the CSCE seminar on democratic institutions in Oslo in November 1991. Experts on national minorities were also scheduled to meet in Geneva in July.

As 1990 turned into 1991 and the Gulf war was fought, the break-up of the Soviet Union and Yugoslavia accelerated, and the CSCE's moment of truth was at hand. In regard to the former, it was the summit of the main industrialized nations; in regard to the latter the European Community, that took the initiative. Despite its key role in helping to redefine the meaning of security, the utility of the Helsinki process was no longer as obvious as it used to be when its progress served to overcome Europe's division. With the division gone and Europe's reintegration high on the agenda, the CSCE's own mission became subject to redefinition.

Because of its rule of unanimity, the CSCE could hardly be expected to serve as the main tool in managing the contentious liquidation of the Soviet and Yugoslav states, which might well require at some stage the use of international military force. Nor could the CSCE, with its anaemic Basket Two, take the lead in advancing Europe's economic integration; with the 1992 single market drawing near, the well-established institutions of the European Communities were available for the task. And as far as the Basket Three agenda, where so much has been done yet a great deal more remains to be done, there was, indeed, much to be said for the Council of Europe taking the lead – not only because of its mechanisms but also because of its special attraction precisely for the potentially refractory states.

Yet its limitations did not render the Helsinki process obsolete. One part of its genius had been its ability to get results in specific cases by generating political pressure. There is unlikely to be a shortage of worthy cases in the future – less overwhelmingly, it may be hoped, in human rights matters and increasingly in diverse other issues, from building international confidence to preserving the environment. Another part of the Helsinki genius pertains to the CSCE's proven ability to anticipate long-term trends by constant exchange of views in an all-inclusive gathering.

The presence in that gathering of even Europe's mini-states has never been more topical as a reminder of the necessity of accommodating in the continent's future security framework the conflicting legitimate needs of its rising minorities. At a time of mounting nationalism, this task alone should keep the new CSCE going for many years to come.

Moreover, the outcome of the Gulf war may have opened for the CSCE new perspectives for extending some of its principles beyond Europe after all. The plight of the Kurdish refugees in Iraq dramatized the familiar connection between security and human rights. It added new dimensions to the unresolved dilemma between minority rights and state sovereignty. And it added unexpected prominence to Turkey as a CSCE member with an Asian base. At the Moscow conference on the human dimension, held in September 1991, the CSCE went farther than ever before in authorizing intervention into the member states' internal affairs for the sake of international stability. With the memory still fresh of the abortive reactionary coup in the Soviet Union, the conference presented the extraordinary sight of the Soviet and the German delegations taking a common stand in devising a mechanism that would facilitate intrusive intervention, with or without the consent of the government involved. Moreover, a decisive break required less than unanimous consent of CSCE members for such action.

At the Moscow conference, the CSCE admitted the newly-independent Baltic states of Lithuania, Latvia, and Estonia. Yet the question of how to deal with other candidates for independence from the former Soviet Union and Yugoslavia, as well as with the protection of minorities in these break-away states, remained unresolved, thus indicating the shortcomings of the CSCE as an institution created to preserve Europe's territorial status quo. There was growing conviction about the need for a radical reform of the Helsinki process to preserve its effectiveness in the rapidly changing international environment.

More than at the time of the overarching east–west conflict, in the post-cold war world the CSCE sets the standards of international behaviour linked with those of the domestic order. Nowhere are those standards elaborated more precisely and comprehensively than in the Helsinki documents, culminating in the Charter of Paris. This is no guarantee against violations. But neither should the enforcement of the standards be more difficult against states far less powerful than the Soviet Union used to be. While not the harbinger of a millennium, the Helsinki process therefore does presage a better world.

REFERENCES

Ferraris, Luigi Vittorio (ed.) 1979: *Report on a Negotiation: Helsinki–Geneva–Helsinki, 1972–1975*. Alphen an den Rijn: Sijthoff & Noordhoff.

Ghebali, Victor Yves 1989: *La Diplomatie de la Détente: La CSCE d'Helsinki à Vienne (1973–1989)*. Brussels: Bruylant.

Maresca, John 1985: *To Helsinki: the Conference on Security and Cooperation in Europe, 1973–1975*. Durham, NC: Duke University Press.

Mastny, Vojtech 1986: *Helsinki, Human Rights, and European Security: Analysis and Documentation*. Durham, NC: Duke University Press.

Sizoo, Jan and Jurrjens, Rudolf 1984: *CSCE Decision-Making: The Madrid Experience*. The Hague: Nijhoff.

Spencer, Robert (ed.) 1984: *Canada and the Conference on Security and Cooperation in Europe*. Toronto: Centre for International Studies, University of Toronto.

Wells, Samuel T., Jr (ed.) 1990: *The Helsinki Process and the Future of Europe*. Washington, DC: Wilson Centre Press.

19

Defence and arms control in a new Europe

Peter Stratmann

The starting point

Whatever the future holds for defence and arms control in Europe, the situation will be fundamentally different from that of the cold war period. That much is inevitable in view of the political upheaval which has taken place in the Soviet Union, and in the central and southern parts of eastern Europe. The old political and military structures have disintegrated, and the traditional lines of confrontation have been made obsolete. New security problems are now emerging. The concepts, strategies and institutions of defence and arms control have for decades borne the imprint of the ideological differences between the two alliances, power politics and military confrontation. As soon as the prospect of the end of the cold war appeared on the horizon, a progressive but radical process of change was set in motion.

In the field of *defence*, the Soviet Union changed its military doctrine, agreed to disband the Warsaw Pact and began the process of completely withdrawing its armies from eastern Europe. The member states of NATO responded by giving an assurance that they would not exploit the situation to gain a strategic advantage, but would instead cooperate with the Soviet Union. They also agreed to revise NATO's strategic concept of flexible response and the associated operational concepts, and reconsider the structures and size of its forces.

The end of the Soviet Union's offensive posture and militarily-backed strong-arm tactics in Europe also led to the first substantial successes in *arms control negotiations*: the Washington Treaty banning medium-range nuclear missiles, the Conventional Forces in Europe Treaty (CFE), and the Confidence and Security Building Measures (CSBM) contained in the Vienna Document of the Conference on Security and Cooperation in Europe (CSCE).

Although the crucial CFE treaty was initially intended to achieve a systematic stabilization of the military relationship between the two alliances, it proved possible during the closing phase of negotiations to adapt the treaty to the new political ground rules in eastern Europe. The treaty commitments to limit certain weapon systems, and the obligations concerning information and verification now apply not just collectively to the Warsaw Pact and NATO, but also individually to each member state. This step foreshadows what is bound to be a political precondition for future European arms control negotiations. The key issues are now the individual security interests and political decisions of each sovereign European state (and, of course, of the North American member states) within the framework of the CSCE. Exactly how this framework can and should be developed further in practice will become clearer during the course of preparations for the 1992 CSCE conference in Helsinki.

The new Soviet foreign and security policy position, the end of the Soviet hegemony of countries in the former Communist bloc, and the continuing process of reform within the former Soviet Union triggered dramatic changes in the military and arms control policies of the major western nations. The United States framed a new national military strategy, which involves drastic reductions in its military presence in Europe over the next few years. In their debates and defence plans, Great Britain, France and Germany respectively foresee cuts in troop levels by the mid 1990s to well below their entitlements under the CFE treaty.

Political developments have thus generated a disarmament momentum, and the consequences within the Soviet Union of the failed coup of August 1991 have further strengthened this trend. One of the results was President Bush's unilateral decision (taken admittedly in the hope of reciprocal concessions from the Soviets) to withdraw all his country's tactical nuclear weapons (Short-range Nuclear Forces: SNF), and ship them back to the US for destruction. American stocks of chemical weapons have already been withdrawn from Europe. Soviet–US cooperation in the destruction of both the chemical and nuclear weapons is likely. These examples suggest that in the future the nature of arms control will, in practice, be quite different from that of the SALT, START, MBFR and CFE negotiations. The matters at issue will in many cases be less extensive, the participants will vary according to the type of weapon considered, and the talks will not necessarily lead to the signing of an international treaty. In short, arms control will become more flexible and will be conducted on a more differentiated basis.

Although the end of the cold war in Europe marks the end of one set of threats and points the way forward to greater pan-European cooperation and drastic disarmament, there is unfortunately another side to the coin. The collapse of the Soviet empire has led to conflicts which raise *new security problems*. Demands for national self-determination and autonomy are breaking up the cohesion of multi-ethnic states and calling existing borders into question. Historical, ethnic, religious and socio-economic tensions and conflicts are again springing up, and are being politically exploited both internally (in the post-communist struggle for power and the search for a new form of government) and externally (in efforts to establish new borders). The civil war in Yugoslavia and the tensions in Caucasia are the most visible and worrying examples of this increasingly widespread problem. Similarly, explosive situations also exist in other regions of the former Soviet Union, eastern Europe and the Balkans. In many western and southern European countries fears are widespread of a growth in autonomist and separatist movements.

The causes and forms of these conflicts cannot be understood in terms of the kind of threats expected in the past or the deterrence-based defence doctrines of the two pacts. What we face today are not the problems of deterring and defending against calculated large-scale offensive operations with a strategic objective, but the limited use of force either within a state or across borders, which could however have serious indirect effects on European security. The possible consequences range from environmental disasters (the explosion of the nuclear reactor at Chernobyl in April 1986 reminded everyone of this kind of potential risk) to mass refugee movements, violations of human rights, the breakdown of the economic and social order, and the rise of extremist anti-democratic regimes.

Events in Yugoslavia have demonstrated that none of the existing international organizations is properly equipped to prevent the outbreak of internal conflicts of this kind, bring them under control or end them once they have started. The limitations of the charter of the CSCE, still in the early stages of institutionalization, have been revealed just as clearly as the limited effectiveness of the European Community (together with the Commission and European Political Cooperation) and the western European Union (WEU). NATO decided that the events did not fall within its responsibilities. The UN could initially do no more than back the EC and the CSCE in their expressions of concern.

The Yugoslavian crisis has demonstrated not only the lack of institutions capable of effective conflict prevention and management, but also the extreme political difficulties faced in setting up this kind of international institution. Whereas during the cold war period every conflict required – and usually resulted in – unified action because of the associated general and existential military risks, in limited and politically-confused conflicts between ethnic groups – as in Yugoslavia – differences in the viewpoints and interests of the other countries come to the fore. Such national divergences restrict the ability of international organizations to intervene effectively if they can only take decisions on a basis of consensus, or if they take the view that the need to ensure internal cohesion is more pressing than the need for intervention.

As, however, further crises and conflicts like those in Yugoslavia could well occur in Europe, one can only hope that this experience will stimulate efforts to establish basic principles of international law and an institutional and procedural instrument for the prevention and management of conflicts within the framework of the CSCE, the EC, NATO's liaison framework and the UN. Considerable emphasis also needs to be placed on these tasks in the future as far as arms control is concerned.

In the west European context the idea is being pursued of organizing a separate European force both for peace keeping and for the enforcement of any sanctions which may be applied. However, the current controversies about setting up such a force, and its institutional relationship to the EC, WEU and NATO, clearly reflect the political obstacles which still need to be overcome. For the moment, it is unclear whether the civil war in Yugoslavia will act as a catalyst for progress along this path, or conversely discourage such efforts and thus lead to political fragmentation.

The future of defence and arms control in the new Europe will also be fundamentally influenced by all developments in Europe's neighbouring regions which carry security implications. The end of the cold war has had diametrically opposed effects on threats faced by Europe from nearby countries, and on those from more distant, strategically important regions.

The tensions and conflicts in the third world which resulted from the global power politics of the two competing superpowers now no longer apply. The days of regional proxy wars and antagonistic global involvement in the states of the Near and Middle East, south-east Asia, Africa and Latin America – in the name of proletarian internationalism or the domino theory – are over.

The drawback, however, is that as the two superpowers no longer exercise control over their client states, the healthy restraint necessary to prevent regional conflicts from getting out of hand and escalating into a major war will no longer be applied. This could encourage some governments to try to achieve their political objectives through military force. Admittedly, they would probably not be successful, to judge from the outcome of the Iraqi invasion of Kuwait, and the successful military action of the international coalition force organized under the aegis of the UN Security Council and placed under US command. With the end of the east–west stalemate and backed by Soviet–US cooperation to overcome long drawn-out regional conflicts, the UN could now be developed into an effective instrument of collective security. The prospect that under UN auspices American diplomacy would not only be able to bring to bear the superior global strategic power of the US, but also the weight of a coalition of major western industrial states and states in the region concerned, should – in the light of Saddam Hussein's experiences – considerably cool down the aggressive tendencies of other political leaders.

However, the case of Iraq in fact reflects special tendencies which – when viewed against the background of a wide range of endogenous political, economic, demographic, ideological, cultural and ecological factors which are conducive to conflict – constitute a significant threat even for Europe: the extension of the ability to produce or obtain both nuclear, biological and chemical weapons of mass destruction and the means with which to deliver them to distant targets. On the southern edge of Europe there is a whole series of states – notably Pakistan, Iran, Iraq, Syria, Libya and Algeria – which may be included in this category.

This does not necessarily mean that there will be a 'new military threat from the south', and it does not alter the fact that Europe must work to achieve security by developing strategies of political, economic and cultural cooperation. However, the possibility of external military security problems in the future cannot be ruled out, and this should be borne in mind as defence and arms control in Europe are developed.

The debate on external dangers for the defence of Europe has primarily revolved around the organization of European forces and their possible missions, command organization and structure. Another precautionary measure concerns the development of a European air defence system to protect also against missiles capable of carrying nuclear, chemical or biological weapons.

There has been a growing call for European intervention forces in the wake of the Gulf war, when most of the European members of NATO provided contingents for the coalition force. This call very quickly became part of the wider debate which has been underway since the end of 1990 about the future of NATO and the development of a (west) European security and defence identity, as part of European Political Union (EPU).

The considerable differences between national interests and objectives on this issue – particularly between the UK (and the US) on the one hand, and France on the other – have clearly emerged in discussions within NATO, at the intergovernmental conference on EPU and in the WEU. The Anglo-American side, whose views are also supported by SHAPE and the NATO General Secretariat, prefers a rapid reaction force integrated with NATO. If, however, the force could not operate under NATO command because the conflict in question was outside the NATO area, a British–Italian proposal would place European units under the flag of a transformed WEU, which would be linked as closely as possible to NATO.

France, on the other hand, favours the development of a genuine European intervention force which would be independent of NATO, also under the aegis of the WEU, but which would operate in accordance with the directives of the European Council, and the Ministerial Council of the European Union. The strength of feeling on these issues emerged again in late 1991 during discussions on the possible intervention of a WEU peace-keeping force in the Yugoslavian civil war.

As long as no workable compromise is reached on the future relations between a reformed NATO and a developing EPU – particularly as regards a common foreign and security policy and approaches to defence – European countries will continue to react to any new external dangers on an ad hoc basis and in conjunction with the USA. Compromise will, however, be even more difficult as the sticking points in fact reflect more basic differences on the future political role and basic purpose of the transatlantic alliance, the institutional form to be taken by future European Union, and the extension of that union to other countries in addition to the twelve. Matters were barely clarified by the November 1991 NATO Summit in Rome and the EC Summit at Maastricht the following month. The treaty text referred to the 'eventual framing of a common (EC) defence policy, which might in time lead to a common defence'.

The future of the project for an extended European air defence system should also be considered from a wider viewpoint. Will the US and the negotiators of the former Soviet Union (i.e. the Commonwealth of Independent States) agree to modify the ABM treaty so as to allow the development of extended air defence systems against limited missile attacks? Would the European states be prepared to provide the funds needed for this purpose? Alternatively, what are the prospects of international treaties and mechanisms effectively controlling the proliferation of biological and chemical weapons, and the means used to deliver them to targets at long range?

For the reasons stated above, conceptions of arms control in Europe must transcend the borders of the region. The unexpectedly advanced development of Iraq's research and production in the field of weapons of mass destruction, and of the related missile technology, underlines the political urgency of intensifying international effort to prevent further proliferation and regulate arms exports and technology transfers. The member states of the CSCE

– including the US and soon no doubt more republics which were once part of the Soviet Union – can bring considerable influence to bear in this matter: the CSCE includes the major nuclear powers and arms exporters (with the exception of China), and each also holds a permanent seat on the UN Security Council. They are in a position to use their collective diplomatic, economic, technological and military muscle to foster the development of effective international mechanisms. They can also lend greater legitimacy to this endeavour by showing restraint and a readiness to disarm in Europe. The agreement between Washington and Moscow on the destruction of their arsenals of chemical weapons, and their unilateral declarations that they are ready to destroy all the warheads of their land-based short-range nuclear systems are major steps in this direction.

The difficulties of making predictions in turbulent times

It is at present very difficult to predict how the new Europe will have developed by the end of the decade, and what role defence and arms control will have played in this process. All the essential political and strategic mechanisms and internal structures are changing at the same time, and all are closely interrelated. One can do no more than speculate about which states, intergovernmental bodies and international organizations will play a key role in the future security of Europe, and which political positions will form the basis for cooperation and integration, or opposition and conflicts.

The trends which can be perceived today are contradictory, which means they cannot be extrapolated to make a prediction. Any forecasts must therefore be based on alternative scenarios.

a)   It is clear that military security issues have become less politically significant and have less impact on structures than they did during the cold war. However, the likelihood of violent military conflicts is increasing; the stabilizing and civilizing effect of the mutual deterrence of the two opposing blocs, which was instrumental in preventing wars, no longer applies. This backward step means that armed struggle has again become a means of political change in countless ethnic and nationalistic confrontations.

b)   This set-back has led to renewed and strengthened efforts to stop the outbreak of conflicts by developing international law and international institutions for cooperative and collective security, and to limit, resolve and if possible end such conflicts through external intervention, which would undoubtedly be a significant step forward in historical terms. But these efforts are resisted by some governments which reject any interference in internal affairs on the grounds of the traditional principle of state sovereignty.

c)   With the end of the confrontation between the two essentially united alliances, security policy and defence in Europe will more clearly bear the stamp of particular national viewpoints and interests not only in the ex-communist bloc but also within NATO. Running counter to this trend is the fact that all countries – with the exception of the US – are obliged by political and financial restrictions to abandon ideas of an autonomous strategic capability. It remains to be seen to what extent the increasing drive towards international cooperation and integration is implemented in political terms, or whether, in fact, the declining military threat persuades governments and parliaments to continue to present the facade of an independent defence policy for internal political reasons, even if this means foregoing necessary rationalization and effectively reducing the capability of coherent military operations.

d)   Another issue which is closely related to national security interests is the future development of the various international organizations which are important for European security and the relationships between them. There is a general verbal consensus that NATO, EPU, WEU, CSCE, the UN and other bodies should remain components of the often mentioned 'framework of overlapping and interlocking institutions', in order to ensure a peaceful, secure, free and united Europe. However, this diverts attention from the fact the preferences of particular governments are different at least to some extent, as competitive national interests and ambitions begin to emerge. It therefore remains to be seen to what extent moves will be blocked by various sides, preventing progress on the reform of NATO, the framing of a common European foreign and security policy (and its defence dimension), and the development of the CSCE into an instrument of cooperative and ultimately collective security, or even leading to the dismantlement of existing organizations. Alternatively, if compromises between the various interests are achieved, the outcome could be the development of a European security system based on a sensible cooperative approach and division of tasks.

Forecasts are made even more difficult because the trends mentioned could be turned in either direction or strengthened by isolated events, such as the break-up of the central power structure in the former Soviet Union or the Yugoslavian civil war. The possible structural effects cannot be determined in advance. Depending on what actually happens, and the political constellations as they exist at that time, the break-up of the Soviet Union, for example, could weaken or strengthen NATO, slow down the CSCE process or accelerate and deepen it, and weaken resolve to achieve a western European defence identity or promote its development.

The future of European defence

Leaving aside the stillborn European Defence Community (EDC), NATO was the only framework for the organization of western security in Europe during the cold war period. Will it continue to hold a monopoly on this role now that the cold war is over? The earlier threat to western Europe from the excessive and offensively organized conventional and nuclear potential of the USSR and the Soviet-dominated Warsaw Pact alliance, used as an instrument of its strong-arm political strategy, meant that stability and security in Europe could only be ensured by the US commitment to NATO. The key components which ensured the effectiveness of the American commitment were the stationing of strong US armed forces in Europe with nuclear weapons both for US and other alliance forces, the integrated multinational command structure, and preparation for multinational forward defence.

In 1968 NATO adopted a 'flexible response' strategy, which was intended to deter attacks by influencing the political and strategic risk calculations of the Soviet leadership in particular. (Détente was also pursued alongside this strategy, to defuse and eliminate possible political crises and causes of conflict.) In the event of an attack, NATO forces were to undertake defence operations, and to seek if necessary to re-establish the deterrent effect through measured escalation, i.e. mainly by the controlled use of nuclear weapons. The objective was to prevent the aggressor from continuing his aggression and ensure the withdrawal of enemy troops from NATO territory.

The sweeping political and military changes in eastern Europe and the USSR since 1989 mean that a Soviet threat of this type is now out of the question. The Warsaw Pact has been disbanded. Poland, Hungary and Czechoslovakia are seeking membership of the EC and NATO. The Soviet armies are losing cohesion and are withdrawing from Europe to the territory of a Soviet Union which no longer bears the same name and which is becoming a loose commonwealth of independent states. The complex internal problems caused by the breakdown of the old political and economic system and the lack of any alternative to extensive long-term western aid means there is no question of the former Soviet Union again becoming a strategic threat to western Europe and NATO. The possibility of a residual Soviet risk has been politically and materially ruled out since the failed putsch of August 1991. The real risks of the future will be of quite a different kind: the possible failure of the political and economic reforms, the uncontrolled splintering of the union, the outbreak of conflicts inside and between the republics (which could spread to neighbouring states), loss of political control over the vast military arsenals, and finally the use of the weapons in internal wars and their international proliferation (particularly in the case of weapons of mass destruction).

In view of the radical changes in NATO's strategic environment which have already taken place or which are still in progress, the alliance will unquestionably have to change its strategy, operational concepts and force posture dramatically. It could even be argued that the purpose of NATO has been fulfilled, and the political justification for its continuing existence is in doubt. As far as we know, no government of a NATO member state has yet drawn this conclusion. What did clearly emerge however from NATO's London Summit in July 1990 was the overriding determination that NATO should not be drawn into the maelstrom generated by the break-up of the Warsaw Pact. At the two plus four talks held to discuss the external implications of German reunification, concern was expressed that Soviet calls for Germany to leave NATO, and for the withdrawal of all forces and nuclear weapons stationed in Germany, could possibly cause the disintegration of NATO.

The alliance governments reacted intelligently to this challenge, by expressing their readiness to reform the strategy and forces of NATO, while safeguarding those structural elements which are of critical importance for its cohesion and capabilities.

On the basis of preparatory agreements, reached in the preceding meetings of the Defence Planning Council (DPC) in Brussels and the NATO Council in Copenhagen, NATO member states agreed on a new strategic concept at the Rome Summit in November 1991. This document and the accompanying

Rome Declaration on Peace and Cooperation demonstrate the political will not only to maintain NATO as a collective transatlantic defence alliance, but also to extend its responsibilities to take account of the new prospects and requirements of European security.

The remaining core functions of NATO include the task to preserve the strategic balance in Europe. Now that the earlier strategic threat has disappeared, this function can, however, be redefined under three headings:

a) guarding against threats to security in the interim period until Soviet forces have been completely withdrawn and reduced in accordance with CFE and other treaty commitments;

b) counterbalancing the massive strategic and sub-strategic nuclear potential remaining in the former USSR;

c) preserving the necessary organizational, infrastructural and industrial base to enable measured rearmament in the event of a long-term resurgence of a threat targeted against western Europe.

These precautionary requirements, which are very much in line with the traditional bipolarity of security issues, will in the future be easier to meet in practice. All that is required is the consolidation of the structural elements and strategic core principles which are essential for NATO's political and military cohesion and its operational capability. Once this base has been confirmed, it is possible to react to the fundamentally modified political and military situation by drastically dismantling and withdrawing NATO forces, modifying the strategic concept and introducing new operational concepts and armed forces structures.

Continuity is what the NATO member states are seeking, by maintaining the conditions which are fundamental in ensuring political solidarity and the collective defence capability. In practice this means:

• that American troops should continue to be stationed in Europe, and that the possibility of bringing in reinforcements from the other side of the Atlantic should be retained;

• continued adherence to an integrated multinational military command structure and integrated troop units;

• continued adherence to the principle of defending close to borders against all attacks on NATO territory;

• continued adherence to the nuclear sharing system, i.e. the stationing of American nuclear weapons and force units in European NATO countries, and the participation of those countries in the formulation of directives concerning the possible use of nuclear weapons, employment planning and nuclear missions.

Some fundamental changes are planned however, particularly in the following areas:

• there will be extensive withdrawals and reductions in NATO's conventional and nuclear capabilities by the mid 1990s (some 50 per cent of conventional forces, and 80 per cent of nuclear weapons);

• the nuclear components of NATO strategy will be revised, particularly in the light of the planned withdrawal from European soil of all American land-based short-range nuclear weapons (SNF); the possible use of nuclear weapons will be regarded as a political and strategic measure of last resort;

- operational concepts, operational planning and the disposition of forces will be fundamentally changed to take account of a situation in which there is no clearly identified enemy, and thus no predetermined direction of attack or front. The policy of establishing detailed operational plans in peacetime for forward defence by NATO forces will be abandoned;

- the structures of the armed forces will be adapted to meet the new requirements, i.e. to demonstrate a collective military presence in the event of crises and to provide effective border defence in the event of attacks on NATO countries, particularly on the southern edge, bearing in mind that the strength of forces in the NATO area as a whole will be much lower.

The outcome of the Rome Summit was globally positive in that it enabled the continuing political existence of the Atlantic alliance despite the end of the cold war, while at the same time eliminating some outdated elements. The cohesion of NATO as a unified security zone has been preserved. The sharing of risks and burdens between the various member states seems to be politically acceptable. The planned structures for NATO forces are extremely flexible, and can thus be adapted to take account of the inevitable further changes in the European security situation.

From a military viewpoint, the planned components of the NATO rapid reaction force provide a remarkably successful example of how this combined approach can be implemented. These multinational troops will have an integrated core formation kept in a high state of readiness. It will be possible to deploy them quickly and over long distances anywhere within the NATO area, and they will be flexible enough to handle the whole spectrum of possible intervention missions whatever the conditions. The concept behind this force is therefore fully in line with the stated political requirement of solidarity, and also reflects the shift of the focus of expected security problems from central Europe to areas on the edge of the NATO zone. If this shift becomes even more pronounced, NATO's new structural concept offers the possibility of further increasing the relative strength of the rapid reaction forces. In this case the main defence forces and augmentation forces, for which mobilization is necessary, could be correspondingly reduced, particularly in NATO's central region.

As noted earlier, the new instabilities and dangers in and for Europe do not amount to a direct and large-scale military threat. What therefore is NATO's future European security role, bearing in mind that it was created and conceived to deal with a specific threat? All the indications are that the likely causes and locations of future threats will lie for the most part outside the borders of NATO territory. Any such crises would only trigger the 'NATO case' (i.e. an attack on the NATO area) at a very late stage if at all, by which time major political, humanitarian, economic or ecological damage may already have been wrought.

NATO's obligations, and its political possibilities, as regards collective military action have always been strictly tied to the 'NATO case'. Under its charter, the alliance cannot provide any security guarantees which extend beyond the NATO area. Calls for NATO to extend its zone of operations

further in order to develop a more broadly defined policy of crisis prevention and management have never been successful in the face of powerful
internal resistance. Yet it is obviously unwise not to make use of the alliance's potential in tackling critically important tasks which may arise in the
future. Any restrictive practice of this sort would undoubtedly seriously
damage NATO's political viability.

During the preparations for the NATO Summit in Rome contrasting fears
were expressed: on the one hand – in the eyes of the French in particular,
and supported by the American and British – efforts to make NATO into a
near-monopolistic institution for all fundamental security problems
throughout Europe and the bordering areas would block progress on the
creation of a (west) European security and defence identity, and the development of the CSCE into a cooperative and ultimately collective security
system; on the other hand, these developments would politically marginalize
NATO and thus threaten its existence. The Rome Declaration and NATO's
new strategic concept contain formulations which at least suggest ways of
overcoming this unproductive polarization of views. The EC Summit in
Maastricht nonetheless indicated the difficulty of moving to more constructive positions. France could be pleased that the WEU was recognized as an
'integral part' of the process of developing a European security identity and
defence role. But Britain ensured that the new arrangements, up for review
again in 1996, would not be incompatible with NATO.

Those who favour a strengthening and broadening of NATO's existing role
decided to introduce compromise formulas playing down fears of a mono-
polistic or dominant NATO, while leaving the way open for pragmatic innovative steps in the preferred direction.

NATO's 'new strategic concept' points out, for example, that in the context
of the radically different security situation, the alliance can pursue its original
aims more effectively than ever before through political means:

> It is now possible to draw all the consequences from the fact that security and
> stability have political, economic, social and environmental elements as well
> as the indispensable defence dimension. Managing the diversity of challenges
> facing the Alliance requires a broad approach to security. This is reflected in
> three mutually reinforcing elements of Allied security policy: dialogue, coop-
> eration, and the maintenance of a collective defence capability.

In similar vein, the Rome Declaration emphasizes that the new challenges
cannot be met by any one institution alone, but can only be dealt with
through a 'framework of interlocking institutions': 'Consequently, we are
working towards a new European security architecture in which NATO, the
CSCE, the European Community, the WEU and the Council of Europe complement each other'.

In line with this approach, the broadening of the process of west European unification in the fields of security policy and defence is viewed in a
reasonably positive and constructive way, as is the institutionalization of
the CSCE process in order to manage crises effectively, and settle disputes
peacefully.

Attempts to extend the influence of NATO, by enabling it to apply a
broadly defined policy of crisis prevention and management in zones outside the NATO area, mainly reflect concerns about the former Warsaw Pact

countries. The 'liaison' concept enables the involvement of the new democracies – including former Soviet republics – in consultations with NATO on issues of security policy. It was decided at the Rome Summit to set up a North Atlantic Cooperation Council at foreign minister and ambassador level. Within this comprehensive framework it should be possible to develop dialogue and practical cooperation between the forces of these countries and the military apparatus of NATO. This will complement the dense network of bilateral relations, and the existing contacts and cooperation in arms control agreement implementation.

Initiatives taken by NATO to enable it to play a stabilizing role through cooperation will of course be welcomed mainly by those governments in central-eastern Europe which are seeking NATO membership. They will view the initiatives as a step towards their objective and as the best possible alternative at the present time. The initiatives supplement the CSCE's Confidence and Security Building Measures (CSBM), and are also fully in line with the almost identical measures envisaged by the WEU.

In seeking to extend its security policy responsibilities to out-of-area regions *outside* Europe, NATO can justify its approach by referring to the contents of the original alliance treaty, and to its established practice of information, consultation and in some cases coordination in respect of developments anywhere in the world. But the critical question is whether and to what extent NATO should and could be a military player in such areas if crises or conflicts arise.

At the present time, such action is not permissible unless the NATO case conditions are met. But the Gulf war demonstrated that individual NATO member states, with a mandate from the UN Security Council, could take part in military operations, while drawing on extensive NATO support in the form of supplies, infrastructure, means of transport and even supporting activities of forces.

An attempt to treat this procedure as a precedent, and to include it in the Rome Declaration as an almost generally applicable option in the NATO catalogue was unsuccessful. Furthermore, the British suggestion that the NATO integrated multinational rapid reaction force under British command could be given a second role in out-of-area intervention under the aegis of the WEU was opposed by other NATO member states.

Despite these unsuccessful attempts to extend at least indirectly both NATO's area of military operations and to broaden the range of conditions under which NATO can intervene, there is no doubt that the alliance's military capability for this role is remarkably strong, provided that its member states grant the political authorization for its use.

NATO's capabilities have been adapted with notable speed to the changed conditions of European security.

- This has been demonstrated by the Gulf war. Though the whole operation was 'out of area', the bulk of the troops, equipment, logistics, and military strategy were supplied by NATO allies. The newly-united Germany, though, was preoccupied with domestic reconstruction, and refused to send troops 'out-of-area'.
- The structures of US forces that will remain stationed in Europe are primarily devised with out-of-area intervention in mind.

- The planned characteristics of the NATO rapid reaction forces, and the restructuring processes which are already underway in the national armed forces of most NATO member states mean that all these forces will be flexible and highly mobile for interventions not only across the borders of the regions within the NATO command area, but also outside this area.
- The 'technical' availability of appropriate intervention forces should also be seen from the viewpoint of NATO's interest – emphasized in the new strategic concept – in having the appropriate military instruments and planning for stage-by-stage intervention in the management of a crisis. This means that mainly political objectives can be pursued, in accordance with political directives.

The limits to arms control in post–1989 Europe

The arms control process in Europe has now come to a parting of the ways. Its development was closely linked with the cold war period. Its concepts and negotiation objectives were determined by the prevailing context of militarized political confrontation, for they were, in fact, instruments of antagonistic strategies as well.

As the new political thinking took hold in Soviet foreign and security policy, more space for manoeuvre became available, enabling substantial progress in the limitation and banning of various types of conventional and nuclear weapons. The whole process was made more transparent through agreements on the exchange of information and the notification of military activities. The agreements on verification, which for the first time included inspections on Soviet territory, marked a major step forward.

However dramatic the progress made in the INF and CFE negotiations may seem when compared with the stagnation and immobility of earlier talks, the structure of the discussions still bore the imprint of the possibility of conflict between the two military alliances. The opposing blocs were seen as the key protagonists, and their confrontation set the ground rules for all calculations and agreements relating to the military balance of power and military options. The fundamental objective, it was felt, was the stabilization of relations between the two alliance systems by balancing their military potentials, primarily by setting equal upper limits on the main categories of heavy military hardware. Even the Confidence and Security Building Measures negotiated at the CSCE were indelibly marked by cold war antagonism.

This is not to detract in any way from the significance of the achievements of the INF and CFE talks. The December 1987 Washington Treaty banning US and Soviet medium range missiles worldwide brought an end to an arms race which had put a particularly heavy political burden on Europe, and the November 1990 CFE Treaty obliged the Soviet Union to reduce asymmetrically the quantitatively overwhelming offensive potential of its heavily equipped land forces, thus defusing the central strategic problem of the European security situation.

As the political changes which made these successes possible have gathered speed and become more radical, their effects have made the political preconditions and principles which characterize this form of arms control obsolete. Independence and democratization in Hungary, Poland, Czecho-slovakia and other ex-Warsaw Pact countries, the disappearance of the German Democratic Republic, and reform and federalization in the former USSR have made the eastern bloc a thing of the past. Politico-ideological and military fortress mentalities and confrontations have disappeared. The impetus for arms control now comes from the motivation to achieve a broad degree of cooperation and the readiness to tackle common problems.

This wholly new political situation is setting the ground rules for future progress on arms control. The institutional and organizational framework for this process is the CSCE, which at present has thirty-eight member states but which a number of others will no doubt be joining. The key issue concerns the widely varying security interests of the various sovereign states. All will be intent on ensuring their independence and obtaining equal rights. Determination and readiness to reach a consensus will therefore determine what kind of arms control agreements, settlements and treaties can be achieved.

In the follow-on from the CFE Ia round and the CSBM talks, the CSCE was also confronted with the urgent matter of devising effective arms control measures, and of incorporating them in a common European security policy. The problems addressed are of longer-range significance for Europe as a whole.

Decisions have to be taken concerning the tasks, responsibilities and organization of the planned new European security forum, and its sub-systems.

The first item on the agenda is undoubtedly to ensure the ratification and implementation of the CFE treaty, which have become problematic because of political reorganization and confrontations within the former USSR. Rapid attempts need also to be made to encourage all CSCE member states to comply with the fundamental rules of the CFE treaty, and, particularly, national limits on armed forces and obligations as regards information, notification and verification. Yet, although public opinion expects faster progress in achieving additional reductions of forces, this seems unlikely to happen.

As far as conventional forces are concerned, the transformations in Europe have reduced the inclination to pursue treaties which reduce the limits set by the CFE. There are several reasons for this:

- concerns about military imbalances have lost their political weight for the reasons outlined above;
- for budgetary reasons further arms reductions are already taking place in most countries on a unilateral basis without any treaty guarantees of reciprocal reductions;
- the financial, economic and social problems of arms reduction are becoming clear, particularly in the former USSR. Disarmament takes time; additional commitments to arms reduction therefore seem unwise;
- military planners are currently disorientated because of the uncertainty about the future tasks, budgets, structures and international regulatory framework relating to armed forces;
- it is practically impossible to work out an acceptable general formula for

setting further national reduction quotas, in view of the heterogeneous security policies of the new system of European states;
- moreover, politically difficult problems, which up to now have been shelved, are liable to emerge during treaty negotiations on further reductions: should the CFE solution ('from the Atlantic to the Urals'?) be extended over the whole territory of the former USSR and likewise to the USA? And should naval forces, which have hitherto been left completely aside, also be included?

All these aspects indicate that conventional arms reduction decisions are more likely in the future to be decided unilaterally in the first instance, probably however within a continuing process of mutual information, consultation and political commitment between countries with security policy links.

This trend can also be discerned in European nuclear arms control, for example in the contrast between the form and content of the Washington INF (Intermediate-Range Nuclear Forces) Treaty, and President Bush's decision to withdraw and destroy all US land-based tactical nuclear weapons. The American step was taken unilaterally, although the Soviets did reciprocate as expected. No treaty obligation was entered into however, and no verification guarantee was provided.

The adoption of these initiatives was informed by a number of considerations:

- changes in the strategic situation in Europe mean that tactical nuclear weapons (SNF) have become dispensable. Their maintenance and su pervision is expensive, and they are politically controversial in the European countries where they are stationed;
- the interest to quickly support the remaining central Soviet power structure, to ensure that it would maintain its political control over the nuclear weapons in the republics;
- global nuclear non-proliferation policy needed to be supported and extended in view of the acute dangers faced in this matter;
- the move prevented talks on SNF from beginning a possible groundswell towards the complete withdrawal of American nuclear weapons, i.e. a denuclearization of Europe.

Under the auspices of NATO, the USA will continue to station in Europe aircraft capable of carrying nuclear weapons, and provide weapons for these aircraft and those of their allies. There is no inclination to bring this remaining component for a minimum deterrent approach into arms reduction negotiations.

The west European nuclear powers, France and Great Britain, would also be reluctant to take part in talks of this kind, because they are concerned about possible spill-overs. If reduced, their national strategic nuclear forces would no longer be operationally viable. As far as SNF are concerned, the British are adopting the same policy as the Americans. France is still holding on to her Hades rockets, but is, in fact, producing them only in small numbers and is not deploying them in operational units. Both countries possess aircraft capable of carrying nuclear weapons (and reserve the right to equip them with a nuclear stand-off capability). Such systems should be available not only for possible sub-strategic employment tasks, but also to increase the flexibility of their strategic potential.

In addition to the question of further arms reduction, European arms control policy in the New Security Forum after Helsinki – hopefully building on a solid base of CFE and CSBM provisions and probably in conjunction with an 'open skies' aerial monitoring system – will probably revolve around the following tasks:

- improving and supplementing information and notification measures, so as to facilitate the transparency of military potential and activities (e.g. by incorporating such aspects as defence budgets, armed forces planning including arms development and procurement, arms exports, as well as mobilization exercises for personnel and equipment, and deployment exercises);
- improving and supplementing stabilizing measures to regulate and limit military activities by adding to the CSBM catalogue and the dispositions of the CFE treaty;
- discussing and regulating the structure of armed forces, in order to limit stability-threatening capabilities for large-scale offensive operations, particularly if they can be launched after only a short period of preparation.

In addition to these familiar arms control tasks, the new political situation in Europe offers the opportunity of developing a far broader network of cooperative military relations. Indeed such relations are already beginning to develop as a result of the requirements of arms control provisions, particularly as regards the exchange of military observers and inspection activities. But they could take on a new dimension, so that in the future the prospect would not consist essentially of mutual monitoring, limitation and confidence building, but would involve military cooperation in the performance of common security tasks (peace-keeping tasks; the application of international sanctions to enforce international law under the aegis of the UN Security Council; training, planning and exercises, and common operations staffs; catastrophe prevention and relief; the safeguarding and destruction of NBC weapon potentials).

It seems, however, that European arms control will have no more than a limited effect on the new instabilities and threats faced in and around Europe.

The prevention of external threats is a task which requires the use of the whole range of instruments of foreign policy. The composition and scope of the international norms, organizations, institutions and cooperation networks which are important for this purpose must have a global dimension. This applies, for example, to preventing the proliferation of weapons of mass destruction, and controlling exports of arms and technology. However, a determined policy on the part of the European nations and their American partners could be crucial for the effectiveness of such world-wide arms control efforts.

As far as Europe's neighbouring regions are concerned, it would be advisable to recommend stability-building rules and agreements in the context of a policy of wide-ranging cooperation, and indeed to work towards concrete agreements between the European and non-European countries concerned.

Another important point is to ensure that the arms control measures which need to be developed within Europe from a security viewpoint should not impair Europe's ability to defend itself against external threats, preserve its interests and carry out its obligations worldwide.

Nor is arms control likely to play any major part in facilitating the prevention and management of conflicts inside and between countries in European crisis zones in the Balkans and eastern Europe. Recent developments in Yugoslavia and the republics of the former Soviet Union have demonstrated that conflicts of this type usually develop and grow within the state itself. They are, moreover, not primarily fought out in a confrontation between regular, heavily armed military units. Up to now, arms control measures have not covered paramilitary units and light weapons, but have been limited to categories of major military equipment and to the balance of forces between states.

Clearly, therefore, a different kind of institutional approach is needed, using other instruments and resources, if stabilization efforts are to succeed. A significant factor here is the consensual development within the CSCE of a code of conduct and provisions of international law which enable effective international crisis prevention, provide mechanisms for the peaceful resolution of disputes, and offer the possibility of imposing sanctions (with UN backing where necessary). The process of arms control could provide support for such political efforts to limit the scope of conflicts, and to prevent internal conflicts from spreading over borders and becoming interstate conflicts.

- One possible approach would be to include the forces of the states concerned in the mechanisms of international cooperation.
- Measures could be taken to increase transparency and boost stability in neighbouring zones (such as mandatory notification of, and restrictions on, military exercises, mobilization and concentrations of forces). This would make it easier to obtain early and unambiguous indications of critical developments, lessen the likelihood of an escalation through misapprehension, and define thresholds at which international crisis mechanisms would come into play.

Yet all of the above depends on the willingness of the states to cooperate in creating a viable security system in a new Europe. This means a readiness to place collective interests before particular concerns of states. In the meantime, the member states of the Atlantic alliance seek continuity, while adapting to the process of unification in western Europe, the transition in the former party-states, and to the potential of the CSCE forces. The security framework of a divided Europe has gone. A new one, for a greater Europe, has yet to be negotiated.

REFERENCES

Binnendijk, Hans 1991: The emerging European security order. *Washington Quarterly*, 14(4), 67–81.
Buzan Barry, Kelstrup Morton, Lemaitre Pierre, Tromer Elzbieta and Waever Ole 1990: *The European Security Order Recast: Scenarios for the Post-Cold War Era*. London. Pinter.
Daalder, Ivo H. 1991: *The CFE Treaty: an Overview and an Assessment*. Washington DC: The Johns Hopkins Foreign Policy Institute.

Hassner, Pierre 1990: Europe beyond partition and unity: disintegration or reconstitution? *International Affairs*, 66(3), 461–75.

Hyde-Price, Adrian 1991: *European Security Beyond the Cold War*. London: Royal Institute of International Affairs, Sage.

Lellouche, Pierre 1992: *Le Nouveau Monde: De l'ordre de Yalta au désordre des nations*. Paris: Grasset.

Walker, Jennone 1991: New thinking about conventional arms control. *Survival*, 33(1), 53–65.

DOCUMENTS

Charter of Paris for a New Europe, an Era of Democracy, Peace and Unity. (Declaration by the Heads of State or Government participating in the Conference on Security and Co-operation in Europe). Paris, 21 November 1991.

Rome Declaration on Peace and Cooperation (by Heads of State and Government taking part in the Extraordinary Meeting of the North Atlantic Council, Rome, 7–8 November 1991). Europe Documents. Brussels: *Agence Internationale d'Information pour la Presse*. Doc. no. 1744, November 1991 art. 3.

Final Communiqué issued by the North Atlantic Council Meeting in Ministerial Session, 19 December 1991 (*Atlantic News* no. 2382, Annex I, 21 December 1991).

North Atlantic Cooperation Council Statement on Dialogue, Partnership and Cooperation, 20 December 1991 (*Atlantic News* no. 2382, Annex II, 21 December 1991).

The Alliance's New Strategic Concept, Europe Documents. Brussels: *Agence Intenationale pour la Presse*. Doc. no. 1742, November 1991, art. 25.

20

Europe's architecture and
the second Russian revolution

Alexander Naumenkov

As if not satisfied with the upbeat pace of radical change in Europe, history chose yet again to accelerate the march of extraordinary events on the continent. The abortive coup attempt in the USSR effectively signed the death warrant of the Soviet empire and ignited an avalanche of dramatic events, the international repercussions of which may be only guessed at. The Soviet Union, or rather what once comprised it, plunged into a transition period of unprecedented proportions. This period overlapped with the transition already underway in Europe in general, shifting the focus of attention on new dimensions of the ongoing pan-European debate.

The whole, once-mighty and menacing Soviet image, as well as the very position of this country in the world are being overturned. For the transitional period the former Soviet Union is unlikely to pursue some kind of an active foreign policy stance, characteristic of a superpower position; it can be expected to be more akin to third world status. In short, the former Soviet Union will find itself on the receiving end of the international–political game, without much room for manoeuvre. In the progressing crisis of national-state identity the economic needs will be taking priority at the expense of political, not to mention military–political interests. The move towards interdependence, which has already materialized in the emergence of Baltic states and the curious entity fielding such varied labels as Union of Commonwealth Republics, or the Confederation of Independent States is bound to cultivate the variability and diversity of actors, establishing themselves on the remnants of the old empire. For example, the Baltics will certainly be looking for deep integration, first and foremost, with west Europe; this can also be said of the other western sovereign republics such as Ukraine and Belorussia. Russia, too, will be attracted westwards, though the necessary qualifications must be made about the potential role of partners geographically elsewhere, most notably Japan. But what about the so called periphery of the late empire? Would it not be correct to predict that they will be turning more to the east and south in their international aspirations, rather than towards Europe, putting faith in what has become popularly known as the South Korean model of development for Kazakhstan, or in Turkey as the patron of Turkish-speaking people? Geographical distances and ethnic empathy do matter, whatever the political rhetoric might be.

Several key considerations could be drawn from all this, when trying to assess the possible impact of the August democratic victory in Russia on the new Europe. These developments in their own way sped up the continental integration process, if only through the quantitative increase of parties involved. The victory of democratic elements in August builds up the premium put on the principle of mutual trust and equality. Institutionally, the impact is clear. The existing pan-European organs, whatever their drawbacks and limitations, are entrusted to cope with the changes only because no other arrangements currently exist. In the new, extremely volatile conditions these organs will feel direct pressure for increased responsibilities that will simultaneously push them towards their own radical reform.

The Baltics have already become fully-fledged members of the CSCE, and NATO is probably next. Even more crucial is the role of the EC: the state of evolution of this organization draws immense interest now as a prototype for economic and other integration among the republics of the former Soviet Union.

The potential benefits on offer to the EC are evident: under their own rules the Communities can hope to establish with time a large market right in their own continental back yard. But there are uncertainties too. The EC in particular will have to deal with a much lengthier queue of states asking for aid and striving for membership – a factor that could overtax its reserves. The EC has yet to settle the problem of eastern Europe and now there are additional numbers to count. There is also a special futuristic note of caution: if indeed the Soviet sovereign republics–states eventually evolve into something along EC lines then they could present a potent competitive threat to the EC itself. In this respect it may become tempting for the EC to follow a selfish, arms-length relationship with its new, but inferior east European partners – i.e. on the one hand not to give away 'too much too soon', but on the other not to ignore them totally, so as to minimize additional sources of instability.

This vortex of political, economic and humanitarian events in Europe was precipitated by the advent of *perestroika* in the Soviet Union, clearing the way for the overhaul of the continental international order, which had been based on postwar bipolarity. Subsequently the sweeping tide of democratic revolutions in central and eastern Europe, the reunification of Germany, the acceleration of the CSCE process have all laid down the cornerstone in the foundation for a future pan-Europe of universally accepted values and ideals.

The transition to this new European entity will by no means be smooth or quick. The main challenge, as in any transitional period, lies in ensuring adequate dynamic stability, in combining continuity with change in a time when the old traditional ends of underpinning the regional system of international relations are quickly becoming obsolete, but have yet to be firmly superseded by new viable mechanisms.

To facilitate the drive towards the new Europe there has been no lack of policy-making visions. Leaving aside the pros and cons of each individual scheme, the current pan-European debate leaves little doubt as to the emerging consensus on the feasibility of Project: United Europe. Emphasis has steadily shifted towards working out practical action blueprints and calculating tangible moves towards achieving this crucial goal.

The concept of a wider Europe could be analytically approached from various angles. Perhaps the most obvious one is alongside the dimensions (or 'baskets') of the CSCE. This is the broad approach pursued below, but some qualifications are necessary. Less attention is paid to the military/ political aspects – an obsessive component of European relations for many years. The emphasis is placed more proportionately on the general institutional architecture, on the economic and on the humanitarian dimensions of a pan-Europe. Finally, the approach below is inevitably biased in the sense that it is informed by a prejudice in favour of the desirability for republics of the former Soviet Union to be a part of the new Europe under construction. It is also informed by an acute appreciation of the dangers for them being excluded to the periphery.

Shaping Europe's common architecture

The late 1980s witnessed major headway in the process of de-ideologizing and de-militarizing the system of international relations in Europe. New political thinking in the Soviet Union, combined with positive attitudes in the west, heralded a radical shift in the disarmament process. The military leverage became subordinate to the political one in the resolution of outstanding issues. As the cold war environment became increasingly obsolete, the threat of military aggression in Europe declined dramatically. Simultaneously, revolutionary changes in the countries of eastern and central Europe have made defunct the category of the 'brotherly socialist community', stripping the Soviet-led alliance of its major asset. As a result of all these new developments, the whole fabric of international political relations on the continent finds itself in a state of flux.

The inherent characteristics of the transitional period on the way to the new Europe, most notably the dynamic flow of events, magnify the importance of preserving the diversity in institutional forms of European interaction and of maintaining a wide institutional landscape on the continent. The near future may hold many delicate twists and turns in the European situation. This or that structure in the emerging common architecture of the new Europe could be quickly elevated to the top of the institutional hierarchy or, quite the opposite, be relegated in relative importance.

The reshaping of Europe's common architecture starts with the development of multilateral instruments. The CSCE acts as a sort of 'umbrella' structure, aimed at ensuring interaction between all member states regardless of their participation in other, narrower institutional arrangements. Moves towards a pan-Europe envisage, quite clearly, substantial changes in the CSCE. Quantitatively, these changes have been manifesting themselves in the galvanization of meetings and discussions within all the respective 'baskets' of the process. Qualitatively, the main direction of change lies in broadening the scope of activity – and especially in further institutionalization – of the CSCE process. In this respect the Paris Summit stands out as a landmark. Apart from signing the Paris charter, CSCE members agreed to set up a small permanent secretariat in Prague to coordinate their activity,

to establish a conflict prevention centre in Vienna and to regularize ministerial meetings.

However, there are obvious limits even for a changed CSCE to assume the
main responsibility for collective security in a wider Europe. For one thing,
the CSCE process is governed by consensus politics. During the cold war
era the quest for consensus was, ironically, more straightforward, the main
objective being to align the views of two hostile country blocs. Sometimes
this proved hard, but still the task was greatly simplified by the relative ease
with which unanimity was achieved within each respective bloc. Perhaps
this was most evident in the east, where the Soviet Union called the shots
in the 'socialist community', with other members 'naturally' zealously agreeing and supporting the Soviet stance. But in the west, too, it was the United
States that took the lead on most crucial issues, since the EC, just as it
was starting to develop as a potent political force, ran into a bout of
'Europessimism'. Any potential disagreement between the west Europeans
and their powerful Atlantic partner was sacrificed on the altar of bloc
solidarity. Thus, the paradox of cold war bipolarity was that, however
detrimental to the international political structure of Europe, it facilitated
the consensus mechanism of the CSCE.

With the disappearance of clear-cut bipolarity, consensus politics, as
practised by the CSCE, acquire new and not necessarily advantageous
features. Today there is a high possibility of the revival of national state
individualism as more and more countries (notably of the former socialist
bloc) start to ascertain their sovereignty externally (Baranovsky, 1990, pp.
6–10). The case can be illustrated by the curious episode that took place
in the run-up to the Paris Summit. Liechtenstein objected to the establishment of a CSCE secretariat in Prague on the rather obscure grounds of old
property claims, and the situation had to be dealt with according to the
consensus principle. Some would shrug off this episode (perhaps justly) as
minor and irrelevant. However, it could be a prelude of much more serious
things to come. In early 1991 the Soviet Union rejected the possibility of
CSCE hearings on human rights abuses in the Baltics, where developments
took a regrettable turn. Similar attitudes might intensify.

So what could be hoped from the CSCE in dealing with the emerging threat
of nationalism in parts of Europe? Would the consensus principle prove
effective in negating this potential danger and providing an adequate level
of security? If this line of argument is pursued, the CSCE comes out with
serious handicaps. Its mechanism will probably evolve primarily to improve
interaction between member states and to work out unified rules of conduct,
rather than negotiate would-be conflicts between participants (Baranovsky,
1990, p. 28).

Another point for deliberation is that consensus, coupled with large membership, makes the CSCE susceptible to the dangers of over-bureaucratization.
In the 1970s and 1980s a feature of the CSCE process was the low efficacy
of adopted decisions because of the lack of an adequate control mechanism
for their implementation. In this regard the further institutionalization and
structuralization of the CSCE is a necessary and timely step. But the crucial
question is how far and to what extent?

The inception of new institutional arrangements must not become an
obsessive aim. Institutionalization should be approached with a dose of

healthy scepticism, always with an open eye for suitable alternatives. Among the latter most viable is the utilization of the existing structures to the benefit of the new Europe. Indulgence in the creation of new institutional arrangements may lead (directly or indirectly) to an undesirable overlap with the functions of other multilateral structures, existing and maturing in Europe. These structures could be ahead of the CSCE in their respective weights of influence. Perhaps the clearest examples to date are to be found beyond the purely military–political dimension of the CSCE.

To take the economic agenda first. The economic aims of a wider Europe can undoubtedly be pursued through the establishment of a special independent 'arm' of the CSCE, which would target priorities in cooperation. In some respects its activity could model that of the OECD and incorporate on an autonomous basis the existing multilateral European economic organizations. However, accepting the long-term feasibility of such a step, it seems premature if placed in the context of the current transitional period in Europe. The process of economic reforms in the east of the continent has yet to run its full course, thus confining the search for wider homogeneity to its infant phases. Moreover, there is still considerable inertia towards the existing system of economic organs in Europe. In these circumstances a completely new role may be awarded, for example, to the Economic Commission for Europe – a regional UN organ with a range of important functions.

Another illustrative case can be drawn from the humanitarian sphere of European cooperation. Here an organization of considerable prominence is the Council of Europe. The latter has comparative advantage over the CSCE, being a more coherent organ with a wide network of institutional arrangements (conventions, agreements etc.). The countries of central and eastern Europe, as well as the republics of the former Soviet Union, are bound to become full members of the Council of Europe at some stage. Why then not gradually shift the bulk of humanitarian aspects of the new Europe towards this structure, making an inventory of CSCE's third 'basket'?

To sum up, progress on the way to the new Europe could be speeded up not through institutionalization of the CSCE proper, but through increasing coordination and consultation between all existing prominent European institutions. Even more important is to work out some common strategic line among them, which would be in tune with the changing Europe. Precisely here the CSCE may step in by cementing ties in its capacity as the widest representative forum on the continent.

As mentioned earlier, the direct consequence of the formation dichotomy in post-war Europe was the emergence on the continent of large, ideologically hostile blocs. NATO and the EC were mirrored by the Warsaw Pact (WTO) and the CMEA respectively. With bipolarity rapidly becoming a historical relic, the overcoming of bloc division is crucial to the political healing of Europe.

The intricate dynamics of NATO and the WTO proper is a separate subject for discussion. The issue of concern here, however, is their role during the transitional period to a new European architecture. NATO has proven its military-political durability and is largely perceived as a much more viable institutional structure. Its eastern counterpart, on the other hand, expired in summer 1991. Changes in central and eastern Europe had hung a large question mark over the WTO's necessity. Nonetheless, the issue of how to salvage the useful functions of the WTO during the transitional period and to formulate appropriate policy options featured prominently in the European debate in its military–political dimension. Suffice it to say here that the general direction of the desired change had been described as democratization of the pact arrangements and its transformation into a purely political organ. The various factors facilitating such a move were enumerated (Karaganov, 1990).

The arguments for the WTO's transformation were based on political rationale. Unfortunately, relations within the WTO were governed not by rationale but by perceptions in member-countries. And the dominant perception, both in public opinion and official circles, was that of the WTO being a crude and outdated instrument of Soviet aims. Historically, this was an understandable price to pay for the damage inflicted on inter-block relations by the 'Brezhnev doctrine' and actions preceding it. So it proved impossible to foster a sense of common interests among pact members in the highly emotional phase of reassessing relationships after the events of 1989–90. To this was added growing doubts that the Soviet Union could retain its integrity and act as a unified entity on the international arena. Not least, the lack of any realistic ideas about transforming the WTO, until it was too late, made the institution's demise inevitable and irrevocable.

Bearing all this in mind, the only correct course of action for the Soviet Union itself seemed to be not to create the impression that it was the most interested party in retaining the WTO (however modified) at all costs. It was more advised to 'let go', facing the short-term consequences and opting for the medium- and especially long-term benefits.

One such potential benefit was that the absence of policy 'straps' on WTO's preservation would put pressure on NATO to transform itself. Furthermore, NATO may feel freer to pursue the aim of becoming a broader European structure and, subsequently, of cementing the future security system on the continent. In this respect, it is interesting to point out that many east European countries expressed the desire to strike some kind of association agreements with NATO – a wish which was in part realized at the November 1991 NATO Summit in Rome. These agreements could evolve into full membership status. For the former republics of the Soviet Union, incorporation into the NATO framework – either directly or via the CSCE – is much more difficult for a variety of reasons. It will have to involve, among other things, massive swings in official perceptions as well as broad public opinion, and not just in the former party-states but most of all among members of the Atlantic alliance.

Another legacy of bipolarity in postwar Europe was the creation of large opposing integration groupings, notably the EC and CMEA. The economic aspects of the European integration process are addressed below. However, there are issues that transcend the purely economic dimension.

In any discussion of the common architecture of the new Europe the role of the EC is paramount. The reasons for this lie both in the economic and political tracks of west European integration (Shenayev and Tsimailo, 1990). Most notably, the impact of the single market on the EC alone would be multidimensional, heralding the gradual transformation of markets from a national to a supranational level, with greater coordination of economic, and ultimately social and foreign, policy. The EC is clearly destined to become the 'centre of gravity' for the emerging international system on the continent, gradually drawing other European states into its orbit. Such scenarios appear to be more and more plausible, and are much more realistic than the options based on utilizing the structures of the CSCE and the Council of Europe. Despite wide and democratic representation these latter structures are inferior to the EC in their operational capabilities, not to mention their economic and financial weight.

Among the multilateral structures NATO and the EC today are a crucial factor in shaping the common architecture of the new Europe. Thus, two main configurations may be seen as constituting the backbone of the new European architecture. Whatever the role of the CSCE, their respectful weights of influence is a serious factor to take into account for the former Soviet Union and its erstwhile allies in entering the new Europe. On the one hand, given the important role of American involvement in European stability and the changing relationship between the USA and the former USSR, it would appear that the primary structure emerges around the USA–NATO–Germany axis. On the other hand, some west European countries favour the notion that ex-Soviet and east European interests will be best pursued through support for the France–EC–Germany axis.

Obviously, these are scenarios on the level of crude perceptions, and a lot will depend on the ability of the parties concerned to face up to the challenges of the new Europe. For the time being, any clear choice can be safely ruled out. But for the former Soviet Union in particular the second scenario appears to have a slight upper edge for two main reasons. First, it is the EC that has the most leverage in influencing the situation in the eastern part of the continent. Second, this scenario opens up new possibilities in fostering links with the WEU, whose role in Europe could increase.

Even if one is to draw the line here as to the key institutional players shaping Europe's common architecture, a mixed projection emerges. Widening the theatre of operations for one infringes on the rights of others. In this respect, any arbitrary actions aimed at the artificial redistribution of existing prerogatives of the relevant actors is at odds with the true interests of the new Europe. It is counter-productive in any way to set one institutional arrangement against the other. In the current volatile environment each supporting bloc in the new European architecture should be laid down individually. In other words, a 'parallel line' approach is needed, when all key institutions should be allowed to strengthen, to develop in their own way without interference and stimulation of a 'tug of war' in terms of functions and responsibilities. Ultimately, these institutions will as certain themselves to the benefit of a streamlined and viable architecture of a new Europe.

It is quite logical that the current debate on Europe's future architecture revolves primarily around the CSCE, NATO, EC and, to an extent, the Council of Europe. This fact, however, should not over-shadow the importance of lower – grassroots – level of institutionalization for the new Europe. This level is complementary to the whole structure of the emerging pan-European architecture.

After the end of World War II Europe witnessed the rapid extension of the network of regional organizations, dealing with virtually every aspect of contemporary society. Their numbers today run into hundreds. Unfortunately, the cold war has left its distinctive mark on the development of these organizations. The 'normal' response during the period for the east was either to 'mirror image' the west by conceiving some exclusive arrangement of its own or to refrain from membership altogether. As a result, at the grassroots level Europe has to cope today with institutional duplication in some spheres, on the one hand, and heavily curtailed functional arrangements, on the other. The continuation of this stance is detrimental to the process of shaping Europe's common architecture, especially if one considers such important sectors as communications, transport, energy, financial services etc. Without achieving a higher degree of homogeneity in them, the new regional institutional system will be hardly complete.

There are huge possibilities for the quick rationalization on the grassroots level of pan-European architecture. The main initiatives should come from the eastern part of the continent. Narrower arrangements are to be abandoned in favour of wider representative ones, either through merger or re-entry. The first signs of this approach have already manifested themselves. In autumn 1990 the International Radio and Television Organization (OIRT), which unites national radio and television networks of former socialist states, expressed the wish to merge with the European Broadcasting Union in the next three to five years. These two organizations were the product of the split in a single institutional arrangement for Europe four decades ago. Now that the reasons for this split no longer exist, the way has been cleared for establishing a single European broadcasting and television organ with membership by all European national organizations. The general assembly of the European Broadcasting Union has already modified its charter so as to enable national networks of former socialist countries to join. Czechoslovakia, Poland and Hungary have exercised this option. Others, the successor states of the Soviet Union inclusive, should follow suit.

Working the economic jigsaw puzzle

Economic aspects of a wider Europe have recently been giving cause for growing concern. It is true, that the new international climate makes the prospects for the economic healing of Europe brighter than ever before. The situation today contrasts sharply with that of the first detente, when the 'enemy image' was the prime official argument for necessitating autarchic trends in then socialist bloc and for constant vigilance on the part of the western alliance. But the new political situation in Europe serves not only to raise hopes for overcoming the economic divide of Europe; it makes crystal clear the vital need of radical economic change within the eastern part of the continent. There are no illusions as to where the economic future lies. The basis of a truly democratic new Europe can only be a uniform market economy, or at least an economy built along similar principles. This is not an aim in itself. If there are to be continuing gaps in prosperity and living standards between the two parts of Europe, then the concept of the free movement of people, goods and capital is considerably undermined. Massive one-way migration for economic reasons may tempt the more prosperous European states to erect barriers to stem the flow of refugees from the east , which estimates put at anywhere from 10 to 30 million in the next few years.

The countries of eastern Europe have been quick to embrace the concept of a market economy. Changing the mix between the public and private sectors to the latter's advantage is inherent in the action programmes of the absolute majority of their political parties and movements. Though there may be variations in the pace and depth of reforms, the 'westernization' of east European countries on economic grounds is already a fact of life.

For the former Soviet Union the turn of events in eastern Europe only accentuated the country's economic difficulties. The absence of a market economy as an integral element of its acceptance in the new Europe could not be compensated by a flurry of diplomatic and political activity. In the military–political dimension the Soviet Union had a lot to offer: the very geopolitical position and the huge nuclear capability ensured a Soviet participation of sorts in the new Europe. Culturally, too, the USSR had long established itself as part of the common European heritage. However, all this was not enough to ensure a place in the future pan-European economic organism. Throughout the 1990–1 debates in the Soviet Union over successive economic plans, there was always a risk that a gap would quickly emerge between the principles governing economic activity in the Soviet Union, and those followed (or accepted) by the rest of the European continent. For most of the postwar period the Soviet Union existed in what has been appropriately labelled as 'quasi-isolation' from the world economy (*Izvestia*, 25 April 1990). However, it was at least able to take comfort in the cushioning effect of the 'socialist economic community'. Throughout 1990–1 the Soviet Union risked complete isolation from the economic mainstream by pledging obsessive loyalty to discredited economic principles.

The basic laws which comprise the market system are universal, and to try to override or distort them will not yield productive results. Naturally, they do not preclude specific country features of economic organization, notably in the public and private mix. The republics of the former Soviet Union are bound to have a very high social welfare component built into any reform package, but the official desire to opt for some third economic way (i.e. 'planned market economy') represented a self-pursued cul-de-sac.

Domestic economic reforms in eastern Europe provided a strong impetus for external change. The retaining of the CMEA lost any sense, following the Soviet-led move to switch to trading in world prices and in convertible currency. By mutual consent it was agreed to formally disband the CMEA in June 1991 and to set up a new structure under the provisional name of the Organization for International Economic Cooperation (OIEC). However, the establishment of this successor organ remained an open question because of contradictions between its potential members regarding the strategic tasks of the organization. The underlying hope is that it will function along internationally accepted principles for bodies of this type. It is quite clear that economic multilateralism cannot and should not be imposed, confining itself only to areas of true common interest.

The rapid switch to payments in hard currency only further entrapped former CMEA members in a web of illusions. Their hard currency reserves were depleted rapidly, and the countries in question prefer to spend them in the west anyway. The situation was complicated also by the confusion in decision-making, brought about by the ongoing reforms of their foreign trade sectors. The overall result: the vacuum which was created by the rapid disintegration of traditional links was not institutionally filled to any satisfactory level.

At the time of the major transitions in the former party-states, there was an awareness that something had to be salvaged from the old system in order to cushion the transition to a market-oriented relationship in foreign trade. For example, suggestions were made to split trade in two parts: to reinstate intergovernmental trade on the basis of bilateral clearing arrangements and, simultaneously, to develop free trade on the level of enterprises (Grinberg and Legay, 1991).

Meanwhile, priority in economic relations between former CMEA members could be given to bilateral forms of cooperation. As the process of 'westernization' of east European countries gathered pace, their foreign trade structure would change accordingly. However, the traditional economic links between them and the former Soviet Union were likely to retain a fair degree of inertia for the coming few years, the former being much more dependent on exogenous factors in their economic security. Simultaneously, one could expect growing differentiation among east European countries in the implementation of their economic restructuring. In these conditions further complications in relations could be avoided if the republics of the former Soviet Union and east European countries negotiated bilateral agreements, establishing areas of free trade. Gradually, as the network of bilateral agreements expanded, the concept of a more comprehensive free trade zone, uniting future OIEC members, could be put on the agenda. A free trade zone is a long-established and historically-tested form of economic cooperation. The proclamation of such an aim and subsequent moves towards it are also important in light of recent arrangements reached by the east European countries with the EC and EFTA.

The pivotal role of the EC in the economy of a wider Europe has been established beyond any doubt. It is the longer-term reaction on the part of the EC that will prove to be crucial in this respect. What is remarkable today is how the EC has taken the issue of eastern Europe on board at a time when it is burdened with the single market programme, and when it is resisting widening (Wallace, 1990, pp. 458–9). Apart from agreeing to channel immediate financial and technical aid, the EC has decided to conclude with the east European countries special association agreements. The creation of a free trade zone has been quoted as one of their prime features. Mutual steps aimed at conceiving such a zone are expected to be asymmetrical in character. Initially, the EC will take the lead in abolishing unilaterally the existing trade restrictions. Later, the countries of eastern Europe will introduce legislative changes so as to comply fully with the economic standards and norms set by the EC. Association agreements are bound to take the countries of eastern Europe into the mainstream of the European economy, but will not necessary culminate in full EC membership.

A further point to be mentioned is that several east European states have managed to sign declarations of economic cooperation with EFTA. Poland and Hungary, in particular, seek to negotiate agreements which would allow entry into the free trade zone. The EFTA members, as in the case of the EC, have expressed willingness to an asymmetrical response during the initial phase of transition to new arrangements. Considering the fact that negotiations between the EC and EFTA on the creation of a European economic area are drawing to a conclusion, then the countries of eastern Europe have every reason for optimism. Their imminent arrangements appear foolproof. They are to have formal association agreements with the EC, backed by similar, though separate, arrangements with EFTA. In the case of the EC and EFTA merging into a common economic area, the countries of eastern Europe are assured active participation from both ends.

A distinctive feature of the current phase in integration tendencies in Europe is the emergence of various sub-regional groupings, membership in which transcends the existing institutional arrangements. Perhaps the most prominent among them is the so called 'pentagonale'. It includes Austria, Hungary, Czechoslovakia, Yugoslavia and Italy. Efforts have been also made to constitute the so called central European trio, to institutionalize co-operation in the Balkans.

These sub-regional organizations have a certain role to play in sorting out the economic jigsaw puzzle of Europe and are likely to portend more comprehensive arrangements. However, their importance should not be exaggerated. Arrangements of this kind are characteristic of a transitional period, and thus are likely to be transitory in nature. The success of sub-regional schemes largely depends on participation by one or two powerful members of the EC and/or EFTA. Likewise, arrangements, involving east Europeans only, are unlikely to hold firmly together. The incentive for the inferior economies to participate in sub-regional schemes is to gain a 'foot-hold' in west European markets and their institutional framework. Such schemes are a means to play through on a minor scale practical scenarios for the future; they enable the east European countries to get valuable experience. Once the institutional outlines of the economy of the new Europe become clearer, the importance of sub-regional arrangements for wider integration is likely to decline, and they will probably confine themselves to facilitating cooperation between neighbouring states.

There is no doubt that the developments outlined above contribute positively to the overcoming of the postwar economic divide of Europe. They are to the benefit of all European states, the former Soviet Union inclusive. The latter, however, has put forward initiatives of its own, namely the concept of 'common European economic space'. It would be unjust not to place it in the debate on a pan-Europe.

There can hardly be objections to the creation of a common European economic space as a long-term ultimate goal. But its achievement implied a readiness to dismantle the structures of the command economy, and embark on the trilogy of reforms for moving to a market system, and that are required by the international institutions. Without a freeing of prices, privatization of state assets, and control over monetary variables and government outlays, the transition to market economies could not be effected.

Two further observations could be made with regard to the Soviet concept of a 'common European economic space'. First, it creates an impression of exclusiveness and is liable for criticism akin to 'Fortress Europe' arguments in the case of the EC's single market. The European economy is part of the world economic system. In other words, there are certain limits to promulgating regional exclusiveness. Moves of the former party-states to enter the economy of wider Europe should be coupled with a more active stance on the world economy. Among other things, the successor states of the Soviet Union would have to aim at joining the IMF and the World Bank, and at ensuring conformity with the basic provisions of GATT.

Secondly, the grandeur of the concept of a 'common European economic space' appears to be somewhat at odds with the immediate tasks of the transitional period to the new Europe. Perhaps intentions should be scaled down, and the search for unanimity conducted on a more modest, sectoral (functional) level. Illustrative of this kind of approach is the idea of Dutch Prime Minister Mr Lubbers, floated in summer 1990, to establish under EC auspices a common energy community for the whole of Europe. Later, bearing in mind the difficulties of the transition period, it was targeted to the adoption of a European Energy Charter. The latter is envisaged as a form of code of conduct for all interested parties (Commission of the European Communities, 1991).

The project was adopted in winter 1991, underlining the fact that the energy sector is the backbone of any economy. In this capacity it may form the first practical link between the old Soviet economy and that of the EC, not only serving to restructure the Russian energy industry, but giving the much-needed push to other branches of industry. It may also provide the initial impetus to wider European economic integration not dissimilar to the seed-bed role that the European Coal and Steel Community had played for deepening west European integration. Thus, Russia, as a country with enormous energy potential, must undertake special efforts through various channels to ensure active participation and an adequate role in finalizing the provisions of the charter.

The human dimension: opening new horizons

Humanitarian issues in general, and human rights in particular, for decades presented a major obstacle to improving east–west relations, let alone striking some common arrangement for the continent as a whole. The situation changed drastically once the countries behind the old iron curtain released the ideological brakes in their societies, proclaiming the subordination of class interests to universal human values. The full democratization of Europe was set on a firm footing. New horizons for humanitarian cooperation opened up as the nations of Europe advanced from the concluding document of Vienna in 1988, through the Paris and Copenhagen conferences under the third 'basket' of the CSCE, to the Paris charter of 1990. Each subsequent step brought with it greater tangibility of practical results.

To facilitate the radical changes in the humanitarian sphere, in summer 1989 the Soviet Union and France jointly put forward the initiative of creating a 'European legal space', which stimulated a favourable response in many quarters. In essence, it closely resembles the aforementioned concept of a common 'economic space': being more a vision of longer-term goals and objectives, the Soviet–French initiative raises new questions, rather than providing answers to existing ones. However, there are positive differences too. Firstly, sheer political will, aimed at realizing this initiative, is likely to yield faster results than in the case of the economy. Secondly, the idea of a 'European legal space' goes far beyond the humanitarian sphere from where it originated. In scope of coverage this idea 'infiltrates' every dimension of pan-European cooperation. A new Europe is in need of gradual rapprochement and mutual adaptation of legislation and legal norms in CSCE members across the board. Thus, progress towards a common legal space becomes an important prerequisite in laying down the firm legal foundation in every dimension of a pan-Europe.

The human dimension proper appears to be the one where progress towards achieving a higher degree of homogeneity could be relatively quick. Because of the variable legal geometry in Europe today, the most urgent task is to target priorities and to introduce appropriate methods of harmonization. The forming of a 'European legal space' in its human dimension could involve moves on two levels – the national and pan-European (supranational) ones respectively.

On the national level the main task is to ensure that domestic legal systems in CSCE states comply with the relevant international accords (notably, the Helsinki Final Act, the Vienna concluding document and the Paris Summit charter). Naturally, success will come only if all concerned states undertake purposeful unilateral measures to this effect.

The successors to the Soviet Union, quite clearly, are expected to take the lead in carrying out the necessary domestic legal reforms so as to discharge their international obligations. Few would deny that with *perestroika* and *glasnost* the Soviet Union had made substantial progress in this direction (Zagorsky and Kashlev, 1990). However, the crucial test of intentions was the legal package, governing the immigration procedure, the right to leave the country and to come back. The prevailing perception was of the Soviet Union dragging its feet on this issue – a perception that became increasingly valid considering the time factor involved. Full compliance of the successor states to the Soviet Union with the Vienna document was made more practicable, following the collapse of authority in the old Soviet Union. But liberalization of their societies remains a task that lies ahead for all of them.

Harmonization of national laws affecting human rights and civil liberties should also involve a comprehensive comparative analysis of legal systems and concepts throughout Europe. This would enable one to keep abreast of the more advanced practices and to exchange experience. Such analysis, in turn, could be greatly assisted by two discretionary factors. Firstly, by the free flow of information. For example, legal harmonization could be accelerated by the introduction of a single computer network, based on the latest achievements in information technology. Computer linkage could be negotiated within the CSCE process and lead to the creation of a relevant institutional framework. A 'seed-bed' role might be played by the already existing structures, such as the Documentation Centre on human rights of the Council of Europe in Strasbourg.

Secondly, within the general framework of comparative analysis it is important to study the numerous instruments of the Council of Europe. They include the European Convention on Human Rights of 1950, the European Social Charter of 1961, the European social security code of 1964, the declaration on the freedom of speech and information of 1982 etc. Perhaps the first of these instruments can be singled out as the most important one. Even though this Convention is restricted by membership in the Council of Europe, it can be safely assumed that this obstacle is of a provisional nature. Joining this convention would bring the successor states of the Soviet Union and the countries of eastern Europe closer to the mainstream of existing European standards and norms on human rights. It would also pave the way for adherence to the already existing (within the framework of the Council of Europe) regional mechanisms for protecting human rights and to the jurisdiction of the European Court on Human Rights, which undertake control functions with regard to regional humanitarian agreements.

The second factor clearly shows that national measures to form a European legal space must be complemented by moves supranational in their character. This level includes the establishment of new political–legal structures for Europe as a whole, as well as the pan-European widening of existing regional bodies and agreements.

REFERENCES

Baranovsky, V. 1990: Europe: emergence of a new international political structure. Moscow: *IMEMO Discussion Paper*, no. 5, August.
Commission of the European Communities, 1991: *Communication from the Commission on European Energy Charter*. Com (91), 36, 14 February.
Grinberg, R. and Legay, K. 1991: Stupeni dezintegratsii: problemi torgovli SSSR s Vostochnoy Evropoy. *Nezavisimaya Gazeta*, 21 May.
Karaganov, S. 1990: Problems of USSR's European Policy. *International Affairs* (Moscow), 7, July, 72–80.
Shenayev, V. and Tsimailo, A. (eds) 1990: *EC na rubezhe 1990-tykh godov*. Izdanye MZNTI.
Wallace, William 1990: The Soviet Union and Eastern Europe. *Futures*, June, 451–61.
Zagorsky, A. and Kashlev, Y. 1990: La dimension humaine en politique. *La Vie Internationale*, 3, March, 68–80.

21

Europe between nostalgia and utopia

Ian Davidson

For nearly fifty years after the end of World War II, Europe was organized on principles which were clear, unmistakable, and apparently stable. With the collapse of the Berlin Wall, those organizing principles have been swept away without reprieve, and Europe is hard put to know what can take their place. In such circumstances, it would be the height of rashness to make firm predictions, let alone firm prescriptions.

One of the unstated assumptions behind this book is that there will be, or at least there should be, a new order to take over from the old; and that it is the task of Europeans to help construct that new order. These assumptions are beset by two opposite but equally dangerous temptations: an apologetic nostalgia for a stable past, and an idealistic hope for a utopian future. Both temptations are understandable, but neither is likely to lead to a reliable path through the maze of uncertainty in the post-cold war era.

No liberal could possibly regret the end of the cold war, the unification of Germany, the recovery of national independence by the countries of eastern Europe, or the declared ambitions of Mikhail Gorbachev to restructure the Soviet Union. And yet there is no mistaking, in many western discussions of the new Europe, a note of nostalgia at the passing of some of the old simplicities. Soviet repression was an evil curse on the people of the eastern half of the continent, and the rigidities of communism imposed terrible economic costs; moreover, the entire continent suffered from the constant fear of nuclear war. And yet one side-effect of the manichean struggle, was that the liberal countries of the west were constantly required to re-examine, and re-affirm, their deepest common values; the democracies of western Europe were virtually compelled to stand together in defence of freedom, and in alliance with their friends from North America. The Soviet threat traumatized two whole generations; but without it there would have been no North Atlantic alliance, and there would have been no Helsinki process for human rights, for arms control and for national reconciliation.

The obverse of this kind of ambivalent nostalgia, is a utopian hope for the future (as well as being also a guilty regret for the past). The west has largely prospered, rich and free, throughout these decades of communist failure and authoritarian repression; now that the iron curtain has collapsed, the time has come for the west to share its advantages, material, political and cultural, with its historic cousins in the other half of Europe. These impulses of philanthropy and fraternity are often reflected in proposals that the countries of eastern Europe should join the countries of western Europe as fellow members of some brave new pan-European organization.

Which pan-European organization would be the most suitable, is a question where opinions differ. The Council of Europe is manifestly an institution which attracts the aspirations of all those governments in the east which wish to prove their democratic and human rights credentials. Equally clearly its functions are rather narrowly focused, and most east European governments appear to regard it primarily as an obligatory staging post on the way to a more rewarding destination. The Conference on Security and Cooperation in Europe (CSCE) offers a larger agenda of pan-European business, starting with the negotiation of arms control in Europe. To some people it appears to offer the potential foundations for a potentially broader European security regime. The fact that the CSCE already includes all the countries of Europe, plus the two superpowers, is an additional recommendation to pan-Europeanists; the fact that all decisions are taken by unanimity in the CSCE suggests that it may not have an easy future as a policy-making institution.

The most utopian believe that all European countries have a natural vocation to become full members of the European Community. They are also joined by those who are hostile to the development of the Community in a more federal direction, and who see the rapid enlargement of the membership as a sufficient safeguard against that danger.

These large organizational schemes do not seem to me the most helpful way of thinking about the new Europe. I do not believe that there is any way of recapturing an old order which has now disappeared, nor that there is any ready-made template for a new pan-European order which can usefully be summoned into service. In its present state, Europe is composed of so many contradictory elements, that it is entirely premature to think about any unitary scheme. Some of these elements may be conducive to the formation of a larger order, but others seem to be leading ineluctably towards a greater disorder; there are factors of strength, but there are also factors of weakness; there are points of similarity, but there are also points of great dissimilarity. If a new European order emerges, it will be as the largely unplanned product of these contradictory cross-currents, and we cannot expect to predict the end of the process.

Some basic principles

On the other hand, we can attempt to identify some of the principal forces which will be at work. I suggest that there are five major vectors which will help determine the future shape of Europe. This is an entirely schematic list which does not pretend to be comprehensive, or indeed anything more than suggestive, for the purposes of argument. There may well be other factors of real importance which I have not taken into account, but at least I would argue that all the following five vectors will be relevant:

Vector 1: the basic players: the nation states

I start with a statement of the obvious: the basic building-block of the new Europe will continue to be the nation-state, because the nation-state is so far the only unit which is in a position to exercise, across the complete gamut of political activity, the essential functions of political organization and legitimacy. Anyone who advocates the erection of a multinational or pan-European scheme must start from this basic building-block. This requirement does not, of course, invalidate the appeal of multinational or international organizations or arrangements, let alone the supranational ambitions of the European Community; but it is obvious that multinational organizations will be designed primarily if not exclusively to satisfy the interests of the nation-states which are members, and not to suit the interests of some other group, let alone those of the world at large. The prospectus of any multinational scheme must explain what will be its advantages to the individual national-states which make it up.

Vector 2: the leaders and the winners: France and Germany

By an extension of the first principle, those European nation-states that are most powerful, most successful, and therefore most necessary to the organization of the whole, will have a disproportionate influence on the organization of Europe. Not merely will they necessarily play a leadership role in the relevant constellation of nation-states, but the arrangements they subscribe to will in the first instance have to satisfy their national interests. It seems obvious that Germany and France must come into this leadership category; it seems possible, but by no means certain, that Britain and Italy may come into it; by its sheer size, the successors to the Soviet Union should be a major force, but it may be incapacitated from any significant influence on the organization of Europe, by the process of domestic economic and political disintegration.

Vector 3: the dominant groupings: the European Community, Western European Union, the Council of Europe

A similar hierarchy applies to the various institutionalized groups of states: the most successful and most powerful groupings will become the most influential vectors for the organization of the future Europe, and their interests will be dominant in the creation of new arrangements. Almost inevitably, the European Community will play a leading part, partly because it has already proved remarkably well-adapted in institutional terms to a rapidly expanding role, but mainly because its member states wish it to have an expanding role. It is important to make this distinction: the vitality of the European Community does not yet have any real endogenous political existence, but still springs almost exclusively from the political will of the member states.

There are other multinational European institutional groupings, which will play significant but secondary roles. They include the Council of Europe, the Western European Union, the Economic Commission for Europe, NATO, the Organization for Economic Cooperation and Development, and the European Free Trade Area. Some have real vitality, and some may look forward to a vital future. What distinguishes the European Community from the others, is the wide range of its competences, and the prospect that these competences will continue to expand almost indefinitely in the future.

Some people believe that the Community will gradually acquire the characteristics of a federation; but the fact remains that the Community is still essentially composed of nation-states, which will continue to have very diverse levels of economic development, and even more diverse political and socio-economic systems. If there is movement towards a federation, it will be a novel kind of federation, which would have to take account, and take care, of these diversities. This idiosyncrasy has been exemplified by the negotiations on economic and monetary union, in which the political need to ensure that all member states remain together, is in a permanent state of tension with the monetary/economic need to hold open the possibility of differentiation between the strong and the weak.

Vector 4: the losers: COMECON, Warsaw Pact, Soviet Union

At the other end of the spectrum, are the institutional groupings which sprang out of the communist system or the cold war or both; their future, and even their very existence must be in jeopardy. The Warsaw Pact is being disbanded; and despite attempts at modernization, it is hard to see any sensible future role for COMECON (the CMEA) as the economic clearing house for the Soviet Union and its former communist allies in east Europe.

By the same token, there must be serious doubt whether the successor states to the Soviet Union can exert much influence over the construction of a new European order. The Soviet Union is the major casualty of the end of the cold war: it has lost its previous ideology, it has lost its 'external' empire, it seems to be in the process of losing its 'internal' empire, and it is having the gravest difficulties in constructing a new future for itself. This is not to say that the Soviet Union, or whatever succeeds it, has become insignificant; far from it. Even if all the peripheral Republics were to break away, the remaining Russian core Republic would be a very large country, whose land mass, population and military power would be decisive in defining the eastern frontier of Europe. But in the wake of a secular political defeat, and in the face of an equally colossal economic failure, the Soviet Union's influence on the re-ordering of the rest of the continent is likely to be marginal, at least until its internal struggles have come to rest.

Vector 5: dominant values: democracy, prosperity, education, health, art, security; and dominant systems: supranationality, interdependence, law, pluralism, devolution, social market economy, free markets and free trade, arms control

This is just an illustrative list of the kind of values and systems which are likely to be salient in the future European dialectic. If it is representative of the issues which may dominate intra-European relations in future, then that may be partly because these are the issues which are already dominating the agenda in the post-cold war world, but mainly because these are issues which correspond to the values and preoccupations of the winners of the cold war, the leaders and the dominant groupings.

If these five categories can reasonably be thought of as the leading vectors in the construction of a new Europe, then there may be some general conclusions of principle which can be drawn. In the first place, it seems plausible that the winners will get stronger, and will be in a powerful position vis-à-vis the weak, at least for a while; this means the leading nation-states (Germany and France), and the dominant groupings (the European Community). In other words, the future of Europe will be determined more by the strong than by the weak. This thought may not be comfortable for the winners, and it will certainly not be popular with the losers; but it is realistic.

By the same token, it is quite likely that these vectors will converge and reinforce one another. The dominant values, systems and issues are those which characterize the leading nation-states and the dominant groupings. Not only have they contributed to the winning of the cold war, but their dominance of the postwar agenda is an almost automatic consequence of that victory.

Even if this list of the primary vectors should be near the mark, however, it would still leave us in some perplexity, because there are so many factors at work, and so many actors at play, that it is not easy to integrate them into a consistent pattern. Many of those who have tried to wrestle with the problem of the future European order, have resorted to images and metaphors as a device for feeling their way through the maze.

One suggestion proposes two opposite images, as metaphors for two fundamentally different approaches towards the future of Europe: they picture the antithesis as one between architects and gardeners. An architect is a man who believes that the collapse of the Soviet empire has created the conditions for such a clean sweep, that it is possible to devise a new grand design from the ground up. A gardener is a man who believes that the only option is to rely on the growth and incremental development of what already exists.

The most striking feature of this evocative pair of images is how American it is, in the sense that it implies an outside actor: a new order will be created from outside by an architect who will build, or nurtured from outside by a gardener who will fertilize. This is the kind of viewpoint which over the past forty-five years has become natural in the capital of the western superpower.

In reality, however, it may be more illuminating to think in terms of internally-oriented images. The probability is that Europe will not be re-ordered from outside by either of the erstwhile superpowers, but from within by the Europeans, in response to the power vectors suggested above. If metaphors are helpful, a more suggestive pairing might be the antithesis between a cooperative cafeteria and a nuclear or extended family.

The notion of the cooperative cafeteria corresponds to one version of the architectural image, in the sense that it implies an all-encompassing arrangement for the whole of Europe. It would be symmetrical and egalitarian, in the sense that everyone could belong on equal terms; it would be an order of modest ambitions, because it would have to take account of the vast differences between different states; it would be an arrangement of very low integrative power, in the sense that there would be little institutional delegation of power to the centre; but it would offer a wide range of choice, in the sense that the participants could pick and choose on an ad hoc basis what they wanted to do, and with whom.

The contrasted image of the nuclear or extended family has quite different connotations. Membership is selective and exclusive and at least partly inherited, not universal; the organization is hierarchical, not egalitarian; the commitment is integrative, wide-ranging and progressive, not optional or selective.

Between these two images, it seems clear to me that the family metaphor corresponds more closely to the lines of force which are present in Europe today. Many European countries, including many of those which are not now members of the European Community – either because they are members of the European Free Trade Area (EFTA) or because they are former satellites of the Soviet empire – would prefer a European order which resembled a cooperative cafeteria. No doubt the United States, Japan or Russia would also prefer a cafeteria Europe, because that is the kind of arrangement which would tend to minimize the coherence and independence of the Europeans, and therefore to maximize their own influence. But the options for the future European order will be drafted primarily by the Europeans, and more by the winners than by the losers; and the winners in Europe are countries which, for the time being, seem to be opting for the family model.

Ever since 1985, the European agenda has been following the family model of integration, first with the programme for the single market of 1992, and then with the accelerating process of negotiation of new treaties on Economic and Monetary Union and Political Union. This process has been driven primarily by the two winners and leaders of the European system, France and Germany. Their long history of conflict and rivalry compels them to seek a new relationship through the mediation of European integration.

But within these broad strategic choices, the detailed agenda for the process of European integration is determined by the values and systems which prevail in those European countries which are dominant in the European integration process. These are the values set out in vector 5 above: democracy, prosperity, education, health, art, security; and the corresponding systems are supranationality, interdependence, law, pluralism, devolution, social market economy, free markets and free trade, arms control.

These fundamental values are essentially driven from below, in response to the demands of voters, consumers, producers, parents, children, individuals; they are not determined arbitrarily by the interests either of states or of rulers of states. Since this is the hierarchy of values which has brought about the renaissance of western Europe and presided over the collapse of the Soviet system, it is logical to assume that it will continue to be dominant in the new era. Since they can only be integrated through a democratic process, it is also logical to assume that they will continue to be expressed primarily through the legitimacy of the democratic nation-state, as a component of a cooperative structure of nation-states.

The three main dimensions of the new Europe: security, politics and economics

In the light of these basic principles, I now propose to discuss how they might interact with the three main dimensions of the new Europe: security, politics and economics. I shall start with security, partly because this is the dimension of Europe which was most important before the fall of the Berlin Wall, partly because it remains salient for a number of European countries in the shadow of the turbulence in the former Soviet Union. I shall then discuss, more briefly, the purely political and economic aspects of Europe. I shall conclude with a composite discussion of these three dimensions as they relate to the European Community.

The security dimension 1: NATO

In the immediate aftermath of the fall of the Berlin Wall, governments of both east and west were particularly preoccupied with questions of defence and security. Military confrontation had for forty-five years been the most intense expression of the division of Europe. It was inevitable, therefore, that security would continue to be an urgent issue. Could existing defence arrangements survive at all? Would they need to be transformed into something more appropriate? Or would it be necessary to construct entirely new arrangements to take their place?

Under vector 4 above, I suggested that the losers in the post-cold war era would be likely to include any institution which owed its existence either to communism or to the cold war, and that the biggest losers would be those institutions which were linked both to communism and to the cold war. By this principle, the Warsaw Pact's demise in the course of 1991 comes as no surprise. But the same principle should also weigh, if less heavily, against NATO, and even against the Conference on Security and Cooperation in Europe (CSCE), otherwise known as the Helsinki process.

First, the questionmark over the future of NATO. The disintegration of the Warsaw Pact, the progressive withdrawal of Soviet forces from eastern Europe, and the Soviet Union's explicit renunciation of any hostile intent towards the west, are all factors which appear to remove the plausibility of a Soviet threat, and thus to undermine the justification for the existence of NATO. But NATO's residual saving grace is that its member governments wish to keep it in being, because they are not yet quite persuaded that the military threat has entirely disappeared for good. In the first place, the successors to the Soviet Union will remain a military great power in terms of conventional as well as nuclear forces, and their future behaviour could not be deduced with any confidence from the reassuring discourse of their leaders.

That discourse is consistent with the sweeping withdrawal of Soviet forces from eastern Europe, which would make it extremely difficult for any deliberate large-scale attack to be mounted against western Europe. It was sustained in the winter of 1990–1 by the Soviet circumvention, on a massive scale, of the spirit of the 1990 Vienna conventional arms reduction agreement, apparently boding ill for the potential future course of Moscow's foreign policy. From April 1991 at the latest, the Soviet Union slid towards domestic political conflict and dismemberment on a scale which would seem to rule out any confident assumptions about the future of Moscow's foreign policy.

NATO's first dilemma, therefore, is that the geostrategic indicators are pointing in contradictory directions. The old Soviet military threat has almost certainly disappeared, and is unlikely to return. At the same time, there could emerge new threats, or at least new risks, from an ex-Soviet Union which is going through a period of turmoil and disruption, and whose future policies are largely unpredictable.

NATO's second dilemma is that its strategy of forward defence with large, militarily integrated ground forces based in Germany, makes no sense once the Soviet Union had withdrawn all its troops from eastern Europe, and the Warsaw Pact had in turn been disbanded. Forward defence implies a threatened eastern frontier; but under the new conditions of détente, NATO's eastern frontier would now face onto a group of east European countries which manifestly pose no threat, and which are in the process of disowning their alliance with Moscow. The new entity emerging in the place of the Soviet Union could again become a committed adversary of western Europe, at least in the long run. If this were to be the case, western Europe would need a new defensive strategy to meet that potential threat, bringing the countries of eastern Europe directly under NATO's wing.

NATO's third dilemma is that it is an alliance of unequal members which has been held together during the past forty years primarily through the intensity of the external threat. With the disappearance of that threat, the bindings of NATO's military and political structures are bound to be loosened and may fall apart. It is not clear that NATO continues to have a pressing military need for integrated military structures with an integrated command; and it is not clear whether integrated military structures with an integrated command will remain possible after all the members of the alliance have sharply reduced their force strengths under the NATO umbrella.

The central issue here is the role of the United States. During the cold war, American leadership of NATO was virtually determined by the scale of the nuclear and conventional military threat from the Soviet superpower; without the backing of US conventional forces based in Germany, and without the ultimate guarantee of the strategic US nuclear deterrent, western European countries did not believe that they could have resisted a determined Soviet push. In practice, American leadership was effectively expressed through the integrated military structures of NATO, with an integrated command exercised by an American general.

In the new conditions of détente, however, the US leadership role in NATO becomes much less self-evident as a matter of operational necessity. The US troop strength in Europe is likely to fall sharply, either because forces deployed from Germany to the Gulf during the course of 1990–1 will not return, or because the federal deficit will require large savings on the defence budget. America's European allies will also reduce their conventional forces, but the overall effect will be a relative decline in the American share of NATO's ground troops, and a general thinning out of all NATO troops on the ground.

It may be possible to retain the principle of military integration, despite this thinning out; but the case for an American commander-in-chief may not answer the same compelling logic in the new circumstances as in the old. And yet it is not clear that the US will be prepared to make a continuing military contribution to NATO's defence of Europe, on any other terms except those, however anachronistic, of leadership and command.

If America is on one side of the NATO medal, France is on the other. America may not be prepared to stay, except on the old terms of leadership and integration; but those terms were part of the reason why France withdrew from NATO's military structures in 1966. If they are maintained unchanged into the new era, they are likely to guarantee that France would continue to stand aside from a modernization of NATO. And yet if NATO is to reconstruct its credibility, so as to compensate for all the new uncertainties, it will be vital for France to become, once more, part of the process.

Given these mutually exclusive points of view, logic would suggest that the NATO equation is insoluble except by the insertion of one or more additional variables. NATO without America would soon cease to exist; NATO without France would, in the new era, seriously lack credibility; therefore, the Europeans and the Americans must look for new security structures going beyond the narrow confines of NATO. Two additional variables which could conceivably answer the purpose are already available: the pan-European Conference on Security and Cooperation in Europe (CSCE), and the nine-nation Western European Union (WEU). Both should have some role to play, but CSCE will necessarily have less of a role than WEU.

The security dimension 2: the CSCE

There are essentially two distinct security functions which could be performed by the CSCE. The first is that of a free-standing, self-contained system providing adequate collective security for the whole of Europe, but also covering the ex-Soviet Union, the US and Canada. The second is that of an ancillary system of reassurance for western Europe, providing a low level security framework for the whole of Europe, but a complementary security regime which would be significant for NATO.

Many people would welcome the first of these two functions, if it were available, because it would imply a qualitative transition from an era of confrontation, defence and armed forces, to an era of cooperation and civilian security. Cynics would argue, on historic principles, that this kind of collective security has never and can never provide genuine security, because it is too utopian: it assumes a readiness by all member governments to live and let live, it denies the many historic examples of aggression, and above all it cannot move into the higher gear of defence if an individual strong country launches the attack. But the immediate objection is that a collective security system can only work with a stable constellation of satisfied states. The ex-Soviet Union, however, is not stable, its component parts are not satisfied and no one can be confident that it would continue to be restrained by the moral obligations of a collective security arrangement. Moreover, it is not clear that all the countries of eastern Europe can be classified as satisfied states, whereas there are ample historical reasons for friction over frontiers and minorities.

It follows that the CSCE cannot, in present circumstances, be a free-standing, self-contained system offering adequate security guarantees for the whole of Europe. It can perform many useful functions as a mediation system between the countries of eastern and western Europe, and it might perhaps perform a useful ancillary function for the security of western Europe. But it cannot by itself perform an effective security function.

The alternative is a low-level security regime for the whole of Europe which would complement other political and military security arrangements, notably the defensive alliance of NATO. Some western strategic analysts believed they could see, in the far-reaching conventional arms reduction treaty negotiated in 1990 in the context of the CSCE, the ingredients of a potential solution to NATO's triple dilemma. This potential solution was based on the proposition that east–west conventional arms control would itself become the starting point for a new defensive strategy, which would enable NATO to renew its existence as a specifically western alliance, but without in any sense calling in question the new principles of east–west cooperation.

This potential new strategy for NATO promised to be the exact opposite of its predecessor. The existing NATO strategy was based on the assumption of east–west confrontation, was intended to provide, in permanent readiness, a credible defence against a potential Soviet *blitzkrieg*, which might be launched at any moment out of the blue; but a replacement strategy, starting from the new assumption of east–west reconciliation and reliable arms control, could be based on the expectation that hostilities would be preceded by long-range warning, running to months or even years.

The west, like the east, would have to run down its forces in place in line with the new arms control agreements. It would be able to do so in perfect security, because the intrusive verification regime of the new arms control regime would ensure that an attempt by any potential aggressor to mobilize forces which would be adequate for an attack, would automatically involve breaking the agreements, and would thus give the rest of the world time to prepare an adequate defence. A long-range warning strategy would even make it possible for the US to withdraw most of its ground forces from Europe, without jeopardizing the security of western Europe or the integrity of the Atlantic alliance, provided that the arms control verification regime was sufficiently watertight, so as to leave time for an American policy of mobilization and transatlantic reinforcement.

The advantage of this potential new strategy was held to be that it need not require the western allies to think or talk in terms of a single pre-designated enemy: they could still keep their defensive alliance, and yet provisionally start to treat the Soviet Union as a supposedly friendly country. There would be a multilateral arms control treaty signed and verified by all CSCE member countries, and there would be an equal level of forces in place, too low to permit a standing-start attack; any country that infringed the treaty would be designating itself as 'the enemy', because it would be giving what was tantamount to a long-distance signal of intent to go on the attack.

Unfortunately, the plausibility of an international security arrangement as the framework for a new defensive strategy for NATO was thrown into disarray even before the 1990 CFE treaty had been signed, by the deliberate decision of the Soviet Union to circumvent the spirit of the treaty on a massive scale. This circumvention coincided, as mentioned in previous chapters, with Gorbachev's alliance in the autumn and winter of 1990–1 with the reactionaries in the party-state apparatus. On the one hand, the Soviet Union appeared determined to retain – admittedly by transferring them to the far side of the Ural mountains – much larger inventories of heavy weaponry than western governments had anticipated. On the other hand, the Soviet Union proposed to exempt substantial military forces from the scope of the treaty by relabelling them as naval units. As a result, therefore, the US administration and Congress were reluctant to ratify the treaty, which therefore could not become a basis for binding international commitments, nor for intrusive verification, nor for a new western defensive strategy.

Of course, in the absence of ratification of the CFE treaty, the west could still hope to assemble some of the ingredients of a new NATO long-range warning strategy, by relying partly on the Soviet withdrawal from eastern Europe, and partly on the countries of eastern Europe as involuntary contributors to the security of the west. Having formed an unwilling glacis for the Soviet Union during the cold war, against the putative threat from the west, they would now become the equally unwilling glacis for the countries of western Europe in the post-cold war era, against a potential threat from the east.

In any case, the countries of eastern Europe progressively negotiated bilateral agreements with Moscow for the removal of Soviet troops; these treaties had the potential of becoming indirect substitutes for the provisions of the CFE treaty. This would not have been a really satisfactory foundation for NATO, however, since these bilateral agreements would put no limits on the presence of Soviet forces in the western military districts of the Soviet union, and would not be subject to verification by western inspectors. By the same token, it would be an even more unsatisfactory security arrangement for the countries of eastern Europe.

In the event, the Soviet Union – following Gorbachev's reconciliation with Yeltsin in April 1991 – made compromise concessions over disputed aspects of its interpretation of the conventional arms control agreement, such that the CFE Treaty could reasonably be ratified by the western powers, and notably by the US Senate. But the more fundamental weakness of a new western long-range warning strategy based on a conventional arms control treaty, however, is that it really depends for its plausibility on the political stability and predictability of 'the other side'. In reality, governments would be individually reluctant, and collectively unable, to agree on the triggering of mobilization and reinforcement measures, simply by a pre-determined infringement of the provisions of an arms control treaty. In reality, they would also want to be able to form strategic judgements in the light of a spectrum of political indicators as well, in which stark intelligence about troop movements would be amplified by assessments of political intentions.

But these essential characteristics of political stability and predictability are exactly what is absent, and likely to be absent from the former Soviet Union for some time to come. In the first place, western governments cannot assess the relative influence of hawks and doves in Moscow, nor can they tell how disgruntled military officers are able to fashion policy. Even more fundamental uncertainties derive from the power struggle over the component parts of the Soviet empire, leading to a redistribution of the components of military power, both nuclear and conventional, and to tensions which in turn could erupt into unpredictable military conflict.

As a result, if NATO is to be transformed in ways which would enable it to survive in the post-cold war era, it would have to assume, and indeed actively promote, cooperation from the Soviet Union's successor states. Any failure to give NATO a peacetime face-lift without cooperation from Russia, would face real problems along two independent axes: the European–American axis, on the one hand, and the political–military axis, on the other.

The security dimension 3: Western European Union

The other factor which can be mobilized as an additional variable for the NATO equation, is Western European Union (WEU). Unlike the CSCE, WEU is a natural partner for NATO, in general because it is by its inheritance a wholly western institution, but specifically because it was the midwife for the creation of NATO: it was the admission of West Germany (and Italy) to WEU in 1954, which opened the door for the inclusion of these two countries in NATO, and thus for the creation of the Atlantic alliance that we know today.

In the very act of creation of NATO, WEU lapsed into a deep trance of inactivity. Periodically, enthusiastic Europeans invoked the idea that WEU should be the vehicle for the expression of a European defence identity; periodically, European governments rhetorically endorsed this idea; in practice, nothing happened for thirty years. In the mid 1980s, however, the European Community entered a new phase of vigorous activity, and at about the same time the member governments started showing an apparently genuine interest in a reactivation of WEU. They held regular joint meetings of Foreign and Defence Ministers, they mobilized WEU in 1987 for the coordination of European naval patrols in the Gulf during the Iran–Iraq War, and they enlarged the membership of WEU from seven to nine, by the admission of Spain and Portugal.

By 1991 a broad-based consensus was emerging that, if western Europe were to develop a specifically European defence identity, Western European union was bound to play a prominent role. But this consensus barely concealed a long list of ambiguities: would the WEU role be primarily political and symbolic, or would it also be military and operational? Would the European Community be the locus for discussions on security, leaving WEU to be the locus for specifically European discussions of defence? Would WEU's defence responsibilities overlap with those of NATO, would they concern non-NATO interests in Europe, or would they be mainly directed outside the European area? Would the WEU be mainly linked to the European Community (as proposed by the French and Germans) or mainly linked to NATO (as proposed by Britain and the Netherlands)?

Some of these ambiguities were disposed of, first at the NATO Summit in

Rome in November 1991, and then more conclusively at the European Community Summit at Maastricht in December. In Rome the idea of a specifically European defence identity was given a more wholehearted endorsement by NATO (and thus by the US administration) than ever before; and in Maastricht the twelve formally agreed that Western European Union would be the body to implement such a European defence policy.

Many uncertainties were left hanging both by the NATO Summit meeting and by the Maastricht treaty summit. Did the western allies, and in particular the US really believe that NATO's new strategic concept would be enough to keep the organization alive? Did the twelve really intend to move towards a common European defence policy, or was this still, for the time being, mainly a rhetorical option? Would the development of a European defence option have the effect of undermining NATO; or would it, on the contrary, prove a constructive contribution to the indispensable reform of NATO, a necessary first step towards the restructuring of the transatlantic relationship between western Europe and North America? If the twelve seriously intended a European defence policy, would the proposal to enlarge and expand the Franco-German brigade become the core of a new European army?

The political dimension: the CSCE and the Council of Europe

If we turn from the security dimension of Europe to the political dimension, it is clear that there already exists a range of possible institutional frameworks with widely varying characteristics. Some, like the Conference on Security and Cooperation in Europe (CSCE), have a comprehensive membership covering the whole of Europe, but an eclectic and cautious range of activities. Others, like the Council of Europe, have a large (and growing) membership extending from western Europe into eastern Europe, but a rather narrowly specialized menu of activities. Others still, like the European Community, have a restricted membership but a comprehensive and growing agenda of functional competences.

The first institution on the list, the CSCE, otherwise identified as the Helsinki Final Act, has two significant strengths, but they are counterbalanced by two substantial weaknesses. Its first strength is its membership roll, which includes not only all the countries of Europe, east and west, but also the United States and Russia: this is a major asset in the eyes of those who hope for the creation of a pan-European structure, since in the CSCE they see a ready-made organization whose membership already fits the bill. Its second strength is that the CSCE has played a significant if subordinate role in the phasing out of the cold war, first in the promotion of human rights as a legitimate demand for the peoples of eastern Europe and the Soviet Union, second as the forum for far-reaching negotiations on east–west arms control.

The weaknesses of the CSCE are just as pronounced as the strengths. In the first place, it is manifestly a child of the cold war, and it is not obvious that it can easily create a new role free from those cold war connotations. In the second place, it has three quite distinct sets of attributes, which may have seemed to cohere together in the cold war context, but which today seem strangely ill assorted.

Its human rights provisions were designed by the west to exert pressure on repressive communist regimes; but as part of their voluntary abandonment of the communist system, most of the countries of eastern Europe are hastening spontaneously to improve their credentials in the fields of human rights, law and pluralistic democracy, and even the Soviet Union claims to be following suit. There is still a large gap in human rights performance between east and west; but with the end of the cold war, Europe may need to reconsider whether the pressure function of the CSCE is after all the best way of closing that gap.

The economic provisions of the CSCE have always been a dead letter, and they will remain a dead letter, because the CSCE is essentially an inter-governmental institution, and such an institution cannot deliver much in the field of multinational economics. It might have been adequate for early experiments in the field, like a simple free-trade area; but the world has moved on, and the competitive pressure of world markets today requires more than that. The gradual development of the European Community has demonstrated that the complex interaction between freedom and regulation, which is needed for the satisfactory operation of a multinational free market, demands a high degree of political integration and pooling of national sover-eignty according to recognized legal procedures. The CSCE does not have these characteristics, and is unlikely to acquire them.

The security provisions of the CSCE would seem to have borne spectacular fruit in the 1990 Vienna CFE conventional arms control treaty, which ought to secure such large reductions in Soviet armaments in the European theatre, as to rule out any prospect of a successful Soviet blitzkrieg attack on western Europe. But that treaty may turn out to be a one-off achievement, which may be over-shadowed by the more effective arms-control implications of a series of narrower agreements, such as the two-plus-four agreement on the unification of Germany, or the bilateral agreements for the withdrawal of Soviet forces from the territory of former east European allies.

Moreover, it is not clear that a negotiating process which is based on the premise of a balance between east and west, can long remain in business once the east–west balance is destroyed by the disintegration of the eastern alliance. No doubt there will continue to be a demand for further progress in conventional arms control, especially from east European countries whose occupation of a security limbo after the collapse of the Warsaw Pact will continue to generate demands for reassurance, in one form or another. But it is not easy to see the counting rules for a new multilateral arms control agreement which would pit Poland against Russia and at the same time against Germany, Hungary against Romania, or member states of the EC over the question of which side to support in the Yugoslav crisis.

In the end, the most serious weakness of the CSCE will be the mirror image of its greatest strength. Many people in east and west have aspired to the establishment of a new pan-European structure to consecrate the ending of the cold war and the division of Europe, and to cement cooperative relations between east and west; and many of them assume that the CSCE must be ready-made for the task. The problem is that this well-meaning aspiration is not necessarily self-explanatory in functional terms: what would a pan-European organization do, and how would it do it?

The Council of Europe has played, since World War II, a central and

historic role in western Europe as the primary common forum for democratic debate in Europe, and as the source of Europe's common jurisprudence in human rights. No doubt it will continue to play this role, and will
increasingly attract those countries of eastern Europe which are willing and
able to prove their credentials in the field of democracy and human rights.
But its activities are not likely to spread much into new fields, or to acquire
an extra integrative power. The eastern European countries which have
become members of the Council of Europe will look elsewhere if they want
to intensify or deepen their institutional links with the rest of Europe, especially with western Europe.

At the beginning of 1990, French President François Mitterrand floated
the idea of a European confederation; President Mikhail Gorbachev had
canvassed his concept of a 'common European home'. Neither leader spelled
out what he intended, however, with the result that it remains impossible
to know whether the proposals had any operational content to match the
rhetoric. Illustrative indications which have emerged from the French
Presidency suggest that 'confederation' may really be a grand word intended
to encompass all forms of ad hoc multilateral cooperation between eastern
and western Europe, as it might be on postal services or railways, on student
exchanges or environment, without any organized institutional commitment.
But the lack of any organic or institutional ingredient in his prescription
suggests that President Mitterrand at least may have been engaged primarily
in a limited holding operation, in which the gesture of goodwill and non-
exclusion is primarily intended to buy time without making any far-reaching
commitments.

One unavowed element in the French holding operation was to gain time
in the face of the growing pressure from many European countries, from
the east as well as from the west, to seek membership in the European
Community. This pressure for admission provoked a sharply polarized debate
inside the Community. Some conservative parties in the Community, such
as the ruling Conservative party in Britain and the Gaullist RPR party in
France, were only too eager to welcome new members, because they believed
that a larger Community would automatically be a looser and less federal
one. The French government, by contrast, became more and more committed
to a federal vision of the Community, especially after German reunification,
and was anxious to defer any consideration of new members until the
Community had taken an irrevocable step towards a more federal future,
in the negotiation of new treaties on economic and monetary union and
political union.

President Mitterrand continued to argue in favour of his concept of a
European confederation right up to the end of 1991. But it was already clear
that the Community could not for long delay serious consideration of admitting new members from western Europe. By December 1991 the twelve
had concluded the agreements at Maastricht which would mark the Community's future development with a politically federal stamp, so that applicant
countries would be forced to take this into account in advance of membership
negotiations. Moreover, these agreements included an advance commitment
to the development of a common foreign and security policy, with the long-
term goal of a common defence policy. So, although the list of applicant
countries was headed by two neutral states, Austria and Sweden, the

Maastricht agreements made it inevitable that membership would entail a profound revision, and perhaps an abandonment of their neutrality.

The political dimension: the European Community

I have tried to argue, or at the very least to suggest, that the next phase in Europe's history will be dominated more by the winners than by the losers, more by the strong than the weak. This is not an original reflection: it has always been true.

In the new circumstances of the end of the cold war, however, it often elicits a reaction of moral revulsion, as if we should expect that this better world was called upon to break free from the tawdry imperatives of *realpolitik*. These are no doubt laudable impulses; yet it seems to me reasonably clear that, if there is to be a new order in Europe, it will be built, first, on the leading nation-states of western Europe, and second, through them, on the European Community.

This is not just because no other institution can fulfil the function, but because the Community is already the dominant force in Europe, and will become even more dominant in future. But it seems to me salutary to keep in mind this dual foundation, of the nation-states and the Community.

In the first place, though the Community is the framework through which the states of western Europe can provide a new European order, it has not even begun to replace the nation-states as the motors of action or as the centres of political mediation. Second, the Community has been shaped very slowly and very painfully by the member states in order to serve their national interests, not in order to offer some altruistic gift for the rest of the world. Third, it is important to stress the ongoing nature of the process: the Community of today is not a finished institution, but is in a continuous process of construction; the treaties now negotiated will mark a qualitative step forward in this process of integration, but there is absolutely no reason to suppose that it will be the last step.

Because of the manifest power and prosperity of the European Community, a growing number of European countries are becoming interested in joining. Already, many voices are raised, expressing the view that these potential applicants have a moral right to join the Community, because they are European; providing, of course, that they satisfy the minimum entrance criteria of democracy and liberal economics. These are, in many cases, the same voices that previously argued that the new European order should be structured round the CSCE, until it became clear that the Helsinki process would not satisfy the demands of the applicants.

In fact, of course, there is no such thing as a moral right to membership of the European Community. The Community is being created by the member states, and is being fashioned to satisfy their common interests. These interests may continue to be satisfied if the membership of the Community is enlarged, but there is nothing self-evident about the proposition. The self-interest of the member states will certainly require them to take account of the interests of non-member states in Europe: as an emerging semi-superpower, the European Community cannot fail to be deeply concerned by what happens on the rest of the European map, since the disintegration of the Soviet empire in eastern Europe involves a degree of uncertainty which could easily jeopardize the security and the stability of the whole of Europe. But this does not mean that the only logical response to this uncertainty is the enlargement of the European Community to include all those European countries which now want to join.

Moreover, when moral arguments are being paraded, it is worth bearing in mind that there may be two sides to the question, and that the list of present and potential applicants is not limited to those countries in eastern Europe which have just been liberated like innocent damsels from Soviet oppression. It also includes countries, like Sweden and Switzerland which, while enjoying all the advantages of membership of the western community, have for many, many years built their freedom and their prosperity on their refusal to accept any obligation of solidarity with their European neighbours. There are also some other candidates, potential and actual, whose moral qualifications for membership in the new Europe of democratic integration are even more questionable. If there is a moral case for demanding that the Community admit new members, (which I contest), then at least none of these countries is in a strong position to lay claim to it.

The existing member states face two sorts of questions: first, they need to decide what kind of Community do they want to build, now and in the future; and only second do they have to decide whether they want to admit new members? Logically, these questions should be asked and answered in that order, because future members will necessarily influence, and may determine, the future nature of the Community.

With the Maastricht agreements, the twelve have answered the first of these questions in terms whose general implications are loud and clear. If the programme of economic and monetary union is carried out, the Community will manifestly be moving towards a federal system of economic government; and if the fixed deadline of 1999 is respected, they will get there much faster than any one had previously expected.

The parallel commitment to develop a common European foreign and security policy is surrounded with much greater ambiguity. This is partly because the ancient countries of western Europe have inherited distinct national policies, interest and customs, but more because it is impossible to prescribe in advance either the procedural or the substantive phases of the development of a common policy. It is safe to assume, therefore, that the convergence of foreign and security policies will be uneven, and may encounter very painful setbacks. But it is almost equally safe to assume that the twelve will be under continuous and growing pressure to move towards common policies; this pressure will come, not just from their new treaty commitments, but from the interactive nature of foreign policy. The twelve member states will progressively lose their freedom to exercise national foreign policies, because the rest of the world will demand common Community policies.

By answering the first question, about the future nature of the Community, the Maastricht agreements have opened the door to the second question, about enlargement; and it seems fairly clear that the reply to this second question will be positive, in the sense that a significant number (perhaps half a dozen) of west European countries may join the Community in the next few years. The paradox of the Maastricht agreements, however, is that a Community of 18–20 states will have to be more integrated and more federal than a Community of twelve members. Unless the Community simply abandons the objectives of the Maastricht treaties, therefore, it will have to go further down the road of majority voting than before.

Membership will not, however, be an available solution for all the countries of Europe which would like to join. In the first place, it will be many years before some of the countries of eastern Europe have attained the necessary degree of economic development and democratic stability. In the second place, even with extensive majority voting the expansion of the number of member states must at some point bring the Community to a complete halt.

On the other hand, it seems clear that the Community must establish increasingly close links with the other countries of Europe, whether as members or non-members, if only because this will be the unavoidable corollary of the Community's growing power. Moreover, it is possible that the Community will develop intermediate structures for its links with the rest of Europe, which would reduce the starkness of the antithesis between membership and exclusion. As it is, some analysts believe that the demands of integration will call into play a model of variable geometry inside the Community. In the case of economic and monetary union, for example, all twelve member states may be members of the governing system, but those which are weaker economically, or more reluctant politically, may be exempted from the full rigours of the practical implementation of EMU. In the same way, some non-member states might become quasi-members of some of the Community's specific activities, without becoming full members of the Community's political organs.

In other words, it is possible to imagine a new European order, which would have at its centre a polyvalent European Community with a tendency to move towards a federal structure with universal political competence; and round it a multi-tiered, variable-speed system in which most other European countries would be more or less deeply embedded. Such a variable-speed Europe might provide a security system which would meet the essential needs of the countries of eastern Europe, but without the conflictual overtones of a formal alliance aimed against any power, including the successor states of the Soviet Union. At the centre, the European Community would gradually move towards the development of a European foreign, security and defence policy, and would equally gradually take over responsibility for its own defence. But indirectly it would also assume an informal responsibility for the security of its European associates, which would be tantamount to a treaty guarantee, or might even take the form of a treaty guarantee.

Conclusion
Europe: from one containment to another

Jonathan Story

The great transformation in world politics during the years 1989–92 brought to an end the structure created after 1945 on the debris of war. Bipolarity was the key element to have disappeared. With the collapse of the party-states, and then of the Soviet Union, the order which had preserved Europe's divide vanished. More than ever, the United States, Japan, and western Europe constituted the three pillars of the world economy. The dollar remained the world's key currency. Fragmentation was accentuated with a further expansion in the number of states in the international system. An inherently unequal world was recorded in a sixty-to-one gap in the average living standard of people in the rich and poor countries (Programme des Nations Unies, 1992).

In the ensuing flux, there was little reason to consider that the dynamics of world affairs would continue to operate in the particular pattern that they had done in the past. Competition on markets between states and corporations continued to bind western Europe into interdependence with the United States or Japan. The United States had to continue to reconcile management of the national with the world economy, setting the context for world interest or exchange rates. The novelty lay in the substitution of the structure of bipolarity with the much looser configuration of a core and periphery. In western Europe, the change generated a competition between projects for more union, accompanied by an accelerated process of disintegration of old structures in central and south-eastern Europe. The forces of fragmentation at work in the Balkans, central Europe or in the former Soviet Union spread out into western Europe, while the dynamics of western European union drew the extended periphery towards the core (Wallace, 1990).

Nor was the rhythm set by the interactions of these dynamics comparable to that of the preceding European and world system. The previous interactions, as discussed in the opening chapter, proceeded at the slow pace of the structure within which they evolved. As processes of competition, emulation and subversion ran within definable bounds, the Europeans had the leisure to build up the society which had set such an overwhelming challenge to the party-states. The collapse of the old structure, and its replacement by open-ended processes, therefore came as a shock. People had to improvise, to follow the tides of change as best they could, and exploit the opportunities available. The initial response of western leaders was one of preservation. Only through cooperation could the system of interdependence built up since the world wars be secured. But the revolutionary changes happening about them occurred at a pace far in excess of the ability of institutions to adapt.

A central stake in the new Europe is the challenge posed by the speed and scope of the changes to national identities. The states, and the European Community, face – as Pierre Hassner writes – the double dilemma of identity, 'the temporal dimension of continuity and change, and the spatial dimension of closure and overture' (Hassner, 1992). The general crisis of collective identities, Hassner goes on to write, derives from the non-coincidence of their two dimensions of optimal size and sentiments of belonging. The states are not generally aware that the two dimensions do not coincide for politics, currency, defence or culture, but when they do, their citizens or governments tend to go on to the defensive, and become nostalgic for a lost or threatened unity. The Community then may become a scapegoat, or seek to redeem itself by trying to reproduce a mythical unity of defence or money and economy at the level of a continent.

It is this interaction between the nostalgia for a lost unity or aspiration to a future substitute, with the great transformation in European and world affairs, which forms the substance of this concluding chapter. The Maastricht Treaty was negotiated by the member states while Europe and the world figuratively changed shape. In method and concept, the design was conservative of Europe's society. But the ambitions to move to unity were constantly undermined by internal differences between the governments and peoples, and by the need to improvise as one new surprise followed on another.

The European union and the great transformation

With the events of 1989–92, the familiar dialectics between east and west, the two Germanies, and the two Europes gave way to a new dialectic provided by the interactions between the conditions of flux in world and European affairs, and the triple moves to integration in western Europe, self-determination in Germany and transition out of Communist Party states in central-eastern and south-eastern Europe, and the former Soviet Union. The military threat faded, to be replaced by disintegration and multiple disorders in Europe's expanding periphery. With the disappearance of the Soviet Union, western unity was challenged as familar landmarks vanished.

The roots of these rearrangements in European affairs and world affairs lay in the combination of two complementary factors. Competitive wooing and prodding of Germany by its western partners and by the Soviet Union to confirm its western identity, or to declare neutrality, helped to sap the foundations of the international structure created after 1945 on the debris of war. Gorbachev's common European home competed as a vision for a future including a neutral and non-nuclear Germany, with Reagan's rhetoric of a world free of nuclear weapons and Washington's iron will for a Germany bound into NATO. Delors launched the EC's internal market as one element of a neo-functional strategy, designed to widen EC competences, and to bind Germany into a westward-oriented European alliance. The prolonged German quest for national self-determination and state unity, culminated in the great transformation of European and world affairs, opening in 1989.

The end of the cold war confirmed the thrust to western European integration, just as the principle of self-determination prevailed in Germany. As William Paterson's chapter testifies, German unity proceeded apace with the move to European union. The principle had been the keystone of the western alliance since the Atlantic Charter of 1941, the Declaration on Liberated Europe, to which Roosevelt and Churchill had won Stalin's momentary assent at Yalta in 1945, and the Deutschland Vertrag of 1955, whereby the western allies renewed their commitment to support German state unity. The counterpart was the anchoring of the Federal Republic westwards. Once the compatibility of German state unity and European integration became evident in the course of 1989–90, German public opinion surged in support of European union. Similarly, about four-fifths of EC people interviewed favoured Germany's move to unity, a level of support which dropped momentarily when, in the course of 1990, Chancellor Kohl prevaricated about the recognition of the Oder–Neisse border between the new Germany and Poland (Eurobarometer, No. 34. Table 24. Annex 26).

The breaching of the Berlin Wall on 9 November 1989, brought together what had been previously divided. Europe's division ebbed away. Markets, previously segregated, were joined. Indeed, the Soviet collapse transformed the structure of the world economy. Countries such as Finland, Poland, India or Vietnam – dependent prior to 1990 on the Soviet Union for 20 to 40 or 80 per cent of total exports – had urgently to redirect their sales to the hard currency markets of the west. Mainland China had led the way in the 1980s. The former Soviet republics now joined the rush. The effect of this widening of the south through the collapse of the old east, to use Hanns Maull's phrase, was a precipitate expansion of the global economy. As all indicators showed Pacific Asia's economic growth as the fastest in the world, the IMF and World Bank spread the gospel of market-friendly policies by governments. The implication was for a more rapid opening of OECD markets to imports from poorer countries, whose comparative advantage to the world's corporations resided primarily in their low relative labour costs. The speed of these changes could be expected to place new burdens on relations between western Europe, the United States and Japan over the distribution between them of the costs of absorbing the inevitable expansion of trade with the wider south.

As Michael Kaser writes, reticence rather than generosity marked the EC's dealings with its central-eastern European neighbours. With low population growth rates, high average unemployment and effective lobbies urging protection on the EC in the lower value-added sectors, the EC appeared first and foremost a fortress to its immediate neighbours. On 16 December 1991, the EC and the countries of central-eastern Europe concluded the 'new generation' association agreements, with the EC offering limited access to their producers of farm, textile, or steel products. Labour migration issues were to be dealt with on a bilateral basis. Much resentment was thereby caused at the discrepancy between the welcome extended by western Europe to their move to political democracy, and the unwillingness to allow their exporters to earn vital hard currencies in the immediate future.

Western Europe was more than ever a figurative island of prosperity in an ocean of poverty to its south and east. The options for EC Europe's eastern and southern neighbours were simple: either export products into the key European markets and keep most of the people home, or run ever-wider trade deficits as their markets for products were opened, and export people. The EC in 1991 already held about 8.2 million legal immigrants, and another 3 million without legal papers. The number of asylum seekers had risen from 70,000 in 1983 to 400,000 in 1990. The prospect was for a further surge in migrants in the light of the forecasts of unemployment in the former COMECON states, amounting to about 50 million by 1994, and the very high birth rates to Europe's south. Over the 1990s, the populations of the countries of the southern Mediterranean were expected to rise by 100 million, while the populations of sub-Saharan Africa would expand by about 200 million. As it was, western European publics were for restrictions on immigration from the two areas. Furthermore, the prospects for growth were poor in a western Europe whose principal states were competing – as the chapter on monetary union indicates – to meet by 1996 the convergence criteria set during the Maastricht negotiations. Labour-market policies and anti-immigrant sentiments promised to introduce a particularly divisive note in the counsels of the new Europe.

Western Europe could not rest isolated from the changes on its eastern periphery. The failures of Soviet-style planning added to the scepticism in western Europe about the ability of governments to reconcile efficiency and equity through dirigiste policies. Nor could the failures of the party-states be divorced from the search for post-communist identity in an interdependent world economy. As the chapters in this volume indicate, on the transitions out of a communist command economy to market capitalism and to western-type democracies, the former member states of COMECON, and the successor states to the Soviet Union, have no option but radical modernization, without any precedent to go by. The risk is therefore of precipitate westernization, or imitation of supposedly western policy formulas, followed, in Russia's case by isolation – as Neil Malcolm points out – or by dictatorships in such post-communist states as the Ukraine and Serbia. Neither precipitate westernization nor the rediscovery of pre-1939 traditions to promote modernization would lead to results, readily compatible with the values of Europe's society of states. The disintegration of the Soviet Union, and the transitions in the former party-states, poses, as Georges Sokoloff writes, one of the west's principal challenges for the 1990s.

Disintegration in the former communist party-states abruptly extended the new Europe's outer periphery eastwards into the Slav successor states to the Soviet Union, and south-eastwards beyond the Balkans and into the Caucasus. As Alexander Naumenkov points out, Gorbachev's policies launched Europe into full democratization. Demands for self-determination, which had occurred after 1945 primarily outside Europe, migrated back to the continent of their origin. Participation in the CSCE increased from thirty-four to fifty-two sovereign states in the course of 1991–2. The principal western institutions scrambled to adapt as best they could: NATO extended its reach eastwards with the creation at Rome in November 1991, of the North Atlantic Cooperation Council, incorporating a gathering number of participants; the Council of Europe, as the guardian of the European Convention on Human Rights, opened its door to new applicants; President of the Commission, Delors, in October 1991 called on member states to prepare for a European Community numbering twenty-four to thirty over the coming decade.

The London NATO summit of July 1990 when the western leaders declared the allied mission accomplished also marked the transformation of the world's military system. This had been predicated in part on nuclear deterrence, contributing to the peace in Europe for forty-five years. The seventy-nine civil wars and twenty-seven international wars fought between 1950 and 1990 occurred outside Europe, and accounted for nearly 20 million deaths (World Bank, 1991). With Iraq's invasion of Kuwait in August 1990, followed by the disintegration of the two multi-ethnic states of the Soviet Union and Yugoslavia, the prospect of war returned to Europe with a vengeance.

European euphoria over the end of the cold war ebbed fast as the individual security interests of each sovereign European state became manifest. No two of the twelve EC member states adopted identical positions over the duration of the crisis in the Gulf, ending in the crushing victory of the United Nations coalition, under the leadership of the United States (Salmon, 1992). Only strong United States action ensured a measure of control over nuclear weapons in the hands of the Russian state, as the heir to the Soviet Union in international relations (Walker, 1992). Bonn's unilateral decision in December 1991 to push the EC into hasty recognition of Slovenia and Croatia, against the preferences of Washington, London, Paris or Madrid, followed the Foreign Ministry's disappointment over the Maastricht Treaty's modest innovations with respect to a common foreign and security policy (Schöllgen, 1992).

The end of the cold war, as Hanns Maull notes, threatened the fabric of interdependence, as conflicts of interests rose in the west. A new hierarchy of states, presided by the United States as the world's sole great power, took shape, where rank was measured more in terms of economic performance than the possession of nuclear weapons. The name of the new world game was the pursuit of wealth, the prerogative of corporations. The United States embarked on a reappraisal of its position in the world. The internationalist argument is spelt out by Henry Nau to the effect that this is not the time to mothball the Atlantic alliance. The allies' original political purpose to create a firmer basis for the construction of a peaceful and prosperous Europe remains incomplete. The main opportunities lie ahead. A similar point is made by Jean-Pierre Lehmann that Japanese–American relations remain a priority for Tokyo. Without cooperation between the two giants, Washington's objective of achieving an Asian Pacific Economic Community (Baker, 1991–92) would be unattainable. Yet the July 1990 London summit coincided with the end of the prolonged western boom, starting in 1982 when the world financial markets shifted from bank lending to capital market activities and the United States acted as a locomotive pulling the world economy into export-led expansion.

As the western recession of the early 1990s deepened, trade frictions sharpened between western Europe, the United States and Japan. Japan's trade surplus with the United States and western Europe mounted. A parallel imbalance developed in terms of foreign direct investment flows. Meanwhile the Asian Pacific economies expanded apace as ever-wider regions were incorporated into world markets. Their wealth within twenty years promised to be comparable to that of North America or Europe. Over a broader canvas of time and space, these developments held major implications for post-cold war Europe. Avoidance of a breakdown in relations between Tokyo and Washington was a precondition to confirming Japan's pre-eminence as the core of the Asian economy. The outcome of the Gulf war indicated the continuing United States commitment to alliance with Saudi Arabia. The end of the communist threat in Europe and the lack of a clear mandate for NATO undermined political support in US public opinion for a continuation of a major US military presence in Europe.

The ambition to forge a European union was driven by a powerful combination of state and corporate interests. There were two novelties which distinguished the relaunch of Europe in the late 1980s from its predecessors. In the past, efforts at European integration had become ensnared in the toils of debate between the supporters of a Europe of the states, and the champions of a federal or supranational Europe. The success attending the implementation of the Single European Act, as Albert Bressand points out, is that the EC's internal market policy operated on 'the new citizenship of mutual recognition'. Simply, member states would mutually recognize each others' different standards and ways of doing things, but that in principle and in the future doing things differently would not be an excuse for protection. And as Stephen Woolcock writes, the EC had moved to internalize much of the multilateral trading process in its emerging regulatory system.

The implications were considerable. The EC's force of attraction had pulled Britain – as Geoffrey Edwards writes – and then Spain, into its orbit. Conclusion in October 1991 of the EC–EFTA talks opened the way for EFTA countries to incorporate the EC's regulations into their domestic legislation. Association agreements with the newly liberated countries of central-eastern Europe were negotiated, as mentioned, by December. As the inner core of a wider Europe, the EC would account for 45 per cent of world trade, and be a major force in setting the agenda for world trade negotiations. Add to that the EC's declared ambition to move to a single currency by the year 1999 at the latest and the old method of EC integration by stealth could no longer describe realities. The EC, driven forward by the complex relations between France and a united Germany, was bidding for a world status on a footing of near equality with the United States. There could be little going back on such an evident aspiration, without the whole enterprise losing momentum and credibility.

The Maastricht Treaty

The Maastricht Treaty, agreed to at the European Council on 9 December 1991, and signed on 7 February 1992 (Presse und Informationsamt der Bundesregierung, 1992), stands in the long line of treaties, protocols, declarations and statements stretching back to the May 1948 Congress of The Hague, the creation of the Council of Europe and the launching of the Coal and Steel Community (Wessels, 1992). The treaty modified the Rome Treaty, and is seventy-two pages in length, containing forty-eight annexes or protocols. The battle of interests and complex of motivations entering the negotiations were burnt into the text. Three pillars were to sustain the European union: the internal market, to which was added the European System of Central Banks; a common foreign and security policy; and home and legal affairs. The union's aims were declared to be:

- The achievement of balanced and lasting economic expansion, along with social progress, through the completion of the internal market, economic policy cooperation, and monetary union, leading 'in the longer term' to a single currency.
- The assertion of an EC identity in foreign policy, 'which in the longer term includes a defence policy'.
- The promotion of the rights and interests of citizens through the creation of a European citizenship.
- The strengthening of cooperation in home and legal affairs, notably on the politically sensitive matters of the struggle against transfrontier crime, or the granting of visas and immigration.
- The maintenance and development of the EC's legal foundations, rooted in the federal jurisprudence of the European Court of Justice.

On the insistence of the British government, reference to the whole enterprise as a 'Union with a federal goal' was dropped. The treaty was defined as 'a stage in the realisation of an ever closer Union between the peoples'. The union, the treaty stated, 'is to have due regard to the national identity of its member states' and is to respect their rights and liberties such as they have developed from their constitutional traditions. Article 3b incorporated the concept of subsidiarity for the first time in treaty form, declaring that the European Community is to act:

> only if and insofar as the objectives of the proposed action cannot be sufficiently achieved by the member states and can therefore, by reason of scale or the effects of the proposed action, be better achieved by the Community. . . . Any action by the Community shall not go beyond what is necessary to achieve the objectives of the Treaty.

Furthermore, the union is beholden to respect the European Convention on Human Rights, which expresses 'the constitutional traditions common to the member states as general principles of Community law'.

The union treaty confirmed the projects' ambitions. Community competences are extended into new areas, including health, education, consumer protection, environmental policy, 'transnational networks', or police cooperation as well as money and defence. But these competences were dispersed, some like the internal market remaining under federal jurisprudence, others such as education located firmly in the domain of the states, while cooperation and coordination were the words invoked for immigration.

Maastricht also introduced institutional modifications. The European Parliament's powers were considerably enhanced – but far less than desired by the federalists. The treaty gave the Parliament a form of 'co-decision' powers through a complex 'negative assent procedure', spelt out in article 189b. The Parliament may negotiate directly with the Council, and reject legislation which fails to take account of its recommendations. The treaty required the assent of the Parliament for structural funds in the EC budget. Parliament's assent was required for measures relating to the rights of union citizenship, or the investiture of the Commission, whose members are possibly to be reduced from seventeen to twelve. Its scrutiny of Commission activities, notably on personnel, was to be enhanced. Both Parliament and Commission were to run concurrently for five years. Britain's contribution was to have agreement for the Parliament to scrutinize EC 'maladministration' and finances. A new advisory group, the Committee of Regions, was to be set up – as the result of pressing demands from the German Länder – with representatives from EC regions and local authorities, appointed by the states. Their opinions were to be heard on regional policy, cultural measures and transnational networks. Finally, a European Environmental Agency was to be created.

A key innovation in the treaty was the member states' 'irreversible' commitment to achieve monetary union by 1997–9, as adumbrated in the monetary union chapter in this volume. A European System of Central Banks – designed on Bundesbank lines – is to be set up, composed of the European Central Bank and the central banks of the member states. The ESCB is to give priority to price stability, and conduct business in full independence of the Council. All six members of the governing body are to hold office for eight years. The most controversial element in the negotiations was the transition to phase three. Before the end of 1996, the Council must agree by qualified majority voting on the basis of a Commission proposal, as to which members would meet the convergence criteria to pass for entry to stage three. If a majority meet these criteria, the Council may agree to take the move. If agreement is not possible, the date for entry for those states meeting the convergence criteria is 1999. Meanwhile, Council and Commission are to supervise the economic policies of member states, and make recommendations. The union may sanction a member state which fails to comply.

Maastricht, as Elfriede Regelsberger's chapter makes clear, holds fewer innovations in the field of the common foreign and security policy. Cooperation is still the operative word. France and Britain, as permanent members of the UN Security Council, without prejudice to their responsibilities in the Charter, are to promote the position and interests of the union. There is the commitment 'in the longer term' to formulate a common defence policy, and the introduction of qualified majority voting on the implemention of a policy decided by unanimity. In addition, the member states associate 'the development and consolidation of democracy' as an indispensable element of their aid and trade policies to poorer countries. Member states nonetheless continue their own aid policies, with only a commitment to 'coordinate' their efforts. The West European Union is declared to be an 'integral part' of the union, its main purpose being 'to strengthen the European pillar of the Atlantic alliance'. As if to confirm the opposite, the text then states that there is to be no competition between the WEU and NATO.

Union citizenship was a considerable innovation. Any person holding the nationality of a member state was declared to be a citizen of the union. The idea was championed in particular by Prime Minister Gonzalez. European citizens were to move freely within the union, enjoy consular protection by one of the member states in third countries, as well as enjoy active and passive voting as citizens in communal and European elections. Borrowing from the German Basic Law, the political importance of European-wide parties was confirmed as favouring European integration. Citizens were to acquire a new right of petition to the European Parliament, as well as the possibility of appeal against administrative abuses to an EC ombudsman. In addition, the treaty was to bring home affairs within the union domain. Though such matters as frontier control or the struggle against crime remained in the realm of unanimity voting, significantly – in view of the political sensitivity of immigration in member states – a common visa policy was to be agreed by the Council on the basis of majority voting after 1996.

In a separate protocol, eleven states other than Britain agreed to adopt common measures on social policy. The eleven signatories were thereby committed to a variety of measures to be adopted by qualified majority voting. These included 'the promotion of employment, improved living and working conditions, proper social protection, dialogue between management and labour, and the development of human resources with a view to lasting high employment'.

Spain had led the poorer member states to insert a protocol for the creation of a 'cohesion fund' by the end of 1993 for transfers from the richer northern countries. Given Germany's budgetary problems, there was no evident source of new funds for this demand. Final conclusion of the European Economic Area discussions, embracing the EFTA countries within the EC's internal market regulatory system, was facilitated by agreement of the EFTA countries to contribute funds to EC budgetary resources in return for the access they enjoyed to southern markets.

France won a partial victory in its bid to win support from member states for an EC-wide industrial policy. References to industry in the text were couched in terms of promoting competition. The political battles between the protagonists of state industrial policies and the supporters of a competitive market subject to federal law, may be expected to revive when the next intergovernmental conference for further Treaty revisions is held in 1996. But extension of the Community domain into 'trans-European networks' – meaning transport, telecommunications and energy sectors – provides a legal basis for industrial cooperation in these fields. The Commission's key powers in trade policy were confirmed notably in trade protection measures against dumping and export subsidies from extra-EC suppliers. But the Commission's servants had reason to believe that the Maastricht Treaty strengthened the states' or Parliament's powers at their expense.

The European union's complexities and ambiguities

The Maastricht Treaty was a complex package deal, where member states injected their preferences into the negotiations, and haggled over the slightest details. The process prompted a competition between differing traditions to fashion the treaty as much as possible after familiar forms. German negotiators, with the support of the Italian government, championed the development of federal institutions and practices. France and Britain, along with the smaller states, ensured the continued centrality of the states at the core of the union's evolving institutions and practices. Whether the ultimate design was perceived as laden with federal intent, or as perpetuating the states' existence in an open-ended process, the concessions made by all parties to the treaty meant that none was satisfied with the result, and that all could claim a partial victory. Yet the concessions involved a challenge to domestic institutions while the partial victories provided further incentives to stay in the game, 'at the heart of Europe'.

The centrality of the states in the European union has been expressed forcibly by President Mitterrand: 'Those who decide economic policy, of which monetary policy is only one instrument, are the politicians elected by universal suffrage, the heads of state and government who make up the European Council' (*Le Monde*, 5 September 1992). At Maastricht, the European Council was confirmed as the union's political authority, laying down the guidelines for policy and charged with ultimate responsibility in overseeing the coordination of activities across the three pillars of the union. Equally the Council of Ministers, and the committee of member states' permanent representatives, have their position enhanced in the shaping of policy. The Economics and Finance Council's say in budgetary policies has been extended, and it shares powers with the ECB over monetary union. The General Affairs Council shapes the union's agenda, along with the Commission, and is the locus for discussing foreign policies. This enhancement of the member states within the union presented, in Prime Minister Major's words, 'a revolutionary change', as it enabled the member states to 'act together in unison without necessarily acting within the framework of Community law' (*Financial Times*, 8 September 1992).

For the federalists, Maastricht was a temporary fudge. The terrain had therefore to be prepared for a next leap towards a federal union in 1996. The arguments are familiar. The European Parliament's powers must be enhanced the better to represent the European electorate. The Commission is to be developed more as Europe's government. Majority voting is to be introduced explicitly into all areas of policy, with the Council sitting as an upper house, representing the member states. Legislative powers would thereby be shared between Parliament and Council. All domains would enter the sphere of the Court of Justice, ensuring the separation of powers between executive, legislature and judiciary on the lines of the United States constitution. Law had to apply uniformly to all citizens. This would require adaptations of national constitutions. Not least, the advisory Committee of Regions could be expected to develop regional loyalties within the member states, and open channels for local authorities to by-pass national governments through the creation of union-wide alliances. Such a federal union would be based on a common citzenship, and an internal market, subject to a federal rule of law; a common monetary and exchange rate policy; it would have to have its own tax base and fiscal policy, alongside those of the member states; it would require a federal police; and it would run its own commercial, foreign and security policy.

This tension between the federalists' aspiration to transform European politics, and the insistence of the member states to preserve their autonomy, lies at the heart of the treaty. The federalists' vision is of a union with the attributes of a state, where government is responsible to a dual legislature composed of the states in Council, and the people's representatives in Parliament. The separation of powers between executive, legislature and judiciary at the centre, is to be complemented by the separation of functions between the central authorities and those of the states. In a federal Europe, all politics become domestic, by abolishing diplomacy between the member states, the traditional and characteristic feature of European affairs. The union, not the member states, would be the central protagonist of global politics. The content of the common foreign and security policy indicates that member states are much more conservative. There is little sign, as the national chapters suggest, that any one of them contemplates bowing out from the world stage.

The Community process, though, prompts the member states to press ahead and form a union, while continuing to disagree as to its ultimate form. As compromises must be struck, no one member state rests entirely satisfied. The result in the meanwhile is greater complexity in procedures, where Maastricht's extension of the union's policy domains promises to make the EC policy process more rather than less cumbersome. The European Parliament's relations are governed by six different procedural devices, while the conciliation device between Parliament and Council is a triumph of complexity. The overlap in fact between the practice of intergovernmental negotiations – in other words, diplomacy – and the making of law by the Council of Ministers – the EC's legislature – risk bringing the law into disrepute as an instrument of particular political interests, rather than a body of doctrine applicable equally to all citizens, firms and governments of the union (Cohen–Tanuggi, 1992).

Maastricht thus stands accused on two accounts: it centralizes legislation in the union's executive, and deprives the member states' parliaments of their legislative and other powers; it lacks democratic legitimacy because the European Parliament's powers, though enhanced, remain restricted to that of assessing Community affairs and of co-negotiating treaties. Maastricht, in short, stands accused of confirming a union of governments and bureaucracies, rather than of peoples.

The tensions within Maastricht are mitigated in part by promise of Europe's imminence. The intergovernmental conference for further treaty revisions is planned for 1996, when the union must decide whether to make the leap into the third stage of monetary union. No leap would be possible without a renewed transfer of powers to the union, involving a major package deal satisfactory to the member states. In Ian Davidson's wording, the treaty proposes a polyvalent EC with tendencies to move to a federal structure and with universal competences. This future orientation is embedded in the textual description of the accords as 'a stage in the realisation of an ever closer Union between the peoples'.

The narrow path towards this open-ended destination is traced by the internal market, underpinned by the federal jurisprudence of the European Court of Justice. But the addition of new policy areas in the treaty multiplied the number of exemptions and derogations, without which the necessary consensus between the states could not have been attained to bring them to sign the document. Much use was made of the future as a place to locate difficult decisions, for lack of unanimity at the time of signing. Britain's opting-out clauses on monetary union and social policy were cases in point. On monetary union, Westminster retained the right to ratify Britain's opting in. But on social policy, Britain's exemptions fragment the EC's legal space. Britain's more flexible labour laws could serve as a continued attraction for corporate investment, and set an example for Spain, Portugal or Ireland.

The treaty underwrites a multi-speed, variable geometry Europe of concentric circles and special relations. Title V, article J.4.(5) is a case in point. While common foreign policy includes all matters relating to European security, with the view 'in the longer term' to define a common defence policy, the article does not stand in the way of cooperation between two or more member states either bilaterally, in the WEU and in the Atlantic alliance. This leaves the inner core of states, led by France and Germany, free to continue to set the agenda for the union's future development, without placing undue strain on German-American relations, as long as – the paragraph specifies – such bi- or multilateral relations do not run contrary to or do not hinder this (European) cooperation. The same holds for monetary union. The convergence criteria for price and exchange rate stability provide the preconditions for member states embarking on the 'irreversible' move to a single currency under the ESCB. An inner core of member states could make the move first, and be joined by the laggards later.

Yet the prevalence of process over structures in the post-cold war world bodes ill for architectural designs, which seek to freeze the future into a timetable. Indeed, the fluidity of events offer opportunities to expand, rather than to restrict the options open to states presented within 'Europe's framework of interlocking institutions'. Prior to the great transformation, European diplomacy ran along familiar lines, with a division of tasks between the various multilateral institutions. The states' ministers and representatives could move between organizations, settle problems in one location while sustaining drama and dissent in another. A position taken in one was invariably tied to discussions in other fora, and more or less loosely according to the subject and political constellation in domestic, European or Atlantic affairs. The neat distinctions drawn between the competences of Europe's 'interlocking institutions' served to preserve appearances: as such and such a topic, the argument ran, had nothing to do with another, disagreements in one sphere could be delineated from continued dialogue in other areas. If EC foreign ministers met under NATO auspices, they could change hats and talk European affairs in caucus; when trade matters were going in an undesired direction, there was always international law derived from the Council of Europe or GATT to fall back on, and in turn shape the debate or the outcome in the EC.

With the return of flux to the European home, the states scrambled to redefine or to extend the tasks and memberships of all the European institutions built up since 1945. The European union was to be the hub, tied in through its trade dimension to GATT; through the new citizenship to the Council of Europe; through the Common Foreign and Security Policy to the WEU, NATO, the CSCE, and the United Nations. Yet were the union to be too jealous of its claims to primacy, the disputes familiar to those organizations could be expected to become internalized within the union. Contrariwise, were the diplomatic processes from the cold war period to be continued after its disappearance, and without the structural constraints which it imposed on participants, the individual interests and political decisions of each sovereign state, which Peter Stratmann identifies as the key feature in the domain of security and arms control, could triumph in all domains.

The European union, as sketched in the Maastricht Treaty, thus risks being overwhelmed by the disputes which its ambitions attract, or torn apart by the opportunities for self-assertion presented to the states in the post-cold war Europe. The half-way house between these two poles is a Europe of many speeds, of multiple geometry and concentric circles. It is the only Europe with the flexibility to survive the prevalent conditions of flux, and the dual tensions of overture and identity.

European union and public opinions

European public opinions formed part of the state of turbulence in world politics, defined as the acceleration and growing complexity of messages from the environment (Rosenau, 1990). Both the Single European Act, launching the internal market, and the Maastricht Treaty, signed on 7 February 1992, were negotiated by elites and then presented for ratification to the parliaments or peoples of the member states. As soon as the European publics became aware in the course of 1988 that their particular interests could be challenged by the creation of the internal market, they mobilized to protect themselves or to project their special interests into EC legislation.

The Maastricht Treaty went further, challenging inherited national identities. Thus, France's shift in the 1980s to become a champion of European integration, bound in a 'community of fate with Germany', was informed by a permanent ambition to defend France's rank, securing France's future *grandeur* in a more exclusive European family, hinging on France's relations with Germany. The implications were extensive. They entailed constitutional revision within France, and challenges to the concept of the 'one and indivisible' Republic. In Germany, European union spelt the abandonment of the DM, the outer symbol of the Federal Republic's success. In Britain, they challenged the conventions of Westminister as the seat of British sovereignty. For Italy, as Cesare Merlini indicates, the end of the cold war accelerated trends to restructure domestic alignments and priorities. Maastricht, in short, pulled on deep-rooted sensibilities and the sensitive 'membranes of convention' (Pfaff, 1989) in the member states.

There is nothing new about the problems confronting the Community in sinking its language and symbols into European soil, as the introductory chapter recalls. Established national cultures, with their pre-modern origins, their saints, heroes and commemorations, were too strong for the protagonists of European union to confront directly (Smith, 1992). That was the lesson of the French National Assembly's rejection of the European Defence Community in 1954. Jean Monnet's was a substitute strategy, where the political substance and aims of European union were thinly veiled in the technical language of markets, or draped in the political jargon of European integration. The Single European Act, ratified by member state parliaments in 1986–7, was the last time that the whole undertaking could be presented to European publics essentially as a series of measures designed to improve the functioning of the European economy.

With German unity, and the collapse of the Soviet empire, the political aims for union could no longer be concealed. Yet the Monnet method, which had served in the past, was applied one more time. Maastricht was a pure product of the marriage between European diplomatic traditions, and neo-functionalist methods. It depends for its content and implementation on the cooperation of the European states. There was no readily available European culture on which the elites who negotiated Maastricht could draw. National cultures commemorated Europe's divisions. Fleeting moments of European unity lay too far in the past, or too tragically within living memory, to be acceptable. European union had to be forged on the foundations of Europe's post-1945 society of states, and on a novel, memoryless project for a future beyond the cold war. 'Never before has a conscience or a sentiment of common destiny been created on the future, on what has not yet happened' (Morin, in *Le Monde*, 14 April 1991).

The treaty thus incorporates the future not only as a location to place problems now unresolvable, but as a binding or implicit commitment to act now in ways compatible with the Union's longer-term aims. As these remain for the moment defined as an ever-closer union rather than as a union with a federal endpoint, and sanctions are restricted to the internal market and economic policy, the implication for the future tone of business is clear. A premium is set on behaviour that complies with procedures or fits with the consensus. Two features of Maastricht Europe are therefore discernible:

1   States whose domestic opinions and interests, or external attachments, run counter to the consensus will have to trade their disagreement on the substance of union policy for the expected cost of isolation from the crowd. The procedures must be sufficiently adaptable to make allowance for the expression of their idiosyncrasies.
2   The lack of transparency in the process and dissatisfaction with the substance of policy proposed may be expected to engender demands to close the gap between the union's activities and the preferences of European publics. As the treaty's aims are to achieve a union which raises expectations or anxieties that the margins of autonomous action by member states are reduced, the eruption of public preferences into the domain of union policies points to the preservation of Europe's diversity, its pre-eminent historical trait.

Indeed, the loyalties of Europeans remained primarily national, and their concerns mainly economic in nature. The launching of the EC's internal market programme was designed in part to meet widespread concern about unemployment. The EC had created no new net jobs between 1973 and 1992, as the recorded jobs created during the boom years of the late 1980s were lost again in the conditions of slower growth in the early 1990s. Given the expansion of world markets, the number of new entrants to world competition, and the differing demographic dynamics at work in each one of the member states, two general theories vied to explain the phenomenon. One saw the roots of unemployment in the conservative nature of macroeconomic policies, under the aegis of the Bundesbank as Europe's de facto central bank. The other emphasized the structural impediments to factor movements embedded in the national legislations of the member states. It was to these that the EC's internal market programme was addressed.

Promotion of the 'social dimension' as a vital accompanying measure was prompted by the prospect of a populist backlash against a liberal market programme. Here at least was an area where the distinctive European endorsement of a social net commanded widespread support (Times Mirror Center, 1991, p. 15). German leadership in tandem with France of a continental alliance in favour of social protection pointed to a showdown with Conservative Britain as the prime protagonist of free factor markets in labour. The campaign served to identify 'Thatcherism' as a common scapegoat, while preserving intact national social systems. This meant in effect restricting competition within labour markets, while negotiating in the EC over Europe-wide regulations which preserved the *acquis national*. The ambiguity was written into the Maastricht Treaty in a separate protocol where eleven states other than Britain agreed to adopt common measures by qualified majority voting on social policy. Unanimous voting is required for matters affecting social security (highly sensitive in France), worker–management negotiations (highly sensitive in Germany), and the conditions of work for immigrants (highly sensitive across western Europe).

Another explanation for the high levels of unemployment across Europe identified the Bundesbank as the principal culprit. Its conservative macroeconomic policies relayed through the exchange rate mechanism to all countries whose currencies were tied to the DM. Growth rates in the rest of Europe, the argument ran, were kept far below potential. Hence, France's bid to create an ESCB, and end the Bundesbank's role as Europe's de facto central bank. As the chapter on monetary policy indicates, the German government agreed on conditions to be worked towards over a time scale, stretching to 1997–9. The conditions of German unity provided one set of arguments to postpone the move to monetary union. Another reason for postponement was the German public's reluctance to abandon the DM, as the symbol of the Federal Republic's success. As Governor Pöhl stated, the German people would be 'sacrificing a hard currency on the European altar without knowing what we would get in return' (*Die Welt*, 4 September 1990). Yet any backsliding by the German government in not moving to union would be tantamount to the Federal Republic breaking an 'irreversible' treaty commitment.

The German government's counter to France's request to sacrifice the DM was to call for a common foreign and security policy. But this was the area where European governments and public opinions were most divergent. The Gulf war, the USSR's disintegration and the collapse of Yugoslavia brought the differences to the fore. The architectural debates, discussed in Part VI of this volume, revealed the depth of western Europe's divisions over security and defence policy. The struggle between the institutions – NATO, WEU, EC or CSCE – merely duplicated the differing priorities and policies of the states. The profusion of public attitudes on defence and security was as great between countries, as was the confusion of public opinions within them. German public opinion in the spring of 1991, following the war in the Gulf, favoured EC responsibility for security and defence matters; was less keen on EC joint decision-making capabilities; and opposed the EC having a joint military intervention force. Both French and British public opinions favoured a common European military intervention force, but French opinion was opposed to joint EC decision-making capability while British public opinion was positively hostile. Only the United Kingdom, followed by Denmark, showed clear majorities expressing confidence in NATO (Euro-barometer, No. 32, pp. 43–5).

Not surprisingly, disenchantment with the EC followed on the elation accompanying the promises of its initial relaunch. Optimism gripped Europe as the cold war faded and growth rates picked up. Greatest overall popular support came from Italy, and Greece – the two countries then with the worst record in implementing the single-market legislation. Portugal, Spain, Ireland and Greece as major recipients of structural funds recorded high satisfaction with the benefits of their country's EC membership. The German public remained relatively supportive. But those German citizens judging that the country benefited by EC membership fell from a peak of 61 per cent polled at the time of the first nationwide elections in December 1990 since November 1932 to 48 per cent by June 1992. This sharp decline paralleled the rise in anxiety in Germany as the costs of unity stretched ever further into the future. The most notable change, though, came in France, the principal protagonist of European union. By June 1992, 48 per cent of those polled expressed indifference or relief if the EC were scrapped, placing the French public alongside the Belgian, British and Danish as the least supportive of the EC. The Danish vote of 2 June, rejecting the Maastricht Treaty by a few thousand votes, was followed by the French referendum of 20 September, with a slender majority voting in favour.

European public opinions, then, continued to support the broad goals of 'European unity', while preserving their own collective identities with respect to the future and to the rest of the world. Attitudes were shaped primarily within the context of the states. Maastricht duplicated these reservations in selecting 1996 as the 'moment of truth' (Tietmeyer, 1992) when key decisions would have to be made for the next intergovernmental conference, and any subsequent steps to monetary union. Disagreements on foreign policy left the United States as prime guarantor for Europe's security, while the convergence criteria sanctioned the Bundesbank's primacy. Given the fluidity of international conditions, this was a frail package. The WEU was declared to be an 'integral part' of the Union, its main purpose being 'to strengthen the European pillar of the Atlantic alliance'. But NATO as a legacy of the cold war was an instrument without a clear mandate. The combination of Germany's high interest rates and budget deficits to finance reconstruction in the new Bundeslander could be expected to exert strong deflationary pressures on business activity across Europe into the mid 1990s. But Germany's priorities were national and could not be presented indefinitely as in Europe's wider interests.

An old Europe in search of the new

Maastricht Europe was a sketch of the new Europe, drawn by the old, and negotiated in a manner not unlike the many diplomatic conferences convened down the centuries of European history. These had been fashioned within the features of the European state system, identified in the first chapter as the propensity of states to live in anarchy, to develop their own purposes, to foster society and to allow for the development of interdependencies. The states had sought to keep their options open, and their external attachments alive, in a competition which regularly had broken out into war. Peace after 1945 had been preserved at the cost of Europe's division, but had allowed for the development of a society anchored in western institutions and practices. Its ideals for world peace and prosperity were those of the United Nations and of the Atlantic alliance.

With the return of flux, unbounded by cold war structures, to world and European affairs, the battle to widen Europe's society of states and peoples, and to embed them in the terrain of a post-cold war Europe, was opened. Yet the world prior to 1989 had gone. Much unsettled business from the early years of the century re-emerged with the collapse of Yugoslavia and the Soviet Union. The wars of 1914–45 remained in vivid memory. As President Mitterrand stated in May 1992, 'many Europeans vacillate on the threshold of a world that they fear' (*Le Monde*, 11 May 1992).

Germany's achievement of state unity marked the re-emergence of a Europe of the great powers. United Germany outweighed all other western European states in demography, and as Europe's prime agricultural and industrial power. The DM was the continent's key currency. Germany was the prime provider of aid and investment to the former party-states, and the main target for their post-communist trade. The end of the cold war spelt the winding down of the allied military presence to one-third of the Bundeswehr's manpower, and the withdrawal of Russian troops from German territory by 1994. The prospect beckoned of a MittelEuropa, hinging on Austro-German cooperation in central and south-eastern Europe. Germany championed the EC's rapid enlargement, while nothing within the EC could be agreed on without Germany's consent. 'In these circumstances', former Prime Minister Thatcher concluded, 'the Community augments Germany's power rather than constraining it' (*The Times*, 18 May 1992).

A Europe of states, envisioned by Secretary of State Baker and Foreign Minister Genscher as a 'Euro-Atlantic union from Vancouver to Vladivostok' (*Neue Zürcher Zeitung*, 5 October 1991), was predicated on linking NATO and the CSCE. The United States would be united Germany's prime ally in the maintenance of the new European balance, characterized by the continued uncertainties in Russia, the problems of transition in central-eastern Europe – as Paul Lewis's chapter records – and the risks of nuclear weapons proliferation or concern in France and Britain about loss of status. A US presence in European security arrangements would reassure smaller states against domination by one, or a combination of European powers. If Germany for the first time in its history was a satisfied power, without internal aspirations to a unity which had been already secured, or to demands on neighbours' territory, that was the achievement of the Atlantic alliance, and in particular of America's commitment to European security.

State unity meant freer hands for Germany. Bonn cited constitutional constraints on the deployment of troops out-of-NATO area to avoid military participation in the Gulf war of August–February 1990–1. Then, Germany – with Austria – emerged as the champion of independence for Slovenia and Croatia. Austria sought to mobilize the CSCE as the appropriate forum to deal with Yugoslavia's dissolution, but – as Vojtech Mastny's chapter indicates – the CSCE process had no effective way of dealing with the secession of nationalities from multi-ethnic states. France backed its traditional ally, Serbia, seeking to maintain the unity of Yugoslavia until minority and human rights had been ensured. In an effort to preserve European unity, the EC in late 1991 vainly attempted to negotiate a ceasefire in the brutal Serbo-Croat war. But German frustration over Maastricht finally prompted Bonn unilaterally to acclaim Slovenia's and Croatia's independence. Simultaneously, the Bundesbank decided to raise interest rates, giving clear priority to national over broader European considerations. The ERM in the course of 1992 was thus caught between the high German short-term interest rates, and the declining dollar, leading to the forced exit of the lira, peseta and pound sterling in September.

These events illustrated that a united Germany could choose to champion a Europe of the states. Were German public opinion to grow confident in a recently confirmed national identity, France's strategy to bind Germany into a European union, as sketched at Maastricht, would entail paying an ever-higher price. As German reticences about Maastricht rose, the German leadership's terms would harden. Germany was being asked to abandon monetary sovereignty. In exchange, nothing short of a federal Europe was acceptable. The future ECB had to be located in Frankfurt or Bonn. The ECB's money market operations would be decentralized, and not located primarily in London. All central banks would have to be independent. Meanwhile, member states had to meet the treaty criteria for convergence. That spelt stabilization across Europe, a marked deterioration in the balance of public finance across the continent, and a sharp decline in public support for European union. Yet it was far from clear that Germany could meet the Maastricht criteria by 1996, given the budgetary problems associated with the transfers to the new Bundeslander.

France's bid to Europeanize the Bundesbank pointed by the end of the decade to a European currency rivalling the dollar. Meanwhile, France invoked time as an ally in framing a European defence for the union. The pull of isolationism in the United States was strong, and could be promoted by French obstinacy on trade negotiations in GATT. The WEU could be built up as an alternative to NATO. References to the compatibility of WEU with NATO, the shared western interest in preventing the proliferation of nuclear weapons in the former Soviet Union, or the reassurance provided to the countries of central-eastern Europe by NATO's new Cooperation Council, no doubt would continue to bind the United States into European security arrangements. Further instabilities across the new Europe, though, could prompt German public opinion to favour the development of a European security policy, engaging German troops under the WEU or the United Nations in areas outside of NATO's remit.

These shades of a return to a balance of power in Europe, and the distant mirage of Europe as a great power on a world scale, coupled with the continued vigour of the forces of fragmentation, illustrated that the scale of the new Europe by far exceded the capabilities of any one of the larger states. This applied with particular vigour to Germany. The counterpart to Germany's prior rank among European states was the rise in the burden of financial demands and psychological strains placed on it, far in excess of its ability to meet them. There were at least two reasons for a united Germany no longer being able to play the role of 'Europayer', as in the past. The first related to the domestic and external costs of German unity. As William Paterson's chapter points out, the prospects for the 1990s were that they would remain a heavy burden for the coming decade. The second related to the use of EC resources for the 1990s. The flow of funds into Community coffers to finance the agricultural or regional policies would be complemented by additional demands for aid to the former communist party-states.

The psychological strains on Germany, too, could be expected to rise, were its many neighbours to suspect that a petulant, and nationalistic Germany was beating its own path to primacy. Indeed, the course of events over the period 1989–92 provided a host of examples to illustrate how much the history of 1870–1945 continued to burden German policy and attitudes. Two may suffice.

France did not concede to Germany's demands for a move to a federal foreign and security policy, which subordinated the WEU to the Atlantic alliance, and to Germany's prior alliance with the United States. Yet France still asked for Germany to sacrifice the DM. As the treaty's German opponents mobilized in early 1992, they vented their resentments at France's 'grand strategy to extract Versailles-style reparations for German unity'. France wanted to act as grave digger for the DM, and was designing a Europe to be run by the 'élites of the *grandes écoles*' (*Wall Street Journal Europe*, 2 June 1992).

Germany's unilateral recognition of Slovenia and Croatia unlocked the vaults of Serbian paranoia. Belgrade denounced Austro-German hostility to its existence as a continuity from the two world wars. Bonn's gesture also antagonized Turkey, which feared destabilization in the Balkans, and for the future of the Moslem populations in Bosnia, Kosovo and Macedonia. Greece favoured Serbia's cause, and insisted that the EC delay recognition of Macedonia and Bosnia. The Croatians and Serbians then fell on the unprotected Moslem populations of Bosnia. Both NATO and the EC rejected calls for military action. Meanwhile, the fundamental principles of Europe's society of states went by default. Serbia and Croatia 'cleansed' their territories of alien minorities in mockery of human or minority rights. External and internal frontiers of the former Yugoslavia were altered by *faits accomplis* or by force, in disregard of the CSCE signatory states' commitment to the inviolability of frontiers.

Indeed, the danger facing Europe is not the emergence of a dominant Germany, but of a new Europe. This is a curious hybrid from the inheritances of pre- and post-1945 Europe. From pre-1945 Europe comes the tendency to a competition between the states through the play of shifting alliances, as well as the distinct but changing structures and purposes of the states. From post-1945 Europe is inherited the complex political and market interdependencies within western Europe, with multiple strands and ties into the rest of the world, and the society established in western Europe on the basis of institutions and values, and now extended at least in principle to the rest of Europe. The end of the cold war has prompted a struggle between the two, one pulling backwards to the renationalization of policies and public opinions, and the other calling for patience and perseverance in establishing a grand compromise for the whole of Europe in a new world.

The paradox of Maastricht is to have been designed in the spirit of a grand compromise, open to further elaboration, but to have been inspired by the renewed competition between states, and to have promoted a partial trend to a renationalization of policies and public opinions. The grand compromise was between two views of a European union, one as the centre to a European periphery, and the other as a wider Europe of states, with Germany as a geographic centre. Both impinged on existing identities, and demanded differing degrees of openness. The first envisaged a union broad enough, and sufficiently constraining on all, to defuse the pre-eminence of any single member. That entailed agreement by all participating states to agree to a condition of semi-sovereignty for each, and a sharing of sovereign powers in agreed domains for all. The second envisaged the emergence of Germany as Europe's leading state, but confronted with other nation-states, firmly rooted in their inherited cultures, and secured through a convivial coexistence with Germany, by ensuring the permanent presence of the United States as a European power.

A Europe of the states would not be able to operate effectively without cooperation between the members, the development of common policies, mutual and agreed adaptation to changing circumstances, and openness to the rest of the world. All of these features are common in Maastricht. Yet a Europe of the states inevitably hinges on Germany and includes Russia, and therefore the United States in a wider security arrangement which turns around NATO and the CSCE. Such an arrangement recieves the support of the countries of central-eastern Europe, or Norway and Turkey, all of whom share common concerns about the turbulence around them. It binds the United States and Canada, at lesser cost into a European security structure.

But it holds a number of key weaknesses. The continuation of the United States presence in Europe may no longer be taken for granted. A Europe of the states places great economic and psychological strains on Germany, allowing Germany's national ambitions to linger in the ambiguities of a post-cold war European security structure. As a Europe of the powers, it widens the gap between larger and smaller states and their responsibilities. Most of all, it functions on the voluntary principle. That principle applied in NATO and EC policies towards Yugoslavia. At most, member states succeeded in preventing the events in the former territories of Yugoslavia from driving a wedge between them. But the use of force in the name of 'ethnic cleansing' went unpunished.

A European union requires member states to cooperate or to develop common policies, but with the difference that it enshrines explicit or implicit coercive rules. It is organized around the core of the EC member states. It is rooted, as Ian Davidson insists with reason, in the states, but the union is predicated also on the principle of multinationality, of a common legal space and citizenship (defined in non-ethnic terms). Given that the coercive aspects of the EC are more implicit than explicit, any attempts at closure unacceptable to most members would not be a viable policy. The dynamics between the states, and their external attachments, ensure the EC's graduated overture to the EFTA countries, to central-eastern Europe, and to the rest of the world. It binds the United States in through the WEU's subordination to NATO, and implies mutual adaptation of military policies by the member states to develop an effective military instrument, to supplement that of trade policy, and perhaps of the currency.

But the union, too, has it weaknesses. Its implementation, however partial, rests on the drive and support of the member states, anchored in their own historical identities, with their particular external attachments and domestic alignments and interests to consider. Its ambitions are a token of the union's weight in the global economy, but internal divisions inhibit, or may enhance, the union's effectiveness in external relations. As there is no final agreement about its destination, the union must meanwhile deal with the extension of Europe's periphery eastwards and the lengthening list of candidates who wish to join. That extension shifts the balance of Europe towards its geographic centre in Germany, away from the EC's own inner periphery of the British isles or southern Europe. It places a great burden on Germany, economically and psychologically, and may be expected to drive up Germany's price for cooperation. It not only challenges, but fosters national identities.

The Maastricht Treaty also hints at a future where the union's identity could be defined against outsiders. This was discernible in the provisions for a common asylum policy, designed in part to prevent an influx of impoverished migrants from south or east, or in the hints at a European defence organization, autonomous of the United States and the Atlantic alliance. In the past, the European project had been presented in contrast to the key protagonists of the cold war. Multiple variants had been played on the theme of Europe as a prospective third force between the two powers, or as a partner of the United States against the Soviet Union. But the Soviet Union was history, and Europe's domestic institutions and markets made it part of the western world, to which the central-eastern European countries aspired to belong fully and whose leader remained the United States. Furthermore, each state continued to be the focus of its own network of regional and global relations. Changes around the world therefore continued to differentiate Europeans from each other, in that an opportunity for one could present a threat to another. The various sources of rupture in world affairs, referred to above, provided as many stimulants for intra-European differences as opportunities to 'speak with one voice'.

There is therefore no certainty that by the year 2000 the union will have helped to consolidate Europe's society. In retrospect, the commentary may run, the great leap into union prompted by the huge transformation of world and European affairs was too ambitious. The union absorbed tasks, previously dispersed about Europe's varied diplomatic fora, without having the legitimacy to act on behalf of its many peoples. Its institutions attracted a rising tide of demands as the scope of its competences widened. They were overwhelmed in the process. The gap between the union's aspirations and performance brought it into ridicule. Strong on principles, the epitaph could read, but weak on delivery.

The Maastricht Treaty evisaged the European Community as the core around which a wider, open Europe would be organized. But the fragmentation from the peripheries of Europe was quite capable of entering the core, destroying the achievements of the past four decades. Europe's society of states had flowered within the confines of the Atlantic alliance. Its rationale of containment disappeared with the Soviet Union. The novelty for Europe thus lay in the opening of a parenthesis in European history, where the continent would be in transition from a containment which had provided it with a degree of unity in opposition to a common enemy, to an as yet undefined polity capable of containing its historic diversity. Europe, in short, is in transition from one containment to another. It triumphed in the first; it has just embarked on the second.

REFERENCES

Baker, James A. III 1991/92: America in Asia: emerging architecture for a Pacific community. *Foreign Affairs*, 70(5), 1–18.
Cohen-Tanuggi, Laurent 1992: *L'Europe en Danger*. Paris: Fayard.
Colombani, Jean-Marie 1991: L'urgence européenne. *Le Monde*, 14 April.
Commission of the European Communities. Eurobarometer. No. 32. December, 1989.
Commission of the European Communities. Eurobarometer. No. 34. December 1990.
Hassner, Pierre 1992: Construction européenne et mutations à l'est. In Jacques Lenoble and Nicole Dewandre (eds), *L'Europe au soir du siècle*. Paris: Editions Esprit.
Pfaff, William 1989: *Le Réveil du Vieux Monde: vers un Nouvel Ordre International*. Paris: Calman-Levy.
Presse und Informationsamt der Bundesregierung 1992: Bulletin. *Vertrag uber die Europäische Union*, Nr 16/S, 113, 12 February. Bonn.
Programme des Nations Unies pour le développement 1992: *Rapport Mondial sur le Développement Humain*.
Rosenau, J. 1990: *Turbulence in World Politics*. Princeton: Princeton University Press.
Salmon, Trevor C. 1992: Cracks in European unity? Testing times for European political cooperation: the Gulf and Yugoslavia, 1990-92. *International Affairs*, 68(2), 233–53.
Schöllgen, Gregor 1992: Deutschlands neue Lage: Die USA, die Bundesrepublik und die Zukunft des westlichen Bündnisses. *Europa Archiv*, Folge 5, 125–32.
Smith, Antony D. 1991: *National Identity*. London: Penguin.
Smith, Antony D. 1992: National identity and the idea of European unity. *International Affairs*, 68(1), 55–76.
Tietmeyer, Hans 1992: Währungsunion – ein weg ohne umkehr. *Integration*, 15 Jg, 1/92, 17–24.
The Times Mirror Center for The People and The Press 1991: *The Pulse of Europe: A Survey of Political and Social Values and Attituds*. Washington DC, September 1991, pp. 43–5.
Walker, William 1992: Nuclear weapons and the former Soviet Republics. *International Affairs*, 68, 2.
Wallace, William (ed.) 1990: *The Dynamics of European Integration*. London: Pinter.
Wessels, Wolfgang 1992: Maastricht: ergebnisse, berwertungen und langzeittrends. *Integration*, 15 Jg, 1/92, 2–15.
World Bank 1991: *World Bank Development Report*. Oxford: Oxford University Press.

Index

NATIONAL UNIVERSITY
LIBRARY ORANGE COUNTY

NATIONAL UNIVERSITY
LIBRARY ORANGE COUNTY

6173